11-1-09

CLOUD NINE

A DREAMER'S DICTIONARY

To Birdlady with love "RO"

CLOUD NINE

A DREAMER'S DICTIONARY

SANDRA A. THOMSON

An Imprint of HarperCollins *Publishers*

Grateful acknowledgment is made to Jeremy M. Tarcher, Inc., for permission to use previously published material from *Dreams That Can Change Your Life* by Alan B. Siegel. Copyright © 1990 by Alan Siegel. Reprinted by permission of the author and the publisher.

HarperCollins books may be purchased for educational, business, or sales promotional use. For information please write: Special Markets Department, HarperCollins Publishers Inc., 10 East 53rd Street, New York, NY 10022.

First Avon trade edition published 1999.

Reprinted in Quill 2003.

Library of Congress Cataloging-in-Publication Data is available.

ISBN 0-380-80889-7

07 08 09 RRD 20 19 18 17 16 15 14 13 12

To Robert,
my dream partner and
my partner in dreaming

The nights are long and dreary, Mr. Sandman.
Can't seem to sleep a wink anymore.
My pillow gets so weary, Mr. Sandman.
Tell me why you pass right by my door.

Haven't I plenty reason to grumble?
Mr. Sandman, you just pass me by.
Never give me a tumble;
Don't seem to hear when I sigh.

Mr. Maker of Dreams,
You've forgotten me, it seems.
Tho' other folks hear when I sigh,
They call me a poor weeping willow.

But I promise that I'll be all right,
If you'll put a dream under my pillow.
And make it a good dream tonight,
And in dreams bring my love back to me.

GOLDIE PHILLIPS
1889–1962

Acknowledgments

I am grateful to those dreamers everywhere who contributed their encouragement, energy, ideas, and dream images to this book, especially my sister *Carol Hand*.

Betty Yenetchi and *Bunny Rosenzweig* painstakingly worked their way through earlier versions of the manuscript, letting me know what worked and what didn't.

The Rev. Carl Yenetchi, of Wayfarers Chapel, Palos Verdes, California, inspired me with his willing and extensive research on the gems used in the foundation stones of the New Jerusalem described in the Book of Revelation.

Sculptress *Maria Leon* took my wisp of a description, molded some clay around in her talented fingers, and created the first three-dimensional Dremmy, another dream quest fulfilled. *Andrew Kovner* and *Robert Mueller* perfected it graphically.

Drs. *Alan Siegel, Stephen LeBarge*, and *Marcia Emery* generously gave permission to use their ideas and offered comments that pertained to their work within the manuscript.

My agent, *Bob Silverstein*, kept after me until my proposal was one to dream about. *Chris Miller*, my editor at Avon Books, dreamt right along with me, albeit editorial pencil in hand, of the day when the book would leave our respective dreamworlds and enter our waking world.

Contents

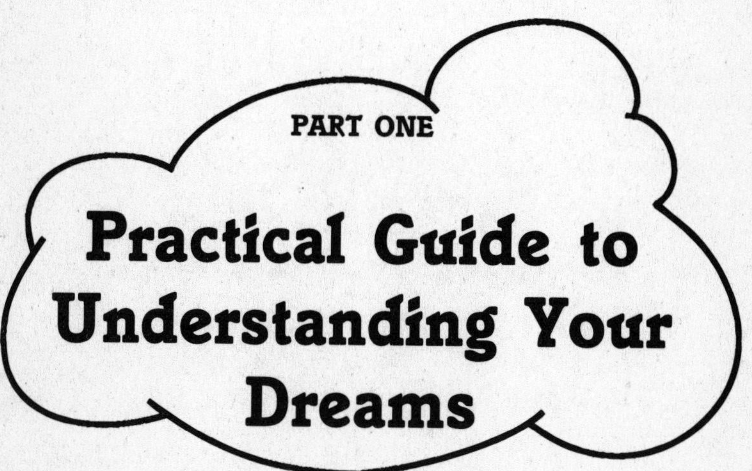

PART ONE

Practical Guide to Understanding Your Dreams

We are such stuff as dreams
are made of.
William Shakespeare

CHAPTER 1

Dreams: Mirrors of Growth

"I had the weirdest dream last night. I can't get it out of my mind. I was in my house, but it wasn't exactly my house, and there was this guy who . . ."

Remember that conversation? Perhaps you had it, or a similar one, just this morning. From the beginnings of recorded history, we have considered dreams fascinating and important. They have figured prominently in our cultural, societal, and religious development.

Dreams were among our first attempts at scientific study and control over our universe. Priests, the scientists of earlier civilizations, believed happenings of nature, triggered by the gods, could, nevertheless, be predicted and organized through dreams.

The first known book on dream interpretation, now called the Chester Beatty papyrus, came from Thebes in Upper Egypt, and is preserved in the British Museum. Recorded around 1250 B.C. by priests of the god Horus, it includes material dating from 2000 B.C. It contains some 200 dreams and distinguishes between good and bad ones. In Babylonia, good dreams were sent by the gods. Bad dreams, sent by demons, often required the enactment of specific protection rituals.

Today we still retain some of that magical feeling about dreams, partly because, for most of us, they are our most unusual, mystifying, and creative productions. Animals speak to us; both we and they possess amazing powers. Surroundings change instantly in ways that defy waking laws of time and space. Within our dreams, we move fluidly between past, present, and future.

Dreams transcend time. Not only are they interwoven with elements of our personal past, present, and future, but, if we are to believe the great dreammaster C. G. Jung, they are interwoven with themes from human experience since the beginning of time, which he called the *collective unconscious*.

Those of us who work with our dreams regularly, cherish and enjoy them. They are signposts of our inner pilgrimage. We have fun recounting them and playing with them. Those who don't, look upon our wonderful creations as something bordering on hallucination.

In 1992 I was hospitalized for the removal of a tumorous kidney. On my release day I was drowsing while I waited for the doctor. I asked the universe for a dream that would tell me what sense I was to make of my surgical experience, and what I was to do next. (This is a form of incubation dream, which you will learn more about in Chapter 5.)

When the doctor entered my room, I was having the following dream:

Chicken Farmer

I am merging into the body of a chicken farmer in Arkansas. I am aware that once I am a part of him, he will know what I know about nephrectomies [yes, that new word was in my dream awareness] and can apply this to his flock. But I'm puzzled about what I am to learn from him.

I recounted my interrupted dream, which I loved immediately. After all, it was my first creation following a week of relative inaction and medicated sleep. I realized from the look on my doctor's face that she was trying to decide whether to release me or call for a psychiatric consult. Finally she said simply, "You have the most unusual dreams. I don't have dreams like that."

Maybe she does, and doesn't remember them. Maybe she's right; she doesn't. But she could. When we become more involved in our own dreamwork, we recall more dreams. As we have more varied life experiences, so, too, do our dream symbols expand and take on richer meanings.

I, for instance, cannot recall, and cannot find in my dream log, which I have been keeping since 1977, a dream about snakes. Yet when I began reading about Greek incubation dreams for this book—and discovered the healing meaning of snakes related to those dreams—I, too, dreamed about snakes.

It was as if my inner dream director, whom I'm sure is French, said, "*Mon Dieu. Mais oui. My, God. Yes, of course.* Now that I know what snakes are all about, I certainly don't want you to be left out of this healing experience. Snakes! Can we have snakes on the dream set? *Immédiatement. Immediately.*"[1]

Whether or not you read that same material, your dream snakes will act differently from mine, as will your cast of characters, depending on your *own* experiences. So what are you and I to do with our respective snake dreams, then? What sense are we to make of them when we look up "snake" in our dream dictionary?

Most of us have been led to believe that each symbol in our dream represents a *thing*—or worse, a prediction—but, in fact, that group of symbols comprising a dream tells part of the tale of our inner striving toward self-development and fulfillment. Not only does a single symbol, even a single dream, represent only one aspect of that story, but it also may have several levels of interpretation.

Dreams show us our conflicts and ways to resolve them; they chronicle our inner strivings. This book, or certainly this chapter, might well have been titled "To dream, perchance to awaken," because of the potential for insight or enlightenment that dreams have to offer.

Dreams can nudge us toward a question that needs to be faced or answered in our conscious life, or a growth direction that needs to be respected. Psychologist and dream expert

---

[1]You'll meet your own inner dream director in Chapter 3.

Patricia Garfield refers to our dream figures as "momentary crystallizations" of life energy.[2] Each dream can be considered a "healing" dream, as well as an inspiration or revelation.

Although writing from the doctor/patient perspective, psychoanalysts Edward Tauber and Maurice Green believe that a dream understanding is not complete until it introduces a new perception, one that liberates our inhibited learning potential and increases spontaneity. Likewise, Jungian analysts Edward Whitmont and Sylvia Perera write that a dream is not fully understood until it casts light on a blind spot, or challenges a one-sided, rigid position.

Psychiatrist Robert Langs believes that when you "decode" a dream, you will always find out something significant—something you weren't consciously aware of—about a waking-life event or situation. Little wonder, then, that Clarissa Pinkola Estés calls them "teaching images."[3]

In my 28 years of practice as a psychotherapist, I have worked with my own dreams and those of others. They are all in some ways similar, which allows me some good guesses about how to get started, and yet, in the end, each is unique, as an individual's personal symbolism becomes comprehensible.

Cloud Nine: A Dreamer's Dictionary helps you make some good starting guesses on your own. It contains guidelines and questions that allow you to participate more fully in understanding your own dream productions or in identifying your growth tasks. Its definitions and dreamwork techniques—dreamercises, I call them—will help you use common or universal ideas as a guide for unscrambling your own inner ciphers.

---

[2]Patricia Garfield, *Pathways to Ecstasy: The Way of the Dream Mandala,* p. 219.

[3]Clarissa Pinkola Estés, *Women Who Run With the Wolves,* p. 458.

HOW TO MAKE THE MOST OF THIS BOOK

Like physical exercise, the dreamercises included in each chapter help you "shape up" your dreamwork skills. They enhance your own dreaming shorthand, so you can make the invisible map of your inner geography visible.

Your goal in any dreamwork is to be able to ultimately answer the questions:

- What is happening within me that is reflected by this dream?
- What do I need to know to take the next step in my growth?

You may need to use more than one dreamercise to arrive at a satisfactory answer to these questions. Since some techniques work better for certain dreams, such as puzzling or scary dreams, than others, you probably won't use the same technique for every dream. You'll also acquire favorite dreamercises—or, more likely, a combination—that consistently work well for you.

Most days you probably won't have time to work with your dream before daily responsibilities pull you away, a good reason for keeping a dream diary or journal. By the end of a hectic day, your dream may be only a vague wisp, if remembered at all. So acquire the habit of writing down your dreams before your busy day begins. Even dream fragments, or "dreamlets," as the Rev. Jeremy Taylor describes them, can provide insight.[4]

Dreamercise #1 gets you started working with your dreams by giving suggestions for keeping a dream journal.

Although some people prefer to record their dreams on cassettes, most dreamwork techniques involve working with

---

[4]Taylor believes dream fragments are often condensed versions of our night's dreaming edited to make "as economic and clear a symbolic statement as possible" (*Dreamwork,* p. 63).

one or more dreams over a period of time, so ultimately writing them down is the better approach.

KEEPING A DREAM JOURNAL

1. *Write your dreams first thing in the morning before getting out of bed.* Even a sketchy outline is better than nothing. Sometimes it's easier to remember the dream if you write while still lying in your dreaming position. Or you may want to sit up slowly, keeping your eyes closed to help you recall the dream. I use a pad of paper that eventually can be three-hole punched and inserted in a notebook.
2. *Keep paper and pen beside your bed.* Making this effort will also help you remember your dreams. Keep your paper or notebook within reach, so you don't have to make large movements to begin recording your dream, and so you can easily roll back into your dreaming position, if necessary, to help your recall. Some people keep a small flashlight beside their bed, or use pens that light in the dark to record dreams during the night.[5]
3. *Before you retire, start a new page, and make some notes* about the day's activities, your actions, state of mind, feelings related to the day, and any issues or situations troubling you.

[5]You can order such a pen, called the Night Writer, from Magellan's, P.O. Box 5485, Santa Barbara, CA 93150-5485, 1-800-962-4943, or Reliable Home Office, P.O. Box 804117, Chicago, IL 60680-9968, 1-800-869-6000.

4. *Write the dream in the present tense as if you were having it as you write.* (In recording my **Chicken Farmer** dream, I wrote "I am merging" not "I was merging.") Describe the setting or scene fully. Include all the characters' actions, the sights, sounds, colors, odors, and tastes. Be sure to include the dominant emotion, or the sequence of emotions, that you felt during the dream.
5. *Date each dream and give it a title,* as in my **Chicken Farmer** dream. This allows you to refer to it easily in future work.
6. *On a separate page, or the back of the same page, write:*
   - how you felt on awakening from the dream
   - how you feel after writing the dream
   - any fantasies the dream stimulates
   - waking-life experiences to which you think the dream relates
7. *Summarize the theme of the dream in a catchy phrase or a sentence or two.*
8. *During the day, think about the fact that you are now keeping a dream journal and remind yourself that you value and will remember your dreams.* Repeat this intention several times before going to sleep each night.

Don't worry if you don't remember a dream right away. Preparing your recording materials before retiring and writing anything you can remember (a fragment or a feeling about a dream) helps you get used to writing dream memories. Scheduling a regular time to work on your dreams by yourself or with others—and knowing that appointment is coming up—is another way to help you remember your dreams. Dreamercise #13, Chapter 3, offers you a remembering ritual you can use. Eventually your dream mind will get the idea that you *do* want to listen to it.

Some people like to have their dreams together in their notebook, so they can read through them sequentially, uninterrupted by artworks or other creations stimulated by their dreams. This has the advantage of later letting you review your dreams over a period of time without distraction (see Dreamercise #15—Dream Flow). If you like this idea, then, in addition to the dream log itself, you may wish to create extra sections in your notebook where you record any subsequent meditations, art, or other productions related to your dream.

You may prefer, however, to have supplemental dreamwork creations follow the dreams that stimulated them. If so, using a notebook binder rather than a bound volume lets you insert dreamwork creations without having to guess how many pages to leave blank.

Although we'll work with nightmares later in this chapter, and again in Chapter 5, at least one study has shown that the very act of regularly writing down nightmares reduces their frequency of occurrence. Psychologist Alan Siegel believes that keeping a dream journal for just two weeks during times of crisis or transition—and identifying feelings, conflicts, and solutions—can help you understand and resolve the emotions stimulated by the crisis situation.

Ira Progoff, a former student of Jung's, once called life an "artwork unfolding." This is akin to Jung's idea of individuation, which refers to the lifelong process of each of us becoming the complete person we were born to be. A dream journal is part of the record of your personal unfoldment. As Canadian analyst Marion Woodman says, "We're not here just to eat and sleep. There is a glory to be expressed."[6]

When you're ready to work on a dream that you've written down, follow the beginning technique outlined in Dreamercise #2. It shows you how to identify images and how to use both your personal associations and the dictionary in Part

---

[6]In an interview with Tami Simon for the Sounds True Recording *Language of the Soul* (see Bibliography).

2 to understand your dreams. Read through the entire dreamercise before you begin your work.

DELVING INTO YOUR DREAM IMAGES

1. Draw a line down the center of a notebook page.
2. In the left column write the first image of your dream. Locations and actions occurring within the dream are considered dream images, as are sensory experiences. A smell or taste, words or noises, feelings or sensations, are all images we can explore for insight.

   In my **Chicken Farmer** dream there are four images: the *action* of merging, the *person* of the chicken farmer, my *feeling* of puzzlement, and *me* (called the "dream ego").

   Alternately, you may wish to begin your work with the image that seems the most important or significant and then continue with other images as they appeal to you. Dr. Lillie Weiss likes to start with the image that is the most incongruous or makes the least sense.
3. In the right column across from the image, record any recent (within the last day or two) thoughts, experiences, or concerns that may have influenced or triggered the dream content, and, following that, any personal past experiences related to it. It may be one or several things; don't limit yourself.
4. Then record any thoughts or ideas you have about what this image may refer to, or mean. If you get stuck, it might be helpful to use one

of Dr. Gayle Delaney's questions and ask yourself, "What is a . . . ?" In my dream, for instance, "What is a chicken farmer?"

5. For further ideas, consult Part 2 dream dictionary entries regarding your particular image. If they don't connect or stimulate you, don't worry. Don't feel you have to use them. Stick with your own ideas.
6. Record any other words or themes—secondary symbols—that now occur to you.
7. Write a brief first statement of what you think your image could mean; who it might represent or how it could be present or active in your waking life.
8. Record any personal experiences related to your secondary symbols, as well as any feelings that now emerge about the dream image.
9. Continue with the second, or next, image. Work in the same way with each dream image, either in its order of appearance or its importance to you.
10. Don't forget to consider any obviously missing or implied images. (In the **Chicken Farmer** dream, the farm and the flock of chickens were implied, but did not actually appear in the dream.) Add your personal references to them and look up possible ideas about their meanings in Part 2.
11. When you have followed items 2–10 above for each image, you should be able to answer one of the following questions:
    - What does my dream director want me to know through this dream?
    - Or, what inner process is this dream expressing?[7]

---

[7]For a continuation of my work with the **Chicken Farmer** dream, see Endnotes at the close of this chapter.

- Or, what issues in my life is this dream directing me to consider?

As you go through your ideas about each image, one of them will connect more than others. It will feel right to you. Jungian analyst Robert Johnson says it "clicks." Psychologist Ann Faraday applies the "tingle test," and for the ever-poetic Jeremy Taylor, it is the "wordless rightness." When you finally connect with the meaning of a dream—your "aha" experience—it will likely be a "moment of wholeness, which serves as a tuning fork of inner reality."[8]

Trust it. If you wait for it and don't force yourself into a reasoning or interpretation you *think* makes sense, your body will teach you your own inner signal that says you have touched an intuitive truth.

If you are satisfied with your dream understanding, and want to acknowledge your dream material in additional ways, select one of the dreamercises from Chapter 6 to pursue, probably later.

If you think there is still more this dream is trying to convey—and you will soon learn to recognize your own body signals that indicate whether you are satisfied or still unresolved—use Dreamercise #3 later in this chapter, or select one of the dreamercises from later chapters and apply it to your dream.

After that, if you still don't have a sense of resolution, put the dream aside for a while. It will percolate in your psyche, and clues or meanings will become apparent in your waking state or through subsequent dreams. If your inner guidance is trying to tell you more, you will have another, related dream. Jeremy Taylor calls this the "self-correcting" process of dreams.

Even if you do arrive at a satisfactory understanding of your dream, don't be surprised if days, months, or even years later, you return to a memorable dream with new or richer associations. This reflects your inner growth. Symbols are

[8]Marion Woodman, *Language of the Soul,* Sounds True Recording.

multilayered, and as we grow or acquire more knowledge, the same symbol can take on enhanced meaning. This is especially true as you learn more about archetypes (**ar**-ki-types)—universal symbols—or symbols from another time or culture. It was not uncommon for Carl Jung to reflect on the same dream for years, amplifying and expanding its meaning as he gained more life experience.

Above all, don't worry. Lighten up. Dream time is fun time. The clichés and puns of your dreams show you at your cleverest. Who but you could come up with such precise personal puns, and who else could so succinctly express those messages? Appreciate yourself; enjoy your unfolding. You have plenty of dreams to play with, learn from, grow by.

AN INNER CAST OF THOUSANDS OR MERELY A SMALL PANTHEON?

The fact that dream dictionaries tend to give the erroneous impression that objects, and sometimes even people, in our dreams are things with one definite, often predictive, meaning stems, in part, from the tradition of early dream manuals and also from daily life wherein objects appear to be immobile, even though physicists tell us differently. The idea also evolved from early Freudian concepts wherein dreams were expressions of repressed sexual instincts. Therefore, any elongated dream object was considered a phallic or masculine symbol; and objects that were round or could contain other objects were disguises for the womb, especially one's mother's womb.

More accurately, we can liken the images and messages in our dreams to an elegantly sprawling spiral staircase, which seems to go forward as much as it spirals upward. The dream story frequently has more than one "level" of meaning. We take our steps; do our dreamwork. At each turn of the spiral, a different view, a new vista of understanding, rises to meet us. We may have to stop awhile and catch our mental breath before proceeding; but ultimately we arrive at an expanded perspective and understanding.

To aid in identifying the multiple-levels of a dream, it is often useful to identify all the characters *and* objects in our dreams as representing different aspects of our inner self. After all, you—or that part of you we're calling your "dream director"—created the dream. Most of us recognize the idea of differing aspects of ourself when we say, in reflection or conversation, "Part of me wants to do that, but part of me doesn't."

Early Egyptian priests, searching for an explanation of nature's forces, personified natural happenings into gods responsible for their occurrence. The same god or goddess was given different aspects, sometimes different names, to express the unique qualities of a particular village or region. While this made it seem as if there was a multitude of gods, most of them were only varied aspects of a small pantheon. Similarly, within the Jungian concept of the Self (wholeness) are many archetypes, which may manifest, or become active, at different times in our daily life and behavior.

Whatever words we use to identify our own cast of characters, when taken together, they, too, comprise our inner state of being, our own small pantheon. Often it is easier to understand our psychological processes if we temporarily personify them and imagine that we have an "inner child," or an "inner mother," and that we can talk to each of them as if they were separate characters waiting backstage for their cues.

For instance, I have an "inner writer," who sometimes resembles Moses carrying the tablets of the Ten Commandments. When I asked him, in inner dialogue, if he really looked like Moses, he replied, "No, but you wouldn't pay attention if I didn't appear this way." Apparently there was no other way at the time that I could so succinctly convey pomp, primal authority, someone I wouldn't dare refuse to listen to, powerful writing, and good editing.

We all use symbolic shorthand to express ideas and processes we can't grasp fully, or explain with mere words. Note, for instance, in Endnote A at the end of this chapter, the number of words it takes for me to explain my **Chicken Farmer** dream compared to the conciseness of the dream images themselves.

Frederick "Fritz" Perls, the father of Gestalt therapy, thought each image in the dream represents an aspect of ourselves that we fail to acknowledge or recognize. By taking its viewpoint, by speaking its message in the present tense, we begin to reclaim it as a part of ourself and express it more appropriately.[9]

We reactivate and personify the image's energy within us so we can utilize it rather than be distressed by it, or deny its existence. As we recognize it as part of our personality, we become a more wholly—and perhaps, holy—integrated person. For psychologist Ernest Rossi, dream objects that are unique, odd, or idiosyncratic express the "growing edge" of our individuality, "the raw material out of which new patterns of awareness may develop."[10]

To begin to reincorporate a dream symbol's energy or process into your waking life, use the following technique adapted from Gestalt therapy.

GIVING YOUR DREAM SYMBOLS THEIR VOICE

Close your eyes and reenter the dream experience. One by one you are going to become one or more objects or characters in your dream.

Speaking in the present tense, describe or introduce yourself, say what your function in the dream is or for the dreamer, and then add anything else that comes to mind. Finally, say what is good and what is bad about being that object/character, and what it wants more than anything else.

It is better to speak aloud than to just "think" the statements in your mind, because sometimes

---

[9] Throughout this book the information about Fritz Perls's dreamwork was taken from my observations of Perls at work, as well as Fagan and Shepherd's *Gestalt Therapy Now* and Perls's *Gestalt Therapy Verbatim* (Moab, Utah: Real People Press, 1969).

[10] E. L. Rossi, *Dreams and the Growth of Personality,* pp. 25, 190.

the act of hearing your own words spoken aloud facilitates insight. You might want to record your work to listen to later.

For example, in the dream reported at the beginning of the chapter, you might first become "the house." Begin speaking by saying, "I am the house. I am two-storied and I have 12 rooms . . . [or whatever it takes to describe *your* dream house]. My function is . . ." Continue until your inner house has said everything it has to say. Then finish: "What's good about being a house is . . . What's bad about being a house is . . . As a house, what I want more than anything else is . . ."

Then become "the guy": "I am the guy. I look like your brother, except that I have more hair and I do not wear as nice clothes as he does. I am here to help you understand your . . ."

Speak as significant dream *objects* first before speaking as your dream characters. (Perls believed that inanimate objects represent the most alienated parts of ourselves.) Then speak as any threatening figures or characters. Be sure to speak also as any wounded persons, missing or wounded body parts, or damaged objects in the dream.

To give you an example of the process: In June 1993 as I was preparing to go to the annual conference of the Association for the Study of Dreams, I had the following dream that I worked on in a variety of ways during the conference.

Lina/Katharine

I am sitting at a round oak table that belonged to my friend Lina when we were in graduate school together, and in the dream, still belongs to her. I am delighted to be at this table again and to see that it still exists. Its presence evokes many memories, which I simply know and feel are a part of me without having to elucidate them. Also at the table are Lina, the actor Michael

Douglas, and a woman whom I cannot quite see. [She is in shadows and represents my shadow.] Michael calls Lina by the name of Katharine. I look more closely and realize that when she has makeup on, she is, in fact, Katharine Hepburn. I am so astonished that I know who Katharine Hepburn really is when she's not acting, and that I have known her for more than 30 years, that I hear very little of what Michael is saying.

I had such emotion about being at that particular table again, [clearly, it lives inside me] that I chose to speak first as the table:

I am the oak table. I am round, old, well used, and cherished. My function is service. Lots of important interactions have occurred around me. Many people have learned new things sitting around me. I have facilitated much pleasure and fun, as well as seriousness. I am here to show you that existence is more than the role you play. It is knowing the character behind the character.

Over time the other characters in the dream had their say also.

Instead of starting with the description, my friend Betty Yenetchi prefers to ask herself, "What would I be saying to myself if I were" . . . a house . . . a waterfall . . . or whatever? Or "What am I trying to say to myself by being" . . . a house . . . a guy . . . etc.?

Not every dream merits the thorough scrutiny of Dreamercise #3, but for those oh, so elusive ones, well, peek behind the curtains of your dream theater and get acquainted with that cast member waiting in the wings to be noticed.

Dreamercise #4 offers you another, shorter peek behind the curtain.

WHOSE DREAM IS IT, ANYWAY?

1. Tell your dream aloud in the present tense, noting how you feel, associated thoughts that occur, and any body sensations you experience while you are speaking.
2. Now tell your dream again from the perspective of another character (or object if there are no other characters). Notice how your feelings, associations, and body sensations change.
3. When you change character, how do "you" appear through the eyes of that "other" character or object?
4. Does this change your understanding of the dream?

And now, maestro, a little dream music, if you please, while we continue our progress toward becoming card-carrying oneirophiliacs (o-**nye**-row-phil-ee-acts), lovers of dreams. Psst, *your* card is on the last page of this book.

ENDNOTES

My associations to the chicken farmer are: hick, earthy (me? I am a Virgo), real father [my father was a chicken farmer in Oklahoma during my teens], inner father.

Turning to my dictionary, I find that the entry **farm(er)** suggests the dream may refer to nurturing, cultivating aspects of myself, to cycles, and to an archetypal theme. The magical "merging" confirms this dream has an archetypal/mythological theme.

I need to acknowledge and utilize both my masculine (animus) and feminine (me) aspects, to enhance healing, which the dream is telling me is both my foremost physical and psychological task. I was, after all, sent here because this chicken farmer really needs me. Perhaps my inner father needs some attention before my flock appears.

Jungians might say the hospital experience has activated my father complex. I tend to operate in a forceful (animus) way for my projects, so I think the dream also was saying that I must modify that behavior to heal. Prior to surgery I had been told that within a week I would be able to work at the computer. In fact, I had neither the stamina to do so, nor the ability to sit upright without pain.

Being puzzled = being blocked, resisting the dream message = not seeing other alternatives?

I realize the male and female in this dream also represent my experiences with the wonderful and creative husband-and-wife team of clinical hypnotherapists, Dr. Norma and Phil Barretta, with whom I worked preparing for surgery.

Although our work together focused on surviving the surgery, and subsequent comfort and healing, one of Norma's hypnotic suggestions was that I would find some way to write about my hospital experience. So it's appropriate they should be central in my first drug-free dream.

If I can be as flexible (merging) as they are and draw on all my experiences and resources, as they did in our work together, I, too, can heal, physically and psychologically, and have a flock of successful ideas. This insight fills me with a surge of energy. It clicks.

As a therapist originally trained in Freudian concepts, I would be remiss, however, if I didn't point out that the dream also relates to "transference," which means transferring onto the therapist feelings derived from earlier, infantile feelings/wishes about family members, especially parents.

The dream says that I wish to occupy the same space as the chicken farmer, now identified as therapists Phil and Norma. In the Freudian view, most dreams are regressive, so the dream expresses the combined wishes to have sex with father Phil and to nurse at the breast of mother Norma. Of course, this relates to childhood wishes regarding my real parents. Although I am consciously ready to leave the hospital, my dream expresses a desire to be "nursed" longer.

The preceding are examples of some of the multilevel meanings a dream can have.

ANNOTATED REFERENCES

I regard Cloud Nine *as a handbook of resources for dreamers, each chapter of Part 1 containing information, dreamercises, and at its end, several annotated references you can consult for additional help or information.*

Garfield, Patricia. *Creative Dreaming*. New York: Simon and Schuster, 1974.

No one has done as much to make dreamwork popular as Dr. Garfield, one of the cofounders in 1983 of the Association for the Study of Dreams. In this, her first book, Garfield introduces the techniques of the Senoi dreamers (a primitive Malaysian tribe first studied by Kilton Stewart), and teaches how to develop dream control through lucid dreaming.

Although Stewart's work was later called into question—specifically, that some of his claims were exaggerated and reflected his theories rather than the Senoi—many of the techniques for confronting dream figures presented in *Creative Dreaming* are still appropriate. And the Senoi/Stewart technique for bringing dreams into daily life and honoring them has been adopted and modified by subsequent dreamworkers. We will learn some of these modifications in Chapter 5.

Reed, Henry. *Dream Solutions. Using Your Dreams to Change Your Life*. San Rafael, Calif.: New World Library, 1991.

In this workbook, Dr. Reed, a psychologist, guides the reader to focus on a problem or question and then develop and test a solution by actively working with the dreams that occur during a 28-day period.

After recording dreams for seven nights, the dreamer spends one study evening working in a variety of specific ways on those dreams, arriving at a "best guess" dream contract to test during the next week of dreams. Reed works with one of his own dreams and shows how much mileage he can get out of an initial 32-word dream.

A dream which is not explained
is like a letter which has
not been read.
THE TALMUD

CHAPTER 2

Last Night I Had the Craziest Dream

Perhaps from our human beginning, certainly from the beginning of recorded time, we have regarded dreams and dreaming as special. When we no longer believed the gods had to be appeased for our dreams, we developed superstitions about them, often contradictory, in an effort to control their effects.

"*Never tell a dream till you've broken your [break]fast,*" but "*To come true, a dream must be told before breakfast.*" "*To dream of things out of season is trouble without reason,*" but perhaps not if it's "*Friday night's dream on a Saturday told, is sure to come true if it's ever so old.*"

Although the more than 260 books on dreams in print today attest to our avid interest, it is not just "dream books" that tout dreams as important and influential. From ancient to modern times, dreams have been included in literature and have enhanced our enjoyment and helped us identify with characters. Indeed, Daphne du Maurier set the entire tone for *Rebecca* with her unforgettable beginning, "Last night I dreamt I went to Manderley again."

The gods brought dreams to the Greeks, so their literature abounds with the appearance of visionary dreams on the eve of battle. The Bible contains a number of dreams and visions—which many biblical scholars now believe to have been dreams—sent by God. Today Marion Woodman regards the dream as given by "the God within," the Jungian concept of the Self.

DREAMS AS A SECOND LANGUAGE

In comparing dreams to myths, Swiss psychiatrist Carl Jung regarded "dream thinking" as the survival of an ancient mode of thought. It employs figurative or metaphorical language to express thoughts, feelings, or concepts that, for societal or personal reasons, cannot be expressed openly.

Erich Fromm called the language of dreams, myths, and fairy tales the one "universal language" we humans have ever developed, being largely the same throughout history and between cultures, with a few variations, which he called "symbolic dialects."

Ignoring the logic of time and space, symbolic language speaks of our inner experiences as if they were sensory experiences (events in the outer world). The ruling categories, according to Fromm, are intensity and association. Events are related to one another not by waking logic but by their "association with the same inner experience."[1] Psychoanalyst Montague Ullman calls dreams "metaphors in motion" and suggests we speak of dream *appreciation* rather than dream interpretation.

What the poet Bruce Vance refers to as the "laws of the dreamscape," psychologists would call "primary process" thinking. Ideas and thoughts are represented by allusion, puns and other wordplay, by rhymes, and by being presented as the opposite of the real concept they are dealing with. They are presented as pictures rather than sentences. Pairs of opposites may be synthesized into one symbol containing both its positive and negative potentialities—Jung called this the "transcendent function" of a symbol.

In an interview for Sounds True Recordings, Jungian analyst Clarissa Pinkola Estés, author of *Women Who Run With the Wolves*, poetically refers to dreams as coming from the

---

[1]Erich Fromm, *The Forgotten Language,* p. 23.

''Riddle Mother,'' who gives us answers in the form of cryptic puzzles to unravel.

To understand our dream metaphors, and to unravel their riddles, we must listen with what psychoanalyst Theodor Reik called our ''third ear,'' an inner voice usually drowned out by conscious thought. When we sharpen our inner acuity and increase our readiness to ''hear,'' we begin to become literate in ''dream-speak.'' We become an initiate in the ways of the Riddle Mother.

PIONEER DREAMWORKERS

Although the forerunner of all subsequent dream books, *The Oneirocritica*, was written in the second century A.D. by the Italian physician Artemidorus Daldianus, the theories of four 20th-century psychotherapists have heavily influenced contemporary dreamwork.

In 1900 Sigmund Freud (1856–1939) published *The Interpretation of Dreams* in an attempt to legitimize our nightly productions as worthy of ''scientific'' study. Although it is still in print today, the book was negatively received by medical reviewers, and ignored by readers. It took eight years to sell the first 600 copies.

Freud considered it his most important work. He revised and amplified it eight times, the last in 1930. Freud believed that all dreams derive from the unconscious, which was composed entirely of infantile sexual wishes incompatible with the conscious, or waking, self. Dreams are expressions of, or attempts to fulfill, repressed sexual wishes. Together with the day residue (recent waking-life happenings), those wishes form the *latent* content of the dream. Because of their societal unacceptability, they must be disguised or distorted—the mind deceiving itself.

According to Freud, dreams serve the dual purpose of allowing us to release or discharge the tension of repressed desires while protecting our conscious mind from their revelation through the *manifest* (actual, but censored and disguised) content of the dream. We create the disguise through various kinds of *symbol* formation, again ''primary process'' thinking as opposed to logical or "secondary" thinking. The most common of these are:

representation—An idea or concept becomes (is represented by) a visual symbol or action. Fear of failure might be expressed by the act of climbing up a hill but never making it to the top.

displacement—Occurring in every dream, it refers to the idea that minor issues/actions/feelings are emphasized in the manifest content, while the latent (repressed) content is only indistinctly represented. Having thus been successfully displaced, what seems to be the major issue in the dream may not be the real-life one.

condensation—Several images in the manifest content may represent one element or person in the latent content or in waking life; or one element of the manifest content may correspond to several elements of the latent content or waking life. (Remember the chicken farmer?) Condensation does not occur in every dream.

secondary elaboration or **revision**—This refers to how we give the dream continuity, how we put it together to form some kind of whole. It is the order that we impose on dreams, so they can be spoken or written.

According to Freudian theory, not every dream is sexual, nor is everything in the dream symbolic. Free association to the manifest content leads us to the latent dream wish, or content, derived largely from the day residue, and that allows us to *infer* the unconscious wish, since, by definition, the unconscious can never be really known. For this reason, psychoanalyst Walter Bonime prefers the term "interpretative hypothesis" rather than interpretation. I am indebted to Dr. Milton Kramer for pointing out that from the Freudian point of view, most modern dreamwork stops after identifying the latent dream thoughts.

Free association enables us to separate what is symbolic from useless daily impressions, thereby revealing the latent dream thoughts. From them, however, we can only make some guesses about the unconscious.

Contemporary psychoanalysts also see dreams as having a

problem-solving function through unconscious decision making. Psychiatrist Werner Mendel writes that dreams occurring after a conscious decision has been made can indicate whether a person has the "emotional means" or development to carry through the decision. For instance, a man consciously decides to confront his supervisor with his angry feelings, but dreams he is a little boy in short pants, shooting paper bullets.[2]

Dreamercise #5 gives you ideas for identifying key attributes of a dream, and for using free association and displacement, or reversals, to delve further into the dream. This and Dreamercise #6 are particularly useful for exploring puzzling or bizarre dreams.

BY THEIR ASSOCIATIONS SHALL YE KNOW THEM

- Write your dream, leaving about two inches of space between *each* sentence, so you can write your associations and insights. Or, as in Dreamercise #2, you can write the dream sentence on the left side of the page and your work on the right side.
- Begin with what you think is the least significant or important sentence, or concept, in the dream, and in the space below that sentence, write your associations (what comes to mind) as you think about it.[3] And what comes next? Where does that first association lead you? And where does the next

[2]Werner Mendel, "The Tactical Use of Dreams in Psychotherapy," pp. 336–337.

[3]For some it is easier to identify the nouns in the sentence and associate to those.

association lead you? Continue until you have a string of associations, probably more connected to one another than to the dream image.

After you have your own associations, look up symbols in the dictionary to see if they add to your understanding, and record that information if appropriate.

- Continue through the other sentences, arriving last at what you think is the most important sentence or concept in the dream.
- As you identify your associations, pay particular attention to those that finally take you to the distant past (childhood) and to those from the very recent past (from the residue of the previous day or the past week).

  How do these ideas connect? Is there a similar conflict, a similar pattern of behavior, or a similar theme? Ask yourself, "What had I not noticed before?" or "What did I miss paying attention to?" Ullman says we need to identify the past/present context so we can understand why we had a particular dream on a particular night and on no other.
- Group all the symbols or images into whatever and however many clusters seem to make sense to you. How do they connect? Where do they direct your thinking?
- Consider the least important action, image, or feeling in the dream. Magnify or reverse it. It might be helpful to put it in sentence form: "If I am doing . . . [state what you are doing in the dream], then I probably really am doing . . . [state the reverse]." Or "If I think the most important symbol in the dream is . . . [state it], then it probably really is . . . [state the reverse]." Does this trigger any new awareness?

- Do the same for the most important sentence, image, or feeling. For human characters ask yourself, "Who do I know who is not like . . . [state the dream character]?" "Who does not act like . . . [the dream character acted]?"
- Consider those dream images that seem particularly novel or unusual. Ask yourself, "How am I like you?" "What within me do you remind me of?"
- If you can't connect yourself to any of the people in the dream, or if they do not seem to make sense to you, reverse their sex and consider their activities as a person of the opposite sex. Does this relate to some aspect of you or to some experience?

Freud called dreams the "royal road to the unconscious"; that is, the pathway to uncovering and identifying those repressed infantile instincts/wishes we all have. So if you look for them, don't be alarmed if you find them. Join the human race.

Dreamercise #6 introduces you to the application of Freudian dream interpretation concepts of sexual symbolism, condensation, and wish fulfillment.

TRAVERSING THE ROYAL ROAD

Use these checkpoints for your own trip down the royal roadway:

- Write your dream, leaving about two inches

of space between each sentence where you will write your associations and insights.

- Be especially aware of any image that brings up a memory that is uncomfortable or embarrassing for you.
- Look for images that relate to taking things in (disguises for oral or feminine sexual impulses); circular/container items, openings, and receptacles (female/mother); and elongated items that may or may not fit into other items (male/father, male sexual impulses).
- Sticky, dirty, repugnant, "yucky" items or dark colors often represent anal impulses; looking at things or images difficult to see can represent voyeuristic impulses.
- Actions wherein you are moving up or down, as in stairs, elevators, or riding animals, often represent having sex. Children in dreams may represent your sexual organs. Losing hair, teeth, or other body parts may represent castration anxiety or punishment for masturbation.
- Consider that a single event in the dream or a single individual may, in fact, represent several occasions or people in waking life. Ask yourself, "If this dream person (or event) were to be divided or sliced like a pie, who else (or what else) in my waking life resembles some part of it?" Look for the commonalities in behavior, attitudes, and feelings.

Carl Jung (1875–1961) viewed the unconscious as self-regulating, emphasizing that dreams are compensatory or complementary. They are the unconscious mind's attempt to balance the ideas and perceptions of our conscious mind.

Dreams provide the psychic equilibrium necessary to create

growth toward wholeness, or individuation, by presenting opposite attitudes or concepts (compensatory function). Where our conscious view is too narrow, or we've ignored certain ideas or processes, the dream adds to and rounds out our viewpoint (complementary function). For Jungian analyst James A. Hall, dreams are a *commentary* from our unconscious. They speak about the state of our waking ego and serve to influence us to change our view of ourselves.

Since the dream expresses those unconscious workings that compensate for our conscious situation, for the dream to make full sense, we need always to consider that waking situation or attitude. Rather than ask "Why?" of a dream, the more important question, "What for?" helps us determine the excessive or inadequate conscious experiences for which compensation is necessary. As Jungian analyst Karen Signell writes, "Whatever is not fulfilled in conscious life becomes an unconscious petitioner at the door."[4]

The Jungian approach to dreams is one of deep respect for the guidance of the Self, that aspect of ourselves that others have referred to variously as the soul, the higher self, inner wisdom, or in Hawaiian Huna concepts, the *uhane*.

Jung likened many dreams to an inner drama, which can be broken down into a definite structure, or plot. Dreamercise #7 will help you do likewise with your own dreams.

THE PLAY'S THE THING

From a Jungian perspective, many dreams can often be divided into four phases. The first, *exposition*, includes a statement of place and the identification of the protagonists or dream characters.

The *plot* develops in the second phase. Complica-

[4]Karen Signell, *Wisdom of the Heart,* p. 272.

tions occur; tension develops between the characters. During *culmination*, the third phase, something decisive happens or changes occur; the action turns.

The fourth phase is the *result*—Jung called it the *"lysis"*—the solution sought by the dreamer. It says, "This is where the energy is trying to go."[5]

- Choose a dream and review it from the point of view of a stage play or film. How would you break it down into its four parts? Is anything missing? What is the next step; where is your inner energy trying to go? If you had to make a guess, for what conscious attitude do you think this dream compensates?
- What is the theme or dilemma of this play? Rosalind Cartwright clarifies the dream theme (see *Crisis Dreaming* in the Bibliography) by identifying the adjectives we use to describe dream scenes and adding their opposites. She calls these opposite pairs "dream dimensions," opposing qualities that reflect the way we organize our perceptions. To arrive at your dream dimensions, consider each adjective in your dream and ask yourself what is its opposite.

  Some common dream dimensions/dilemmas delineated by Cartwright, Calvin Hall, and Montague Ullman include: authentic/false, old/young, right/wrong, active/passive, defiant/compliant (or obedient), independent or self-reliant/dependent, adequate/inadequate, freedom/security, closeness (or intimacy)/keeping our distance (or abandonment), self-definition/defined by others, being/having, trust/betrayal, generous/stingy, giving/withholding, male/female, life/death, good/bad, love/hate, and obese/slender.

[5]C. G. Jung, *Dreams*, pp. 80–81.

Cartwright suggests you review past dreams, making a list of your dream dimensions, especially those you've used more than three times. Then observe how and when they express themselves in future dreams.

- What is the action taking place in the dream, and what role, or part, do you play in that action?
- Can you now identify more clearly a conscious attitude for which the dream is compensating or attempting to balance?

If you have trouble identifying the theme, action, or plot of your dream, use a trick I employ in psychotherapy to help a client achieve insight: Tell or write the dream as if it were a story happening to someone else ("There was this woman who was packing things for a move when . . .").

Jung believed that the unconscious was also the repository for timeless world knowledge or spirit—the primal source—which he called the "collective unconscious." Its contents are the "archetypes," qualities, principles, or patterns of instinctual behavior that exist in the collective psyches of the human race.

Archetypes determine our basic functioning as human beings. Each archetype is part of our vital inner energy and can be galvanized into action or expression. They are one of our connections to all humans, past and present, and suggest that psychically we are all not really so different after all. As expressions of universal human struggles and, therefore, of our universal self, archetypal dreams compensate for the one-sidedness of our personal lives and help us become whole persons, a process Jung called "individuation."

Archetypes are timeless and appear as primordial symbols or motifs not only in our dreams, but in art, religion, and myths. Like a master mental pattern, they connect us with all humanity. Although ancient, they are still alive in our psyches; and we, too, can locate ourselves in myth (or in the

Tarot cards, which some consider a systematic form for organizing archetypes).

Although "pure" archetypal dreams are rare, there is often an archetypal element in even "small" dreams. For instance, if you dream about your father, at a more profound level, which you may not understand until later, you are also dreaming about your relationship to the archetypal father, the Wise Old Man.

The more you understand, accept, and utilize dream material in your waking life, the closer you come to the archetypal world, which Marion Woodman says is where the real healing occurs. Dreams that are quite detailed most often relate to our personal world, while pure archetypal dreams usually are characterized by sparse details and simple images, although not necessarily.

"Big" or numinous dreams come from the collective unconscious. Jungian psychiatrist Lionel Corbett describes them as having an uncanny, fascinating, and awesome quality, often making it clear we are part of something larger than ourselves. They cannot be analyzed, only experienced intensely. Hard to ignore, the numinous dream often alters, dramatically and unquestionably, some part of our belief system.

To recognize archetypal thinking in your dreams, review them for the elements listed in Dreamercise #8.

BIGGER THAN LIFE

1. Look for an expression of one or more of the four basic archetypes in every dream. They are the dream ego, the shadow, the anima (for males) or animus (for females), and the Self. See the dream dictionary, Part 2, for an elaboration of these concepts.

2. Other archetypal figures or "image guides" that often appear in dreams are the Cosmic Christ (not Jesus, but the principles he and other historical religious leaders stood for), the devil, the trickster, the hero/prince, and the heroine/princess/maiden.
3. The archetypal mother figure can appear in many versions, which include Mother Earth, the Great or primordial Mother, the mystic mother, the Madonna, the Black Madonna, the Wise Old Woman (priestess, witch, sorceress, crone), and the terrible, devouring mother. She can appear in the guise of any female wisdom/healing figure, such as teacher/professor, grandmother, judge, queen.
4. Versions of the archetypal father/wisdom figure include: the Wise Old Man, the chief or warrior, the priest; the magician, the mighty ruler, the wanderer, the hermit. This archetype can appear in the guise of any male authority/wisdom figure, such as priest, minister, doctor, tribal elder, grandfather, king.
5. Archetypal child figures include the child hero, the divine child, the wonder child, the magnificent child, the eternal boy (representing spontaneity and freedom).
6. Certain actions, themes, or motifs, as mythologists call them, are also considered archetypal. They include:
    a. death/rebirth
    b. the night sea journey, which is linked to the death/rebirth motif. In mythology it is sometimes called the whale-dragon myth (Remember Jonah and the whale?), and represents the process of depression or confusion, which directs us to pay attention to unconscious material and to become whole.

c. the Golden Age or lost paradise
d. the battle of opposites
e. the wishing tree or well
f. the hidden treasure
g. the walled garden
h. the World Axis, World Tree, or World Mountain
i. the mandala

7. Magical, heroic, mythical, royal, and divine characters in dreams usually represent archetypal patterns, but they also can be expressed through quite simple characters who have great insight. Archetypal patterns are sometimes represented through unknown persons who have great significance or prominence in the dream (if the same sex of the dreamer = the shadow; if the opposite sex = the anima or animus), certain geometric patterns (especially circles and squares), and certain numbers, especially one, two, three, and four.
8. Look for mythical themes in dreams where people/objects behave in impossible ways: People change shapes or merge into other people/objects; animals become other animals; people become animals; animals become people; inanimate objects/animals speak and behave with the abilities of human beings.
9. All archetypal constellations are bipolar. They have both positive and negative meanings.

Oftentimes we do not recognize the archetypal structure expressing itself until we consider a number of dreams over a period of time (see Dreamercise #15—Dream Flow) and can see the repetition, development or expansion, or return to simplicity of a geometric pattern or a person—all the more reason why we should keep track of our dreams (Dreamercise

#1) and become familiar with our personal dream vocabulary (Dreamercise #14).

Another important Jungian concept is synchronicity, the match of outer and inner conditions. With respect to dreams this means that something that occurs in the dream also occurs the next day, or soon after the dreaming. However, Jung's concept of synchronicity is different from foresight or prediction.

Synchronicity between dream and reality usually occurs in association with situations in which archetypal powers or patterns have been activated; the inner energy of the dream tends to appear in outer reality. Synchronistic happenings are, thus, another clue to the archetypal nature of the dream. If we attend to them, we may gain a new insight about our inner state, or reaffirm the dream message.

Unlike Freud's idea of association wherein the dream image was the first idea and your associations led you along a train of ideas, Jung believed that all associations to a dream image should refer to the original image rather than be chained to one another. Ideas, especially mythical ones, that others had about a particular image might also be helpful in understanding a dream or its images. The process of enlarging a dream image through material gathered from folklore, mythology, or religious symbology, Jung termed "symbol amplification." It is one of his many unique contributions to dreamwork. Dreamercise #9 will help you use it with your dreams.

IMAGE AMPLIFICATION

1. Start with what you think is the most important image in your dream. Explore and expand its meaning by writing down as many personal associations as you can to that particular

image. Then add associations determined by your culture. Don't look in the dream dictionary at this point.

2. Don't build on your associations (create a list of associations, each chained to the one preceding it) as in Freud's free association. Rather, return to the original image each time you finish a previous association until you have a list of associations that exhausts your knowledge and attitudes about that image.
3. Continue with each image or action, or cluster of images/actions, in the dream.
4. Now begin to expand your knowledge about each image by looking in the dream dictionary and in mythology or folklore anthologies.[6]
5. What story does all this tell you about your life, or a current waking situation or relationship?
6. Consider most important the material/associations from your personal history, then consider associations or knowledge that is unique to your culture. Finally, consider mythological and archetypal meanings.
7. Over time, observe how this expanded symbology appears in subsequent dreams, and eventually select these dreams to work on as a series (as in Dreamercise #15—Dream Flow).

---

[6]For instance, *Funk & Wagnalls Standard Dictionary of Folklore, Mythology, and Legend;* Barbara Walker's *The Woman's Encyclopedia of Myths and Secrets;* almost any of Joseph Campbell's or Mircea Eliade's books on mythology in general, and books specific to the mythology of different cultures that attract or have meaning for you.

HISTORIC DREAMWORKERS

A forefather of what is now called *cognitive therapy,* Alfred Adler (1870–1937) had a goal-oriented psychiatric approach. Although he was not particularly interested in dreams (he once wrote: "Very courageous people dream rarely, for they deal adequately with their situation in the daytime"[7]), his approach was to consider how the dream applied to the dreamer's goals, daily life, and "lifestyle" (defined in Adlerian terms as a unifying pattern or construct that governs the direction of our behavior). The more our goals agree with reality, and the more we have fulfilled our infantile claims or desires for power, the less we will dream.

Since dreams serve to support our lifestyle and to justify goals within that lifestyle, Adler's interest was directed toward the role of the dreamer. Was he or she the action taker or the victim, the main character or an observer? How is it with your own dreams?

The Adlerian approach to dream interpretation also guides dreamers to become more conscious of their motivations, and of the private logic (cognitive/perceptual distortions) that blocks goal achievement and interferes with interpersonal relationships. Dreams produce the pictures that arouse the feelings and emotions we need for solving our problems.

Because dreams represent unfinished business, we continue to wrestle with our waking preoccupations during dreams. It is, therefore, important in the Adlerian approach, as well as in others, to know what happened during the day prior to the dream. (Remember the "day residue"?)

After Jung, rebel psychoanalyst Karen Horney (1885–1952) was one of the first contemporary therapists to purport that we are everyone and everything in our dream. Horney (**Horn**-eye) saw dreams as "giving voice to our strivings,"[8] and as our attempts to resolve conflicts in either healthy or unhealthy ways. She categorized people's behavior as moving toward

---

[7]H. and L. Ansbacher, *The Individual Psychology of Alfred Adler,* p. 359.

[8]Karen Horney, *Self-Analysis,* p. 178.

others, moving away from, and moving against, which actions can be identified in our dreams.

If we connect our dreams with the situations that provoked them, we can identify the kinds of experiences that represent a threat to us. For Horney, dreams express our wish or search for a solution. They are our creative efforts to capture the essence of "previously unspoken or inexpressible aspects of ourselves."[9]

Psychiatrist Fritz Perls (1894–1970) believed that each of the components of our dreams represents "projections," aspects of ourself that we have "cast out" and refuse to identify as parts of ourself. For us to become whole, they must once again be reclaimed and assimilated into conscious awareness.

Use Dreamercise #10 to reacquaint yourself with parts of yourself just waiting for their chance onstage. It is especially helpful in identifying personal symbolism or puzzling images.

WE NEED TO TALK MORE

Choose an object, animal, or person from your dream that you want to understand more fully, and have a conversation with it. Or choose the most obvious or central image and begin with that, letting other images have their own voice later.

Your dialogue can be spoken—in which case you may want to record the experience for later—or written. If you choose to write the dialogue, allow it to unfold without judgment or censorship.

Some people like to dramatize the dialogue, just as if it were a scene from a play. If you do this, be sure to move from your cue spot to the one where

[9] S. Knapp, "Dreaming: Horney, Kelman, and Shainberg," p. 345.

the other character has to stand when you speak his/her part. Experiment with changing your posture and voice to fit the dream image, or re-creating some of its key physical movements. For instance, if the image is short and squatty, squat down and make yourself short. If it is lopsided, make yourself lopsided. Tighten or loosen muscles to fit the dream image.

In therapy sessions Fritz Perls used two chairs, and you can, too, if you like. Sit in the chair designated as yours when you speak as yourself. When you speak as the other, move into the second chair. Moving and changing body posture helps you bring into awareness more of the unconscious nature of this aspect of yourself. It also helps you break up any bodily posture or tension (what Reichian therapists call "body armor") associated with each role or aspect of yourself. In other words, it helps you express yourself more fully, so let yourself be animated.

Say anything you wish to the dream image—no more than two or three sentences at a time—and allow it a chance to respond before you speak again. Be sure to ask it to clarify anything you don't understand.

If your dream image is reluctant to speak to you, or belligerent, assure it that while you may have ignored it in the past, you really do want to get to know it now.[10] If it still refuses to speak to you, have a conversation with another image in your dream and return to this one later.

As you progress in the conversation, you may

[10] The more difficulty you have speaking as a particular character or object in your dream, the more you can be certain it is an alienated (or projected, or shadow) aspect of yourself. In *Gestalt Therapy Verbatim,* Perls gives a number of suggestions for becoming more sensitive to your own blocks.

want to ask your dream image some of the following questions, in your own words, of course:

- What do you represent within me?
- What do you want to show or tell me?
- How do you apply to my waking life?
- Do you help me move toward, away from, or against people?
- Why are you appearing in my dreams *now*?
- Why did you behave the way you did?
- Why haven't you appeared before?
- How can we work together better in the future?

Be alert to your feelings as you begin the dialogue. It is not unusual that during the dialogue you may experience some feelings of confusion, but not necessarily so. When a shift in feeling, a flush of understanding, occurs, that is a signal that you have begun to reintegrate into your psyche the cut-off energy behind this character or image.

Close your dialogue by thanking your dream image and adding any other closure appropriate for the "two" of you.

You can also talk to your dream process directly. For instance, if you have trouble remembering your dreams, Perls suggests you ask them, "Dreams, where are you?" or "Dreams, why are you avoiding me?" Likewise, you might ask your nightmares, "Dreams, why are you trying to frighten me?"

Use Dreamercise #9 to give voice to the major emotion or feeling (fear, anger, frustration) of a dream. "Fear, what are you trying to accomplish?"

Perls suspected that sometimes we end a dream just before we are to get its significant message. Dreamercise #11 combines the Jungian concept of active imagination with Gestalt ideas so you can "finish" a dream, whether or not you initially think is it complete. It's another good exercise for working with disturbing dreams or nightmares.

AND THEY LIVED HAPPILY EVER AFTER

In your waking state, finish the dream. Write out, or record, the ending you think you might have dreamed if you hadn't awakened when you did. Even if the dream seems finished to you, write out an ending that takes the dream into the next one or two scenes or interactions.

Now write out the dream ending you would like to have. Especially for unpleasant dreams, consider how you could change its ending to make it come out better.

How do the two differ? Does this give you any new insight about the dream's message?

If you're working with a nightmare, feel free to change not only the ending but any other part of the dream you wish to make it more pleasant for you.

Barry Krakow and Joseph Neidhardt, authors of *Conquering Bad Dreams & Nightmares*, suggest you rehearse the new dream (walk yourself through it in your mind's eye) to be sure it feels just right. If not, make additional changes until it does. During the day rehearse the *new* dream at least twice more. According to Drs. Krakow and Neidhardt, continuing rehearsal of the new dream three times a day for three days often ends the nightmare.

As you no doubt have already discovered from reading Chapters 1 and 2, Gertrude Stein notwithstanding, a rose is seldom just a rose, at least not when it appears in a dream. Chapter 3 presents some ideas to help you understand how and why our dream roses grow.

ANNOTATED REFERENCES

Horney, Karen. *Self-Analysis*. New York: W. W. Norton & Co., Inc., 1942.

This book contains more of Horney's ideas on dreams than any of her other writings. She shows how even a simple dream may have various interpretations; thus the "correct" interpretation must be made in light of personal knowledge. Functions of dreams include: providing confirmation of an assumption, filling a gap in self-knowledge, or opening up new or unexpected leads in the pursuit of self-knowledge.

Jung, C. G. *Dreams*. Princeton, N.J.: Princeton University Press, 1974.

A part of the larger Bollingen series, this book, translated by R. F. C. Hull, extracts writings specific to dreams from various volumes of the *Collected Works of C. G. Jung*.

Krakow, Barry, and Neidhardt, Joseph. *Conquering Bad Dreams & Nightmares*. New York: Berkley Books, 1992.

Krakow, a professor of emergency medicine, and Neidhardt, a psychiatrist, give numerous examples of nightmares and present an organized method for getting rid of them, which involves imagery work, or imagination. They also discuss sleep and dream disorders and include a chapter on children's nightmares.

Mythology is nearly always the ritual and the symbolism of a Mystery school.
MANLY P. HALL

Dream is the personalized myth. Myth the depersonalized dream.
JOSEPH CAMPBELL

CHAPTER 3

It Took All Day to Get Ready for This

Here's a riddle for you:

> *We spend a third of our lives doing it, yet we don't know why. What is it?*

The answer, of course, is sleep. It may surprise you to know that although we have been sleeping—and dreaming—since the beginning of our existence, scientists still do not know exactly what sleep is or why we need it.

What they *have* learned, in the more than 150 sleep laboratories around the country, are the characteristics of our sleep patterns—sleep's autograph—and what helps or hinders sleeping. Those of us who enjoy successful sleep wonder what all the fuss is about; but for the 40 million Americans with one or more of the 84 identified sleep disorders, the continuing search to answer the what and why of sleep might, and often does, spell r-e-l-i-e-f.[1]

[1]For information or brochures about sleep problems or to find a sleep disorders specialist in your area, write: National Sleep Founda-

OUR INNER PACEMAKER

Almost every living thing, even the smallest one-celled organism, has a personal circadian rhythm—an inner pacemaker—and, therefore, a sleep-wake cycle. Our circadian pacemaker controls rest and activity by controlling such physical functions as body temperature, hormone production, hunger, alertness, sleepiness, and countless other characteristics.

A minuscule group of nerve cells in the hypothalamus, known as the *suprachiasmatic nucleus*, or SCN, are connected to light-sensing cells in the eye's retina. The SCN sends information about day-night cycles to our pineal gland, a small, white, pinecone-shaped structure in the middle of the brain, which adjusts our typical 25-hour personal cycle to fit the 24-hour environmental day. It does this by translating nerve signals from the SCN into chemical signals that produce the sleep-inducing hormone melatonin during darkness, and cease its production with the onset of bright light.

WHY WE SLEEP

Although researchers think they know how sleepiness and alertness are produced by the brain, they still have a number of competing theories as to *why* we need to sleep.

One explanation suggests that we sleep to rest various chemical systems that stimulate waking brain functions. Another suggests that electrical charges in the brain determine when and why we sleep. Still other researchers theorize that certain brain activation during sleep reinforces (a) all the learning/data already stored in our brain, and/or (b) our genetically determined programming.

"The anatomy of sleep is a can of worms," said psychologist Dr. Robert Ogilve in a 1993 interview for *The Monitor*, a monthly publication of the American Psychological Association.[2]

What is certain is that the more scientists learn about sleep

---

tion, 122 South Robertson Blvd., Third Floor, Los Angeles, CA 90048.

[2]Tina Adler, "Scientists have clearer view of body's descent into sleep," *The Monitor,* Vol. 24, #9, September 1993.

and dreaming, the more they realize there is no simplistic explanation for the biology and function of sleep.

SLEEP'S SIGNATURE

While busy conjecturing about why we need to sleep and what controls it, scientists have, in the meantime, learned a great deal about what sleep looks like.

Tonight as you snuggle down under the covers, it will take you, typically, 10 to 15 minutes to fall asleep. Faster if you're even the least bit sleep-deprived.

Your body temperature and blood pressure will become lower; your breathing and heart rate will slow. Gradually you'll begin to have slow, rolling eye movements. They signal stage 1 sleep, a transitional phase between waking and sleeping that usually lasts several minutes.

Then your muscle tension reduces considerably and your brain produces large, slow waves overlapping with occasional bursts of rapid waves called *sleep spindles*. You are now in stage 2 sleep, which many scientists consider the actual onset of sleep. It takes up more than half of your total sleeping time.

In 10 to 15 minutes your brain starts producing even slower brain waves, called *delta waves*. When they occupy between 20 and 50 percent of your sleep time, you are in stage 3; when they occur about 50 percent of the time, you will have reached stage 4 sleep. Stages 3 and 4 taken together constitute delta, or deep, sleep.

After about an hour of deep sleep, you emerge back into stages 3 and 2 briefly; and then the doors to your psychic elevator open and you begin REM sleep—visible to an observer as rapid eye movements, hence its name. Stepping off that elevator, you enter a land where time and logic follow no rules. Scenes can change instantly; you talk to cats and they talk back; with an upward surge you can float or fly. You are dreaming.

Although your muscles are limp—the brain has inhibited their movement—your breathing and pulse quicken and your blood pressure rises. Whether or not you're dreaming a sexual dream, if you are a male, you probably will have an erection;

and if you're female, your clitoris becomes engorged. Blood flow to the vagina increases and vaginal walls lubricate.

Following your REM sleep, you will again settle into the progression through phases 2, 3, and 4. Then, once more, your sleep lightens backward through the phases into another REM period. Throughout the rest of the night non-REM (stages 2, 3, 4) and REM sleep follow each other in this 90-minute cyclical pattern.

You will have about three to five dreams during the night, each lasting a little longer than the preceding one. Your first dream will probably last about 10 minutes, while your final one—early in the morning just before waking—may last as long as 45 minutes.

Sleep research conducted in the 1950s and 1960s indicated that dreaming occurred only in the REM stage. This fact, so widely reported, became, for a time, one of the myths of dreaming. Although dreams seem to be recalled better when persons are awakened from REM sleep, later research indicates that people awakened from non-REM sleep also report dreaming.

REM dreams exhibit the typical characteristics of primary process thinking (see Chapter 2). They are longer, more bizarre, vivid, emotional, and involve more activity than non-REM dreams, which lack vivid imagery and resemble waking thought. Seeming more plausible, non-REM dreams tend to focus on contemporary situations and sometimes consist of only a single phrase or sentence.

WHY WE DREAM

Since we know researchers don't agree on the whys of sleep, it won't surprise you to learn they also don't agree about why we dream. Earlier sleep research indicated that people deprived of REM sleep became ill, and when they were able to sleep undisturbed, made up for it with more time than usual devoted to REM sleep—"REM rebound." This suggested that dreams might be essential for our overall physical and mental health. Later studies, however, showed that the same rebound effect held true for non-REM sleep. When allowed to sleep, persons totally deprived of sleep spent most of their time in non-REM sleep, especially phase 4.

One English sleep specialist maintains that REM sleep is an evolutionary vestige from the developmental stage of reptiles, and no longer serves any purpose in mammals. We do know that in REM sleep the brain stem (considered our oldest brain in evolutionary terms) activates itself rather than being activated from outside stimuli. So some scientists speculate that dreams are simply the brain's attempt to create a story in response to the brain stem's random firing of electrical impulses, which stimulate nerves and muscles in the eyes, ear, and memory-storing parts of the brain. Others theorize that it isn't electrical impulses but changing chemicals in the brain that control or change the various stages of sleep and dreaming.

Another theory is that since REM brain wave patterns resemble waking patterns, and since short periods of wakefulness frequently occur at the end of a REM sleep period, this stage originally served to allow animals to check their surroundings periodically for signs of danger.

Some scientists suggest that we dream in order to sort out and forget extraneous or distracting information, while others believe that it is in dreaming that we sort and process information we weren't able to get through during the day. Some Swiss theorists propose that the "functional regressions" that occur during dreaming provide access to earlier experiences and strategies that can be used on current problems.

A great deal of research continues to develop around the effects of REM sleep and various aspects of information processing and memory. We do know that the combination of neurotransmitters that are present or absent during REM sleep alters the brain chemically in a way that allows it—or forces it—to process information differently.

Research conducted in Israel in 1992 indicated that REM sleep helps people remember "how-to" tasks but not factual ("what") knowledge. This suggests that certain physical skills might be more effectively taught during afternoon or evening hours prior to a REM nap or evening sleep.

Aside from the physiological mechanisms of dreaming, many psychologists still hold that dreams are, nevertheless, personally meaningful. They have speculated that we dream in order to:

- release the accumulated energy required to repress personal or socially unacceptable emotions
- restore or stimulate the psychological impoverishment that results from societal prohibitions
- bring to our attention previously unnoticed or unrecognized skills or abilities
- integrate or assimilate contemporary problems or stresses with earlier ways of adapting that we've worked out during our development

Pioneer dream researcher Montague Ullman believes that dreams can be healing when they point to issues from our past that are still active and need to be resolved—and which have been stirred by a present situation—or when they mobilize pertinent information from the past, giving us more insight about who we are. Psychologist Rosalind Cartwright, director of Chicago's Rush Presbyterian–St. Luke's Hospital Sleep Disorders Service and Research Center, believes that dreams reinforce our sense of self. They're messages that tell us who we are and how we're doing.

THE DREAMING EYE

Marion Woodman likens dreams to a camera focused on the unconscious. You snap the picture, and the dream tells you how the unconscious saw what was going on during the day. It tells you what you didn't realize about a situation in conscious life, what Jungian analyst Marie-Louise von Franz calls an unconscious reaction to a conscious situation. Psychiatrist Robert Langs believes a dream is our response to a situation that we have unconsciously perceived as dangerous.

According to von Franz, dreams can also (1) describe a conflict between the conscious and the unconscious, (2) represent the unconscious working to change a conscious attitude, or (3) represent unconscious processes that our consciousness does not yet recognize.

Ann Faraday writes of the "three faces" or functions of dreaming: to bring our attention to something we have failed to notice, to reflect attitudes and prejudices, and to give us a message about the state of our inner world.

It should be clear by now that there are a number of physiological and psychological views about the formation, meaning, and use of dreams. Most of them suggest that it can be not only fun but meaningful to acknowledge our trips into dreamland. The following guided-imagery dreamercise allows you to celebrate and personalize that process by creating, and honoring, your own dream director.

There are two ways to approach Dreamercise #12. You can read it through first and then re-create it in your mind from memory. If there's anything in the exercise that doesn't seem to fit you, don't create it in your mind's eye. Make whatever changes seem to better apply to you.

Or you might wish to read and record Dreamercise #12 on a tape. Then close your eyes and listen to it. Where there are series of dots in Dreamercise #12, be sure to pause on your tape and allow your mind's eye time to notice and fill in details.

Whatever approach you use, allow plenty of time—15 to 20 minutes at least—to complete the dreamercise uninterrupted, allowing you to move from your busy waking state into one of receptivity and creativity. Sit or recline so you are comfortable.

THE ENVELOPE, PLEASE

Close your eyes and take several deep breaths, sighing as you exhale. Move your body in any way you need to become more comfortable.

It is early evening. You are seated in a large auditorium. You are happy to be inside as night begins to fall and you know that outside it is becoming dark.

There are other people around you, but they are exactly the right closeness to or distance from you. You are elegantly dressed, as are the others in the room, and you feel so good to be here. . . . Everything is just right: the way you look . . . the people you are with . . . the temperature . . . the lights . . . the sounds in the room. . . .

You look around and notice the room's decor. There are elements of Victorian decoration, some Art Deco furnishings, and a few modern touches. . . . On the stage in front of you, plush velvet drapes, royal blue, are closed. As you look around, you are aware of the long and varied history this room has experienced. You feel very snug and satisfied. You are glad to be here, to be a part of this time, this experience.

The lights dim and an orchestra you had not noticed before now begins to play softly. As the sound increases, you realize the orchestra is playing a bedtime song or lullaby you loved as a child. . . . You smile and look around. Others begin smiling as they recognize it, too. Everyone begins to quiet and to settle more comfortably in the chairs. You are pleased and excited that the evening's events are about to begin.

The curtains part, with a slow, swishing sound. On a table at the side of the stage are a number of bronze plaques lined up side by side. You know they are "Dremmys," Dream Emmys. The oval plaque depicts the winged god Hypnos, god of sleep, pouring a sleeping draft into the cup of his winged son Morpheus, bringer of dreams to humans. At his feet, already asleep, are two of his most well-known cherub sons, Phobetus and Phantasos, who bring dreams to animals and inanimate objects.

A woman in evening clothes comes to the front of the stage and is surrounded by a spotlight. . . .

The music stops and the room becomes even more quiet.

In a throaty voice, she announces, "Ladies and gentlemen, each of you is here tonight to recognize the accomplishments of a special person, *your dream director,* and to honor your director for the never-ending and imaginative scenes that have enriched your nighttime adventures over the years."

The mistress of ceremonies looks at you and points, and a second spotlight illuminates you. She says, "To begin, you"—and she calls out your name—"have been selected to present the first Dremmy to your dream director."

Amid applause, you confidently leave your seat and walk onto the stage. You move to the table holding the Dremmys and pick up the first one.

The orchestra begins to softly play once again as a person emerges from the wings. It is your own personal dream director. Although you feel you know each other rather well, this is actually the first time you've seen one another. Take all the time you need to look at your director and fill in appearance details. . . .

When you are satisfied that your dream director looks exactly the way you want, place the Dremmy in your director's hands, saying, "This is for you, for your special efforts, and to honor our work together."

Your dream director accepts the award and bows to the audience, who applaud. Then your director turns to you, saying, "And I have a gift for you." Accept the wrapped gift your director hands you, but don't open it yet.

Now the mistress of ceremonies steps forward and announces, "Our first couple will now retire to rooms we have backstage to spend some time together getting better acquainted, while the rest of you present your awards."

You and your dream director walk backstage and enter a lavishly decorated room. Take time to look around and decorate the room exactly as you want it to be. Just imagine it, and it *will* be there. . . .

Now you and your dream director can relax and talk, or whatever it is you want to do. Be sure to unwrap the gift from your director and ask how to use it. Take all the time you need to have a satisfactory interaction with your dream director. You may wish to arrange for future meetings. . . .

When you are ready, bid your dream director good-bye and, taking all the time you need, return your awareness to your present surroundings.

When you have finished Dreamercise #12, take time to stretch and return to full awareness. You might want to record your experience in your dream notebook.

Now that you and your dream director have met, you may meet with him or her at any time you wish. Just close your eyes, create the scene, and have your conversation or other interaction. Or you might like to have a dialogue with your director, patterned after Dreamercise #10 in Chapter 2.

AMERICA'S MOUNTING SLEEP DEFICIT

Many of us seem to be, or think we are, just too busy to get a full night's sleep. Perhaps that's traditional in a Judeo-Christian society, since the Old Testament counsels us that sleep is not to be treasured:

> Love not sleep, lest you come to poverty; open your eyes, and you will have plenty of bread (Proverbs 20:13).

Both spiritual and esoteric teachers often refer to the unenlightened or uninitiated as "asleep." In Eastern and Western religions the term "awakening" signifies having entered a new state of enlightenment or dedication.

With all these subtle suggestions about the negativity of sleep, it is little wonder that the American Sleep Disorders Association estimates that some 70 million Americans regularly fail to get a full night's sleep. Couple that with the fact that our industrialized days offer little opportunity for a nap—even though the brain wants to sleep twice a day[3]—and it is little wonder that many of us are sleeping 60 to 90 minutes less than our body thinks we should.

DIETARY LULLABY

What can you do to help yourself sleep and dream well? Some things that have been found to encourage sleep and dreaming include:

1. Avoiding barbiturates and benzodiazepine (Valium) medications; drug-induced sleep is not the same as natural sleep. Although drugs sometimes help insomnia tem-

[3]According to Dr. Roger Broughton, pioneer nap researcher at the University of Ottawa, our need for a nap, which most of us have learned to ignore, is highest about 12 hours after the middle of the previous night's sleep.

porarily, in the long run, they disturb the pattern needed for dreaming sleep. Antidepressants and alcohol lower your chances of REM sleep. However, if you are on doctor-prescribed medication, don't stop taking it without consulting your physician.

2. Within six hours of bedtime, avoid stimulants such as nicotine or caffeine and foods containing them: coffee, tea, chocolate, many soft drinks, cocoa, and a variety of medications, including some sleeping pills.
3. If you drink a bedtime beverage, make it a warm one. Cold drinks force the stomach to work harder and disturb your system more. Some herb teas, especially chamomile, are reputed to facilitate sleep and dreaming.
4. Have a regular rising and bedtime and take time to wind down before going to bed.
5. Avoid eating a large meal just before going to bed, although a high-carbohydrate snack—rice, potatoes, bread, breakfast cereals, fruit—about 45 to 60 minutes before bedtime often helps induce sleep.

   Complex carbohydrates contain glucose (sugar), which helps speed the animo acid tryptophan to the brain, where it is converted to serotonin, a sleep-inducing neurotransmitter, which, ironically, is absent during REM sleep. Proteins (milk, meat, fish, poultry, eggs, and cheese) interfere with the transfer process and help maintain alertness.
6. Don't get your sugar boost from cookies, cakes, or other sweets. They tend to raise blood sugar levels rapidly and cause them to plummet just as rapidly, promoting wakefulness.
7. Have a room temperature of about 68 degrees Fahrenheit.
8. Keep your bedroom dark, with low noise levels. The quiet hum of a fan or air conditioner may mask environmental noises. Recordings of natural sounds, such as rain or the ocean, may offer mental distraction from worry.

9. Don't exercise right before sleep—it raises your body temperature—although a walk or other light exercise at least three hours before retiring may help you relax.
10. The fragrances of certain herbs or their oil essences also seems to promote sleep and dreaming for some people. These include lavender, chamomile, bergamot, and sandalwood. Place these on a cloth near or beneath your pillow, but don't place them on your tongue or skin.

The absolute best way to sleep well and become a good "oneironaut" (o-**nye**-row-not), or dream explorer, is to eat a well-balanced diet during the day. Vitamin B-3 or niacin (found in fish, poultry, peanuts, legumes, milk, and eggs) enhances the effect of tryptophan and prolongs REM sleep. Calcium (found in milk, cheese, sunflower seeds, walnuts, sardines, legumes, peanuts, kale, and broccoli) is a natural relaxant. Likewise, magnesium (found in potatoes, whole-grain bread, milk, meat, fish, poultry, eggs, legumes, dark green leafy vegetables, yellow vegetables, citrus fruits, apricots, apples, and dates) is a natural sedative.

Deficiencies in iron and copper can produce changes in sleep patterns. Copper is found in whole-grain cereals and breads, shellfish, nuts, poultry, dried beans and peas, and dark green leafy vegetables. Iron is found in dark green leafy vegetables, beef, sardines, prunes and other dried fruits, peas, and lima beans.

If you don't need to restrict your salt intake for health reasons, you might try adding a little more salt to your diet. A 1989 study of men in their 20s showed that those on a low-sodium diet woke up nearly twice as often and got about 10 percent less sleep than when they were on normal diets.

An attitude of wanting to remember your dreams and placing a notebook or other recording device by your bed is one way to signal your psyche or dream director that you consider dreams important enough to remember. Dreamercise #13 offers an imagery experience you can use to establish a relaxing, dream-inviting routine. Please feel free to change it in any way to better suit you.

REMEMBERING RITUAL

As you get ready to go to bed, place your dream-recording materials beside the bed, exactly where you want them. If they're already there, consciously check them, even touch them, to reaffirm to your unconscious that you are ready to record your dreams.

Once in bed, close your eyes and stretch to relax all your muscles. If any one muscle seems tighter than another, direct your attention to that muscle. Tighten it, hold the tension for a few seconds, and then release it, feeling it relax and become warm.

Tell yourself, "I want to remember my dreams and I will pay attention to them when remembered."

Then imagine and visualize yourself awakening in the morning, remembering your dream and entering it in your notebook. See yourself enjoying this activity; feel the comfort and residual warmth of the bed as you write; hear the sound the pen or pencil makes on the paper and feel it in your hand.

To finish the ritual and enter sleep, imagine yourself walking along the dreamway path and sense the ease with which you move . . . so effortless, almost like floating. Take plenty of time to notice the various sights and sounds along the way. They are exactly the way you want them and they are very comforting—everything you need along the way to help you dream and remember. . . .

Gradually you become more aware of the varying shades of green in the bushes, trees, and plants. Blue flowers are everywhere. The sky has a distinctly silver cast, blending its glow over the entire landscape.

Herbs known to assist dreaming, especially chamomile and lavender, grow along the pathway, often trailing onto it. As you walk along, you can't help but brush against them, releasing their gentle fragrance. You may even pick some to carry along with you. The sound of water flowing somewhere in the distance is very comforting, and helps you relax even more. . . .

As the path meanders and turns slightly, you get a glimpse in the distance of the dream temple where you will enter and welcome your dreams. Continuing along, you whisper to yourself once again, "I do value my dreams. I will remember and record them."

Once more, notice how comfortable your body feels, and make any adjustments you need to. Let go and let the bed support you; you don't have to do any work at all. "Oneiros, god of dreams, I am ready."

Today's experiences, your dreams in the making, are about to be translated into the language of the night. What will it be this time?

ANNOTATED REFERENCES

Jung, C. G. *Memories, Dreams, Reflections*. New York: Vintage Books, 1989.

Although this is essentially Jung's autobiography, his reflections on dreams and dreamwork are scattered throughout the book within the context of his life.

Johnson, Robert A. *Owning Your Own Shadow*. San Francisco: Harper, 1991.

Jungian analyst Johnson presents a simple and succinct argument for honoring the shadow aspect of ourselves: It's not good mental health to ignore it, and acknowledging it prepares us for spiritual development. His book suggests ways we can face our shadow safely.

The dream is a spontaneous
self-portrayal, in symbolic form,
of the actual situation in the unconscious.
C. G. JUNG

CHAPTER 4

Make That Dream Count

There is no doubt that men and women are different, so it probably won't surprise you to know that their dreams are different, too. It has long been understood that this difference was inherent in the gender. But thanks to continuing research, begun in the 1980s by a Canadian social psychologist, Dr. Monique Lortie-Lussier, we are beginning to realize that this is likely another myth of dreaming. While there may indeed be some inherent gender differences, it is now apparent that certain portrayals of ourselves in dreams are definitely affected by the changing roles of men and women.

Some dreamworkers have suggested that men's and women's dreams differ much more even than those of dreamers from different cultures. However, when the husband-and-wife anthropology team of Barbara and Douglas Tedlock began training to understand the dream divination system of the Quiché Maya of Guatemala, they were told by their shaman teacher that many of their dreams were inappropriate. They needed to, and did, learn to dream differently.

Fortunately, *you* don't have to learn to dream differently. However, you may find it helpful to compare how your dreams are similar or different from those of your mate, friend, or child and what to expect if you're about to become a parent, a working mother, or a new father whose wife is about to go to work.

MEN'S DREAMS

Men tend to dream more active dreams than women. Their interactions are predominantly with other men and they are aggressive; they fight. The appearance of unfamiliar characters and settings, which are more often outdoors than are the settings of women's dreams, are not unusual in men's dreams.

Men are more prone to identify dream characters on the basis of their occupational status. They dream more about automobiles, tools, weapons, and sexual interactions than women do. Men also appear naked and find money more often.

Psychologist dreamworker Dr. Gayle Delaney finds that men's sexual dreams are more overt and aggressive than women's. Their dream women are passionately ready for sex; and there are more hot, sweaty scenes than in women's dreams.

In the first trimester of his wife's pregnancy, an "expectant" father may have more dreams about sexual experiences/adventures and about being nurtured. Themes of being a nurturing and protective person; of being left out, rejected, deprived, or threatened; "water" dreams; and dreams about being pregnant himself begin to appear in the second trimester.

By his wife's third trimester, a man has many dreams involving his wife's pregnancy, anxiety that something may go wrong, and dreams containing varied symbols of birth (for more information on men's dreams during their wives' pregnancies, see Siegel's *Dreams That Can Change Your Life*).

Dr. Lortie-Lussier's research shows that as more wives/mothers become wage earners, and men become more active in family roles (through necessity or desire), "family" characters and roles appear more often in their dreams than previously.

WOMEN'S DREAMS

Women have more interactions and conversations in their dreams than do men. They have about equal numbers of male and female characters in their dreams, although some preliminary research by psychologist Robert Van de Castle suggests that women with brothers may have more males in their dreams than women without brothers.

They dream more about household objects, flowers, mammals, and small domesticated animals like cats and dogs. Their dream characters have familiar roles or are known to the dreamer (mothers, family members, children, babies); but full-time homemakers (with college degrees) have more incidents of misfortune related to their children than do working mothers. This may reflect anxiety about their ability or performance as wives/mothers or feelings of low self-esteem that research has shown is prevalent in homebound mothers.

Women pay more attention to clothing and jewelry in dreams and usually have more detailed descriptions of a dream character's face, hair, and eyes. Their sexual dreams involve romance and having plenty of time for foreplay and sex.

For a number of years studies showed that there was less friendliness and less aggression in women's dreams than in the dreams of men. With changing roles, the content of women's dreams changes also, becoming more like the dreams of working males in some ways. Women are now reported being more assertive and aggressive than previously, but that behavior is still more likely to be verbal than physical.

Dr. Lortie-Lussier's research shows that achievement strivings and unpleasant emotions (especially anxiety and sadness) increased for a group of Canadian working women who were also mothers, as did characters from their vocational life. Their dreams had fewer "home" settings than those of homemakers.

Women either are more aware of their feelings in reporting dreams, or have dreams in which more feelings are expressed and experienced than in men's dreams. They seem to have more nightmares than men and also more recurring themes. More often than men, women dream of being pursued.

During ovulation women often dream of jewels, eggs, and round or fragile things; and during menstruation their male characters tend to become unfriendly or hostile. Women also have less recall during and immediately prior to their menstrual periods.

As you might expect, a pregnant woman's dreams reflect her changing body and anxieties about how her life will change after the birth. Dr. Van de Castle, in his foreword to Eileen Stukane's book on dreams during pregnancy, reports that career women sometimes forget where they left their dream babies.

If this is her first baby, a woman may have anxiety dreams about giving birth and may rehearse it in her dreams, which some studies show make for an easier, shorter delivery. In the first trimester a woman's dreams often become more creative. She frequently dreams of fuzzy, cuddly animals and "tiny" creatures (Van de Castle).

She grows, or is around, flowers, fruit, water—growing things or life-giving things, all symbols of fertility. Architectural structures (a known symbol for the body) become more prominent; rooms, windows, and tunnels appear.

In the second trimester she begins to have dreams that symbolize her anxiety about being a competent mother—even if this is not her first child—and about having a normal baby. Actual dream babies replace animals; but often the mother can't find her baby. It has disappeared.

Near the third trimester, the expectant mother begins to dream about her own mother. Some researchers have theorized this helps her resolve unfinished conflicts so she can cease to be a child and truly become a mother, or, if she was dissatisfied with the way she was mothered, so she can be a different kind of mother.

She also has dreams that symbolically express her feelings about her changed body, as well as dreams in which she is, somehow, the center of attention—unique, rare, royalty. Other typical dreams include being able to view the baby or take it out to see it, and dreams of having already delivered it.

For more information on the themes of women's dreams throughout their life, see the books by Patricia Garfield and Karen Signell (Annotated References at the end of this chapter). For additional information on dreams during pregnancy, see the books by Maybruck, Stukane, and Siegel in the Bibliography.

CHILDREN'S DREAMS

Young children tend to have relatively simple dreams, usually with animal characters and themes of playing or eating, until they are about five or six years old. At this time dreams become longer; simple story lines and conflicts begin to appear. Settings are home and recreational ones. For the most part events happen to or about the child. The male child is a relatively passive character, while girls begin to assume slightly more active roles. (This evens out at above age seven.) In frightening dreams, the "bad" character is still an animal or a "monster," and children remember their nightmares easier than "good" dreams. Another common dream is of being physically hurt or experiencing some bodily injury. According to the American Sleep Disorder Association, nightmares are most frequent for children between three and six years old, and then they gradually begin to decline.

Until they are about five, children think dreams "come from outside" rather than recognizing them as an internal production. Somewhere between five and seven, they begin to realize dreams come from inside themselves and are not real. One seven-year-old told researchers Augusta Gross and June Rousso that a dream was like a "surprise mind."[1] Dreams now begin to have complicated stories in which the child takes an active part.

From about seven on, as language and thinking skills mature, dreams become more complex but, for the most part, are straightforward and not yet disguised. More often the dreamer is a victim rather than the aggressor. Children get lost; they are chased. They are powerless in many ways, but they also begin to be part of a community, especially their family. When their dreams contain animals, they tend to be large ones for boys (lions, tigers) and small ones (dogs, cats, rats) in girls' dreams. Boys are more likely to dream about dragons than are girls.

As human characters begin to enter into children's dreams, they are who they actually are in waking life. Children sometimes still have difficulty distinguishing the dream from real-

[1] "What Children Really Think About Their Dreams," p. 196.

ity, as they do also with their waking wishes and fantasies. (For additional information on children's dreams, see Garfield's *Your Child's Dreams.*)

With adolescence, all that changes. As children grow and engage in age-appropriate developmental tasks, their dream content, again, reflects those concerns. More and more dreams begin to resemble adult dreams, with special attention to sexual or romantic themes, bodily concerns, interpersonal and peer relationships, role identity, and, for males, an increase in hostility or aggressive actions.

PERSONAL DREAM VOCABULARY

Although the preceding are some common dream themes, even typical dreams are still colored by the issues and events of your personal life and by your attempt to cope with your own feelings and issues as you understand them.

You are the creator of your dreams. I said earlier that this book can give you some good guesses, and some different techniques for working with your dreams, but ultimately *you* are the best expert about the contents of your dreams. Therefore, at some time you likely will want to develop a personal dream dictionary.

Personal symbology arises from your life experiences: your particular occupation, hobbies, lifestyle, family, culture, and special interests that you have studied. All add your special touch to dream symbology.

A personal dream dictionary allows you to observe how a particular symbol expands and develops as your life experiences and self-awareness progress. It prepares you to recognize your crisis or turning-point symbols (see Turning-Point Dreams section later in this chapter) and to identify "dreamsigns," your signals that you are having a dream (see Lucid Dreaming section, Chapter 5).

Dreamercise #14 helps you to start and expand your personal dream symbol dictionary.

IT MEANS WHAT I SAY IT MEANS

To create a personal dictionary, buy some alphabetized tabs and add them to the back of your dream journal, or place them in a separate notebook.

When you experience images (characters, locations, actions, emotions, conflicts) that seem especially important in your dreams or that repeat, and you have determined at least one or more personal meanings for those images that differ from *Cloud Nine* meanings, enter *your* meaning in your personal dream dictionary.

When the images are known persons, include their relationship to you, the emotion they evoke when you think of them, and associations to the idea of how they may be resources for you.

Write the names and dates of dreams that include a given image/symbol, plus any other relevant information, so you can refer to it again when you are exploring future dreams, examining dream series, or looking for patterns in your dreams.

In future dreams containing the same or similar images, refer to your dictionary *first* before consulting *Cloud Nine*'s dictionary.

"Dreamsigns," a term coined by lucid dream expert Stephen LaBerge, are unusual things that happen in your dreams that could never happen in waking life, something that is definitely odd or out of place like last night's dream in which I walked out into a cold, pouring rain in my stocking feet and experienced no discomfort. Identifying and cataloging them will help you realize that you *are* dreaming if you decide you want to learn lucid dreaming (see Dreamercise #21).

LaBerge divides dreamsigns into four categories:

1. Inner awareness—Things you perceive happening to you, such as exceptionally strong emotions, acute hearing or sight, unusual abilities (thinking yourself through a door, wishing something to happen and having it occur).
2. Form—A character or object is unusually formed; you, or someone you know, is noticeably different from usual.
3. Action—Characters or objects malfunction or do something not possible in waking life. Your car accelerates and the brakes don't work; you're able to breathe and talk underwater.
4. Context—The place or situation of the dream is strange, objects or characters are out of place, or the dream takes place in the past or future (you're on Mars, back in junior high school, or starring in a movie).

Include a list of your dreamsigns in your journal. Those that appear the most will become your target dreamsigns to alert you that you are dreaming. Personally, I love to take one gentle step and float through the entire drugstore.

Identifying your own personal symbols over a period of time—and especially during illnesses or surgery—also makes it possible in the future for you to pinpoint symbols forewarning of illness, as well as healing and wellness symbols for psychological and physical health. Healing dream images deliberately remembered during painful or stressful waking times—Garfield calls these "refocusing images"; I call them *restorative icons*—can be especially calming or comforting.

SERIES DREAMS

Two of the earliest neo-Freudians to work with dream series were Erika Fromm and her colleague Thomas French. They believed that dreams—especially a network of dreams—assist us in solving a current interpersonal conflict (called the "focal conflict") by substituting analogous earlier problems that identify defensive and integrative techniques.

John Sanford, Jungian analyst and Episcopal priest, likens our unconscious life to a movie in which *each* dream is only one isolated scene. To look at one scene, one dream, is like coming in on the middle of a movie. It may or may not make a whole lot of sense, but when we add other scenes (dreams) to it, the plot becomes clear. As in a detective story, we have the opportunity to correct bad guesses and to expand earlier good hunches.

Dreams can monitor our progress. Jung wrote that whenever a psychological process had reached culmination—or we have gleaned all the insights we can from it—our dreams sometimes show regression; that is, a reversion to earlier symbols. By the same token, however, if we've missed an important unconscious message, dreams also may revert to sending us earlier, simpler symbols.

Although we can only begin our dreamwork by working on one dream at a time as it appears, the dream does not stand by itself, says Marion Woodman. It is part of a continual process going on in the unconscious that, if attended to, can open our lives and take us in directions we can't imagine. This is one of the reasons we often cannot take in the full meaning of a dream when we have it.

Later dreams may show more clearly what earlier dreams were only alluding to. Jung wrote, for instance, that the dream actions of anima or animus figures (see definitions in Part 2) are often "anticipatory." They do something in advance that the dreamer will do in later dreams.

We are able also to see the development of symbols throughout a series. For instance, in the dream series of one of Jung's male clients,[2] a hat appears in the first dream. Its

[2]"Individual Dream Symbolism in Relation to Alchemy," reprinted in C. G. Jung, *Dreams* (see Bibliography).

circularity suggests it is a precursor to later mandalas, an archetypal symbol of the Self. Sure enough, the hat appears again in dream thirty-five, this time smashed and clearly forming a simple mandala.

Without the series, and the development of the dreams in between, a valuable understanding not only of that symbol, but of the individuation process itself, would have been lost. This may be true for you, too. As you work on your dreams and live your life, you may return to earlier dreams with new insights and appreciation now that subsequent experiences have rendered you capable of understanding the fullness of their message.

Whitmont and Perera suggest that a dream birth may refer to some process that began around nine months earlier. A dream theme followed over time often gives the impression that an earlier dream almost seemed "to know" what a later dream or dreams reveal, and "prepared" us with preliminary hints or insights.[3]

Ira Progoff, a onetime student of Jung, has developed an extensive process of keeping a personal journal, which he calls the *Intensive Journal*. Ultimately work in any one of the 27 sections of the journal, including working with dreams, leads you to work in other sections.

Two sections of that notebook are called the "dream log" and "dream enlargements." In Intensive Journal work, the dream itself is recorded in the dream log section, but no interpretations or feelings are entered there. They are placed in the dream enlargements section, where the work on dreams is done. This allows a person to later read through dreams to observe the "moving continuity" of their life.

Progoff believes that dreams carry the "seed-nature" of a person and that over time, especially, they show the unfolding of life patterns and purposes. They are the "expressions of experiences that are seeking to become real in the future."[4]

During the course of writing this book, I could track my

---

[3]Edwin Whitmont and Sylvia Perera, *Dreams, a Portal to the Source,* p. 120.

[4]Ira Progoff writing on "Waking Dream and Living Myth" in Joseph Campbell's *Myths, Dreams, and Religion,* p. 182.

progress through my dreams. While trying to decide whether or not to write the book, I dreamed I was putting the finished manuscript in a mail box. Shortly after I began writing it, I dreamed of being in a business suit—not my usual writing attire—walking into an office and finding there a new baby that was clearly mine. I hugged it, loved it, and played with it.

I literally lived with this book day and night. Throughout the writing there were many dreams that gave me new insights into the dreaming process or dream symbology. One day I decided to remove the word "guardian" from the dictionary, thinking it related too closely to "caretaker" and "parent." That night I dreamed about stone lions guarding a walkway and recognized a new element. While working on the Ws, a "voice" told me that "woman was the direct line to God." I like it, but I haven't yet figured out how to use it in the dictionary.

At a time when the project was getting a little monotonous, I dreamed I was applying for a new job at a newspaper where one of my former journalism teachers worked. I had to accomplish a task that involved the word "hopple." When I recorded the dream, I thought the word was nonsensical, but looked it up anyway and discovered it was the same as "hobble," which means to be fettered or to go unsteadily, awkwardly, or haltingly. I changed my working style and took some needed time off from writing to do some waiting research.

Based on the work of Progoff and Jung, Dreamercise #15 gives you several ways to explore and elaborate on the seed-nature of a dream series.

DREAM FLOW

1. Begin by either deliberately choosing a time period—such as Alan Siegel's two-week crisis period (see Turning-Point Dreams later in this

chapter) or any other period in your life—or a group of dreams that you know you want to work on. If you have no such apparent need, then quiet yourself for a while thinking about and remembering dreams until one comes to you.

2. To experience their *continuity*, locate the chosen dream or dreams in your notebook. Read through it/them, ignoring any interpretations. If you have allowed a dream to come to you, begin by reading the two or three dreams that precede and follow it.
3. What ideas, thoughts, feelings, images, stir in you as you read these dreams? Progoff calls these "dream leads." Record them and any follow-through of ideas, thoughts, and feelings that occur to you.
4. Then look for the motifs, themes, or conflicts in each dream and whether or not there are changes in them. Consider the possibility of a continuing story or the continuity of a particular theme. Especially look for the progression and extension of a central theme or action over several nights' dreams.
5. Look for the recurrence of similar or identical symbology or dream characters over time.
6. If the series you've chosen is a short one, consider what these dreams tell you about decisions and choices you made, about the expansion of your personal symbols, about conflict or conflict resolution, and about your own growth and self-awareness.
7. If the series is a long one, possibly extending over years, consider what plan or sequence you can derive from the dream motifs that tells of your personal process of development.
8. Look especially for any symbols that, with later knowledge and insight, you now believe to be

archetypal ones, but that you didn't recognize as such originally.

Consider also symbols that you may have missed earlier but now believe express movement, change, ignored issues, or enlightenment.

9. Record your insights. Write a summary of what you have learned about your long- or short-term development and any strategies for change that you may have developed through your insight.

Jung sometimes worked with series dreams by choosing a dream whose meaning he thought he understood. Then he tried to verify this by examining preceding dreams as amplifying its content, especially if they contained recurring motifs. He considered the interpretation correct if subsequent dreams showed continued development. If not, he considered they were correcting the invalid interpretation.

TURNING-POINT DREAMS

Psychologist Alan Siegel, author of *Dreams That Can Change Your Life*, has made a career out of working with turning-point dreams, those dreams that occur at major life transitions or crises: marriage, pregnancy, separation/divorce, death, accidents and other trauma. During these times, the number and intensity of our dreams increase dramatically, and dreaming begins sooner in our sleep.

Apparently dreaming is an important part of our recovery or adjustment process. According to Siegel, our dreams focus on the conflict we are trying to resolve and help us by pointing out its relationship to past experiences. They give us clues about our progress, or impasse.

During life's passages, including positive ones, nightmares or anxiety dreams increase and are actually characteristics of a healthy emotional response. Keeping track of, and working with, the series of dreams that occurs during this time allows them to act as "touchstones" for revealing how the event/trauma aggravated hidden (earlier) fears and conflict, pinpointing lingering anxieties, *and* showing growth opportunities. Unchanging nightmares and unresolved dreams, especially those that dwell on the past or portray the dreamer as a victim, likely indicate being emotionally stuck. The dreamer may need the help of a support group, friends, or a therapist.

As the crisis passes and recovery ensues, our dreams begin to include partially resolved endings. Eventually they express new strengths, show new capabilities, and may even serve as rehearsals for new behavior. Siegel reports that many people have found comfort and encouragement by keeping in mind the message from a significant recovery dream as they approach new opportunities.

With his permission, Dreamercise #16 presents Dr. Siegel's technique.

POLISHING A DREAM'S FACETS

Siegel uses the acronym FACETS as a guide for working with crisis or turning-point dreams:

1. **F**eelings. After recording your dream, make a specific note of the positive and negative emotions expressed in it.
2. **A**ssociations. Write associations, hunches, and insights you have about what the dream could be about, no matter how odd or irrelevant they may seem.
3. **C**haracters. Write your associations, hunches, insights, and awareness regarding the dream's characters and how you're relating to them.

4. **E**nding. Consider the degree of resolution (unresolved, partially or totally resolved) in the dream. Usually it correlates to the stage you have reached in resolving the waking dilemma.
5. **T**itle. Title the dream by including a crucial element from it.
6. **S**ummary and **S**trategies for Change. Summarize the main theme(s) and list what ideas for change you think it suggests.

Once you have completed Dreamercise #16, you may want to allow its insights to direct you to work with any of the other dreamercises in Part 1. Siegel's book (see Bibliography) contains a 14-day program for using dreams to help resolve emotional challenges and stressful events.

DREAM GROUPS

One way of working with your dreams that's becoming increasingly popular is that of exploring them with a group. It is often a good way to help you uncover the multiple meanings of your dreams, but it is definitely not a psychotherapy group. While the group's central activity is that of sharing and exploring one another's dreams, some dream groups have also developed celebrations and rituals for special times.

One of the originators of group dreamwork was Dr. Montague Ullman. Following in his footsteps, many dreamworkers, notably Rev. Jeremy Taylor and Dr. Gayle Delaney, have developed styles of working to facilitate awareness of the dream's meaning and guidelines to prevent the exploitation or violation of a member's dreams. Some of these are presented in Dreamercise #17.

If you're interested in joining or forming a dream group, the Association for the Study of Dreams will be happy to help you connect with a dream group in your area, or to assist you with ideas for starting your own oneironautical explorations. (See their address in footnote 2, Chapter 6).

UNITED, WE DREAM

1. Opening: Taylor suggests a regularly meeting group might open by members saying something about their internal/emotional state and/or do a group centering/focusing/grounding exercise to evoke intuition. He suggests each member also briefly tell a dream before the group selects one to work on.
2. The Dream: In Drs. Delaney's and Ullman's groups, the group opens and work begins when a member volunteers a dream and tells it in the present tense, uninterrupted. When the dreamer is finished, other members may ask questions to clarify the dream images or narration only. These instructions hold for almost every style of dream group described in the literature.
3. Dreamwork: Whatever the group style, members of the group never interpret another's dream. In Dr. Ullman's groups, they serve as resources by making the dream their own and speaking to one another, but not the dreamer, about what the dream says, or would mean, if each of them had dreamed it ("If this were my dream . . .").

   In Dr. Delaney's groups, however, this technique is not used because she thinks it detracts from focusing on the dreamer and does not achieve her goal of teaching dreamers to be good interviewers of themselves and others. Instead, in her groups, the dreamer chooses someone to "interview" him/her about the dream.

4. One of Dr. Delaney's favorite, and most well-known, interview questions is to ask the dreamer to explain an object as if the questioner is from another planet and doesn't understand what it is.[5]
5. In Dr. Ullman's group, the dreamer responds to the group's remarks and then members are allowed to ask open-ended questions to help the dreamer focus on a particular aspect of the dream ("What is it like to be a carved, wooden bowl?"). Other dreamworkers move from the telling of the dream directly into this activity (example: "You were so specific about the fact that the dream bowl was carved of wood that I'm curious about what it means to you. Can you say more about it?"). This is also the time to connect the dream with its immediate or past waking context.
7. If Dr. Ullman's group members see a connection or relationship between the dream and any of the discussion, they can offer it, but it must be made clear that this is the member's projection or fantasy, which the dreamer is free to accept or reject.
8. If the dreamer is drawing a blank, Rev. Taylor says that having someone else read the dream aloud sometimes triggers new awareness or insight.

[5]For a list of 14 additional questions that Dr. Delaney believes constitute a good "cue card" for dream interviewers, see *Living Your Dreams*, pp. 55–57.

TONIGHT, TONIGHT, I'LL DREAM MY THEME TONIGHT

It has been suggested that dreams occurring earlier in the night are more affected by the day's happenings, while later dreams are longer, more complex, and often refer to more remote past experiences. There is no confirming evidence of this, and some research suggests that dreams throughout the night do not significantly differ from one another.

There is more evidence from dream researchers to indicate that dreams occurring during the same night extend, or elaborate on, the same theme—another reason why it is helpful to be able to wake up after a dream and record it. Rosalind Cartwright presents many of these types of dreams in *Crisis Dreaming*. After interpreting each dream separately, Jung sometimes tried to weave together the dreams of one night into a single story line.

Taken together, one night's production of dreams often seems to amplify that night's theme. However, some researchers hypothesize that earlier dreams are simply serving as "residue" material for later dreams.

Psychologist Mary Watkins suggests that just as we have incorporated the day residue into the work of understanding dreams, we need also to consider that the waking day is infiltrated with, or composed of, "dream residue."

For instance, take a dream in which you chase someone in a car, are stopped by a policeman, and end up apologizing to all the dream characters. What images in the dream carry over into your waking behavior? How do you chase yourself round and round, or speed through the day or tasks? When and where do you feel you're out of control? How does your relationship with, or attitude toward, authority (mother? father? boss?) limit you? How do you ticket (judge?) yourself and call a halt to possibly creative or ambitious actions? How and when do you depend on others to set limits (priorities?) for you? And how does this (forced?) apologetic aspect of yourself make itself known in your waking life?

Day residue, dream residue. How do you know when you've done enough? Dreamercise #18 presents some guidelines to help you consider whether you're finished working with a dream, at least for a while. You may, of course, still return to it at any time for further work.

ENOUGH, ALREADY

_____ Working with your associations has brought forgotten memories, thoughts, or ideas into play.

_____ Your "aha" insight is startling or unexpected. You feel an inner flush; you wonder why you didn't see the explanation before. Gayle Delany calls this a quality of "sureness."

_____ Your conclusions make sense to you, fit with other facts and ideas about the situation, and give you a genuinely different slant or approach to consider, or an awareness you didn't know you had.

_____ The information is new and does not repeat what you already know. It is a genuine insight.

_____ Nothing is left hanging. Every element/image in the dream fits. You understand how it contributes to the total dream, and how it fits your current life situation.

_____ You can answer at least one of the following questions:

a. What is happening within me as reflected by this dream?
b. What is happening in my waking life that brings up the issues expressed in this dream (or series)?
c. What have I learned that will help me take the next step in my growth?

In other words, how can you apply the dream's message to yourself?

Gayle Delaney considers a dream ''well interpreted'' when it

- opens your eyes to a new aspect of yourself
- solves a problem; offers a novel idea
- provides you with a new experience or appreciation of qualities of being (joy, compassion, acceptance, responsibility, peace)

By now you've probably realized that you're not always helpless in your dream boat. You can ''row, row, row your boat, gently down the stream,'' or you can paddle furiously through the rapids. But no matter, for when you awaken, you're going to know something more about yourself and your life adventure.

In the next chapter you will discover that many contemporary dreammasters believe there's more to do in dreams than watch them sail by and interpret them later. There are ways you can take charge, have more fun, and even get ideas for new projects or a new career. And all the while, there you are, getting a good night's rest.

ANNOTATED REFERENCES

Garfield, Patricia. *Women's Bodies, Women's Dreams.* New York: Ballantine Books, 1988.

''Women's dreams mirror the tides that move the fluids of their bodies.'' With that introductory sentence, Dr. Garfield launches into an *extensive* review of the unique patterns expressed in women's dreams and the changes that occur with aging. Her information was acquired from interviews with 50 women ranging from ages 20 to 90. It's a good and thorough guide to what's usual, unusual, and what's coming in a woman's dream life.

Hopcke, Robert H. *Men's Dreams, Men's Healing*. Boston & London: Shambhala, 1990.

There are very few books about male dreaming and the therapeutic process. Hopcke, a Jungian-oriented therapist, presents his work with two clients, one homosexual, one heterosexual, using their dreams as the key to their healing. Each chapter begins with a dream and shows how working with it, and subsequent dreams, brings up issues of male psychology, including recognizing and acknowledging feelings, sex roles, fatherhood, and the development of one's true or inner "authority" rather than adopting that of the father or others.

Signell, Karen A. *Wisdom of the Heart. Working with Women's Dreams*. New York: Bantam Books, 1990.

Dr. Signell, a Jungian analyst, uses the dreams of her analysands to show women how their feminine nature and feminine issues are expressed in dreams. She begins with how the Self is expressed in women's dreams and then presents what women's dreams say about aggression, vulnerability, protection, and strength. One chapter deals with the shadow aspect, how dreams can alert women to their own shadow as well as to that of others. Two chapters deal with relationships and sex, and the last, "the wise heart," considers what happens to the dreams of women as they age.

You may be an undigested bit of beef,
a blot of mustard,
a crumb of cheese,
a fragment of an underdone potato.
EBENEZER SCROOGE

CHAPTER 5

Midnight Messages

Although you now know that each dream can be approached as the next conversation in the ongoing dialogue between your conscious awareness and your unconscious Self, it is sometimes helpful to know that sometimes we're all having the same conversation.

JOIN THE CROWD

A number of authors and journalists[1] have come up with lists of "universal" dream themes, although the particulars of each theme will vary according to your own life experiences. Apparently there are quite a few similar pathways we all have traversed at some time or another in dreamland. How many appear in your dreams?

_____ missing a plane, train, or bus
_____ taking a test or examination, or forgetting to take it
_____ arriving too late[2]

[1]See articles by Allen, by Ward, Beck, and Rascoe, and the book by Gutheil, all listed in the Bibliography.

[2]In *Dream Work in Psychotherapy and Self-Change,* experiential psychologist Alvin Mahrer enchantingly describes these first three types of dreams as displaying the "secret delight of saying no, the wickedness of not doing it . . . sweet defiance and rebelliousness . . . a sense of nasty devilishness" (p. 91).

For other explanations, see **fear** entry in Part 2.

_____ falling dreams (falling through space, off high places, etc.)
_____ sexual experiences
_____ being chased or pursued
_____ achieving or accomplishing something great
_____ flying dreams, (including floating, or having difficulty flying on your own power)
_____ paralyzed (being unable to move, run, or scream)
_____ being naked in public
_____ having something happen to your teeth
_____ finding money
_____ being lost
_____ passing through a narrow space

So, dreamer, the next time you find yourself in one of these fourteen situations, look around. Some of the rest of us will be right there along with you.

NATIONAL NIGHTMARES

A creak in the dark; a shadow fills your dream window. Oh, God, it's about to happen again. . . .

Nightmares are often the most repetitive dreams we have. Krakow and Neidhardt estimate that as many as 12 million adults in the United States alone suffer from chronic nightmares. For many, their nightmares disappear as adults—children tend to have more nightmares than adults—but when they don't, they're often related to childhood fears. According to a 1980s survey, dreams of falling were the most common adult nightmare, with dreams of seeing a loved one in danger and dreams of being chased or attacked ranking second and third. Nightmares tend to occur in the early morning rather than in the first half of sleep.

Nightmare expert Dr. Ernest Hartmann was the first to separate night terrors[3] from nightmares and to distinguish between

---

[3]Usually occurring in early childhood, night terrors are often considered a "disorder of arousal," rather than a sleep disorder. They are not dreams because they occur in stage 4, non-REM sleep; are shorter than nightmares, which *are* dreams; and are characterized by more anxiety and panic than nightmares. They are seldom remembered, and upon awakening, the person is much more confused than when awakening from a dream.

usual nightmares and those caused by post-traumatic stress disorder (PTSD). PTSD dreams occur as a result of having experienced or seen something horrible or terrifying, such as a wartime experience, natural disaster, or bodily attack. They usually are vivid re-creations of the experience; and it is likely that their repetition helps the ego begin to overcome the original feelings of helplessness and/or passivity.

Jungian analyst and psychiatrist Harry Wilmer identifies three stages in the PTSD dreams of Vietnam combat veterans. In the beginning dreams are unchanging and replay events pretty much as they happened. In stage two the traumatic event begins to be mixed with events from other periods in the dreamer's life. Stage three dreams are more like ordinary nightmares, mixing and combining many images/characters from the present with the combat location.

Therapeutically, nightmares have been helpful in identifying repressed physical or sexual abuse. The nightmares of those who have been abused are often more explicitly violent than those of people who have not been abused. Although dreaming is reduced for alcoholics and addicts, they may, nevertheless, have what psychologist Kathleen O'Connell calls "attention-getting" nightmares, dramatic intense dreams of danger, dying, or destruction, which serve to propel them into the recovery process.

We tend to have more nightmares when we are mentally stressed or fatigued, or have a fever. Withdrawal from sleeping pills, tranquilizers, and tricyclic antidepressants often produces nightmares, as will taking medications to which we are allergic. Medications for hypertension (high blood pressure), Parkinson's disease, heart disease or angina (beta blockers), and others can also stimulate nightmares.

Jung suggested that the feeling of helplessness so prevalent in nightmares might be a racial memory inherited from ancient ancestors who awoke in panic to find a live animal in their dark cave. Modern authorities think we need not search that far back, but only to our own infancy when we were unable to tell which of the objects looming over our crib were helpful and which were harmful.

Nightmares can also be caused by anxiety regarding upcoming events or changes, especially ones we're not sure about or the consequences of which are yet unknown. These often relate to our feelings about various forms of responsibility: achievement, fear of success or failure, independence. Several studies have shown, however, that in some instances nightmares are the cause of waking anxiety rather than being a reflection of it. Stopping the nightmare stops the anxiety.

Jungians Whitmont and Perera believe nightmares are the Self's efforts to direct our attention to material or issues that we have denied or ignored. Accordingly, nightmares can point to new problems (intruders) or spoiling elements of your personality (monsters), and can expose outgrown limitations or support the death of currently held egoistic viewpoints (dying and dismemberment dreams).

To work on your own nightmares, you first need to begin recording your dreams, if you have not already done so. In one study the act of merely recording the dream ended the nightmares of almost half the group.

Then review your dream and its symbols to see if it applies to a waking situation that you need to, and can, change. If that's not evident, rewrite your dream and image the new dream according to directions in and immediately following Dreamercise #11 (Chapter 2).

Dreamercise #19 presents additional helpful techniques for dealing with frightening images or recurring nightmares.

BANISHING BAD DREAMS

- For recurring nightmares, take some time during the day, or before you fall asleep, to review the dream. Appreciate and congratulate yourself on your extraordinary creativity in making this dream exactly as you have. Tell yourself that you can also use your imagination to behave differently in the dream, and plan at least one way you could change your action in the dream.

One woman decided that if the dogs who chased her nightly were merely her imagination, she would turn on them and brandish an imaginary, invisible sword. I would have made the sword visible, but it worked for her. The dogs were so amazed—perhaps at her audacity—that they sat back on their haunches and stared as she turned and sauntered away.

- Have a dialogue with the scary elements of your dream (see Dreamercise #10) to see what their helpful or positive function is. It is *important* that you: (1) reassure them you can, and will, utilize that function more in your waking life (and be sure you do); (2) thank them; (3) request a gift from them that will aid you in the future (if you're not clear how to use it, ask); and (4) let them know you appreciate their resourcefulness in reminding you in such a unique manner of what you need to pay attention to.
- In whatever dreamwork you do, don't try to rid yourself of a nightmare monster by killing it. Its energy will return to haunt you in some other way because you're still ignoring its message.
- Let the dream's own nightmarish quality, or the impossibility of it, serve as a cue to yourself while you are still dreaming that you *are* dreaming. Then change the dream (see the Lucid Dreaming section later in this chapter).
- Dr. Gayle Delaney suggests you tell yourself before you go to sleep that you will face your threatening figures in the dream and ask them, "What do you want?" or "What do you represent?"

If you explore your nightmares according to the dreamercises in this book and find you still cannot relate them to your waking life, past or present, then you may be someone who, according to the Association for the Study of Dreams, is more creative, sensitive, trusting, and emotionally vulnerable than average.

Mystery writer Sue Grafton told San Francisco radio host and author Naomi Epel that her nightmares are "wonderful," because she draws upon them to create the physical reactions she needs when her private eye heroine Kinsey Millhone is in danger. Like Grafton, learn to appreciate your dream information, and consider turning those nightmarish images into something you *can* deal with.

If you need additional help in handling your nightmares, or those of your child, consult Cartwright and Lamberg (see annotated references, this chapter), and the books by Krakow and Neidhardt (annotated references, Chapter 2), Anne Wiseman, and Denyse Beaudet (Bibliography).

PROBLEM-SOLVING AND HEALING DREAMS

Involved in a situation that's puzzling you? Don't understand why something is, or isn't, happening in your waking life? Need a new strategy for handling a particular situation? Dr. Gayle Delaney, author of *Living Your Dreams*, suggests you incubate a dream and find the answer.

From the time of the Egyptians, people have gone to the temples for dream incubation. In earlier times it was usually to request and invoke a healing dream that would reveal a special ritual or treatment for cure. In some cases, the dream itself would result in a cure.

The Greeks and Romans placed their dream temples near "healing" waterways, where a purification ritual was often performed, as well as various other rituals or procedures designed to prepare the dreamer both physically and psychologically. Special priests helped the dreamer understand the dream. Among the more famous of the Greek dream temples were those dedicated to Asclepias, who lived around 1100 B.C.

In Babylonia certain priests could be designated to receive the dream instead of the person. While in Babylonia, Alexander the Great sent his generals to the temple to dream for him. The Hawaiian *kahuna* (priest) would dream for a patient, receiving treatment methods from his *aumakua* (deified ancestors). Some Mediterranean and African countries still practice dream incubation.

Contemporary dreamers who believe in and are used to working with spirit guides (human or animal aspects of their higher or wise self) are often "visited." However, you don't have to develop a spirit guide or even send your relatives to Africa in order to request information through a dream. Use the tips from Dreamercise #20 to get your questions answered through your dreams. If you *do* decide you want a dream guide, ask to meet one using the techniques of the dreamercise.

PUT A DREAM UNDER MY PILLOW

People who incubated dreams in ancient times were required to participate in a certain amount of ritual and preparation. Sometimes they might spend a month or more[4] at a temple waiting for the right time to have their dream. What this actu-

[4]In *Spiritual Dimensions,* Ania Teillard writes of the 20th-century experience of Sita Lakshmi, who spent six months at a temple in India dedicated to the goddess Parvathi, giver of children to barren women. She ate one meal a day, made the rounds of the temple 108 times morning and night, and performed other rituals until temple priests told her she was ready. She dreamed of four coconuts, one of which was broken as it was handed to her, which correctly foretold that she would have four children, one of whom would die young.

ally means is that during that time, they were doing a lot of mental work on the situation and really preparing themselves to receive, and accept, an answer. So, to begin your work:

1. Choose a problem or situation that has been worrying or concerning you. Shortly before you go to bed, think about everything you know about this situation and write it down. Include: (a) the facts as you see them; (b) the role you think your attitudes play; (c) solutions you've already tried (and what happened) or rejected; (d) and whether or not you are really ready to accept a solution.

   Ask yourself what you will do, how you will be/feel if the situation is resolved, and how you will be/feel if it's not. What prevents you from resolving the issue or having what you want right now? Obviously you need to think about these questions seriously and answer truthfully.

   When you believe you have looked at all the possible aspects of the situation—which may take one evening or a period of time—you're ready for the next step.

2. Compose a succinct, concise question that relates to the issue. Do not ask "Why?" Instead ask questions that begin with "how or "what":

   How can I take care of . . . ?
   How can I handle . . . ?
   What do I need to know about . . . ?
   What do I need to do to . . . ?
   How can I be more [the characteristic you desire] in X situation . . . ?
   What have I missed regarding the issue of . . . ?

   Write your question as the final entry on your work paper.

3. Turn out the lights and, as you go to sleep, repeat your question over and over, like a man-

tra. And like a mantra, if you become distracted, just return to repeating your question.

4. When you awaken, record your dreams with as much detail as you can. Even if you only remember a fragment, record it. Rewrite your question at the top of the page on which you've written your dream(s).
5. If you don't have an immediate realization, put your dream aside. Think about it during the day, considering its possible relationship to your question. Jot down any ideas that come to mind.
6. If the answer to your question is not readily apparent, work on the dream with any dreamercises that seem appropriate. When all of the pieces of the dream fit together, can you answer the question "How does this dream relate to, or answer, my dream incubation question?"
7. What have you learned that you can use in solving your problem or resolving your issue?
8. If one night's dreaming doesn't seem to give you an understandable answer, write down any new information acquired as you've worked on the dream with the preceding steps. Continue to think about, and review, your question/situation during the day and each evening before retiring. Add any new material to your original worksheet.
9. Although for many people the answer comes quite soon and easily, it also is possible that you may acquire several pages of written material. Until you're satisfied you have your answer, at the end of each day's review and writing of new material, take a fresh page for your journal and write your question at the top of it. This will remind your unconscious that you are still working on your question and need additional dreams.

Some research suggests that dream material occurring between five to seven days after the problem is introduced may be more effective in offering solutions or understanding than same-night dreams.

Be careful you don't ignore the answer you receive, just because it doesn't appeal to you. Dr. Delaney cautions that if you don't make an effort to understand the answer from your dreams, you may get the same dream a second time, or a reminder that you already have the answer.[5]

As you become experienced in asking your dreams for answers or insights, and trusting the dream incubation process, most likely you'll develop a shorter, more concise method that works for you. For some this means doing the preliminary work mentally and then simply asking the question.

When interviewed by talk-show host Naomi Epel, Amy Tan, author of *The Kitchen God's Wife*, told Epel that when she is stuck on an ending, she takes the story to bed with her and dreams an ending. Social worker Carol Warner believes that dream incubation can help recovering addicts take some of their power back and feel more in control.

In her book *Dreams & Healing*, Joan Ruth Windsor identifies three kinds of healing dreams. The first are those, incubated or not, that give us advice about our internal personal health, including things that need to be recognized or taken care of and remedies. Dr. Robert L. Van de Castle calls these "prodromal" dreams. They have even been known to give clues as to the status of a fetus during pregnancy.

The other two kinds of healing dreams are those containing insights about another person, and the shared dreams of a group related to one of its members, a form of telepathic dreaming that Windsor believes is particularly potent.

To invoke healing dreams, Windsor suggests that after stat-

---

[5]Dr. Gayle Delaney, *Living Your Dreams,* p. 128.

ing the problem clearly and concisely, and writing it down, request information about the mental *and* physical origins of the symptoms or disease, and specific modes of treatment. Upon awakening, record all information and impressions and especially attend to your personal symbology.

One of the most comprehensive books on the relationship of dreams to healing is Patricia Garfield's *The Healing Power of Dreams*. It contains numerous insights and exercises for paying attention to your dream symbolism in order to identify hidden health problems, speed recovery from traumatic events, evaluate your healing progress, and for promoting physical and psychological health. Dr. Montague Ullman believes that *all* dreams play some part in the healing process in that their having been remembered suggests the dreamer is ready to confront or resolve the issue being dreamed about.

SHAMANISTIC DREAMING

Shamanistic dreaming is quite different from our usual nighttime dreaming, and is used for different purposes. The shaman doesn't consider dreams as psychological events to be interpreted or understood. Rather, they are the training ground where the sorcerer learns to perceive and function differently, or where he/she receives healing gifts, powers, or information.

In one Zulu tribe, the *Inyanga* (shaman) becomes a "house of dreams," according to ethnopsychologist Holger Kalweit, while in another the impetus to become a shaman arises as a result of a "sickness" characterized in part by dramatic dreams. Chemehuevi healers receive their helping spirits from dreams. In his book about the worlds of shamans, Kalweit has an entire chapter on spirit husbands and wives who come to the healer or shaman during dreams and may, or may not, allow earthly spouses.

A basic premise of the sorcerer is that there is more to the world than we have been led to believe, i.e., that we have been coerced by our life experiences into a certain belief system. The shaman must learn to give up or suspend that belief system and to perceive the world differently.

Sorcerers of the Yaqui tradition, made famous by Carlos

Castaneda, see human bodies as egg-shaped luminous bodies—called the energetic body—which extend about an arm's length around our physical body.[6] The energetic body is interlaced with fibers, which are organized at an "assemblage point."

Approximately the size of a tennis ball and surrounded by its own luminosity, the assemblage point is usually located about a foot outside our body (but still within the egg-shaped luminous, energetic body), behind the right shoulder blade. The point fluctuates or shifts when we dream, so the shaman uses dreams and dreaming—called "second attention"—as his or her training ground to learn to perceive the world differently. In shamanistic terms, the energetic body makes forays into second attention.

It is also during dreaming that the sorcerer learns to "see" the energy of inorganic beings and bring those energies into the real world to serve the sorcerer.

For more information on shamanistic dreaming, see the writings of Kalweit *(Dreamtime & Inner Space),* Donner *(Being-In-Dreaming),* and Castaneda *(The Art of Dreaming)* in the Bibliography.

Although it is not likely that you will want to spend the extensive time and dedication it takes to become a shaman, the description of some shamanistic dreaming resembles lucid dreaming, which you *can* master.

LUCID DREAMING

For many people, encountering something weird or unusual is their signal they are dreaming. Then the fun begins. "I push off into the air, knowing I can go anywhere and do anything," says one dreamer.

Lucid dreaming, as you've probably deduced, refers to realizing that you're dreaming and then being able to change your behavior while still dreaming. Dream reports show that

---

[6]The Yaqui information was presented by Florinda Donner during a lecture, Being-In-Dreaming, delivered at the Philosophical Research Society in Los Angeles, September 13, 1991. Much of it has since appeared in Castadena's *The Art of Dreaming.*

being in the midst of a lucid dream allows dreamers to explore and engage in behaviors they might not otherwise, knowing they will ultimately be safe because they have realized "I'm dreaming." Jeremy Taylor continues his dreaming in the face of fearful images by reminding himself, "This is a dream, and no physical harm or pain will come to me."

Few people outside of Tibetan Buddhist communities had ever heard of lucid dreaming before Patricia Garfield's 1974 publication of *Creative Dreaming*, yet Saint Augustine wrote of it in the third century, according to psychologist Stephen LaBerge, who has made a career of studying lucid dreaming.

In 1867 French professor Hervey de Saint-Denys wrote about being able to control his dreams, but it was not until 1913, when Dutch psychiatrist Frederik Willems van Eeden delivered a paper to the Society for Psychical Research, that the term "lucid" dreaming was used. Ann Faraday refers to them as "dreams of knowledge," while for German psychologist Paul Tholey, they are "clear" dreams.

For a time researchers questioned whether lucid dreams could occur during REM sleep, thinking they might be brief periods of hallucinatory wakefulness. But LaBerge, who began studying lucid dreams in 1977 for a doctoral dissertation, showed they *do* occur during REM sleep.

Lucid dreamers have described changing the content of nightmares, questioning nightmare figures during the dream about the meaning of their presence, modifying scary incidents in recurring dreams, and practicing athletic performances.

Besides being just plain fun, lucid dreams have also been credited with giving insights into the working process, providing ideas or actual material for new projects, and demonstrating techniques for working more effectively or differently.

Although it takes time to learn, once learned, it is also possible to increase the frequency of lucid dreaming. It's easier to have a lucid dream early in the morning after you've had several hours of deep sleep, during an afternoon nap, or even better, during a morning nap. LaBerge suggests that waking up two hours earlier, doing some work, and then going back to sleep significantly increases your chances of having a lucid dream.

Allow strange or bizarre elements/occurrences that would be impossible in waking life (remember those ''dreamsigns'' from Dreamercise #14?), or the fact that you're frightened in a dream, to become the cue that triggers the awareness that you are dreaming. Sometimes the recognition that you're having a dream you've had before can transform it into a lucid one.

Flying or floating dreams are a common gateway to the lucid dream. On the other hand, many lucid dreamers report that one of the most thrilling consequences of lucid dreaming is that they can fly deliberately. When a lucid dreamer wants something to happen, or change, often he or she needs only command it, aloud or telepathically, and the change occurs. Whee!

For the first few lucid dreams you have, that realization—especially the sense of excitement with your first lucid dream—may cause you to awaken. As you become more skilled, however, you can prolong your lucid dreaming experience.

Although there are several books with extensive instructions for learning to dream lucidly (see the books by LaBerge and Rheingold, Gackenbach and Bosveld, and Harary and Weintraub in the Bibliography), the undisputed master is Dr. LaBerge. The major components of his MILD (Mnemonic Induction of Lucid Dreams) method are included, with his permission, in Dreamercise #21.

LOOK, MA, I'M DREAMING

1. Before attempting to learn lucid dreaming, you should be able to remember at least one dream per night—otherwise you won't remember your lucid dream either—and your dream jour-

nal should contain a number of personal dreamsigns (see Dreamercise #14).

2. When you awaken from a dream period, especially an early morning dream, think about the details of the dream. Memorize them.
3. While still in bed, spend 10 to 15 minutes reading or engaging in any other activity (writing about your dream and identifying your dreamsigns?) that requires full wakefulness. If you have a sleeping partner, it will be okay to get up and go into another room during this time.
4. Lie back in the bed, or return to bed, and tell yourself, "Next time I'm dreaming, I want to recognize that I'm dreaming."
5. Imagine yourself asleep. See yourself in the dream you just memorized realizing that you are dreaming. Find a dreamsign in your imagery and when you see it, say to yourself, "I'm dreaming." Then imagine something you might want to deliberately do once you realize you are dreaming.
6. Alternate steps 4 and 5 until you feel your intention to recognize you are dreaming is firmly fixed in your mind. Allow yourself to return to sleep.

LaBerge says that if it takes you a longer time to fall asleep than usual employing the MILD technique, don't worry, because the longer you are awake, the more times you will be able to repeat the technique and reinforce your intention.

According to the Lucidity Institute,[7] one common way to

[7] A membership organization, established by Dr. LaBerge, that studies and reports on lucid dreaming research. Their address is P.O. Box 2364, Stanford, CA 94309, 415-851-0252.

stimulate lucid dreaming is to question or test reality during the day. As you go about your daily activities, ask yourself, "Am I awake or dreaming?" so you will be able to ask this also while dreaming. Recognize when you are awake or dreaming. Question your surroundings by reading some words. Looking away, will them to change. If they have changed when you look back, you're dreaming.

Some research from the Institute suggests that morning naps taken on the same morning that dreamers awakened 90 minutes earlier than usual were more effective in promoting lucid dreaming than afternoon naps.

Under much different circumstances, psychologist Arnold Mindell reports it's not uncommon for people who are near death to have lucid dreams in which they see, hear, or feel things that are occurring in distant places. But be assured, having a lucid dream does not mean you are near death. Quite the contrary. You may never feel so exhilarated.

Reports from dreamers suggest that lucid dreams are more vivid, colors brighter and feelings more intense. So get ready to push off. And if you need a boost, *Exploring the World of Lucid Dreaming,* by Dr. LaBerge and Howard Rheingold, contains a number of exercises for perfecting your technique.

PSYCHIC OR PSI DREAMING

Mankind has a long history of experiencing dreams that bring messages or warnings of things to come. Believing that psi—a general term applied to all psychic phenomena—or psychic dreaming is possible and that you can do it is a *major* factor in having, or developing, this dreaming skill. Practice also promotes psychic dreaming for some.

If you are a nonbeliever, your chances of having a psychic dream are less likely, although some psychic dreams have come unbidden and changed hardened skeptics into surprised believers. The life of chemist Rita Dwyer, former president of the Association for the Study of Dreams, was saved by an associate who several times dreamed of pulling her out of a fire. When Dwyer's laboratory exploded, the friend knew she was inside because of his dreams, and was able to rescue her.

This is an example of the psychic dream we know the

most about, the precognitive dream. In it someone sees, or has some insight into, future occurrences, although sometimes this is simply the result of our unconscious having put together some signals or clues that we noticed but ignored.

If you have a seemingly precognitive dream, consider first if the dream is telling you there are some negative elements occurring in your life that you need to especially notice, or take action about, to diminish their future effect.

Some people include Jung's notion of synchronistic dreams in the precognitive category, but Jung was emphatic that they were not. Rather, he thought of them as meaningful "coincidences" clustering around a highly charged emotional, archetypal situation.

One of the most prolific writers about precognitive dream skills is parapsychologist Alan Vaughan. Stimulated by his material, Michigan psychologist Marcia Emery began studying precognitive dreaming after the death of her mother. Reviewing her dream diary, Dr. Emery discovered three dreams some four months earlier that she believed mirrored the events of her mother's death.

Subsequent work with her own and the precognitive dreams of others has led Dr. Emery to characterize them as vivid, often with sensuous impact, and as having an awesome quality. They *feel* bigger, more powerful than usual. When you're learning to have precognitive dreams, however, it may be relatively easy to pay little notice until a later experience reminds you of your dream.

Some dreamers acquire characters or images that signal the dream is a precognitive one, such as an animal—one woman sees a white dove, another an eagle, and a third sees one or more deer—a certain color (sparkling or bright white light), or even a famous person. For instance, the actress Jane Seymour appeared in the precognitive dream of one of Dr. Emery's students.

Emery has begun to acquire some evidence suggesting that precognitive dreams may correlate with astrological timing, namely, that more precognitive dreams will occur when the moon passes through the fourth, eighth, ninth, and twelfth houses of your horoscope, and conjuncts with planets Neptune and Uranus, as well as entering the houses ruled by them.[8]

When you are ready to try precognitive dreaming, relax and prepare for bed according to your own method, or suggestions offered elsewhere in this book. Place your dream-recording materials within reach. Then follow the instructions in Dreamercise #22, based on Alan Vaughan's and Marcia Emery's techniques for developing your own personal signal of a precognitive dream, and for programming the appearance of a precognitive dream.

PRECOGNITIVE DREAMING

1. When you're comfortable in bed, say to yourself, "Dear Higher Mind [or Inner Mind/Intuitive Self/Inner Dream Director], I thank you for any direction you have to offer me about any future event. Please send me a signal for a precognitive dream, so I will know that this dream represents an occurrence that can go forward in time."
2. An alternative request used by Emery, modified from suggestions given by Alan Vaughan in his book *The Edge of Tomorrow*, can be: "Dear Inner Dream Director [Higher Mind, Inner Mind, Intuitive Self],[9] I need advice and guidance. I

[8]Personal communication, June 1993.

[9]Alan Vaughan addresses his "dream tiger." Derived from one of Vaughan's own dreams, "dream tiger" is his term for the remnant of a primitive aspect of our inner selves. Vaughan hypothesizes that it sent premonitory dreams to our earliest ancestors when a dangerous animal was near at hand, awakening them and saving them from death.

need a dream that will answer my question . . . [state your question]. Please give me a simple picture that I can understand. I will arise early in the morning with the dream picture fresh in my mind. I shall be able to remember it easily and write it down. Its meaning will become clear to me. I shall follow its advice."

3. When you record your dream, according to Dreamercise #1, pay special attention to the emotions in this dream. If your dream question can be answered with a "yes" or "no," consider whether the positive emotions in the dream signal a yes answer and the negative ones signal a no answer. If the emotion seems to be stronger or greater than the dream scene implies, it may be a precognitive dream, according to Vaughan.
4. Indicate whether the dream was very clear and whether you were unusually tired, drained, or feeling emotional during the preceding 24 hours, which will give you clues as to the state that promotes precognitive dreaming for you.
5. Vaughan's other clues that the dream may be precognitive include: elements that seem particularly bizarre or don't make sense, things that have never happened, people you've never met, situations you've never before encountered.[10]
6. If you know your horoscope, record which psi-favorable times appeared in your horoscope at the time of the dream.

Telepathic dreams are another well-known type of psi dream. The dreamer receives messages from someone else, from another's dreams, or seems to pick up another's

[10]Alan Vaughan, *Patterns of Prophecy,* p. 132.

thoughts and express them as a dream. Dreams of ghosts, apparitions, and those recently dead, who speak to you telepathically, also fall into this category. The strength of the emotional link is an important factor in telepathic dreams.

Out-of-body dreams, in which you "float" up and look down upon yourself or upon another location, are a third type of psi dream. During the fourth type, clairvoyant dreams, you accurately view—some psychics claim they actually visit—other, actual locations, often ones that you've never seen.

If psychic dreaming sparks your interest, you might want to consult the books by Aerbach and Ullman (Annotated References below) and those by Tanous and Gray, and Vaughan (see Bibliography).

ANNOTATED REFERENCES

Auerbach, Loyd. *Psychic Dreaming. A Parapsychologist's Handbook*. New York: Warner Books, 1991.

This primer, written by a magician and student of parapsychology, is a good introduction to the kinds of psychic dreaming that are possible. It includes: a chapter on the way other times and cultures, especially American Indians, have used dreams; interviews with three dreamworkers who believe in psychic dreaming; and exercises you can try.

Cartwright, Rosalind, and Lamberg, Lynne. *Crisis Dreaming*. New York: HarperCollins, 1992.

Dr. Cartwright, director of the Sleep Disorder Service and Research Center at Rush–Presbyterian–St. Luke's Medical Center in Chicago, offers effective tips for understanding and changing anxiety dreams, dreams that occur during life crises, and nightmares.

The book presents a number of exercises for learning to handle unpleasant dreams through a procedure she calls "RISC," for: **R**ecognizing when you're having a bad dream, **I**dentifying components of the dream that make you feel bad or that have gone wrong, learning to **S**top the dream action while it's still in progress, and identifying and Changing negative dream dimensions (see Dreamercise #17) into positive ones.

Ullman, Montague, and Krippner, Stanley, with Vaughan, Alan. *Dream Telepathy. Experiments in Nocturnal ESP*. Baltimore: Penguin Books, 1973.

Detailed descriptions of the experiments and explorations in affecting dreams through telepathy conducted at the Maimonides Medical Center in Brooklyn in the 1960s. It contains excellent examples of how the symbols from artwork or other articles are transformed into personal dream symbols. Now in a second edition, published in 1989 by McFarland & Co., North Carolina, it also presents a history of others' earlier attempts or experiences in the 1940s and 1950s with dream telepathy.

Deep into that darkness peering,
Long I stood there wondering, fearing,
Doubting, dreaming dreams
no mortal ever dared to dream before.
EDGAR ALLAN POE

CHAPTER 6

The Dream Quest

In addition to their compensatory function, Jung thought that dreams also had a "prospective" function, which occurred when a dream's content outlined the solution to a conflict or problem. He likened it to a sketch or plan roughed out in advance. There are many well-known accounts of this kind of dream.

The Russian chemist Dmitry Mendeleyev discovered the order of the elements through a dream, while German chemist Friedrich Kekulé von Stradonitz similarly discovered the structure of the benzene molecule. Albert Einstein attributed his theory of relativity to ruminations about a dream he had as a teenager in which he was flying a sled through the sky at faster and faster speeds. When he reached a certain speed, the stars changed shapes and achieved fantastic colors. Elias Howe invented the sewing machine needle after a dream in which he was attacked by natives brandishing spears with holes in the ends.

Freud's hunch about the nature and relationship of dreams and neurosis led to his theories of psychoanalysis; and Jung's own idea of the collective unconscious derived from one of his dreams of entering a basement. It is important to realize, however, that for none of these men did the solution spring from out of nowhere to be expressed as a dream. Rather the dreams occurred after, or during, periods of intense mental concentration.

AGELESS INSPIRATIONS

In addition to having prompted inventions and theories, dreams have heavily influenced and enriched the literature of all countries by expressing important ideas or themes. In the classic literature of India, *nested* dreams (scenes that chain from one dream image to the next) have been aptly used to simultaneously convey the concepts that life is an illusion, and that we must recognize our shadow side; the karmic results of our behavior; and the differences between internal/dream time and reality.

It is well known that dreams have inspired many literary works, including Dante's *The Divine Comedy,* Mary Bysshe Shelley's *Frankenstein,* and Robert Louis Stevenson's *The Strange Case of Dr. Jekyll and Mr. Hyde.* Poems based on dreams were popular in the Middle Ages. "The Nun's Tale" in *The Canterbury Tales* was derived from one of Chaucer's dreams.

Other authors who have indicated they use their dreams for inspiration include Jack Kerouac, Graham Greene, and Sylvia Plath. San Francisco radio host Naomi Epel interviewed 26 well-known novelists, including Stephen King, Anne Rice, Sue Grafton, Amy Tan, and William Styron, all of whom recounted ways dreams influence their writings. Pulitzer Prize winner William Meredith works the content of his dream images into his poetry.

The Koran is said to have been delivered to Mohammed in dreams, even though he later forbade the practice of dream interpretation. Mohammed was apparently a great archetypal dreamer. No less than the Archangel Gabriel served as his guide during the heavenly travel experiences and conversations with Abraham, Moses, and Jesus that became the contents of his Night Journey manuscript, the *Lailatal-Miraj.* There are at least 20 dreams/visions in the Old and New Testaments of the Bible.

Dreams have even influenced the content of films. Shadowy dream sequences were an integral part of the film noir genre of the 1940s. Swedish filmmaker Ingmar Bergman delves into his own dreams for movie themes. By bringing his dreamworld into waking life, Bergman says he confronts and heals his own fears, developing new meanings and understandings of life. He uses film to connect his symbolic world with ours.

Like others before you, honoring your dream symbolism and bringing it into form in your waking life is one way to enhance your dream life and explore your unconscious. According to Meier, Asclepias frequently required a literary production as an offering of thanks for a successful healing dream, thus making him the patron of learned men and artists.

To bring a dream into another form honors it; continues your work with its message, and anchors the dream into your waking life, making its message more accessible. While I was working on this book, doctors identified (mistakenly) a mass in an acquaintance's liver. That night in one of my dreams I saw an invisible baseball field bordered by a line of bright energy, open at one end. It formed the shape of a V and matched the shape of a string of red hearts that hangs over my bed.

Since energy lines appear so seldom in my dreams, I took this as an important dream and a signal to do further work with it. One result was the following poem, which has the same title as the one I gave the dream, and plays around with the significant shape within the dream:

Viewpoint

I know you're worried.
You don't ask for reassurance,
  so I dream enough for both of us.

An invisible baseball field,
  enclosed by bright lines of energy,
  matches the hearts strung
  above my bed.

Like point.
perspective single
lines a
they from
open close
or

game? ???????? anger?
the our
change transform
we we
Can

Into
loving
energy
fields
opening
ourselves
to
the
world?

Clearly this poem is far from priceless and not even close to prizewinning, but it *is* precious to me. The point is that poetry derived from your dreams doesn't have to be perfect, follow traditional rules, or even have great artistic merit for you to play around with it, magnify it, and possibly acquire additional insight into the dream's message. The poetry is for you, not someone else, although in some instances your writing may help others. Following a lengthy and harrowing ordeal with a misdiagnosed broken wrist, psychologist Patricia Garfield wrote *The Healing Power of Dreams* as her gift to others who might experience traumatic injuries or experiences.

ACTUALIZING YOUR DREAMS

Dreamercises #23 and #24 offer suggestions for ways you can do something tangible to integrate your dream experience into conscious life. Jungians call this "actualizing the dream.'' It also helps further the dreaming process. So let your dreams stir you.

SAY IT YOUR WAY

1. Patricia Garfield suggests that when you understand the life situation your dream is referring to, write out a plan of action; or, at the very least, write down a decision you have made as a result of the dream.
2. Garfield also finds it helpful to use the dream content or message to create proverbs that express your life values. You might want to make this a section of your dream journal. You can also include key phrases or affirmations stimulated by the dream.
3. Whether or not you consider yourself a poet, you may find it pleasurable or insightful to take images from a recent dream and write a two- or four-line poem—certainly more if you wish—that embodies the symbology and/or message of your dream. It doesn't have to rhyme, if that's your idea of poetry. Rather you are trying to capture the dream's essence.
4. Form the dream's message into a plot for a short story. Who or what's missing? What do you think needs to happen?
5. Research the creatures (animals, insects), characters, countries, or other images that appear in your dreams. Then observe how these images change over time as your inner horizon expands.

If writing isn't your interest, perhaps you, like Chef Roland Passot of La Folie restaurant in San Francisco, would enjoy dreaming about food and creating new dishes from those dreams.[1]

For many people and cultures, dreams give them songs and ideas for artworks. According to von Franz, religion for the Labradorian Naskapi tribe consists of giving their dreams permanent form through singing and painting. They believe each person possesses Mistap'eo, the Great Man in the Heart, who sends the dreams.

In ancient Hawaii songs and dance movements for the hula were often experienced first in dreams. Powerful dream songs that could bring rain, heal the sick, and ensure a good crop were received by Papago Indians. It was in a dream that composer Richard Wagner heard the initial chord of *Das Rheingold*, the first opera in his *Der Ring des Nibelungen*.

Jung believed that since the unconscious works in images, image has power and value of its own and should be honored. He carved, sculpted, and painted many of his dream images into the stonework of his Bollingen retreat on Lake Zurich. Much of the art of Australian aborigines, presented as layered circles, spirals, and other geometric shapes, is "dreamtime" events or maps *(churinga)* as "seen" by the spiritual essence of the artist.

Modern Mayan women still get their weaving designs from dreams. "It came to my heart in a dream," says one woman in the National Geographic television special on Mayan culture, "Lost Kingdoms of the Maya."

Dreamercise #24 suggests additional ways you can honor the Great Man or Woman in your heart and keep your dream images active in waking life.

---

[1]Caroline Bates, "Spécialités de la Maison, California" (restaurant review section), *Gourmet*, February 1991, p. 56.

DREAM TREASURES

1. Jungian analyst Clarissa Pinkola Estés believes that dreams carry the possibility of healing our psychic wounds if we transform their symbols into waking actions that reverse the dream injury. For instance, if an animal (representing you) feels helpless in the dream, do something in your waking world that results in your feeling more powerful or creative.
2. Some people make a kind of talisman from their dreams. Use cardboard, clay, or whatever medium is handy or appeals to you. Worn or carried with you, or displayed where you can see it, your dream message continues to influence your waking consciousness.
3. Whatever your artistic skills or hobbies, translate your dream into those mediums: drawings, paintings, watercolors, clay or plasticine modeling paste, collages, engravings, carvings, needlework. Even if you think you have no talent in these areas, pick one and re-create the essence, or some other aspect, of your dream. After all, the activity is for you alone, no one else.
4. Dance your dream; choreograph its movement.
5. Instead of telling a dream's content as you normally might, deliver it like a magnificent oration.
6. Act the role of storyteller. Tell your dream as if it were a piece of tribal heritage and you were instructing the other members of the

tribe, especially the children, adding bits of wisdom or reminders here and there.[2]

7. Retell your dream as if it were a fairy tale, using fairy-tale castles, forests, rescuing characters, wicked stepmothers or witches—whatever is appropriate to your dream. Krippner and Feinstein use this technique to discover a person's personal myth.
8. Create a three- or five-word mantra from the dream's theme and meditate on it. Repeat or chant it, observing whatever images come into your mind's eye, or allowing the mantra to change as you repeat it over and over. As an alternative, pick an image from the dream and meditate, or concentrate on it, observing what comes and allowing it to change in whatever way it seems to want to.

Jungian analyst Marion Woodman says that creating from a dream is like saying *YES* to the soul. It is an acknowledgment of yourself at a most profound level.

As part of that acknowledgment, Jung painted images from his dreams throughout his life. He believed that when we give a dream image visible form, we clarify and widen our understanding of our unconscious processes. We enhance both waking and dreaming life. Creating from your dreams can enable you to awaken the ecstatic dimension in your life,

[2]If you are interested in learning of others nationwide who value their dreams, contact the Association for the Study of Dreams (ASD), P.O. Box 1600, Vienna, VA 22183, or the Dream Network, 1337 Powerhouse Lane, Suite 22, Moab, Utah 84532.

The Dream Network is a grassroots organization that publishes a quarterly newletter/journal. ASD is an international organization that publishes a quarterly newsletter, quarterly research journal, and holds annual meetings where current research from all disciplines (literature, film, anthropology, psychology) and how-to workshops are presented.

which Jungian analyst Robert Johnson believes we all require.[3]

THE EVER-EXPANDING IMAGE

Circular designs like the sun, wheel, and spiral are prominent in the drawings and structures of every culture. Jung named this universal form the mandala, and considered it to be the basic expression or reflection of the Self, and of dream content.

A Sanskrit word, mandala (correctly pronounced **mun**-deh-leh or **mun**-duh-luh, but more commonly mispronounced man-**dah**-lah in English) means circle or center. Jung wrote that the mandala format reduces confusion and expresses "order, balance, and wholeness,"[4] even when our conscious mind doesn't necessarily understand its content.

Dreamercise #25 teaches you to draw mandalas for individual dreams—or to create a mandala from several dreams—as a way of honoring your dream and of stimulating new ones. On days when you can't remember a dream, drawing a mandala may reflect your state of being after a night of forgotten dreams, and may spawn the next night's dreams.

You can draw single mandalas for each dream or day, or you can draw one major mandala that reflects your dream themes and process over time, as Patricia Garfield does in her *Pathway to Ecstasy*.

---

[3]Johnson expressed this idea in an interview for Volume 3 ("A World of Dreams") of the video series *The Wisdom of the Dream*, produced in 1989 by Border Television and Stephen Segaller.

[4]C. G. Jung, *Archetypes and the Collective Unconscious*, p. 361.

JOURNEY TO THE CENTER

Although mandalas can be made of any material—flowers, sand, leather, cloth—it might be easier for you to start by drawing or painting your mandalas. In her book *Creating Mandalas*, art therapist Susanne Fincher suggests you begin by using colored chalk, colored markers, or oil pastels on drawing paper. You can make the circular form by drawing around a paper plate, but in my workshops I have also used the paper plate itself as the form, drawing right on the plate.

When you have set aside some uninterrupted time to create your mandala, have gathered your materials, and are ready to begin, follow the instructions below:

1. Reread your dream, or dream series. Close your eyes and, without judgment, let the dream images stir within you.
2. When you are ready, open your eyes and select a color. Draw your circle freehand, use the paper plate for an outline, or draw on the plate itself.[5]
3. Using some symbol or color that seems to relate to the dream—or feels right—draw a ring, or boundary, around the inner edge of your circle, of whatever thickness seems right to you.

---

[5]If you prefer to use a more stylized Tibetan form, filling in images within already created lines and spaces, Garfield has one suitable for duplication on p. 228 of *Pathway to Ecstasy.*

Although many of the mandalas shown in Jung's writings do not have such a ring, Garfield suggests that the creation of this ring acts in a similar fashion to temple walls, defining and protecting an area of sacred power.

4. Allow the movement of the dream, or dream series, to guide you in filling in the form with whatever colors, patterns, or images—or combinations of these—seem appropriate and meaningful to you. You can work from the outer boundary inward or from the center outward, or even randomly. There is no right way.
5. Taking all the time you need, let the color or design emerge and clarify itself. It becomes what it wants to be.
6. When you have finished, turn the drawing around and look at it from different angles and positions. Mark the top with a T.
8. Date your mandala, so that in the future you can know your sequence of production.
9. If you don't feel finished when you have completed one mandala, draw another, now or later in the day. Be sure to indicate that it is the second, third, or whatever for that given date. If you feel you'd like to add something to your first mandala, it is better to draw a second mandala rather than change the first one.
10. If you've used pastels or chalk, you may want to spray artists' fixative, or unscented hair spray, on the mandala to keep it from smearing.

HOME

According to Dineh (Navaho) tradition, it is Changing Woman, the living principle of life, who brings stories. And it is our stories that connect us to the centers of both our outer and inner worlds: our home, our Self. Myths and dreams can tell us when we're home, when we're grounded within ourselves, when we're centered and connected with all other beings in our world. They give us what anthropologist David Maybury-Lewis, in his television series "Millennium," called the "wisdom of the different yet common." A Dineh woman in that series says, "If you know where home is, you know all things."

The creative dream quest is a continuing journey home. It occurs anew each waking and dreaming moment. The resulting creation/self-realization is both an individual and a communal journey. Occurring in present time, it must also take us back into earlier time, renewing our connection with ancient images and concerns.

It is a thematic quest: the death/rebirth struggle, the battle with, and integration of, opposites, learning to live with paradox, the search for our inner treasure—in short, the hero and heroine's journey. It is the inward dream and the outward activity of the present and the future.

In the final analysis, our dreams are a link to one another and a mechanism for achieving wholeness and oneness within ourselves and with all mankind. Not only are we linked by the fact that we all dream, but by their archetypal content, our dreams intertwine us with the psychic themes of all people. Dreams are one doorway for experiencing our lives within a universal context.

Dreams tell us who we are. When we attune to them, we become sensitive to the "common yet different" that we share with all peoples and all cultures, past and present. In our psyches, where our holiness resides and presides, we move into one consciousness.

Welcome home, dreamer.

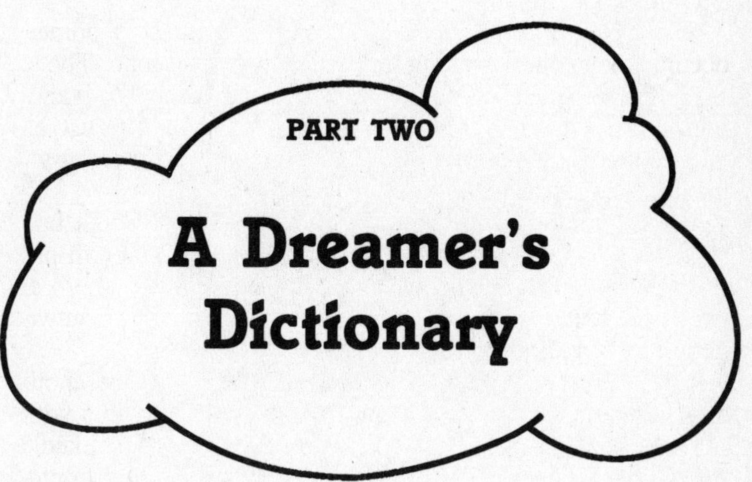

PART TWO

A Dreamer's Dictionary

HOW TO USE THIS DICTIONARY

Cloud Nine dreamer's dictionary takes the next step in the evolution of dream dictionaries. Since the second century, other dictionaries have told dreamers that a specific symbol or dream had a given and distinct meaning, often a prediction.

Rather than limit the meanings of dream symbols/images, *Cloud Nine* entries suggest material that may be developing in your psyche, or psychological energy calling for the recognition it needs so growth can occur. Even if it's not included in the dictionary entry, always consider that a dream symbol may have the opposite meaning from the one given, since every symbol has both a positive and a negative aspect.

Cloud Nine entries include questions, clichés, and puns to suggest individual pathways your psychic development might be trying to take through your "dreamscapes." Names in parentheses indicate a reference in the Bibliography and refer to information compiled by that researcher or dreamworker.

Consider the meanings in Part 2 as suggestions pointing to ideas that might not have occurred to you or that might trigger or amplify your own ideas. If they don't connect for you, don't worry and don't try to force them to connect. Although there are some common themes among dreamers, your dreams are *yours and yours alone*. While they may seem mysterious in one sense, on another level, you know more about your dreams than anyone else. Ultimately it is you who will have to decide how they apply to your life.

The dictionary will be more useful to you if, before you look up an image, you jot down what it means to you, given your personal and unique history. It's likely that words that relate to your profession, special skills, or avocations will have much more elaborate meanings for you than those given in the dictionary. Consider those meanings first. (See Dreamercise #14, Part 1, to create a personal dream dictionary.)

Dream symbolism can be a reflection of personal idioms, puns, or slang with which you're familiar. Names of cities, people, or objects can be puns that give you clues or break down into smaller images, as in being in the city of Liverpool (liver/pool) or Los Angeles (the angels), or being on a boat named the *Bright Lady* (light/woman). Sometimes dream actions are puns. Avoiding something in a dream may relate to "a void," or something that's apparent in a dream may relate to "a parent."

While many symbols are singular in the dictionary (an otter), plurals, or more than one (otters, a group of otters), may signal special emphasis or a compounding of a situation. A specific number (say, nine otters) may reflect the symbology of that number (nines = triple victory) or your personal symbology to the number, perhaps from a nursery rhyme ("nine/ten do it again").

A number of clichés are included in the dictionary because that's the kind of "logic" the unconscious uses. If a particular cliché doesn't seem to exactly fit your dream, let it float around in your mind to see if it applies in another way, or stimulates another, more applicable one.

Where an image was also a symbol or attribute of a god or goddess, you may want to review the story attached to that deity in order to check whether it pertains to a mythology active in your own life, or an energy attempting to manifest itself within your psyche. Good books for this include: Funk & Wagnalls *Folklore, Mythology, and Legend,* Davidson's *Gods and Myths of Northern Europe,* Crossley-Holland's *The Norse Myths,* Walker's *The Woman's Encyclopedia of Myths and Secrets,* and Bolen's *Goddesses in Everywoman* and *Gods in Everyman.*

If you think a dream indicates a medical condition, don't hesitate to consult a doctor, even if only to rule out the possibility so you can return to a symbolic message.

Remember, dreams are your productions, your gateway to your inner state of being. Their symbols are the hieroglyphs of your unconscious; therefore, if the definitions in Part 2 don't satisfy or seem to make sense, work on the dream with one or more of the dreamercises in Part 1.

The "right" interpretation of a dream is the one that makes sense to you *and* gives you a new understanding or insight into previously hidden or unacknowledged aspects of yourself. By approaching your dream images playfully and with no prejudicial forethought, you free your creativity to explore new possibilities along the dream path and to enhance your inner journey.

Symbology from A to Z

abandon(ed)

If you were the one abandoned, how old were you? Check for feelings of being lost/overwhelmed regarding a current situation, possibly rooted in the past at the age you were in the dream, or a situation that began that many years ago. Otherwise, it can suggest feelings of being misguided/misled, possibly reflecting present or old situations with respect to your family, especially if you're working to separate yourself from family experiences/situations. It can also signal estrangement from your unconscious; having lost sight of your spirit, your greater life goals, or your life purpose.

If you did the abandoning, check for feelings of relief or guilt. Is this a new or typical action for you? Is there a situation in your life you wish you could handle by "reckless abandon," especially an oppressive or sexual one? Dr. Rosalind Cartwright, who has done extensive studies on the dreams of divorcing people, writes that abandonment is a common theme for people experiencing severe depression after separation; it can signal the need for therapeutic help.

See **alone; labyrinth/maze**.

abbey

Religious beliefs/aspirations; need to escape for spiritual renewal; need to be a part of a community for your own support or to support the efforts of others; identification with a larger/higher goal, possibly related to public or charitable service.

See **monastery**.

abdomen

As part of the lower body, the abdomen represents natural instincts and repressed emotions, the physical world, as contrasted to intellectual ideas. If exposed or decorated, the belly, as the vulnerable underside, can represent trust, or desire to express our primal emotions/instincts. If wounded, the fear of such expression, or of intimacy. Who did the wounding and what aspect of yourself might he/she represent? If swollen, it may represent the womb and be related to pregnancy or fertility.

As part of the digestive process, the abdomen may refer to being unable to digest or accept something, or to assimilating new ideas/attitudes. It may represent complaining (''bellyaching''), being disgusted or finished with something/someone (''I've had a bellyful of you''), immobility, or fear or cowardice (''don't have the guts'').

See **body; stomach**.

abducted

See **kidnapped/captured/abducted**.

abnormal

Although many things appear abnormal/unusual in dreams, pay special attention to those that seem particularly strange or unusual. Whether they are part of you, another, or the environment, assume they reflect some aspect of you, or your life functioning. Use Dreamercise #3, Chapter 1, Part 1, to determine the message of the distortion.

Abnormal *objects* are often used to ward off malevolence, evil spirits, or your shadow side.

See **amulet(s); body; shadow**.

aborigine/aboriginal

The ancient, primitive aspect of ourself, possibly sexual urges; the struggle to cope with, subdue, or dominate your instincts or waking-life surroundings/situation. Depending on behavior and dress, it could be an archetypal symbol for contact with higher inner wisdom, sometimes represented as a shaman or guide (Wise Old Man). It might represent connection with the mother archetype (Mother Earth) or current feelings/activities related to community/world ecology.

See **Africa/African; American Indian; person, dark or dark-skinned; Wise Old Man**.

abortion

If pertaining to an actual situation, pay attention to your feelings in the dream and after you awaken. Are they unfinished and need to be recognized and responded to?

If not an actual situation, is there a present situation that you have a wish/need to end abruptly; wish you could get out of, yet feel helpless to do so; fear/feel there will be a miscarriage of justice? Are you not allowing some situation or emotion to come "full term"?

See **baby**.

above

If looking down at another or a location, may reflect feeling/wishing you are "above it all," aloof or superior toward some person/situation. Perhaps you're concerned about a situation wherein you wish things were more revealing/honest ("aboveboard"). It may also be a disguise for feeling just the reverse (see **below**).

See **ascend(ing); flying; high/height; mountain(s); position(s); standing above**.

abroad/traveling abroad

Is this a wish to travel, or anxiety about traveling, to a particular place; or does it reflect an actual place you have visited? If the latter, check your feelings/reactions to that place and its people. Could they, and any architecture, represent some aspect of yourself or characteristics you wish you had? Perhaps it's some characteristic you do have but haven't recognized (still "foreign" to you). Possibly you need these characteristics to deal with a present situation. Is some person/situation making you feel like "a broad," put down, or sleazy?

See **architecture; foreign country; travel(ing)/journey**.

abscess

Something trying to come to a head and be expressed; physical or psychological toxins (prejudices, attitudes, negative emotions) attempting to be released. Consider the symbolism of the body area where the sore/abscess is located and how you, or someone else, took care of it. Are there emotional toxins still festering, waiting to be acknowledged and cleansed? What are you sore about?

See **body; disease; infection; swelling; teeth**.

abuse

If not referring to actual abuse, consider the symbology of the body area(s) being hurt, and the way you respond.

Whether you are the abused or the abuser, the action symbolizes hostile, possibly self-destructive, feelings. If you're an actual abuser of persons/drugs, you may not dream about abuse to yourself but rather will disguise it as behavior toward animals, houses (the body), and other inanimate objects.

See **addict(ed); alcohol/alcoholic**.

abyss

The unknown; the depths; the source of life and wisdom; readiness to change your concept of God. Your location with respect to the abyss and your feelings in the dream are particularly important as to whether this is seen as a fearful experience (losing control/ability), or as an adventure (exploring new abilities; going beyond the bounds of present knowledge/behavior). It can be the archetype of both the good (nurturing) and bad (terrifying or engulfing) mother. In mythology, the Great Abyss can represent the underworld, or the archetypal Great Mother. Many ethnic legends describe the world as emerging from a great abyss, symbolizing new life and development, potential.

See **above; descend(ing); falling** (if applicable); **standing above**.

acacia tree

Often a symbol of the sun because of its golden blossoms, the acacia was sacred to the Egyptian sun god and to Horus. In Old Testament tradition acacia wood is the wood of life.

access

Look to the ease/difficulty with which you gain access to suggest your feelings about a waking situation, or life attitude. To identify the issue/situation, consider the symbolism of the place of access and of any of the characters/objects helping or hindering you.

accident

An accident may be a way of preventing/postponing your taking some action, making some decision, or taking personal responsibility. It can reflect self-punishment for real/imagined guilt; hostility for which you need take no responsibility if someone else is hurt ("accidentally on purpose"); a message that you need to slow down and attend to happenings, integrate feelings or experiences. Are you afraid you're "making a wreck of things"?

account(s)

Record keeping; a "count"

(point) for/against you; something you need to answer for; an elevation of prestige or prestigious person (a count). Are you "a-count-able" for something, or unable to count (lowered self-esteem)? How do your accounts/relationships stand? Accounts also have to do with keeping the "right order," an attribute of the Egyptian goddess Ma'at, whose name is frequently mistakenly translated as simply "truth" (Norman), and whose headdress was composed of a single feather. Therefore, accounts/keeping correct accounts may symbolize the order/structure of your life or, archetypally, the entire order/structure of creation.

See **bookkeeping; feather; royalty**.

ace

The ability/energy to accomplish some task quite well ("you're the best"); a reminder that you have unused resources upon which to draw ("have an ace up your sleeve") or that you "haven't played all your cards yet." If you've been perceiving yourself as rather lowly in status/skills, the dream may be a wish fulfillment to be more accomplished, or a compensatory dream to establish balance.

If applicable, see **cards/playing cards**.

ache

If you're certain this doesn't refer to an actual physical ailment about to appear, then it may symbolize stored energy or emotion needing to be recognized; or unresolved feelings. Consider that part of the body that aches for clarification.

See **armor; body; pain**.

acid

Assuming this is not a drug-related dream, acid eats away at surfaces, but is too destructive a process to be considered positive. So acid can symbolize something negative that's "eating away" at your core (possibly self-destructive impulses/actions), or at a relationship. Consider the symbology of the specific object/body part for clues about what message or infantile/unacknowledged emotion might be trying to emerge and reveal itself. Do you need to use the old "acid test" to get at or face the truth?

Mild acid is sometimes used as a cleansing agent, especially on hard metals. Are you being so hardheaded about something that it takes acid to get to you and begin the cleansing/enlightening process?

acorn

What's happening to the

acorn and where is it located in the dream? It may signify potential growth; wisdom waiting to be activated/discovered; something you, or someone, is being a little "nutty" about. Do you wish you were a mighty oak, but, in fact, feel like a tiny acorn? What's the next word that comes to mind when you think of acorn?

See **seed(s); squirrel; tree(s)**.

acrobat

Precision; carefulness; balance. Acrobats are often perceived as fearless risk takers. Is there something in your life about which you need to be more, or are already being too, adventurous? Archetypally the acrobat can symbolize inversion or reversal, upsetting the established order. In ancient Crete acrobats jumped over large/fierce animals to indicate that death was being overcome and life being renewed. As a reversal, acrobat can also symbolize the turning of opposites.

See **balance(d)/balancing; circus; opposites; trickster; x**.

actor/actress

Look at me; look at me. If actor/actress is not your profession/avocation, it can signal a need for attention/recognition; a fiction you're maintaining; some drama you're attempting to introduce into waking life. Is there a situation wherein you're trying to convince yourself/another that you are truly sincere, when, in fact, you're playing a role? (See **mask(s); persona**.)

What role do you play in the dream? Are you overemphasizing those characteristics in waking life, or do you need to incorporate/activate them to accomplish some task ("act the part")? Do the characteristics of the actor/actress point to an actual person or relationship?

Perhaps you or another have recently been "caught in the act," as you were "acting up." Have you been "playing the fool"? Do you need to "get your act together," "act your age," or "get in on the act"?

If you dream about a known actor/actress, you may wish to connect with his or her fame—especially if you dream you are a part of the person's family or entourage—or wish to have those characteristics of the person that you especially admire. To be close to the person may mean secrets will be revealed to you, which will make you special in some way. Look for any puns included in the name. (See How to Use This Dictionary at the beginning of Part 2.)

See **applause; audience; person, famous; roles; secret; stage; theater**.

Adam

Adam, our tribal father, can signify a process of curiosity about, or need to return to/examine, your roots, beginnings, or past. For a male, it may represent "the first" of any masculine experience, especially sexual. Edinger says the creation of Eve from Adam symbolizes human nature becoming separated from its wholeness, which brings awareness of opposites (a new consciousness) and the beginning of psychic development (see **thief/theft**). Together Adam and Eve also symbolize the birth of consciousness (by eating of the fruit from the tree of the knowledge of good and evil). They personify the dual powers or energies (opposites) of the world.

See **Eden, Garden of; Eve; father; history**.

addict(ed)

If you're not an addict, dreaming of being addicted can represent fear that you have lost control; that some person/thing has more power over you than you'd like; a need to avoid some harmful/dangerous situation; feeling that your life is meaningless and you're seeking the spirit within. If you abstain from the tempting situation, it suggests you have new strength/power or, possibly, more than you've given yourself credit for.

If you have been addicted and are in recovery/abstinence, first-phase dreams have little to do with addiction and are, typically, dreams of violence, mutilation, and persecution (Morrison). Second-phase dreams (20–90 days into recovery) deal with struggles for control. Third-phase dreams (30–120 days) depict new living spaces, ownership, and positive self-identification. In fourth-phase dreams (60–150+ days) you're once again in situations in which you're using drugs. [One dreamer told me that the dream is so real, it's hard to tell the difference, especially if you wake up with symptoms that mimic your addiction. He regards it as a warning reminding him how easy it is to give up control.] Fifth-phase dreams (90–180 days) show ownership, new discoveries, new and positive behaviors, and symbols of wholeness. The recovering addict then cycles through these dreams again and again, making the thematic hero's journey (Morrison).

See **alcohol/alcoholic; drink(ing); drug(s)/taking a drug; medicine/medication; vampire**.

address

If an address where you once lived, consider your age and any successes or failures you had when living at that address. The house/address may represent you at that age. Is there something you missed or something that occurred then that's related to a present situation?

If a current address, it may be a message about your psychological "space"; anxieties you have about protecting it; or someone who's intruding into your emotional space.

If not an address where you once lived, consider the symbolism of the numbers of the address; any pun on the street name; and any traits of the person living at that address. Do you need/wish you had those traits for a current situation? Or is the dream calling you to activate them?

An address can be a pun regarding your ability to address (face) an issue/relationship, or to deliver your message. How easy or difficult a time were you having? To forget/lose your address suggests aspects of yourself you don't want to face; that you've lost psychological direction (goals, aims?).

See **childhood home; home; lost**.

adolescent/adolescence

If you're beyond adolescence, yet you are still the adolescent in the dream, it can symbolize immature feelings; sexual instincts; an aspect of yourself that still needs developing in order to achieve fulfillment; a struggle for independence. Consider your feelings during/following the dream. Can you connect them to feelings/experiences you had as an adolescent, perhaps awakened by some present situation?

If not you, it still may represent you, but could also be someone in waking life you regard as responding in immature ways. How you interact may offer clues to your actual feelings.

See **appearance**. If an exact age, see **number(s)**.

adore(d)/adoration

Strong feelings/emotions. If you're being adored, it may reflect a need to raise your esteem; therefore, low self-esteem. If you're the adoring one, you may be losing yourself (your ideals/integrity?) to an idea/emotion; or you may have projected aspects of yourself onto the other and are ignoring that you have those qualities too. Use Dreamercise #3, Part 1, to attend to/acknowledge this awareness, so you can become a more whole person.

See **worship**.

adultery

See **sex**.

advertisement

The nature/location of the advertisement determines whether it is a self-aggrandizing or negative message; possibly a need to be noticed. If about you, it can be a form of self-reflection, but one that puts distance between you and the recognition; therefore, a repressed, or little acknowledged, feeling/instinct seeking to emerge. Are you "advertising your (sexual?) wares" or did you do something "in-ad-vert-ently"?

See **mirror; reflection**.

advice/advise

Are you advising, or receiving advice? Does this say something about your current role with respect to authority or knowledge, feelings of power/helplessness, or convictions? Depending on who is advising you, it may represent a message from your Self, shadow, or superego (conscience).

See **voice**.

affair

See **sex**.

afraid

See **emotion(s); fear**.

Africa/African

Inasmuch as Africa is currently considered the birthplace of man, to dream of Africa may represent the primal tribe; your need to identify with the tribe or some group/community (are you accepted or not?); primitive sexual urges. Consider the symbolism of any special characteristics/clothing/behavior, especially if different from your own. Although modern travel has allowed us to learn more about Africa, it was once known as the "dark continent," and may, therefore, represent your unconscious or shadow aspect.

If you're African-American, Africa may represent issues related to your heritage and belongingness, and may be associated with your personal myths. If you're white, an African dream character first represents your knowledge, ideas, or biases about Africans. An African can also represent an archetypal (shadow) figure, or a shaman (magical) figure. If the character is your same sex, it may be your anima/animus.

See **aborigine/aboriginal; anima; animus; Black Madonna; person, dark or dark-skinned; shadow**. If applicable, see **magic; magician**.

age

See **number(s)**.

aggression

Hostility toward some person/idea, possibly feelings you've repressed during waking. How do you react in the dream and how do you feel about your reaction? Is this typical waking behavior, or a way you wish you could be? Are you feeling vulnerable and in need of protection?

See **fear; roles**.

AIDS

A dream sex partner with AIDS, especially in a woman's dream, suggests that a waking relationship may be terminal or destructive (Delaney). Whitmont and Perera suggest that AIDS as a metaphor may reflect your inability to defend your psychological integrity.

aim

Aims often refer to goals, so aiming at a target may express life goals/direction and your abilities; your intent toward someone; preparing for something ("taking aim"). Is your aim "straight as an arrow," or is it that you "can't hit the side of a barn"?

See **arrow(s); bow and arrow; gun(s); target**.

air

One of the four elements, air symbolizes life and is considered a "masculine" or active element, often *the* primary element. Air can symbolize inner/universal spirit; the creative "breath of life"; your own creative energy. Are you "breathing easy" or suffocating in your life situations?

Be alert to emphasis on this image evoking memories of flight, lightness, heat or coldness as related to waking experiences, or other dreams, to help clarify its personal meaning for you.

The Roman goddess Juno (female counterpart of Jupiter) was the personification of air. Identified with the Greek goddess Hera, she, likewise, was the queen of heaven, the protectress of women and of marriage. Her bird was the peacock.

See **breath/breathe; peacock; wind(s)**.

airplane

You're "flying high," and whatever happens can reflect wishes/anxieties/progress regarding your life or professional progress, possibly your ability to "rise above it all" (be careful this is not denial); risk-taking abilities/attitudes. Are you the pilot, in charge but isolated from the rest of the group? Difficulty boarding the plane may reflect anxieties about, or reluctance in, pursuing a particular plan, although missing a plane is a common anxiety dream. An accident suggests the perils of pursuing a particular goal or route, possibly a fall in self-esteem/confidence.

See **flying**.

airport

The point of departure for an unusual/new opportunity; a change in goals. What is your experience in the airport? Do you traverse this challenge with ease, or is it entirely too crowded and you are one of many (self-esteem issue?)?

If applicable, see **crowd**.

alarm

A common alarm dream occurs when dreamers' own clocks are ringing to awaken them. If this is not the case, it may be a signal that it's "time to wake up and smell the coffee," i.e., time to attend to, notice, acknowledge something you've been ignoring or, possibly, are frightened (alarmed) about.

See **fear** (if applicable); **clock**.

albatross

An unusual bird, the albatross is an expression of the concepts/feelings you have about it transferred onto a waking situation/person. Is it a gooney bird or a burden? Does it have a lot of endurance? Since all birds have in common the symbolization of spiritual aspirations/development, are you "having a hard time getting yours off the ground," or are you "all at sea"?

See **bird(s)**. If you think the dream is about an emotional issue, see **air; water**.

alcohol/alcoholic

Drinking liquor, say, at a party, suggests you may be working too hard and need to add some relaxation/fun to your life. Consider how your waking behavior is when you have consumed alcohol and whether you need more or less of this behavior in a current situation (more or less inhibited, more or less negative or positive feelings?). Does your dream behavior indicate you are in, or out of, control?

Since alcohol is sometimes called a "spirit," and since an altered state of awareness often permits us to commune with spirits, alcohol can be considered a symbol for releasing unconscious material, especially the shadow side, or for an expression of your spiritual state. It may indicate you are seeking to find meaning in your life (Jung). Also called "firewater," alcohol can represent a conjunction/union of opposites (Jung). Alchemically, it represented the divine spirit in man.

Dreams of being an alcoholic are symbolic, or result from associated anxiety, because actual alcoholics don't dream well or often. (Alcohol inhibits dreaming.) If you're a recovering alcoholic and dream of getting drunk, it may signal success in ceasing to "act out" your needs, a positive shift in your ability to be in control. Choi found that 83 percent of alcoholics in recovery for more than a year had dreamed about relapsing at least once. He believes that alcoholics who can satisfy their need to drink through dreams can be abstinent longer than those who don't.

See **addict(ed); drink(ing); opposites; water; wine**.

alien(s)

An alien/foreign part of yourself, i.e., one you have failed to recognize and possibly projected onto others (see them as having it). Therefore, it may represent unconscious material about to emerge and be elevated (as in a UFO vision), or a negative or shadow aspect of yourself. For additional cues, consider how you interact with, or are treated by, the aliens; whether they are less evolved than humans (say, reptilian and, therefore, primitive emotions/urges), or more evolved (higher beings = an idealized inner goal or inner creativity?). What part of you is like the alien? How have you rejected or ignored that part? What would change if you accepted/acknowledged it?

See **UFO**.

alike

See **double/duplicate; twins**.

alley

What does an alley represent to you: the back way, a shortcut, sleazy, dirty, sneaking around? Consider the characteristics of your particular alley. How is it related to your waking attitudes/behavior—are you an "alley cat"; is something "right up your alley"; or are you not on the main street (trying to take a shortcut, or have lost sight of your goals)?

alligator

Hidden instincts, which may feel potentially dangerous and destructive. It may be a signal for you to take a new perspective, since in mythology and folk belief the alligator has been both dreaded and venerated. Alligator teeth are often considered to have magical healing powers. What needs to be healed?

See **animal(s); crocodile; reptile(s)**.

alone

Is this a comforting or frightening way to be in your dream? In a positive sense, being alone can express independence, the ability to think for yourself. Negatively, it could represent loneliness or isolation. It can signal being overwhelmed in your waking life and needing time for retreat, restoration, or healing; time to "get in touch" with your innermost needs.

See **abandon(ed); hermit**.

altar/alter

Either word can be a pun for the other. Is there something you need to alter, which is expressed in your dream as an altar? If not a play on words, altar usually has sacred, spiritual, or religious meanings. It can symbolize something that needs to be healed or transformed (altered, as in the Eucharist and Communion). In ancient times an altar was a place for sacrifice. Have you been too self-sacrificing? It's also a place to focus your energy, or where higher energy is focused. Is there something you need to direct more attention toward, possibly your spiritual development?

amber

As a gemstone that's also the fossilized resin of pine trees, it is related to trees and to once-flowing sap (a life source), which has now ceased. Has something in your life become rigid and inflexible? Related to antiquity, amber may refer to old, possibly archaic, ideas/values. Its golden color, and the fact that it often contains bits of ancient material, make it a symbol for eternity; earthiness; preservation.

See **color(s); gem(s); gold(en); tree(s)**.

ambulance

Depends on whether you're the driver (in control?); a paramedic (care-giving ability to deal with emergencies?); or the patient (need to be taken care of; dependent; overwhelmed?). It can signal that some aspect of your psyche is injured and needs to be nurtured and attended to.

See **accident; vehicle(s)**.

America/American

Your values/perceptions about America, possibly freedom and the ability to develop your potential. If you're American, it could represent values of patriotism/loyalty regarding a waking situation; other "American" values you need to awaken for some situation. If an American, are you in the process of weighing/comparing values, perhaps fighting, or reaffirming, your own cultural values?

If applicable, see **abroad/traveling abroad**.

American Indian

That part of yourself in touch with primitive instincts or a more natural (earthy?) way of living. Being in touch with the spirits and relying on native information can symbolize being in contact with/relying on your unconscious knowledge. Metaphysically, it may signal you are on the path of the warrior. However, if you regard American Indians as "savages," they may be your personal symbol for fearful, repressed feelings/instincts; or they may represent other outdated perceptions.

See **aborigine/aboriginal; fear** (if applicable); **hero/heroine**.

amethyst

In gemstone lore, amethyst brings peace of mind and is the birthstone of someone born in January. Because of its purple color, it is considered a sign of humility in Christian symbolism. It can signify a spiritual foundation or spiritual growth, since it is the twelfth foundation stone of the New Jerusalem described in the Book of Revelation. It represents the tribe of Benjamin.

See **color(s); gem(s); purple**.

amnesia

If total amnesia, and you don't know who you are, it suggests the lure to escape from demanding situations; the need or wish to wipe out the past (values, attitudes, family?), accompanied by the belief/fear that you don't have the power to change the past without drastic, possibly self-destructive, measures.

If a temporary amnesia (as in forgetting some relationship, then remembering it later in the dream), it represents the ease with which we can slight others or wipe out their needs in our own narcissistic pursuit of pleasure. What are you trying to ignore or forget about? What have you been careless about attending to?

If applicable, see **accident; fear**.

amputation

Consider the specific body part that has been or was being amputated to determine the kind of power/energy/expression you've lost, or fear you will lose. If already amputated, it may indicate a serious emotional scar (trauma?); loss of confidence or self-esteem. If some part of an animal, consider that animal and its quality/characteristics. How do you need to bring more of that quality into your life?

See **animal(s); body**.

amulet(s)

Since antiquity, amulets have been associated with magical, protective powers, and, in folklore, with the power to succeed in the journey, or complete the required growth tasks. Often given by wisdom/power figures, they represent magical or improbable power that we can draw on to succeed in our venture/quest; reserve energy; or unrecognized unconscious resources. Amulets/talismans are reminders of knowledge that's felt or known but not seen, intuition (Estés).

To elaborate on its meaning, consider any symbolism for the shape, size, and part of the body over which it is worn (if not around the neck), any gemstones or animals associated with it, and any significant number related to it. These may tell you what you fear, or what you are aligned with, and its place in your waking life.

See **fear; magic; stone(s); Wise Old Man**.

amusement park

An amusement park with people, lights, rides, and games may be a call to distraction, or a signal that you need to consider adding enjoyment, expansion, and variety to your life. It may represent a current challenge or a need to push/challenge yourself a little more. Consider everything in the park as expressing some aspect of yourself, and have some fun getting to know your many subtleties and talents. If dark, quiet, and empty, it may be time to open yourself to more fun and adventure.

See **arcade; carnival**.

analyst

If you're not in therapy, this may represent your need for, or your ability to be, analytical about yourself, to make an assessment and become more self-aware; also an inner, therapeutic aspect of yourself. If in therapy, it expresses some feeling about your own analyst. Many people in therapy dream telepathic dreams about ideas/actions their analysts are considering, so check it out.

ancestors

Ancestors, especially ones you've never met, symbolize family traditions and myths; attitudes, prejudices, limitations we have inherited/learned from our family; long-buried traits, or other aspects of the self, now craving expression. Archetypally they may represent the collective unconscious.

See **ancient; family**.

anchor

If an object anchored to the earth, it suggests coming from a solid, secure place where you're able to support others, or, conversely, feeling insecure and needing some strong support. It may reflect a need to collect or hold on to things, possibly because of anxiety about running out of material possessions—and, ultimately, love.

If on a boat or in the water, and in good shape, it can represent your ability to use and grow from unconscious material, or to trust your intuition/inner awareness. If rusty, it suggests some potential problems—possibly from the past, or long-standing—that need to be cleaned up.

ancient

Anything ancient/old likely represents our past, especially valuable/revered experiences; the wisdom of the ages and sages; possibly memories from the collective unconscious. Ancient peoples/buildings may represent family tradition; family stories; family members and their ways, especially grandparents/elderly relatives. How might you need that input or influence now? Are you unwittingly carrying on certain behaviors? With what satisfaction or anxiety?

See **old**.

anesthetic/anesthesia

If not dreamt shortly before/after surgery, which would be related to actual surgical experience, it may represent a part of you that is deadened to certain feelings/ideas; a "false" or magic sleep, as induced in fairy tales; a need to escape present responsibilities. Who or what does it take to awaken you? Are you waiting for Prince Charming?

See **awake(n)**.

angel(s)

In its best sense, the appearance of an angel often precedes a revelation/insight and heralds the need for, or represents the active process of, spiritual transformation; a wisdom message.

Angels represent invisible energy forces at work, which have become temporarily visible; therefore, unconscious material coming into consciousness. In metaphysics, angels have become *devas*, natural energy forces that also bring wisdom messages, often related to gardening or ecology but not necessarily limited to those subjects. Angels, or other winged humans, may represent high or spirited ideals; lofty goals; religious aspirations; feeling a need for guidance.

In early Christianity, angels symbolized the death, or repression, of animal instincts, which may be what is now coming into your conscious awareness. They can also symbolize someone who has died, and in that sense, represent eternity; or kinship with God. In Christian symbolism the evangelist Matthew is represented as an angel.

If applicable, see **climbing a ladder**. (Angels often ascend/descend on ladders.)

anger

The feeling you have toward something/someone in waking life, but are unwilling or unable, because of circumstances, to recognize or express. If your dream anger results in aggressive action, consider whether that action is positive and self-protective, which may indicate growing strength/power (if this is new behavior), or hostility/destruction. How do you feel about expressing anger in the dream? With what ease/difficulty do you accept the dream experience as an aspect of yourself, both in the dream and in waking life? Anger can be a disguise for fear, so check for waking feelings of fear. Recurring anger dreams following a waking crisis suggest you may be having trouble resolving the situation.

See **emotion(s); fear; impasse**.

anima

This archetypal concept changed over Jung's lifetime, and some contemporary Jungians have subsequently come to view it differently as well. Originally Jung considered it the ultimate feminine life principle of the collective unconscious and the feminine aspects of the male personality (sense of worth/value, ability to feel). Later he came to consider it as the personified image of a man's soul, and, still later, as the personification of a man's psyche, which is still sometimes indistinguishable from "soul" in Jung's writings.

She may appear in a man's dream when he has failed to attend to/acknowledge his feminine qualities. She is the introspective side of life and part of the shadow archetype, thus she may appear as an unknown, but extremely significant or noticeable, woman.

The anima develops out of a man's relationship with his personal mother, his own inborn femininity, and his particular cultural "mythology" of all that is feminine. Therefore, contemporary Jungians are aware that to a certain extent, she can be the bearer of cultural/patriarchal sexism (Hopcke). For this reason, some of them would rather focus on the fact that the anima figure/process is that which bridges or connects the conscious with the unconscious. The anima bears important messages about the state of the Self and the self-growth process.

Although Jung considered the anima to always appear as a female, Hopcke has found that in homosexual men, the anima may appear as a masculine figure.

In traditional fairy tales, the anima is often represented as the "fair maiden," or the "damsel in distress," who is awakened/rescued by the hero. (Remember Sleeping Beauty?)

See **animus; Great Mother; Mary, Virgin; moon/moonlight; mother; Self; water; woman/women; Wise Old Woman**.

animal(s)

Animals usually represent some aspect of ourselves, especially instinctual/biological ("bestial") feelings/wishes from the unconscious. What specific instinct/emotion/urge may be made more clear by your personal associations to your dream animal?

In Jungian dream psychology, the more primitive the animal, the deeper the layers of the unconscious it represents; or the more fundamental/undifferentiated are the feelings or instincts it represents (Signell). More frightening animals represent fearful attitudes toward instinctual or unconscious material, while helpful animals represent ideas/concepts closer to consciousness. Animals that are a combination of human and animal (see **mermaid; Minotaur**) can represent a transitional phase in your developing consciousness (Taylor). Mammals appear in the dreams of women throughout their lives and may express their connection as milk-giving creatures, or may represent themselves (Van de Castle). Sometimes, however, the characteristics of a particular animal refer to someone in your waking life with similar characteristics. During pregnancy both the expectant mother *and* father dream more frequently of animals.

Animals can also represent incredibly strong (active?) divine/cosmic forces. Taming an animal refers to the desire or concern (depending on dream feeling) to tame one's own instincts or unconscious. An injured/wounded animal represents some way in which you are instinctually/psychically wounded. Consider the animal's qualities/injuries. How do they relate to waking functions/feelings?

Who is in control in the dream, you or the animal? If the animal is controlling you, it might represent something that is controlling you in your waking life (Krakow and Neidhardt).

If you have trouble getting an exact meaning for a specific animal, become the animal. What are its major characteristics? Move and behave as you think that animal behaves. How is the action/emotion similar to, or different from, your typical behavior/feelings? Do you need more or less of it in your waking life?

A talking animal is an archetype for the Self. Notice its age, attributes (a kitten or a tiger?), and sex (a message from the anima or animus, depending on the dreamer's sex). Its message is often some form of wisdom. For animals who speak and display superior knowledge, see also **Wise Old Man**.

See entries for specific animals. For animal skins, see **skin; tail**.

animus

The ultimate masculine life principle of the collective unconscious. Appearing only in a woman's dream, he represents her masculine aspects, and his presence often indicates she has failed to attend to/acknowledge her masculine side. The animus develops out of a woman's relationship with her personal father and her particular cultural ''mythology'' of all that is masculine.

In its positive, classical sense the dream figure may represent a source of analytical ability, judgment, and convictions, while the negative presentation is a harsh, stubborn, or opinionated person.

Modern Jungian analysts, like Clarissa Pinkola Estés, have moved away from the idea that the animus is patterned after culturally derived masculine behavior. Rather, Estés believes that the animus is the masculine ''bridging force'' that helps a woman act on or express—manifest—in concrete ways her inner thoughts, ideas, and impulses.

See **anima; man/men; Self; Wise Old Man**.

ant

Because of their tininess, ants can symbolize pettiness and annoyance. Because of their food-gathering activity, they can symbolize diligence and foresight. They may suggest a larger, ordered community, possibly one in which you're just like everyone else, and too busy, or are relatively insignificant. The word is also a pun on family relatives (aunt).

Ants play a part in the mythology of every culture, and their meaning differs considerably depending on the culture. They are associated with Ceres, the Italian goddess of grains and harvests, and were used in soothsaying, so if the ants speak or guide you someplace (the Aztecs believe they showed Quetzalcoatl the place where corn grows), attend to their message. In Indian mythology the Arimasps were giant ants who dug up gold, i.e., wisdom and emotional richness. Ants helped

Psyche sort a huge pile of mixed seeds, leading Johnson to suggest that the "ant nature" of a woman is her ability for both inner and outer sorting.

See **aunt; insects**.

antelope

A bounding antelope suggests a need to avoid/flee from something that scares/threatens you. Perhaps there's a waking situation in which you need to be alert/on guard. In mythology and folklore, the antelope is a medicine animal, so pay attention to how your antelope relates to you, or any healing message/gift it gives you.

See **animal(s)**.

antique(s)

If you like and appreciate antiques, they can represent time-honored values/wisdom; something genuine or proven; tradition; authentic truth. If you don't value them, then you may be moving away from outdated childhood conditioning or training (a positive move), or discarding/rejecting something valued that, in fact, you should heed. Is there some situation/relationship wherein you have anxiety about its deterioration, or in which you may need to do some restoration or repair?

See **ancient; old**.

anus

Your anus is connected with: your concepts about giving/withholding; negative emotions (something is "shitty"); power; self-expression or the withholding of it; generosity/stinginess, therefore money/gifts; sexual or traumatic experiences. Have you, or another, been behaving like an "asshole"? Who or what is the "pain in your ass"? Is there something you need to expel?

See **ass; body; excrement; hole; sex**.

anxiety

See **fear**.

ape

Our animal nature; basic instincts; primitive impulses related to power or mothering (depending on the sex of the ape); being part of a family complex with its securities/anxieties; a need to be involved with family and ancestors; cunningness. What aspect of you is almost, but not quite, human? Perhaps there has been some waking situation in which you have pounded your chest too much (stood out), and the dream is saying you need to quiet down and be part of the team.

In many mythologies apes are wisdom figures. In ancient Egypt, the ape/baboon was an attribute of the god Thoth, who was later connected to Hermes, and in this sense is a symbol of higher wisdom, transformational secrets. In the zodiac it corresponds to Sagittarius and can represent someone born under that sign (November 23–December 22).

See **animal(s); hair(y); monkey; primates**.

apparitions

See **ghost(s)**.

appearance

Consider the sex, age, and any decorative (or tattered) clothing/jewelry of dream characters. Their facial expression may suggest feelings being expressed. Look to the symbolism of especially emphasized parts of the body.

Who or what traits in waking life could the person whose appearance is emphasized resemble? What aspects (strengths or weaknesses) of yourself is the dream suggesting you have problems with, or need to recognize (superficiality, societal expectations, what others think?)?

The same/similar dream character appearing over time can document unfinished emotional business; previous messages not listened to; growth and progress. (See Dreamercise #15, Part 1, for ideas of how to work with a dream series.)

See **decorate/decoration**.

applause

Need/desire for, or giving oneself, recognition/encouragement. Do you deserve it, or is it to soothe some anxiety? Who gives you the applause? How does this correspond to some known person (including yourself) or situation?

See **actor/actress; approval; audience; rejected; roles; stage**.

apple(s)

In folklore/mythology, the apple is considered a symbol of fertility; a love token (the "apple of someone's eye"); a sacred or magical fruit. In Christian lore it has come to wrongly represent temptation and the permanent loss of innocence, although, in fact, the apple is never mentioned in the biblical story of Adam and Eve's expulsion from the Garden of Eden. To pluck the apple of paradise may refer to a sexual experience/fantasy. Psychologically, the Eden apple symbolizes becoming more conscious/aware of unconscious impulses; developing consciousness, rational thinking, and worldly wisdom.

If someone is in a "doctor," or authority, position with you, perhaps you're dreaming "an apple a day" to keep the doctor away. Is there an admonition/fear/wish to "upset the apple cart," or a need to keep things in "apple-pie order"? Is there "one rotten apple who may spoil the whole barrel"?

See **Eden, Garden of; five; sex**.

appointment

Keeping an appointment may relate to an actual appointment/meeting about which you have concern/anxiety. Many people have dreamed of an appointment as a way to remind themselves about a meeting, or as a wish that a fearful meeting were already over. There is a pun in the word, "a-point-*meant*," so perhaps you mean, or need, to make your point more clearly, or have misunderstood a point made.

approval

Be especially alert to the person who gives you, or the situation wherein you receive, approval, to determine whether it reflects a wish/need, a reversal (in fact, disapproval), or whether some aspect of yourself is giving you recognition, which you have ignored. What are your feelings, and how do you handle the approval? How is your dream behavior like, or different from, waking behavior?

See **rejected**.

apron

Who wears the apron and how is it decorated? Is someone now making the commitment to work on a task, particularly a family or nurturing one? If worn by a woman, she may be a mother/grandmother symbol, or an archetype for the Great Mother. Are you still tied to some female's apron strings, or keeping someone tied to yours? The apron's symbolism may relate to attitudes about food and to female/mother stereotypes. Aprons sometimes symbolize protection; or secrecy, as in the white apron of Freemasonry. Because they cover the lower body, they can symbolize modesty; hiding/denying sexuality.

See **clothes/clothing; lower body**.

arcade

A need to let off steam, to relax and let some of your childish aspects come out; playing too many games in a relationship. Perhaps too many people are playing games with you, and you're feeling overwhelmed.

See **game(s)**.

arch

Strength; support; the rainbow or the universal heavenly arch. In folklore, arches protect against evil spirits and sometimes represent the green bough of nature; therefore, primordial (basic) protection and shelter.

See **architecture; rainbow**.

archeology

Something old (repressed); something ancient (wisdom?) to which you have not paid attention or that is now safe for you to dig into, uncover, and consider; buried issues; the past; your heritage; personal/cultural tradition. If discovering a hidden treasure, it can represent creativity, buried within and now ready to be exposed; the Self.

If applicable, see **dig(ging); museum**.

archer

See **bow and arrow; hunter/huntress; target**.

architecture

Buildings/structures often represent ourselves, or some aspect of ourselves. How high you are in the building suggests rising or higher awareness/consciousness. Lower areas can represent more base attitudes, or sexuality. Is the architecture modern, outdated, fancy or plain? What could the style of architecture be expressing about your attitudes/approach to an issue/relationship? Ask yourself, "If this were a part of me, what would I be saying about myself and my needs?"

Dreams of damaged architecture are common for pregnant women approaching labor and may reflect their concerns about damage that might occur during delivery (Siegel).

Structures can also represent values/ideals. Are they sturdy or crumbling? What is your relationship to the structure in the dream? For persons recovering from life-threatening illnesses, buildings that are being renovated may reflect their triumph and the return of their energy and creative powers.

See **abroad/traveling abroad; cave; childhood home; church; house**.

arena/amphitheater

Are you in the audience or a performer? Can you relate any of the occurring action (performance, fight?) to a waking situation? Are you overwhelmed by too much action? Do you need to focus your attention more or need more attention? Perhaps you need, and have the capacity, to combine more information than you're presently considering to arrive at a decision. Or are you outside your arena of influence?

See **actor/actress; stage**.

argue/argument

Anger/tension that you've been ignoring or repressing, which is now making itself known. Consider the symbolism of the person with whom you are arguing. Does he/she represent some person/situation in waking life, or some aspect of yourself? Does the argument show you how to resolve a situation, or emphasize feelings of helplessness?

ark

Noah's ark, or one similar, suggests preservation of our animal instincts; maintaining life as you know it; holding on to important values or ideals. The Ark of the Covenant symbolizes your relationship to the universal spirit and to treasured ancient wisdom. The ark is also related to the hero/heroine myth and to the tests we each must undergo to become whole.

See **hero/heroine**.

arm(s)

As part of the body, arms symbolize the capacity to: move toward people; embrace and contact people/ideas; extend yourself; withdraw; carry burdens; fight aggressively; defend; wrestle with a challenge. It may be time for you to "reach out" toward some person/goal. If an arm is especially decorated/injured, notice whether it is the left (feminine) or right (masculine). Would you "give your right arm"—give away your masculine energy—for something? Or can you accomplish it with "one arm behind your back"? Which type of energy do you fail to use?

Hand/arm gestures are a universal nonverbal language and can indicate such actions/feelings as: anger ("up in arms"), giving, receiving, conquest, supplication, acknowledgment of authority, and worship or adoration.

As a pun, it can also symbolize an act of aggression or protection as you "arm yourself" with weapons, or "take up arms."

See **body; hand(s); hold (ing); restrain/restraint**.

armor

Entire books have been written on the way we express emotional and intellectual rigidity in our muscles/posture, called "body armor." Adjust your body to the dream position for possible clues.

Armor can symbolize a need for personal protection or defense, accompanied by a feeling that you are, or are about to be, under attack. Are you misreading someone's intentions or is this a customary, outdated stance, which needs to be replaced with more modern ways of perceiving/interacting?

See **antique(s)**.

army

Your own experience in the army will definitely affect your

symbolism. If you've never been in the army, then it can signify belonging or a wish to belong; protection issues; feelings about authority/control, discipline, and restriction; physical conflict; possibly, destructive or conflicting (warring?) wishes attempting to emerge from your unconscious. It can symbolize the ongoing battle between regulation/discipline and the wishes or needs of the impulses/personality. Metaphysically, it may signal you are on the path of the knight/warrior (see **knight**).

See **battle; soldier(s); war**.

arrested

A need for control/restraint; fear that you're being overly controlled/restrained; some part of your personality has been arrested/stunted in its development toward maturity; morality/values and related guilt. The person who arrests you may represent an authority figure in your present/past life, or your attitude toward authority in general.

See **police**.

arriving too late

See **late**.

arrow(s)

Like the spear, the arrow is a masculine symbol of energy direction and of penetration. In what direction it is pointing (left, right, up, down)? Whether you're male or female, what does this say about your prowess and development intellectually, psychically, sexually? Whether the arrow was aimed at a person or a target may give you clues about sexuality or aggression. Has someone or some situation pierced (wounded) you?

Arrows also symbolize swiftness; love (Cupid's arrow); the sacred sound *Om* that penetrates ignorance (in Buddhism and Hinduism). An arrow piercing a heart symbolizes the reconciliation of opposites; unification of the masculine and feminine within the self. The archer/arrow represents Sagittarius (person born November 23–December 22), and was the weapon of Apollo and Diana (goddess of the hunt), but the arrows of Apollo often sent plagues (the negative, wounding aspect of arrows).

See **anima; animus** (if a god or goddess appears in your dream); **bow and arrow; direction(s)** (if applicable); **hunter/huntress; target**.

art

Ideas/concepts/emotions; creative potential; your unconscious; a part of yourself that may take a long time for you to recognize and give its proper due. Consider whether its shape is feminine (round, container) or masculine (sharp edges, elongated) and whether this represents you or the opposite, which you may need to tap into. Earthenware vessels or pottery might represent your body. If on display, do you need to reveal more, or have you revealed too much already? What happens to the art piece, i.e., is it fragile, admired, rejected? Are you having to explain it?

See **artist; painting**.

artist

Artists have been the carriers of symbolism throughout time and cultures, so dreaming you're an artist, or engaged in an artistic project, indicates that aspect of yourself that's in contact with unconscious energy. In Jungian terms, a male artist may represent the animus for a female dreamer, and vice versa for a male dreamer. The anima/animus may also appear as an art gallery owner or manager. If possible, actually create the artistic dream project in some form (see Chapter 6, Part 1).

See **anima; animus; art**.

ascend(ing)

Meanings differ somewhat depending on whether the ascension is nonphysical (floating upward) or physical (by escalator/elevator/climbing).

Nonphysical ascension can signify a wish for a spiritual gift/reward; a need to be elevated in someone's eyes without doing the necessary work to make it happen.

Physically ascending suggests reaching beyond one's presently perceived limitations—either you have or you can; desires regarding sexual intercourse, particularly if you're ascending with, or to, someone desirable and/or ordinarily inaccessible; a search/need for a different perspective (the person/place you're ascending to may represent that perspective); sublimation of instinctual energies to "higher" purposes.

Esoterically, ascending often signifies becoming more aware/enlightened, or participating in a psychological or spiritual initiation. In Jungian terms it's the process of individuation. It can represent the upward flow of kundalini or spiritual energy, and is a common signal that you're about to enter the lucid dreaming state (Garfield; LaBerge).

See **descend(ing); elevator; flying, ladder; up**.

ashes

Transformation; humility; penance; purification; the death/ending of some situation. If the ashes are on your or another's body, consider the symbolism of that body part and/or the ceremony in which you may have received them. Do you place or receive the ashes, which speaks of your power or subjugation? Were you "raking over the ashes," trying to search for or save something from a past/present situation? Is your unconscious trying to tell you it is time to let go of dead values, or of a relationship that has died, and to move on or change? If the remains of a deceased person, cremains, they may reflect your feelings about that person or about cremation; issues related to his/her death; anxiety/concerns about your own aging and death.

See **fire; urn**.

asleep

Dreaming that you're asleep suggests a need/wish: for healing; to relive the infantile nursing situation (nurturance needs); for magic to be at work; for a better waking than usual. It may reflect lack of awareness of your emotions/needs; avoidance of issues/aspects symbolized by other persons/actions in the dream, or comfort with them. Is your dream suggesting that there's no reason to "lose sleep over" a current situation, or that there's an issue you "need to sleep on"?

See **awake(n); dream within a dream/dreaming you are dreaming**.

aspirin

See **medicine/medication**.

ass

The ass is a burden carrier (plodding), as well as a carrier of biblical and mythical personalities (a liberator). In Christianity, it is a sacred symbol because it carried Jesus into Jerusalem. It sometimes symbolizes sacrifice, but also stupidity. Have you been in a situation in which you have "made an ass of yourself"? In Greek mythology, the ass is related to the uninhibited, insatiable Dionysus (Roman, Bacchus); therefore, it can represent unconscious impulses; sexual acting out. In slang, it represents the anus.

See **animal(s); anus; lower body**.

astrological images

One at a time, these can represent people/dates that fall under specific astrological signs, especially if you're familiar with astrology. Together they represent the flow of time. Each astrological image is also an archetypal symbol.

See **planet(s); zodiac**.

atom bomb

During the 1950s and 1960s, to dream of an atom bomb was often an expression of anxiety about death and powerlessness at the hands of world leaders. Today it more likely speaks of personal existential anxiety about death; feelings of helplessness; hostility/rage of destructive magnitude; a desire to wipe out some aspect of yourself; the end of something crucial or especially precious to you; fear of losing control. It is, therefore, a common dream during times of crisis. It can represent the *intensity* of the emotions you experience or expect to experience with an impending loss. How you cope with the situation may point out strengths and resources you haven't previously realized.

See **bomb/bombed; destruction; end of the world**.

attack

Are you the aggressor or the one attacked? If being attacked, how you respond can tell you something about your own feelings of power/helplessness, or suggest a waking stressful incident/situation in which you feel "under attack." Attack, especially by animals, may represent your own instincts or aggression, which you're not recognizing.

If you are attacking, most likely you're expressing aggression against some person/situation, possibly in defense of ideas/projects that were recently attacked; also, the ability to defend yourself. How successful or clever are you?

Being attacked is one of the most frequent recurrent dreams. If yours is a repetitive dream, consider creating an imagery to practice just before sleep, wherein you deflate the attack/attacker in some way, or change your behavior so you take a more successful stance (see Dreamercise #11, Part 1).

See **battle; fight/fighter; war**.

attention

Receiving, or not receiving, attention may be saying something about your current level of self-esteem, or your need to receive attention from a certain person/group. If someone else is receiving attention, that person may represent an aspect of yourself to which you have been giving too much, or too little, attention. Also something you need to attend to.

attic

Since houses can represent ourselves, the attic may represent your mind; thoughts or conscious intellectual processes; higher ideals/aspirations; your superego or conscience, and therefore, a storehouse of rules, admonitions, guilt. Is your attic dirty, dusty, little-used, or do you have "bats in your belfry" (disordered thoughts)? Do you find some forgotten/neglected treasures there? If there are objects/animals in your attic, see their specific symbolism.

See **body; head; house(s)**.

attorney

See **lawyer**.

audience

Are you a member of the audience or in front of it? In one sense, an audience represents more passive behavior; vicarious participation in an event or in the enjoyment and sensations associated with it, without commitment; voyeuristic needs; reviewing aspects/issues of your life. It also represents a group of people who give or withhold attention/approval, who make judgments, thus community/societal or professional values (especially if you're part of, or appearing before, a particular professional group). Where in your waking life do you need to become more active or need more approval/acceptance? Who—or what aspect of yourself—is being too judgmental (rigid)?

See **actor/actress; applause; arena/amphitheater; roles; theater**.

aunt

Family characteristics/values; connection with your heritage; aspects of yourself that you like/dislike; possibly a substitute mother.

See **ant; relatives**.

aura

An aura or light surrounding a person/animal says you are connecting with the energy field of that figure; therefore, this is someone with whom you will interact on a different, higher (possibly more spiritual or universal) level. In metaphysics the aura represents the etheric body, which is the energy in which ideas/concepts are generated before becoming manifest; hence, a source of developing creativity/realization. Archetypally it can symbolize the Self.

See **egg(s); halo; light; luminous; Self; shine/shiny**.

automobile

See **car**.

autumn

Middle life; a metaphor for whatever are your own emotions about this season or time of life; your psyche signaling some process is almost complete; time to slow down. It can be related to satisfactions or regrets. Some people think of this season as "fall," with all the puns that implies. Others think of it as a time when certain animals store up winter hoards, so the dream could reflect some emotions, emotional energy, or resources that you're "gathering in" to protect, or for protection.

See **seasons**.

avalanche

If snow, frozen emotions in

the unconscious; repressed emotions as big as boulders (if rock). Do you escape or is it about to be set loose to engulf you? When we begin to recognize repressed emotions, it often feels like an overwhelming experience, buried alive in feelings. But somewhere in the dream is also a safety symbol.

awake(n)

Mythologically, to awaken, or an awakening, refers to initiation/rebirth (with resultant access to secret/magical knowledge), either spiritually or instinctually (the awakening of masculine/feminine energy)—to become whole. Archetypally this has to do with awakening to your full potential, to the ability to be who you are; the development of the Self.

The symbolism of who/what awakens you may tell you what's missing in your waking life. Be careful that you're not waiting for an outside prince to awaken you, when you need to awaken and accept your own dormant princely attributes (whatever your sex).

award

Consider who's receiving the award, for what, and how you feel about it to help you decide whether you're honoring yourself; have a wish for recognition; or could get an award if you emulated the characteristics of the person receiving it. Could the dream be saying you've been abandoned or are alone—orphaned ("a ward") in some way?

See **abandon(ed)** (if applicable); **prize; trophy**.

aware(ness)

From an Adlerian viewpoint, being aware that you're dreaming may signal unwillingness to give up the "logic" being expressed in the dream. Awareness that you're dreaming is also a characteristic of lucid dreams. Consider the symbolism of things of which you are more aware in the dream. Is some insight/wisdom revealed to you?

See **dream within a dream/dreaming you are dreaming**.

awesome

Any aspect of a dream that is awe-inspiring, especially nature or water scenes, can represent the archetypal mother.

See **Great Mother**.

ax

As a tool dating from the Stone Age, it may symbolize craftsmanship; creativity; growth of knowledge. Do you "have an ax to grind" with someone, or are you afraid of being "axed" (fired)? In the United States there are a number of superstitions about axes. Did your family teach you one?

An ax can symbolize power/rank; archetypal masculine energy (remember Paul Bunyan's ax?); the power of light or cosmic illumination; the liberation of cosmic secrets (an ax penetrating a geometrical figure). In the Bible, the ax symbolizes Divine Truth (Matthew). In East Indian/Greek mythologies the twin-bladed or doubled-headed ax is associated with sacrifice, the labyrinth, and with Dionysus. A double-headed ax was dedicated to Apollo at Delphi; its duality also associates it with Gemini, possibly someone born under that sign (May 22—June 21).

See **labyrinth/maze; weapon(s)**.

axis mundi

See **world tree**.

baboon

See **ape**.

baby

A desire for a child; innocent or infantile aspects of the Self calling for attention/recognition; acknowledgment of a needy inner child; an expression of infantile desires you're not quite ready to abandon; concern about, caring for, or protecting someone younger, less competent, or less mature than you; new possibilities; a new project; a psychological/spiritual birth of any kind, now ready to be nurtured.

It can suggest feelings of vulnerability or a wish to return to a totally cared-for state; therefore, a wish to escape responsibilities/perceived burdens. Are you feeling as inexperienced or lost as "a babe in the woods"? It may reflect a recent separation and suggests a longing for, or wish to still be connected with, that situation/person. A pregnant woman who sees her baby already born, or even several years old, may be attempting to skip the anxiety of labor and the adjustments of parenting a newborn (Siegel).

See **birth; child/children**.

bachelor

If you're a married man dreaming you are a bachelor, you may be wishing to return to the single state with its freedom and/or decreased responsibility; possibly, you're still reserving/withholding part of yourself from full commitment. (There *is* an outlet.) If your wife is pregnant, it may be associated with all the anxieties/responsibilities that come from expanding your family.

If you're a single woman dreaming of a bachelor, this may reflect a wish to find your Prince Charming. (What are his characteristics?) A married woman dreaming of a bachelor may be expressing a need for more romance in her life. For both women, this may be an archetypal expression of their animus. How does he treat you and how do you treat him?

If applicable, see **sex**.

back

The back, as a body part, often reflects our posture (attitude) or stance in the world, our strengths and burdens. We can "carry" people, "turn our back" on them, or "get back at them." Sometimes it reflects pressure, as when you want someone to "get off your back," or someone is "breaking your back." Relationships are reflected in a "stab in the back"; someone "speaking behind your back"; or "you scratch my back and I'll scratch yours." Are you in a situation in which you feel your "back is against the wall" or is it "back to the salt mines" and "backbreaking labor"? Do you need to "back away"?

Back can also reflect concerns about things that are occurring "behind your back." Dreams of falling behind, being at the back of the room, or at the back of the line may relate to feelings of inadequacy/low self-esteem. Hostility may be indicated in a "backhanded" compliment. Emphasis on the lower back may represent blocked sexual feelings.

As a position, back is the reverse of front and, therefore, related to duality and reversals ("backsliding"). Being behind (back of) objects or buildings ("behind the barn") relates to secrets or repressed feelings, probably sexual, as in things kept in the "back room."

Back also can refer to time (go back) and may represent a need/wish to return to earlier/better times (childhood?); or movement, i.e., to back up, slow down, review events.

See **backbone; behind; body; front/in front; left behind**.

backbone

Specific emphasis on the backbone/spine can relate to feelings of fear ("spineless"); rigid attitudes; flexibility; strength and courage (she "has a lot of backbone"). Metaphysically, it refers to spiritual aspiration and alignment with higher, spiritual energies. Kundalini (spiritual energy) rises along the spine. Chakras, sacred energy centers, are considered to be located either along the spine or in nearby alignment to it.

See **ascend(ing); back; bones**.

bag

Its style and contents—or whether you can determine the contents—will help clarify its meaning. Bags can represent the womb; secret possessions or ideas; withholding/hiding something from someone; saving or protecting.

The elaborateness/simplicity of the bag says something about the value of the contents. A simple bag may suggest something of little importance; basic values, something important that you don't want others to recognize/value. An elaborate bag can symbolize an ostentatious facade; something you wish were more important than it seems to be.

Do you regard someone as an "old bag," or is some deal "in the bag"?

See **clothes/clothing; container; knapsack; luggage; purse/wallet; suitcase**.

bag person

See **beggar; homeless**.

baggage

Do you need to clean your emotional house and, in the words of Professor Higgins (*My Fair Lady*), "throw the baggage out"? Are *you* "just so much baggage" (a self-esteem issue)? Consider how much unfinished business (excess baggage) you're carrying around or are bringing into a new situation/relationship.

See **luggage**.

baker/bakery/baking

Fertility and creation. Being the baker relates to your creative abilities; your ability to connect with the divine spark within you. If making a round loaf/pastry, it may symbolize the Self. In Freudian symbology, working the dough may symbolize playing with/exploring your feces.

Baking/bakeries suggest transformation; growth and development; available (or forbidden) riches/goodies; home; nurturing.

balance(d)/balancing

Something/someone balancing or being balanced suggests that you have—usually for only a brief time—achieved psychic equilibrium. It is the creative synthesis that occurs when we have been able to temporarily take ourselves out of the battle of opposites (Johnson). To trip, stumble, or otherwise lose your balance suggests a situation in which you've been thrown off balance emotionally.

See **account(s); acrobat; juggler/juggling; justice; mandorla; opposites; scales of justice**.

ball

In sexual slang, balls represent male testicles, and therefore, possibly the desire to have sex; feeling threatened or immobilized (someone "has you by the balls"). How you "play the game" will give you clues as to your inner perception of your prowess, sexually as well as in other interactions. Is someone pressuring you at work or elsewhere to cooperate in something you think is unethical/sleazy ("play ball"); waiting for you to respond, or even make the first move ("the ball is in your court")? Do you need to be more focused ("keep your eye on the ball"); or is there a challenge or new perspective awaiting ("a whole new ball game")?

A ball also refers to an elegant dance. If you're female, is the princess (heroine) part of you being prevented from going to the ball?

See **baseball; circle; football; game(s); sporting events**.

ballet

See **actor/actress; dance/dancing**.

balloon(s)

A festive mood; a need to play more and acknowledge your inner child; breasts (shape); the womb (container); a condom (especially if made of rubber). Consider its decoration, number, color, shape (if not round), for more clues. Is something or someone threatening to "burst your balloon" of trust/illusion/fantasy?

For a hot-air balloon, see **ascend(ing); flying**.

bamboo

Flexibility (sways in the wind); youth (because the plant is always green). If you remember when fishing poles were made of cane, which resembles bamboo, then it may symbolize a need for more fun, or escape for renewal. In India it symbolizes friendship, while in many primitive tribes, it's used for ritual magic. In Eastern traditions, bamboo symbolizes the pathway to spiritual development. In cultures/mythologies in which cremation is practiced, new bamboo plants often grow from the ashes; therefore, it is also a symbol of cycles; birth/death/rebirth motifs; eternity.

banana

Feelings/attitudes about a male, maleness, the male sexual organ, or sexual experiences with a male. Eating a banana may refer to oral or exotic sex. What state is the banana in: just ripening/spoiling? A cluster of bananas (see bunch) can reflect complex feelings, while the "top banana" suggests superiority. Does the number of bananas offer additional cues?

See **fruit(s); penis/phallus; yellow**.

band

A musical band can symbolize a professional group/community; a sense of belonging. Consider whether they are playing harmoniously/discordantly, and whether you're an observer, player, or leader.

A band can also be an armband, which indicates status or emotion (mourning). Issues about relationship can be considered in a wedding band ("a band of gold"), or in needing to "band together."

See **music/musician**.

bandage

A badge of action and courage; a symbol of having been emotionally wounded, which we all have experienced in our growing. Does this wound pertain to the past (consider the specific body part for additional cues) or to the present? Is there an aspect of you calling out to be healed or protected, perhaps one that's been seriously neglected (dirty, ragged bandage)?

banjo

Because of its shape, it suggests both feminine and masculine symbolism. It can, therefore, succinctly express the incorporation of both aspects, or difficulty incorporating both, into your psyche.

See **music/musician**.

bank(er)

Your treasures and wealth, possibly internal wisdom; the psyche; trust or expectation (something you can "bank on"). Have you been adding to your stores (making a deposit) or withdrawing too heavily, which may call for a rest? A bank shares some of the same symbolism as money (energy; issues of retention, hoarding, or saving).

An overbearing banker may symbolize your superego or conscience. The vaults suggest fertility (a womb, a sperm bank?). Do you have difficulty with, or are you, a teller—a pun for someone who has a message for you or a sign that you/another talk too much? Archetypally a teller could symbolize a tribal storyteller, a keeper of tradition. Is there a big windfall you're counting on, hoping to "break the bank"?

See **anus; horde/hoard; money**.

banner

An announcement or focus—pay attention to the message, where the banner is located, and its condition. Because of recent experiences, are you "flying the banner of success," or wishing for success? Do you need to be noticed; or is your psyche telling you that you've ignored some important point, or aspect of yourself?

baptism

Acceptance into, commitment/dedication to, a path/direction or a new cause (spiritual or otherwise); purification/cleansing (if water is used); initiation into spiritual ways; spiritual rebirth/awakening; acquiring truth and ending illusion; a new potential awakened (or now acknowledged) within you. Depending on the appearance of the person who baptizes you and feelings associated with the dream, it could be an archetypal theme signaling an important step in your hero/heroine journey and development of the Self.

See **Christ**.

bar

Your feelings about a bar and your dream actions will suggest the most appropriate symbolism from among: recreation; companionship and socializing; sleazy or low-class attitudes/feelings; a need for (sexual?) companionship/adventure; indulgence; something that is off-limits. Is some situation/person barring you from joining or continuing toward a particular goal/direction?

See **alcohol/alcoholic; drink(ing); restrain/restraint**.

barber/hairdresser

Since hair is associated with power and masculine energy, to be one who cuts hair is to be in an extraordinarily powerful and controlling situation, or to place yourself in the hands of someone like that. It's the taming of barbaric energy. Negatively it could symbolize castration (remember Samson?). In some ancient stories, to have one's hair cut was the punishment for dishonor. Reverse the sex of the barber to see if it makes sense.

Women often change their hairstyles immediately before/after a major decision, so going to the barber could symbolize the imminent solution to a problem/situation; change; need for a new image.

See **appearance; castrate; hair(y)**.

barn

Where animals (instincts) are kept, and therefore, the unconscious; possibly, holding back (containing) instinctual action. In what condition is the barn? Consider the animals/objects within for additional cues.

See **stable**.

barricade

An obstacle (attitudes, habits, unfinished business?) to emotional growth; resistance to change. A barricade can also be a person barring your way or preventing you from continuing. Consider his/her age and appearance for clues about the waking age or number of years ago when your personal obstacle may have occurred.

baseball

As a game, baseball can symbolize camaraderie; team effort; group organization; play and fun; power; masculine aspects (shape of the bat) in opposition to feminine aspects (ball; ballpark); and sublimation (safe and acceptable expression of aggression). If you're a woman whose husband immerses himself in baseball, it may have negative connotations, especially related to isolation, loneliness, or rejection; or, conversely, freedom.

See **ball; game(s); sporting events; victor/victory**.

basement

Female genitals; sexual feelings and rules/prohibitions; an archetypal symbol for the unconscious. Is the room scary (repressed or instinctual material?) or a playroom? Consider what is stored/found in the basement (cluttered = time to set priorities and clean up past issues?), its condition (well-kept or covered in cobwebs), and whether it's in good shape or needs repair (pay attention; do some work here with guilt, denial, or other unresolved issues). Leaky or cracked walls suggest a damage to your psyche, and the possibility of being flooded with emotion. If dark (little explored), you may need to do some inner work and become more en-*light*-ened?

See **architecture; cellar; house; sex**.

basket

A container, therefore, a feminine symbol; fruitfulness and fertility, especially when filled with fruit/seeds; the personal womb; the maternal womb. Consider its condition/contents for more clues. In many mythologies a baby was saved by being put in a basket that was then put into a river. Do you need to save (attend to) some newly emerging aspect of yourself?

See **birth; container; water**.

bat [mammal]

A creature with ambivalent and varying symbolisms, its meaning is greatly dependent on your own beliefs/feelings about bats. As creatures of the night (lunar symbol) that sleep in caves, they can symbolize the unconscious, or signal that you're avoiding/ignoring something (''blind as a bat'').

In some myths and cultures, the bat is a symbol for eternity. They also are associated with vampirism (see **vampire**); sex and seduction (bloodsucking); and evil (enemies of light). They can represent irrational ideas/thoughts (''bats in your belfry''), and speed (''go like a bat out of hell''). If you're ecologically minded, you know that bats eat insects and are extremely valuable, gentle creatures. Your personal symbolism will reflect that awareness.

See **black; flying; x**. For a quite different meaning, see **baseball; sporting events**.

bath(ing)

Cleansing in preparation for a greater group, religious, or spiritual experience—a healing, baptism (voluntary death/rebirth), or initiation. An elaborate container may signal a need to luxuriate or take time for special care/pampering of yourself. It may suggest an experience in which you need to ''come clean,'' washing away old secrets/pains/guilt. Perhaps now is the time to acknowledge and release them. You may be dealing with some finished or ''wasted'' experience, washing it away and sending it ''down the drain.''

See **clean(ing)/cleansing; water**.

bathroom

As this is the place where natural functions occur, thoughts/feelings related to instinctual urges are associated with the bathroom and its furnishings. In Jungian psychology it represents images from the collective unconscious, especially the anima/animus. Since our early learnings about bathroom activities are usually taught by parents, it can reflect early training/conditioning, which you accept or rebel against; therefore, also issues of control, rebellion, independence. As a place where washing our bodies occurs, it can symbolize preparation; purification; regeneration; luxuriating indulgence (soaking in a bath of oil/bubbles). Are you experiencing/holding on to some feelings/burdens and need to ''relieve yourself''?

See **toilet**.

battery

Life energy; therefore, a dead/bad battery in a car or other vehicle suggests you're running low on emotional energy. Time to recharge your batteries with rest, play, or relaxation. A flashlight battery is related to light; inspiration; goals; the ability to find your way. Trouble in these areas could be represented by a dead flashlight. A clock battery relates to the passage of time, so a stopped battery in a clock could refer to anxiety about: aging or death; the time (no more?) left to accomplish a task/project; regrets that you've let time pass without accomplishing certain ambitions/goals.

battle

An attempt to suppress instinctual elements of yourself; warring aspects of yourself; the archetypal conflict between two opposites, especially the conscious and unconscious. Truth/enlightenment lies somewhere in the battle; look for it.

See **balance(d)/balancing; opposites**.

bay

Its crescent shape pertains to the moon, therefore to the feminine and to sexuality; the emergence of instinctual/unconscious material that's safer (less turbulent) than aggressive/hostile impulses. What emotions can you now safely acknowledge/express? Consider what activities are occurring (sunbathing, swimming, picnicking, boating?) for additional cues. Conversely, it might reflect a feeling that you are "at bay" or being "held at bay" (trapped; cornered) by someone or by the fear of emerging feelings, which you may need to "keep at bay."

See **moon/moonlight; water**.

bayonet

In its positive sense, a bayonet can cut away illusion. What illusion does the person you use the bayonet on represent? Or do you fail to use it and need to maintain that illusion a little longer? Alternatively, as an instrument of aggression/death/war, it can symbolize the threat of being overcome by feelings, especially anger/hostility; feeling a need to defend yourself (associated with a waking situation in which you feel under attack?). In Freudian terms, it is certainly phallic.

See **battle; knife; sword(s)**.

beach

Related to a body of water, beach is not as desolate a symbol as a desert and may, therefore, relate to ambivalence (water versus sand); the conjunction of opposites (unconscious versus conscious); a need for rest/recreation; a symbol of cycles ("the sands of time"); being on the brink of developing new qualities or clarifying emotions. Consider who/how many people are on the beach and their appearances for additional meanings. Are you a "beach bunny," who comes to the beach mostly to be seen/admired? If you're a woman, what part of you needs more attention? If a man, do you need to pay more attention to your feminine aspects? A beached whale suggests that a large part of you (your emotions?) has been left ignored and dying ("high and dry").

See **sand; sea; water**.

beacon

Shares some of the same symbolism as light, especially enlightenment when associated with a lighthouse (house of light, God's candle). Also constancy; safety or, conversely, the presence of danger; a signal for attention. Consider the quality of the light (on and off; steady; bright; dark; working; not working?) and the surroundings (water; cliffs; grass?) for additional cues.

See **lighthouse; tower**.

bear(s)

Because they hibernate, bears can symbolize cycles; birth/death/awakening motif; power or overpowering ("big as a bear"); your own cyclic activity/ability. Is it time for you to awaken into activity, or to hibernate and renew your energy? Mythologically, bears represent mothering—the archetype of the Great Bear. In Greek mythology the bear is associated with Artemis (Roman, Diana), goddess of the moon and woods (fertility and the unconscious), and was associated with the Virgin Mary in medieval writings (von Franz). Bearskins have protective and magical power, hence the fearless Nordic warriors, were originally known as "bearsarks," because of their bearskin shirts.

What "bearish" aspect of yourself do you need to recognize? As a pun, it can refer to something that is "hard to bear"; an overbearing person; a need to bare yourself (exposure) or your soul (truth/lies/trust-distrust issues?); having a difficult time "getting your bearings" (need for a sense of direction/guidance).

See **animal(s)**. If you think your dream refers to "bare," see **naked/being naked**.

beard

Masculinity; strength; maturity;

automatic talking or thoughts that bubble up from the unconscious (von Franz). A long beard, especially a white one, can symbolize wisdom; the passage of time. A pointed beard may symbolize the devil. Consider its color and condition (well-kept; scruffy) for clues.

Seeing yourself with a beard, when you don't actually have one, suggests a change of face; a need for a mask/disguise; a different facet of your identity. People who have a weak chin, or can't "take it on the chin," sometimes grow beards to cover their vulnerability. Does this apply to you or someone you know?

See **hair(y)**.

beaten/battered

If replaying an actual experience that you are now out of, you're probably reliving the trauma for healing. If not out of the situation, it reflects continuing anxiety.

If not an actual experience, it may reflect concern with a situation—or too many situations all at once—in which you feel emotionally battered. Have you been struggling unsuccessfully to resolve some situation in which you feel someone has gotten the better ("beaten") of you; or have you been "beaten at your own game"? If you're someone who can't allow yourself full pleasure with a successful experience, you may need to disguise a recent joy.

beauty/beautiful

A beautiful person/object/scene can symbolize a flowering of the psyche, possibly your feminine aspect. If you've recently experienced a traumatic event/injury, it's a definite sign that you're on the road to recovery.

beaver

Have you been "busy as a beaver," overextended yourself, or haven't been busy enough and need to "get down to business"? Perhaps you need to adopt the attitude of being "eager as a beaver." As a water animal, the beaver is especially symbolic of the workings of the unconscious, or can represent a damming up of emotions. In North American Indian tales the beaver is often associated with the porcupine, both trickster figures. In sexual slang beaver refers to a woman's genitals.

See **animal(s); trickster**.

bed

A bed, or actions in bed, can symbolize you; your unconscious (where dreams originate); possibly your shadow (if you have nightmares); sex and/or sexual relationships (the marriage bed); the way you're living your life ("bed of roses"; "bed of nails"); the consequences of decision ("You made your bed, now lie in it"). Consider who shares your bed; any patterns on the covers.

See **bedroom; house; womb**. If you're in bed dreaming, see **dream within a dream/dreaming you are dreaming**.

bedroom

If your own bedroom, it may reflect a need for rest; intimacy/sex/withdrawal (interpersonal issues); dropping your societal mask; possibly your shadow aspect. If exploring someone else's bedroom, it may indicate voyeurism/curiosity, especially about sexual matters (perhaps remembered childhood curiosity about parental sex, triggered by some recent situation). Since sleep is one of the ways we get in touch with unconscious messages, entering/exploring a bedroom may also indicate curiosity about your unconscious or instinctual workings and a need to become more aware of them.

See **bed; house**.

bee(s)

Like ants, bees can represent a need to belong to a community; a feeling that you need to organize your life; a desire/concern that you will become "busy as a bee"; signify your identification with an organization/group. Their well-known industriousness can signal new energy or emerging creativity. A single buzzing bee may reflect a small but ominous annoyance; many suggests gossiping women.

Bees can symbolize higher emotions; the production of food for the soul (honey). They are related to wax, which can make candles for celebration, worship, or enlightenment.

In ancient lore, bees were messengers from the gods. In India's love poetry, they are associated with eroticism and form the bowstring of Kama, the god of love/lust. They plunge into flowers oozing with sap. In ancient Egypt the hieroglyph for bee denoted royalty. Are you, or do you need to be, the "queen bee"?

Bees can signal a connection with the divine, since in ancient Greek teaching, bees represented souls; and a bee was the sacred attribute of several gods/goddesses (Demeter, goddess of fertility; Zeus, the Great Father god).

Honey, made by bees, often symbolizes the elixir of life—manna, food from heaven. If you were eating honey, or trying to get it (with how much difficulty?), perhaps you need to incorporate more sweetness in your life, or strengthen your connection with higher, spiritual powers.

As a pun, a bee could reflect issues of identity ("to be or not to be").

See **honey; insects**.

beer

See **alcohol/alcoholic; bottle**.

beggar

Feelings of failure; outcast; financial anxiety; humility. Consider the opposite (haughty?). If haughtiness has been your recent waking expression, the dream beggar may be the shadow's attempt at balance. Hungry dream characters can represent aspects of yourself that you've neglected to feed. What has "gone begging" in your emotional/physical life? Perhaps there's some situation that requires a choice/decision, and your finances or lowered self-esteem make it seem that "beggars can't be choosers." Do you have feelings about having to "bend your knee" to some situation/person more powerful than you?

See **appearance; homeless**.

behind

Who or what are you behind? As a position, behind can symbolize fear/recognition that you're being "left behind" or are in trouble ("behind the eight ball"). Are you afraid you'll never catch up? Because behind can represent something "unseen," it may symbolize emerging unconscious material, especially shadow aspects (if something seems to be lurking); secrets or forbidden activities (sex, smoking, which occurs "behind the barn"); forbidden or childhood urges.

It can suggest that you're "behind the times" and need to adopt some new attitudes/behavior. If you're "behind bars," consider who or what relationship/situation has you feeling trapped or immobilized. Is there some situation in which your intuition suggests more is going on than is obvious, or in which you need to do some additional work or repair "behind the scenes"? Behind is also slang for the buttocks.

See **back; buttocks; position(s)**.

bell(s)

Consider their size, number, and whether or not they're ringing. Bells can have spiritual symbolism (hanging in a church bell tower, midway between heaven and earth); ritual or celebratory symbolism (wedding bells; call to worship); reflect a need for protection (they are said to ward off misfortune);

convey lightheartedness ("bells on her toes"). In a play on words, a bell can represent a popular, desirable woman, or your wish to be the "belle of the ball" (Cinderella motif?).

"Belle" is the name for the beautiful young woman in the French tale of *Beauty and the Beast*, so consider the possibility of the archetypal theme wherein a woman must learn to see beyond the superficial (the persona) and accept/love her basic ("bestial") instincts (shadow) to achieve wholeness.

belly

See **abdomen, body, stomach, womb**.

below

If you're below something, looking up, it may relate to lowered self-esteem or, conversely, may be compensating for feeling too superior ("high and mighty"). Something below *you* may relate to a situation/attitude/relationship you feel is "beneath you," "below your standards," or "beneath your contempt." If threatening or difficult to see, it may refer to your shadow; unconscious/instinctual needs.

See **above; position(s)**.

belt

A constricted flow of life energy; separation between the top/upper (intellectual; consciousness) and the bottom/lower (instinctual; unconscious); moral beliefs or restrictions. What would happen—how would those beliefs change—if you removed the belt and let these two aspects of your personality connect? In Christian symbology, a belt (girdle) often symbolizes protection or virginity. Its opposite is the belt of Venus, associated with eroticism. Consider the comfort/discomfort of the belt and any decorations (especially fancy buckles) for additional cues.

See **appearance; buckle; clothes/clothing; opposites**. For "belt" as a strong, quick drink, see **alcohol/alcoholic**.

berries

Ideas/concepts coming to fruition ("the time is ripe"). If inedible, they may represent false hope; possibly wishing for an activity/project to be finished before its time, or a fear that it has no substance (if for decoration only). Wild berries often attract birds. Are you afraid your idea is "for the birds" or too flighty?

See **fruit(s)**.

beside

Standing/sitting beside someone is the most common dream position, and may have little significance. If emphasized, it suggests equality ("side by side"); someone who can serve as a support ("side with you") or resource for you, unless you're "on the wrong side."

See **position(s); side**.

Bible

Depending on your own religious training/feelings, the Bible can represent divine authority; the presence of God or divine wisdom; patriarchal values; genealogical information and tribal wisdom/mythology; laws/morals/ethics, which you may have discarded and of which you need to be reminded. It can signal that the dream message (especially if a particular book or verse is indicated) is one of great spiritual importance, or is pointing you in a profound direction to pursue. Consider where the Bible is located (church, altar, home?) and whether it is open or closed (needs to be opened?).

If you have negative experiences associated with the Bible, or people who preached from it, it may represent those persons/ideas; conflict with or turning from authority; a shadow aspect of yourself, which it is now time to face.

bicycle

Are you able to progress through the world on your own power, or are you having trouble riding the bicycle (anxieties about success and making it on your own)? A bicycle can also symbolize recreational needs; issues of emotional or spiritual balance. If someone is interfering with your bicycle riding, consider that person's characteristics for insight into what attitudes within yourself/another are keeping you "off balance."

See **vehicle(s)**.

big

Who/what is especially big? If known to you, you may be: expressing an inflated opinion about him/her; feeling small in comparison (a big monster); experiencing a need, or inability, to exert dominance over some actual person/situation. Big figures/objects often signal the appearance of archetypal material.

See **large; power/powerful/powerless; size**.

bill

What is still unpaid and owing emotionally? It's now due; time to pay up, i.e., resolve it. If from someone known, it may be an obligation you have incurred that's weighing on your mind. It could also be a pun for someone named Bill/William.

binoculars

A new perspective/viewpoint; having limited/restricted vision;

a need to distance yourself from a situation/person, possibly because you perceive a threat. Is there a waking situation in which you're so far out of touch, or being kept at a distance, that you need binoculars to see what's happening?

See **distance/distant/in the distance**.

bird(s)

In general, thoughts and ideals, especially insightful, "far-seeing," or spiritual ones; the capacity to use your mental abilities to escape being hurt/overwhelmed ("flights of fancy"). Small/tiny birds may symbolize troubles/irritants. A singer considered finches as the "birds of worry" that flew around her head (mind). In mythology birds often represent the soul. The hero often understands the speech of the birds (divine wisdom; listening to the inner self) at decisive moments.

As winged creatures, birds represent the element of air and are of heaven. A flock of birds may emphasize, or express the negative. The symbolism of the number of birds may add to or change the meaning. Birds and snakes/serpents together symbolize opposites: above/below, sky/earth. In Hindu mythology, the mythical bird that slays serpents is Garuda. A giant bird is a symbol for a solar bird, a cosmic or divine messenger.

Our proverbs/idioms associate birds with communication ("a little bird told me"); a sweet-talking person can "charm the birds from the trees." Issues of trust and/or desertion/commitment are reflected in the idioms "the bird has flown the coop" and "free as a bird." "A bird in the hand is worth two in the bush" and "that's for the birds" suggest issues of thrift/value, while "a sly old bird" suggests cleverness, possibly duplicity. Any idiom/proverb that comes to your mind suggests connection with homespun wisdom and can relate to family/ancestors/early training. Bird and chick are sometimes used as sexual slang for a woman.

A birdhouse or nest and whatever's occurring there likely refers to your own home/family issues.

See listings for specific birds and **opposites; snake(s); wings/winged**.

birth

If you're not pregnant, to dream of having a baby can symbolize the birth of a new attitude/viewpoint; new project; new recognition/acceptance of your inner child. It can also refer to separating from some recent relationship; release from an old relationship; anticipation of a new future. If you dream of your actual child, it may indicate a wish to return to earlier times (and the reactivation of whatever feelings you have about those times); to go back and change the past; a wish that you still had that kind of power/control over your child.

Birth may also be expressed in dreams symbolically as going in and out of holes, caves, or tunnels; swimming, boating, or otherwise navigating through narrow canals.

If you *are* pregnant, birthing dreams are typical throughout your pregnancy and may reflect anxiety about your readiness to be a mother (in the first trimester). During the third trimester, they may serve to actually make your delivery easier. (See the section on Women's Dreams, Chapter 4, Part 1.)

See **baby; canal; channel; grief**.

birth control

See **contraceptive**.

birthday

Whose birthday is it and how do you feel about it? Birthdays can symbolize the passage of time (cycles); a return to better times (if an earlier birthday); family festivity, celebration, and connection; an expression of individuality and growth. Dreams of *birth*-day parties, which might be wild celebrations or where the father might be rejected, are often prominent dreams for expectant fathers (Siegel).

See **birth**.

bite

Biting something/someone or being bitten (by a person/animal) can be either an expression of, or fear of, anger. If there's fear in the dream, look for hidden anger. If anger, look for hidden fear. An insect bite suggests either a minor or major (if allergic) annoyance; also something venomous/poisonous, i.e., infected with some idea/attitude that's unhealthy/toxic. Consider the animal/insect for additional symbolism.

Esoterically, the bite (or, more specifically, the prints left by the bite) can symbolize the imprint of the spirit upon the flesh. Negatively, it can symbolize the emergence of "dangerous" or primitive instincts/wishes, with the subsequent fear that you may be overwhelmed.

The dream bite can also symbolize an idea that "has bite to it"; or one that you've failed to recognize has "bitten the dust" and you're still holding on to it. Are you "biting your tongue" about something you should be saying, or are you withholding in a relationship? You could be feeling overwhelmed or low in confidence, having "bitten off more than you can chew." Did you "bite the hand that feeds you" (issues of support, dependency, guilt, obligation?)? Perhaps you need to persevere and "bite the bullet"?

See **anger; hunger/hungry; mouth/lips; teeth**.

black

Mystery; secrecy; unenlightened; underground, therefore the underworld and/or descent; death/mourning; emotional darkness; primordial chaos; hidden desires/instincts; the unconscious, which may appear as a black animal. Black undergarments suggest sexual instincts/urges. Archetypally a figure dressed in black may represent the shadow. In alchemy, black, or blackening, was the first color in the transformation process and therefore holds within it the promise of something to come (growth, change, insight?).

See **animal(s); clothes/clothing**; (if applicable); **color(s); individuation; shadow**.

blackbird

Since all birds can represent thoughts (sometimes anxieties or fears) and fantasies, the blackbird's color relates it to the unconscious, possibly your shadow, or, if a male dreamer, possibly your anima. Consider how the blackbird behaves and your actions toward it (do you scare it away; feed it; cage it; tame it?) for additional cues.

See **bird(s); raven(s)**.

Black Madonna

Long revered in cult mythology and early European Christianity, her appearance is a signal that your old life is being reversed. You're moving in, or into, a different dimension, a different energy, that's both sacred and sexual (Woodman). She may appear as a dark-skinned woman. She is the shadow archetype, the earthy, lusty balance to the virgin white goddess/Madonna (in Christianity, Mary, the mother of Jesus), and once recognized/accepted, holds the potential to release creativity and energy. Together the black and white Madonna energies form the primal or Great Mother.

See **Mary, Virgin; person, dark or dark-skinned**.

blessed/blessing

A sign of acceptance; initiation (the introduction to spiritual or esoteric learning); a talisman for safety (do you feel in waking danger?); a bond or ongoing relationship between the spiritual and the physical. Depending on who gives you the blessing, it can symbolize a student/teacher relationship, a superior/inferior relationship; a transfer of energy from your spiritual aspect (possibly unconscious) to your physical (conscious); a confirmation of your inner work.

If an object is blessed, it may symbolize something that's being, or needs to be, elevated by sanctification.

blind(ness)

Have you "lost sight of something" important or are denying something about which you should "see the light"? It suggests there is an area/situation in your life in which you have a "blind spot" and need to shift your focus to gain new perspective or "in-sight." In esoteric/Christian symbolism, being blind refers to the time before one became aware of, or awakened to, the "teaching" and in that sense is similar to being asleep (spiritual darkness). Archetypally, blind men, especially old ones, often symbolize inner wisdom, but blindness was also a punishment/sacrifice for transgressions. Does this dream refer to a guilt issue, or urge you to turn inward?

See **eye(s); light; look(ing)/looked at; see(ing)**.

blister

A relatively small annoyance/disturbance in your consciousness that's nevertheless sapping energy; also a situation that is healing or festering (depending on other dream images). For additional cues, consider where it's located on the body and how you got it, i.e., hard work (effort?), a burn (emotion?), or by pursuing recreation or a hobby (evidence of success?).

See **abscess**.

blond

Archetypally, a blond woman can represent the appearance of a goddess, divine wisdom. In United States slang, however, blondes are often considered "dizzy" (a little crazy) or "dumb" (ignorant), but very desirable ("gentlemen prefer blondes") and sexy ("blond bombshell"; "blondes have more fun"). Is your blond presenting a spiritual, or a physical (sex), message? If you're a male dreamer, she may represent your anima (see **anima**).

blood/bleeding

Life energy. If a particular part of your body is bleeding, consider the symbolism of that part, but also consider that you may want to have a medical checkup. Women often dream of blood, or of someone bleeding, shortly before, or during, their periods, and when they are pregnant (Garfield). Drops of blood in the snow (red and white) represent the need to unite the masculine (red) and feminine (white) principles (Jung and von Franz).

See **body; menstruation; wound(s)/wounded**.

blouse

Consider your associations to its color (a favorite one or inappropriate for the dream situation?), style (conservative, sexy?), and fit (loose, constricting?) for your first cues. It shares some of the same meanings as shirt.

The top of a military uniform is often called a blouse. Are you at war with a person or aspect of yourself; or is there a situation in which more discipline is called for?

Clothes can express your confidence, or lack of it, with respect to a particular situation/relationship, so consider whether the blouse is related to one that, possibly, involves your femininity or mothering. Is some aspect of these qualities now exposed (sheer material)? How does the blouse affect your interaction in the dream?

See **appearance; clothes/clothing; shirt; upper body**.

blue

Blue is the third most common color in dreams, behind black and white. Some of the traditional symbolisms for light blue include: spirit or the divine (heaven); intuition; purity (the color of Mary's robe); your relationship to/feelings about the Virgin Mary, which also relates to feelings/issues about the archetypal mother and your personal mother. The darker the blue gets, the more it relates to sadness (''blue funk'') or depression (''have the blues,'' ''blue Monday''), but can also represent clear thinking; royalty (''blue blood'') or superiority (''blue ribbon''); frozen ideas/emotions (''turning blue''); something that appears unexpectedly (''out of the blue'').

In ancient Egypt, blue and/or a starry blue cloak were symbols of Nut, the sky goddess. In Greece blue symbolized Jupiter and Juno, the god and goddess of heaven. Because it can represent both the sky and the sea, blue can symbolize vertical alignment in a spiritual sense (alignment of the personal soul with the overshadowing/God soul); the concept of height/depth; the metaphysical/alchemical concept ''as above, so below.''

It may also be a pun on the verb ''to blow,'' with all the idioms that relate to it: blew a fuse; blew my stack; blew my cool; an idea that blew your mind; or a secret revealed (blew the lid off; blew the whistle on).

A blue flower can sometimes be an allusion to the "golden flower of alchemy," thereby symbolizing the beginning of the process of transformation/individuation (Jung).

See **breath/breathe, color(s), sky** (if applicable); **wind(s)**.

boar

From ancient times a sacrificial animal, therefore the creativity/release that arises from sacrifice and subsequent victory of the spiritual/higher self over primitive instincts. Vishnu created the world through his sacrifice/incarnation into a boar and his lengthy battle/victory over a sea demon. Also, anxiety that instinctual/lower behavior will overcome the higher self. (Both the Scandinavian goddess Frey and the Greek god Adonis were killed by boars.)

The Scandinavian god Heimdall, son of nine sea giantesses (waves of emotion?) and guardian of the rainbow bridge between heaven and earth, was fathered by a boar and carried boar blood. Thus the boar is a perpetual watcher (Heimdall never needs sleep) between the upper/lower realms (conscious/unconscious) and, once again, a creator (Heimdall sired the three classes of men: noblemen, farmers, and thralls/slaves).

It may also be a pun for a person/situation that "bores" you.

See **animal(s); pig(s)**.

boat

The relationship of your conscious life with unconscious motivations. Is it "smooth sailing"; are you drifting aimlessly; or are you "rocking the boat"? If you "missed the boat," you may be failing to attend to messages (intuition) from your unconscious, or you may be experiencing regret over lost opportunities. Are you just "skimming the surface," or is your boat nicely settled in the water and progressing steadily?

See **sailing; ship/shipwreck; submarine; vehicle(s)**. If a boat without oars, see **oar**.

body

The dreamer's body represents the dream ego; your conscious identity. Consider whether your dream behaviors ("ego actions") are different from daily life. Compare what you're doing in the dream to what you might be doing in waking life. Do you need to make a change? Information about dream ego actions is especially relevant when collected and compared over time (see Dreamercise #15, Part 1).

Other persons in the dream may represent various "bodies" of knowledge. Specific body parts/clothing are only significant if they're different than usual, i.e., missing, injured, more elaborate or decorative, or otherwise emphasized. Then see the specific part or article of clothing. If you're clinically (severely) depressed, it's possible that your body won't appear in your dreams until you're in remission.

See **dreamer/dream ego; left side of body; lower body; right side of body; upper body**.

bog

All water symbols relate to the unconscious or to emotions in some way. Perhaps yours are "bogged down," or you're sluggish in your intentions. In what way are you stuck, and what would you need to add to the dream to get unstuck (see Dreamercise #11, Part 1)?

See **marsh; quicksand; water**.

boil(ing)

Boiling something symbolizes transformation; sacrifice; incorporation of certain traits/characteristics if boiling something to eat. If water is boiling, it may symbolize emotions/feelings in turmoil ("boiling mad") or ready to rise from the unconscious, be recognized, and be assimilated into conscious knowledge. Is there some experience you may need to "boil down" to get at the heart of it, or to retain the essence or lesson learned?

For the boil that appears on the body, see **abscess; blister**. See also **cook(s)/cooking**.

bomb/bombed

A bomb exploding is a dramatic signal, possibly of an ending and new beginning. Changes/repairs have to be made. An unexploded bomb could signal that potentially dangerous emotions (rage?), or a destructive situation, are ready to explode/erupt. Do you have anxieties about how you "bombed" in some project/relationship, or are you getting ready to "drop a bomb" on someone? Is there some potentially explosive situation you need to defuse?

See **atom bomb; destruction**.

bones

The past; "digging up" and discovering personal, family, or cultural secrets; underlying structure/strength; a need to "dig deeper." Knuckle bones and animal vertebrae have been used in a number of cultures as divination devices and can symbolize higher wisdom; anxiety about the future. (If applicable, see **fortune-teller/fortune-telling.**)

Do the bones form a skeleton (lost energy, patterns of the past?), or do they need to be straightened out and put in order? Are they human or animal (depleted instinctual energy)? They can also indicate nothing hidden; something scanty ("bare bones") that you need to "flesh out"; food/weight anxieties and the need to "put some meat on those bones," which may be true or may be one of those now-outdated childhood admonitions.

In the Jewish tradition the bone of Luz, a spinal bone, is believed to be indestructible. From it the body can be re-created. Similarly, in Jungian archetypal symbology, bones refer to our indestructible force (Estés). The bones of some saints are thought to have curative powers; but in ancient Scandinavia bones were hurled at lawbreakers for humiliation/punishment.

Consider the particular body part formed by the bone for additional clues. Breaking bones ("taking a break"?) is a definite signal of some situation/relationship you should attend to, or review its status ("bone up on"?), before an actual break occurs. Are you about to "take a false step" (broken foot or toe)? Do you have an ethical problem with something "underhanded" (broken hand), something you can't quite "put your finger on" (broken finger), or something you "can't stand" (broken leg)? Is someone or some project being a "pain in the ass" (broken hip)?

If applicable, see **archeology; backbone; skeleton**.

book(s)/ looking at books

History, both societal and personal; the book of life, and therefore, you; memories; attitudes about learning, and therefore, possibly school/education/authority issues; knowledge/wisdom; esoteric secrets (the book with seven seals in the Book of Revelation); openness/honesty ("my life is an open book"); the power of knowledge; the law (the tablets of the commandments given to Moses). Reading a specific chapter may refer to a particular section of your life. (Consider the chapter number for the age or number of years passed.) Are there chapters in your life that haven't been brought to a close (unfinished business?)? Looking at books can symbolize a passive attitude toward action/change without having to put forth effort. Consider the condition of the book for additional clues (well-kept/tattered; old/new; common/rare?).

See **read(ing)**.

bookkeeping

Financial matters; holding your emotions in "check"; keeping track of the emotional rights/wrongs in your life; attempting to balance the emotional/mental aspects of your psyche ("balance the books")—and, of course, how you feel about any of these.

See **account(s); balance(d)/balancing; checks**.

boss

Unfinished business with your own boss; feelings about authority; power/dominance and dependence or self-confidence issues. Dreaming about a past boss may suggest a way to handle a current situation. Are you or another being "too bossy"?

Cows are sometimes called "bossy." If you know this, it's possible to have a dream cow represent one of the above situations/issues. It can also be slang for something that's valued ("it's boss").

bottle

A feminine symbol, possibly sexual intercourse (if something is being inserted). A bottle of alcohol, or drinking from it, can symbolize nursing at the breast; a desire to return to infancy/dependency. Perhaps a "bottleneck" is causing you to "bottle up your emotions," or hold back in a relationship. If you uncork the bottle and let out the genie (primitive emotions/wishes), will you be overwhelmed?

See **alcohol/alcoholic; shadow**.

boundaries

Limits; restrictions; a need to restrain your actions/feelings or keep them in check ("setting boundaries"). Consider the strength of the boundaries, their collapsibility, and whether or not they need repair. Are you feeling "hemmed in" by present/early parental prohibitions? Is it time to break out of those boundaries and look to an unending horizon? Or you could be "staking your claim," taking ownership of some aspect of your life/personality.

See **fence; line**.

bow(ing)

Respect; honor; admiration; recognition of authority; subjugation; humility or humiliation. Consider the sex/age of the person and whether or not known to you. Is there someone you wish would bow down before you? Have you been too haughty and need to remember your more humble aspects?

bow and arrow

The bow often represents the combining of female (the arch/crescent of the bow) and male (the strength needed to release the arrow) energies. It can symbolize recreation; aggression; tension; life energy; competition; "aiming for perfection." Consider also whether it's aimed at a person, animal, or target. Depending on his/her appearance, the archer could be an archetypal symbol for the anima/animus; Diana, goddess of the hunt, or someone named likewise. In mythology/folklore, the archer is often associated with love (Cupid) or lust (Apollo). Therefore, the bow and arrow may represent directed libido (sexual energy).

See **arrow(s); hunter/huntress; lance; target** (if applicable).

bow(s)

Feminine aspect, unless a bow tie (emphasis on the neck as a place of separation between mental/physical functions). Consider its color, number (if more than one), and where placed (in the hair, on a dress or shoes?). Is its function to restrict; tame; focus attention; decorate?

See **appearance; hair(y)**.

bowl

A feminine symbol; the womb. Decorations on the bowl, as well as the contents (if any), may offer additional cues. Consider its condition and how it is treated/handled in the dream. Is it cracked, dropped, caressed, regarded as the center of attention, sitting unnoticed, packed away, used for everyday activities—any one of which may express how you feel you're treated in a particular relationship?

See **art; artist; container; womb**.

box

A feminine symbol; sexual slang for a woman's vagina; something hidden (secrets, instincts, unconscious material?); destructive impulses (Pandora's box, originally a vase); wisdom/truth not yet revealed (closed box). Esoterically, boxes are often used to preserve/protect/control/amplify the energy of whatever they contain. Consider the number of boxes, their shape and decoration.

See **container**.

boy

At its most positive, if you are

an adult male, he can indicate your playful, innocent, childlike nature; your inner child; or whatever other positive aspect the child expresses. He can also symbolize an immature aspect of yourself that needs to grow; some aspect of yourself at the dream age that you've ignored and need to recognize/acknowledge; demands from your inner child.

If you're female, he can indicate your developing masculine aspect (animus); feelings about some boy who is important to you; your son, if you have one. Consider how the boy is dressed and acts for additional cues.

In folklore the boy, or boy-judge, because of his unique perspective, often has more wisdom/insight than his elders. One of the most famous mythological boys, possibly a dwarf, is Telesphorus, an associate of Asclepias. Dressed in a hooded cloak with a point at the top, he was the sender of "true" dreams, *oneirata telesphora*. Like the hermit, Telesphorus was often depicted carrying a lantern and was, therefore, considered by Jung to be a "pointer of the way."

In Jungian theory, a boy appearing in the dreams of males or females can represent the spirit. In men's dreams, if positive, he represents higher aspects of the Self; if negative, the shadow.

See **animus; brother; child/children; family; girl; Self; son**.

bracelet(s)

As an aspect of appearance, they (consider the number) may be expressing a personal sense of value, worth, or preciousness—especially if containing jewels (see the specific jewel). If broken, it may symbolize loss of value or of a relationship. (Consider who gave you the bracelet.) Psychologically, bracelets can cut off energy to the hands and may prevent action, including reaching out/touching. In slang bracelets refer to handcuffs and can symbolize being a prisoner or being enslaved by some idea/attitude/behavior.

See **appearance; arm(s); hands; jewelry**.

brain

Consciousness; the ego; severe intellectual stress ("beat your brains out"). As the repository of knowledge and creative ideas, it can also symbolize our problem-solving abilities or resources ("pick someone's brain"); intellectual abilities; concerns about teaching/transmitting your knowledge. Have your ideas received enough attention/ validation?

See **head**.

brass

As an alloy of copper and zinc, brass can represent a conjunction of opposites. When well cared for, it is shiny, reflective, yellowish, golden. For both these reasons, it may symbolize the unconscious or your inner growth process. Because it has to be polished regularly, it could symbolize work needing to be done. What part of you needs polish?

Is it time for you to "get down to brass tacks"? In military slang "the brass" refers to officers/authority. Bigwigs in any field are considered the "top brass," "big brass," and "brass hats." So your dream may be related to a personal authority issue, a person in authority, or to a higher position you've been considering. Have you had recent contact with someone who's cheap, brazen, harsh, loud, insensitive ("brassy"), or a braggart ("showing off his brass")? Consider the meaning/ shape of the brass object.

brassiere

A need to know the truth or to get at something covered/hidden. How much real support is needed/available in some waking situation?

See **breast(s); underwear**.

bread

We all know the saying that bread is the "staff of life"; therefore, it's little wonder that bread symbolizes both physical and spiritual nourishment; basic needs. In some form, bread has been a sacrificial token since ancient times. Is there a waking-life issue regarding sacrifice, or connection with the divine? Bread can have sacred/religious symbolism (Jesus was considered "the living bread"; the bread or wafer of the Eucharist or Communion), even if you are not actively religious. It can also symbolize community/ family ("break bread together"). Consider what kind of bread (unique, ordinary?), how it is used in the dream, and its quality (fresh, moldy?). Both bread and dough are slang for money. Is your dream related to a financial situation/issue?

See **eating; food**. If applicable, see **baker/bakery/baking**.

break(ing)/broken

Does the dream express the action of breaking something (who performs the action?), or has the break already occurred (how do you respond?)? If the fracture/splintering of an object, especially a fragile one, it might symbolize shattered hopes/ideals. If a break in the earth, it can symbolize unconscious material attempting to move into consciousness, perhaps a "breakthrough." Breakers are crashing waves with a strong undertow, another symbol for unconscious activity.

Consider whether the break could be physical or spiritual. Perhaps you need to "take a break" before you break down, especially if bones or body parts are broken. It may relate to a situation you need to "break away" from or "break out of." As a pun, it might also mean to brake or discontinue some activity/relationship.

If the break refers to money ("break the bank") or treasures ("break in"), the dream may refer to your psychic energy (its expenditure/loss/increase).

See **glass** (if applicable).

breakdown

A vehicle (your body) breaking down suggests you may be pushing too hard and heading for physical difficulty/illness. Take care; reexamine the route you've chosen for missed alternatives.

See **vehicle(s)**.

breast(s)

Primal nourishment; needing to be nursed/cared for; your personal mother; infantile dependence; female identity/appearance issues; anxieties about being a woman/mother (in a woman's dream); anxieties about being overwhelmed (in a man's dream). For both men and women, breasts can symbolize sexual arousal/energy.

See **appearance; brassiere; chest; sex**.

breath/breathe

Breath/breathing is one of the most evident symbols of life/life energy, and is related to all our life goals, but it is usually not emphasized except by performing special breathing exercises, having difficulty, or being able to breathe in unusual atmospheres. Breathing/speaking underwater signals a mythological theme. Difficulty breathing may symbolize difficulty in incorporating the spiritual realm, but is also not uncommon in the dreams of abused women (Garfield). Heavy/excessive breathing may symbolize the presence and/or release of toxic energy (unfinished business) or negative emotions.

Breath/breathing issues can be represented as wind (see **wind(s)**). As a function that we don't ordinarily perform consciously, it may symbolize unconscious activity.

Since our breathing changes with excitement, fear, or stress (faster breathing; holding our breath, followed by a big sigh), consider the style of breathing for clues to the emotional content of the dream. Breathing in may refer to receiving inspiration; taking in ideas. Exhaling suggests expelling toxins; letting go. Holding your breath suggests exerting conscious willpower, but holding it underwater may symbolize a return to the womb state.

Archetypally, breathing symbolizes the breath of life from God; the in-breath/out-breath of God, the rhythm of the universe. It can symbolize the divine spirit within us; a way of incorporating spiritual power (Yogic breathing) or of building energy to use in spiritual work (Hawaiian Huna).

See **body; lungs; nose**.

bride

Beginning a new path/direction; turning your back on old ideas; the feminine quality in a relationship; for a man, his anima; for a woman, her Self. Her presence may signal a need to attend more to your feminine energy (or intuition?), in order to have a successful union, possibly with respect to a particular relationship/project. Being a bride is a common ''wish fulfillment'' dream for unmarried women, or a frequent anxiety dream (if things go wrong) for women about to marry (Siegel).

See **bridegroom; wedding**.

bridegroom

Change of direction/focus; the masculine quality in a relationship; for a woman, her animus; for a man, his Self; anxiety about an impending wedding (especially if things go wrong). His presence may signal you need to bring more consciousness and willpower (masculine energies?) into play, with respect to a particular relationship/project.

See **bride; wedding**.

bridge

Going under a bridge suggests delving into unconscious material; a need/fear (depending on the feeling of the dream) of dealing with instinctual material. Crossing a bridge over water may be a way to avoid unconscious material or may symbolize using the intellect to arrive at a decision/behavior; sexual intercourse (Freudian). A bridge can symbolize a need or willingness to: overcome obstacles; make a connection between one point/idea and another; make a transition between two conditions in your life (unite the past/present, the spiritual/material?).

It can symbolize a crossroads or a decision you need to make. A collapsing bridge may represent repressed feelings, or can indicate that your psyche took some incident more seriously than you did consciously.

Consider how easy/difficult it is to cross the bridge and its condition (rickety/stable, small/narrow, huge/heavy?). Are you closing off alternatives/resources you may need in the future ("burning your bridges behind you")? Or are you avoiding a decision, waiting to "cross that bridge when I come to it"?

A rainbow is a common symbol for bridging heaven and earth. Since a dream itself is a bridge between the conscious and unconscious, a bridge, or activity on the bridge, may symbolize your dreaming/dreamwork process.

See **crossing; rainbow; water**.

briefs

Since legal briefs are memos citing authorities (previous, applicable laws/decisions) to help attorneys make their cases or win their arguments, they can represent past authorities; resources; a point of view. They can also be a pun for underwear, or vice versa.

See **underwear**.

bright

See **light; luminous**.

broom

Time to clean up your act; sweep out (resolve) unfinished business/past issues and discard what's no longer useful. Brooms can symbolize the establishment of a household, or the inner hearth. Associated with witches/crones in folklore, broomsticks may refer to your witch aspect—usually a part of a woman's shadow, but a source of power or vitalizing energy if recognized. Brooms have a long association with sexual imagery, especially female masturbation.

See **witch/witchcraft**.

brother

If an actual family member, he may symbolize some aspect of your relationship, or serve to remind you that someone in your waking life has certain characteristics/behavior similar to your brother's. Also issues related to: caring/protection/overprotection roles; sibling rivalry; your role in the family; kinship/belongingness or unity ("blood brothers").

If not your brother, he may symbolize characteristics of yourself; ones you need to activate ("big brother"?); the animus in a woman's dream. For a male dreamer without a brother, he may symbolize the Self. Negatively, he can symbolize oppressive authority ("big brother is watching you"). A "brother" is also a religious person and may symbolize spiritual issues.

See **boy; family; man/men**.

brown

Earthiness; practicality; fertility; excrement (therefore, anal wishes/anxiety and the collecting of money/material objects). Does something in your life need to be organized or controlled? Are you responding to someone in a subservient way ("brownnosing")? In New Age terms brown can reflect a need to "ground" yourself, to balance/steady yourself and connect with your inner core. Sometimes it can signal an impending physical illness (Hoss), so consider carefully the symbolism of the object or body part where brown appears.

See **color(s); excrement**.

bubble

Wishes; unrealistic expectations; illusion; a fragile isolation. Has some person/situation shaken your fantasy or naïveté ("burst your bubble")? Someone stepping from a beautiful bubble suggests you now have the capacity to realize some fantasy or ideal. In Buddhism the bubble signifies the transitoriness of thought/life. A child blowing bubbles may symbolize an immature/undeveloped aspect of yourself. Consider any numbers in the dream, or the child's age, for clues about when this aspect of yourself may have stopped developing, or how long ago the illusion may have begun to develop.

buckle

A modern symbol of the shield, it represents self-defense; protection of your center (navel). It splits the body in half and separates the upper (consciousness) from the lower (unconscious). Is there a particularly vulnerable issue in waking life that needs nurturing, or one in which you need to "buckle down"? Perhaps a split, or a battle of opposites, needs to be reconciled/united.

See **belt; lower body; upper body**.

bud(s)

New life, energy, or ideas; cycles; a tender/vulnerable project/relationship; potential; the season of spring (revival and renewal).

See **flower(s); tree(s)**.

buffalo

An old/primal instinct/wish, which has been, or may once again be, a burden (hump) to bear; someone who's trying to outmaneuver you; feelings of confusion or lack of understanding.

See **animal(s)**.

bug

Sexual thoughts; worries/anxieties; nudges from your conscience; strong emotional involvement or attraction to an interest/career/profession ("bitten by the bug"); gossip or special information ("put a bug in someone's ear"). What's bugging you?

See **insects**.

building(s)

See **architecture**.

bull(s)

Fertility; a need for sexual contact; kingship/authority; stubbornness ("bullheaded"); clumsiness ("bull in a china shop"); solar/masculine energy. In some cultures, the bull is a lunar symbol because of the shape of its horns. It can: suggest that it's time to take action ("take the bull by the horns"); identify insincerity or bragging ("shoot the bull"); signal that you've been given incorrect/inaccurate information ("given a bum steer"). Because all animals can represent unconscious emotion, a raging bull may signify unacknowledged rage. Astrologically the bull is identified with Taurus and may represent someone born under that sign (April 21–May 21).

In Christian symbolism, the bull (sometimes the steer) is associated with the evangelist Luke. The bull has been a symbol for a number of deities: Anu, the Sumerian father of all gods; the Roman war god Mars; and Zeus (Roman, Jupiter/Jove), the supreme patriarch of Mount Olympus. In Egypt he was associated with Apis, a fertility god; Serapis, a god of healing; and Min, the male moon god.

See **animal(s); sun/sunlight**.

bullet

Aggression/anger (directed at you or another?); the penis; sexual intercourse. Perhaps you need to brace yourself, persevere, and "bite the bullet." Are you sidestepping issues by "dodging bullets"?

See **gun(s); marksman; penis/phallus; wound(s)/wounded**.

bum

See **derelict**.

bunch

In Christian symbolism bunched fruit, especially grapes, symbolizes Christ and spiritual organization. It is related to the sheaf (of grain) and refers to the integration of psychic processes, the development of psychological order.

Being bunched in with others strips you of your specialness. It suggests that your uniqueness is being ignored, or that you're being required to give up certain aspects of yourself in order to be "one of the bunch."

See **sheaf**.

burden

See **load**.

burglar/burglary

See **intruder; thief/theft**.

burial/buried

The end of a situation/relationship; letting go of something (an attitude, perception, or memory that's now "dead and buried"?); finishing some unfinished business. Perhaps you need to make peace and "bury the hatchet." Dreaming of someone buried may represent repressed anger or other "unacceptable" feelings toward that person, or characteristics you have and are denying. Dreaming of buried treasure or uncovering/recovering something precious (the Self) frequently symbolizes emerging unconscious material.

See **death; funeral**.

burn(ing)

Intense emotions, especially sexual passion ("burning with desire") or anger ("that burns me up"); purification; a signal that you need to relax and stop "burning the midnight oil," especially if you've been "burning the candle at both ends." Is there an issue you can no longer avoid ("burning question")?

See **fire; sex**.

bus

Your perceptions about your experience/relationship with a group/organization. Are you carrying too heavy or too light a load, or do you need to be carried for a while? Perhaps you've failed to do/perceive something important ("missed the bus"); or the dream is warning you it could still happen if you're not vigilant. In sexual slang a "buss" refers to a kiss. This could be a sexual dream, or it could be saying you've been "kissed off."

See **vehicle(s)**.

bush

Inasmuch as trees often symbolize the Self, a bush may be an early symbol of growth; change; the individuation process. Consider its characteristics for further cues (well-trimmed, scruffy, blossoming, dormant?). In Judaism and Christianity, the burning bush symbolizes divine fire/energy that can burn within us without consuming. In sexual slang, "bush" refers to a woman's pubic hair/genital area.

business/work

If a present business/work situation, your dream behavior/feelings are your best clues as to whether the dream is compensating for feelings of inadequacy/egotism—or other feelings that are the opposite of the dream feeling—or whether it is signaling that you're on the right track and it's "business as usual." It can suggest anxiety about a task/project. Perhaps you need to "get back to work" or "get to the business at hand," which could relate to waking situations (actual work/relationships) or inner work.

To dream of a past business/work situation may signify that there was a message to be learned from that situation, which you failed to see but now need to recognize (insight?), especially as it may apply to a present situation. Is there still some kind of emotional connection with a person from that past situation, or with certain aspects of his/her personality? It may also be an attempt to repair past business/work transgressions or inadequate behavior. Training someone else to take your place says you're moving on, with respect to some task/business/inner development. You need to, and can, leave behind old attitudes and look to future creations.

If business/work aspects of a dream (locale, colleagues, clothes, occupation) don't pertain to an actual business, they may pertain to psychological business, which most likely will be clarified through your associations to other images in the dream.

butterfly

Depending on the culture/myth, butterflies frequently symbolize transformation; the soul; freedom; carefreeness; lightness; beauty; rebirth. A butterfly can symbolize your inner psyche, since the name of the goddess Psyche was taken from the Greek word for butterfly. In China two butterflies symbolize union/marital bliss. Consider the activities of the butterfly and its color, especially idiosyncratic changes from its usual color to an unusual color, for additional cues.

Could the dream be telling you that you're too much of a social butterfly, or flitting about too much? Do you need to settle down, make/attend to commitments?

See **insects**.

buttocks

Instincts and urges. Buttocks

are the "seat" of those instincts related to sex/elimination. Are the buttocks deformed (undeveloped or wounded aspects of the psyche), decorated (pay attention), or is there some difficulty with functions? Are you "sitting down on the job," "sitting on" some issue, or are you "at the bottom of the stack"? Perhaps after much effort, you are able to "sit back" or are "sitting pretty." Or you may be "sitting tight" (either immobility or waiting), or tackling some job/issue "by the seat of your pants" and not feeling too secure.

See **body; lower body**.

cabinet

Feminine symbol; female body; hiding place for family/personal secrets; storage for various ideas, or aspects of yourself. (Are they still useful, or outdated and need to be discarded?) Consider the cabinet's contents, age, and condition for additional clues.

cactus

Ouch! Be careful. A cactus can refer to a need to protect/defend yourself (vulnerability?), or to distance yourself from some situation/relationship. Depending on its condition and size, it also can symbolize strength/endurance. A blooming cactus has more positive connotations than a dying one (see **flower(s)**). If your cactus is host to any birds, consider their symbolism.

See **desert**.

cage

Are you outside or inside; alone or with someone else; struggling to get out or put someone in? Or is the empty cage merely someplace in the dream as a potential threat/reserve in case of necessity? You may be needing to restrain yourself or another's interaction with you.

A cage may reflect your feelings about an experience/struggle in your life, and feelings of being imprisoned in or by it. It may serve to remind you of your own or another's perceived limitations, but remember, perceived limitations are not necessarily actual ones. The cage can suggest confined impulses; a feeling of being out of control; a wish for confinement of your emotions/actions; guilt or other feelings related to accusations.

See **cell; restrain/restraint**.

cake

Celebration; anniversaries (birthday) and rituals (baptism, wedding), and therefore, the passage of time and cycles. Food is often an allusion to feelings/emotional situations. What emotions does cake evoke for you? Perhaps some waking situation is, or will be, like a bonus (''icing on the cake''), or you wish something were going more smoothly (''a piece of cake''). Is there something you're more surprised about than you've realized or haven't really acknowledged its positive nature (it ''takes the cake'')? Maybe you're feeling deprived and need more sensual sweetness/enjoyment/reward. Rich, sensual experiences are sometimes a disguise for sexual needs/desires. In ancient times cakes of all shapes and flavors, especially honey cakes, were used to propitiate the gods. Is there guilt hidden in the meaning of this dream, or a need to attend to your spiritual development?

See **eating; food; sugar/sweets/candy**.

calendar

Cycles; passage of time; aging; reminder of an appointment or an anniversary (also of some ended or unhappy relationship?); a need to make plans. Pay particular attention to numbers/months indicated. If the dream takes place in the past, review previous dreams to see if there was some process that began at that time.

See **time; zodiac**.

calf/calves

A suckling animal, and therefore, an immature aspect of yourself; a desire/need to be nurtured; part of the herd, and therefore, belonging/protection, or lack of awareness/independence (just ''following the herd''). In ancient times, calves were often animals of sacrifice, but the biblical Golden Calf symbolizes the worshiping of idols/valuing material possessions. It may, then, refer to having placed more value on a situation/person than is merited—hero worship—or letting the monetary value (the ''fatted calf'') of a situation blind you to its other aspects.

The animal may be a pun for the lower leg and symbolize movement. Keeping your calves/herd together or attempting to, may refer to female modesty.

See **body; cow(s); leg(s)**.

camel

In North African symbology, it represents obstinacy and pride. As an animal, it symbolizes long, hard journeys ("the ship of the desert"); plodding energy; carrying burdens; endurance and sustenance, inasmuch as a camel can provide meat, milk, and protective clothing (skin). If you've been to countries where camels are used, it may represent your feelings about that experience, perhaps now awakened by a current situation.

Cirlot says the camel is related to the dragon in that, according to the Zohar (a mystical Jewish commentary that forms one basis of the cabala), the serpent in the Garden of Eden was a kind of "flying camel." There is a current saying that "a camel is a horse created by a committee," so perhaps your camel represents misguided effort, or impossible action ("a camel going through the eye of a needle"). In folktales the camel, representing stupidity, is often tricked by birds/animals.

See **animal(s); desert; dragon; sand**.

camera

As an instrument for recording and keeping track of past experiences/memories, the camera can symbolize the process that lets you relive/review experiences. It may be keeping track of your self-growth or identity if appearing in several dreams. The eye of the camera never lies, so it can symbolize truth; something that needs to be noticed; something noticed by your unconscious when your consciousness didn't pay attention; something you need to view with a new perspective or focus in on. In primitive mythology, the camera, through its photographs, can capture the soul of a person; therefore, imprisoned/inhibited spiritual development; loss of identity; control by another.

See **photograph; picture; voodoo**.

camouflage

A need to hide/disappear; putting on a false front or act; possibly feeling attacked/vulnerable. Consider the symbolism of the concealed person/object and how effective the camouflage is.

camper/camping

Wanting to be more in touch with nature; being independent/self-sufficient; self-survival; recognition of basic needs; a quest/initiation. Camping vehicles/vans may symbolize a gypsy/adventurer attitude; holding open the option of moving on if a situation doesn't fit you. A "tent city" may symbolize a sense of homelessness/lack of belonging; loss of security.

can

The womb (consider the container's contents); the feminine; nurturance; buttocks; groundedness/stability or lack of it ("get knocked on your can"); something that's in a mess or mixed up ("can of worms"). It is also slang for the bathroom/toilet and associated activities. It may be a pun for skills/ability ("I can"), lack of them (empty can), or for lost opportunity ("get canned").

See **container**.

canal

Feminine symbol; the birth canal; passageway; direction; access to inner emotions or goals. How are you progressing along the canal: on your own, in a vehicle guided/pulled by another, with ease/difficulty? Some believe that dreams in which you're having difficulty traversing a canal reflect memories of your birth experience. Is your creativity momentarily stuck in its birthing?

See **vehicle(s); water** (if applicable).

cancel(ing)/cancellation

To cancel an appointment, or have it canceled, may express anxiety about keeping an actual appointment. Whatever you're canceling may relate to a situation/relationship that you'd like to cancel or get out of. If canceling a wedding or major event, it may be an expression of anxiety about the life change you're about to undergo and any loss of identity, privacy, or whatever, you may anticipate. Remember that every major change, no matter how positive, also involves loss, which has to be acknowledged. A canceled check may refer to a waking-life financial issue, or it may be saying that you have canceled—hastily or not, wisely or not—some checks and balances in your life. Wordplay suggests that, indeed, you "can sell."

cancer

As a malignant growth, it may be a disguise for some terrifying event/memory that you've incorporated into your unconscious, possibly repressed, that's eating away at you; some aspect of your life that's out of control; anxiety about the disease. Consider the symbolism for the body area where the cancer occurs. Persons with cancer have dreams depicting upheaval and crumbling, or contain pollution, contamination, or poisoning situations (Siegel).

Cancer, the fourth sign of the zodiac, is represented by the crab and can represent someone born June 22–July 23.

See **body; crab(s); disease; fear; moon/moonlight; water; zodiac**.

candle(s)

Earlier times; individual light of your personality; your personal awareness; life energy; insight; spiritual awareness/knowledge; the soul; the relationship between God and man; reverence; ritual; mystery. Candles are often used at ceremonies/celebrations and may, therefore, symbolize relationships; cycles; the passage of time; creating the mood for romance; and past ("an old flame") or present romance ("my new flame"). Ritually used, they can create the safe, magic circle, which denotes another state of being.

It can reflect feelings of inferiority ("can't hold a candle to"), or too much activity ("burning your candle at both ends"). An unlit candle suggests untapped inner resources. A burnt-out/blown-out candle may symbolize lack of awareness; an issue you can't, or don't want to, face.

In Freudian terms it is a phallic symbol, so consider how it burns or what you do with the candle (light it, put it out, put it in a drawer?). Esoterically, the wax candle is related to the bees that come from paradise.

See **bee(s); fire; flame(s); light; sex**.

candy

See **cake; sugar/sweets/candy**.

cane

A Freudian phallic symbol, possibly hostile/aggressive if used to hit someone. If used as support/aid, consider in what way you're wounded/incapacitated—or view yourself that way—and need someone (a male?) to come to your aid, or need more time to resolve something. What prevents you from throwing away your cane and standing on your own? Consider any decorations on the cane for additional clues.

In Mohave Indian tradition the cane is related to creation/creativity. Mastamho, one of two sons born to Sky and Earth, used a cane made from his breath and spit to strike the earth and create the first river. Twisting his boat through the river, he created the earth's canyons.

See **staff**.

cannibal

To eat another person is to incorporate those characteristics into yourself. Use Dreamercise

#3, Part 1, to play the roles of cannibal and victim to determine how both are necessary for your survival.

See **jungle**.

cannon

See **gun(s)**.

canyon

Fertility; female genitals; the depth of the unconscious, especially if there's a stream flowing in the canyon; the passage of time; inner nature/history revealed. Negatively it can convey being walled in, stuck. Grand Canyon is an archetypal (magnified) expression of Mother Earth, and the aspect of mothering that can be overwhelming.

See **abyss; canal; vagina**.

cap/hat

Your head, or more likely, your intellect/intellectual activity ("put on your thinking cap"); mental attitudes/beliefs/ideas, especially fancy ones if decorative. If round, it may represent the sun or the Self. It can symbolize secrets ("keep it under your hat"); an attitude of humility and obedience to God or authority (if worn to church); feelings that you need to approach someone with your "cap in hand." If it bears a name or insignia, it may represent your interest/affiliation with a particular group.

Metaphysically, it may represent the "cap of maintenance," which was worn before nobility to show respect, or worn by nobility, underneath the crown, to show they maintained their spiritual alignment with higher powers/deities. In sexual slang, it may refer to a condom.

See **clothes/clothing**.

captain

Authority; wisdom of experience; worldly awareness; father figure/leader; control/independence issues; someone who knows the direction of life. If on land, it may represent that aspect of yourself that knows the spiritual/inner path. If the captain of a ship, it may represent that aspect which can guide or set new directions through unconscious (intuitive; emotional?) material.

See **boss; leader/lead(ing); roles**.

captured

See **caught; kidnapped/captured/abducted**.

car

Often your body, or your way of moving through life/approaching situations, although it can also represent someone else. It may be a message to "shift gears." If you're in the backseat of the car, are you being a "backseat driver," or are you "taking a backseat" to someone else? Are you directing your life (the driver) or just going along (a passenger) with someone else's lead/ideas? Perhaps the dream is reminding you not to let yourself be "taken for a ride."

Consider the make of the car and what that particular brand means to you (safety, prestige, recreation, freedom, luxury?). A car that needs repair, lacks horsepower (energy), runs out of gas, or malfunctions may represent a health problem and could be signaling that it's time to stop ignoring some symptom and see your doctor. It can also signal that you need to turn your energies/efforts elsewhere for more success. A stolen car may indicate that some person/situation is robbing you of energy, has distracted you, or is preventing you from attending to long-range goals. Don't forget the goddess Car or Kore (the maiden; Persephone), after whom Chartres was named (see **core**).

See **vehicle(s)**.

carbon copy/ word-processing copy

Sameness; duplication; concern with fitting in; emphasizing similarities rather than differences. Negatively, it could indicate lack of originality or uniqueness, as well as low self-esteem. (You didn't rate an original.)

See **double/duplicate; twin(s)**.

cards/playing cards

As with all games, card games can symbolize camaraderie; team/partner cooperation; competition. It may give you clues about your strategy/behavior in a waking situation. Your opponents, or partners, are aspects of yourself whom you will need to deal with to be more successful in the game of life. Depending on how the game goes, someone in your life game may be "stacking the deck," or "dealing from the bottom of the deck." If your associations don't connect with anyone in present waking life, consider someone from your past, or the shadow (sabotaging) aspect of your inner self.

The game can make you aware of fatalistic ("it's in the cards") or reckless ("playing for high stakes") attitudes. Red suits represent the female/feminine energy/life (blood); black suits represent the male/masculine energy/death.

Modern playing cards evolved from the Tarot deck and are esoterically related, therefore, to ancient spiritual or religious (usually non-Christian) mysteries. Many consider the 22 Tarot Major Arcana as archetypal symbols, although the joker (see **trickster**) is the only one to have remained in modern bridge decks.

See **fortune-teller/fortune-telling; game(s)**.

caretaker

Consider how the caretaker is doing (adequate; inadequate?), who or what is being taken care of, and whether the caretaker connects with anyone in your past/present life (parent, nanny, baby-sitter?). If you're the caretaker, consider whether you are playing a healthy/supportive or dysfunctional/enabling role. Is it time to take on, or to give up, this role? If you're not the caretaker, then, in addition to any of the above, he/she may symbolize your inner caretaker—the qualities/abilities you have for taking care of yourself. What part of you needs to be taken care of, protected, or nurtured?

carnival

If the kind of carnival that accompanies a circus/fair, it may symbolize a need for fun; the chance to compete or show your prowess; the opportunity to view freaks or distorted aspects of yourself at the sideshow. It can symbolize surges of energy/excitement; the "ups and downs" of life; frivolity; letting down inhibitions; or the goddess Car (Kore, Persephone), patroness of carnivals.

If a Mardi Gras–type carnival, it may be the archetypal symbol for a Bacchic communal celebration in which lack of restraint, sexual freedom, the shedding of one aspect of your persona and showing another, prevail. In some European communities, groups deliberately choose to represent/display shadow or demon aspects of human personality as a way of acknowledging and bringing balance to our lives during the rest of the year. Do you need to release some inhibitions; try on a new role; or get better acquainted with shadow aspects calling for recognition? Where are you out of balance?

See **circus; fair**.

carpenter

Building; rebuilding; repairing the body (structure) or the personality. Consider the symbolism of the specific object. It could also represent Joseph or Jesus.

carpet

Consider its condition and any special designs. Do you need to "roll out the carpet" for yourself, or is someone "walking all over you"? A carpet may represent a way you insulate yourself from cold, hard reality, but it can also represent luxury, comfort, or the lack of it (threadbare rugs, bare floors). Are you/another "sweeping something under the carpet"? A magic carpet may reflect wishes to escape a situation/relationship/current responsibilities, and is one form of a flying dream.

carriage

While sharing the general symbolism of vehicles, a carriage, drawn by an animal, may relate to more primitive emotions or biological drives, and how you're coping with them. If an ancient carriage, and the dream story occurs in ancient times, it may relate to issues from your past, or to family values.

Consider the state of the carriage, the ease or difficulty of the ride, and whether you're on the outside looking in (viewing the past, unconscious material, voyeuristic issues?), or on the inside looking out (or being looked at?). What's occurring in the carriage: loneliness, haughtiness, romance?

Is your carriage a pumpkin in disguise, signifying that the heart of the issue is really something else, or that there is an issue/relationship to which you are reacting as if it were a fairy tale? Are you living out the Cinderella theme—or possibly that of royalty—in some situation?

A baby carriage may refer to a need/desire to be mothered/nurtured, or to a new project/relationship that needs to be nurtured, a new pathway.

Because carriage also refers to posture/movement/balance, the dream carriage may symbolize issues related to any of these, i.e., back/lower body problems; an issue that's keeping you off balance; a need to set priorities.

See **vehicle(s)**.

carry(ing)/carried

Are *you* carrying or being carried? If not a person, what is being carried?

Regarding some waking situation/relationship, consider your feelings/anxieties about being a burden ("carry your own weight"), being responsible, or giving up. "Carrying" can relate to romance or athletic ability ("carrying a torch"); something you desire. Negatively, it can refer to burdensome persons/situations; emotional baggage—"carrying a chip on your shoulder"—that you're holding on to (anger, grudge, hate, resentment?). What prevents you from putting these down? Is there something in your waking life that you are "carried away" with; now realize has been "carried too far"; or in which you wish you could "carry the day"?

carving

Carving a cooked animal may refer to trying to rid yourself of (cut away) certain feelings (chicken, cowardly?). It may reflect feelings about someone (he's a turkey), or that some person/situation is violating (taking a slice out of) your life. It may mean you have distanced yourself from your emotions (cooked them) and want to cut them apart and analyze them. Are you worrying about carving a niche for yourself at work; carving up a project (who gets the treasure, or the lion's share?); or that your personal "kingdom" is being carved up and power taken away from you?

If carving an art object, see **art; artist; craft(s)**.

case

As a container, a case can be a feminine symbol, or a symbol of female genitals. Consider its shape, contents, and decoration. If a suitcase, consider the symbolism of the clothes within. If a briefcase, what kind of documents are contained in it and how do they affect you? People-helpers carry a caseload, and a client is often referred to as a case (are you feeling depersonalized?). If you're familiar with this language, consider who, besides yourself, "the case" might represent.

See **container; suitcase**.

cash

See **money**.

castle

With its moat and towers, a castle can symbolize an aspect of yourself that's walled off or on the watch for attack; your psychological defenses (are they strong as a fortress or crumbling?). How limited is your psychological/emotional movement, your choice of direction? How powerful/vulnerable do you feel; are you secure or under siege?

A castle can represent feelings about yourself (royal, special) or your family; security; relationships ("a man's home is his castle"); that you're living a fantasy; some aspect of your fantasy life, especially with respect to the future and future relationships—the fulfillment of wishes (someday I'll be carried away and taken care of?).

One of the most famous

mythological castles was the castle of the Grail. Visible only to the true knight, it disappeared when a false one appeared; therefore, it was a symbol of right thinking and the ultimate in spiritual or self-development. Where are you on your quest?

See **architecture; Grail; house**.

castrate

If you're male, most likely you won't dream of your actual castration, but will dream of other images, possibly double images, that face damage/destruction. Consider especially any games where balls are used, nuts/eggs are eaten, rotted, or destroyed. These, or animal castration, dreams deal with issues of your basic identity; your role in a relationship; loss of creative power; anxiety about sexual prowess. If you're a woman, they may express attitudes toward men and your internal animus.

See **barber/hairdresser**.

cat/kitten

Instinctual energy that's been tamed and is relatively close to consciousness; feminine power/energy; the feminine archetype; the immature or coy feminine (kitten); female genitals (pussy). Other characteristics/aspects of yourself/another that cats may symbolize include: devouring/playful; snugly/independent; graceful; lazy/pouncing; stalking; patient; snide (''catty''). Traditionally cats are the ''familiars'' of witches (the shadow or crone aspect), but in ancient times they were often associated with goddesses/divine powers. In Egypt the feline-headed goddesses Bastet, goddess of pleasure, and Sekhmet, a terrible-mother goddess (bringer of epidemics but also a goddess of healing/healers) represented various feminine attributes. A cat elevated to its most powerful expression of energy (possibly hostility/danger) is, of course, a lion or tiger.

See **lion(s)**.

cataclysm

See **destruction**.

catacomb

Your path to the inner world; finding the way through your psyche and/or the fear that you will get lost therein; buried or ancient attitudes/training.

See **labyrinth/maze; tomb**.

caterpillar

Having a lot of feet (resources) to stand on; mobility; rhythm; fluidity in thinking/action. After a period of inner work or development (bursting through the cocoon of limitation), the caterpillar becomes the butterfly. Thus, its presence may signal a need for the kind of personal work/introspection that results in transformation, or may represent ongoing inner work. The caterpillar promises future freedom from being earthbound (restricted by your instincts), and points to a time when your self-development will send you soaring into the realm of the divine. A caterpillar can symbolize a smaller version of a snake with all its symbolic attributes. Its undulating motion may symbolize sexual activity.

See **butterfly; insects; snake(s)**.

cattle

See **bull(s); calf/calves; cow(s)**.

caught

Psychically immobilized; limited choices; guilt issues (fear of being caught); sexual issues ("caught in the act"); trapped by your innocence/lack of knowledge/issues from your past.

See **trap(ped)**.

cauldron

See **cup(s)**.

cave

In Jungian terms, a cave symbolizes the unconscious (dark, secret). To enter and explore is to begin the process of awareness/transformation/individuation. As a dark place to enter/leave, cave is also a symbol of the womb, and can represent mother; the feminine; the vagina; sex; the birth process. In myth it sometimes symbolizes a place of initiation/rebirth, where one learns secrets/finds truths that lead to growth/enlightenment.

The cave was the symbol of Demeter, Greek goddess of earth/fertility (corn, fruits). Her symbolic animal was the pig. Demeter was one form of the Great Mother, and the mother of Persephone, condemned to live part of the year in the underworld (the unconscious). Persephone's cyclic emergence is a rebirth symbol.

Metaphysically, "the cave" refers to a created location within the head that serves as access to the higher self or universal creative energies, the doorway to the soul.

See **catacomb; pig(s); tunnel**.

celebration

Another level of growth achieved; a goal, or the path, gained; recognition of developed/acquired insight/wisdom; the joy and honoring of victory/success/accomplishment; freedom dom from restraint, and therefore, emotional release. A celebration can also represent cycles and the passage of time (birthdays, anniversaries, holidays); family/social connections; anxieties about any of these. Party and celebration dreams are common when there are upcoming actual turning points/events (Siegel).

About 50 percent of the expectant fathers Siegel studied had dreams of initiatory ceremonies/celebrations, especially birthday parties, which often involved elaborate food preparation eating, and drinking.

See **ceremony; drink(ing); eating; food**.

cell

If in a jail cell, attitudes/behaviors/ideas, possibly feelings of guilt, that hold you prisoner and prevent your growth. Thus, successfully breaking out suggests you've liberated some part of yourself and resumed your growth process. A cell can represent a situation/relationship in which you're not free to be yourself or to "speak your mind."

In a physiological/cosmic sense, the cell represents the beginning—and the restrictions—of life; the container of all we have and are; basic identity. Potential growth of yourself or a fetus may be expressed by observing cells (ovum, sperm, other tissue?) through a microscope.

If you have a malignant growth or terminal illness, that process will most likely be expressed through destructive symbols, especially fire, holocaust, or other devastation, rather than the actual growth of cells. Once you've acknowledged your illness, your dreams will resume their progress toward individuation and wholeness (von Franz).

See **cage; prison/prisoner**.

cellar

The unconscious; the womb/vagina; stored or buried (repressed) feelings, horrors/fears, especially if you once heard stories of a "bogeyman" who lived in the cellar. If you live in tornado country, the cellar may symbolize a place of safety; anxiety about sudden, unpredictable destruction. If you have knowledge of food cellars where "grandmothers" kept preserves/staples/supplies, the cellar may represent a place of ancient, "stored" wisdom/treasure/nourishment. In ancient times or in mythology, it often represents a place of initiation, of discovering truths that promote transformation.

See **basement**.

cemetery

Family/societal heritage; connection with the past; anxieties/attitudes about death; possibly the collective unconscious. Look for archetypal designs within the cemetery. As the door to the underworld, it can also represent the unconscious, especially repressed ("dead and buried") emotions, values, or relationships. Consider the experiences you have in the cemetery, specific people who are there. More generally, a cemetery is a symbol of transition; movement into a new phase. It may represent a return to Mother Earth, i.e., to more natural/earthy ways of being.

See **death; funeral; grave**.

center

If you're in the center of a crowd or group, or the "center of attention," consider whether people are honoring (need for recognition?), threatening (fear of being found out or punished?), or restricting (family or societal values?) you. Are you satisfied in this situation, or need to break out? Your dream may be expressing a need to center yourself, to contact your own core feelings/values and respond to them. The center of the circle, or a point (dot) in the center of a circle, is an ancient symbol for God. It can also represent the Self. The vertical axis (*axis mundi*) of the world always grows from the center, where all creation takes place.

See **circle; dot; middle; navel; Self; world tree**.

ceremony

If participating: change; movement or entrance into a new phase/way of life; growth; cyclic forces; establishment of a beginning/ending; defining/solidifying purposes. If creating a ceremony is emphasized, you may be expressing a need to organize/control your surroundings for predictability or stability. If observing, see **audience**.

See **celebration; rite/ritual; zodiac**.

chain(s)/chained

Chains/being chained can represent the idea that you're an essential "link in a chain" (family, work?) and are necessary/important to some situation/relationship, even though it may sometimes be restrictive/rigid. It can also symbolize a "chain of events," which you may perceive as unalterable, or which may provide insight. Review earlier events/dreams to see when this process might have begun (see Dreamercise #14, Part 1).

Being chained puts you in the position of being a prisoner or in bondage. How are you restrained in your life, or need more control/impact? If you're in bondage, it may reflect a sexual situation; your feelings about a person/relationship; a need to awaken and release your sexual feelings. Chains are related to other types of bindings (the "chain that binds"), all of which symbolize social/psychic integration/toughness. A golden chain can symbolize a reward for work well done (inner or otherwise). In Christian symbolism, prayer has often been depicted as a golden chain to God.

See **gold(en)**, if applicable.

chair

The chair of power, and therefore, an authority/leader; your personal power; controlling/guiding aspects of your personality; support; refuge; comfort. Could it represent your attitude/feelings about a waking situation (comfortable, enveloping, worn-out, sagging, inviting, restful?)?

See **rocking chair; throne; wheelchair** if applicable.

chalice

The eternal symbol of the quest for the perfected self; therefore, the Self and the individuation process (Jung). It can be a symbol for spiritual nourishment; communion with God (the chalice of the mass); or the Grail—the hero/heroine's journey through life. One special chalice, hard to obtain, may symbolize the child archetype; the healer; the bringer of wholeness.

See **cup(s); Grail**.

champagne

The launching/completion of a new project or phase of your life; "bubbly," happy feelings; a signal for celebration.

See **alcohol/alcoholic; celebration; drink(ing)**.

champion

A wish/need for victory or to be the best; therefore, you may have been experiencing feelings of inadequacy. Also standing behind judgments/values, possibly undervalued ones ("championing a cause"). Archetypally, it may signal the hero/heroine-journey theme.

See **first; victor/victory**.

channel

Female genitals/the vagina; access to inner wisdom or the unconscious. Traveling along a water-filled channel can represent the birth of a new project/life direction, or the delivery process if you're pregnant. A channel, or channels, can represent one or more of the five senses by which we take in information and through which we try to express ourselves.

See **canal; tunnel**.

chapel

See **church**.

charging ahead

An anxiety or compulsive need to accomplish things; being caught up in a physical/emotional thrust forward; a surge of emotion. It may signal that you need to step aside and catch your breath, or think through some waking issue/relationship that's moving too fast for you.

chariot

Action; conquest; competition. It is related to the hero's/heroine's journey and to any physical/mental journey we must make. In the spiritual "Swing Low, Sweet Chariot," it is the vehicle that carries you home, and can, therefore, symbolize death; inner awakening. The solar chariot of mythology represents life-giving energy; connection with the divine. As one of the symbols of Aphrodite (Roman, Venus), Greek goddess of love, it may be an archetypal representation of the Self, especially if round wheels (mandala) can be seen on the chariot.

See **vehicle**(s).

charm(s)

The need to manipulate energies, gain power or focus your own power, organize unconscious energies. Originally charms were often sung; therefore, the power/mystery of self-development through music. Is there a situation in which you need to develop the ability to "charm the honey from the bees," or has someone "charming" entered your life? Perhaps you wish you were more charming. A charm from a bracelet can relate to past experiences/issues still active; or to memories revived by a waking situation.

See **amulet**(s).

chase(d)

One of the most frequent types of recurrent nightmare/anxiety dream, being chased sometimes can be traced back to waking situations in which you felt caught/vulnerable, acted passively, or in which you "gave in" (Mahrer). Some researchers connect it to a stressful situation dating from childhood/adolescence, the memory of which is often repressed. Being chased by animals/demons can represent your own unexpressed/unacknowledged anger/aggression, which is being "projected" onto the chaser. Being chased and caught, especially by a man, may be birth-process memories (Hopkins). Consider it as a possible sexual pun for "chaste"—being "chaste" and not caught. If you're the chaser, what you're chasing may represent a goal, or a solution to a waking issue. With what ease/difficulty are you pursuing it?

See **escape; fear**.

chasm

Fear of being swallowed/enveloped, especially sexually or in a sexual relationship; fearing the disappearance of your personality/integrity; a door to your underworld/unconscious.

See **abyss; canyon; vagina; valley(s)**.

chauffeur

If you're the chauffeur, it may symbolize attitudes about a waking situation in which you are required to be at someone's call, or are responsible for his/her welfare and time commitments. (Your time is subservient to theirs.) Are you feeling unacknowledged for your efforts? If you have a chauffeur, someone else is driving you and you're not traversing life under your own power, or choosing your own direction. What part of you is paying, or what are you paying, to avoid responsibility?

See **vehicle(s)**.

cheap

A "cheap" person can represent some way in which you are feeling inadequate/undervalued/sexually denigrated. Purchasing a cheap product, or getting something of value at a cheaper price, may symbolize some aspect of yourself that you, or another, undervalue. Consider the symbolism of the item itself and how you feel in the dream. Are you putting forth less effort than you really think you should; are you, or someone else, getting away with something? By choosing to be cheap, do you cheat others, or yourself, out of things of value, i.e., a way of withholding the best of you or of failing to recognize/honor your own worth?

checks

Access to energy/power/creativity that's "banked" or stored in the unconscious. Consider the amount and the situation in which you write a check for additional cues. Psychological equilibrium is implied in the idiom "checks and balances." Is there a situation that needs to be checked on, and balanced?

See **account(s); bookkeeping; money**.

cheek(s)

Cheeks emphasized (decorated, war paint, wounded?) may represent attitudes of courage; passiveness or nonviolent action ("turn the other cheek"); commitment/closeness ("cheek to cheek"). "Rosy-cheeked" suggests life energy; enthusiasm; vitality. Cheeks can represent impertinence; being opinionated ("has a lot of cheek"); strength of character ("high cheeks"); withholding yourself ("frozen expression"). Since cheeks change with almost every major facial expression, they may represent your ability to have an effect on someone else. In sexual slang, cheeks are buttocks.

See **body; buttocks; face; head**.

chef

See **cook(s)/cooking**.

chemical(s)

Combining chemicals, or the energy they represent, can produce a potion (love potion?) or an explosion; thus, chemicals/working with chemicals may symbolize creativity; magical or intellectual power derived from formulas; conscious manipulation/conversion. Alchemically, the use/presence of chemicals implies transformation and is related to the Self/individuation process (your "chemistry"). What ingredients/elements in your life need to be remixed for more satisfaction?

See **chemist/chemistry**.

chemist/chemistry

What aspect of you is working with, or knows about, the power of chemicals? If the chemist is your same sex, it may represent your Self. If the chemist is doing something negative, it may represent your shadow. It can represent an associated chemistry experience (in school?), or someone you know connected with chemistry. It can also symbolize the union of opposites; attraction; a relationship (make or have "good chemistry" together). In Britain and other European countries, "chemist" is another name for druggist. If you know/use this, then the chemist/druggist may represent a healing aspect of yourself; a part of you that's drugged, out of control, not attending to conscious details. In what situations are you searching for solutions or a formula for success? Do you need to bring your body chemistry under control?

See **chemical(s); magician**.

cherry

Like any fruit, it symbolizes fertility; abundance; cycles—in this case, spring. As a red fruit, it symbolizes the Virgin Goddess. In early Christianity, the cherry symbolized forbidden fruit. Out of that developed the sexual symbolism of the cherry as a virgin woman with an intact hymen. In North America, many folk remedies have been made from parts of the tree and its fruit, thus it may also symbolize healing—especially natural healing—or the old ways/wisdom; even superstition in its negative sense. In Japan the cherry symbolizes self-discovery; its blossoms symbolize purity and beauty. What's preventing your life from being a bowl of cherries?

See **fruit(s)**. If the tree, see **tree(s)**.

chess

Mastery; achievement; the need/ability (depending on your success) to tackle demanding intellectual activities or to think through your actions before ''moving'' toward your goals; ''black and white'' thinking; the confrontation of opposites.

See **game(s)**.

chest

A feminine symbol (container), but if heavy/rough, it may symbolize overdevelopment or overemphasis on masculine aspects for a female dreamer. If beautifully decorated, it may symbolize false pride (negative); self-esteem (positive); or be related to breasts and sexuality. As a place where treasure/jewels are kept, it can symbolize the unconscious, or the Self, for male or female dreamers.

If part of the body, or acting as a symbol for the body, it can represent male confidence; conquest; virility (''hairy chest''); triumph (''beating on the chest''). Is there some emotion you've been storing that you need to ''get off your chest''? As the cavern surrounding the lungs, the chest is related to breathing; therefore, to basic life energy/instincts, and anxieties about them. It is the place where ''inspiration'' occurs.

In Egyptian mythology, the beautifully decorated chest/coffin is the one in which Osiris's (solar, active, divine light symbol) body was cast into the Nile by Typhon. Isis (Great Mother archetype, lunar/universal nature symbol) then began her search for him—the union of opposites and death/rebirth themes.

See **body; breast(s); breath/breathe**.

chicken

Historically chickens have been favorite sacrificial tokens, so your dream could symbolize a request for a message, or for propitiation.

Is there something you're being cowardly or "chicken" about? Are you being warned ("don't count your chickens before they're hatched")? Perhaps you're feeling anxious about the consequences of some action ("chickens coming home to roost"). Or do you need to set some goals/priorities for yourself and stop "running around like a chicken with its head cut off"? Maybe you think your efforts aren't being rewarded sufficiently and you're receiving "chicken feed."

Soft, vulnerable chicks can represent your present state, or the potential of a project, both of which need to be cuddled/nurtured.

"Chick" is sexual slang for a female, but as she becomes older, she's "no spring chicken," which may symbolize anxieties about diminishing sexual attractiveness/ability, or other skills.

See **cock; hen**.

child/children

If not your own child, it may represent your inner child; unfinished growth processes within you; a childish part of you that's reacting to a waking situation. It can represent your own child and wishes for that child; perceptions about your child; your own childhood needs awakened by actions of your real child.

An archetypal child, which may appear as a wonder or divine child, represents the collective unconscious—the "treasure hard to obtain" (Jung). It is our potential, our urge to be all that we can; therefore, the archetypal child represents a healer, a bringer of wholeness. In folklore, the motif may be expressed by the appearance of a dwarf/elf.

Children can symbolize innocence; the future; growth; spontaneity; carefreeness; fearlessness. The child's age may represent some experience/issue that occurred around that age, or a process that began that number of years ago. If the child's age is not readily apparent, make a guess.

See **boy; daughter; dwarf(s); family; girl; son**.

childbirth

See **birth**.

childhood

Returning to your childhood, becoming a child again, or taking on childhood traits can be a wish to return to a life wherein you had little responsibility and were taken care of by others. Also, infantile innocence; losing your way; infantile contents of the psyche that haven't yet been integrated into the adult personality. What childhood anxieties have you carried into adult life? Are you missing the fun, the playing? Are you so busy gathering your toys that you don't have time to play with them?

childhood home

Refuge; security if positive memories; or a punitive, abusive place if you have negative memories, or you were abused. It can symbolize beginning/new steps toward independence/responsibility; childhood experiences/feelings awakened by a current situation; aspects of yourself that developed while you lived in that home. It's closely related to early identity; parental love; anxieties about getting lost, or losing your way. Many people can still remember that first address and their parents' emphasis on remembering it, even when they have forgotten others.

See **home; house**.

chimney

Definitely a phallic symbol because of its shape. The collapse of a chimney is a common symbol of impotence. Yet, because of its hollowness and connection with the hearth, it can be a feminine symbol (birth canal?), and may symbolize "keeping the home fires burning." Children who live in happy homes—or wish they did—usually draw a chimney with smoke coming out of it, even when they have no fireplace in their actual house. Rising smoke from the earth/hearth into the air/spiritual realm can symbolize a search for, or connection with, higher aspects of yourself, or the divine.

See **fireplace; smoke**.

china closet

See **closet(s); furniture/furnishings**.

choice(s)

Making, or feeling you have, a choice—or not—may represent a situation/relationship that you need to reexamine or about which you need to establish a new (more appropriate?) value. It can reflect a situation in which you've been too passive/active and need to take the opposite action. It may be saying it's time to make a decision, take a stand. It can reflect a new feeling of freedom/empowerment, or a feeling of imprisonment/helplessness (no choice). Consider the symbolism of the person/object related to the choice you make. Women often have dreams in which they're called upon to choose between something/someone who represents a passive or cultural lifestyle and something that represents their own inner or self-growth.

See **crossroads**.

choir

Harmony; seeking the divine in music; "making sweet music together." If you're singing in the choir: camaraderie; belongingness; a sense of community. If you're leaving a choir, it may represent discord/discontent with some group/organization to which you belong. If watching/listening, it may represent enjoying—possibly wishing for—more harmony in your life.

See **music/musician**.

choke

If choking on something, what's "hard to swallow"? Is someone trying to "stuff something down your throat"? You may be trying to cut off the expression of emotions, especially anger/sadness ("all choked up"). Choking someone else suggests feelings of aggression or, more benevolently, perhaps you're just trying to stop a flow of words. If you're being choked, consider what situation/person or aspect of yourself is trying to disrupt your life flow, your progress toward self-fulfillment.

See **neck**.

Christ

As the historical Jesus, he often symbolizes our ability/need to achieve self-fulfillment through love; the rules/conventions of organized religion; your relationship with a church/congregation. In Jungian terms, Christ is an archetypal figure who represents the questions we all seek to answer; the process toward understanding the nature of life, our relationship with the cosmos or the unknown divine, and our ultimate destiny. He is the Great Wisdom figure who initiates us into a higher realm of inner development/individuation. He can represent the union of cosmic consciousness (the wisdom mysteries) with personal consciousness. Alchemically/metaphysically, he is the materialization of the son (sun/fire), the divine within. His presence/action speaks of/sparks our own transformative process.

See **Jesus**.

Christmas tree

If your dream occurs in December, it may refer to expected pleasures/responsibilities/anxieties you have about the upcoming holiday. If not in December, it may symbolize family celebration; connectedness; demands; anxiety about family relationships; the passage of time; cycles. Do you need to be more of a Santa to yourself, supplying those gifts you'd like to receive; or do you need more twinkle and tinsel in your life? Wrapped gifts under the tree may represent unconscious material waiting to be explored. If it's a tree without roots, it may symbolize a precarious mental/physical situation you're going through.

In Christian symbology, the tree with its lights symbolizes the birth of Christ, the "light of the world." Presents represent the gifts of the wise men; therefore, the Christmas tree can represent your spiritual, religious, or self-development; issues about birth/rebirth and becoming whole/healed. In Jungian psychology it symbolizes everdeveloping inner awareness in which new lights are seen (von Franz).

See **king/prince; tree(s)**.

chrysalis

A need for privacy, especially to plan/consider goals; growth that seems dormant but is moving at its proper pace. Negatively, it might indicate withdrawal; avoidance of issues that will eventually need to be addressed.

See **butterfly**.

church

Churches with elaborate towers/spires may reflect a particular man in your life; your attitude about men in general. They may appear when you have some apprehension about a sexual relationship. Or perhaps the tower is not elaborate enough for you?

A church can also represent religious beliefs; your attitude about dogma (authority, religious freedom); connection with the divine or with a community/congregation. It may represent your need to listen to your own inner wisdom/soul; a need/time to meditate/pray/withdraw temporarily. If your association to a church is sanctuary, or you're in the sanctuary of the church, it may be a message that you need to protect yourself; take extra care of your physical/psychic life. A chapel may represent that inner place where you go for healing or to listen to that small, inner voice of intuition/faith.

If special ceremonies are occurring (wedding, baptism, funeral?), the church may be the embodiment of cycles; passage of time; or may refer to your connection, or lack of it, with family. (See also the symbolism of those events.)

Walking by a church, or being outside of it, may represent the loss of religion/spirituality, and your feelings about it; lack of connection to higher beliefs, values, ideals.

cigar

Although in Freudian terms a cigar is a phallic symbol, it was

Freud himself—an inveterate cigar smoker—who said that sometimes a cigar is just a cigar. Still, it can represent achievement; male power; camaraderie—since it is a traditional signal of a new birth/promotion. If cigar smoke annoys you in waking life, you may perceive a cigar smoker as overbearing or insensitive; thus, the dream cigar may signify these qualities as they apply to a waking situation/person.

cigarette

Cigarettes share some of the same meanings as cigars. More than cigars, however, cigarettes are what adolescents try in order to defy their parents or to have a sense of peer belongingness. Thus, they can be related to themes of defiance/submission; peer identification; addiction; habit versus willpower. As the relationship to cancer becomes more definite each day, cigarettes may be related to, or act as expressions of, self-destructive impulses. They are also related to the buildup and release of tension without insight, and may signal that you're more tense than you realized about some issue, or that you're ignoring its real meaning.

If you've recently given up smoking, your dreams may follow phases similar to those described under **addict(ed)**.

See **cigar; smoke**.

cinema

See **movie**.

circle

A "magic" circle, or circular action, may relate to a developing secret. If you're in the center, it may indicate that you're beginning to acknowledge what is holy/sacred within yourself. It can represent a safe place, one that wards off danger when you're inside; a place that's uniquely yours or you; the Self. Archetypally it may be an early form of the mandala; therefore, a sign of developing inner growth. Circular movement is often connected with a feeling of tension, associated with change/development (Jung). Is there a situation in which you feel you've "come full circle"? Will you go round and round again, or change gears and move to a higher turn on the spiral?

See **center; dot; spiral; uroboros**.

circus

The acceptance/enjoyment of your basic instincts/primitive passions, which are available to you but may still be controlled by the discipline of the parade, the animal trainers, or the constraints of the ring. A childhood fantasy for many people, which may be reflected in some aspect of your dream, is to run away with the circus. This reflects the desire to shed inhibitions, cast off societal restraints, and live the roving or Gypsy life; possibly symbolizing ridding yourself of pressures at home or in a relationship. In reality, a circus community is a tight-knit group that's not very accepting of outsiders, so your circus may represent affiliation with a special, exclusive community—or feelings of being excluded. Are you part of the circus or merely an observer (not quite ready, but considering it)? What part of you is represented by each person/animal/action? Perhaps your circus act is merely a front/mask to please your audience.

See **acrobat; audience; clown; dwarf(s); trickster**.

city/cities

To know a city is to know the different parts of yourself—to have visited the high, snobbish places and the low, squalid, base parts of yourself—and to have survived. How did you make it through your city—with ease/difficulty, with/without a map? If the city is laid out in an obvious square or circular pattern, or has a town square, it can be a symbol of the Self. Towns/cities/buildings in the distance suggest you have a ways to go before reaching your goal.

If applicable, see **walled city**.

clam(s)

Closed off; inviolate; a need for privacy or to protect your personal space; avoidance of emerging unconscious material or insight. What's occurring that raises a need to withdraw or "clam up"?

claws

Feelings of vulnerability and a need to defend/protect; feelings of hostility and a need to attack. Are you "clawing your way to the top"?

clay

Clay, or working with clay, is symbolic of the first, divine creation (Adam) and, therefore, of creativity/creation in general. It can indicate a need to formulate (mold) goals/plans/ideals. It represents the basic human, who has yet to grow, and who is still naïve/innocent. From a Freudian viewpoint, it can also represent feces.

See **art; artist; craft(s); excrement**.

clean(ing)/cleansing

Purification; removing obstacles; preparing for initiation, hence a new stage in your life. If cleaning an object, it may represent an aspect of yourself that doesn't work as well as it might. Cleaning inside or behind appliances (ovens, refrigerators) suggests you're getting to the core of a situation, perhaps discarding old rules/attitudes/training. However, it may also suggest negative feelings about the female role, or an inferior position in which you feel you've been stuck in waking life. Clearing/cleaning a desk, or your calendar, may represent ridding yourself of burdens; acknowledging new choices/freedom in arranging your inner/outer life's work. In what way is it time to "clean up your act"?

See **grief; housework/housekeeper; soap**.

cliff

Have you come to the edge/boundary of a situation and need to consider a change of direction? Perhaps a waking situation suggests danger/unfinished business ("a cliffhanger") or that you've made it to the heights. Do you now have, or is it, the time to consider a wider perspective? If you're looking down, it may represent inner work or an acknowledgment of unconscious needs, especially if the cliffs are seaside. Being at the bottom of a cliff may suggest the heights you need to scale/overcome to resolve an issue. What helpful possibilities/resources does the dream include? The cliff may also be a pun for a man's name.

See **abyss; canyon; edge**.

climb(ing)

Goals to achieve; efforts (mental/physical) toward achievement; progress or its interference (depending on how easy/difficult the climb is). The workaholic needs to "climb *every* mountain."

See **hill; ladder; mountain(s)**.

climbing a ladder

Implicit in the climb is the fact that you'll have to come down again. In Freudian terms "up and down" themes relate to sexual intercourse; in Jungian, the "ups and downs" of steps/ladders refer to the psychological growth process. It can also represent spiritual initiation; connection with higher realms.

See **ladder**.

cloak

A long cloak often symbolizes hiding/secrecy; royalty (dignity/rank); the wise man or woman; the seer; and may relate to the search for or acquisition of special/concealed wisdom.

See **coat**.

clock

The passage of time; cycles. If it has a circular face, which is emphasized, it may represent a form of the mandala (Self). A huge, heavy clock suggests the stability or burdens of time (your heritage, physical health?); possibly a looming deadline. Consider the symbolism of a particular number/time if emphasized. Are you out of time with respect to some situation/relationship?

Clocks/stopped clocks are common in the dreams of terminally ill or dying people (Siegel; von Franz).

See **battery; mandala** (if circular); **number(s)** (if applicable); **time**.

close

Short-term goals; a nearsighted/shortsighted perspective; a need for more, or feeling you don't have enough, intimacy in a relationship. Perhaps you are, or someone else is, ''too close for comfort.''

See **distance/distant/in the distance; position(s)**.

closed

Depending on the object that's closed, it could represent some aspect of your life or an opportunity that is closed off to you; an inability to consider alternatives; prejudice/bias (''a closed mind''); lack of ability to progress; feelings of inadequacy/frustration; adult/sexual secrets or activities.

closet(s)

As dark, enclosed places, they can symbolize the womb/the feminine; hidden (shadow) aspects of ourselves, negative (''skeletons in the closet'') or positive (capabilities). ''Coming out of the closet'' is a modern term for declaring previously hidden homosexuality/transsexuality. If you're not homosexual or transsexual, it may refer to recognition of an opposite aspect of yourself (masculine/feminine), depending on your own sex—or a need to draw more upon that part of yourself.

Since we put away our clothes (appearance) in closets, they can symbolize stored aspects/roles of our personality. Collective aspects—and the collected best—of our persona may be displayed, and protected, in the china closet, usually made of glass for everyone to see/admire.

clothes/clothing

Attitudes and levels of consciousness; your persona or some aspect of it; a need for attention or to conceal your true self. Work clothes may refer to a persona/attitude with respect to work/business, or may identify a dream as related to your occupation. If you're changing your style of clothing, or buying new clothes, it may reflect a need to change your persona, or inner feelings. It could also signal that you're recovering from a crisis such as a death/divorce/depression. Dreams in which you're shopping for, or buying, clothes, or in which you/another appear inappropriately dressed, are common during times of crisis/transition. They may reflect anxiety about "trying to fit in" or being "well-suited" for your new/changing role (Siegel). In myths, homespun clothes symbolize a continuing connection or strong ties with home, mother; therefore, they can represent a kind of innocence/immaturity, naïveté.

See **appearance; persona**. Also specific garments and types of clothing, i.e., **underwear; work clothes**.

clouds/cloudy

Dreams; fantasies/wishes ("having your head in the clouds"); lack of insight ("clouded vision"). Rain clouds often symbolize fertility/the feminine. Storm clouds may symbolize an impending eruption of emotion. In mythology, clouds were often the dwelling place of the gods, and in European churches angels are often depicted on clouds, so clouds can symbolize connection with the divine or messages from the divine. From antiquity, black clouds have represented the lack of wisdom or the confusion that precedes growth; therefore, also the beginning of the alchemical/individuation process.

See **fog/mist; rain; sky; storm**.

clown

Putting things in a different perspective; sometimes your alter ego or an immature viewpoint. In mythology, the clown is the inversion of the king, especially a foolish king, and thus is a kind of wisdom figure. A clown can also be a disguise for something serious; therefore, "topsy-turvy"—things are not as they seem, a secret; playing a comic role to hide your true feelings (Pagliacci). During celebrations, especially pre-Lenten events, the clown is allowed to portray—thereby "commenting" upon and releasing the energy of—the erotic, repressed, or usually inexpressible (shadow) aspects of humankind. The clown brings the psychic world back into balance. Often in mythology the clown, in the form of the trickster figure, guards the threshold/gateway between two worlds, usually the world of the living and the underworld, and is related to boundaries/restrictions.

See **acrobat; trickster**.

club(s)

As an instrument of play (baseball bat, golf clubs?), it can symbolize feelings about play/recreation (perhaps you need to add more to your life), competition, aggression.

As an organization to which you can belong, it can symbolize exclusivity; honor; status (having arrived, been admitted to the club); relationships; camaraderie; a sense of community or service—and, of course, the negative of any of these, i.e., rejection.

If a symbol on a playing card, it may be a pun for any of the above. Don't forget to consider the symbolism of the number of the card.

See **cards/playing cards; game(s)**.

coat

Love; protection, possibly by a man (husband/father) or by God (especially if a sheepskin coat); integrity; self-respect. A coat that's shabby, too short, or ill-fitting may symbolize negative feelings about yourself, or may relate to feelings about a particular situation/relationship. (It doesn't fit right.) As a body covering, the coat can represent the persona; your feelings about the adequacy/inadequacy of your mask/appearance. A multicolored coat may reflect a changeable nature; distracted/splattered attention or energy; the ability to tap into a variety of energies/resources. Consider any color/decoration for additional clues.

See **appearance; cloak; clothes/clothing**.

cock

The male chicken or rooster, the cock heralds/summons the sun, and is considered a solar symbol. The word is a slang term for penis and can symbolize male strutting; pride; conceit ("cock of the walk"). In Tibetan symbolism the cock represents lust. Because he symbolizes fertility, the cock was often used as a sacrificial animal in ancient times and, indeed, was the offering preferred by Asclepias after a successful healing dream had been received. In Christianity the cock symbolizes the resurrection. The weather cock symbolizes Christ's victory, light reigning over darkness.

See **chicken**.

cocoon

See **chrysalis**.

coerce(d)

See **force(ing)/forced**.

coffee

Coffee break: a need for a shift in routine; time out for a pick-me-up; an outlet for communication/camaraderie (if with others). Having/needing your morning coffee may signal that you need to put yourself together; be uplifted from a down mood; establish a routine; build up energy to tackle some project/relationship; gain insight ("wake up and smell the coffee"). Drinking coffee with someone special suggests stimulating feelings.

See **food; tea**.

coffin

As a container that goes into the earth, the coffin is the quintessential Earth Mother/womb symbol. Consider any decoration on it for additional clues. "Putting someone to rest" indicates it may be time to end a situation/relationship. It may already be dead and you're just now realizing it. Metaphysically the coffin is a symbol of the completion of one life, or lifestyle, and opening into another. It may be an expression of opportunity, or of the archetypal death/rebirth theme.

See **cemetery; death; funeral; transformation**.

cog/cogwheel

The union of the masculine (tooth) and feminine (groove) to make the world (a relationship/project) go round; perceiving yourself as a small but essential part of a project/situation/relationship; feeling that someone regards you as just part of the machinery.

See **wheel**.

coins

Stacked coins represent masculine power/energy. Gold coins represent success. "Coins of the realm" suggest unconscious energy available to you. Flipping a coin represents a casual attitude toward making a decision; failing to take responsibility for your decision and projecting it onto fate or luck; being in the hands of unknown forces/power (which may also be the unconscious) rather than using conscious, rational thought.

See **money**.

cold

Dressed warmly and out in the cold could be saying you've taken care of yourself in an environment that's not supportive. Cold hands suggest you're "out of touch" with some situation/relationship. Is there a situation in which you have been, or you fear you might be, "given the cold shoulder" or "left out in the cold"? Having "cold feet" signals having second thoughts about some situation/issue, possibly needing to get out of it. A cold-blooded animal/creature may indicate blocked instincts/emotions.

See **reptile(s); warm/warmth**.

colonel

Feelings/attitudes about authority, including parents or the military; issues of obedience versus rebelliousness, or ambition/success. As a pun, it can represent a "kernel" of truth, related to a desire for wisdom/knowledge; archetypal Wise Old Man. It may reflect your concern about an academic situation or your intellectual needs.

color(s)

More than half of our dreams are in color, and the longer the dream, the greater are its chances of being in color. However, our recall of dream colors fades even more rapidly than memory of their content. Colors can symbolize moods or emotional processes; but specific color symbolism exists, and has been used, in all cultures, literature, religion, and alchemy. Consider first what the color says to you and how you feel about it. Sometimes several colors are inextricably linked, as in the seven colors of the rainbow or red/white/green/black representing the four directions of the world. Fourfoldedness in colors, especially the four primary colors (red/blue/yellow/green), represents wholeness; the missing color suggests what you need in order to create stability (Hoss).

Drab colors may reflect lack of/depressed emotion. Pastels suggest an emotion you're not totally recognizing/dealing with, while fluorescent colors—because of the light behind them—suggest a new awareness (Hoss).

See **four** and specific colors: **black; blue; brown; green; indigo; orange** [color]; **pink; purple; red; violet** [color]; **white; yellow;** also **rainbow**, if applicable.

comb

Comb is related to the symbolism of hair/head. It may reflect a need to organize (get the tangles out of) your thoughts. Combing can reflect a search/need for elements that aren't clear to you in a situation/relationship.

See **hair(y); head**.

combat

If you've never been in combat, it may reflect feeling under mortal attack in a waking situation, and a need to counterattack, shore up your defenses, or develop a strategy. Can you relate these feelings, or this experience, to earlier childhood experiences/relationships? For the nightmare phases that combat veterans with post-traumatic stress disorder (PTSD) experience, see the section titled National Nightmares in Chapter 5, Part 1.

compass

A need for direction/guidance; a signal that it's time to check your direction/goals, which could be associated with a sense of wandering/drifting in your life, or of following another's plans for you.

See **direction(s)** and, if applicable, specific directions: **east; north; south; west**.

competitor/competition

Challenge; an invitation to grow/expand. Seeing yourself competing may signal you need to expand your endurance/perseverance. Perhaps you've been too passive in some situation and need to become more active/assertive. Is there a competitive situation in your waking life that you haven't really acknowledged? Winning a competition suggests you have the skills to accomplish a waking task, or that a crisis in your life is now, or will soon be, over. Time to rejoin the human race.

In a 1993 presentation to the Association for the Study of Dreams, the esteemed psychoanalyst Dr. Walter Bonime suggested that we use or substitute competition in place of developing our own and others' potential to the fullest. Did a recent situation thwart your development in some way or remind you that you haven't lived up to your potential?

See **game(s)** and specific games if applicable.

composite creature

See **mermaid; Minotaur**.

compulsive/compulsion

Your compulsive behavior, or another's, may signal an emotion that's unacknowledged and trying to emerge. It can represent a situation in which repetition/perseverance is called for; or one in which it's not working and you need to consider alternatives. In what way, or in what waking situation, are you driven or have lost control?

computer(s)

If you've just acquired a computer or are learning to use one, the dream may reflect your present frustration/anxiety about that waking experience. A computer can suggest that you're behaving in too automated a way. Perhaps you haven't taken time to listen to your heart/intuition regarding some situation. It may suggest you need to learn another's language in order to communicate, or to adopt a new (more modern or updated?) perspective. Perhaps you need to take more notice of something that "doesn't compute" in waking life.

condemned

A judgmental situation/issue is often involved with condemnation. Your dream may reflect negative judgments about yourself that others have applied to you in the past; feelings of guilt; feelings of being misjudged without a proper trial/hearing. Consider the situation/person who's condemning you for additional clues. If someone or something else is condemned, it may reflect feelings of anger/revenge toward whomever or whatever they symbolize. It might be a signal that you've been too judgmental about someone (if known to you in the dream), or some aspect of yourself (if an unknown person), and need to reconsider.

condom

See **contraceptive**.

confession/ going to confession

Feelings of guilt; a need to be blamed/punished. Because confession releases the energy required to keep secrets, it is, for some, the first step in healing.

conjurer

See **magician**.

construction

Construction of anything, but especially buildings/houses, represents a surge of new energy/ambition; renewed confidence.

See **architecture**.

container

As an object that holds things, containers symbolize the feminine/the womb. If you're a woman, it may symbolize you. Consider its contents and quality for clues regarding the state of your ego, or your physical body. Is there some aspect of yourself that needs to be contained?

If the container is closed, or has a lid on it, it may represent protection; feelings of being closed off or emotionally suffocated; heightened awareness of your internal state; not enough outside input.

contraceptive

Anxiety about pregnancy or sexually transmitted diseases; willingness to take responsibility for consequences of sexual behavior; the attitude of not allowing anything to emerge/escape, or not allowing any outside input/viewpoint. If you're having sex and wonder if you or your partner have used a condom, it may be a signal that you haven't protected yourself emotionally in a waking situation (Delaney).

control/controlled/ out of control

Issues/anxiety about being in control/out of control/needing control. They may also be reflected in images where you're in the air, possibly falling, and are not grounded; where you're unable to get a hold on something concrete (earth, walls, mountains); or where you're in vehicles or situations that you're powerless to stop. Lack of control may appear during times: of crisis when you're attempting to cope with emotional trauma/changes; when you fear you're being pushed into a decision that doesn't support your innermost being; when a support you thought you could count on doesn't seem to be there; when you fear you are, or will be, at the mercy of waking actions already set in motion. Control dreams also can reflect new inner strength; issues of adequacy, self-esteem, independence/dependence, helplessness; and may occur when these states are high or low.

See **magic**.

cook(s)/cooking

Being the cook suggests you have the capacity to choose the recipe for life's pleasures/nourishment, or to "cook up" what others want. You have the experience/talents/abilities to choose what's going to be on the menu of life, and what you're going to "dish out." There may be something in your life you need to make more digestible, or are having trouble digesting. The cook is related to the chemist/alchemist and, therefore, to change/transformation/creativity. "What's cooking" in your life?

See **food; kitchen; magician; roles**.

cooperate/help

Working with/helping someone (opening a door, helping him/her on with a coat, working on a task?) represents the combining of talents/energies to reach a mutual goal. It can represent giving up a personal stance for a greater accomplishment, or be related to issues of dependence/independence. Consider characters/images, to determine whether it pertains to a merging of opposites, possibly masculine/feminine energies.

cord

If you're tied by a cord, it may refer to anxiety about being controlled; or a situation in which you need to assert some control/restraint. It could be a play on "chord," referring to harmony/discord in your life. Tying a box/gift/object with a cord may represent: a need to secure some waking feeling/situation; "wrapping up" some situation; "tying up loose ends." Our primal cord, of course, is the umbilicus, so any cord/rope in a dream may relate to it and to the ideas of relationship; connectedness; involvement with the personal mother/the cosmic or Great Mother/the creative spirit. In many traditions the personal soul is bound to the higher spirit, or overshadowing soul, by a silver or golden cord.

A cord with knots often symbolizes membership in a community. In Hawaiian mythology the *aha* was a strong, braided cord, which represented being braided into/connected with the mutual purposes of an assembly/group. Therefore, the dream cord can be related to issues of authority/obedience; independence/dependence; or can indicate a situation/relationship in which you need to "cut the cord."

See **birth**. See **silver** for the metaphysical cord.

core

The core of something can represent your creative foundation; the seeds of the future (core of fruit). Getting at the core of anything, or revealing the core, refers to the center, the Self. The Greek goddess Kore means maiden, and in its cultural variations (Kar/Ker in Egypt; Car/Carna in Rome) has come to represent the feminine creative spirit of the universe; the Earth Mother; the virgin mother. In Greek mythology Kore is another name for Persephone; hence, you need to ask how this myth is active in your life.

See **body; center; Self**.

corn/cornfield

Fertility; development of potential; a solar symbol, and therefore, a symbol of light/consciousness. Being in a cornfield may represent being surrounded by so many choices/options that it's difficult to see your way clear. An ear of corn can be a pun symbolizing the ear of the body. There may be some situation/relationship that is, or in which you've been, "too corny."

See **gold(en); sun/sunlight; yellow**; if applicable, see **ear(s)**.

corner(ed)

Corners/being cornered may

relate to waking issues about which you have guilt (standing in the corner) or in which you fear you'll be trapped or "backed into a corner." To "turn a corner" refers to change; the unexpected; opportunity—and to your anxiety/excitement about those kinds of situations. Corners may relate to decision/indecision issues; represent the "hard corners" or rigid thinking/attitudes that remain in your psyche and need to be resolved before you can become more flexible. Consider whether some waking situation has frightened you, or made you feel weak (inadequate, incompetent?); and you're responding by stiffening your corners.

cornerstone

Laying/viewing the cornerstone of a building/structure can represent establishing the basic nature/foundation of a situation/relationship/belief. Consider other persons in the dream and any messages on the cornerstone. One of the most famous cornerstones is that which Jacob placed in the temple following his "ladder" dream. He had used it as a pillow (as was customary in dream incubation rituals) during the night.

corpse

See **death**.

corridor

See **hall(way)**.

cosmetics

Changing the face/mask/persona you show to the world; adding a new mask/role to your repertoire (buying cosmetics); changing your identity or "making up your mind"; a superficial change requiring little inner work; hiding your true self; a situation/relationship in which you suspect/fear there's been a cover-up.

See **mask(s)**.

cosmic

See **galaxy**.

cost

Considering the cost of something, or focusing on cost/money, refers to value, i.e., recognizing value, realizing your worth and getting it. You may be considering the emotional cost of a waking relationship/situation.

See **money**.

costume

See **disguise; mask(s)**.

counterfeit

Low self-esteem; someone/something that's phony; placing value on the wrong things; a relationship/situation in which what you thought was of value turns out to be worthless.

country/countryside

A need for escape/relaxation; possibly a return to more basic/natural values; listening to your own natural wisdom or hearing the wisdom of your own nature; getting in touch with the real you.

See **landscapes/settings**. If applicable, see **farm(er); field(s)**.

court

If you're in court/a courtroom, consider, first, what role you play: judge, attorney (defense or prosecuting?), the accused, a witness, a jury member; spectator. It could be related to your ability to make judgments/decisions; aspects of your behavior/attitudes you think need defending; some person/situation you need to defend. If you're the criminal/defendant, could this relate to unresolved issues with your parents or other known authority: guilt, punishment, defying authority, needing to win? If the plaintiff, is there an issue you would like to complain about and haven't? If a witness, is there some waking issue in which you need someone to see it your way, or wherein you think you see the real issue? What's at stake here?

Court or "to court" is related to courting/courtship; therefore, the dream may represent a relationship issue and your position within that.

See **courthouse; judge/judging/judgment; jury; justice; lawyer; scales of justice**.

courthouse

Records; looking for your/another's; a need (possibly based on a waking suspicion) to uncover hidden/undisclosed evidence/secrets; anxiety about a legal/moral issue.

See **court**.

cover(s)

Being uncovered can reflect feelings of exposure; fear that secrets/indiscretions will be revealed; anxiety about how successfully you have covered up something. It can refer to a willingness to be open in expressing/revealing emotions, or, conversely, a need to cover them up. Perhaps something is occurring that you need to "put a lid on." The dream may be related to issues of the facade/disguise you present to the world, as in being a "cover girl," or in "going undercover." Covers can also relate to feelings of warmth/safety, the need for them, and parental caring. Could you use some tucking in?

If applicable, see **bed**.

cow(s)

Maternal instincts; desire to be suckled/nursed. What project/relationship needs to be nurtured? As a herd animal, the cow can symbolize the need to belong; the burden/anonymity of belonging. In ancient Egypt the cow symbolized Hathor, a sky goddess and wife of the sun, and Nut, the "sky cow"; therefore, the divine mother/maternal spirit—both renewal symbols. White cows in India are considered the sacred representation of Kali, consort of Siva and the supreme mother goddess.

In slang, a cow can be an unattractive woman. Often called "bossy" on farms, your dream cow could be a pun for someone who's bossy. Or do you have the persistence to "wait till the cows come home"?

See **animal(s); boss.**

cowboy

The Wild West, and therefore, nature/emotions turned loose; being more in tune with nature; surviving natural/emotional phenomena; that part of you that's rough and tough; rugged individualism; archetypal masculinity; the ability to tame/control nature/emotions; the need/potential to cut loose, let go, and be totally caught up in the hedonistic life when appropriate.

See **horse(s).**

crab(s)

As the astrological symbol for Cancer, it may symbolize someone born in that sign (June 22–July 23). It is a common symbol for female genitalia. Because it sheds its shell, the crab can also symbolize resurrection/rebirth; in Christianity it sometimes symbolizes Christ. As a shellfish, it may represent defensiveness; hiding behind a shell; or suggest that your expression is a "mere shell of yourself." It can reflect something eating away at you (repressed emotions, guilt?), which may make you "crabby." Archetypally, the crab is a lunar symbol related to primal waters/the ocean; therefore, to emotions. Able to move in all directions, the crab may symbolize the flexibility/capacity to consider all options. In sexual slang, "crabs" are sexually transmitted lice and may represent anxiety about sex/sexual feelings; the negative consequences (annoyances?) of having sex. Having your skeleton on the outside reflects the need to create an inner skeleton/backbone; to build from the inside out; or a need to create armor to protect yourself; feelings of basic vulnerability.

See **lice; moon/moonlight; ocean; water.**

craft(s)

Any kind of handicraft or craft work suggests attempts to sublimate/subdue life energy/instincts; transforming unconscious energy into conscious awareness; drawing on creative energy/resources.

crane

Justice; diligence; purity (white feathers). As a migratory bird, the crane is related to spring and cycles. Associated with the number 1,000 in Eastern symbology, the crane represents longevity. Among the Greeks/Romans, cranes represented love/lust, largely because of the male's elaborate courting ritual.

See **bird(s)**.

crash(ing)

Being in a vehicle that's about to, or does, crash suggests that some aspect of your life (emotions?) is out of control; losing control. Is some situation/relationship in your life about to take a "crash dive"? Perhaps you "need to crash," i.e., take a rest. Is there a situation in which you feel like you "crashed the party"?

See **vehicle(s)**.

crater/caldera

An old hurt/trauma, especially to your feminine aspect, which may simply be there, or which may be threatening to erupt/collapse again. If steam/moisture is escaping through a crater opening, it can represent the threat of emerging unconscious material/strong feelings. As a half-circular shape in a cone or in the earth—possibly filled with water or grass—it is related to the feminine, i.e., to the archetypes of the Wise Old Woman; the crone; the nurturing/devouring aspects of the Earth Mother, the cauldrons of mythology.

See **volcano**. For relationship to cauldron, see **cup(s)**.

crawl(ing)

Crawling out of a wreck, or dangerous situation, suggests you have the heroic willpower to survive trauma. If you're in a waking crisis situation, you may soon "get back on your feet." Traffic jams or crawling insects may represent situations that are progressing too slowly ("at a crawl") for you. There may be a waking situation in which you wish someone would "crawl to you" or would "come crawling back" so you would have power, control, revenge, superiority, approval. You have to crawl before you can walk, so you may be making the psychological preparations, or gathering the internal resources, that will allow you to take those baby steps toward growth.

crazy

Bizarre/unusual behavior suggests concerns that your judgments/perceptions don't match customary/accepted (by society, your profession, or another subgroup?) ones. Have you lost a frame of reference (person, relationship?) you once depended on? Perhaps you've lost sight of your own goals, or are not attending to the voice of your inner guidance.

create(ing)/creative

A need to express yourself in a new way; forming new ideas/insights about yourself or a relationship; self-growth or the creative work of living; getting in touch with how you have been created/formed (by God, parents, society?). Creating refers to shaping matter in some way; therefore, the dream may be referring to your ability to shape what matters in your own life or your need to shape/reshape your life so it matters more.

See **art; artist; baby; craft(s); painting**.

credit cards

Your worth/value; your credibility. Depending on your waking experiences, they may also symbolize being in debt (having used up available energy), or be related to your attitudes about work/money/thrift. If you've lost them, consider issues of carelessness and how this relates to your waking or emotional life. If they're stolen from you, consider what within yourself (determined by your associations to the thief) is robbing you of vital energy.

cricket

The cricket's chirping suggests safety, since crickets become silent when danger is near. Crickets are a longtime symbol of good luck and may represent your own feelings/attitudes about luck. The Chinese create elaborate cages for their crickets, and if you know this, the dream may be asking if your luck is caged. The idiom that's "not cricket" suggests there may be an issue in your waking life that has, or has not, been approached in an appropriate or legal way. The "cricket on the hearth" has become an archetypal symbol for hearth/home; thus, your dream may refer to family issues.

For the possible meaning of cricket as a game, see **game(s)**.

crime/criminal

An expression of negative emotions/impulses/wishes with

subsequent disapproval ("breaking the law"); defiance of authority; feelings of guilt; you or someone in your waking life behaving in a way that you consider criminal, even though not actually breaking any laws. The criminal in a dream may represent the shadow aspect of yourself.

See **shadow**.

crime and punishment

See **punish(ment)**.

crippled

See **disabled; immobile/paralyzed**.

crochet

Crocheting consists of making a pattern from one long string; therefore, it may represent the thread of life, the pattern of your life. Consider the shape of what's being crocheted for additional clues. (Round doilies may refer to mandalas.) Often articles are crocheted by elderly relatives or passed down through families, in which case they relate to family connections/values/heritage; possibly old-fashioned ways.

See **craft(s); thread**. If applicable, see **mandala**.

crocodile

Some aspect of your nature (also a situation/relationship) that needs feeding or threatens to devour you. Depending on its location/behavior, the crocodile can represent obstacles you need to overcome/avoid; the dark aspects of feminine energy (crocodiles feed in water)—possibly because in biblical symbology a crocodile represents lower desires/passions, which in medieval Christianity were attributed to women. It may reflect insincerity/false grief (crocodile tears); any superstitions you have about crocodiles. They are akin to serpents, lizards, alligators, and other creatures that would suck out the lifeblood that wants to transform and grow (Woodman).

crone

In Jungian thought, she is the third aspect of the female/mother archetype (after the maiden/virgin and mother). As with all archetypal energies, she has a dual nature. On the benevolent side, she is a nurturing wisdom figure, sometimes depicted as a Wise Old Woman or green mother, who can bring life or save abandoned babies. She may be depicted negatively as a hag, witch, or devouring mother and can be symbolized by objects/images that are: secret, dark, hidden, terrifying, inescapable, or that seduce or poison.

Jung called her the "loving and terrible mother."

See **Great Mother; Mary, Virgin; mother; virgin**.

cross

Spiritual beliefs/feelings; connection with the divine; the developing spiritual aspects of your life; connection with your inner Christ/love consciousness. More generally, it is a symbol of the tree of life, or world tree, and may represent a stabilizing influence in your life, or a need to find one. It also can symbolize emotional/physical burdens ("my cross to bear").

See **crossing; shape(s); world tree**.

crossing

Change; transition; a decision point; or turning point. A river to be crossed, with its distant bank, often symbolizes emotional growth. If you're crossing a river, abyss—whatever—consider the ease/difficulty and the manner in which you cross for additional clues.

In many myths, crossing a bridge represents the passage from life to death and into whatever is your conception of life beyond. This, or other crossings, would be a typical kind of dream for someone who is terminally ill or close to death.

It can represent feelings of denial/avoidance ("cross that bridge when I come to it"); having been crossed by someone; or sincerity ("cross my heart").

See **crossroads**.

crossroads

Ambivalence; the time or possibility for decision/choice; the union of opposites. For Jung "union" frequently implied the mother, so if you're a woman, your crossroads might relate to feelings about motherhood; mothering (present/past); your personal mother; your ability to mother. If you're a male, crossroads could symbolize your anima; your personal mother; a time of stress in which you might need more mothering.

In Greek mythology, crossroads, especially triple ones, are associated with Hecate, one aspect of the triple goddess, for women dreamers. Hecate is associated with the old crone (wisdom figure) and the underworld. (In one version of the myth she accompanied Persephone into Hades.) She was also the goddess of magic. For men, the god is Hermes, often associated with sacred male sexual energy.

See **x**.

crouch

Being in a crouched position

can represent feelings of defensiveness; the fetal position, and therefore, wishing/needing to be nurtured or escape responsibility; needing to hide/protect yourself; feeling/being restricted. If crouching preparatory to a race competition, it can represent feelings/issues with respect to competition, challenge, victory; activating/utilizing your potential. Crouching animals relate to your instincts/urges/passions; also feelings of vulnerability/power.

If applicable, see **animal(s)**.

crow(s)

Crows and ravens share similar symbolism. Often a symbol of death, because of its black color, most likely the crow doesn't represent your own death, but whatever death means for you; or the death of some situation/relationship in your waking life and subsequent new, creative beginnings. Crows can refer to communication about accomplishments (''something to crow about''), or to gossip (''sound like a bunch of old crows''). It may signal that you need to be more direct about an issue or take more direct action (''as the crow flies'').

See **black; death; raven(s)**.

crowd

How you feel/act in the crowd provides clues about its symbolism. A crowd can symbolize feeling crowded/unnoticed (just ''one of the crowd''); taking leadership/action and its opposite, passivity; the potential for getting caught up in others' needs/ideas. It may be related to guilt/fear in the sense of representing a need not to stand out and be caught/discovered; or a feeling that you don't stand out and are not special (a self-esteem issue).

Archetypally, for a woman a crowd may represent the animus, especially if, as Woodman says, it is composed largely of men and if some man/men gradually become clear. The crowd may represent various aspects of yourself, and together, your total personality. Choose someone from your crowd whom you disliked, who was unlikable, or whom you fear as an unacknowledged aspect of yourself. Work with him/her using Dreamercise #3 or #10, Part 1.

See **group(s)**.

crown

Success; recognition; acceptance of authority; leadership; awareness or spiritual awareness (especially if gold or shining). In some instances it can represent solar (soul?) energy, or the Self (because of its circular shape and the adornment of jewels). A gold crown may represent masculine aspects; willpower; healing. A silver one represents feminine aspects; creativity; receptivity; forgiveness; nurturing.

Metaphysically a crown can refer to the crown chakra, the highest spiritual/energy center, located halfway inside and halfway outside the top of the head. It can represent the halo/energy field around the head.

See **halo; king; prince; princess; queen; royalty**.

crucifixion

Feelings of being victimized/unjustly accused/punished; feelings of guilt; an extreme need for, or fear of, punishment/retaliation. Are you sacrificing too much?

See **Christ; cross**.

cruel/cruelty

Being cruel—striking out verbally/physically for no reason—may represent the release of pent-up hostility/anger; the need to acknowledge/examine the tyrannical/shadow aspects of your personality. Being the victim of cruelty may be a call for you to develop your inner/outer strengths, to become emotionally powerful.

See **shadow**.

crutch

Being supportive; needing emotional or economic support; being emotionally wounded; perceived inabilities. It is also related to issues of security independence/dependence—a need to lean/count on someone/something. Notice what body part is disabled and consider the symbolism of that part, i.e., foot (understanding?), leg (''not having a leg to stand on''?), knee (need?).

crying

See **emotion(s)**.

crypt

See **catacomb; labyrinth/maze; tomb**.

crystal

Transparent crystals symbolize the union of spirit and matter (it exists but appears as if it did not, according to Cirlot); hence, the crystal can also represent transformation; a straightforward message (''crystal-clear''); the spirit. Circular/hexagonal crystals or crystal patterns represent the Self. If colored, see the specific color.

See **gem(s); minerals; quartz**.

crystal ball

The crystal ball—or gems that perform the same function as a crystal ball—symbolizes the ability/capacity to view the unconscious; contact with unconscious material and a readiness to attend to its message. As one form of oracle, it may symbolize contact with the divine or archetypal; or it may represent the Self (because of its circular shape).

See **fortune-teller/fortune-telling; medium**.

cube

Shares the symbolism of the square and represents earth/earthiness; material/worldly issues as opposed to spiritual/divine issues; solidity and stability.

See **square**.

cuckoo

In early times the cuckoo was the bird of May and represented the lascivious, promiscuous May games. From which the word *cuckold* is derived; thus, sexual needs/wishes; nontraditional sexual attitudes/behavior; someone who's crazy. Often associated with a clock, the cuckoo, or its sound, can, then, represent the passage of time; a timely reminder; or any time-related issues.

See **bird(s); sex**.

cul-de-sac

The vagina and sexual relations; but as a semicircle, it also can be an early, primitive form of the circle, and therefore, of the Self, or efforts at individuation. It may represent a situation in which you feel blocked/trapped, or that does not appear to offer the possibilities/opportunities (openings) you originally hoped/believed were there.

See **alley; trap(ped); vagina**.

cup(s)

Nurturance (the breast); receptiveness; the womb; the body as the vessel of life; transcendence into a realm of higher consciousness. Is your cup half-full, half-empty, or does your "cup runneth over" (abundance)? Consider the cup's contents/decoration, or lack thereof, for additional clues. In Greek mythology the *Krater* or cup held the matrix of creation. The cup is also related to the cauldron, whose contents often hold the potential for magic, healing, transformation, rejuvenation, and wisdom, as did the "Hermetic Vessel" of the alchemists and, in Greek mythology, Medea's cauldron, which rejuvenated Jason.

See **breast(s); drink(ing); food; Grail; womb**.

curtain

See **veil**.

curve

A curve on the road can represent an unexpected turn of events that has happened or that you fear might happen and, therefore, with which you must deal. Consider how you handle it for clues as to your strength/weakness/resources.

cut(s)

A cut on some part of the body may represent a woman's genitalia; sexuality; female attitudes toward sex.

See **wound(s)/wounded**.

cypress

As a conifer/evergreen, it symbolizes long life; immortality. However, its branches and sprigs also have symbolized death/mourning because the Romans connected it to Pluto, the god of the underworld who abducted Persephone. It could be a pun for the island of Cyprus, and your knowledge/feelings about that particular island, its people, Greece/Greeks, Greek mythology. Mythology/legend has it that Cupid's arrows, Jove's scepters, the pillars of Solomon's temple, and Jesus' cross were all made of cypress wood.

See **tree(s)**.

dairy

The source of milk, and therefore, nurturing/creative instincts, possibly the primal/archetypal mother; mother's breast; or the need for many breasts. Perhaps you can't get enough, or need more, mothering, or, to the contrary, you're overwhelmed or stifled by too much of it. A dairy is also a place where there is lots of manure, which can be positive (fertilization; creativity) or negative (a lot of crap), depending on your associations.

See **animal(s); barn; cow(s); farm(er); manure; milk**.

dam

Is the dam strong/vulnerable? Are you withholding unexpressed emotions, which are safely contained, or are they building up and threatening to break through? Dams often refer to a need for control; therefore, they can be a reflection of feeling out of control. Consider also menstrual difficulties/anxieties.

If animal-made (a beaver dam?), it may relate to endeavors, accomplishments, performance, and/or fears related to those. Are you involved in a task that seems unending, or about which you have strong emotions?

A broken dam suggests that although something within/without may have been deteriorating or threatening to break through (emotions?), you need to assess the damage and make repairs.

See **beaver; water**.

damage/damaged

Damage to objects represents spoiling (breaking?) whatever that object symbolizes to you, perhaps a part of your body, a damaged/wounded psychological aspect of yourself, or of a relationship. If you create the damage, it could relate to: aggression; a lifestyle wherein you spoil/ruin things for yourself; responsibility or lack of it (depending on how you handle the situation).

Damage or wounds/injury to the body may indicate an impending physical problem. If the dream is a recurring one, you might wish to see a physician.

See **wound(s)/wounded**.

dance/dancing

Sexual activity/needs/wishes; sensuousness or sensuality; the "dance of life," i.e., creation/life movement; ecstasy and altered states; celebration. Ritual dances are attempts to evoke the gods or contact the spirit within, or spirits without. If your dancing is easy/effortless, it may mean being in balance/harmony with yourself. If ballet and you are on your toes or in the air, it could suggest an attempt to reach the divine or the spirit; that you are not well-grounded emotionally; or, conversely, that you need to be more on your toes with respect to some situation/relationship.

If applicable, see **actor/actress; audience**.

dancer

Often a symbol of the immature Self in female dreams and of the anima in the dreams of males. In folktales the dancer is linked with the maiden who has to die because her immaturity hinders development. Dancing with linked arms symbolizes connectedness or union (male/female, heaven/earth, divine/human). Shiva represents God as the cosmic dancer. As Lord of the Dance, Shiva dispels fear, assists us to dwell in the bliss of the Self, and is considered a god of transformation.

Dancers in a circle or weaving around a Maypole suggest spring, a mandala, cycles (see **world tree; zodiac**).

danger

Anxiety about yourself/another; emotional threats to the ego or personality. Intensely dangerous situations may appear in the dreams of addicts/alcoholics not yet in the recovery process. For more information on how to work with anxiety dreams/nightmares, see Chapters 5 and 6, Part 1.

dark/darkness

The womb; the unconscious;

primal yearnings/urges (especially dark waters), hence the instincts; undeveloped potentiality out of which light (consciousness) arises; creativity; the cosmic nothingness out of which creation arose. It can symbolize a stage of ignorance/unknowing, psychologically blind ("in the dark"); or hope ("it's always darkest before the dawn"). Perhaps there's some issue to which you're not attending. (Consider other images for clues as to what it might be.)

Mythologically, darkness often symbolizes the underworld/death and is related to rebirth and to Persephone and her experiences (Hillman). Dark locations/areas and black spots can symbolize death (von Franz). If you're in a dark tunnel but can see light, it may symbolize an actual birth memory, impending death, or simply that there's a way out of a current dilemma ("a light at the end of the tunnel"). Although dark/darkness dreams may be present during depression, dreams of the clinically depressed are more often simply bland and not very lively.

See **black; color(s); death; grief; night; person, dark or dark-skinned; shadow; tunnel**.

darn(ing)

A situation you're perturbed about. Consider what you're darning for clues.

See **mend(ing); sew(ing)**.

dating

If you're an adolescent, or a single adult who's dating, it may reflect a desire for someone known in your waking life. Or it may reflect anxieties about dating/relationships/acceptance. Married or not, if you don't know the person, consider whether he/she represents some aspect of yourself (or someone else) that you should woo or give a more prominent place in your awareness.

daughter

For a man or woman, she may represent your own daughter and concerns about her. For a mother, she may represent yourself when you were the dream age; possibly what you wanted for yourself then. Conflicts your actual daughter is having—with you or others—may awaken conflicts *you* had when you were a daughter. For a father, she may represent protective urges or the development of the feminine (feelings?) within. When a father dreams he has sex with his daughter, it usually does not reflect an actual desire for incest, but rather symbolizes an emotional need to awaken/incorporate aspects of her into his own psychological development.

See **family; relatives**.

dawn

Rebirth; renewal; hope; solitude; creativity; intuition ("it dawned on me"); "dawning" insight/awareness; a new beginning or phase in your life; the beginning of a situation/relationship.

See **morning**.

day

Light; consciousness; awareness ("I've seen the light of day"); clarity of thought. An overcast day may represent a dark mood/depression. If the dream time extends beyond one day, it may represent the passage of time, past or present. The three times of day (morning, midday, afternoon) often represent the seasons of spring, summer, autumn, respectively.

Consider the symbolism of the number of days. If a particular hour of the day is emphasized, it can have personal symbolism related to a present attitude or past happening. It may serve as a reminder of something that needs to be done or an appointment. "D Day" or the "eleventh hour" may represent some deadline. The time of day can also refer to your age or the "time" (phase/cycle) of life you're in; or, for women, "that time of the month."

See **autumn; dark/darkness; light; night; seasons; spring** [season]; **summer; sun/sunlight; time**.

dead end

See **alley; cul-de-sac**.

dead people

See **person, dead**.

deaf

Inability to hear; or ignoring pertinent information; being ignored; allowing something illegal/immoral to be done without taking a stand ("turn a deaf ear"), which may relate to feelings of guilt, or lack of responsibility. Freud believed our superego/conscience was mostly auditory. Is there some situation in which you're trying not to listen to parental prohibitions or your conscience?

See **ear(s)**.

death

Transformation; there's now room in the psyche for a new way of life; a need to revise your self-image; the end of one type of inner personification. When we are truly about to die, our dreams contain symbols/images other than those of our death. However, as we age, we may explore death/transition more in our dreams, i.e., meeting symbolic figures of death. Dreaming of yourself as dead reflects a wish to get out of a situation/responsibility. Often the dream ego is still alive and watching the funeral. Consider the behavior of those attending the funeral for additional clues of how you behaved and their opinions of you. Each of them is, most likely, another, or wished-for, aspect of yourself. Death can also represent an attempt to repress/kill off some aspect of yourself.

Dreaming of someone else's death/funeral may be a message that your feelings about that person are dead; that a significant change/loss is occurring in the relationship; a wish to complete/end/repress that aspect of yourself represented by the other; anxiety (if the other is known to be ill); aggression toward the other (if not ill). It's not uncommon to dream of someone close to you who recently died, although frequently you'll dream of him/her as still alive.

Death/rebirth is an archetypal theme, and dreams of this nature may have to do with initiation/quest; search for the spiritual in your life; growth/change; loss of power/identity. After the symbolic death, look for symbols of escape/rebirth in the same/later dreams: i.e., fertility/womb symbols, including caves; the season of spring; seeds; new plants; trees; dawn; water; a snake; a bird, especially one resembling the phoenix; a pearl. Intensely dramatic/emotional death/dying dreams may occur for the addict/alcoholic not yet committed to the recovery process.

See **asleep; cemetery; crossing; evening; funeral; grief; person, dead; sunset**.

decorate/decoration

Whether the decoration relates to a person or an object, consider the symbolism of its specific shape/color for additional clues. Is it frivolous or beautiful; something you already own or want to possess; something you never had or need to have to be complete? Does it bring some dream person/object into balance? The dream decoration might suggest that you feel incomplete without it; that it's an essential part of you (related to your self-esteem), or a social facade you put on, possibly to attract sexual interest.

See **appearance**. If applicable, see **clothes/clothing; jewelry; necklace; tattoo**.

deep

Going/being deep within a place represents going into the unconscious. Consider clues in the surroundings to help determine whether this is your personal unconscious (i.e., lost/discarded personal or family possessions in a cellar) or the collective unconscious (architectural diggings; ancient artifacts; gems; skeletons). It can symbolize the womb, or, archetypally, the Great Mother, where you may enter for divine nourishment, or may be devoured. Perhaps deep water leaves you "no ground to stand on," or surrounded by emotions.

See **descend(ing)**.

deer

Some aspect of yourself that you value (and possibly keep private) or someone in your life whom you hold dear. If the deer is frightened or under attack, it can reflect a situation in which you feel you're threatened and must defend yourself, although perhaps you're feeling as skittish as a deer. In Christian symbolism and Grail stories, a white stag represents the soul's thirst for spiritual knowledge/wholeness, or Jesus, the Christ archetype. The stag's appearance in Celtic-Arthurian literature heralds change and a call to the spiritual/inner quest.

See **animal(s)**.

defecate

Getting rid of unwanted garbage in your life; sorting out/separating your own attitudes from those of others (parents, society), which you once had to digest. If you defecate on someone, however, it's usually an expression of anger/hostility. If done to you, or smeared on you, it can represent feelings of guilt, of being unclean/unworthy—lowered self-esteem. Having diarrhea suggests urges out of control, while constipation indicates holding on to inner material, possibly an unwillingness to make it known. In Freudian terms anal activity is related to feelings of pride (I made this myself), shame, disgust. What, in your waking life, may have triggered these feelings?

See **bathroom; excrement; toilet**.

defend(er)

Are you the one being defended, or are you the defender? What part of you is being attacked/needs protecting? Are you rescuing, or need to protect, material aspects of yourself (territory/land), emotional aspects (rules; laws; internal kingdom), the queen/princess (feminine awareness), or the king/prince (masculine authority/power)? Does the dream imply there's a safe place for you, a refuge, or are you absolutely vulnerable? Is your defender some aspect of yourself that makes it safe for you to grow or that's protecting new growth (strength)? Consider the sex and number of your defenders for additional clues.

See **peace/peaceful; warrior**.

deformed

Undeveloped aspects of yourself that you may have ignored and that may be especially creative, or that, in the negative sense, may be sabotaging your waking activities.

See **disabled; dwarf(s)**.

deliver/delivery person

See **messenger**. If delivery refers to childbirth, see **birth**.

deluge

See **flood; destruction**.

demolition

See **destruction**.

demon(s)

The Freudian view is that most demons represent repressed infantile sexual feelings, likely incestuous ones toward our parents. For Jungians, they represent a projected negative aspect of the anima/animus, i.e., someone whom you perceive as a threat and are attempting, or wish, to avoid, when, in fact, that power/energy is also a part of you. For more insight, take the part of the demon in Dreamercise #3, Part 1.

See **monster(s)**.

dentist

Many people feel vulnerable when they're at the dentist or think about seeing a dentist, so is there some situation in your waking life—possibly related to nurturance or to aggression—in which you're feeling threatened? A friendly visit/interaction with a dentist suggests a need to become more confident or polish up your aggressive, protective skills, or you're becoming more able/less threatened.

See **teeth**.

depart(ing)/departure

Breaking away from your usual attitudes/patterns of behavior; growth; change; anxiety if you were "left holding the bag"; anxiety about being left alone ("left in the lurch"; "left at the altar"), hence anxiety about survival/independence/loneliness. Examine your feelings in the dream for clues as to whether its symbolism is toward growth or toward anxiety.

See **vehicle(s)**.

derelict

Negative, possibly ignored, aspect of yourself (Whitmont

and Perera); not facing responsibility or being "derelict in your duty"; your shadow; anxiety about your adequacy/ability, a self-esteem issue.

descend(ing)

Meanings differ depending on whether the descent is by means of an object (elevator, stairs) or by falling. Descending by stairs/ elevator can symbolize getting more realistic ("down to earth"). Going below a building (basement, cellar, secret room) often represents unconscious material ready to emerge, but it can represent depression ("down in the dumps"). Descending into the earth (into a cave; "going down into the depths") may represent the womb and a desire to return to more infantile times; concern about giving birth (if you're pregnant); getting in touch with what is essential; an initiation and reception of wisdom (also related to unconscious material). "Going downhill" may symbolize physical changes occurring in your health; aging; loss of intellectual/sexual prowess. In mythology we descend into the underworld for enlightenment/ rebirth, hence up/down is thematically related to other opposites such as death/rebirth; night/day.

See **ascend(ing); dark/darkness; deep; elevator; fall(ing); stairs; under/underneath**.

desert

Many people perceive the desert as barren, hot, dry, so it often symbolizes a barren, dry creative/emotional (loss of spirit) state. What aspect of yourself is withering? Time to find an oasis—the healing waters of your soul/psyche—and restore yourself.

Yet a desert is teeming with life if you but look for it, and may symbolize the unusual, or hidden gifts/creativity for which you have to look a little harder, or take a second look, to recognize. Deserts were once lush, often underwater, locales, and in that sense represent change (possibly aging); cycles; a lost paradise; historical perspective.

In various religious views, the desert is seen as both a place of retreat/meditation/divine revelation (where one can be close to God) and a place of temptation (where demons dwell). Wandering in the desert may symbolize a sense of being lost; a search for meaning. Consider any animals/creatures you encounter for additional clues. It can be a pun on the feeling that you've been deserted by someone.

See **sun/sunlight**.

design

See **pattern/design**.

desk

Work; ideas; possibly authority. As a place where information is stored, it may symbolize knowledge; family history; professional reputation; secrets waiting to be discovered. In sexual slang, drawers = panties, so the drawers, or the entire desk, may symbolize feminine aspects of yourself; sexual desire; a current woman or women (there usually are several drawers in a desk); mother. Consider the desk's tidiness/messiness (time to get rid of old ideas?); particular papers/objects on/in it; the owner of the desk (if not your own); and the style of the desk for additional clues.

destination

How easy/difficult is it to reach the dream destination? Are you distracted/thwarted, and in what ways? How near/far is it and how is your energy level? If you're having trouble, the dream may speak of waking difficulties in determining/arriving at your goals. It may be a dream with the hero/heroine journey motif, the quest, especially if you can see lights (awareness) in the distance. If you've arrived at your destination, consider how you feel and the surrounding images for additional clues.

See **crossroads; travel(ing)/journey**.

destruction

Destruction dreams suggest the psyche has experienced some sort of conflict, or overwhelming anxiety threatens the boundary between the unconscious and the ego. It's a breakdown of old ways (attitudes, perceptions), a major reorganization of outer/inner life. Destruction dreams can represent the loss of an "old" identity or relationship during times of crisis/transition (Siegel). Often the threat is of a magnitude to constitute an archetypal theme. The good news is that frequently in destruction dreams there's a key to how you can save yourself (repair/reduce the threat), which is also presented in symbolic terms. After destruction comes rebirth, especially if the destruction is by water (fertile symbol); thus, destruction can also symbolize the final phase of a cycle. Destruction may appear in the dreams of alcoholics/addicts not yet in the recovery process (O'Connell).

If applicable, see **atom bomb; bomb/bombed**.

detour

Time to change direction; need for a new perspective; feelings of being lost/misguided. Where have you lost sight of your goals?

devil

Regression; negative/denied/rigid aspects of yourself; an avoidance of responsibility ("the devil made me do it"); guilt; temptation. Use Dreamercise #3 or #10, Part 1, for more insight into what aspect of yourself this figure might represent. Freudian symbolism suggests that the devil, and other "evil" creatures, represent repressed infantile sexual feelings, especially those toward parents.

See **shadow**.

devour(ed)/devouring

Are you not dealing with some issue, and it's "eating you up"? Consider the symbolism of who/what is trying to devour you. If you're the one doing the devouring, it could represent hostility; greed; a need to incorporate the mother/nurturing (Freud) or some other aspect of what you're devouring; your sexual appetite.

Our primal fear that Mother will devour us, which is also a fear of incest, is expressed in fairy-tale motifs of witches (Hansel and Gretel) and wolves (Little Red Riding Hood) who devour children. Archetypally, it's related to the night-sea-journey motif (Jonah and the whale), and to the ultimate swallowing up by death—fear of death.

See **digestion; eating; vampire**.

dew

Renewal; fertility; enlightenment or the spiritual search/development, because of its glistening quality in the sun.

See **dawn; morning; pearl(s); water**.

diamond [shape]

Information, possibly danger and/or a need for caution (as in road signs); the quaternary, and therefore, anything with fourfold quality (man, directions). The shape may also be related to baseball (see **baseball**).

See **four; shape(s)**.

diamond(s)

Purity; strength of character; attitudes of being hard/irrefutable. It's the birthstone of someone born in April. It also symbolizes something (message/attitude/emotion) enduring/valuable; therefore, it may relate to the spiritual aspect of your life; or to treasures (skills) lying dormant in your unconscious ("a diamond in the rough"); the Self (Jung). Consider what happens to the diamond for additional clues.

See **gem(s); jewel(s); Self; treasure**.

diary

Self-expression; the need to record/understand your own actions/motivations; passing time (cycles, aging); hopes/dreams; the desire to pass along information about yourself and your achievements to others, but in a personal, private way. Consider whether you might need to be more public about this in waking life. The diary might also symbolize your dream journal.

dice

A gamble, taking a chance; luck; Lady Luck, therefore a symbol of divine/magical intervention; the depiction of yourself as a winner/loser; a pair. A single die can represent decision; rigidity; bravery in the face of the inevitable; fate (''the die is cast''); the quest. Often used in board games, dice can symbolize family/social interaction; challenge; competition; the ultimate ''game of life.'' Consider the symbology of the numbers that are thrown.

See **dot; gamble/gambling; game(s); lose/losing something; victor/victory**.

dig(ging)

Unconscious material ready to emerge; seeking a connection with your personal mother/the Earth Mother. If you're digging for buried treasure, it can symbolize work that needs to be done with respect to self—growth; creativity. Consider what you find (possibly unrecognized urges/drives?). How easy/difficult is the task? Are you digging into something or digging your way out (possibly a birth memory; a need to extricate yourself from some actual/potential situation)? Perhaps you're turning over ground (ideas) to create/replant a garden (a new project, fertility, your own growth?). It may represent a chance to grow what you need, or bury what you need to get rid of.

See **archeology; dirt(y); garden**.

digestion

Mastery; assimilation; incorporating certain values/beliefs, or having difficulty doing so (indigestion). In alchemy, digestion is associated with transformation, the dragon, the color green. Cosmically, it's related to death.

See **dragon; eating; food; green; stomach; transformation**.

dining

See **eating**.

dining room

Basic needs; appetites, including sexual ones; support; comfort; family connection. Is there something you need to incorporate into your life? Consider the symbolism of other images in the room for additional clues.

See **eating; house**.

dinosaur

An outdated attitude/part of yourself, which you may need to discard; fear of becoming extinct/unnecessary; a primordial part of yourself, hence unconscious urges/instincts.

See **death; monsters**.

direction(s)

Your need/ability to take instruction/criticism, which may be related to feelings about authority; lack of, or the search for, purpose; goals; aims; going around in circles. Consider whether you're giving/taking/seeking direction and how this relates to a waking situation. Do you need a map/guide? Are you being distracted, thwarted, turned away, or otherwise prevented from reaching your goal? This often relates to the difficulties of the hero/heroine's journey toward self-realization and the triumph of consciousness over the unconscious. Consider the symbolism of what's blocking you: a person, fence, object, washed-out/flooded road.

Metaphysically, vertical direction symbolizes inner/spiritual alignment with the overshadowing soul or the divine, while horizontal direction reflects the relationship of your personal soul, or inner divinity, to matter/the material world.

Where applicable see **choice(s); detour; down; east; forward; left** [direction]; **movement; north; right; south; west; up**.

director

Authority; feeling/taking responsibility for others' behavior; taking, or needing to take, action to bring various aspects of yourself into a unified whole. Are you feeling overwhelmed and need an inner director?

See **actor/actress; boss; direction(s); movie; theater**.

dirt(y)

Mother Earth; fertility; creativity. It can represent dark/shadow aspects, such as dirty (forbidden/sexual) thoughts/behavior (masturbation?) and guilt/shame related to them. Do you need to "clean up your act"; have you been "dishing the dirt" (gossip); or is there something in your life that has lost its value ("dirt-cheap")? It can represent anxiety about death; transition/transitoriness, especially if you associate it to the biblical saying "Dust thou art and unto dust shalt thou return." Perhaps you need to "get your hands dirty," i.e., involve yourself in some mental/physical work you've been postponing. Dirt that has become mud may refer to being stuck in anger/resentment, or to feces.

See **death; dig(ging); earth; mud/muddy; shadow**.

disabled

Lowered self-esteem; lost power/direction; not drawing on all your skills; loss of abilities/capacities. What part of you isn't working to full capacity; and how do you feel about that? Consider the symbolism of those parts of your body, or another's, that are disabled.

See **immobile/paralyzed**.

disappear(ance)

Who/what disappears; and what aspect of yourself that you've lost touch with could this represent? It can symbolize lost awareness; a need to get away from/avoid some distressing situation/issue; loss of control/power, unless you're causing the disappearance; feelings of inadequacy/lack of importance.

See **magic; magician; vanish(ed)/vanishing**.

disaster

See **danger; destruction**.

discharge

Release; loss of energy; ejaculation; ridding yourself of abilities/attitudes no longer useful. If the "discharge" refers to a wound/lesion, consider the symbolism of that part of the body from which it is emitted, and see **wound(s)/wounded**. If it relates to a weapon, see **gun(s); weapon(s)**.

discipline

Taking/gaining control, inwardly or outwardly; a sense of order; attitudes about authority/parents. Esoterically, it may refer to learning life's secrets or performing exercises/meditations that train you spiritually.

discover

See **find/discover**.

disease

The emergence of repressed feelings; fear of being overwhelmed; not at ease (dis-ease) with some aspect of yourself or your way of being; a conflict between an archetypal motif and the ego, i.e., a psychological crisis that has not yet been understood and assimilated (Whitmont and Perera).

See **illness**.

disfigure/disfigured

If the threat of disfigurement is to you, it suggests anxiety about losing your identity/persona. If someone else is disfigured, what aspect of yourself has been wounded? Also, ugly/unacceptable aspects of yourself.

disguise

Concealing the truth; hidden agenda; trying on a new role; putting on an act; developing a little-used aspect of yourself. It may relate to the idea of withholding/protecting aspects of yourself, or being a hidden observer/watcher.

See **appearance; mask(s)**.

dish(es)

If filled, emotional nourishment; fate ("what's been dished up for you"). If empty, a barren aspect of your life; the potential for nurturance. (Every meal begins with an empty dish.) Shards of old dishes, especially pottery, can represent a positive link with the past, or broken relationships. Are you having trouble "taking what's dished out"? Were you cautioned as a child to "eat everything on your plate," an admonition now evoked by some waking situation? In sexual slang, a dish is an attractive/sexy woman—possibly something you wish for, or fear.

See **container; eating**.

dishonest

Unacceptable emotions/actions, i.e., the shadow aspect; feeling cheated; possibly some waking situation that you suspect is not "on the up and up," or in which you've been too trusting.

disinfect

Cleaning up negative aspects of yourself or your waking life; purifying; needing to put distance between you and your unconscious urges/feelings, especially ones you think are negative/unacceptable.

See **clean(ing)/cleansing; dirt(y)**.

dislike

Someone in your dream whom you dislike is most likely a projection of some disliked/denied aspect of yourself—or something you *think* you should dislike (possibly because of someone else's opinion); some part of yourself with which you're out of harmony, especially a body part. (Look to its particular symbolism.) It can remind you of a situation/person you should avoid in waking life, or the reverse, i.e., someone to whom you're really attracted.

distance/distant/ in the distance

Goals; aims; the future; need for a new/different perspective; need to protect yourself from emotions or separate yourself from your own/another's feelings; need to move away from a waking situation. It also suggests feelings of inadequacy/disappointment, or that you're not yet prepared enough (if objects/people are out of reach).

See **binoculars; position(s)**.

distorted/distortion

All dreams are distorted, in that they contain images that could not occur in waking life. However, if something/someone in your waking life is distorted in a dream, it's a definite signal to pay attention to its symbolism or to your feelings about that particular person/relationship, or to consider what aspect of that distortion is like you (if an unknown person). It can symbolize a misperception of outer/inner behavior/motives; a signal that someone's waking-life behavior is not all that it seems.

dive/diving

Diving into water symbolizes delving into or working on unconscious material; seeking hidden aspects (treasure) of yourself; courage to face your fears/emotions; taking a risk. It can refer to immersing yourself in a project, positive action/energy; an adventurous attitude ("dive right into it"); the potential for danger/disaster or the need to develop inner/outer skills (if unsuccessful).

See **fall(ing); swimming**.

divide/division

A situation/relationship that's breaking apart; separation anxiety or a need to separate; divided feelings within yourself; growth. Anxiety about learning division, or math/statistical anxiety, if related to a waking educational situation.

See **double/duplicate; half**.

divorce

Most authorities agree that dreams during divorce show the stress of that experience. Long after the divorce, stress that has elements similar to what you went through during the divorce—often a situation in which you wonder if you've made a mistake, or in which you're treated similarly as in your divorce—may retrigger divorce dreams. Divorce not related to an earlier divorce and its trauma may signal transition: something changing in your inner/outer life; time to change, discard old, or acquire new goals/directions; time to heal a current relationship/marriage. What aspect of your life is ready to develop a new outlook? It can represent separating your inner masculine (wisdom, power, intellect) from your inner feminine (intuition; feelings), or utilizing one of these aspects of yourself too much. You may need this temporary separation for a new perspective; or your dream may signal that this is a long-standing problem that needs repair. (How long have you been divorced in the dream?)

dock

Consider whether you're leaving (finishing some aspect of your life; ending a project?) or arriving (the beginning of a new project/phase of your life?), and with what ease/difficulty. If you're meeting someone else or seeing him/her off, what aspects of that person are similar to you? Are you tied to the dock, or do you want/need to go to sea and explore the unconscious? Docking a spaceship may symbolize sexual intercourse; the union of masculine/feminine aspects.

If you're fishing from a dock, see **fish/fishing**. See also **boat; ship/shipwreck; water**.

doctor

An authority figure; possibly a wisdom archetype (the Wise Old Man), depending on the doctor's appearance/behavior. Is there an incident in your waking life that has triggered feelings about authority? Is the doctor a disguise for an expert in another field from your waking life? Perhaps there's an aspect of your life that needs attending to so healing can occur. It may be your own inner healer making his/her presence felt. It could be saying that you need to trust your inner authority, or need to assert more authority/healing in waking life.

dog/puppy

Loyalty/fidelity, especially to your own values/intentions; therefore, your ability to go forward in the world from a strong internal base. Dogs guard treasures, so their appearance may indicate a treasure (skill, knowledge) you've ignored/forgotten that needs to be activated, or has the potential to be activated (pregnant dog); some idea, or aspect of yourself, that you need to guard more carefully. Is something happening in your waking life that you need to "be on guard" about or need to "guard against"? Is something threatening you, and you are, or need to be, "guarding your territory"? Consider whether there's something in your waking life that you're doggedly pursuing, or that you're feeling hounded about. If you're a woman dreaming of a pregnant dog, it may symbolize your own sexual/maternal instincts.

Dogs have a keen sense of smell to ''nose out'' matters, so they can symbolize intuition. If the dog is a pet, it may represent a need/wish for love; caring; pampering; no responsibility. If wild/dangerous, it suggests primitive instincts.

In mythology, dogs are often guides into another world; therefore, they are related to birth/death, and sometimes represent the souls of dead heroes. The dog was one of the animal attributes of the healer god Asclepias, his father, Apollo, Artemis, goddess of birth, and Selene, goddess of the moon. In alchemy the dog was associated with *the* primal material and, therefore, was essential to transformation.

Look to the number, breed (if it's one you have personal knowledge/ideas about), and color (if unusual) for additional clues. The number of puppies may tell you how long ago a current idea began developing, or how long it will take to come to fruition.

See **animal(s)**.

doll

Dolls can represent part of our creative instinctual nature—the inner spirit—and are related to the symbolism of elemental beings (Estés). Negatively, a doll can represent an aspect of you that's rigid or fragile (''china doll''); an unacceptable part of yourself (especially feelings) that's projected onto the doll; a helpless part of yourself, particularly if anger or violence is inflicted on the doll; the way you feel, or are treated, in a relationship. A rag doll may symbolize a loss of energy/power/individuality. ''Doll'' is sexual slang for a female.

It's normal for a pregnant woman to have doll dreams, especially in the first trimester when her baby may resemble, or change into, a doll, and especially if this is a first pregnancy.

See **baby; elemental being; toy; voodoo** (if applicable).

donkey

See **ass; animal(s)**.

door

A transition symbol leading to new/different feelings/perceptions. Often the search for our center/Self begins with the opening of a door or being confronted with a door that we have difficulty getting through. (Remember *Alice's Adventures in Wonderland*?)

A closed door may symbolize a secret; hidden knowledge; the entrance to the unconscious (especially a hidden/strange door); the sacred (an elaborate door). It can represent something you don't want to know or from which you want to protect yourself; being/feeling "closed off." From a Freudian perspective, a closed door can represent denied entry into the parental bedroom, related to feelings of being excluded. However, "opportunity knocks" (at the door). Swinging doors suggest flexibility; options open; or in sexual slang, someone who "swings both ways."

In Freudian terms, both the door and its keyhole represent the vagina; therefore, opening a door may indicate sexual intercourse. The back door of a house may symbolize the anus. The front door is our connection with the world, our public self/persona, while the back door may be our hidden self/the shadow.

See **architecture; bridge; house; threshold**.

dot

One of the three (along with the line and circle) most primitive fundamental symbols. By itself it represents universal consciousness; truth; heaven; the first breath or emanation of God. Placed in the center of a circle, the dot represents God, or the soul, and together with the rest of the circle, is an archetypal symbol for the mandala, the Self. Metaphysically, the dot in the center represents our will. The space between the dot and the periphery represents consciousness/awareness, while the boundary represents the limits of personal influence. All of this can be represented by a dream woman named Dot or an actual person by that name.

double/duplicate

Our double (*doppelgänger*) is our mirror image and appears in dreams as another appearance of ourself—sometimes the same, sometimes reversed in size, shape, skin color, clothing. It's often difficult to distinguish it from the dream ego and the shadow until you have some experience exploring your dreams.

If the dream double is not an opposite/mirror image, but rather, two close or twin figures, it can reflect an idea/concept from the unconscious that's approaching consciousness; the act of conscious realization itself—for Jung says that at a certain moment unconscious material splits into two halves: conscious/unconscious. It can demonstrate a new level of self-reflection, a "critical" personality change wherein a new nature/side of our personality is emerging (Rossi). It may serve as a basis for homosexual men's relationship with their inner masculine and, as a soul guide, may lead them deeper into themselves (Hopcke).

See **shadow; twin(s); two**.

dough

See **baker/bakery/baking; bread; money**.

dove

The soul; peace; the Holy Ghost in Christianity. A dove mates for life, and therefore, it can symbolize your mate; love; marriage; commitment; or wanting any of these.

See **bird(s)**.

down

Downward movements can signal that you're feeling low or "down in the dumps," although an actual dump may signal emotional garbage that needs to be cleaned up. Down can symbolize that you're currently intellectually or emotionally impoverished ("down and out"; "going down for the count"). Look to the dream or the next night's dream to give you clues for change. Are you perceiving someone as "low-down"?

Going down into the earth can suggest going back in time, into history; searching your origins for insight or to repair wounded aspects of yourself. Or perhaps you're coming "down to earth" from a lofty position.

See **descend(ing); fall(ing); movement; position(s)**.

drag(ging)

What/who is being dragged? Are you "dragging your heels" regarding making a decision about some issue? Perhaps you're "being a drag" (no fun) or "dragging out" some relationship/project longer than you should? Someone "in drag" (homosexual, transvestite) may symbolize some aspect of yourself you need to acknowledge, or the archetypal union of the masculine/feminine (androgynous).

If you're in/pondering a drag race, what feelings does this evoke (excitement; fear; sense of competition?)? If you're not a driver, how do your feelings/actions relate to your feelings/behavior regarding a waking situation, i.e., assisting (pit crew), watching (passive or vicarious excitement/danger) owner/boss?

See **vehicle(s)**.

dragon

Animal instincts to be conquered, hence the battles of Saint George and Saint Michael with "the Dragon." The dragon fight is related to the archetypal themes of search/quest, the hero/heroine, and, in more modern terms, separating ourselves from the collective values of our parents/ancestors. The dragon can symbolize a guardian or guarding quality; something that needs to be guarded/protected in your life/psyche. As a devouring creature, it may represent negative aspects of the mother archetype. It shares much of the same symbolism as the snake, and both can symbolize the developing Self. In many cultures/legends, the dragon symbolizes wisdom and strength. Because of its hidden knowledge, the dragon often possesses supernatural/magical powers.

See **fire; serpent(s); snake(s); uroboros**.

drama

See **movie; theater**. See also defining the dream as a drama, Part 1, Chapter 2, Dreamercise #7.

draw(ing)

Like any form of art, drawing may symbolize creative expression; the emergence of unconscious material. If architectural plans, you may need to draw plans for your self-development or your future, to put new order in your life. Do you need to find a different perspective from which to view a waking scene; are you "drawing a blank"; or do you need to "draw upon"/"draw out" some aspect of yourself or another? "To draw blood" may signal hostility; vulnerability; some issue/situation that's draining your energy; or the classic competition situation in which the winner is the one who draws blood first. Perhaps there's some issue in your life wherein you need "to draw the line," or an unfinished situation that you need to "draw to a close." Is there some hidden aspect of your life that you've "drawn a veil over"?

If you're drawing cards, see **cards/playing cards; game(s)**.

drawbridge

If closed, it may indicate defensiveness or something/someone in waking life whom you feel you need to strongly defend against, or not allow into your life; outmoded/outdated feelings/attitudes (sexual?), possibly ones developed in childhood that now can be modernized. If open, it can indicate mental/emotional/sexual receptiveness. Because a drawbridge is usually associated with a castle, it can refer to an archetypal/fairy-tale motif, and especially the division between our inner/outer or conscious/unconscious worlds.

See **castle; vagina**.

dreamer/dream ego

Your dream ego is your self-image, your sense of self, the "I" in the dream. You can obtain information about how you deal with life by observing/reviewing your dream ego's actions over time (see Dreamercise #15, Part 1). Usually we don't appear alone in dreams; rather, we interact with some person/image, and talking and listening are the most common modes of interaction. We seldom appear distorted or as we were in childhood.

For each dream, consider whether you play an active role—that is, you're in the middle of events, things are happening to you—or whether you're an observer, watching things happen. If you're an observer, consider whether you're watching aspects/characteristics of yourself that you need to acknowledge or include more actively in your life. Or perhaps the dream is a rehearsal, and you're watching to see how you might perform in these roles, thereby expanding your image of yourself.

Consider how your dream behavior is similar to/different from your waking behavior, and how it might relate to your self-esteem/self-image. Is it appropriate for you to make changes, or practice some new waking behavior, based on your dream behavior?

From a Jungian perspective, if you're behaving as you do in waking life, that may be "the problem," and other characters can show you the solution. If you're not acting as you customarily do in waking life, possibly you're portraying a solution to consider (Sullivan), a new way to behave based on psychological growth.

dream within a dream/dreaming you are dreaming

Freudians suggest that the contents of the dream-within-a-dream are the true, undisguised message. Sometimes it's also a safer, more acceptable, way to recognize material from the unconscious, or information you've been ignoring. It may signal a dominant/important life pattern or reflect a hidden but crucial issue (Whitmont and Perera).

dresser/dressing table

Putting on your social image/mask/persona. The contents of the dresser can symbolize various aspects of your public personality, or aspects hidden away in drawers. If the drawers are closed, use a waking imagery to look inside for additional cues (see Dreamercises #3 and #10, Part 1). In the imagery, don't forget to look for a message taped on the bottom of a drawer.

See **bedroom; furniture/furnishings**.

drink(ing)

Consider the way you're drinking (in/out of control), what/why you're drinking. Do you need more attention in your waking life? Feeling out of control in waking life can precipitate drinking dreams for recovering alcoholics. "Drinking the waters of life" may symbolize renewal, rebirth, or a need for it. Drinking milk may say you're in need of nurturing, or wish you could escape responsibility and return to an earlier state. Ritual drinking may be honoring the gods or the spirit within. Drinking alcohol/spirits may symbolize seeking connection with the divine (Jung). Consider the characteristics of the people you're drinking with, the number of drinks, and the location where you're drinking. It's not uncommon for expectant fathers to dream about parties/ceremonies in which there is elaborate eating/drinking (Siegel).

See **addict(ed); alcohol/alcoholic; celebration**. If applicable, see **coffee; milk; tea**.

drive/driving

How are you progressing through life? With a lot of drive/ambition; or are you being driven by others and by past attitudes and self- or family-imposed restrictions?

See **car; chauffeur; vehicle(s)**.

drown(ing)

Anxiety; fear of being overwhelmed by repressed emotions, or by feelings stimulated in a waking experience. If you have a lung/breathing disorder, it may be time to consult a physician to determine if water is building up in your lungs.

See **death; water**.

drugs/taking a drug

See **addict(ed); alcohol/alcoholic; medicine/medication; pain medication**.

drum(ming)

Often associated with primitive rites/rituals/dances, a drum or a drumming rhythm could be expressing a need for more ritual in your life, or a need to connect with the divine. (Drumming is sometimes thought to attract, or call down, the gods.) It may represent your own internal rhythms, or the rhythm of life. Drumming is associated with initiation, and with producing an altered state of consciousness; therefore, it can represent a change in perception, a need to make such a change. For many tribes, the drum's sound was the primal sound, which can induce shamans into an altered state in which they can enter/repeat their first cosmic journey (expanded awareness, union with the divine). Depending on the complexity of the rhythm (especially if you're the drummer), it can represent creativity and self-expression ("marching to a different drummer").

See **initiation; music/musician**.

drunk/drunk driving

Loss of control; loss of spirit in your life; a wish to give up responsibility and return to more immature or infantile stages of your life; a need to be nurtured by your mother/a mother figure/ the Great Mother.

See **alcohol/alcoholic; drink(ing); drive/driving**.

duck(s)

The duck is at home on top of the water, in the air, and below the water, where it finds nourishment, so it can represent a comfortable dip into the unconscious; the conjunction of conscious (air) and unconscious (water) information. Are you "skimming the surface" or "on top of it all"? A duck and a drake together often symbolize marital happiness. It could be a pun for "ducking out" (escaping responsibility or a relationship issue), "ducking an issue" (avoidance), "ducking your head" (guilt, shyness?), or the fact that you're a "shy duck." In England, of course, "ducks" and "ducky" are the equivalent terms of endearment to "honey" or "sweetie" elsewhere. Inasmuch as female ducks are excellent mothers, it could relate to maternal instincts, especially if there are goslings.

dusk

See **evening**.

dwarf(s)

Childish/immature conditions of your personality; hidden/ growing creative impulses; aspects of yourself that you've never developed. Dwarf gods like the Cabiri and the Dactyls were gods of invention (smiths, craftsmen, musicians), personifications of creative impulses, and also represented elemental powers of nature. In Hawaii they are represented by the lost race of Menehune. Dwarfs, especially those wearing pointed hats (phallic and upward in direction), may refer to small but significant creative energy from the unconscious (Jung). The Egyptian dwarf god Bes, as the protector of roads and byways, was often invoked to protect dreamers from the dangers of the unknown. In esoteric/metaphysical thought, the dwarf sometimes represents earth spirits.

See **boy; child/children; elemental being**.

dying

See **death**.

eagle

Soaring; free; majestic; grandeur; independence; height; one's inner spirit/spirituality (close to heaven). Are you "flying high"? The eagle is a bird of light—messages made clear—as opposed to birds of the night/shadow. As a solar bird, it symbolizes self-renewal. In the Middle Ages and in alchemy, it was equated with the phoenix, also a symbol of regeneration/eternity.

The eagle may suggest that you're able to see large vistas—the whole picture—at once, and within that, to be selective/focused, utilizing your "eagle eye." For United States citizens, it's a symbol of patriotism/nationality; therefore, of belongingness/community/identity. It appears as a symbol of sovereignty in the emblems of many countries. In Indian folklore, the eagle is often a symbol of power/leadership. In Greek mythology it's the bird of Zeus—and can, therefore, symbolize the archetypal father. In Christian symbology, the eagle represents the evangelist John.

See **bird(s); flying; phoenix**.

ear(s)

Receptivity to outer or inner guidance (be "all ears"); needing to be receptive ("lend an ear"); immaturity/lack of experience ("wet behind the ears"); intuition or relying on your own judgment ("play it by ear"); obedience. Are you "turning a deaf ear" to something to which you should attend? Ears may relate to a need for more sensuous experience.

See **body; deaf; head**.

earth

Our origins; our home; the cosmic or personal womb. ''Earthy'' symbolizes instincts or instinctual behavior; naturalness; sexy. It may also symbolize that you're too ''up in the air'' and need to be more ''grounded,'' or to come ''down to earth.'' It can symbolize the concepts of union and of opposites, as in heaven/earth, divine/mundane, birth/death. Although in mythology the earth often symbolizes the primordial feminine or Great Mother, in ancient Europe there was the *Green Man* as the embodiment of nature. Today he symbolizes the depths of masculinity (Crawford). During the Renaissance, the earth was personified as the goddess Cybele (Demeter).

See **dirt(y); Great Mother; heaven; opposites; sky**.

earthquake

This is likely to be an anxiety dream if you live in an area where earthquakes have occurred recently, or if you worry about them. If not, then an earthquake may symbolize upheaval or sudden change in your psychic/personal life. It may represent unleashed, destructive feminine energy (Krakow and Neidhardt). Earthquakes or earth tremors are common for women in their third trimester of pregnancy (Cartwright and Lamberg).

east

The direction east is related to all solar symbolism (see **sun/sunlight**). It can symbolize a need to dedicate yourself to something (knowledge, wisdom?) that's very old; a new beginning; the birth/rebirth motif; mystery; spiritual enlightenment; the Eastern mystical tradition/approach to inner wisdom/knowledge. In its most spiritual sense, it symbolizes the very first emanation from God. East is related to the direction right and can suggest that you're taking a right (correct) direction.

See **direction(s); lily; right**.

Easter

See **holiday(s)**.

eating

Eating is a way that we incorporate things into us, so you may be eating food that represents qualities you think you need/desire. Eating is nourishment and may represent emotional/maternal nourishment, especially if you're eating/drinking milk products, warm/sweet foods, or especially satisfying foods your mother made. Eating undesirable foods, or foods you ordinarily don't like, may symbolize a need to recognize/acknowledge a negative/shadow aspect of yourself. Difficulty eating may represent difficulty taking in reality (Woodman); in assimilating information/energy that you need to make a change. Sharing food with another or feeding another suggests nurturing, closeness. Overeating may relate to issues of greed/emotional neediness; trying to fill an internal void; attempting to satisfy/fulfill other sensual needs. Eating can be a disguise for sensual/erotic experiences. Perhaps you need more sensual/sexual stimulation in your waking life.

Consider what aspects of yourself you're nurturing, symbolized by whomever you are eating with or feeding. There's always the chance that you're "eating your heart out" over some person/situation, or that you wish you had someone "eating out of your hand." Then again, because of your behavior in, or attitude about, a situation/person, you may need to "eat humble pie," "eat your hat," or "eat your words."

Eating with a family/group reflects family/social pleasure and connection (or a need for it). Eating alone can reflect independence needs; feelings about exclusion; rejection or loss of family/social ties; no one but yourself to nurture you.

See **celebration; digestion; food; teeth**.

Eden, Garden of

Pleasure; freedom; lack of responsibility; primitive instincts; a longing to return to innocent times, possibly early nursing situations (an oasis); the infant struggle between good mother/bad mother. As the cosmic garden of Christianity, it is an archetypal symbol for the pull of opposites (innocence and its loss, obedience/disobedience) and the wish for the primal parents (treasures difficult to come by).

See **Adam; Eve; garden**.

edge

What is the dream telling you that you're on the edge of: a dangerous situation, freedom, a discovery? Consider how you feel (scared, excited, happy, sad?) for additional cues. In what direction are you looking (up, down, straight ahead?)? If you're on the edge of a canyon/channel, is there some opposite aspect of yourself, or quality, you need to reconcile, or are having trouble reconciling? Perhaps there's a waking situation in which you've not consciously realized you're "on edge" or one that you're "edgy" about.

What has you feeling tense, anxious, or excited? Could the dream be telling you that if you don't change your behavior or reconsider a decision, you're "going over the edge"?

See **abyss; canyon; cliff**.

egg(s)

An ancient fertility symbol (especially Easter eggs), a symbol of new life. It represents potentiality, a wealth of possibilities waiting to be tapped; a quest; the act of seeking knowledge/solutions. It may symbolize being closed in, unable to escape. As a nest egg, it could symbolize hoarding, or something treasured you're worried about. Could your meaning be found in the idioms "egg someone on," "rotten egg," "laid an egg"?

In early Christian times, the egg symbolized Christ and was, therefore, a symbol of resurrection and perfection. Mythologically, it's related to the world/cosmic egg, which gave of itself at the primal beginning, thus suggesting the beginning of the process of inner growth. Esoterically, it represents a person's aura/energy field, and the "ring-pass-not," which defines the limits of your inner/outer world.

What are you seeking to protect or to express? What confines are you trying to outgrow? What potentials are waiting to be born, or beginning their development?

See **aura; chicken; hen**.

ego

See **dreamer/dream ego**.

Egypt

Ancient Egypt was the place to go for initiation into "the mysteries," so Egypt may symbolize esoteric knowledge/wisdom, or the search for it. Many Western magical/metaphysical traditions have their roots in Egyptian culture, as did Greek philosophy and science, so it may symbolize heritage; the passing on of tradition; a link with the past. In Judeo-Christian symbology, Egypt represents the sensual and material life that one leaves behind to go toward the promised land.

If applicable, see **abroad/traveling abroad; desert; magic; pyramid(s); sphinx**.

eight

In numerology eight is related to possessions; status; achievement (time for action; the pattern/idea put into form); balance. Placed on its side, it resembles the lemniscate, symbol of infinity/timelessness. Jung considered eight a symbol for wholeness/completion/totality—and, therefore, a symbol for the Self—because it's the double of four and because the tension between the divine Trinity and the four earthly elements calls for the eighth. Eight ends the process of evolution and becomes an "eternal static state," eternity (von Franz).

Eight is associated with the Buddhist wheel, thus the mandala and the wheel of life. It is also associated with the Hindu god Vishnu, whose eight arms symbolize the eight guardians of the world.

Because it is the first cubic number, the cube becomes the geometric symbol associated with eight. When unfolded, the cube represents the Christian cross, a symbol of the human body. Metaphysically, then, it also reflects and is related to the alchemical "three into four" symbolism (the three horizontal squares of the crossing arm and the four vertical squares of the upright staff of the cross).

See **mandala; number(s); Self; three; wheel**.

ejaculation

Ejaculation dreams, with/without the actual emission of semen, are common in men. They may be an expression of sexual needs. The woman in the dream may represent the man's anima, or idealized woman, and may point to a need to recognize/develop this inner archetype. It may be that someone in waking life is stimulating the archetypal image. The ease/difficulty with which ejaculation occurs and under what circumstances can provide clues as to how you perceive your role in sexual/love relationships.

See **orgasm; sex**.

elastic

The ability to rebound or bounce back, or its opposite, depending on the elastic's condition. Is there some waking situation in which you've been too rigid and need to adopt a more flexible attitude? Possibly you need to stretch your limits and consider more options.

elbow

In Freudian terms limbs equal phallus; therefore, a wound to the elbow, such that you cannot move it, could relate to feelings of impotence with respect to sex or, more likely, to another waking situation. If it's the left elbow, it may refer to the shadow aspect; undeveloped characteristics; passive action (possibly inaction?). The right elbow would relate to a moral/ethical problem/situation, or to the kind of action you have taken (possibly too aggressive?). Still, perhaps you weren't really aware that someone has "given you the elbow," or that you need more "elbow room" to function. You may need/fear to make a space/place for yourself ("elbow in") in some waking situation.

See **arm(s); body**.

electrician/electricity

See **engine; engineer**.

elemental being

Whether they be fairies, gnomes, dwarfs, the cobbler's elves, Irish leprechauns, or Iceland's *huldufólk* ("hidden people," who still appear regularly in the dreams of some Icelanders), elemental beings in fairy tales/myths always possess extraordinary or unusual powers/forces (negative and positive). They therefore symbolize primitive/unrecognized bits of energy acting within us. They represent latent potentialities or resources waiting to be drawn upon (positive), or to spring upon us unawares (negative). In Jungian terms, the land where they live symbolizes the collective unconscious, another type of resource available to us all.

See **angel(s); child/children; dwarf(s)**.

elements

See **air; earth; fire; water**.

elephant

Strength; endurance; with an upturned trunk, good luck. In ancient times, the shape of an elephant in geological or cloud formations represented the world axis. Probably the most well-known elephants are the cartoon Dumbo, which may symbolize immaturity or the ability to escape the mundane by flying, and the Hindu god Ganesh, son of Shiva, who symbolizes our ability to overcome obstacles (also symbolized by Dumbo, who turned his enormous ears into an advantage). Honoring Ganesh is said to bring prosperity, in general, and wealth, specifically. In some parts of Asia he is also the patron of artists/academics.

See **animal(s)**.

elevator

An elevator can symbolize being "uplifted"; achieving a higher state of mind, or wishing to do so; a feeling of being deflated/"down." The movement of an elevator between floors often symbolizes the transition between two states of consciousness/awareness. An elevator rising from the basement suggests material rising from the unconscious into consciousness. As with stairs, up/down movements can symbolize sexual feelings (rising passion).

See **ascend(ing); descend(ing); direction(s); down; falling; stairs; up**. If you can't get out of the elevator, see **cage; enclosed/enclosure**.

eleven

Numerologically, eleven symbolizes transition—thus a common number for magic/sorcery—as well as conflict/struggle as a new cycle begins (10 + 1). It doubles the symbolism of one, hence, is related to doubles/twins.

In Cabalistic tradition, existence came into being through ten emanations from the One, which metaphysics calls the ten states of consciousness/energy. We need to incorporate these ten energies into ourselves to become complete persons. The Cabalistic tree of life (map of energies operating in the universe) depicts these ten emanations, as well as a place for Daath, an eleventh, invisible emanation, which acts as the gateway to incorporating the other energies and to the divine world. Daath is the bridge over the abyss that separates the mundane from the divine. Hence it, and eleven, are related to death/rebirth and quest themes. Daath also symbolizes the initiate who is studying the Cabalistic wisdom/mysteries.

See **double/duplicate; one; twins; x**.

elf/elves

See **elemental being**.

elixir

See **magic drink**.

embarrass/embarrassed

See **emotion(s)**.

embroidery

If this is a hobby/skill that you once did, but no longer, it may suggest an era in your life that you need to review to determine its relation to a present situation. It may be that you're being asked to play a more traditional female role in some relationship. It could suggest that you've been "embroidering the truth." Consider the scene/objects that are being embroidered.

See **craft(s); decorate/decoration; sew(ing)**.

embryo

To dream of an embryo or fetus is common for a pregnant woman in her third trimester, or for her husband. If you're not pregnant, the dream may refer to: an idea you are "hatching"; unconscious material about to emerge; an early stage in your inner growth process. It may refer to your need to be protected, hence, feelings of vulnerability.

See **baby; egg(s); mother**.

emerald(s)

Tranquillity; fertility; a lunar/feminine symbol. As the fourth foundation stone of the New Jerusalem (Book of Revelation), it is related to the tribe of Asher and to doing service to the community/society. Christian symbolisms of the emerald include faith; immortality; purity.

According to medieval/legendary writings, when Lucifer fell from grace, the emerald that signified ancient wisdom also fell from his crown. Coming in contact with matter, it became, first, a stone, then a sword, a spear, and finally the Grail cup—the four hallows of the Grail legend/quest, and the four suits of the Tarot deck. Likewise, the tablet of Hermes Trismegistus, the founder of alchemy, was reputedly made of an emerald. Thus, the emerald is related to the reconciliation of opposites (the famous dictum of Hermes) and to the discovery/perfection of the Self. It is the birthstone of someone born in May.

See **gem(s); green; jewel(s)**.

emotion(s)

Fear/anxiety are the emotions most often experienced in dreams. Anger ranks next, followed by friendliness. Fear, anger, and sadness occur twice as much as pleasant emotions. According to psychiatrist Walter Bonime, the emotions/feelings we experience in a dream do not serve as symbols of something else. They are always our authentic response to something in our waking life and may be emotions we didn't feel safe to express at that time.

On the other hand, emotions can be, and often are, expressed/symbolized by images (landscape, persons) and actions in our dreams. For instance, dark clouds, dark houses, or mud might symbolize depression or anger, while a spring day might refer to feelings of lightheartedness, happiness, or energy. Textures (soft, fuzzy, rough, hard) can express intimate or distant feelings (Signell). For additional clues or insight, ask yourself; "When have I felt this way before?" "Is there a similarity between the way I felt in the dream and some waking-life situation?"

Dreams with intense affect, especially awe or ecstasy, often signal archetypal dreams.

See **anger; fear; impasse; love; water**.

emotionless

The most common emotional tone in dreams is one of blandness. However, a definite feeling of coldness/indifference could be a signal that you've closed off, or are repressing, your emotions about a particular person/situation. It could be saying that you're neglecting, or need to pay attention to, your emotional life. If your associations, or the dream images themselves, suggest the dream refers to mourning that should have been over years ago, then it may be a signal that it's time to let go of that situation/relationship. If you are, in fact, in a current mourning process, emotions reawaken in their own good time as the ego can handle the loss, but for a while you may feel empty inside. Don't rush it; look for future dreams that indicate you're moving through the mourning process and have begun to reconnect with the life force. Attending to absent or significantly diminished emotions in an experience that would ordinarily evoke emotion may give you an idea of conflicts/issues the dream is expressing.

See **emotion(s)**. For a dream that begins without feeling and moves to full feeling, see **transformation**.

emperor

An emperor/ruler may symbolize the supreme/archetypal male authority, or he may simply be a figurehead for psychological energy operating within you. His presence can suggest the dream is saying something important about your feelings/attitudes toward your personal father, or a current father substitute/authority. Perhaps someone in your life is acting like an emperor, and you feel like a loyal/rebellious subject.

See **empress; royalty**.

empress

An empress may symbolize an archetypal female authority, or she may simply be a figurehead for psychological energy attempting to express itself. Her presence can suggest the dream is a message about your personal mother, your inner mothering process, or a present mother substitute/authority. She can represent someone in your waking life who's behaving like an empress, or is the "power behind the throne." Are you a loyal subject or planning a coup?

See **emperor; royalty**.

empty

Consider the symbolism of what is empty for additional clues. Are you, or someone, not thinking enough or not attending to your conscious knowledge ("empty-headed")? Does the dream refer to something that was never there, or something that you've lost? Something that's empty can refer to a feeling of loss; depression; lack of fulfillment; fear that internally there's a void; suppression of feelings. Perhaps you're "running on empty" regarding some situation/relationship and need to restore yourself. Feeling empty can also be a defense/protection against too much pain.

See **emotion(s); emotionless**.

enclosed/enclosure

An enclosure (room, building?) can represent being walled off for defensive or protective purposes. What situation in your waking life arouses a need to protect/defend yourself, or someone else? Who/what is restraining you, or in what situation do you feel confined? If made of glass or bubblelike, perhaps some aspect of you is ready to express itself or come into action. Alternatively, you may be too critical about a person/situation, or you're being regarded critically. ("People who live in glass houses shouldn't throw stones.") Some dream experts believe this type of dream can refer to birth memories/trauma. It may represent your actual/perceived limitations; the testing of boundaries, which can lead to growth.

See **bubble; cage; prison/ prisoner; wall(s); walled city**.

encyclopedia

Knowledge; consciousness; worldly wisdom; need for learning/education; seeking answers. Is there some waking situation in which you don't have enough answers, need more facts?

end of the world

Not predictive of the actual end of the world nor of death, dreams that the end of the world is coming/occurring usually signify a momentous change taking place within. They are dramatic/ emotional. Often dreamed by seriously ill people and by uprooted refugees or others forced to make extensive life changes (Siegel), they may indicate the end of one kind of lifestyle and the beginning of another.

See **atom bomb; destruction**.

engaged

During an engagement and approaching wedding, it's not uncommon to dream you're attracted to another but suddenly remember that you are engaged. These dreams are often "rehearsals" for maintaining self-control in the soon-to-be exclusive sexual arrangement (Siegel). If you're not engaged, the dream may reflect sexual/relationship needs; an attempt to resolve feelings of aloneness; issues of commitment stimulated by a waking situation.

See **sex; wedding**.

engine

Energy or motivation, sexual or otherwise; that which is driving you to achieve your goals; your life philosophy/attitude; life power; a desire/skills to take charge and run things. It can represent automatic behavior (instincts); physiology (breathing, aging); learned (mechanical) behavior, which may need to be repaired/replaced if it's no longer working for you (engine trouble). Anxiety about any part of your body and its functioning may be reflected as engine trouble. What part of you needs maintenance?

See **vehicle(s)**.

engineer

The person who runs the engine (nervous system?) or body, i.e., you, and whoever else shapes your goals or the structure of your life; becoming aware of the different levels of your life. How are you doing; what difficulties, if any, are you having; and how do you feel in the dream? Can you connect these with a work/interpersonal/health situation? You may need to see a doctor, if only to reassure yourself about a health issue; or it may be time to reexamine your goals/directions.

See **engine; emotion(s)**.

enjoy

See **emotion(s)**.

enter/entryway

See **door**.

epidemic

Fear of being caught up in the negative attitudes/opinions of others—possibly a specific group to which you belong or are being pressured to join—and of losing your uniqueness/identity; being at the mercy of, or overwhelmed by, your own/others' emotions.

See **destruction; disease**.

escalator

See **ascend(ing); descend(ing); elevator; stairs**.

escape

A wish to get out of a current inner/outer situation; time to move in a new direction, take new action, make new plans. If you're unable to escape from a recurrent frightening situation, use Dreamercise #11, Part 1, to change the situation.

See **enclosed/enclosure; prison/prisoner**.

Eve

Eve, our primordial mother, is

the prototype of all women and is related, archetypally, to the Great Mother. She symbolizes the material aspect of women, while Mary, the mother of Jesus, often symbolizes the spiritual aspect. Eve can be an expression of the undeveloped Self for a woman, the anima for a man. She also symbolizes sexual duality that has been integrated, the coming together of the masculine/feminine in each of us.

See **Adam; Eden, Garden of; Great Mother; history; mother**.

evening

The end of a cycle; aging; death. Archetypally, it can be the preparation for the dark, i.e., preparation to encounter the personal or collective unconscious.

See **dark/darkness; morning; night**.

evicted

If this is not anxiety/fear about an actual situation, then being evicted suggests that a present situation/relationship may be evoking feelings such as helplessness or loss of power (not having a chance to defend yourself), lowered self-esteem, not belonging. You may be feeling unfairly treated, or you may not be living up to your contractual agreements (inner or outer).

evil

To dream of someone/something that's evil may refer to a repressed, possibly forbidden, aspect of yourself; or it may be the personalized form of a strong emotion (hate, rage?). It could be your shadow aspect seeking recognition/expression. It may reflect the feeling that you gave in to base/selfish desires when you "should" have behaved with better/higher intentions.

See **devil; shadow; voodoo**.

ex-spouse/ex-mate/ex-lover

Dreaming of an ex-spouse may be a way of alerting you to the same/similar behavior in a new spouse/lover, especially during times of stress (Garfield). Love affairs with former lovers/mates are common dreams of women in their second trimester of pregnancy and may reflect appearance concerns and a need to be reassured that they're still attractive. One of Rosalind Cartwright's studies showed that divorcing women who dreamed, even angrily, about their soon-to-be "exes" got over the loss of separation sooner. If the separation/divorce is a recent one, the "ex" character may be helping you through the mourning/ending process. If the separation/divorce is an old one, the presence of the ex, especially in a positive way, may remind you that this is a quality you need to incorporate into your present life/relationship. The dream could be suggesting that what you learned from a previous relationship may need to be applied in a present one; that you're repeating the same mistake; that feelings/attitudes you have about an ex (especially as they apply to men/women in general) are being transferred onto a present relationship. What part of you is an "ex," or is some part of you being "x'd out"?

See **x**.

exam(s)/examination

If you're late for a school exam or realize you haven't studied for one (a common anxiety dream), it may represent something in your life that you've failed—or fear you've failed—to prepare for. It may represent feeling that you've gotten yourself into a situation, or you're being asked by someone else to do something, that you don't feel totally capable/qualified to do—again, anxiety about failing. You may be in, or about to enter, a waking situation in which you will, once again, be tested, or in which your self-confidence is wavering, especially about your ability to handle new responsibilities (Freud). One study showed that men have this dream more often than women do.

examined

If you're being physically examined, as in a medical examination, the image may suggest that you need to reveal more of yourself, or, conversely, anxiety that you've already revealed too much. It may relate to a waking doctor/patient relationship, possibly an unsatisfactory one. Consider any emphasized body part and the interaction for additional clues.

See **body; doctor**.

excited/excitement

See **emotion(s)**.

excrement

Aspects of yourself that are dirty or that you believe to be undesirable/repulsive. Is there someone in your life whom you regard as a "turd"? In a positive sense, excrement refers to creative processes that have yet to find their appropriate form/expression.

In Freudian terms excrement, and any anal activity, can be related to possession/withholding, to money, to aggressive acts.

See **defecate; mud/muddy; toilet**.

executive

Your appearance as an executive or engaging in executive activities symbolizes the need, and your capacity/readiness, to make important decisions or take decisive action. The level of the position/action suggests just how ready you are.

See **boss; business/work**.

existential dreams

See **grief**.

explosion

Something (feelings, knowledge that you've ignored?) that's emerging dramatically into your conscious awareness; a need to "explode" and express yourself more fully; your response to some piece of news that consciously you hadn't realized was so devastating. The explosion, or its aftermath, may also provide you with a solution for some waking situation.

See **atom bomb; bomb/bombed; destruction**.

extraterrestrial

See **alien(s); UFO**.

eye(s)

Enlightenment; understanding/comprehension ("I saw it with my own eyes"); intellectual awareness/consciousness; inner vision (the third eye); unconscious material becoming conscious. Are you, or are you not, "seeing eye to eye" with someone, perhaps an authority; or do you need to look at something more carefully? The eye can also represent the "I," the dreamer's ego, as well as the opportunity/process of seeing oneself or becoming "enlightened" with self-knowledge (insight) or spiritual knowledge (the inner eye of God). Another of its aspects is the passage of time, which occurs in the "blink of an eye."

The pupil of the eye can be a pun on the student/teacher relationship—you're still a "pupil," a student in your own eyes or someone else's. Woodman says if you see yourself reflected in the pupils of someone else's eyes, especially those of a teacher, it can be a way of saying you are being loved for what is within you, your potential.

There is also the "evil eye," related to negative powers (the shadow) and magic. Deliberately failing to make eye contact suggests avoidance of intimacy. Closed eyes/blindness symbolizes not wanting to see ("you must be blind").

An eye in the palm of a hand is a well-known symbol for clairvoyance, and divine creative wisdom. In Christian art, an eye surrounded by sun rays symbolizes God, the omnipresent Eye. In Egyptian mythology, the right eye of Horus represents the sun, while the left eye represents the moon. Many mythologies refer to a one-eyed person, usually one who sacrifices an eye to attain a special knowledge. The most famous of these is Odin. One eye might also symbolize a one-sided viewpoint.

See **body; dreamer/dream ego; iris; look(ing)/looked at; see(ing)**.

eyeglasses

How are they decorated? Who might they have originally belonged to? They can symbolize that you haven't got your own eyes yet and are looking at the world through someone else's ideas/attitudes/beliefs (Woodman), or even through "rose-colored glasses." Dream glasses may offer "clear sight," or you may be too "nearsighted"/"farsighted" about a situation. Glasses for farsightedness suggest a need to examine a situation more closely, or, conversely, not wanting to see what's before you. Glasses for nearsightedness suggest an inability to look ahead, or not wanting to see the future. Unless, of course, you have recently made a *spectacle* of yourself, or someone you care about has.

If you've just received your first pair of glasses, it would not be unusual to dream about them as you incorporate them into your image of yourself, or as they reflect ideas about your changing/aging body.

See **eye(s); vision**.

face

Mask or front (''poker face'') we put on for the world (persona); vanity; visible reputation; reflection of societal expectations (''save face,'' ''lose face''). Some idioms suggest that face can symbolize our willingness to deal with issues (''face the music,'' ''let's face it''); truth (''face the facts''); confrontation (''face up to it'') or its avoidance (''do an about-face''). Something in your personality, or elements of a waking relationship, may be deceitful (''two-faced''), not all that it seems. Is someone not being up front about feelings? Pimples/blemishes can represent erupting emotions, or a flaw in your persona/mask.

See **body; mask(s); persona**.

failure

Feeling unsuccessful, failing to take action or to succeed, in a dream suggests feeling/perceiving yourself as inadequate. How have you failed to honor/acknowledge your needs/feelings, or someone else's? How has another failed to acknowledge you? By whose comparison/standards have you failed? If the dream is one of compensation, you may have been too inflated about a recent success, and the dream is bringing your ego into balance.

fair

Celebration; the passage of time and marking of cycles (once-a-year county/state fair); continuity; community/basic connections/wisdom; a situation that's "not fair" to you. As a place where people exhibit handcrafts or animals, it can symbolize a willingness to share your insights and inner resources/ knowledge (or to learn from elders), but also competition; honor; recognition (or lack of it). If a carnival accompanies the fair, see **carnival**.

See **person, fair-skinned**.

fairy/fairies

See **elemental being**.

falcon

In ancient Egypt, the falcon symbolized the sun and the sky, solar consciousness; therefore, it can also symbolize sharpness; alertness; awareness.

See **bird(s)**.

falling

One of the most common dream happenings to occur, especially in nightmares, falling has quite varied meanings. It can refer to the tendency to give up or to escape from some demanding situation, or the perception that you have failed and "fallen from grace" (a self-esteem issue). Falling can be considered one form, albeit dramatic, of descent dreams. In Jungian terms it is a dream happening that leads toward the death/rebirth motif, which may be acted out in waking activities. It can compensate for an egotistical waking situation, or may serve as a warning to change waking attitudes ("pride goeth before a fall"). Falling propels us toward Mother Earth (the primordial feminine/maternal) and can represent issues/fears relating to the personal feminine/maternal, and to the primordial/archetypal mother. Consider what you're falling toward or away from for additional clues. A falling dream may give you clues as to waking situations in which you feel in, or out of, control—depending on how much control you have in the fall. Related to control is also the experience of "falling in love," and your feelings about that.

See **abyss; control/controlled/ out of control; descend(ing); flying**.

family

In general, dreaming of a family member represents the relationship between you and that person. It can reflect worries about the relationship; disharmony; interpersonal tensions; projections (aspects of yourself) you've directed onto your relative. Parents may represent your attitudes toward authority; wisdom/rules/attitudes you've been taught; ways in which you are like your parents.

Being at a family gathering suggests your background and life experience (personal history); feelings of connection with a line of heritage. Singling out a particular person at the gathering may indicate some quality that you now need to utilize/develop within yourself. It may signal that feelings similar to those you have about your relative have been awakened by a present situation, although you may not have consciously recognized it. Depending on his/her dream behavior, a brother/sister can sometimes represent your anima/animus (depending on your sex), or your shadow.

See the specific member of your family: **brother; daughter; father; grandparents; husband; mother; parents; relatives; sister; son; uncle; wife**.

famous people

See **person, famous**.

fare/toll

The price we pay to travel life's highway. Consider the ease/difficulty you're having with your fare. How much toll is some present situation taking? It may be a pun on whether or not you perceive some waking situation as "fair."

See **fair; ticket; vehicle(s)**.

farm(er)

Nurturing, cultivating aspects of yourself. You're sowing and reaping, have the capacity to, or the time is ripe for some project/idea to reach fruition/harvest.

As the modern equivalent of the guardian of cycles and regenerative forces, the farmer can represent a primal, archetypal pattern at work.

If the farm is not in good shape, your dream may be calling for attention to, and adjustment of, the cycles of your life—possibly sleep/work/menstrual cycles.

See **animal(s)** and specific animals, if applicable.

fast

Fast refers to the speed of action in your dream, or to your need/urgency to go faster. What's the hurry? Is the need or action typical of your waking behavior? If you need to do something faster (run, skate, drive) to escape danger, consider whether there isn't a more effective solution and practice it in waking life (see Dreamercise #11, Chapter 2, Part 1). If in a vehicle that's going too fast, consider what aspect of your life is out of control, scary, or overwhelming (depending on dream feelings).

See **speed**.

fasting

Fasting is considered an effective form of purification and a way to prepare for a spiritual experience, so you may be preparing for the next stage in your individuation process. It may signal unconscious material ready to emerge (intuition/insight); your attempt/need to rid yourself of physical/mental negativity, possibly remaining from childhood.

fast food

This largely depends on your attitude about fast food, whether it is fun (recreational eating), junk, convenient, unhealthful, the best, etc. The dream image could be telling you that you have the same attitude about some waking situation/relationship—or are treating someone, or being treated, that way.

See **drink(ing)** (if applicable); **food; eating**.

fat/fat person/being fat

It's normal for pregnant women to dream of themselves, or others, as fat, which usually reflects concern with their changing bodies. If you're not fat or pregnant, it may represent vulnerabilities you need to insulate/protect. Is there a waking situation in which you think you're carrying more weight than you should, or in which you desire to "carry your own weight"?

See **body**.

fate

Attitudes about fate could appear as situations in which you gamble, play cards, engage in dangerous/reckless actions ("tempting fate"), or as a message that, somehow, cannot be altered (perhaps carved in stone). Issues about fate may be expressed when there are three women in your dream (the three fates, the three Norns of Norse mythology). Two are often benevolent, and one evil/angry, or in some way negates the others' behavior. In fairy tales (Sleeping Beauty), they often appear as godmothers.

See **game(s)**.

father

Traditional values; religious philosophy; patriarchal values, as opposed to personal masculine power/energy; issues/relationship with your personal father. Archetypally, he can represent Jung's collective consciousness, our cultural/societal awareness and spirit.

See **Adam; family; parents; Wise Old Man**.

faucet

The ability to turn your emotions on and off; self-control or lack of it, and, possibly, being overwhelmed by your emotions (broken faucet; unable to stop running water).

FAX

See **telephone**.

fear

Fearful dreams, or anxiety dreams, are among the most common nightmares. They are caused by a threat of "functional bankruptcy" (Bonime), i.e., doubt about, or threat to, your self-sufficiency or competency. Feelings that are scary for you, either positive or negative, can promote anxiety dreams, as well as perceived threats to your own control or to your ability to manipulate others. Anger often masquerades as fear, so don't forget to look for issues about which you're angry.

The ego often selects our next direction for growth from something we fear. Consider, then, that the dream may identify your next area of self-growth. Anxiety dreams become more intense and fearful during life crises and the first year of bereavement.

See **anger; emotion(s); grief**.

feather

The realm of the birds, thus, the heavens; flight; the wind. Wearing/receiving feathers may reflect a need to awaken the power/symbolism of that particular bird, which most likely was the token bird of a deity—another way the feather can symbolize connection with the divine. In ancient Egypt the headdress of the goddess Ma'at was a single feather, which came to represent her. Ma'at's function is frequently translated to mean "truth," but more correctly means "the right order" (Norman). A single feather, then, could suggest it's time to get your life in order, i.e., to establish priorities; clarify your ambitions; plan goals; fulfill your dreams. It may be time to "feather your nest," or you may need "a feather in your cap." Is there a part of you that would like to "take flight"?

See **bird(s); flying; wind(s)**.

feces

See **defecate; excrement**.

feelings

See **emotion(s)**.

fence

Restrictions ("don't fence me in"); rules (family, societal); boundaries; inhibitions; self-control or consciousness (if wild animals are fenced in); obstacles; indecision ("sitting on the fence"). A pretty or decorative fence around a house may say you want/need privacy. Or do you need to "mend your fences" (rickety or broken fence)?

See **boundaries**.

ferry

As a water vehicle, a ferry can signal that you're attempting to acknowledge/resolve an emotion or information from your unconscious. It suggests that you're attempting to bring together/connect opposing forces in your life, or to bring about some other change. However, unless you're the ferry operator, you are not totally in charge and may be too passive in a current situation.

See **boat; bridge; water, vehicle(s)**.

field(s)

Freedom; fertility (flowers/grasses in the field); openness (a need for more?); your basic nature (especially if there are animals in the field); hopes/dreams; unlimited potentiality. If plowed, it may represent the *potential* for fertility/creativity (physical/mental); new growth; the womb. Is there some knowledge/sophistication you need to acquire or someone you need to cultivate? Wildflowers growing in the field often represent a release of restrictions/inhibitions.

The field may relate to your professional field/specialty. Consider the field's condition, action you take within it (or perhaps you're merely observing), and what you feel in the dream. A river, stream, pond, or spring in the field symbolizes unconscious or inner depths. Are the waters flowing, dammed in (controlled?), or filled with debris that disrupts the flow?

See **farm(er)** (if applicable); **landscapes/settings.**

fig/fig tree

Figs have been sacred and revered in many cultures. The fruit and tree (and its sap) symbolize fertility; a life-giving, nurturing element; abundance. Ripe, soft, and luscious, fruit can represent a female/female genitals. The tree has been a symbol for male genitals since ancient times. Fig leaves, which Adam and Eve used to cover themselves, may symbolize modesty; forbidden (sexual?) behavior; disobedience or defiance of authority, which sets the hero/heroine on the journey toward self-fulfillment. It can represent spiritual wisdom/insight, or the search/need for it, inasmuch as it was a fig tree *(Ficus religiosa)* under which the Buddha achieved enlightenment *(bodhi)*. Merlin Stone believes the sycamore *(Ficus sicomorus)* was the tree of the knowledge of good and evil in the Garden of Eden.

See **food; fruit(s)**.

fight/fighter

Inner turmoil; some aspect of

yourself at odds with another aspect of yourself, possibly an unacknowledged aspect fighting for its right to be heard. Is there a waking situation in which you're fighting for your space, ideals, your emotional, physical, or psychological survival? It may be an expression of anger toward present/past situations. (Dream figures should give a clue here.) If watching others fight, it suggests you may be unwilling to acknowledge your own turmoil or your role in a waking conflict.

See **attack; battle; hero/heroine; warrior**.

figure changes into someone else

See **transformation**.

film

See **movie**.

film star

See **person, famous**.

find/discover

To find something is to come in contact with some part of your psyche, or your past, that you've previously repressed, not acknowledged (inner qualities?), or not developed (new strengths?). Consider the symbolism of the specific object(s) you find; whether it is positive/negative, a lot/little, or a specific number; how easy/difficult it was for you to find (a statement about your efforts/abilities?). Perhaps it magically appeared, suggesting an archetypal motif.

In daily conversation we often say, "I find myself . . . [in the midst of, or feeling . . .]" What does your action/discovery say about your efforts in a current situation and your place in it? Perhaps you need to "find your bearings" psychologically/emotionally, or you may need to "find it in your heart" to take some action. Finding jewels/treasure can represent identifying something precious within yourself. Finding money reflects new energy; finding people suggests recognizing new resources or new aspects of yourself; identifying new facets of a relationship. The "find" or "treasure that is hidden" often relates to the development of the inner Self (Jung).

See **archeology; dig(ging); search(ing); Self; treasure**.

finger(s)

Finger/hand gestures have positive and negative meanings in all cultures. They are one form of signal for nonverbal communication (where the action is) or manipulation (get someone to do what you want).

Fingers can point (direction/authority issue), beckon (come closer), or dig deeper. They can symbolize physical/mental dexterity. Hands/fingers can hold, grip, release, and may be related to those actions as they apply to inner attitudes or outer situations. The ring finger, associated with love/marriage, can point to a relationship issue.

In some cultural dances, hand/finger gestures enhance the story told by the song/dance. In Eastern cultures, hand gestures (mudras) are related to spiritual ideas. If you're going to lose a finger, consider what that particular finger means to you; what it says about you; in what way your lifestyle or future actions will be hampered if you lose it. The fingers that helped the goddess Rhea give birth to Zeus became the Dactyls; hence fingers can symbolize small helpers of the unconscious (Jung). Since the hand has five fingers, fingers are related to the symbolisms of five/ten.

See **body; dwarf(s); hand(s).** If applicable, see **five; ring(s); ten**.

finish(ing)/finished

What are your feelings about finishing/completing something? At a loss, happy, satisfied? A dream finish could relate to: competition issues; procrastination and a reminder of something you need to finish; perseverance; financial/professional affairs ("I'm finished"); or to a relationship/project that has ended, or needs to be ended. If a race, are you in the audience, racing (need to slow down?), or are others using their energy (engines, horsepower?) to pass you by?

Finish can also relate to the exterior color/protection put on a piece of furniture, car, other object (if you were that object, what would the dream be saying about you?); or to "finishing school," where we add charm/poise to our exterior personas.

See **persona; lose/losing something; victor/victory**.

fire

One of the four basic elements, fire is considered a masculine, active symbol, and a representative of our spirit or energy. It can represent immortality; resurrection; destructive, consuming forces (especially when out of control); a source of nurturance and growth (fireplace, cooking). It sometimes represents powerful/overwhelming emotion (psychic intensity) or motivation (psychic energy), which can bring en-*lighten*-ment or destruction; hence, it is related to birth/death and renewal motifs. As a symbol of transformation, it may refer to the maturation process; the growth of spirituality (if flames are in the sky, or reaching toward it). Associated with the god Vulcan, it is related to volcanoes.

Menopausal women dream of fires more often than before menopause. People with AIDS and cancer may dream of spreading wildfires, reflecting the disease process (Siegel).

See **ashes; candle(s); fire engine; fireman; flame(s); volcano**.

fire engine

Resources available to fight whatever your dream fire symbolizes (out-of-control emotions?). Since we fight fire (masculine) with water (feminine), it may signal an attempt to: balance some inner issue or actual relationship; draw on your feminine aspect to help resolve a situation in which you've exerted too much masculine energy/effort; balance consciousness/reason (fire) with the unconscious/intuition (water).

See **fire; fireman**.

fireman

Since a fireman usually controls, or puts out, fires, your dream fireman may be attempting to control/quash an intense emotion (anger; lust?) you have ignited. He/she may be attempting to give you some needed "breathing space," or may represent cultural values/restrictions with which you are in conflict. It may be your psyche's way of attempting to balance an intense situation, or to tell you that your feelings about a relationship have become soggy or turned to ashes.

See **fire; fire engine**.

fireplace

The modern image of the archetypal "hearth," which refers to a place of emotional warmth; the heart of the home; family connectedness; the womb. If ashes in the fireplace, the dream may represent emotional barrenness; feelings that have died. Do you need to "light a fire" under yourself regarding some issue/relationship in which you've been procrastinating?

See **fire; home**.

first

First can be a position, an announcement of a date or the passage of time; a reflection of victory (a win/lose theme?) If you're first in line, first in a crowd, etc., this can refer to your being valued/undervalued in a waking situation. Did you have to fight your way there or did you simply "take first place"? It may relate to your birth order and symbolize all that goes with being the "first-born" in your family (responsibilities?). It can refer to ambition; your "need to get ahead" or your fears that you won't; issues of competition; academic skills ("first honors"). Conversely, it may be dealing with an issue of "last." It can represent feelings/anxieties about being judged.

See **competitor/competition; last; victor/victory**.

fish/fishing

For Jung, fish were symbols of some content from the unconscious, emotions, or life energy that's been stirring around in the unconscious from the beginning of our life. Therefore, fishing represents the search for, or process of becoming aware of, material from the unconscious. In this way fish can also symbolize the Self, or the inner Christ.

If the above doesn't seem to fit, consider a situation in which you/another have been acting like a "cold fish," or a "big fish in a little pond." You/another may have been "fishing for compliments" or other information; or behaving like "a fish out of water." Is there "something fishy" about some situation; or is someone more of a "queer fish" than you've realized?

Perhaps it's time to get a little rest and hang up a "gone fishing" sign in your window. If you *are* fishing, it can symbolize a wish to relieve present stress; a need to get away and ponder some situation; delving into the waters of the unconscious for insight/wisdom (especially deep-sea fishing). Eating fish would be incorporating new realizations or spiritual feelings/knowledge. If you're in the water, being eaten/swallowed by a large fish, this is the archetypal theme of the night-sea-journey (see Dreamercise #8, Chapter 2, Part 1).

Fish may suggest you need to look to earlier situations (experiences from younger years) for guidance in a present situation. Twin/double fishes can represent the astrological sign for Pisces, possibly someone born under that sign (February 20–March 21). Tiny fish in a bowl/container may represent sperm, a wish for sex or pregnancy. In many cultures, fish represent fertility and the preservation of life.

See **dock; hook; water**.

fist

Often a sign of aggression/hostility, a fist can also symbolize victory/triumph; emphasis, i.e., making a point you need to acknowledge. Perhaps you're feeling that someone isn't listening to you; or you're not listening to some aspect of yourself, and it's attempting to make itself known. Is some part of you "tight-fisted"?

In your mind's eye, review the dream. Have the person with the fist open it to see what may be contained inside or what happens (see Dreamercise #11, Part 1).

See **body; finger(s); hand(s)**.

five

Five is the symbol of humans and of their senses, and can symbolize an issue related to one or more of your five senses, or to an awakening of the senses and change. Five's related geometric symbol is the five-pointed star. In ancient Egypt, stars on the ceiling of a tomb represented the soul; therefore, archetypally, five is related to eternity; change; transformation; life/death and birth/rebirth issues. Consider the symbology of whatever appears in fives for additional clues.

Five and star are related to the apple, because when you cut an apple in half horizontally, the five seeds form the shape of a star, which also was the symbol of the goddess Kore (note the pun), an early female spirit representing the primal universe and feminine creation.

See **apple(s); number(s); star(s)**.

flag

A flag is a special signal ("flag it") to which you need to pay attention. Consider the designs/colors on the flag and its condition. If the flag of a company/country, consider what that country/company means to you. Flags are nonverbal messages of experience; affiliation; allegiance; patriotism; loyalty; and pride, so consider whether you have recently received a message, especially a nonverbal one, related to any of these concerns, or are pondering issues related to them. Flags are often regarded as feminine ("long may she wave"). Is it possible that your dream flag relates to yourself (if a female dreamer); a woman in your waking life; a cycle of time; your feminine aspect (if a male dreamer); or someone with the last name of Flag?

flame(s)

Sharing the symbolism of fire, flames that are smaller or reduced versions (as in candle flames) may be considered a potential, as opposed to a full-blown, fire. Is there a situation in which you're "adding fuel to the flames" by your behavior, or by keeping some emotion alive? It may refer to a present romantic situation (my "new flame")—that has the potential to get out of control?—or to past love relationships (my "old flame"), issues, memories, regrets, or missed opportunities.

See **candle(s); fire**.

flashlight

Searching; questioning—especially related to unconscious material or issues about which you're "in the dark." Mental illumination; sudden awareness; insight/intuition—a flash of light. As an elongated tool (male symbol) searching in a dark place, it can represent sexual intercourse.

float(ing)

If you're floating in water, in its positive sense, it can represent relaxation; taking it easy; the light feeling that results after releasing heavy emotions/issues. When your life is in balance (in whatever way you define that), you may experience "the incredible lightness of being." Perhaps it's a time when you need a respite from dipping into psychological issues.

Negatively, it may represent indecision; avoiding taking action (as opposed to swimming); a need for grounding and letting go of fantasy ("get your feet on the ground"); a situation in which you're drifting ("all afloat"); a financial issue ("float a loan"); a responsibility issue ("keep the business afloat"). Floating in the sky is related to flying, but again, a situation in which you're less active and take less responsibility.

See **flying; swimming; water**. If you're floating upward, see **ascend(ing); direction(s); up**.

flood

The release of emotions from the unconscious; intense emotions (positive/negative) that may seem overwhelming. Pregnant women, women on the verge of starting their menstrual periods, and people with lung problems often dream of floods/flooding (Garfield).

See **destruction; flow(ing); rain; water**.

flow(ing)

Flowing water can symbolize change; mobility; acceptance ("go with the flow"); the flow of wisdom, or of inner or collective knowledge. If, during its flowing, water becomes more dangerous, it suggests a change in emotion; however, water that changes its nature/depth/movement is typical in the dreams of pregnant women. Water or any fluid that's flowing/overflowing is a common symbol for menstrual blood and may occur immediately prior to/during a woman's period (Garfield).

See **water**.

flower(s)

Women tend to have more dreams about flowers than men. They may symbolize the woman herself; her budding sexuality; the first sexual act (to be "deflowered"); the flowering of new energies/ideas. Some flowers resemble women's sexual organs, while many resemble a mandala, the symbol of the Self.

Consider how you feel about flowers in general and what you feel/know about your particular flower. For instance, if you're allergic to flowers, they most likely have a negative meaning for you (some person or situation to which you are allergic, or should be). Or you may be, magically, nonallergic in the dream, in which case flower(s) may symbolize a part of you that has begun to bloom.

Flowers in a field can represent uninhibited emotions and letting your passion run wild, whereas flowers in a bouquet/vase indicate more control/restriction. Dying/dead flowers suggest some aspect of you is dying and needs more attention. Specific flowers and wreaths of flowers are widespread symbols for life after death; thus, the flower is often a symbol for the soul (von Franz).

Pregnant women often dream of exotic or richly blooming flowers in all kinds of unusual situations, symbolizing the body's creative power at this time (Siegel).

See **bee(s); color(s); garden;** and the specific flower.

flute

Since flute music has often been used to portray haunting, mystical, luring attractions, especially from the forest, the flute has come to be associated with, and can represent, mystical/supernatural/elemental beings; the forest; enchantment (fantasy, magic); the mysterious—especially hidden rites/rituals (expressions of natural instincts, primitive sexual behavior, or relationships with divinity). It can also represent the presence of "forbidden" things (emotions behavior, relationships?) toward which we are drawn.

Because of its elongated shape, the flute can represent masculine aspects, and from its ancient uses, it may represent male initiation rites; courtship; procreation. The traditional instrument of shepherds, it's related to the role of the peasant—or natural aspects of human (as opposed to royal or haughty)—to solitude; the symbolism of sheep; Jesus as the cosmic shepherd.

See **elemental being; forest; magic; sheep**.

fly

As an insect, a fly is a small irritant; a minor annoyance; "a fly in the ointment." As carriers of "dis-ease," their message can grow into something major if ignored.

See **infection; insects**.

flying

For most of us, flying dreams mean our body rises from the earth, but flying can also be symbolized by being inside flying vehicles (airplanes, helicopters, hot-air balloons?), in which case you're usually not flying under your own power. In the Freudian view, flying represents exhibitionistic wishes/tendencies; sexual pleasure; the desire to recapture childhood experiences of being rocked or of swinging. For Jungians, flying represents having a raised consciousness; seeing/needing a new perspective. Flying can represent a false sense of inflation; acting in a manner not true to yourself; not being grounded, hence split in your energy or intentions (flighty); "flying off the handle." Perhaps you need to "rise above it all." If your dream body is that of a young boy/girl, it may represent the desire to remain a child and not face responsibility (Peter Pan); immaturity. If flying in outer space, it may signal you're developing, or need to develop, the ability to look at yourself in relationship to the whole world, or the entire universe. You may be expanding your spiritual life, since flying can also represent a union of spirit/matter.

Consider the ease/difficulty with which you fly, what you see (your viewpoint) while flying, and what you do. What do you gain by adopting or maintaining this perspective? Don't forget to look down and see what you're flying over (some aspect of yourself you're ignoring/denying?).

See **ascend(ing)**.

flying saucer

See **UFO**.

fog/mist

Fertility; growth and renewal. As "upper waters," fog and mist represent the spirit/divine realm. Ethereal and intermediary (not quite clouds, not quite rain), fog or mist may represent the unconscious; anything that's hidden/obscure in your life; a stage of transition. It may refer to a situation in which you're feeling gray/gloomy, "waiting for the fog to clear," or about which you "haven't the foggiest idea." You may be expressing a fear that someone/something in your waking life is not solid enough, or a wish that you'd like to disappear for a while.

follow(er)

The dream could be telling you that this is a characteristic way you behave in certain situations and that you need to become more of a leader; or by way of compensation, that you've been leading too much and need to take a less active or powerful role. You may be wishing to give up certain leadership responsibilities.

It may be a message to "follow your . . . instincts . . . dreams . . . heart . . . star/destiny." Whomever/whatever you're following may be a message that you are "being led on" sexually (following a man?); your instincts rather than your intellect are ruling (following an animal?); or that you are following, or need to follow, old rules/beliefs (an elderly/authoritative leader, a parent).

See **followed; lead; leader/leading**.

followed

Being followed can be an assertion of leadership, which can be gratifying or scary. It may say you're ready to take control or leadership, or, conversely, that you're not ready. The person/animal following you can represent unfinished business: repressed emotions, old memories/situations, regrets. If a nightmare, use the dream changing/confronting techniques from dreamercises in Part 1 (see Dreamercises #3, #11, #19).

See **pursued/pursuer/pursuing**.

food

For many of us, food symbolizes caring; nurturing; security. Consider the kind of food and the action you're taking with respect to it (eating, feeding someone, being fed, preparing/serving a meal?). Is this typical waking behavior, or is it expressing a deficiency/need? Liquids, milk, soft/mushy foods, or being fed may symbolize a need to be a baby (less responsible) again; possibly a need to regress for renewal. If you have foods you especially eat during stressful times—comfort foods—and they appear in your dream, it may signal that you need to take care of yourself or your inner child. Because we take in food through, and speak with, the mouth, food can symbolize nurturing your ability or right to self-expression—or the opposite, inhibiting or preventing your expression (depending on dream action).

Food can represent an offering of unconscious energy; intellectual wisdom ("food for thought"); as well as have religious/traditional/familial symbolism in that a particular food is always served at certain sacred or family gatherings. If you're dieting, food can symbolize temptation. Feeding an animal suggests you're nurturing/developing your unconscious instincts or a more primitive aspect of yourself. Storing food may relate to feelings of emptiness/neediness or to hoarding needs (I'll never get enough).

See **eating** and specific foods.

fool

See **clown; trickster**.

foot/feet

Feet symbolize our foundation; stability; our "under-standing." They can represent your roots; basic/earthy knowledge; your "standing" in a community/group; your need/fear to "take a stand" or to get "down to earth." Injury to the foot can reflect anxiety about any of the preceding. Do you have your "feet on the ground," need to "stand on your own two feet," or do you, or someone else, have "feet of clay"?

Are you receiving enough support or experiencing anxiety about some lack of support? Perhaps you need to get back on your feet psychologically and the dream is showing you how. Are you "dragging your feet"? Issues of freedom/spontaneity may be involved in being fearful of stepping forward or out. Do you wish you could be more "footloose and fancy-free"? Feet can also represent mobility and direction through life ("on the right path," "going in the wrong direction").

The sole of the foot may be a pun on being/feeling like the sole (only) support of some person/situation; or it may refer to a need to connect with your soul, or inner spirit. The Achilles' heel is particularly vulnerable, but the heel may also suggest a need for healing.

See **body; footprint(s); shoes; walk(ing)**.

football

Shares some of the same symbolism as baseball. In addition, football can symbolize anger/hostility; pent-up energy needing expression; feelings of being kicked around. The two opposing teams may represent opposing aspects of yourself that need to be reconciled, possibly top-dog/underdog. Ball changes could represent your vacillation about making a decision. If observing a football game, it may represent your inability/reluctance to become involved in some "battle," or lack of team cooperation. As with all games, there may be some conflict in your life that you're attempting to make less of, or deny its importance, by turning it into a game.

See **baseball; game(s); sporting events; victor/victory**.

footprint(s)

Footprints hint of something missed; an idea/energy/path to follow; someone who is never quite there for you. Perhaps you're following in someone's footsteps (or someone is following in yours), which may represent pride; heritage; transmission of special knowledge/skills; lack of originality; or your feelings about any of those situations. Footprints can also beckon you to follow a particular path.

See **follow(er); foot/feet**.

force(ing)/forced

If forcing someone to do something, it suggests power; strength; dominion; issues related to feelings of power (overpowering?), competition, and victory. Someone forcing you to do something can reflect the same issues, but may also help you come into contact with inner messages about weakness, inability, helplessness/powerlessness. Trying to force a lock may reflect an impasse; knowledge/insight closed off to you; the need to change direction and find the key. Unknown forces most likely represent emotions/energies within you seeking expression.

forces of nature

Instincts; feelings; the power of the unknown (the unconscious); remnants of childhood feelings when we were powerless with respect to adults; anxieties about destructive natural occurrences, especially if you've been in a tornado, earthquake, etc. Dreams involving a destructive or powerful force of nature at work are common during crises or transitional times, and may represent the emotional upheaval/change occurring (Siegel).

See **destruction; earthquake; end of the world**.

forehead

If wrinkled, it may symbolize worries/burdens; an active thinking process; pride in your intellectual capacities. In Eastern tradition, the forehead is the location of the third eye (the ajna center/chakra), symbolic of psychic and spiritual opening, inner or higher awareness.

foreign country

A foreign/unknown aspect of yourself or your psyche; your associations to a particular country or someone from that country/heritage.

See **abroad/traveling abroad; person, foreign**.

foreigner

See **person, foreign**.

foreplay

Certainly foreplay can refer to actual sexual feelings concerning someone in your waking life, but it can also represent some project/relationship that needs more preparation before completion. It can represent "pregame" options available to you; a need to arouse interest toward some waking situation; warming up to someone/something (not "starting out cold"); a developing passion/excitement about a project; anticipation of the fulfillment of some relationship/project.

See **sex**.

forest

The unconscious; the unknown; the hidden/mysterious; secrets; fertility. It may contain, or represent, wild animals (instincts, your wildest dreams?), fairies/elemental beings (unconscious energy), the potential for physical or spiritual healing, i.e., inner guides, nature (natural?) priests/priestesses. It can refer to innocence (a "babe in the woods") or to a situation not yet resolved ("not out of the woods yet"). You may be so bogged down in some issue that you "can't see the forest for the trees." The sacred grove, a uterine symbol, always had a pillar or stone inside it, representing the male element for balance/unity.

See **tree(s)**. If applicable, see **animal(s); dark/darkness; elemental being**.

forget/forgot

Dreaming that you forgot an appointment may be your unconscious helpfully reminding you of an engagement, or something related to time that you need to remember/consider. Often in exam dreams you realize you've forgotten to study or attend class, which suggests stresses/anxieties about a current situation/project. Forgetting your purse, wallet, or other items linked to your identity can reflect changes in your life role, and insecurities/anxieties about that; perhaps you're not yet recognizing clearly who you are in the new situation.

During pregnancy, it's not uncommon, especially for working mothers, to dream of forgetting the now-born dream baby. Such dreams can represent fears about one's adequacy as a parent and are positive if they serve as a stimulus to seek emotional support (Siegel).

fork

Although an eating utensil, the fork often represents other issues such as force/coercion; being robbed of something emotionally important to you ("fork it over"); a fork in the road related to a new opportunity/choice and/or fear about having to make a decision.

If applicable, see **crossroads**.

fort/fortress

Earlier, wilder times; defenses against strong emotions, which may be threatening to break through into your awareness.

See **castle**.

fortune-teller/ fortune-telling

Fears/anxieties about the future; wishes to know the unknown; attitudes about control, or lack of it; fate/hope issues ("it's in the cards"). If a Gypsy fortune-teller, she may represent foreign (repressed, unacknowledged) or exotic aspects of yourself calling for expression.

See **Gypsy**.

forward

Moving forward suggests moving toward the future and the accomplishment of your goals; not restricted; confident. Moving forward slowly or with hesitancy may reflect caution, uncertainty, indecision—possibly fear—about a commitment issue or other waking situation/relationship.

See **foot/feet; direction(s); move(ing); movement**.

fountain

Spurting or flowing water can relate to ejaculation or to menstrual fluid, respectively. The fountain's shape may suggest a womb. It can represent the flow of the life process. Depending on the experiences in, or around, the fountain, it may reflect anxieties about aging ("seeking the fountain of youth"), or regrets. If circular, or in the center of a town square, it may represent the Self (Jung).

See **flow(ing); water**.

four

Connected with the four-sided square in geometry, four is the pattern for the building/ordering of the psyche (individuation) and the world: four elements (air, earth, fire, water), directions, seasons, phases of the moon, four parts of the Jewish name for God (Joh-Heh-Vau-Heh), four New Testament evangelists (Matthew, Mark, Luke, and John), four prophets of the Old Testament (Isaiah, Jeremiah, Ezekiel, Hosea), and the phases of the alchemical process (see **black; gold(en); red; white**).

When four appears in your dreams, it symbolizes your orientation to reality; you should examine, or are examining, the boundaries of your world and your place within it.

Four is always an important signal that concerns you personally and should not be ignored (Jung). It often marks the beginning of a new cycle in your creative energy. In alchemy as in numerology, it is said that one joins three to form four, a synthesis. Therefore, four is a psychological sign of the growth of consciousness or the striving toward wholeness.

If four appears as a square, consider the relationship of the square in the formation of a mandala, which represents the ever-unfolding Self. In alchemy, the squaring of the circle was one of the methods for producing the philosopher's stone, the lapis/Self (Jung).

Considered a feminine number, four may represent feminine aspects/needs. Pay particular attention to the fourth person in a dream, as he/she may represent your anima/animus, or shadow.

See **emperor; mandala; square; three**.

fox

Folklore foxes are often portrayed as clever, trickster figures, so a dream fox may represent the cunning, "sly as a fox" aspects of you/another. A reddish fox may represent a redheaded person in your life, especially one who also has "foxy" or sexy attributes, or your own desire to be foxy. Is there a situation in your life in which you need to be resourceful ("smart as a fox," "crazy like a fox")? If your association is that of a fox hunt, or being chased, it may represent competition, especially at work; a situation in which someone is after your position, or in which you have to "stay ahead of the game." Is there some situation/relationship in which: you feel you have to "run for your life"; your emotional/physical life is being threatened; you feel like you're being pursued relentlessly without regard to your feelings?

See **animal(s); chase(d)** (if applicable); **follow(er); followed** (if applicable).

free/freedom

Having new opportunities available; removal of emotional restrictions; the success of personal growth (''free to be yourself''); the ending, or approaching resolution, of a waking conflict/crisis; a new, more expansive role/position, or a need for one; a wish/need to escape (''free as a bird'').

See **cage; chain(s)/chained; escape; isolated; prison/prisoner**.

friend(s)

If known, but the dream situation doesn't reflect an actual waking situation, the image/character may represent characteristics you need to incorporate/recognize in yourself. If unknown, it can represent inner support; newly developing inner resources.

See **person, known**.

frog(s)

Fertility; creativity; resurrection. Since it is a lunar/water creature, those symbols (see **moon/moonlight; water**) may also apply to the understanding of your dream. Like a butterfly, a frog can represent transformation; a signal that you're ready for another leap from one stage of life into another. According to von Franz, frogs represent the ending of a stage of psychological sterility; an unconscious impulse that has a tendency to become conscious (von Franz).

As a tadpole, it can represent immaturity; unresolved childhood issues. Tadpoles can symbolize sperm and/or future growth potential, and sometimes appear in dreams at or around the time of conception (Garfield). They are common in the first-trimester dreams of pregnant women.

A dream focus around a frog can express the fairy-tale motif about the frog who has to be kissed before he can return to being the prince he really is; therefore, issues about who you really are; wholeness; inner beauty versus outer appearance; acceptance. Frogs sometimes represent communication problems (''a frog in your throat'').

See **moon/moonlight; reptile(s); water**.

front/in front

The front of a body/house/car can represent your own front, the facade/persona you put on for public life (''putting up a good front''). If you're in front of a group, it can represent leadership strength/difficulty, or relate to communication/honesty issues (''being up front''). Something that's in front of you can represent an obstacle; a situation that needs to be confronted; future opportunities. Considered more vulnerable (soft) than the back/spine, the front of the body may relate to an issue/relationship in which you feel vulnerable. Have you been insulted or experienced a real/imaginary affront?

See **back; face; leader/leading); position(s); victor/victory**.

frozen

Shut-off/repressed feelings, which could reflect your lifestyle and personality, or could have occurred as a result of trauma and, therefore, be temporarily protective; sexually uncaring, aloof, or frigid; defensiveness; the end of a relationship; lack of inner mobility/creativity, hence rigidity ("frozen stiff") in dealing with a situation/relationship.

See **cold; ice; thaw(ing)**.

fruit(s)

Ripeness; abundance; fertility; earthly desires; a project that's finally "bearing fruit." It's related to the egg because at its center is the seed of the future. When cut open, some fruits (bananas, cucumbers, melons) exhibit the archetypal mandala shape (symbol of the Self) in the center. Forbidden/unreachable fruits may symbolize temptation. Consider the number of fruits, their shape (masculine or feminine imagery), and the specific kind of fruit.

Round fruits may represent the breast. Luscious, soft fruits can symbolize females, female sexuality, female genitals. Pregnant women often dream of ripening or burstingly ripe fruit, as do women on the verge of having their menstrual period (Garfield). Elongated fruit (banana) can symbolize males, male sexuality, the penis.

See **egg(s); mandala**.

fuel

Life energy. If coal (comes from the ground), it may represent unconscious instincts, while gasoline may represent the more refined/civilized aspects of those energies. Consider how it's being used/wasted; whether it's being contained/spilled; the kind of vehicle (if any) it's powering. Food is sometimes referred to as fuel for the body, so dream fuel can relate to food, nourishment, or addiction issues.

See **food; vehicle(s)**.

full moon

See **moon/moonlight**.

fun

Having fun, or watching others have fun, may signal that

you need to include more fun in your waking life; excitement or the anticipation of a soon-to-be exciting event; a release from negativity; resolution of a waking issue/conflict.

If applicable, see **amusement park; celebration; laugh/laughter**.

funeral

Whether you are close to death or not, a fairly common funeral dream is one in which you're a mourner watching other mourners. If you're nearing death, a funeral dream may relate to your feelings about your own death and what happens afterwards. If you're not physically ill/dying, the dream may be helping you deal with/recognize dead or repressed aspects of yourself. Or perhaps it's time for you to join the living, and acknowledge/express some not-quite-buried feelings.

If attending someone else's funeral, consider what aspects of that person are, or might be, like you. The dream could represent the death of a relationship or way of life; or some feeling (resentment, anger, hostility toward someone?) that you're clinging to, but that, for your growth, needs to be ''dead and buried.'' If a funeral for a still-living parent, you may be expressing a need to separate from him/her, or from parental restrictions/training. It may be easier to see that parent dead than do the appropriate growth work; or the symbolic death may give you the courage to take the next step in your inner work. If the funeral of a recently deceased parent, it may be part of your necessary mourning process.

See **burial/buried; death; person, dead**.

furniture/furnishings

Household furniture/furnishings are closely related to the way we feel about ourselves and our family relationships. They may be comfortable pieces, which fit so well, and are related to our body image. They may be worn-out pieces that we need to discard. Old/antique pieces can represent outdated attitudes/feelings, or feelings about past family/home relationships, your heritage.

See also the specific piece of furniture.

furry

Pregnant women often dream of small, furry mammals (puppies, seals, kittens). If you're not pregnant, it may symbolize a new, creative project.

gag

Restricted communication; a suspicion that you're not receiving the whole truth ("gag order"); your own inability to express yourself as well as you'd like. Gag also suggests being nauseous, so it may refer to some situation that's difficult for you to swallow/accept.

See **vomit(ing)**.

galaxy

Traveling in/to another galaxy, or seeing one, speaks of expanding horizons; new worlds open to you; transcending old ways. If you've been doing spiritual growth work, it may represent developing wholeness; a new awareness of yourself; a feeling of oneness with divinity/spirit—or the search for these. It may represent involvement with an ecological group/plan.

See **star(s); sun/sunlight; UFO; universe; world**.

gamble/gambling

Taking risks; tempting/relying on fate; courting Lady Luck; not taking responsibility for your decisions; feelings/attitudes about good/bad luck; self-esteem (winner, loser, victim?); obsessive traits you can't give up. If you're an uptight/restricted person, the dream may be saying you need to take a chance, or let up on yourself. If not, it may be telling you that you should reconsider some issue/situation and get more information, not rely on fate.

See **cards/playing cards; game(s)**.

game(s)

Depending on the game, it can symbolize competition with others/yourself; an opportunity (''fair game''); team cooperation/planning; vicarious experience/adventure; sublimation of sexuality/aggression (especially team sports); willingness to enter into some situation (''I'm game''). Life is sometimes referred to as a game, so the dream game can symbolize your life's pathway; the rules you ''play'' by (a clean or dirty game); your success/struggles in resolving opposing aspects of yourself (your opponents). Is there some situation in which you're ''playing the waiting game''? You may need to examine some issue/relationship/project more thoroughly in order to ''know the name of the game,'' or to ''beat someone at his own game.'' Perhaps you've been, or fear you'll be, found out (''the game's up'').

See specific games: **baseball; cards/playing cards; football; tennis**. Also **competitor/competition; lose/losing something; sporting events; victor/victory**.

game warden

Your conscience; society's rules/restrictions; that aspect of you that watches and controls instinctual/wild behavior. It lets you have only so much (your quota) and no more. Consider how the game warden is treating you for additional clues. If too restrictive, or your quota is too low, you may need to work on self-esteem issues.

See **hunt(ing); police**.

gangsters

The ''bad guy'' part of you, perhaps angry, hostile feelings, or rebellious/defiant ones; your shadow aspect. If you're at the mercy of gangsters, pent-up feelings may be holding you hostage, i.e., threatening to emerge and overwhelm you (''shoot you down''?). Who/what is ''ganging up on'' you?

garage

If containing a car, it suggests energy/goals at rest or not being used; reserve energy you can draw on (especially if spare batteries or auto supplies are kept there also). Consider the state of the garage (well cared for, leaky?). If you have difficulty getting into the garage, it may be a signal that everything else comes first before rest/recreation (a workaholic?). Some garages are places where men pursue a hobby or store their tools; therefore, a symbol of creativity; fertility; sexuality; masculine competency. Garages can symbolize resources; compulsive/anal tendencies (where everything you can't give up is stored). Are old, outdated modes of thinking/beliefs/attitudes/values stored in that garage?

See **car; vehicle(s)**.

garbage

Although it may seem apparent that this probably symbolizes useless, leftover "stuff" from your past, it may also be saying that someone/something in your present life isn't as nice (up front, honest, special?) as you may have thought at first. It may be a signal that things are being stirred up in your psyche; a first step toward transformation (compost heap).

garden

How does your garden grow? If flowering and well cared for, it may symbolize fertility; creativity; ideas you're cultivating; the flourishing of your inner life. If not, it may represent an aspect of yourself that needs to be cultivated/fertilized/tended to. What do you need to weed out?

A formal garden may symbolize order/symmetry; following the rules. If square/round, it may symbolize a mandala, hence the blossoming of the Self. A walled garden may symbolize private parts of yourself that you're keeping secret or protecting from others. Especially in the dreams of pubescent girls, a small mound/hill in the garden may symbolize the mons veneris, the area where pubic hair grows (Garfield).

Gardens also symbolize balance/harmony; the divine order (to garden is to get in touch with the spirit of the land); the union of the divine and the material; mastery over nature, hence over instincts. Consider your personal symbolism of the plants growing in the garden for additional clues.

It's common for pregnant women to dream of incredibly fertile gardens with exotic or richly blooming flowers and luscious fruits, all symbolizing the body's creative powers during this time (Siegel).

See **circle; Eden, Garden of; gate; square; wall(s)**.

gardener

The wise or nurturing part of yourself that helps ground you and aids you in growing/flourishing. Archetypally, it may be an expression of the Self.

See **caretaker; garden**.

garland

Linkage/connection; victory; festivity/celebration. When presented as a circle, a garland is also the symbol of the feminine and the mandala.

See **celebration; game(s); mandala**.

garnet

See **ruby**.

gasoline

Something that has the power to motivate or get you going, but also has the potential to be explosive/dangerous; personal energy/drive, or the lack of it (depending on dream situation); reserve energy (a full tank); potentially inflaming thoughts/emotions.

gate

An opening/entryway, and therefore, entry into a new stage/way of life; the threshold between conscious/unconscious material. If you're able to open the gate and enter, it suggests readiness and success, perhaps the end of a crisis time. If you have difficulty opening it, where are you stuck? If the gate is barred, it suggests that you're being denied access to whatever is on the other side (paradise? freedom?). How are you restricting yourself? A rusted gate may symbolize resources within yourself that you've not drawn upon for a long time.

See **door; fence; wall(s)**.

gazelle

A traditional symbol of the soul. Associated with the heart chakra, it's also related to issues of love/relationship ("heart problems"). It would also not be unusual for someone who's having physical heart symptoms (palpitations, chest pain) to dream of a gazelle.

gem(s)

Gems/precious stones suggest something valued/treasured, often the Self. In gemology lore, each stone is considered to give off certain vibrations/energy and, therefore, to offer certain protection, cures, or promote certain attitudes.

See **jewel(s)** and the particular gem; **Self.**

genitals

Most often genitals will appear as other images according to their shape: containers, abyss, canal, canyon for female genitals; elongated, pointed objects for male genitals. Usually when actual genitals appear, the rest of the body appears also (as in having sex, or appearing nude in public). Emphasis on genitals refers to your sexuality; how you feel about it; and current/changing attitudes toward masculinity/femininity; issues of commitment, pleasure, and their relationship to one another in your value system.

See **body; ejaculation; orgasm; penis/phallus; sex; vagina**.

ghost(s)

Primordial form of the spirit (soul); embodiment of the image-creating activity of the unconscious. Depending on its message/wisdom, it may represent the archetypal Wise Old Man or Woman. The spirit may also appear as a gnome, boy, or talking animal. Is there something in your life that has about it a sense of being unreal?

The ghost may be an expression of outdated modes of behavior/memories/regrets that are still haunting you. The dream may be expressing a feeling/fear that you "don't have a ghost of a chance" in some situation/relationship. Freud thought that dream ghosts represented infantile memories of a mother figure (in a white nightgown?) who looked in on her "sleeping" child.

See **boy; gnome; Wise Old Man; Wise Old Woman**.

giant

Primordial feelings; unbridled passion; the tremendous force/energy of the unconscious. The presence of a giant may serve to amplify anything else in the dream, or signal the mythical, archetypal quality of the dream. He/she may represent earlier dreaded (if threatening) or loved (if protective) adults. Are there numbers or other clues to guide you to what time or part of your past the giant may represent?

The giant can also be the guardian of the treasure that is the unconscious or the Self. As a guardian, giants are related to serpents/dragons. The mythological giant is often a guardian of higher realms who must be overcome/bypassed before we can have access to divine secrets. In Jungian theory he is linked with the precious (extraordinary) child motif and can, therefore, represent the yet-to-be-realized childhood aspect of the collective psyche—the "childhood" that's greater than your personal childhood. In esoteric/metaphysical thought, giants often represent elemental spirits (see **elemental being**) related to, or of, air/wind (see **air; wind(s)**).

See **dwarf(s)**. If applicable, see **dragon; serpent**.

gift/giving

Since all aspects of the dream are yourself, to get or to give a gift means you're attending to/acknowledging yourself in some way. Consider what aspect of yourself is giving and what aspect is receiving, as well as the nature of the gift. It can refer to talents/skills that you've yet to realize/utilize. If you receive the gift, in your waking associations, ask yourself, "If I could place this gift anywhere in my body, where would it go and how should I use it?" This may give you additional clues as to its meaning.

If the giver/receiver is someone you know in waking life, then the symbolism also relates to elements of that relationship: needing/receiving support; giving yourself to another (which may reflect openness/genuineness or impulsiveness/recklessness); the "give and take" of a relationship or its sexual aspects.

If the gift is negative, consider whether: someone has given you away (betrayed you); you've given yourself away (exposed a secret); you feel emotionally discarded/discounted. The gift may relate to issues you have about acceptance (of yourself/others); what you/another have to offer; neediness/independence issues.

See **Christmas tree**.

girl

If you're an adult female, she can indicate your playful, innocent, childlike nature; your inner child; other positive aspects the dream girl expresses; an immature aspect of yourself that needs to grow; some aspect of yourself at the dream age that you've ignored and now need to recognize.

If you're a male, she can reflect an underdeveloped or developing feminine aspect (anima) of yourself; your feelings about some girl who's important to you and exhibits similar or opposite physical/psychological characteristics as the dream figure. Consider how she's dressed and acts for additional clues.

For both sexes, she can represent your daughter, if you have one.

See **anima; boy; child/children; daughter; family; Self; sister**.

glacier

Some aspect of yourself that's frozen/repressed, but that you fear holds the potential for destruction if released.

See **frozen; ice**.

glass

Because of its transparency, glass is often a symbol of light; openness; nondefensiveness. Yet it can also represent an invisible emotional barrier you've put around yourself. Have you needed to activate this lately, or is it always with you? Deliberately breaking glass may indicate a new openness or feeling of security/confidence. If you're looking through a glass window, there may be a person in waking life you need to "see through," or a situation/relationship you need to examine more closely. Opaque/dirty glass that you can't see through may indicate secrets; confusion; privacy; someone you suspect is keeping something from you.

If applicable, see **break(ing)/ broken; look(ing)/looked at; window(s)**.

glasses

See **eyeglasses**.

globe

Ecology issues; feeling connected to something larger than your ego; the ability to stand outside yourself and examine an issue; the Self. The dreams and hallucinatory experiences of dying persons often take the shape of a luminous globe of light, sometimes with stretchable arms and legs, that has come to help the transition process (Moody).

See **earth; planet(s); world**.

gloves

Their symbolism is closely related to that of the hands. They can be used for decoration; protection; aggression (boxing). They may refer to a situation that you need to "handle with kid gloves"; a situation in which you've been threatened ("throw down the gauntlet") or feel you need to protect/take care of yourself, possibly by being more assertive.

See **clothes/clothing; fight/ fighter** (if applicable); **hand(s)**.

gnats

Minor disturbances, which, if left unattended to, have the potential to fly together and become major annoyances.

See **insects**.

gnome

Jung speculated that gnome-like creatures, especially in the dreams of women, represented their inner spirit or animus; the capability for conscious spiritual effort. In the dreams of men, a gnome may represent the higher personality; that aspect of the personality capable of higher development (if positive); the infantile shadow aspect (if negative).

See **boy; elemental being**.

goat

Fertility; nurturing; aspirations/competition (king of the mountain); someone who's made lecherous approaches ("an old goat"); sacrifice (the goat was often a sacrificial animal); a situation involving anger/frustration ("get someone's goat"); someone born under the astrological sign for Capricorn (December 23–January 20).

See **animal(s)**.

goddess

For a female dreamer, try to determine if the goddess, or a woman who has goddesslike attributes, is a specific goddess, and consider the myth related to her. (For help, see Bolen or Walker in the bibliography.) She could represent the activation of, or need to activate, a particular kind of archetypal energy in your life, since, according to von Franz, each god/goddess represents a specific pattern of behavior. Then again, it may mean you're feeling demeaned and need to elevate yourself. If you're a man, the goddess can represent your anima, or ideal woman.

going to confession

See **confession/going to confession**.

gold(en)

Something precious, perhaps royal; therefore, your own worth/high value; another's value; a signal that you should reconsider the value of a relationship/situation. Gold is a solar (see **sun/sunlight**) symbol and relates to cycles; eternity; the divine or cosmic spirit/intelligence. In alchemy, it represented the final stage of transformation, *rubedo*.

See **color(s); individuation; money; Self**.

goose/geese

Probably one of the most well-known archetypal images for most of us is Mother Goose, a benevolent witch/midwife, who represented the Great Mother. The goose was one of the symbols of the Egyptian god Amon, from whom we derive our word *amen*. The Nile goose, which laid the golden egg of the sun, was one of the forms in which the goddess Hathor appeared. In the fairy tale "Jack and the Beanstalk," Jack stole a goose that laid golden eggs, representing that Jack had undertaken the hero's quest and found his inner, precious Self.

More mundanely, there may be some waking situation in which you're being "a silly goose." If you've ever seen a goose on a farm, then you know they can be quite aggressive and may, therefore, represent an attacker/threat in your waking life. However, if you've seen geese migrating, you realize that they also may reflect leadership; precision; and organization.

See **bird(s)**.

gossip

Consider whether you're a part of the gossip "grapevine," or outside it, which will show your active/passive relationship to the message. Dream gossip may also be related to issues (anxiety?) about secrecy, privacy, exposure, and trust.

graduation

If there's a pending graduation in waking life, the dream may reflect the anxieties/excitement associated with that event, as well as the changes that will occur—the disruption of old ways as a result of growth/progress. If it's a past graduation of yours or isn't related to someone you know, then, depending on what part you play in the scene, it may reflect a time of transition; growth; new or added responsibilities/opportunities; a sense of accomplishment/completion.

See **initiation**.

Grail

It's unlikely that "the Grail" itself will appear in your dreams—except as a cup/chalice—but you may dream of many images that relate to the Grail, for the Grail search is a metaphor for every person's search for/movement toward realization of potential, spiritual growth, wholeness (Jung). It's the bridge between consciousness and the unconscious, the journey from ignorance to enlightenment.

See **chalice, cup(s)**.

grain(s)

Grains—especially wheat, barley, seeding grasses—symbolize the continuation/renewal of life. However, when one is dying or close to death, it's not uncommon to dream of fields of grain, of fires destroying them, or of them being mowed and harvested (von Franz). Poppies and pomegranates are associated with grain because they were sacred to the Greek Grain Mother, Demeter (Roman, Cybele), who has the ability to induce sleep and dreams, and is one metaphorical image of the Self.

See **bunch; vegetation**.

grandparents

Heritage; ancient or outdated characteristics/behaviors. Your personal grandfather, or any grandfather/elder, may symbolize the Wise Old Man archetype, your inner spirit. His message may provide needed insight/wisdom. A grandmother/female elder may represent your personal grandmother; the Great Mother, the crone aspect of female personality.

Grandparents often gave us a kind of unrestricted love we didn't get from parents, so the appearance of a grandparent may suggest that this is a present need. Or if you receive it in the dream, it may be a reassurance that you're okay.

See **crone; family; relatives; Wise Old Man**.

grape(s)

Fertility, especially when seen in bunches; the raw material of transformation. They also carry associations/meanings similar to wine and vine.

See **fruit(s); gossip; vine(s); wine**.

grass

Fertility; growth; the passage of time; cycles, especially if dead, dying, or brown. If wild grass, it shares some of the same symbology as fields. Lawn grass, well-kept and mowed, suggests feelings/personal growth that's controlled and/or attended to. If overgrown/neglected, it may symbolize emotions or passions that are out of control and need tending. In Jungian terms green grass represents our vegetative processes, i.e., the automatic functioning of our various bodily systems; basic life functioning.

See **field(s); green**.

grave

The earth mother; the womb. The dream may be a signal that: you've lost contact with your feminine spirit/energy; there's a "grave matter" to which you need to attend; there's a waking situation you wish you could end. Grave dreams are often turning-point dreams if their message suggests this is your last chance. If you have a continuing series of similar dreams over a period of time, you may be stuck in an impasse or depression, and the dream is a signal that you need to seek therapy/counseling.

See **burial/buried; cemetery; death; gravestone; tomb; vault**.

gravestone

People who are terminally ill may dream of their gravestone and what they want it to say/reflect. If you're not ill, consider whose gravestone it is and the message or symbols on it for more clues. It can reflect a statement about your life, or some forgotten/buried aspect of yourself, which now needs to be identified/acknowledged.

See **cemetery; grave**.

graveyard

See **cemetery**.

gray

Depression; sad feelings; energy that's shut off/inaccessible. Although it's also a color of humility/penitence, it can just as easily represent neutrality; indifference; inertia.

See **color(s); fog/mist**.

Great Mother

An archetypal figure who symbolizes our origins; our own body; the womb; nature; our unconscious life; the collective unconscious; the matrix/original pattern; foundations; the source. She is the mother of life/death and is related to the cosmic waters out of which life emerged originally. She may appear as an Earth Mother or earthy woman; and when she does, things are going to happen—a new development is occurring or on the way. In Hinduism she is Śakti, the source, the breath, the goddess of the spoken word.

See **mother**.

Greek/Greece

If you're not associated with Greece or its people, the symbolism definitely resides in your own associations, especially ones you've derived from reading/movies. For many, the archetypal Greek is the literary/movie character Zorba. If true for you, your Greek may signal that you're worrying too much and need to live more in the here and now, get more in touch with your inner self, your feelings. Or perhaps you should "beware of Greeks bearing gifts."

Greece also represents for many an early seat of learning, therefore consciousness. As it is the historical location for well-known oracles, your dream may be a signal to attend to your wisdom messages, or the Greek character may be the equivalent of your Wise Old Man archetype, or any Greek god/goddess archetype. It could also be saying you need to explore your own divinity or begin a spiritual search.

Many Jungians believe that the themes of Greek mythology are still active in our personal lives/culture. Thus, to dream of anything related to Greece may be a signal that you need to consider the nature of your own personal myth, or how a particular Greek myth is active in your own life. It may signal an issue about which you're confused ("it's Greek to me").

See **abroad/traveling abroad; person, foreign; travel(ing)/journey**.

green

In color symbologies, green represents nature/fertility; feelings/sensation; individualism; life/growth; divinity. Ecclesiastically, it symbolizes the Holy

Ghost. It is the attribute of the Greek love goddess Venus (Aphrodite). Negatively, it can reflect being "green with envy." In alchemy, green represented the second stage in the process of transformation, often associated with the tail of the peacock.

See **color(s); emerald(s); grass; growth/growing**.

gremlin(s)

See **elemental being**.

grief

When you're in the mourning process and resolving your grief, dreams are often more vivid because the unconscious has been activated. Kennedy defines grief stages as shock, descent (longest phase), and emergence. Shock-stage dreams offer comfort. (The deceased may appear alive in the dream.) Descent-stage dreams contain much dark symbolism, cleaning activities (objects, rooms), and images that in some way give you courage to keep going. Emergence-stage dreams (occurring about one year after death) depict moving into a new sense of yourself or a new life. Something new is born or appears in the dream.

Kuiken reports that in adjusting to loss, the type of dream most likely to occur was associated with the dreamer's psychological reaction to the loss. Anxiety dreams (associated with feelings of psychological numbness) were more frequent during the first year following loss. Existential dreams (depicting explicit sadness, separation and loss, distinct emotional shifts within the dream) became more frequent after one to five years; transcendent dreams (magical, ecstatic, the dreamer having extraordinary powers) can begin to occur from three to five years after loss. While all three may produce affective insight, it's more prominent with existential dreaming.

See **emotion(s); impasse**.

grind(ing)

Consider the symbolism of the object being ground. If a weapon, for instance, grinding and shaping it can refer to feelings of defensiveness; a need to protect or be ready. It can refer to a need to sharpen your senses, awareness, or interaction. Grinding grain suggests ripe opportunities; getting down to the essence/kernel of your labors.

It may mean that you need to polish or grind off some rough elements in a relationship/situation to make it work more smoothly. Perhaps you need to become more smooth in your interactions. It may also be a pun for your work, the "daily grind."

grocery store

See **marketplace/grocery store**.

ground

See **dirt(y); earth**.

group(s)

Social skills or roles; your place within society (importance/insignificance of it); professional stature; leader or follower issues or roles, hence feelings about authority; dependence/independence issues; the collective unconscious.

See **center; crowd**.

growth/growing

Images of growing plants/animals can symbolize inner growth; cycles; fertility; change. If you're pregnant, it would not be unusual to dream of growing things, inside or outside of your body. Monstrous/ugly things that are growing, possibly out of control, may symbolize emotions; a relationship out of control or turning ugly; the growth of disease within you—and anxieties about that—if you've been diagnosed as having cancer or another progressive disease.

guard(ing)

Are you guarding or being guarded? It can represent protection, as well as restriction/obstruction toward a goal. In imagination, play both roles (see Dreamercise #3, Part 1) and determine what aspects of yourself they're expressing (caretaking; aggression; overbearing; possessive; firm stance?). To be "guarded" can relate to feelings that you need to be careful with respect to verbal expression/behavior in some situation. What aspect of you needs to be more controlled, or nurtured/protected? Consider also the symbolism of who/what is being guarded (if not you) and your waking relationship to it. Live or stone guardians, especially lions, often signal an important pathway that needs to be followed; however, for access you may need to do something more to overcome difficulties in your inner/waking life.

See **kidnapped/captured/abducted; prison/prisoner**.

guide/guidance

Meeting a guide/teacher or receiving guidance can symbolize feelings that you're overwhelmed and need help. If an actual former teacher, it may represent a situation in which you feel you're being tested again, or depict how you're grading (judging) yourself. It can represent a wisdom message from your inner/higher self—also referred to variously as your soul, Self, the God within. This is especially true if the guide appears as a talking animal, a shining being, Christ, other spiritual figures. It may reflect/confirm a new pathway, or initiation toward change/self-development.

See **initiation; teacher**.

guillotine

Anger; hostility; something you've "lost your head" over; possibly the eruption/appearance of strong emotions, or a situation in which you've failed to use good judgment.

See **head**.

guilt(y)

Someone who's guilty of something may represent repressed, negative, or undisclosed feelings you have about yourself, or someone in your waking life. Feelings of guilt are frequently associated with failure/success or competence/incompetence issues. Guilt is related to real/imagined insults or emotional wounding that concerns you. Is there a relationship/situation in which you're "guilty by association"? Consider other images in the dream for clues regarding the source of your inner guilt.

See **emotion(s)**.

gun(s)

Traditionally guns are symbols of aggression/anger toward others if you're using the gun, or turned inward if you are being shot at. They can represent the penis; male sexual drive; ejaculation; issues of passiveness/aggressiveness, attack/defense, power/impotence, authority/dependence, masculine/feminine. Perhaps a waking situation has opened up old wounds related to any of these issues, especially if someone from your past is in the dream. Consider the symbolism of what you're shooting at.

See **penis/phallis; sex; weapon(s)**.

guru

See **guide/guidance**.

Gypsy

Most of us have learned what we know about Gypsies from stories/movies (Marlene Dietrich wearing the golden earrings; Maria Ouespenska foretelling the werewolf fate of Lon Chaney, Jr.), so be sure to consider your own associations first. For some, Gypsy suggests a person who roams about and has more freedom than most people, so your dream may be suggesting how confined/restricted you're feeling. Gypsies are often considered secret-bearers and fortune-tellers. Perhaps you're experiencing anxiety about your future, or about the consequences of present actions on your future. If your dream Gypsy has darkened skin, he/she may represent your shadow/trickster aspect.

See **fortune-teller/fortune-telling; magic; shadow; trickster**.

hag

See **crone**.

hair(y)

Longstanding biblical/fairy-tale symbolism equates hair with masculine power/energy (Samson and Delilah). When associated with the head, hair can reflect intellectual processes; the projection of unconscious involuntary thoughts/fantasies (von Franz). It may represent someone you know who's particularly hairy, or someone named "Harry." Consider its condition (unkempt = misuse of energy or frazzled thinking?), body location, and color for additional clues. If on an animal, see **animal(s)**

See **body; head**.

half

Something that's cut in half, or that you can only partially see, suggests something in your waking life that's incomplete/unresolved; feelings/attitudes/memories only partially available to you ("half-forgotten"); limitations imposed by you/others, possibly by the way they raised/treated you in the past. What aspects of yourself have you buried so you're only half-alive? There may be something hidden in your psyche or waking life that you're only now catching glimpses of. Someone known in your waking life who's partially/half-hidden suggests that at some level you realize there's "more than meets the eye." Someone/something in a halfway position (on the stairs, caught in an elevator?) suggests:

a situation that calls for compromise; putting only partial/limited energy into something (''half-assed''); midway in a situation/relationship; an opportunity for choice.

hall(way)

If many doors, consider whether the hall represents opportunities awaiting exploration, or ones that have already been closed off. How you feel in the hallway may be saying something about your general approach to life or life's passages/transitions, or about a particular waking situation. Narrow-passageway dreams are common for pregnant women nearing delivery and likely represent the birth canal (Garfield).

See **door; opening; threshold**.

Halloween

Cycles, especially autumn; ritual and celebration; the abandonment/freedom of expression associated with festivals. In medieval times Halloween was a night of magic/divination. As All Hallows' Eve or All Souls' Eve (preceding All Saints' Day), it's related to death; the underworld; ancestors and family heritage (the ghosts or souls of family were said to arise from their tombs); spiritual heritage. Since masks/costumes are often worn for Halloween, it's related to: disguise that protects or facilitates release of inhibitions; temporary adoption of a new persona; and, archetypally, to transformation. What personas/characteristics were being presented in your dream?

See **celebration; ghost(s); holiday(s); mask(s); trickster**.

halo

The divine; connection with, or awakening to, spiritual aspects of your life; enlightenment; growing consciousness. In medieval art, saints/heavenly beings were often painted with halos; therefore, the dream may be expressing your own need to be more ''saintly.'' It may represent your perception that someone else is too virtuous, possibly phony; or that you've elevated/honored that person in your own sights, which may be appropriate/inappropriate.

See **aura; luminous; mandorla**.

hammer

A powerful/forceful weapon; therefore, by shape and meaning, a symbol of masculine attitudes. It could also represent something in your life that you've been ''hammering away'' at, as well as inner battles. As a tool, it could represent new growth/construction; building from the foundation (culture, family) up; the penis and sexual need.

In Scandinavia, making the sign of Thor's hammer (similar to the sign of the cross) over objects/people was a form of blessing/consecration. It was common to wear an amulet in the shape of Thor's hammer for protection. In myth, the hammer is associated with the smith; he, and his hammer, are usually endowed with magical—especially creative—powers.

See **nail; thunder/lightning; tool(s); weapon(s)**.

hand(s)

Hands connect us with people, with the world, and are used in creative projects. If emphasized in a dream, consider their position, potential action, and any special decoration for additional clues. In Jungian theory left hands symbolize feminine/receptive attributes, right hands symbolize masculine/active attributes. They are the agency of consciousness and any injury; therefore, they could represent wounding/impotency of the ego/consciousness (Edinger).

The many idioms associated with hands tell us that hands are definitely a form of communication and can symbolize a number of messages. Do you need a "handout," or need to "lend a helping hand" to another or to some aspect of yourself? Is your waking policy one of "hands off"? Perhaps there's some person/situation you need to "handle with kid gloves." Something that's "handed down" or "handed over" to you, or clothes that are "hand-me-downs," offer messages about your family situation, self-esteem, or impoverished aspects of yourself that need more recognition. Is there a verbal message in the dream that's changed/negated by hand placement/movement? For instance, hands folded across the body can indicate defensiveness/protection. Is there something you need to "take hold of"?

See **arm(s); body; finger(s); five; hold(ing); ten**.

handbag

See **purse/wallet**.

handcuffs

Your ability to reach out—to connect and relate—is, or has been, restricted. Opportunities/alternatives are closed off to you; or you've lost power/authority ("my hands are tied"). Perhaps your actions/emotions are threatening to overwhelm you, and you need some restraint.

If applicable, see **police; prison/prisoner**.

handicrafts

See **craft(s)**.

handle(s)

Do you have, or need to get, "a grip on" something ("handle" it)? Broken handles suggest some situation in which you've lost, or feel you have no, control. Handles can refer to issues of power; control; competency; mediation ("let me handle this"); holding on to something that it's time to give up or that you're afraid of losing. Consider what you're carrying/holding on to for additional clues. Perhaps there's a situation you need to "get a handle on"; or maybe it's time to let go and get on with the next phase of your life (especially if you're holding on to excess baggage or unfinished business).

See **baggage; carry(ing)/carried; luggage**.

hang(ing)

Hanging/swinging symbols in myths/fairy tales relate to the tension associated with unfulfilled expectations/longings (Jung). Perhaps there's some situation in which you think you've been "left hanging," or think that if you "hang in there," something will change.

If a person hanging, it suggests life as you know it is over and you're now moving into a different dimension; a new vision/idea. If hanging upside down, it relates to a change in perception/viewpoint ("it's all in the way you look at it"); rebirth; enlightenment; a mystical isolation that can result in magical/special wisdom, as when Odin hung upside down on Yggdrasil, the Norse world tree, to discover the runes and their spells.

happy

See **emotion(s)**.

harbor

Harbors can represent changes (partings, greetings); hence, the beginnings/endings of situations/relationships/issues. Often the first association people have is that of "safe harbor," in which case it can represent: feelings of/need for safety (danger implied); the personal home; the primordial home (rocked in the bosom of "Mother Water"); need for escape and regeneration. Harbor lights may represent romance or a goal to be achieved.

See **boat; dock; vehicle(s); water**.

hare

See **rabbits**.

harness

Usually used for animals, the harness may, thus, represent harnessing/domesticating/civilizing your animal instincts/urges; mobilizing/directing your energy, possibly into more fertile/creative projects (especially if harnessing an animal to plow a field).

See **animal(s)**.

harp

Divine harmony; the spiritual aspect of yourself. In Greek mythology the handheld lyre was associated with many gods. The lyre of Orpheus could charm inanimate objects (trees, stones) to dance (bringing cold feelings to life). However, it could also tame wild beasts; therefore, it may symbolize the need to soothe/control your instincts/passionate feelings. Orphic followers believed that dreams were prophetic, so pay special attention to any dream in which a lyre/harp appears. The lyre was a major attribute of Apollo, god of youth and music, also associated with oracular wisdom (Delphi).

As a pun, a harp could represent a "harpy" (grasping, shrewish person); or be related to the mythological harpies, winged maidens who plucked away souls, hence, some person/situation that's robbing you of energy.

See **angels; music/musician**.

hat

See **cap/hat**.

hate

See **emotion(s)**.

hauling

Emotional burdens; work; life's efforts ("it's a long haul"). Consider also what you're hauling, and in what kind of vehicle. The dream could relate to some relationship/attitudes/feelings that are dead and need to be "hauled away." In some instances, it may relate to speed/urgency ("haul ass").

See **carry(ing)/carried; move(ing)**.

haunted

Early unpleasant memories; anxieties/fears/guilt about past thoughts/activities; past hurts/traumas. A haunted house is filled with unfinished emotional business, possibly related to: your childhood family, dead relatives, repressed/unacknowledged memories/feelings.

See **ghost(s); Halloween**.

hawk

Hawk symbolism is closely

related to that of the eagle. In early Scandinavian tradition, hawks were associated with Odin, ruler of cosmic order. An eagle with a hawk perched on its forehead guarded the topmost branches of the Norse world tree, Yggdrasil; thus, hawks can symbolize farsightedness; guardianship; tenacity. The Norse trickster god Loki often took the shape of a hawk, so consider mischievousness as one possible message.

See **bird(s); eagle; trickster**.

hay

Depending on childhood experiences/superstitions, hay can represent bad/good luck. In southern/southwestern United States, to wish on a field/load of hay (and not look back) is to have your wish come true. If you know this custom, your dream may relate to luck; wishes; a feeling that only magical/supernatural/mysterious intervention can correct, or bring about, some situation. Is there a situation/issue about which you feel rather hopeless, or wish it were concluded? It may represent the hard work needed to harvest your ideas; a previously unrecognized opportunity ("make hay while the sun shines"); something that has more consequence/value than you have previously attributed to it ("it ain't hay").

Hay is used to feed farm animals and is, therefore, related to nurturing your inner needs/instincts in general, as well as to maternal/feminine instincts (cows), masculine energy (horses), sexual urges ("a roll in the hay"), and romance (hayride).

See **barn; farm(er); straw**.

head

The seat of understanding; the rational/thinking part of you; consciousness; wisdom; memories. Is there a waking situation in which you're "heading in the wrong direction"; have/need to "keep your head above water"; need to "head off" trouble? Consider any special decoration to the head/face, or special coverings for the head, for additional clues.

In Eastern philosophy and metaphysical/esoteric tradition, the head is related to the ajna (third eye) and crown chakras (energy centers) and to the inner cave, all of which are crucial in gaining spiritual insight—and refer to a quite different kind of "thinking."

See **body; cave; face**.

headstone

See **gravestone**.

hearing

See **deaf; ear(s); voice**.

hearse

As with all death-related images, it's related to cycles; transformation; moving into a new phase. It may reflect a need to carry away/bury unfinished business that is really a "dead issue." Consider whether you're the driver (taking charge) or an observer, which suggests you're aware of the situation but have yet to act on it.

See **cemetery; coffin; death; funeral; vehicle(s)**.

heart(s)

Dreams in which the physical heart, or heart shapes, figure prominently suggest a need to explore your feelings, since we often think of the heart as the seat of feelings. The dream action may refer to ways in which you do, or don't, recognize/express your feelings; to feelings about a situation that's giving you a "heartache," a "broken heart," or wherein you've "given your heart away." Hearts can refer to something basic (the "heart of the matter," "at the heart of it") that you need to recognize/acknowledge.

See **body**.

hearth

See **fireplace**.

heat

See **hot; melt**.

heaven

Consider the contents and formation of your dream heaven, for those are all heavenly aspects (resources) of yourself, which you can draw upon for inspiration. To acknowledge/reincorporate those aspects of yourself, it might be helpful to actually create one of the objects from your dream, or do one of the other activities suggested in Dreamercises #23 and #24, Chapter 6, Part 1.

See **angel(s)**.

heavy

While someone or something heavy in a dream may represent a burden, it can also represent misconceived responsibility; that is, emotionally taking on responsibility when you don't really have the power/stamina to carry through. Heavy objects can represent stability; earthiness; solid values (in contrast to flightiness); sadness/sorrow (a "heavy heart"); power (a "heavy hitter").

hedge

If well-kept/trimmed, it can represent a need for control/organization; a need to protect yourself or your territory while appearing socially acceptable. Other possibilities include: wanting to distance/separate yourself from some situation/relationship; withholding communication (or suspicion that it's been withheld from you); feeling "hedged in" and not free to be yourself or to do what you need/want to do; a need to "hedge your bets" against an impending/feared loss. A wild/neglected hedge may represent loss of ability; difficulty related to any of the preceding ideas; awareness that you need to "shape up" some situation/relationship.

heirloom

See **antique(s)**.

hell

Traditionally hell equals the underworld, and therefore, the unconscious; the shadow aspect; guilt feelings. But hell is conceived/perceived by individuals in many different ways, so this is one certain case in which everything in your dream hell is a projection of your inner world; therefore, of aspects of yourself. Any dream in which hell in all its variations appears is a good one to explore using Dreamercise #3, Part 1.

See **devil**.

helm

A need to feel or be in control; therefore, you may not feel in charge of, or may be feeling helpless in, some aspect/situation of your waking life. It can be related to issues of independence/dependence and freedom/restraint. Consider making some small waking choice that will allow you, once again, to feel you have some control. From there you can expand.

helmet

Wearing a helmet may represent feelings or expectations of aggression/confrontation (as for battle). It suggests a need to protect your ideas/beliefs, which you may be perceiving as so vulnerable/threatened that you need something more substantial than a cap/hat.

See **cap/hat**.

help

See **cooperate/help**.

helpless

Feeling helpless suggests difficulty confronting whatever is symbolized by the image that's prompting you to feel helpless. For clues as to whether it's a typical or long-standing behavior/issue, consider whether the image is an old/recurring one, or a person you once knew (aspects of yourself symbolized by that person?). Take charge of the situation by: (1) doing something "powerful" in waking life (some activity wherein you don't feel helpless—it need not be major, only successfully accomplished) and acknowledging/enjoying your feeling of accomplishment; (2) creating something from the dream (see Dreamercises #23 and #24); (3) confronting the image (Dreamercises #10, #11, or #19).

hen

Although mother hens are good mothers, we've come to think of them as overbearing or unreasonably protective. Is this occurring in your present life, possibly taking the form of guilt?

A hen can symbolize your perceptions of your relationship with an actual female authority. Are you outgrowing your need to be mothered, or do you need to attend to your internal mother?

"An old hen,'' or a group of hens, can refer to gossip, which you may need to take care of; your inclusion in a feminine group. The hen may symbolize unexpressed anger (''mad as a wet hen'').

As the mother of the egg, the hen is related to the primal mother and primal birth symbol—some potential that's growing but not yet manifest. Take care to feed and protect your flock.

See **chicken, cock, egg(s)**.

herb

See **spice**.

herd

A herd of cattle/animals can represent your need for belongingness (the herding instinct); a situation in which you're following blindly, without taking time to listen to yourself; a need to be ''heard'' or to ''round up'' some elusive stray ideas and corral them into something workable. Like all animals, the herd is related to your basic instincts, and may represent urges from the collective unconscious.

See **animal(s); bull(s); cow(s); calf/calves; horse(s)**.

hermit

When related to the Jungian archetype of the Wise Old Man, a hermit is a spiritual figure and can be the personification of your own inner spirit/wisdom; the aloneness of the individuation process (Edinger). If carrying a lamp, he may represent inward light or enlightenment (insight); the shedding of new light on a situation. More mundanely, it may relate to: a need to retreat due to feeling under attack or burdened in waking life; privacy needs. (Possibly your personal space/integrity has been violated.)

See **Wise Old Man**.

hero/heroine

This archetypal/mythological motif depicts our own journey/struggle to release our creativity and to become all that we can be. Hero/heroine images deal with issues about the quality of our life; ideals/goals; mastery/success; and all efforts to reach our full potential. Therefore, they are ultimately related to transformation, wholeness, and the tests we must survive for their achievement.

It is the hero's/heroine's task to transcend whatever threatens, to penetrate the realm of our hidden nature and separate good from bad. That often involves conflict with/between our higher (conscious reasoning) and lower (unconscious, animal instincts) aspects, as in the myths of Heracles and the lion, Androcles and the lion, and the biblical story of Samson riding the lion. Egyptian hieroglyphs depict the king/priest (hero) as one who, having fought and won the battle, earned the right to wear the animal skin.

Whether or not you're the hero/heroine in your dreams, the progression of your dream behavior over time gives you another view of your own life quest.

See **Self**.

hexagon

See **six**.

hexagram

See **six**.

hidden room(s)

Searching for/finding hidden rooms that are richly decorated or full of treasures symbolizes a hidden, creative aspect of yourself, possibly even your core Self. How well or deeply hidden these aspects are may be shown in the ease/difficulty you have in finding the room.

See **house**.

hiding

Hiding an object relates to secrets; withholding of information; not facing issues/emotions. Yet hiding is tied to revelation. Perhaps there's something you're getting ready to reveal/confess, or are afraid someone else will find out. If a person hiding, it may represent a need for the security represented by the womb (especially if the hiding place is deep/dark); or a need for protection. Is there a dangerous situation in your waking life? Hiding from policemen or other authorities (parents?) is probably associated with feelings of guilt, possibly with respect to sexual behavior/attitudes.

high/height

Dreaming of someone/something that's excessively tall or is placed up high may represent haughtiness ("looking down on"); an inflated evaluation of yourself/another ("put on a pedestal"); feelings of inferiority, isolation, or meanness ("lowdown"); need for control/power/domination; authority. Consider who is tall or high up, and who is short or below. As with all extremes, reverse the position. Place yourself high up if you're low in the dream, or vice versa, to determine which more aptly applies to a waking attitude. A high mountain/pathway may represent aspirations; a challenge; feelings of being overwhelmed; your life process ("it's an uphill battle").

See **ascend(ing); giant** (if applicable); **mountain(s); tower**.

high-rise building

See **tower**.

highway

See **road**.

hill

Similar in meaning to a mountain, a hill represents goals/aspirations, probably more short-term than those associated with a mountain. Depending on how you're relating to the hill, it can symbolize obstacles; making progress (climbing); confidence in your ability; the successful conclusion of a project or other work (on top of the hill); present struggles/attitudes ("it's an uphill battle"). In Scandinavian mythology, hills/mounds were often the homes of land-protecting spirits (see **elemental being**) with supernatural powers, and ancestral dwelling places.

See **ascend(ing); descend(ing); mountain(s)**.

history

History/historical figures most likely relate to your personal past (old feelings that need to be dealt with, old-fashioned values?); your family heritage. If you dream of a historical figure whom you've admired, it may be an expression of those same feelings toward yourself or a need to activate them in a waking situation.

See **ancestors; ancient**.

hoe(ing)

A need for order/organization; preparation for a creative project; weeding out undesirable elements (unfinished business, nonproductive attitudes/behavior?); straightening out a waking situation.

See **farm(er); garden; gardener**.

hog

See **pig(s)**.

hold(ing)

Someone holding, or having difficulty holding, something can relate to: control over oneself ("get hold of yourself"; "holding in") or another ("have a hold over someone"); ownership/possession ("I'll hold it for you); withholding emotions or other aspects of yourself ("hold back"); responsibility ("take hold of" the situation"); rigidity or inability to give up old feelings/relationships; a sense of urgency/vulnerability ("hold on"); reaching out in an intimate or grasping/clutching way; caring, as in holding a baby/small animal.

See **hand(s); hollow**. For an *object* that holds something, see **container**.

hole

In Freudian terminology, a hole relates to the vagina, therefore to birth; fertility; the feminine aspect. Spiritually it may be an opening/gateway into a higher realm, thereby symbolizing the double function of (1) admittance into (2) a more whole/balanced state. It can represent a place where animals live or store food (instinctual/emotional issues?), or where secrets are kept. Do you need to gather some kind of energy for yourself; have you been holding on to some secret too long; or do you need to "hole up" for privacy/withdrawal?

A hole in the ground suggests entry into the underworld or realm of the unconscious, and therefore, repressed material trying to emerge into awareness; change; return to the primal mother (Mother Earth). It can represent the anus, especially if muddy, and relate to eroticism; gathering or hoarding needs/anxiety.

Holes in objects/clothing may reflect weaknesses; incomplete thinking; some aspect of your inner life that needs to be repaired. Is some situation "full of holes," or is there a hole in some aspect of your waking "logic"? The word can be a pun on "whole" and your attempts to achieve wholeness, or the message that you need to consider a situation in its entirety, examine all its aspects.

If appropriate, see **anus; tunnel; vagina**.

holiday(s)

A need for a break/rest; expectations/anxiety about an upcoming holiday; release from responsibility or increased labor (depending on personal experience). Consider the symbolism of specific persons/activities, the ease/difficulty surrounding the holiday, to determine whether they relate to feelings of worth/worthlessness (I don't deserve this); family issues; other typical attitudes to which you need to attend. If a specific holiday, consider personal/family meanings, as well as cultural/religious ones.

See **celebration; vacation**.

hollow

Anything that's hollow, allowing objects to be placed within, represents the womb and is related to the symbolism of mother/mothering; fertility; secrets. If it's empty, it may be because it is a waiting/receptive time in your life, or a barren one. It may reflect a feeling of emptiness, or of not mattering in your life. Some people feel that at their innermost being there's nothing, a void, and a hollow vessel may represent this fear or sense of worthlessness. Consider the characteristics of the specific object that's hollow for additional clues.

See **container; womb**.

holy man/person

See **Christ; guide/guidance; hermit; Wise Old Man; Wise Old Woman**.

homage

Paying homage to someone/something could be a compensation dream to remind you that you've not been acknowledging the spiritual aspects of your life enough. If you're paying homage to someone in your waking life, consider whether the opposite might be applicable, i.e., that you have been looking down on him/her. It could also signal that you're caught up in a case of inappropriate "hero" worship.

See **idol**.

home

If your current home, it may reflect whatever feelings/needs you have about it (security, safety?). Your home may be an image for anything that's basic to you: your values, goals; family/love relationships ("home is where the heart is").

Past homes, especially childhood ones, may reflect aspects of yourself that were prominent during the occupancy of that home; attitudes you developed at that time; old, possibly repetitive, feelings; family feelings; unfinished emotional business evoked and now surfacing because of some waking situation, or because you're handling a situation in "old" ways.

See **architecture; childhood home; house**.

homeless

Anxieties related to present

economic situation; feelings of/fear of being robbed/deprived of basic needs or of an expressive outlet; feelings of rejection by important family members. What aspect of yourself are you not making a home for?

See **derelict**.

homosexual

Homosexual dreams by heterosexuals may represent secret fears/anxieties about masculine/feminine aspects or passive/aggressive issues, or an attraction toward aspects needed to complete the personality. Dreams of homosexual encounters, or of being accused of being a homosexual, are common for expectant fathers (Siegel). If occurring in dreams prior to an upcoming wedding, anxiety about your changing situation may be expressed as a "fantasy alternative" (Natterson and Gordon). From a Freudian perspective, guilt about sexual feelings may also lead to homosexual dreams.

honey

In early literary works, honey often symbolizes virility/lust; however, often considered a pure food by some, it also can symbolize spirituality; healing; plentifulness. Honey cakes were fed to serpents, the chthonic (earthly) aspects of deities; therefore, honey is symbolically associated with prophecy, with spiritual/divine messages revealed. It can represent someone who is especially, or overly, sweet, or a love/sex partner ("your honey").

See **bee(s); cake; sugar/sweets/candy; sex**.

honor(ing)

Recognition (consider whether the person "deserves" it or not); a person who represents your own morals/values/ideals. Depending on who receives the honor (you/another), it may reflect your own feelings of worth/worthlessness; be related to issues of competition/winning/losing, success/failure, or to your standing in a family/community/profession.

See **idol**.

hook

Catching something with a hook suggests something missing in your self-image that you think you need; a need to acknowledge/incorporate its characteristics into yourself. Or, if negative, fear that it already *is* a part of you. It can relate to a love/sexual relationship, or intimacy issues if you're hoping to "hook someone." The person/object may represent you, or some aspect of you, someone in waking life whom you're "hooked on." Hook is related to acquisition/materialistic needs and may, therefore, be related to feelings of deprivation. Catching a monster on a hook can represent emerging unconscious energy/emotions.

If applicable, see **fish/fishing; monster(s)**.

horde/hoard

Either of these images may act as a pun for the other. Horde is related to crowd and can represent your feelings/anxiety about group membership; identity/recognition issues; rising instincts or emotions (if animals, insects) that feel overwhelming.

To hoard something or find a hoard (cache) can relate to feelings of emotional impoverishment/neediness; the discovery of resources you didn't realize you possessed; concerns/anxieties you have about emotional/economic hard times in the future. Consider the symbolism of what you find (food, jewels/treasure, money, insects?). Is there something you fear you'll never have enough of, or that you're afraid to lose?

If applicable, see **animal(s); crowd; herd; insects**. Or see **food; jewel(s); money**.

hornets

See **insects**.

horns

Many gods/goddesses were depicted with horns, so horns can relate to issues of divinity; spirituality; awesome power. Horned female deities (notably Hathor, the Egyptian mother goddess) were often related to the moon or lunar aspects of the personality. If associated with a male or animal, they may relate to male vitality/sexual energy; possibly fear/need to protect yourself, depending on what character has the horns and how it interacts with you. In Christian theology, horns are associated with the devil and may relate to feelings of guilt, or your ideas about evil. In sexual vernacular "horny" means sexual arousal or needing sex, arising from the lustfulness of the devil, known as Ould Hornie in Scotland (Walker).

Horns may relate to issues of power ("lock horns with"); confrontation/action ("take the bull by the horns"); a situation in which you're "on the horns of a dilemma"; a need to curb your aggression/forcefulness ("pull in your horns").

See **moon/moonlight**.

horoscope

See **zodiac**.

horse(s)

"Horsepower" is energy or power. A horse often represents

our instinctual side; animal/sexual impulses arising from the lower part of the body; sexual libido or energy; male prowess; the ability to be fleet/swift; the daily grind or "horse race." Perhaps you've been feeling like a "workhorse" or been "working like a horse."

Riding a horse can symbolize sex (especially for teenage girls), and masturbation (especially for young boys). Or it may symbolize properly channeled/controlled instincts. The horse/rider together can symbolize the relationship or workings of the psyche (rider) and the unconscious (horse). In Greek mythology, horses had the ability to heal, or ward off, evil.

See **animal(s); lower body**. If the horse is winged, see **wings/winged**.

hose

In a Freudian sense, anything long with a watery output represents the penis and ejaculation, so consider whether your dream is a sexual one. It may relate to fertility; cultivation of inner growth or new ideas (a hose can water plants/vegetation); an outpouring of emotions (water), although the fireman's hose can be used to put out passionate emotion (fire).

See **penis/phallus; sex; water**. If applicable, see **garden; gardener**.

hospital

Anxieties about your health; an existing medical situation; an upcoming medical experience (surgery?); an ailing friend/family member. Occurrences in the hospital may reflect your feelings about past/present medical care. If there's no medical situation in your waking life, they may refer to your own inner ability to take care of yourself physically/emotionally; independent/dependency issues; anxiety about aging or physical deterioration. A hospital can reflect a nonmedical situation that needs to be fixed/mended, or your need to be healed. Consider the symbolism of any specific injured/ailing body parts for additional clues. A mental hospital indicates a wound to the psyche, a present emotional state.

See **architecture; doctor; nurse**. If applicable, **needle; syringe**.

hostility

See **anger**.

hot

Passion; emotion; sexuality/lust for another; seething anger ("hot under the collar"); a situation that's potentially dangerous ("too hot to handle") and should be "dropped like a hot potato."

See **cold; fire** (if applicable).

hotel/motel

Transition; a time in your life when things are moving/changing; a temporary situation; a feeling of not belonging, possibly of being uprooted; diminished feelings of security. Consider the condition of the hotel and the activities occurring for additional clues.

See **architecture**. If applicable, see **holiday(s); vacation**.

hours

The passage of time; your age; reminder of an appointment; personal symbolism related to a particular number; superstitions/folk ideas associated with particular times; i.e., the magic hour (between sunset/dark); the witching hour (midnight); high noon (a turning point or confrontation); the eleventh hour (the time before disaster/confrontation).

See **time**.

house

If you're actually involved in house-hunting or buying activities, a dream about a house would not be unusual and could reflect your current hopes/anxiety. A house can symbolize the psyche; the physical body; your lifestyle; or sometimes the Self. It may be a message about a relationship or about a current view(point). How the house is kept, activities occurring within it, rooms present and missing, all give clues to your attitudes toward yourself and whether or not you need to "put your house in order." Various levels of the house may symbolize layers of awareness, or of your personality. A new house can indicate a new beginning. One falling down may indicate personal change; stress; physical problems. The basement frequently symbolizes unconscious/deeper aspects of yourself, although archetypally it may signify the underworld. Discovered treasures suggest parts of yourself that need to be developed, or the Self (care of your personality). In one of Jung's dreams, entering a dark and ancient room below the basement helped him deduce the idea of the collective unconscious. For Freud, rooms in a house represented women; entering a room symbolized sexual intercourse.

See **architecture; castle; home; Self;** and specific rooms.

housework/housekeeper

Housework rarely appears in dreams, so when it does, it takes on unusual significance. Doing housework, spring cleaning, or having a housekeeper suggests that it's time to: put some order in your life; clean up unfinished business; rid yourself of old dust/debris (outmoded ways of feeling/behaving?); put your soul/spirit life in order. It may relate to feelings of inadequacy or low self-esteem (I'm *just* a housekeeper); success issues; new ideas being born; the feeling/fear that you're locked into endless drudgery. Since many consider housework a "thankless" task, is there some aspect of your recent life wherein you've not received enough recognition?

See **clean(ing)/cleansing**.

hull

Protection against being overwhelmed by unconscious material; the condition of the hull suggests the state of your defenses. If damaged, it suggests that you have access to more unconscious material than you desire at present and need to make repairs, so you can once more glide smoothly along, accessing material when it is safe or to your benefit.

See **boat; ship/shipwreck; water**.

hummingbird

Flighty thoughts, ones that are hard to hold on to; ideas/concepts/messages that are small but possess a lot of energy/power; frivolous ideas, or frivolity in general; a need to connect with many ideas or to link many together; a signal that your dream deals with sexual issues; a playboy in your life or playboy attitudes (flitting from flower to flower).

hunger/hungry

Having a temporary emptiness that needs to be fulfilled/nourished (needs for nurturance, relationship/companionship, relaxation/renewal, spiritual connection?); a need to create something or to listen to your inner self. Because hunger is related to one of the five senses, it can reflect a need for more sensual stimulation/gratification.

Stealing food may represent trying to acquire something that's not yet rightfully yours, i.e., perhaps part of you has not developed enough or done the work to fulfill a particular need. Or it may represent a feeling that you should have what you desire without having to do the internal work. For additional insight, have a dialogue with your inner hunger or your inner mother, as in Dreamercise #3 or #10, Part 1.

See **cook(s)/cooking; eating; food**.

hunt(ing)

Hunting/searching for something/someone is related to the symbolism of the specific thing that can't be found. For instance, lost objects/persons may relate to lost values (valuables), aspects of your identity (wallet, credit cards, etc.), unfinished business. You may have lost sight of your goals/direction (keys).

See **hunter/huntress; lost**.

hunter/huntress

The theme of the hunter/huntress is a common archetypal one, and can represent seeking out unrealized/unconscious aspects of yourself. If the hunter is dark/sinister, it can represent the shadow. Consider what's being hunted; what the hunter part of you is trying to make contact with—animals (instincts or urges?), people (missing attributes?)—and whether it's to collect, capture, or kill. Hunting "game" can refer to the game of life or to your professional/business life; hence, to issues of success, competition, advancement.

In mythology, the hunter often makes a new, or breaks an existing, relationship by his successful "capture." Is there some relationship in which the aggressive/stalking behavior of someone is altering/threatening to destroy that relationship? Consider also the symbology of the weapons used.

If applicable, see **animal(s); arrow(s); bow and arrow; competitor/competition; game(s); gun(s); lance; victor/victory**.

hurricane

See **storm**.

hurt

Consider, first, the symbolism of the specific part of your body, or another's, that's been hurt in order to determine the nature of a possible emotional wound. If you hurt someone known in waking life, do you harbor unrecognized anger/revenge feelings? Consider how you handle the hurt/wound and whether this reflects typical behavior or offers you a waking alternative. What part of you needs to be healed?

See **wound(s)/wounded**. If applicable, see **doctor; hospital; nurse**.

husband

If a woman, dreaming of your own husband may relate to issues you're unsatisfied with in your relationship. Consider how each of you behaves in the dream for clues as to the roles each may be playing that enhance/interfere with trust/closeness. Dreaming of having a husband when you don't, or aren't engaged, could relate to needing any of the following in your life: stability, romance, closeness, protection, assertion—whatever are the characteristics you associate with a husband. A husband can be a reflection of your animus; suggest a need to activate/acknowledge within yourself characteristics you associate with a husband (a need for balance?).

In a man's dream, it may also represent issues in your marital relationship, as well as insight into the various roles you play as a husband and the feelings you have about them.

See **wedding**.

hut

As a small shelter related to a home, a hut suggests protection from basic instincts; providing for only basic comforts; a need to simplify your life and get back to the basics; access to childhood feelings; a need to withdraw and renew your inner self or your creativity, especially if the hut is in a natural setting.

See **home; house**.

hymn

Self-expression; reflection of a heightened religious or spiritual experience/relationship; a need to "sing your own praises" or those of another; your connection with a religious or "vocal" group/community organization. Then again, it may refer to "him," the glorious man in your life.

See **music/musician; song(s)**.

I

See **dreamer/dream ego**.

ice

Emotional coldness; rigid attitudes. It may be up to you to "break the ice." If melting, it could indicate emotional release, or a situation/relationship in which you feel you're "walking on thin ice."

See **cold; iceberg**.

iceberg

Frozen or unacknowledged potential; rejection of primal emotions; a wish to distance yourself from some person/situation.

There's more to some situation/issue/aspect of yourself than you're aware of or have considered ("more here than meets the eye"), and it may have dangerous potential.

See **ice**.

idol

If a statue, picture, or icon, it can represent the *idea* of love/valuation, rather than actually experiencing and developing it in a relationship; false/immature love. If a religious icon, it may represent relationship with divinity, or a need/wish to take on/develop spiritual characteristics associated with the icon. If the idol is a person, it can represent the projection outward of those inward values/characteristics that are really yours but that you attribute to the idolized one. Or it may reflect the emulation of someone whose views you believe in/value; and can be related to a role model, or a need for uplift/support of your own position. It can suggest a safe way to experience/express erotic feelings without having to actually act on them. Have you recently put someone on a pedestal?

igloo

If your conception of an igloo is that of a cold, inhospitable place to live, then your igloo suggests feelings of coldness/isolation in your family/home. If you perceive an igloo as the warm refuge it in fact is, then your image could relate to issues within your family/home relationship in which you feel cramped or don't have enough room to express yourself.

See **home**.

ignored

If you're ignoring, or being ignored by, someone presently known, consider whether you are feeling ignored by that person in waking life, or whether, for your part, you've paid that person too much attention recently. If it's someone from your distant past or not known to you, then the person could represent some aspect of yourself to which you are not paying enough attention.

illegal

See **crime/criminal**.

illness

Consider whether the dream illness is pointing to an actual physical condition whose symptoms you have ignored, or an emotional illness (loss of spirit). Also consider the particular location of the body the illness deals with for clues as to any perceptions/attitudes/judgments that are promoting "dis-ease."

See **body; disease; epidemic** (if applicable); **infection; injury**.

immobile/paralyzed

Although our muscles are paralyzed during REM sleep, this refers to the feeling in a dream that you can't do anything, can't change anything, or are a "helpless" observer. It probably refers to a waking situation, and feelings/anxiety about having no power to change/affect it; some way that you're "handicapped" in waking life. It may represent a habitual passive response, possibly learned when you were a child and could do little else; feeling emotionally paralyzed; inability to get in touch with/express feelings following a traumatic or grief/loss experience.

Another kind of immobilization dream occurs when we're pursued/threatened, are unable to move, and can only get out of the situation by awakening. From a Freudian view, these dreams occur when there are two conflicting wishes/desires—one to remain, one to stay. Frequently this involves the "attraction" of a secret/hidden sexual desire and the desire to avoid/deny it.

See **disabled**.

impasse

Some sort of impasse, human or otherwise, blocking your way or your movement may represent unexpressed emotions of anger or grief related to a life crisis (Siegel).

imprisoned

Being imprisoned or seeing prisoners—especially in basements, cellars, dungeons, or other deep, dark places—represents repressed/unacceptable, possibly shadow, aspects of yourself, which must be released and integrated into your personality before you can become whole again. Use Dreamercises #3 and #10, Part 1, to discover their function. It can represent the need to go inward for the sake of developing insight/creativity.

See **guilt(y); prison/prisoner**.

incest

If you've never participated in incest, then dreaming of it likely suggests a need to incorporate the *values* associated with that family member into your own life; intense feelings about, and need to be close to/identified with, a particular family member. Remember, societal taboos don't exist in the unconscious. It may reflect a need to awaken more masculine or feminine (depending on the sex of the family member) archetypal energy into your life for balance.

It can represent a need to control that person or a feeling/fear that he/she is out of control. It may relate to a situation—not necessarily sexual—in your waking life that has stimulated shocking/objectionable feelings. Or it may pinpoint difficulties in a waking life sexual relationship, i.e., that one or the other of you is still too attached in an infantile sexual way with a parent. (Remember, the unconscious will not consider this strange or unusual; it's only the conscious ego that will censor it.)

See **sex**. If applicable, see **rape**.

Indian

If American Indian, see **aborigine/aboriginal**.

If Eastern Indian, see **person, dark or dark-skinned; person, foreign**.

indifferent

See **emotionless**.

indigestion

See **digestion**.

indigo

If the color is more on the deep blue side, see **blue**. If more on the violet side, see **violet** [color].

See **color(s)**.

individuation

C. G. Jung often referred to the alchemical changes of alchemy (the process of transforming base metal into gold, or, psychologically, the purification of the soul) as depicting the individuation process (the psyche's push toward bringing unconscious material into consciousness for the development of the Self). In one sense, then, our inner development can be likened to an alchemical drama, which Jung believed the ancient alchemists were symbolically portraying in their writings. The alchemical procedure had a varying number of stages, with varying names, depending on the text. All stages were designated by colors. Sometimes there were 12, more often seven, four, or three, which Jung ultimately focused on.

Our immature personality was the *prima materia* (the prime material, base matter), which needed, through conscious effort (the alchemical process), to be transformed into "golden knowing," symbolized by the lapis, or the philosopher's stone.

According to Jungian analyst Robert Bosnak, dreams of the first stage—*nigredo*, blackening—contain "dark," chaotic, or desolate images (stormy weather, night, rot/decay, black birds/animals; venomous/blood-sucking creatures). Although the images are often bleak, this stage is the necessary initial phase of transformation, holding the promise of something to come. In the whitening (*albedo*) phase—illumination—that promise becomes new knowing. Bosnak says typical images might include: moonlight, reflections in water/mirrors, ice/snow, ambiguous images, cleansing action/images, white animals/creatures. The reddening/*rubedo* stage foretells the completion of inner work. In dreams it's often portrayed in sexual images, passions of various sorts, blood, fire, battles of opposites, high mountains, emphasis on red or pointed objects, manic/emotional actions. As purification is achieved—symbolized in alchemy by achieving the transformation of lead into gold—dream images include extremely precious metals, golden objects/creatures, lions, sun/sunlight images, the season of summer, understanding the essence of anything.

Individuation occurs slowly over our lifetime—it is a process, not a realized goal (Edinger)—so it may best be observed in a series of dreams (see Dreamercise #15, Part 1). Typically the stages repeat over and over as we struggle with issues and gain insight/inner knowledge over time.

See **Self**.

infant

See **baby**.

infection

Negative thoughts; rumors or feelings about rumors, which are a form of emotional contagion; reminders/feelings of guilt about engaging in careless waking/sexual behavior that can spread contagion; a need to avoid something/someone you consider harmful/dangerous, but may not have consciously acknowledged it.

See **abscess; blister; disease**.

initiation

An initiation dream could take the form of an actual initiation ceremony, but might also be reflected in any life passage ceremony: bar or bat mitzvah, graduation, wedding. Initiation dreams refer to acceptance in, or affiliation with, a certain community; a feeling of having "come of age" or having "come into your own"; honor/recognition, especially as it might relate to a difficult test/task that's been mastered; life cycles; new directions; spiritual/emotional transformation; accessibility to the mysteries of life (the wisdom pathway); the process of individuation/self-development.

See **ceremony; graduation; guide/guidance; rite/ritual; wedding**.

injection

If for healthful reasons, as an inoculation, it could represent the development, incorporation of, or need for healing ideas/attitudes/behavior; protection by an authority figure. If unhealthful, or forced upon you, it may refer to negative attitudes about a particular situation; recognition of an attempt by some person/group to force negative or unwelcome attitudes/values/behavior on you (peer pressure?). If a sedative or painkiller that makes you drowsy or "spacey," it may refer to a need/wish to avoid an issue/situation that's causing emotional pain, or to avoid some impending responsibility/decision, i.e., to be an infant again and have an authority (parent) take care of (nurse) you.

If the injection refers to street/addictive drugs, see **addict(ed)**.

See also **disease; doctor; infection**. See **syringe** for the sexual implications of an injection.

injury

If to your body, it suggests a need for change. Its severity may give clues to the extent (major, minor?) of the change necessary. Consider the symbolism of the particular body part. Do you wish others would change (injury to other characters?)? A self-inflicted injury may indicate awareness of a need for inner change, or represent anger/hostility directed toward the self. If you're a different age than presently, it may suggest the age at which you were wounded/traumatized, or how long you've been carrying inner hurt/pain that has prevented change/growth. An injury being healed suggests you're doing the needed work and gaining new abilities. From a Freudian perspective, injury to a male dreamer's body represents castration anxiety.

See **wound(s)/wounded**.

ink

Ink that's dark (blue, black) may represent negative/depressed feelings; old/past issues that need to be resolved. Depending on how it's used in the dream, ink can represent attempts at communication that are successful/unsuccessful (spilled/splattered ink); confession; unfulfilled potential (self-expression) that you may now be ready to recognize/utilize (if using ink for writing/drawing). Invisible ink relates to secrets. If colored inks, include the symbolism of their particular colors. They suggest creativity; uniqueness; the expression of more energetic feelings than those represented by darker inks.

See **individuation**.

innocent

Someone especially innocent/naïve may be a signal that you're being too guileless in a waking situation; or may represent earlier, innocent aspects of yourself, your inner child. Consider how that character is being treated for additional clues as to what you may be experiencing or need to take care of.

insects

Traditional interpretations suggest that insects represent annoyances; minutia that creeps into our awareness and "bugs" us; feelings of insignificance. Irritable, complaining women are sometimes said to have a "waspish" tongue, but any stinging insect may reflect insults/stinging remarks.

Still, in fairy tales, insects are

often portrayed as precise, organized, and alert/sensitive to details, so they could reflect a need to sort out your values/attitudes/position with conscious preciseness. Wildlife rehabilitator Joanne Hobbs suggests that our interpretations or personal symbology will change dramatically when we view "creepy crawlers" as divine messengers—as do many tribal people—and take time to learn about the actual insects that appear in our dreams.

See **ant; bee(s); bite; bug; butterfly; moth; roaches; spider(s)**.

intercourse

See **sex**.

intruder

Unconscious material attempting to make itself known, especially knowledge that you've feared. Look to the qualities of the intruder for more awareness about your fears. It may also represent aspects of yourself that you've denied. If a recurring nightmare, use one of the dreamercises (especially #3, #9, #10, #17) in Part 1 for relief.

According to von Franz, an intruder, an unknown sinister person, or someone unfamiliar who unexpectedly enters the dream scene may represent the nearness of death; however, intruder dreams are also common for pregnant women, and in that case, usually symbolize the fetus (Garfield).

See **thief/theft**.

invalid

Some situation/aspect of yourself that's not thriving or getting enough attention. It may represent an idea/attitude that's *invalid*/no longer applicable.

invasion

See **war**. If applicable, see **alien(s); UFO**.

invent/inventor

Inventing something relates to your desires/abilities to create, meet challenges, and overcome obstacles; a desire to succeed/feel competent; issues of self-confidence and persistence. It can reflect a surge of new, creative energy; remind you not to overlook anything (take a different perspective) or to appreciate the uniqueness of a person/situation.

See **patent**.

invisible

Being invisible may derive from earlier times in your life when you felt your needs were not being recognized or you were otherwise being ignored/neglected; counting for nothing (no-thing). Has some present situation reawakened those feelings? It can represent repressed material; look to other aspects of the dream for clues as to the nature of the material. From a Freudian perspective, invisibility relates to behavior/wishes that are taboo and need to be concealed.

Invisibility can represent a change in your attitudes or relationship with another. In fairy tales, an invisible character often refers to inner experience, so consider whether the nature of the character/object expresses an unacknowledged/unrecognized inner asset, or other psychic/inner processes.

iris

If you raise irises, the dream may be related to feelings about your gardening efforts; images of yourself as a gardener (caring, neglectful, successful, unsuccessful?); someone you know who raises iris. In Greek, iris means rainbow. The Greek goddess Iris was the embodiment of the rainbow, as well as a virgin goddess; therefore, the maiden aspect of yourself. The iris was also one of the symbols of the Nordic god Odin. Irises, then, may reflect your relationship with the spirit/divine, or may be a reflection of your Self. It may be a pun for the iris of your eye, and therefore a dream about irises may relate to inner sight (intuition), or to some new understanding/viewpoint.

See **eye(s); garden; gardener; rainbow; Self**.

iron

Strength; durability; determination ("iron will"); but also emotional rigidity/inflexibility; a need for control or domination. If rusted, it may relate to neglected/wounded aspects of yourself or unfinished emotional business, which needs to be acknowledged and cleaned up. Mythologically iron is often used to ward off evil/supernatural spirits/happenings.

If applicable, see **wound(s)/wounded**.

island

Emotional (water) isolation; separation; difficulties coping with life (deserted island), but also integrity; self-containment; a special place/need for emotional refuge/renewal, especially if there's a lot of green growth and flowing waterfalls. Consider your feelings and activities on the island for additional clues.

If known to you, it may represent your feelings about a certain culture; a relationship with someone from that culture; issues raised/stimulated when you traveled to that island.

A number of islands are the result of present/past volcanic activity and may, therefore, relate to volatile or dormant/dead emotions. Islands such as Bali, Hawaii, and Iceland, which result from rifts in the ocean floor, are actually the tops of submerged mountain chains and have a joint symbolism.

Many mythologies contain some form of the "island of the blessed," a paradise where the souls of the good reside after death; hence, your dream image may refer to change or a need to be rewarded.

Being in the Mother Womb (water), an island may relate to issues of birth/rebirth or dependence/independence; being protected emotionally. It might suggest a state of being submerged/overwhelmed by unconscious material and a need to pay more attention to conscious material/reality.

See **water**. If applicable, see **mountain(s); volcano**.

isolated

Being isolated from, or being restricted within, a relationship/person/job—or allowed only limited response—calls for a reappraisal of your goals/wishes, a search for freedom; a time of incubation/repair to allow inner hurts to be healed and inner problems to be solved (von Franz). Also "ice-related"; rejected; out in the cold; issues of aloneness/abandonment/rejection/being ignored.

ivory

Strength; power; something endangered, possibly forbidden (because of its association with elephants); impractical or detached intellectualism ("ivory tower"); some extremely rare/valuable/precious aspect of yourself; therefore, an image for the Self.

ivy

Its more ancient meanings include immortality; friendship; fidelity. It may represent someone who's clinging in/to a relationship. Like all green, growing things, it can represent our basic vegetative functions, so consider its condition. Ivy may represent something that needs to be, or is being, covered in the sense of being hidden, protected, or made less harsh. Ivy is considered a feminine symbol and can sometimes represent fertility; also someone of that name.

See **green; vegetation**.

jacket

See **clothes/clothing; coat**.

jade

A sacred stone in Eastern traditions, it represents male energy; truth; immortality. In Central America it symbolizes the soul. Often carved, it may symbolize creativity; the shaping of the personality.

See **gem(s); green** (if applicable).

jail

See **cage; cell; imprisoned; jailer; prison/prisoner**.

jailer

Those aspects of yourself (attitudes, anxieties, biases, rigidities) that restrict or hold you back; mental/emotional inflexibility; someone in your past/present life who has treated you as if you were, or made you feel, limited in some way.

See **caught; handcuffs** (if applicable); **kidnapped/captured/abducted.**

jar

As a container, it's feminine. Depending on its shape, it can represent female genitals or the womb. If it contains food, it could relate to: nurturance issues; anxiety about being "canned"; a need to "preserve" some aspect of your heritage or a relationship. If containing perfume/lotion, it may represent concern about your appearance; a need to "make a good showing." It can refer to a need to hoard/gather emotional supplies and, therefore, to issues of "running out" of things; neediness; security; readiness.

See **container** and, if applicable, **appearance; horde/hoard**.

jaw

Someone with a prominent/jutting jaw may represent attitudes of determination/stubbornness/forcefulness; needing or having willpower; fortitude. Where in your waking life are you experiencing too much, or need more, of any of these characteristics? Emphasis on the jaw can represent strength; a need to dominate; feeling helpless and, therefore, needing strength. Is there some situation you're "clenched up" about? Tight jaws can represent unexpressed anger or other feelings that you fear expressing and are holding back.

See **body; face**.

jell/jelly/gelatin

Some suspicion/insight, or some issue/situation you were wondering about, that has now jelled and taken a shape you can understand. It can also relate to preserving/maintaining a sweet relationship; someone in your past/present life who makes jelly/preserves. Consider any symbolism related to the shape, color, or fruit used.

See **eating; food; sugar/sweets/candy** (if applicable).

jellyfish

In one sense a jellyfish can represent having no backbone; passive; spineless; feeling exposed; feeling inadequate; or other lowered self-esteem issues. Perhaps there's some situation in which you feel unable to assert yourself. Yet, while looking innocuous, a jellyfish can deliver a painful sting, thus representing hidden/unexpected capability, hostility, or aggression; painful memories emerging, or ready to emerge, from the unconscious.

See **fish/fishing; ocean; sea**.

Jesus

The need to dedicate yourself to/connect with something that has traditional value; looking up to/admiring someone honorable in your life; the need to establish/emulate leadership abilities; the need to incorporate missing spiritual values into your life; recognition of your uniqueness/specialness.

See **Christ**.

jewel(s)

Special/superior knowledge; spiritual truths; that which is precious within; your personality/identity. One special jewel, especially one hard to obtain, or a single pearl, may symbolize the child within, the child archetype, i.e., the childhood aspect of the collective unconscious (Jung). If you lose jewels, consider what emotional loss you may have sustained in a waking situation, or fear you will sustain in an upcoming event. In sexual slang, "family jewels" refer to the male genitals.

See **gem(s); treasure**. If applicable, see specific jewels: **diamond(s); emerald(s); opal; quartz; ruby; sapphire**.

jewelry

Special status; preciousness; material riches. Wearing flashy/stunning/valuable jewelry may reflect a need for recognition of your wealth (inner or outer); a wish to be in the spotlight, have attention paid to you, or otherwise be attended to/admired. Depending on its shape and the stones in the jewelry, it could represent feelings about yourself; psychological riches; possibly the Self.

A particular piece of jewelry from waking life may symbolize aspects of a waking relationship. Antique jewelry can represent old learnings/relationships that still have value for you. Heirloom jewelry may relate to feelings about family/tradition, possibly a relationship with the giver of the jewelry and feelings about it.

If applicable, see **appearance; bracelet(s); gem(s); jewel(s); necklace; ring(s)**.

job

See **business/work**.

jockey

A need to control your own animal instincts, or to assert your will/strength in overcoming obstacles. It is also related to competition and the race/struggle to meet your goals. Consider the dream image's relationship to a waking situation in which you feel somewhat inadequate, possibly frustrated in your ability to be in charge or to "jockey" into the position you desire. If successful, the dream may be telling you that you have the skills to accomplish some impending task.

See **horse(s)**.

journey

See **abroad/traveling abroad; travel(ing)/journey; vehicle(s)**.

joy

See **emotion(s)**.

judge/judging/judgment

Conscience; guilt; issues with authority or the law; issues about obedience, avoiding trouble or blame, adhering to or maintaining family, social, or a particular group's morality, or the natural order of things. These images all have to do with the ease/difficulty of decision making—making a judgment call about what to do and living with the consequences. They may reflect a wish for more guidance; a feeling that someone is being too restrictive toward you or that you're too restrictive of someone else ("sit in judgment"); a feeling that a particular person is unfairly/inadequately judging you ("judge and jury").

Judging is related to the "tyranny of the shoulds," a concept created by the late Karen Horney, that reflects the way we judge ourselves against imagined "shoulds" that are unachievable. We therefore always come up lacking. Is there some way in which you are similarly tyrannizing yourself with an impossible should?

As the Last Judgment, it can relate to: the death/rebirth theme; liberation; insight; release from illusion. It may reflect a new way of being, a new ability to integrate unconscious material into consciousness.

See **court; jury; justice**.

juggler/juggling

Do you "have too many balls in the air" and need to establish some priorities? Perhaps there's some situation (finances?) in which you're constantly having to "juggle things around." Depending on the success of the juggling, there may be a waking situation in which you are, or wish you were, competent, or in which you may be "off balance."

See **balance(d)/balancing**.

jump(ing)

Taking a risk, with possible feelings of anxiety/excitement; confronting/avoiding danger or a potentially dangerous situation (depending on the nature of the jump); anxiety/excitement about a new situation ("jumping-off place"); a need for more excitement or independence/freedom in your life. It may relate to a situation in which you feel you're constrained/restricted and need to break away or take a chance; issues of rashness/impulsiveness; enthusiasm ("jump on the bandwagon"); anxiety about premature ejaculation ("jump the gun"). If you jump over an abyss, gap, etc., it may reflect a need to avoid/overcome extreme "mothering," or a sexual situation with a female. It can reflect a desire for sex ("jump on your bones"), or there may be some person/situation wherein you need, or have anxiety about your ability, to stay "one jump ahead." Then again, perhaps you have recently "jumped to conclusions" you think might not be quite accurate or about which you now have ambivalent/guilt feelings.

See **movement; posture(s)** and the symbolism of the particular object over or onto which you jump.

junction

See **crossroads; threshold**.

jungle

Instincts; the unconscious; uncivilized feelings/thoughts; feelings of being overwhelmed; your attitude toward the unknown or exploring new experiences/relationships. Consider the symbolism of any specific creatures/people you met; your actions (confident, stumbling?); how you felt during the dream (safe, afraid?). Cannibals may represent a situation/relationship in which you fear you've "lost your head." Pygmies, related to dwarfs, may represent childish/undeveloped aspects of your personality. The jungle can symbolize ambition/competition (the "law of the jungle"); your feelings about job/career/the workplace ("it's a jungle out there").

If applicable, see **aborigine/aboriginal; dwarf(s)** and specific birds, insects, or animals.

junk

Superfluous or outdated ideals/attitudes you're carrying around; unfinished business you're hanging on to or unable to resolve; a situation in which you've taken on someone else's mental or physical junk/tasks.

jury

Juries are related to judgment and may reflect issues of responsibility, accountability, and blame/guilt. Is there some situation/behavior about which you feel strongly; have a lot of anxiety; or are afraid that you will be found guilty? The guilt may relate to feelings from your childhood, and you may need to end this trial. If you're someone who's afraid to be criticized, your jury may reflect your careful shaping of your waking behavior so you won't be found guilty and are, therefore, not free to create/behave as you would really like.

See **court; judge/judging/judgment**.

justice

Suggests you may need to work toward bringing more equality ("balance the scales"), harmony, or stability into a waking-life situation/relationship. There may be a situation involving ethical issues. Because justice is often depicted as blind, consider whether there's some situation/relationship in which you're not seeing all that you might. Perhaps more investigation is needed; or you need to more carefully weigh the issues involved.

Justice is concerned with seeking balance within ourselves or in a relationship; acting on our ethical beliefs; asserting our own rights and those of others. In its negative sense, it's related to issues of bigotry/bias.

See **balance(d)/balancing; court; judge/judging/judgment; jury; scales of justice**.

keel

Basic support or emotional strength; therefore, emphasis on the keel of a boat likely suggests you have more of this to rely on than you think. However, depending on the condition of the keel, it could mean that you need to do some growth work and develop more emotional resources. Is there some waking situation in which you need more courage?

See **backbone; boat; ship/shipwreck; water**.

kennel

As a place where animals are kept, a kennel can represent powerful instinctual energy that's beginning to be felt; or instinctual energy that needs to be controlled lest it overcome. Whether this is a positive or negative dream depends on the kinds of animals kept in the kennel; whether they're caged or not (exercising?), tame or vicious; how they're being cared for (fed, starving, well-groomed?); and any other activities occurring.

See **animal(s); dog/puppy** and the symbolism of particular animals if other than dogs.

key/keyhole

A key part of yourself; the crux of an issue. Consider the characteristics/condition of the key (shape, simple/elaborate, decorative, bent?). Ask yourself, "What in my life [or what part of my life] is like this?"

In European mythology/fairy tales, keys often unlock the doors of mystery; expose hidden/secret knowledge (positive and negative); lead to awareness/growth. They can represent release/freedom from entrapment; power ("turn the key"); authority ("keys of the kingdom"); honor ("key to the city"). In Freudian terminology, key and lock (or keyhole) represent the penis/vagina. Together or singly they can represent sexual intercourse. In Jungian psychology, they represent the union of opposites; therefore, the reduction of tension.

See **door; lock(ed); opposites; sex**.

kick

Aggression; defensiveness/protectiveness; assertion ("kick ass"); rejection ("kick someone out").

See **anger**.

kidnapped/captured/abducted

Fear of entrapment or feelings of being trapped. Your abductors/captors may represent some person/situation that has diverted you from your own growth tasks, or is restricting your growth. Are you really captured or merely captivated? If you're doing the capturing, consider what you might be holding on to. Whether you're the kidnapper or the kidnapped, what aspects of you are like both persons (see Dreamercise #3, Part 1)?

See **imprisoned; ransom; thief/theft**.

kill(ing)/killed/killer

Killing could reflect some aspect of yourself (represented by the person/animal being killed), possibly your shadow nature, that you're trying to "kill off," or that you feel someone else is trying to destroy/control; some feeling that you're trying to suppress/repress. Are you in a waking situation in which you're losing your identity, or your uniqueness is being ignored/undermined?

See **anger; emotion(s); hunting); hunter/huntress; murder(er)**.

king

The patriarchal value system; a need for control, possibly of others or regarding your own feelings/behavior; issues related to achievement/recognition of status, mastery, domination, power—or lack of it—which possibly refers to ways you felt inadequate in childhood and, therefore, to unfinished business about the way your parents treated you.

In mythology the future king, as a prince, is often wounded or transformed into an ugly beast, who cannot realize his throne (potential) until he is loved (accepts his feminine aspect). In some fairy tales, the prince is someone with great insight, or realization of the truth, possessing the ability/perseverance to complete the task required to bring it into fruition. In Christian symbology, the three kings or Wise Men who visited the newborn Jesus represent our soul, mind, and body.

See **prince; royalty**. If applicable, see **castle; throne**.

kiss

Depending on who/what is being kissed, it can represent spiritual devotion or reverence; worldly emotion/passion; respect and chivalry (kissing a woman's hand); betrayal (the Judas kiss); a malevolent influence (''kiss of death''); hostility (''kiss off''). In fairy tales a kiss can bring forgetfulness, or transformation/awakening (the prince kisses Sleeping Beauty).

See **sex**.

kitchen

A kitchen is a place of creativity, nurturing (emotional or physical), and may, for some, be a place where the family gathers; hence, the repository of family heritage/connection. If you have negative feelings about a kitchen, such as a place of drudgery, then those feelings will most likely apply to *your* kitchen imagery. As with all rooms, consider its condition (tidy, disorganized?); who's within; what actions are occurring. Archetypally, the kitchen—related to cooking/eating/digestion—can symbolize transformation.

Depending on the activities occurring, see **cook(s)/cooking; eating; food; home; house; room(s)**.

kite

Exultant feelings (''flying high''); alcohol/drug issues (''high as a kite''); needs for freedom or to break away, or other issues of control. As an object in the sky, it may represent a need for union with divinity or the spiritual realm. Consider the kite's colors/shapes and the ease/difficulty of flying it.

See **flying**.

knapsack

How light/heavy is the knapsack and how easy/difficult is it to carry? If there are no problems, it may represent your ability/capacity/willingness to shoulder responsibilities. Otherwise, it may represent activities/relationships that you feel are a burden; perceiving yourself as carrying a heavy load on your back. Additional symbolism may relate to the knapsack's contents. Food and positive objects may represent your ability to nurture or take care of yourself; resources on which you can rely; your ability to be self-sufficient/independent. The knapsack of the American Indian god Kokopelli contains gifts for seducing girls, while those in the knapsack of Santa Claus reward good boys and girls.

See **baggage; luggage**. If applicable, see **camper/camping; walk(ing)**.

knee(s)

Feeling highly emotional, possibly scared or inadequate ("weak in the knees"); being involved more than is comfortable ("knee-deep"); issues of power/control ("bring them to their knees").

kneel

From what perspective are you kneeling (in homage, submission, prayer?)? If kneeling before some object or person you don't know, ask what aspect of yourself feels subservient to, or is being suppressed for, other characteristics of yourself; what behavior/feelings need to be controlled. Kneeling suggests there may be a cause you've selected to serve; a person whom you've begun to revere; possibly feeling inferior/inadequate in some association/relationship; a need to belong and be accepted, possibly by a professional group. There may be someone in your life whom you feel you need to support more adequately, or conversely, from whom you need more support. Kneeling in prayer relates to spiritual needs; connection/need for union with a higher being/values; time to attend to your own inner wisdom.

See **knee(s); posture(s)**. If applicable, see **idol**.

knife

In Freudian terminology a knife, which is a weapon and also cuts/thrusts, can represent the penis/sexual activity. It can be related to issues of power/inadequacy, protection/defensiveness; or it can represent betrayal (a "knife in the back"). There are many superstitions about giving/receiving knives, and if known to you, your dream may relate to one of those. From a Jungian point of view, a knife can cut away the superficial/nonessential/obscure and get to the heart/core of the matter. It is, thus, related to hidden knowledge/insight. It can signal the willingness to make clear endings and carve new beginnings (Estés).

See **scissors; sex; sword; weapon**.

knight

In fairy tales/mythology, the knight is the hero/warrior, often the protector of maidens or guardian of spiritual objects. He carries the ideals and represents honor; mastering instincts (mounted on the horse); the quest toward wholeness. In a woman's dream, he could relate to her male ideal (animus); the wish to be swept off her feet by a "knight on a white horse" (or a waking-life relationship that "feels" like that's happening, perhaps going too fast?); her logical values. In a man's dream, he could represent the heroic aspect of the dreamer; the journey toward wholeness; an impetuous/adventuring aspect of the personality; anxiety about a situation in which honor in general, or personal honor, is at stake.

Metaphysically knights symbolize a person who's at the level of "working disciple" in understanding the mysteries/archetypal energies/spiritual aspects of life.

If applicable to your dream, see: **armor; Grail; horse(s); king; prince; shield; sword(s)**.

knit(ting)

Feelings about present/past family members who knit; your relationship with, or emulation of, someone who taught you to knit; feelings about relaxation/hobbies/social recreation (suggesting a need for time out from your regular routine); creativity; accomplishment; repairing ("knit together") relationships/differences; spinning a plot/intrigue (if negative). It's related to weaving/spinning/needlework, which can simultaneously be relaxing, demanding, require/develop patience (von Franz). Consider also the symbolism of the object being made.

See **clothes/clothing**, if applicable; **craft(s)**.

knob

As something to hold on to, a knob can represent the penis. In sexual slang, knobs refer to breasts. Usually round, and especially if a doorknob, it can symbolize a primitive mandala and represent the beginnings of individuation, the opening of another door in the journey toward wholeness.

See **key/keyhole**, if applicable.

knock(ing)

Knocking signals our presence, requests entry/recognition, and is a noise that focuses our attention. Therefore, a dream with a knocking noise in it suggests that some aspect of yourself, or some waking situation, calls for more of your attention, or needs more looking into.

It can be related to anxiety about pregnancy ("knock up"), physical abuse ("knock around"), or appearance ("she's a knockout"); an expression of aggression (a "knock-down, drag-out," "knockout"); something that has lost its value (the price has been knocked down) or isn't what it seems ("knockoff").

Knocking on wood to ward off bad luck (from boasting; pride) is a popular superstition. Your dream may be saying that you have an inflated view of yourself. In sexual slang, "knockers" refer to breasts.

If applicable, see **boat; door; sex; vehicle(s); water**.

knot(s)

Knots can symbolize unity; community; physical, but more likely psychological, bondage ("tied up in knots"); anxiety ("my stomach is in knots"); a complex issue (Gordian knot). Knots may represent binding/holding, positively or negatively (marriage is sometimes referred to as "tying the knot"); unchanging situations. If released/undone, they may reflect freedom; lack of restraint; the unraveling of an issue. They can reflect feelings of confusion ("tangled up"); powerlessness; a need to take charge.

Many handmade rosaries or prayer "beads" are made by tying knots in a particularly symbolic way; thus, knots formed in a rhythmic order and pattern can be related to devotion. However, in many cultures knots tied in a specific order and pattern, and under certain conditions, are believed to have magical powers.

Knots are related to the labyrinth in that many mazes and mazelike designs were portrayed by a series of knots. When one reaches the center, the knots of particular beliefs are unraveled (Conty). The Gordian knot is a long-standing symbol for the labyrinth; to undo it is to find the center, or in Jungian terms, the Self (Cirlot).

See **labyrinth/maze; rope**.

label

Identification; receiving/imparting knowledge; ownership; the way you see yourself or think others see you.

labyrinth/maze

A labyrinth or maze may symbolize feelings of being lost ("life is like a maze"); or suggest it's time to find a new way/direction. Perhaps you need more patience/fortitude in some situation in order to reach your goal, even though you can't see the center at the moment.

In ancient times, labyrinthine rites symbolized death and rebirth (as in the one that contained the Minotaur); initiation (as in the British turf labyrinths); a spiritual journey/pilgrimage (the labyrinths of European pilgrimage churches, notably Chartres Cathedral, France). Seen from above, a labyrinth is a spiral, and represents the involvements/illusions we must go through in the search for truth/self-development. In medieval times the philosopher's stone (Jungian concept of the Self) was sometimes portrayed as being hidden at the center of a maze, making it clear that to traverse the maze/labyrinth was equivalent to our personal journey ("treading the maze") of transformation toward our center/wholeness.

Labyrinths have often been portrayed ornamentally by a series of knots made in a single string, representing complexity and simplicity simultaneously. There are always varying perspectives within the maze. A dream with a maze in it may be one you return to for many years as you gain perspective and understand more about paradox.

See **knot(s); mandala; spiral; Self**.

ladder

Goals/ambitions (''at the top of the ladder''); professional or work-related effort/skills (''climbing the ladder of success''); attitudes about challenge or hard work; having sex; death/rebirth themes; access to, or union with, the divine (Jacob's ladder). Individual rungs may represent various goals/levels of achievement; your place in your profession/society; difficulties or negative attitudes/actions that are holding you back (especially if damaged).

See **ascend(ing); climb(ing) a ladder; stairs; step(s)**.

lagoon

Like all bodies of water, a lagoon relates to unconscious material; the womb; maternal waters. Lagoons are usually well-protected, safe havens for relaxation (''sleepy lagoon''). Your dream may relate to a need to escape from burdensome waking activities; or it may refer to intimacy/sexual needs/issues.

See **harbor; water**.

lake

Lakes, as common places of purification/initiation, can represent a change in your way of life; emerging unconscious material that will promote growth. Like all bodies of water, it can represent the womb; pregnancy; a desire/need to return to mothering waters and be nourished or escape responsibility; knowledge that's deep/mysterious, possibly occult/metaphysical; your inner world of feelings/emotions. If the surface is mirrorlike, it may symbolize reflection that leads to awareness. If a *constructed* lake/pond, it may refer to the personal unconscious rather than the collective unconscious, often symbolized by the ocean/sea (J. Hall).

See **boat; mirror** (if applicable); **water**.

lamb

Innocence; vulnerability. Consider whether there's some person/situation wherein either of these characteristics is apparent, or wherein you should exert more protection of yourself/another. It may reflect a situation in which you're behaving ''meek as a lamb'' (typical or unusual for you?), or in which you feel ''like a lamb being led to the slaughter.'' Perhaps you suspect someone is trying to ''pull the wool over your eyes.''

In Christian symbology, lambs often represents the flock (of Christians), or a single lamb represents the ''stray'' Christian, looked after/found by Christ, the shepherd. In Latin, *agnus dei* means "lamb of God" and applies to the name Agnes.

See **animal(s); sheep**.

lame/lameness/ limp(ing)

Feeling inadequate; uncertain/ unsure (not surefooted); lack of confidence/assertiveness ("just barely limping along"); needing help and being afraid to ask for it. You may be trying, unsuccessfully, to escape from a waking situation, or perhaps you're having trouble facing responsibility and, in either case, may have only a "lame excuse."

See **body; disabled; foot/feet; leg(s); walk(ing); wound(s)/ wounded.**

lamp/lantern

A situation/relationship in which you need to acquire answers/insight ("shed some light on"); light and hope, which is also related to finding your direction or to new direction; wisdom, possibly of a higher nature or your own internal wisdom; consciousness; action based on reflection and analytical thought.

See **dark/darkness; light**.

lance

As a spear or weapon, a lance represents the need to defend/ protect yourself, to keep yourself at a distance. A broken lance could represent anxieties about protecting, or your inability to protect, yourself.

Medically, to lance an infected area refers to releasing the poisons/toxins and could relate to a situation/relationship that needs to be healed, or needs to be opened—possibly through communication—and examined more carefully.

landscapes/settings

Landscapes, the settings/backgrounds of your dreams, can suggest where you are in your life or relationships, and how you're viewing the world and your place in it, so always take time to derive your own association/meaning about the setting. Jung believed scene changes within the same dream were causal rather than random. They may show psychological transitions/development/progress, while Edinger, a Jungian analyst, thinks that several scenes are varying ways of describing the same central idea.

Review a dream series considering only the setting to determine how frequently you have the same landscape (inflexibility, habitual attitudes, unfinished business, security?) and what a progression of settings may be saying about: where you are emotionally, the chronology of your life's journey, or the state of your concerns/feelings. For Freud, déjà vu landscapes—you feel you've been there before—represent your mother's genitals; however, from a Jungian point of view, it may represent a recurring situation/life drama that you've failed to recognize consciously.

Sunny days suggest a lighter, more optimistic viewpoint than cloudy/gloomy days. Daytime suggests more active control than dreams with a nighttime setting; but they may also be related to inner masculine (sun) or feminine (moon) issues. Nocturnal landscapes can relate to unconscious material, while a scene that changes from night to day could represent becoming more aware of unconscious material, becoming more enlightened/aware/alert. In general, inside locations often speak of psychological work. Outdoor settings have to do with spiritual values or with expanding viewpoints, and, often in the United States, with escape/freedom/recreation. If you come from a country (or participate in activities) where nature/the outdoors is valued and very much in evidence (such as one of the Scandinavian countries), nature/outdoor dreams are quite common.

If your dream has more than one scene, it may be helpful to consider each of them as "varying ways to describe the same central idea" (Edinger, p. 23). However, changing scenes/settings can, in general, refer to various stages in your life, the layout of your life.

lane

Roads pertain to your direction in life. Like pathways, lanes tend to be smaller, shorter, and sometimes hidden among trees or between buildings. They suggest short-term goals; shortcuts; more intimate situations or relationships ("down lovers' lane"); possibly secrets. They may reflect a need to find your own way, or a different way that's out of the ordinary or not expected by others (peers, parents?). Often they have charming or prosaic names, which can reflect their symbolism.

See **road**.

language

An emphasis on language, especially one that's foreign or strange to you, suggests a message you're not receiving or a situation to which you are not giving enough attention; an attempt to make you more aware with respect to a waking situation, or possibly to your own internal signals; a need to be an authority with respect to special/

esoteric information not everyone can understand.

If you're learning a foreign language, the dream may reflect your efforts/anxiety. It is said that you haven't fully learned a language until you're able to dream in it.

lapis

In gem lore, the lapis stone, which can bear any color in the blue or blue-violet range, is a profound symbol related to higher spiritual vibrations/aspirations. Jung speculated that lapis was probably the philosopher's stone, representing the Self.

Lapis can represent inner development, which may be reflected in a surge of growth or creative activity based on inner confidence. It could indicate that you have the skills to take on some task/challenge, including resolving old issues, and successfully complete it.

Lapis is not a single mineral, but a mixture of several. If you know this, it may relate to something that's not "pure" but is, nevertheless, valued because of its combinations. It may refer to the ability to see the potential wealth/value in variety/differences.

See **blue; gem(s)**.

larder

See **food; horde/hoard; pantry**.

large

A large, possibly looming, figure often represents authority/power, menacing or helpful depending on the dream action. Large/oversized figures/animals, possibly monsters, in an adult dream may represent childhood memories/fears, or buried traumatic experiences. They can also signal an archetypal figure/theme.

See **big; giant; size**.

last

Being last in a situation can refer to your self-image: You don't count for much, or someone in a relationship puts other priorities before you. It may be related to being caught up in the past, as opposed to being in front and looking to the future. If you've been feeling proud/successful (egotistical) during waking life, the dream may be a compensating/balancing one.

Could this dream reflect your perception of yourself in a work project/professional situation?

We have many idioms that suggest that last is better or more valued ("last but not least," "and the last shall be first"). Often the last person in relay competitions repairs, or builds on, what the others have done. The last runner in a relay race is the fastest; can make up for others' slowness; and is the one who will actually cross the finish line. Likewise, some of our idioms refer to having another kind of victory ("last laugh," "last word").

See **first; lose/losing something**.

late

To dream of being late may remind you of an appointment. It can relate to anxiety about your adequacy or ability to perform tasks, or an avoidance of responsibility; regret/concern about having missed certain life experiences; feelings of being left out of some situation. Arriving too late to catch the train/plane/other conveyance suggests anxiety about your ability to reach your goals. From a Freudian perspective, this may be an immoral, sexual goal, and at some level, the dreamer realizes that it's too late, the plan cannot be realized. "Arriving-too-late" dreams may occur during times when you have ambivalence about a situation/project/goal. They can signal that you're reaching the limit of your physical strength, especially if part of a number of other frustrating dreams.

See **time**. For late in the day, see **evening**.

laugh/laughter

Laughing may reflect that your daily activities have become too heavy and you need to: become more carefree ("laughter is the best medicine"); take more time out to play/have fun/acknowledge your inner child. It may be an additional release of tension, which is one of the functions of dreams.

If being laughed *at*, especially with derision, it may reflect feelings of inadequacy with respect to a particular situation/relationship; fear/anxiety about being shamed or made to feel guilty. If an unknown person, consider that the image may, nevertheless, represent someone from your past, particularly a person in authority. Disguised or not, you may be laughing at yourself, which can reflect inner guilt (conscience) or derision. If the laughter is not hostile, it could be a message from your inner self that you're taking yourself too seriously and need to laugh at your human foibles.

launch

Related to the symbolism of boat/ship, a launch, or the actual action of launching a boat, may reflect concerns/ideas about beginning/creating something new in your own life (a relationship, project, business?).

See **boat; ship/shipwreck; water**.

laundry

Clothes represent our persona, the roles we play, so doing laundry could represent an attempt to "clean up your act" or change your image; concerns about how you appear to others. If your clothes are hanging outside for all to see, how do you feel in the dream: happy, embarrassed (too many holes in your image?); or are you "airing your dirty laundry in public"? If your laundry is underclothes, it may be related to a sexual relationship; body image; sexual issues/attitudes.

See **clothes/clothing; persona** and specific garments.

lava

Meaning varies depending on whether the lava is hot/flowing (strong emotions such as anger, passion, or lust?) or has cooled (repressed/deadened feelings; unfinished business that prevents growth; rigid attitudes?). If covered with green growth/mosses, it may represent the possibility of new life/ability, but those dangerous past experiences/feelings still lie beneath that plush surface. If the lava has broken down into black sand, perhaps your unconscious (water) is chipping away at negative/shadow material. Persons with a life-threatening illness or high fever may dream of magma or lava (Siegel).

See **destruction; fire; flow(ing); sex; volcano**. Depending on the color, see **black; red**.

lavatory

See **bathroom; toilet**.

lawyer

Lawyer is related to laws, justice/injustice, judgments, evaluations; and any situation in which they are present, absent, or in which you think they're not functioning. If you've been involved in a recent legal situation, your dream may reflect feelings/anxieties related to that. An attorney can represent a situation requiring a decision, especially one in which fairness/injustice plays a part; a decision in which you feel you were treated unfairly or cheated; your conscience (family and social laws); an authority/parent figure (who makes the laws). Is there some situation in which you need to defend yourself, or need another to defend you? Are you ignoring, fighting, or trying to change the natural order of things?

See **court; judge/judging/judgment; justice; scales of justice**.

lead

An issue/situation/relationship that weighs heavily on you, or is toxic; depression; the "weighting" down of creative energy or unconscious insight. You may be in a situation in which blame/guilt is being heaped on you by yourself/another.

Lead symbolizes the first alchemical stage *(nigredo)*. Since the alchemical process—which really related to the psychological process of growth—was to change lead into gold, it may signal you need to begin, or are undertaking beginning stages of, psychological or emotional growth (see **individuation**). Awareness, reviewing the past for old guilt, and/or self-forgiveness may be the first steps.

See **gold(en)**.

leader/lead(ing)

Leading a group, or emphasis on a leader, relates to your need/ability to guide others or to assert your ideas, or any fearful/reluctant feelings you have about that. Consider whether there has been a waking situation in which you've been too passive; and the dream is telling you that you have (and are ignoring?) the capacity for more assertive action. Perhaps the dream is showing that you need to, and can, take some leadership action (some new control over your life or behavior?) to activate your dormant capacity. The dream image can be related to waking issues regarding responsibility; independence/dependence; active/passive; to feelings/issues about authority. (Therefore, the leader could reflect your relationship with a parent.)

See **follow(er)**. If applicable, see **crowd; last**.

leaf/leaves

If a particular leaf, or the leaves of a particular tree, consider the symbolism of its/their shape, color, and type of tree. It may be a wish, or recognition, that you stand out among others; a wish/need to be among others, socialize more, or have more companionship.

Spring leaves and blossoms relate to energy; growth; ambitions; new projects or ideas. Summer leaves relate to fruition; fulfillment of goals/ambitions. Autumn or falling leaves relate to the end of a cycle/project; low energy that needs to be replenished; aging; concerns you have about death.

See **tree(s)** and the applicable season: **autumn; spring** [season]; **summer; winter**.

leave/leaving

See **depart(ing)/departure**.

left [direction]

Movement toward the left in a counterclockwise direction symbolizes movement into the unconscious. Sometimes going/turning left indicates movement backward in time or emotion; an issue involving feminine or more passive/receptive aspects, traits, or concerns.

See **direction(s); movement; right**.

left behind

An inability to keep up (''fall behind''); feelings of inadequacy/incompetency; feelings of being overwhelmed by work/responsibilities, possibly because you have difficulty setting priorities; a wish to avoid responsibility; an inability/need to complete some emotional issue and ''put it all behind you.'' It can relate to competition; promotion; success issues in your work/profession. Being left behind, or leaving someone behind, share some of the same symbolism as being abandoned or being late.

See **abandon(ed); late; lost**.

left side of body

Often considered the ''feminine/receptive'' side, it can represent passive action (especially if you're right-handed); feelings/emotions; intuition; female influence (mother or other adult females). Healing energy is considered to enter the left hand and emerge from the right (power) hand.

See **body**.

leg(s)

Overall the leg relates to balance in your life; the ability to navigate through life; your stance (''don't have a leg to stand on'') or emotional position (''on your last leg''). The leg below the knee refers to abilities/confidence (internal support), while thighs refer to stamina/endurance.

Consider whether there's a situation offering too much, or not enough, independence/autonomy; one in which you feel you're doing too much ''legwork'' without enough credit; or is it time to get on with some situation/project (''shake a leg'')? Perhaps the dream is alerting you that someone is ''pulling your leg''?

See **body; calf/calves**.

lemon

Usually our first association is to sourness/tartness, so your dream may be saying there's something wrong in a waking situation/relationship that you have not fully recognized—possibly related to a woman (tart?)—or one in which your feelings have soured. Lemons may relate to past/present resentment; a need to shock someone into awareness. Many people are familiar with the phrase ''When life gives you lemons, make lemonade,'' and if you are, then your dream may be saying you need to consider the opportunities, or how you can make opportunities, from a situation that otherwise looks quite sour.

See **fruit(s)**.

lens

The need to see an issue/relationship from a different perspective. It may be that you're not getting enough recognition/attention. Perhaps you need to focus more on some situation, or change your focus/viewpoint.

If applicable, see **binoculars; camera; eye(s)**.

leopard

Wild animals relate to instinctual energy, but large cats also reflect the wild woman archetype/energy, according to Clarissa Pinkola Estés in *Women Who Run With the Wolves*. It is a creative energy that, if acknowledged, allows a woman to become more fully female. You may have been doing the kind of growth work that's now allowing your inner leopard to emerge; or you may be experiencing a lack of freedom/autonomy in your life, and a need to break free. Is there some way in which you're feeling oppressed or stalked?

letter

If not from someone known, perhaps some aspect of yourself is trying to send you a message; therefore, consider also the symbolism of the sender. Sometimes we receive information from our inner wisdom/intuition through letters.

If from a known person, the letter, or behavior related to the letter, may reflect feelings you haven't acknowledged about this person; issues you haven't realized existed; characteristics about yourself represented by that person. An unopened letter can relate to defensiveness; a need to ignore, or the fact that you are ignoring, certain messages in your waking life. It can point out that you have resources available that you're not using, or that you're not listening to your intuition. The letter may be a pun on mail/male or ''let her'' and the activities related to it, and then would refer to some waking situation/relationship, possibly sexual.

See **mail**.

letter carrier

See **letter; mail; messenger**.

librarian/library

A need to take charge of, organize, or put things right; wanting to know about/acquire knowledge/wisdom; digging into the past and allowing forgotten memories/feelings to emerge; utilizing/needing additional inner/outer resources; tapping into the collective unconscious. Feelings emerging from your unconscious, or related to a waking situation, might be creating a sense of chaos/turmoil, accompanied by the wish that you could sort them out and shelve them for a while. There may be some waking situation in which you've been overly orderly/meticulous, or have not been careful/methodical enough. A library is also a place where we must be quiet. Is there some situation you have been too loud about?

See **book(s)/looking at books**.

lice

Anxiety/anger about sexual experiences; expression of an aversion toward some person/situation (he's a louse), and a need to distance yourself; feelings of guilt, possibly of feeling "unclean" emotionally/physically; a fear that you're in a parasitical situation/relationship in which you'll be used.

See **crab(s); insects**.

light

Consciousness/awareness ("shed light on the subject"); an enlightened state; an expression/recognition of spirit or spiritual material; protection; insight ("let there be light"); happiness ("trip the light fantastic"); synthesis. Bright light dreams are sometimes common for dying persons. However, if you're not dying, bright light may signal that you need, or are ready to shift to, a new level of feeling/awareness.

Dim/insufficient light suggests the inability to "see the light," or to examine a situation in the "cold light of day"; lack of insight; that you're "hiding your light." Don't forget that "every light has its shadow" aspect. Lights that are flickering or going out may pertain to feelings you're unable to express in waking life (Estés).

Consider the light's shape and position for additional clues; whether it's related to your body, someone else's, or not to a body at all; whether it's surrounding you (protection? encouragement? preparation?), invading you (reflecting chaos/disorientation prior to achieving new meaning?), or whether you're suffused by the light (the coming together of confusion into recognition and alignment with your higher or inner self?). The latter state is sometimes expressed by a fountain of light.

See **angel(s); aura; candle(s); dark/darkness; lamp/lantern; luminous; shadow**.

lighthouse

As a light in the dark and a "tower" with windows, it can symbolize consciousness; enlightenment; a need to focus your attention or awareness (vigilance). Because of its association with water and with the tower, it may be a signal/warning that you're acting too much from your unconscious and need to think things through more clearly.

See **beacon; tower**.

lightning

See **thunder/lightning**.

lily

It's often used as a symbol of the mystical or Eastern wisdom approach. If white, it may reflect purity; virginity; any concerns you have related to sexual issues. Usually considered a feminine symbol, and one of royalty, it therefore can represent the Self for a female dreamer. It's also a symbol of the Roman Great Mother goddess Juno (Greek, Hera). Using her sacred lily, Juno conceived Mars and is, thus, another blessed/sacred virgin.

See **flower(s); virgin.**

limp(ing)

See **lame/lameness/limp(ing)**.

line

In metaphysical symbolism, a line takes you from one point/position to another, and is related to duality and the number two. It's also related to movement/nonmovement ("hold the line"), and limits/boundaries (don't cross the line"). Emphasis on a line of people/objects (cars, pennants, long straight road) suggests you need to enhance your awareness of some situation/relationship by considering more carefully the opposites of movement, and the direction/boundaries involved in the dream.

See **boundaries; two**.

link

Links in a fence, necklace, or bracelet relate to connectedness (see the symbolism of the particular object). If broken, it may refer to a relationship that is ended; feelings of loneliness or of not being connected with any group. Are you a "weak link," or concerned about/needing to recognize one in a waking situation? Broken links in a chain-link fence may serve to point out the possibility of invasion, or escape from an oppressive/burdensome situation.

If applicable, see **chain(s)/chained; jewelry**.

lion(s)

A classic symbol of power/kingship, lions can, therefore, represent a male authority figure, possibly your father. Consider whether there's a waking situation/relationship in which you need to exert more power/responsibility, or in which you're feeling dominated, possibly overpowered.

In ancient Egypt, lions represented the horizon and the sun and were guardians of the sacred. Astrologically it can symbolize a person born under the sign of Leo (July 24–August 23). In Christian symbolism, it represents the evangelist Mark; in Jewish tradition, the lion signifies the tribe of Judah.

People who've become depressed because they're frustrated in the fulfillment of wild, excessive, demanding, or outlandish desires may dream of lions (von Franz).

See **animal(s); leopard** (for the feminine symbolism).

lion tamer

Taming the instinctual nature; being in charge; having/taking control.

lips

See **mouth/lips**.

liquid

A time of transition/change; a need to let your life follow its natural flow, especially if flowing water or liquid that's being poured. If poured into a container, it may represent a need to control/contain your emotions. However, it may also represent unexpressed emotions that need to be acknowledged and poured out. If the liquid is milk, it can represent a desire for maternal nourishment; sex (semen) and a need for sexual expression/intimacy; regrets ("spilt milk"). A volatile liquid may relate to aggression/frightening emotions.

See **alcohol/alcoholic; flow(ing); milk; water**.

liquor

See **alcohol/alcoholic**.

little

Perhaps there's some psychological position or waking situation/relationship that you've outgrown and that's now too little for you; feelings of being insignificant/helpless (self-esteem issues). Is there a waking situation in which you've said something or behaved in a way that made you ashamed? Could the dream be compensating for waking feelings of aggrandizement/egotism?

See **size; small**.

little people

See **dwarf(s)**.

liver

Emphasis on your own/another's liver suggests the possibility of a physical disorder, perhaps related to alcohol. The dream might be a warning, based on your own anxieties, to reduce your consumption of alcohol. The liver is a detoxifying organ; therefore, the dream could relate to toxic relationships in waking life, i.e., people who don't have your best interests at heart, give you messages that confuse you, or leave you feeling bad/belittled/angry/negative after being with them. For Jung, the liver, or any allusion to it (Liverpool), represented the seat of life; the life process and its healing function.

See **alcohol/alcoholic** (if applicable); **body**.

living room

Its name gives it all away. It's where we live; our conscious processes; our persona, the identity we put on for others. Is the living room a closed-off place, or part of yourself, used only for guests, as in the old-fashioned parlor? How well kept the living room is, the people found there, and the colors of the room/furniture will give you additional clues as to your symbolism.

See **house**.

lizard(s)

Lizards share some of the same symbolism as snakes and dragons, only as a smaller/lesser version. As with all reptiles, the lizard represents earlier, more primitive instincts/reactions (need for sex, food), especially those deriving from our lower brain stem. Thus, it suggests an awareness of, or anxiety about, these functions.

Because of the wonderous diversity of their shapes/sizes and their ability to regenerate parts of their bodies, lizards can represent emerging creativity; access to creative functions; any form of renewal/revitalization. A lizard may represent someone in your life who has a chameleonlike personality, i.e., alters moods/behavior, is elusive or slips away from issues easily.

If you associate lizards with being cold-blooded, thick-skinned, and fearful, they may represent someone who possesses these characteristics; repressed feelings; a need to warm up to some situation/relationship. In esoteric/metaphysical thought, lizards/salamanders often symbolize elemental spirits related to fire.

See **dragon; reptile(s); serpent(s); snake(s)**.

load

If carrying a heavy load, you may be expressing feelings of being oppressed or having to carry too heavy a burden. Conversely, it can suggest that you have not been carrying your load/share and need to do so. It can relate to drinking habits ("getting loaded), or financial issues ("he's loaded").

lobster

Because of its shell and claws, a lobster often represents a need for protection related to feelings of threat/vulnerability. It can represent aggressiveness/hostility; male genitalia. If emerging from water, it suggests emerging feelings/instincts, particularly of a more primitive nature, or conversely, consciousness (victory over being overwhelmed by unconscious material); painful memories from the past.

See **claws; crab(s); shellfish; water**.

lock(ed)

Being locked up can have the same meaning as being imprisoned, i.e., alienated/unacceptable aspects of yourself. It may relate to ideas/aspects of yourself you're protecting "under lock and key"; locking up your feelings or having difficulty getting in touch with them ("locked out"). Consider the symbolism of where the lock is. For instance, if you're locked out of a garden gate, it may relate to frigidity, or a lack of inner flourishing. In Freudian terms locks and keys, or either separately, are usually considered sex-related, referring to sexual intercourse, genitalia, or a sexual relationship. If you repeatedly dream of being locked out, consider using Dreamercise #3, #4, #11, #19 or #20, Part 1, for more understanding of your personal message.

See **cage; force(ing)/forced; imprisoned; key/keyhole; prison/prisoner**.

locomotive

See **engine; train(s); vehicle(s)**.

loft

The higher you go in a house, the more it refers to matters of the mind, i.e., thinking; remembering; drawing on inner, intellectual resources/

abilities. Hence, the dream loft may refer to any of these capacities, especially memories—or wisdom from past experience if you discover a loft you didn't know existed. It can relate to finding new ideas; "lofty" or inflated feelings/ideals that may be inhibiting you. If you're in the loft looking down, you may be compensating for feelings of inadequacy and need to raise your self-esteem. If there's a bed in the loft, your dream may relate to a sexual relationship. Looking out a loft window suggests a more expansive or higher perspective; connection with the cosmos or the divine. Hiding in a loft/attic may reflect guilt or a concern with avoiding blame/being noticed, keeping a low profile. The loft shares much of the same symbolism as the attic.

See **architecture; attic; house; sex** (if applicable).

long

Anything long/elongated refers to the penis. It may also reflect comparison/evaluation issues; prowess; some situation/relationship that's gone on too long.

See **size.**

look(ing)/looked at

If you're watching the action of others (a bystander), consider those characters and their actions as some aspect of yourself you need to recognize; also resources or new behaviors you need to consider. Is there some situation you need to "look over" more carefully, or some aspect of your behavior you've "lost sight of"?

Perhaps you're avoiding responsibility for a situation or refusing to acknowledge your role in it. Looking rather than acting implies a more passive stance, which may be typical of your waking behavior. If not, the dream may be saying you need to bide your time, "look before you leap."

Others looking at you suggests anxiety/pride (depending on dream feeling) about being watched; a need for another viewpoint/perspective. To get at that perspective, use Dreamercise #4, Part 1.

See **see(ing).**

looking back

Looking back into the past; a signal that the dream relates to something in your past to which you need to attend (unfinished business); inhibiting or restrictive memories; unresolved grief. Perhaps you need to look to past events for insight/help in resolving a current issue.

lookout

If in a tower, consider the meaning of the surrounding landscape/setting. The dream may be pointing out that you have anxiety about whether or not you've overlooked something; that you have, in fact, overlooked it; or that you need to overlook it. If in a ranger lookout, consider how it might be related to passion (fire), or form a warning pun (look out).

See **guard(ing); landscapes/settings; tower** (if applicable).

lose/losing something

Losing in a competition suggests a waking anxiety you have about whether you're going to be successful in some relationship/venture. If a recurrent dream, it may be related to self-esteem, confidence, or inner security. Losing some object in a dream suggests anxiety or unresolved grief regarding the object and whatever it symbolizes.

See the symbolism of the specific object lost, and, if applicable, see **competitor/competition; game(s); victory**.

lost

Losing your way suggests losing your direction in life or that you've lost sight of your goals. Without plans/goals, you may be feeling insecure. Or perhaps you're still trying to find your way in a new waking situation or one in which the rules/conditions are changing.

lotus

The lotus, like its companion the water lily, is considered a symbol for the Self (Jung).

See **lily**.

loud/loudspeaker

A message to which you have not attended—your psyche is calling it to your attention; anxiety about having been too loud/emphatic/demanding in a recent situation; a need to "toot your own horn," or make your point more clearly.

love

To dream of love/loving/being loved suggests intense feelings about a waking relationship, or, conversely, that you're presently not getting enough love in your waking life. An earlier love suggests unfinished business/unresolved issues related to that specific relationship; that a present relationship is awakening some of those same issues; that you have a need to bring more of what characterized that relationship into your waking life.

See **emotion(s); sex**.

low

If you're repeatedly in a low position below someone, or are in what you consider a lowly occupation, it suggests a self-esteem issue, feelings of inferiority ("low man on the totem pole"). Is there a waking situation in which you're feeling under the domination/control of another? Low positions can refer to feeling of guilt/embarrassment/depression; or may be compensating for too much egotism or for looking down on someone in waking life.

See **high/height; position(s)**.

lower body

The lower body is related to our more basic, or base, physical needs and to sexual needs/conflicts.

See **digestion; sex** and specific lower body parts.

luck

See **gamble/gambling**.

luggage

It holds needed resources—such as makeup, clothes (therefore, public roles, attitudes); support, or can be excess baggage (unfinished business, burdensome reduce attitudes/behaviors).

Lost luggage relates to feelings of anxiety/helplessness when we don't have access to the familiar elements contained in our luggage; anxiety about travel.

See **baggage; clothes/clothing**.

lumber

How is the lumber being, or going to be, used? Lumber can relate to building/organizing your life. As cut trees, it can relate to unconscious ideas/material; a precious part of yourself that has been cut down. However, it can also refer to transformation; regeneration; a new direction in life; new consciousness/awareness, i.e., not allowing the unconscious (the forest) to rule. In Freudian terms a log is a symbol of the penis, so your dream could be related to sexual needs.

See **construction; forest; tree(s); sex** (if applicable).

luminous

Most simply, the need to honor/affiliate with a person/cause you consider admirable. Luminosity relates to divinity; the spirit realm; higher consciousness; archetypes and archetypal motifs. When luminosity appears in a dream, honor it with one of the dreamercises in Chapter 6, Part 1.

See **aura; globe; halo; light**.

lungs

Lungs are intimately associated with breathing; therefore,

with air. They are related to inspiration, insight; creativity. In waking life one of the first responses to a stressful situation is a change in our breathing, so your dream can be related to waking stress; to a lung/breathing disorder; to a situation/relationship in which you feel suffocated.

See **air; breath/breathe; body**. If applicable, see **drown(ing)**.

lying down

See **prone**.

machine

Habits; mechanical behavior (acting/responding without thinking); mechanical attitude (diminished feeling capacity) toward life; a need to organize (mechanize) or control something in your life; a rigid, unemotional approach to situations/relationships. You may be feeling unstable in some situation and need to add more order (precision) to your life/surroundings. Depending on the machinery and its activities, it may represent sexual activity, possibly too mechanical or unimaginative for you. A breakdown in machinery can relate to a breakdown in your body or to relationship difficulties. Taking the machine apart, attempting to discover what's wrong, or repairing it suggests a need to delve more deeply into some situation for insight and understanding of its dynamics.

See **engine; mechanic**.

mad

See **anger; emotion(s)**.

madness

Aspects of yourself that are out of control or have a quite different perspective; an expression of a unique creativity; an unstable or absurd (''that's crazy'') element in your life.

Madonna

See **Black Madonna; Mary, Virgin**.

maggots

Anxieties about death; a problem/issue that's ''eating away'' at you and destroying your equilibrium. There are usually strong feelings of rejection or disgust associated with maggots. Is there a present/past situation that evokes similar feelings?

See **body; death**.

magic

Having magical powers represents the capacity to get what you want, to make your dreams come true. It may represent your own special, unique abilities; a reaction to feelings of powerlessness in waking life; a need for control (over the elements, your inner nature?); the infantile wish to get what you want without having to work for it. Magical abilities often identify the dream as an archetypal one.

Dreams with magical happenings that result in feelings of ecstasy/exhilaration—called *transcendent dreams* by Canadian psychologist Don Kuiken—may occur three to five years after the death of a loved one.

See **magician; witch/witchcraft**.

magic circle

See **candle(s); circle**.

magic drink

Often a symbol of heightened consciousness; carries some of the same symbolism of **magic**.

magician

Someone who has done a "vanishing act" in relationship to you or who's not quite what he/she seems; an element of duplicity. As a person who manipulates illusion/reality, the magician can represent our ability to fool ourselves, thus, related to our perceptions about a relationship/situation/issue.

Archetypally, the magician brings things into reality and can be a symbol of creativity, fertility, revelation; represents connection with the controlling forces of nature (our own and the natural world). Seeming to have control over supernatural/cosmic forces, the magician harnesses primordial creative energy and helps us transform ourselves.

As magic is a "power" that often needs to be approached through ritual, the magician represents activities that mystify us. In the pun "sleight (slight?) of hand," the magician could equal a small person from your waking life, or newly developing creativity, which may need some attention.

Mythically, he is one representation of the Wise Old Man or father archetype and, therefore, incorporates issues of order, support, and traditional guidance. An evil magician could represent the negative aspects or polarity of the father archetype.

Merlin is an archetypal magician image. Born of an earthly mother and "otherworld" (possibly underworld) father, he is a mediator between the two realms (spirit/matter; conscious/unconscious) and can facilitate their connection. He is a gateway, as are all "sacred" (as opposed to stage) magicians.

See **father; trickster**.

magnet

An existing/developing strong influence/attraction; a wish to be able to exert such an influence/attraction; envy of someone who seems to have more charisma than you. Is there some situation in which you've not asserted yourself to your satisfaction? A bar magnet, having the qualities of positive and negative, represents duality and the union of opposites, possibly a paradox/dichotomy in your waking life or an ambivalent situation, in which you feel both attracted and repelled.

magnify/ magnifying glass

Emphasis/focus so you'll get the point of the dream; a need to make more of an issue than is there; needing to look into/examine the small, possibly hidden, details of a situation (take a closer look).

maid

Depressed women going through a divorce often dream they are maids (Cartwright), which is an issue of lowered self-esteem. It can reflect a waking need for emotional/physical tidiness and order—everything cleaned up and in its place.

mail

Mail has to do with messages; therefore, the dream may relate to messages from your unconscious or inner wisdom. It may relate to your need to communicate with others; pass on your ideas; teach your concepts/beliefs; maintain/reestablish contact with someone from your present/past. Is there a situation in which you haven't said all that you'd like to say? The mail or mail carrier may represent a "male" in your life.

See **letter**.

mail carrier

See **messenger**.

main street

See **road**.

makeup

Perhaps a pun for a need to "make up with" or "make up to" someone. Otherwise, see **cosmetics**.

man/men

The meaning of a particular man, or men, in your dreams varies considerably with the setting, other characters, action, and any other apparent symbology in the dream. If known to you, a male can refer directly to concerns/issues/feelings you have regarding him; or he could represent another, possibly new, man in your life with similar aspects that you may need to consider. An unknown man and his actions can represent your ideal man (animus) if you're a woman; aspects of yourself, possibly inner resources (whether you're male or female) such as assertiveness, fortitude, business acumen. A man's behavior toward you can also highlight anxieties/feelings about that aspect of your own behavior, possibly within a relationship, but not necessarily.

mandala

An important symbol that appears in dreams, or drawings related to dream symbolism, to express the formation/development of the center of the total personality, which Jung called the "Self" to distinguish it from the ego of the conscious. Its early appearance may be as something circular being worn, a circular object, or a circular action being performed. As the individuation process continues and the Self develops, mandalas become more complex.

See **circle; labyrinth/maze; Self**.

mandorla

An almond-shaped outline popularly used in Christian art as a frame/halo for figures of divinity. Earlier, however, it was considered a fertility symbol (almond shape = female vagina). In Oriental art, it represents the *divine* female genitalia (Walker). The mandorla is the space/form that occurs when two circles are drawn partly overlapping, sometimes called the overlap of heaven and earth. For this reason, Jungian Robert Johnson thinks it's the perfect symbol to indicate the healing of the split between our conscious ego and our shadow aspects; hence, the symbol of conflict resolution; union.

mansion

A need to raise yourself to a higher social status or to perceive yourself—or appear—as better, more elegant than you may be feeling; a need to acquire wealth/possessions. If you've been feeling inadequate in waking life, the dream may be pointing out inner wealth, resources, possibilities. It can be a reflection of your religious beliefs or those about life after death. ("In my house, there are many mansions.")

See **architecture; home; house**.

manure

Negatively, it may symbolize some situation/relationship that in waking life you would describe as "full of shit," stinks, or in which there's a lot of bullshit being bandied about. In a positive sense, manure is used as fertilizer, thus related to new growth, transformation, fertility. It is related to the dung beetle (Egyptian scarab). Because the beetle laid its eggs in dung, causing its newborns to "miraculously" emerge from the dung, it became a sign of immortality.

If applicable, see **defecate; excrement; garden; gardener** and any appropriate animal.

map

Maps show us the way through physical (goals, ambitions), cosmic, and psychic realities and prevent us from getting lost. They help us traverse time/space, move up/down (the world axis) through archetypal symbolism. Their appearance suggests any of the above; also, a need for more structure/direction in your life (time to set new goals?). If you're guiding someone else with a map, you may want/need more control, authority, power. Perhaps you've not recognized/acknowledged your expertise; been acknowledged by another; or acknowledged another.

If applicable, see **road; travel(ing)/journey; vehicle(s)**.

march(ing)

Inner movement; growth; progress. If marching in a group, it can represent a need for belonging/camaraderie; a need for order/preciseness; the discipline required to obtain them. Although related to walking, marching doesn't reflect the same amount of independence. Usually you must coordinate your actions with those of others, under the direction of another, which could be related to issues of authority and independence/dependence.

Perhaps you've been involved in a waking situation that requires teamwork, and the dream reflects your feelings about it. Perhaps you need to "step more lively"; have anxieties about or need to march to a different tune. Marching and march music frequently stir strong feelings in people, so your dream may be saying you need to awaken/acknowledge your emotions, or you need to have more emotional experiences.

See **band; parade; procession** (if applicable); **walk(ing)**.

marigold

See **flower(s); Mary, Virgin**.

mark

An identification, sometimes negative ("mark of Cain"); a sign of belonging to a group, distinguished by your membership in, or exclusion from, it. Possibly a wound (scar).

marketplace/ grocery store

The repository of physical or emotional needs—and resources—so consider the specific items you're shopping for (or can't find); the role(s) you're playing; and what you select/reject. It can be related to acquisition needs; difficulties obtaining what you want/need; the variety of choices available. Acquiring/ purchasing food suggests a need for sustenance; nurturance needs are not being met in waking life.

If you're a clerk/salesperson, it may refer to your need to give service. If you consider yourself in a demeaning position, that may be expressing feelings of inadequacy, or balancing waking feelings of superiority.

marksman

If you're learning to shoot, your dream may be an expression of your developing skills and any anxiety you have about your performance or about competition. Otherwise, it likely represents a need to be an expert in some sexual (gun is a phallic symbol) or other expressive situation, perhaps a need for more aggression. Is there some waking situation in which you need to "take aim," be more assertive, or develop a better focus?

See **competitor/competition**, if applicable; **gun(s); target**.

marriage

See **wedding**.

marsh

Old attitudes; unfinished business; a present situation that has you "bogged down"; an emotional mess or confusion; feeling overwhelmed/overburdened ("swamped") by waking situations/relationships or by unconscious material (feelings, attitudes); feeling immobilized and unable to function properly.

See **bog; quicksand**.

martyr

Is there some waking situation in which you feel oppressed, that you're losing your identity, or that your hard work/dedication is unappreciated? Perhaps you're making too great a sacrifice in a relationship or giving too much time/money to some organization, even though it seems to you to be a worthy cause. This dream can reflect an inability to stand up for yourself.

marigold

In medieval art, it was an attribute of the Virgin Mary.

marionette

Someone else is in control or pulling the strings; feeling at the mercy of another; feelings of powerlessness/dependency; lack of purpose or willpower.

See **puppet**.

Mary, Virgin

Personal or societal feelings/ideas/values about motherhood. In Jungian psychology the three aspects of the female psyche are the virgin or maiden (Kore, Persephone), the mother, and the old crone/Wise Old Woman. Mary, the virgin mother, combines two of those aspects and, in Jungian psychology, is considered a contemporary archetypal figure of the Great Goddess or Great Mother. She represents quintessential feminine energy, as it is expressed in sex, love, motherhood. Some believe that the life of the Christian Mary was actually derived over time from the myths or beliefs regarding the Great Goddesses, making it easy for pagans to attend to her and to apply some of the same titles to her as to earlier virgin goddesses.

See **virgin**.

massage

You may not have been receiving enough sensual or sexual stimulation in your waking life; a need to acknowledge your body more or take better care of it; a need for more nurturing and comfort; or a new/recognized need or ability to let go of some of your defensive body armor.

See **body**.

mask(s)

Our persona/facade; a temporary identity you'd like to try on; an inability to show, or lack of recognition of, your true/inner self; a need to hide some aspect of yourself. During pre-Lenten European/South American festivals, masks are often used to boldly portray shadow aspects, thereby allowing us to express socially what would otherwise not be acceptable. In Bali, as in many other countries, masks/dancers are blessed before a performance. Once the dancer dons the mask, the corresponding spirit is considered to have entered him/her and will, of course, influence the performance, reflecting intimate contact with divine intervention/inspiration.

See **beard; persona; shadow**.

mass

Whatever your religion, dreaming of attending/observing a mass suggests deep religious/spiritual needs. It may be time to examine your spiritual situation, to commune with your higher self about your potential. Such a dream can indicate that your inner strength/beliefs are low, or that you need more ritual/reverence in your life. Depending on the dream's contents, you may receive needed strength from it.

See **rite/ritual**.

masseuse/masseur

See **massage**.

masturbation

If masturbation is something you reject or have guilt about, it may, like sexual intercourse, be reflected in your dreams in totally symbolic situations, frequently involving pumping, up/down movements, other rhythmic motions.

Dreaming of yourself actually masturbating may reflect unacknowledged/unexpressed sexual needs; a need to take care of/stimulate yourself in emotional or sensual ways (not necessarily sexual); anxiety/concern about waking-life inhibitions (again, not necessarily sexual); a reflection that something in your waking life is not as satisfying as it might be. Perhaps a relationship needs a little more effort on your part.

Psychoanalysts believe that any sexual dream has a manifest (obvious) meaning and a deeper meaning; therefore, you have to consider both what the dream says and what it conceals (Natterson and Gordon).

See **ejaculation; orgasm; sex**.

matador

Taking charge of your unconscious emotions; power; masculine or "macho" image; a need for control and discipline, or recognition that you have more than you think; need for attention ("look at me") and approval (applause); need to challenge a masculine authority (do you win or lose?).

See **bull(s)**.

mathematics

The order of things; logic; a need to organize some aspect of your waking life. The numbers may have symbolic meaning.

See **account(s); bookkeeping**.

mattress

The present status of your life: whether you feel it's comfortable, hard, doesn't have enough support, needs reorganizing (scruffy or losing stuffing). A featherbed/feather mattress suggests old-fashioned ways, possibly a need for truthfulness (see **feather**).

See **bed**.

Maypole

The Maypole is considered a phallic symbol, so it's likely this dream is related to sexual experiences/relationships/needs. Dancing around a Maypole is an ancient fertility rite. Your dream could also reflect a need to be a part of a group endeavor/ceremony. The Maypole itself represents the *axis mundi* (world tree). Dancing around it symbolizes the universal cycle of time; therefore, your dream could also have a cosmic/archetypal motif, possibly of a birth/rebirth nature.

See **celebration; dance/dancing; rite/ritual; world tree**.

maze

See **labyrinth/maze**.

meal

See **eating; food**.

measurement

Comparison; evaluation of, decisions about, your inner growth/status/abilities; taking the measurement (worth) of someone else; determining if you "measure up" to a task/situation. Is it time to "take stock"?

See **size**. If applicable, see particular measurements: **big; deep; high/height; little; long; low; narrow; short**.

meat

Our animal/physical nature; sexual slang for the penis. If raw, it can reflect our untamed, basic nature (raw emotions); if cooked, civilizing influences. As a food, it can represent our physical satisfactions/emotional needs.

See **eating; food**.

mechanic

Concern with/skills for taking care of/preserving/repairing the engine (the body, your goals, other waking-life structures?). Possibly you need to take time for yourself or need more nurturing. You may have anxiety about some situation/relationship that's "coming apart." Do you need to become more critical/analytical and "take something apart"? What needs to be fixed/ restored in your waking life?

See **engine; engineer**.

medicine/medication

A concern with taking care of some aspect of yourself, or another; nurturing; getting well physically/psychologically; a situation that's left "a bad taste in your mouth"; the need to face up to/accept certain situations/ consequences ("take your medicine") that may ultimately lead to more positive results. It may be related to fear about getting, or a wish to give someone, "a taste of your own medicine." Is there some situation in your waking life that's a "bitter pill" or "hard to swallow"?

If applicable, see **doctor; nurse; pain medication**.

meditation

A need to: take some time out from waking-life activities; connect with/revive your spiritual connections; listen to your inner/ higher self.

medium

A need for contact with the unconscious (intuition); unconscious material about to break through into awareness. In one sense, it can symbolize union/ unity, i.e., the meshing of two boundaries, as consciousness and the unconscious. It can represent anxiety about the future or about death; a need to understand your own/another's motivations; unresolved grief/guilt regarding a deceased person.

See **crystal ball; fortune-teller/fortune-telling; séance**.

melon(s)

See **fruit(s)**.

melt

Transformation; change; a need to become closer or more involved, i.e., to melt boundaries and "warm up" to another person/situation; creating new relationships/situations; closer bonds with friends, colleagues. Negatively, it may refer to not having sufficient willpower or endurance.

See **fire**.

mend(ing)

A need to preserve, repair ("mend your fences"), maintain old attitudes or some aspect of a (possibly long-standing) relationship/situation. (Consider what you're mending.) Is there a waking situation that you'd like to keep predictable or in its present state? Do you need to change your behavior ("mend your ways")?

See **sew(ing)**.

menhir(s)

See **stone(s)**.

menstruation

Most women don't dream directly of menstruation during their periods; rather, their dream images change depending on the stages of their monthly cycle. While actually menstruating, dream content is likely to include the color red, receptacles/containers overflowing with water or other fluids, flowing images such as rivers or streams, images of enclosed spaces or containers, and themes of injury, destruction, even dying (Garfield). Those images recede as a woman progresses through her cycle. If you dream of menstruating when it's not yet time, it can indicate anxiety about your cycle or the occurrence of periods. Sometimes it heralds an unexpected/early period.

mermaid

For a male dreamer, she may represent his anima, while in a woman's dream, she may represent unconscious (water) feminine aspects yet to be acknowledged/realized. As a composite creature, she represents the conscious and unconscious, and our attempt at union; material that has emerged and been tamed/humanized (the human upper body), and as yet untamed (unconscious) material (the tail and her relationship to water).

For another composite creature, see **Minotaur**.

merry-go-round

A need for fun/frivolity; feeling oppressed, overwhelmed, or overburdened. "Going around in circles and not getting anywhere"; repressed sexual urges; possibly a mandala.

If applicable, see **amusement park; horse(s)**.

mess

Disorder/chaos in your emotional/physical life; a signal that you've "messed up" with respect to some situation; guilt about "messing around." Time to "clean up your act."

message

See **messenger; voice; write/writing**.

messenger

The messenger motif is an ancient and archetypal one. In biblical stories/fairy tales, the messenger, often a stranger, represents divine wisdom; gifts from the divine (or from sacred or higher aspects of yourself); messages from the Self. As divinity in disguise, the messenger is related to alchemy and symbolizes that aspect of yourself that you need to work with to understand/transform your ego/consciousness into a more authentic state of being.

metal

Valuable, enduring, strong aspects of ourselves (''his mettle''); the transforming or growth process, individuation—the shamans or magicians of myths were often blacksmiths, who shaped metal (formed the Self). In Jungian symbology, it can sometimes represent sexual/basic urges that need refining/purifying (civilizing).

microscope

Examining a situation from a new, perhaps sharpened, perspective; introspection; heightening your awareness about the dynamics of a situation; something in waking life that you need to take another/closer look at; a possibility that ''bears looking into.'' Negatively, it could refer to amplifying some aspect of yourself (egotism) or another (adoration); to making more of an issue than it warrants. Consider also the symbolism of what you see in the microscope.

See **binoculars; magnify/magnifying glass**.

midday

See **noon**.

middle

As a position, it can reflect feelings of: taking a neutral stance; unwillingness to make a commitment; being crowded or not having enough personal/emotional space; not being special enough; an issue that exists in the present rather than the past.

For something that's being divided ''down the middle,'' see **divide/division**. For ''middle of the road,'' see **road**.

mighty

Power/control (''might is right''); physical and emotional strength/endurance. If you have been feeling inadequate recently, this dream may be compensating for that. Excessive might could indicate an archetypal image.

military

Feelings about your own military experience, possibly an attempt to resolve trauma about it. Whether or not you've served in the military, it could symbolize feelings activated in a waking situation with respect to issues of discipline/laxness; order/control; authority; obedience/disobedience; dependence/independence. It could represent a need to belong to a structured community in a time of disruption; feelings that you've lost your individuality/uniqueness.

See **warrior**.

milk

Mother's milk, the primal nourishment. Feeding/giving another milk may symbolize giving basic life energy, nurturing at an elemental/primal level; a need to restore yourself in some basic ways. Milk suggests that a present situation may have awakened some old, early fears/anxieties/needs. Perhaps you're "milking" a situation, i.e., being too greedy or prolonging it. Thin/runny milk may represent poor nurturing; starving for support; semen (therefore, related to fertility or sex needs/issues).

See **cow(s); mother; sex**.

mill

If a grain mill, it may refer to extracting the essence of an experience; the work we have to do (grinding) before we can clearly understand the impact/value of a situation. A lumber mill suggests processing ideas; transformation; and the shaving off of our rough exterior to reach our growth potential.

See **grind(ing); lumber**.

mine

The unconscious and the unrefined emotions/potentials within. It can also be a pun for declaring your ownership of something.

See **cave; dig(ging); hole; jewel(s); minerals**.

minerals

Minerals/ore can represent your precious inner resources/potential, which can be refined (transformed) and combined in many ways for creativity; ideas waiting to be mined.

See **crystal; jewel(s) mine**.

minister/pastor

If you're not a minister, the dream may be an expression of your spiritual nature or need to acknowledge/develop it; your ability to minister to (acknowledge/support) your inner needs; positive/negative attitudes about religious authority/tradition. Consider whether there's a situation in which you're preaching too much when you should be listening or offering other emotional support.

See **priest**.

Minotaur

Dark, destructive forces/emotions that prevent growth and enlightenment (as the Minotaur in the Minos labyrinth); shadow aspects. As a composite creature with a human body and steer's head, he represents the conscious and unconscious and our attempt at union (untamed bestial/primitive impulses in the upper animal part; civilized conscious material grounded by Mother Earth in the human body).

For another composite creature, see **mermaid**.

mirror

Mirrors are complex symbols and in Jungian terms are related to a number of motifs. They can symbolize the intellect, namely, our thoughts (reflections); so looking into a mirror can symbolize reflection in general or, especially, self-reflection (appraisal). It may represent coming "face-to-face" with an inner or worldly issue. What you see may be related to your persona, and a need to strengthen/change it (putting on makeup; adjusting your appearance). Zen priests often speak of the inner mirror, which is the Buddha- or God-mind—the Self, in Jungian terms.

Seeing images in the mirror may be a safer way to consider material from the unconscious (similar to a dream within a dream); an expression of material ready to emerge into conscious awareness. Mirrors symbolize the imagination, another link/door between the unconscious and conscious worlds (as when Alice goes through the looking glass).

In fairy tales, mirrors are often magic (connecting us to various aspects of ourselves, as does the mirror in "Beauty and the Beast"); or relate to issues of truth/self-deception and vanity (the wicked queen's mirror in "Snow White"). They are linked to self-aggrandizement, as in the myth of Narcissus, and to the twin theme. As a reversal, mirror images can be linked to the shadow and to opposites or opposing forces (their battle and their union).

See **face; persona; reflection**.

miscarriage

If you've miscarried previously and are once again pregnant, it may represent anxiety about carrying the fetus to full term. If you're not pregnant, but have miscarried in the past, it may be a healing dream similar to post-traumatic stress dreams (see Part 1, Chapter 5, National Nightmares section). If you're not pregnant and have never miscarried, then the dream suggests a waking situation that has gone wrong or that you fear won't be successful; a miscarriage of justice.

See **abortion**.

mist

See **fog/mist**.

moat

Defensiveness; a need to protect/distance yourself from some person/situation; surrounded (overwhelmed?) by unconscious urges/instincts. Perhaps there's a waking situation in which you feel your integrity has been attacked.

See **castle; drawbridge; water**.

model

If an object, consider the symbolism of the specific object. In general, a model represents a scaled-down version of a problem/situation, possibly in an attempt to make less of it or to get it down to a size with which you can cope. It represents skill/preciseness, so the dream may be reminding you that you have these attributes available for some waking situation (see **craft(s)**).

If a person, consider what masculine/feminine aspects of yourself he/she displays, as well as a need to "show off" or be admired. It may represent anxiety about your own figure. What aspect of you needs to "shape up"? Is there some situation in which, if you don't shape up, you're going to be shipped out?

See **body**.

mold

When related to constructing art/products, it may represent consistency; a lack of creativity (rigidity, following the same old pattern). A broken mold can represent a need to break away from old patterns and try new ways; uniqueness ("they broke the mold after they created you"); helplessness; a need for structure.

Mold as an organism can refer to something that's fallen into disuse or has been ignored; dying and/or transformation—out of the old comes a new kind of growth.

Either of the above can serve as a pun for the other.

monastery

A need to withdraw, possibly for rest, spiritual review, or self-examination; a need to restrain your emotions or your sexual expression; a wish to avoid social, family, professional responsibilities.

See **architecture; monk**.

money

Personal energy; inner resources; acquisition or materialistic issues; the cost of a relationship/situation; a need to be regarded as worthwhile. If you lose money, consider what emotional losses you may have incurred, or fear you will incur, in a waking situation. Finding money suggests you're feeling inadequate, deprived, or impoverished (mentally or physically) and need more energy/resources; or, conversely, you have new/replenished strengths. A money dream can occur if you're feeling a financial crunch, or are unable to acquire something important to you (emotional or physical). Coins ("change") may represent a need/desire to change.

See **coins; gold(en)**.

monk

The reverential or introspective aspect of yourself; a need for celibacy or emotional withdrawal; a need for belonging to a group/situation in which there's more structure/order than you presently experience; the archetype of the Wise Old Man.

See **hermit; monastery**.

monkey

Silliness; lack of inhibition; spontaneous, funny behavior. Have you been "monkeying with" something you shouldn't have? Perhaps you suspect that someone is engaged in some "monkey business," or your own behavior strikes you in some way as frivolous/foolish. Did some person/situation "make a monkey out of you"?

Monkeys symbolize human foibles to which we cling, unable to give them up, but that, most likely, we should laugh at. They nearly always throw a "monkey wrench" into the best-laid plans. In China, monkeys grant good health and protection; they're related to sorcerers and fairies. In Hindu mythology the archetypal monkey is Hanuman (from the *Ramayana*), the monkey-general who demonstrates vitality, service, and protection.

See **ape; dwarf(s); magician; trickster; primates**.

monogram

Identity; wealth/possessions; self-satisfaction; a desire for recognition/appreciation.

Perhaps something in waking life has made you feel you need to declare yourself more.

monster(s)

At their simplest, monsters/grotesque creatures may reflect upsetting or scary features/qualities about yourself, or another. They can represent "monstrous" energy from the unconscious; energy that has not yet differentiated itself (grown into expression) into other figures, but likely contains some quite creative possibilities (Jung), or some violently assaultive wishes (Freud).

Observe the kinds of figures/actions that appear in subsequent dreams as the energy becomes more differentiated.

Monsters can symbolize something (a person, job, issue) in waking life that's taking on "monstrous" proportions or behaving "monstrously." Is there any person/thing in your dream to help you? If not, reimagine the dream in waking life (see Dreamercise #11, Part 1), inserting help.

In myths/fairy tales, monsters often symbolize the tasks/difficulties in life that we, the heros/heroines on our quest, must overcome to achieve inner development/insight.

If applicable, see **dragon; giant; serpent(s); snake(s)**.

moon/moonlight

The moon has long been a feminine symbol and the symbol of certain goddesses (Ishtar, Hathor, Artemis), although in some cultures (Iceland, India, Maori of New Zealand, Eskimo) and religions (Japanese Shinto), the moon is masculine (Egyptian god Min). It represents emotional flux, cycles, and may refer to a woman's monthly cycle. Moonlight is related to a need for rest, withdrawal/contemplation, romance, and magic. In metaphysics the moon often represents the astral plane. A new moon signals change/potential. A full moon suggests completion; ripeness; emotionality; tension; unconscious urges; passion/romance. The crescent moon signals movement through a cycle; progress and renewal, hence, feminine creativity, or creating through the feminine aspect of yourself.

See **night; shape(s)**.

morning

A time of potential and enthusiasm; a new beginning; the season of spring; the youthful phase in your life or another's.

See **dawn; day; sun/sunlight**.

mortuary

See **death; funeral; mourning**.

mosaic

The need to analyze a situation/relationship and consider all its elements; putting the pieces together to get the whole picture; creativeness that occurs when a variety of resources/talents are pooled; the need to break down emotional barriers and create closeness. Are you viewing (introspection, a new perspective?) or creating (putting together the elements of your life?) the mosaic?

See **art; artist** (if applicable); **craft(s)**.

motel

See **hotel/motel**.

moth

The lunar or dark aspect of the butterfly, and therefore, the creative aspect of the shadow; seeking spirituality or wholeness (the light); a waking situation/relationship to which you are inexorably drawn even though you know it may be disastrous (addictive behavior?).

mother

Your personal mother and any psychological or unfinished issues related to her; archetypal images buried when we are born, hence, the collective unconscious (Jung); the anima of a male dreamer; the place of origin; paradise; the womb.

When we dream of mother during physical illness, she can represent our basic physiological/somatic functions, and therefore be a message from our psyche about the nature or progress of the "dis-ease." She can also represent the need for comfort, nurturance, or nursing (in the sense of caretaking or drinking at the breasts).

See **child/children; family; Great Mother; Mary, Virgin**.

motorcycle

Energy; freedom; sexuality (mechanical horse); need for escape/adventure.

See **horse(s); road; vehicle(s)**.

mountain(s)

Depending on dream experience/actions, mountains can symbolize a barricade/obstacle or a challenge; something looming; a tall person whom you desire to emulate; high goals to which you aspire (a lofty spire); something misperceived or exaggerated ("making a mountain out of a molehill"); tackling new emotional/psychological realms.

They can symbolize spiritual energy; renewal; ancient values (the old ways). Do you need to "climb every mountain" or only the "highest mountain"? Are you at the peak of your life or profession? Peaks imply valleys, and peaks and valleys have to do with progress toward goals; cycles; ups and downs. The mountain as the *goal* of the climb can symbolize the Self, but where you are on the mountain can symbolize levels of accomplishment or skills still needed before you can achieve the peak (ultimate wisdom?).

See **climb(ing); hill; valley(s); world mountain**.

mourning

Holding on to regrets; feelings of depression or unresolved

grief; the loss of old ways; sorrow over something missed.

See **death; funeral**.

mouse

Timidity and the absence of assertiveness or courage ("are you a man or a mouse?"), which may be related to feelings of inadequacy or low self-esteem. It sometimes symbolizes introspection.

See **animal(s); rodent**.

mouth/lips

Communication ability (or inability, if damaged); what we hunger for; taking some quality/characteristic into ourselves; life support; dependency or nurturing needs; vagina/labia. They can suggest you need to "button your lip" if you've been "badmouthing" someone or "have a big mouth." They can symbolize treachery if you've been "speaking out of both sides of your mouth." But remember that wisdom/insight comes "out of the mouth of babes."

See **body; face; teeth; tongue**.

move(ing)

Moving out, or away from, some situation reflects a need/desire for change, possibly the end of a situation/relationship. It can also represent aggression (the military command "move out"); having influence ("movers and shakers") or determination ("move heaven and earth"); withdrawal; dependence/independence issues. Inability to move your body suggests rigidity in attitudes/behavior, possibly physical/mental constipation; passivity.

If applicable, see **run(ning); walk(ing)**.

movement

One out of three dreams contains some kind of movement, including changing locations within the dream.

Movement to the left (turning left, taking the left-hand road) can represent concerns with the past; needing to activate feminine aspects of yourself; active unconscious material/conflict. Movement toward the right suggests activating masculine aspects of yourself; freeing yourself from past issues that have held you back; moving toward integrating unconscious material into consciousness. Upward movement may reflect a breakthrough, downward movement a need to explore your inner depths (Epstein).

Forward movement indicates orientation toward the future and toward achieving your goals, especially if you know where you are going. It may also reflect attraction/repulsion issues. Standing still, moving in no direction, may indicate ambivalence about a waking situation/project; lack of confidence; indecision about your next step; waiting for inner/outer guidance or direction. Moving away from something can relate to issues that have been completed, are being ignored/avoided/rejected, or involve feelings about leaving/separation.

From a Freudian perspective, movement—especially conflicts about movement—can refer to intestinal activity and bowel movements; therefore, being afraid to move may be related to constipation and to opening up emotionally (Natterson and Gordon).

See **crossroads; direction(s); posture(s)**. For circular movement, see **circle**.

movie

Viewing a movie in a dream suggests that you're watching an already understood situation (Jung). It has been organized and edited; listen to its message.

Viewing a movie in which you have a part may have a meaning similar to that of the double or twins, and may signal that significant material is emerging or ready to emerge from the unconscious. It may represent memories of images/scenes from your past.

Are you watching life pass by, or living vicariously through others' actions? Perhaps the feelings/actions expressed in the movie are distant and removed from you, suggesting that you're protecting yourself from experiencing them.

If you're participating in the making of a movie, its story may be dealing with an archetypal theme and offer a message as to where you are in relation to it. Whatever your role, consider all the characters in the movie as personifications of various aspects of yourself.

See **actor/actress; person, famous**.

movie projectionist

The animus, which can mediate between the conscious and unconscious, transmitting its pictures (Jung).

mud/muddy

In Freudian terms anything dark and slippery may refer to feces and to unconscious feelings of anger; resentment; shame; guilt; withholding; attitudes about money/possessions.

Several idioms in our language refer to behaving negatively toward someone (''mudslinging,'' ''drag someone's name through the mud,'' ''his name is mud''), so consider what's happening to you inwardly/outwardly with respect to your identity or ego. You may need to take a respite from a situation/relationship; consider another way of behaving; or perhaps your dream is warning you of possible difficulties (''detour, there's a muddy road ahead''). A mud bath may imply a need for healing.

See **defecate; dirt(y); excrement**.

mummy

Preservation of old, possibly outdated, ways; death/rebirth themes; immortality issues; feeling yourself immobile and unable to assert yourself or make any difference in a waking situation; ignoring your ''gut reactions'' to a situation; a situation that's ''all wrapped up''; a pun for your mother or another's, especially her ineffective aspects. Your dream could be saying that your inner mothering aspect is dead. If you're superstitious, it may represent anxiety about a recent curse/threat, or danger related to prohibited behavior.

See **death; Egypt; preserved**.

murder(er)

If you've actually witnessed a murder, your dream may be a replay for healing purposes and may recur a number of times (see Part 1, Chapter 5, National Nightmares section), as in post-traumatic stress dreams. Otherwise, it may represent deep-seated feelings of anger/rage toward someone symbolized by the victim. Consider that the victim may represent some aspect of yourself you want to destroy or, perhaps, that you feel is being destroyed (not respected?) by someone else.

See **anger; kill(ing)/killed/killer**.

museum

Ancestral connections; your personal past; memories; the collective unconscious (depending on the complexity of the museum).

music/musician

Inner harmony; balance; divine influence or vibrations; needing to ''make more music'' in your life or in a relationship (''make beautiful music together''); self-expression; the rhythm of the universe. Conversely, it may represent anxiety about ''facing the music,'' fear that it's time to ''pay the piper,'' i.e., take the consequences of your behavior; possibly death anxiety. Musical instruments can represent sensual or creative achievements, or aspects of yourself, including sexual organs. Playing musical chairs suggests an unconscious awareness/anxiety about some shuffling around going on in your waking life, or about achieving a new perspective.

See **orchestra; rhythm**.

mystery/mysterious

Secrets; something that's not obvious. It may refer to bodily processes, puberty, societal roles/expectations, since in primitive tribes there are male/female mysteries that are revealed when a youth has reached a certain age. Something in a dream that hints of mystery, or of being mysterious, can relate to the archetypal (shadow, anima/animus?) or mythical level; to initiation and the revelation of esoteric/mystical/metaphysical secrets.

See **secret**.

nail

Holding something together; connecting or connectedness; construction/building, therefore new energy, especially male/phallic. It could refer to accurate insight; the ability to hone in on a central issue/point ("hit the nail on the head"); an attitude of toughness or coldness ("tough as nails," "hard as nails"); a way that you/another are slowly wounding or depleting yourself ("a nail in my coffin"). Is there something or someone you need to "nail down"?

See **construction; hammer**.

naked/being naked

Hall says a nakedness dream without embarrassment may mean you need to develop a more adequate persona. It can, however, mean that you feel comfortable being natural, being yourself, or that you're shedding an old role (represented by clothes) for a new one. It may refer to anxiety about revealing intimate details; fearing exposure from, or feeling exposed (vulnerable) regarding, a certain person/situation, especially a new job. (Maybe they'll find out I'm not so great after all.) During times of crisis/transition, nudity dreams are common and may represent the discovery/adoption of new roles/identities (Siegel). From a Freudian perspective, they can represent daring to expose/show yourself; the infantile desire to violate the rules.

name(s)

If the name is not someone you know, consider first your own associations to, and feelings about, the name itself; what you might think of someone who bears that name. What kind of person would he/she be? Do you have, or need, those characteristics someplace in your personality? Also look for a pun, or piece of advice incorporated in a name applied to any dream image.

If the name of someone famous, see **person, famous**. See **person, known; person, unknown**.

narrow

If a passageway, it may refer to feelings of being restricted, limited, or hemmed in (limited alternatives), but consider how you feel in the passageway, because it may also be quite comfortable (''just your size''). Do you need to grow bigger/smaller to fit; are you having difficulty navigating through it? It can refer to some person/idea that reflects a narrow-minded view; the narrowness of the vagina/birth passage/anus (related to creation or to retention/storing).

See **canal; hall(way); tunnel**.

native(s)

See **aborigine/aboriginal; Africa/African; person, dark or dark-skinned**.

nature

Changes in nature reflect changes in our life process and the cycles of our life/projects/relationships. Actions of nature often reflect our emotions, while objects of nature can reflect us, attitudes, or almost any aspect of a waking situation.

See the specific natural object/occurrence elsewhere in the dictionary. If its meaning is still not clear, ask yourself, ''If I were a . . . what would I be trying to tell myself?'' or ''What's it like to be a . . . ?''

Being in outdoor scenes can, depending on the locale, reflect needs to escape; replenish yourself; connect with your spirit/soul; break free of societal restrictions; assert your independence/individuality. People who live closer to nature (Scandinavians) or work with nature have more nature images in their dreams.

navel

Our origin; our center; our connection with the primal/material source; the beginning of a process.

For cosmic symbology, see **center; world tree**.

navy

Emotional conflict because of association with military (warriors) and water (unconscious/feelings). However, since a ship is also a female/womb symbol, it may relate to a female relationship issue or a need for mothering. If you've been in the navy, conflicts you experienced there may have been awakened/stimulated by some recent situation.

See **military**.

near

Although there's no good evidence for it, some believe that the nearer/closer you are to dream objects, the less they are a symbol and the closer they are to becoming conscious information, or the more they serve as a conscious resource/concept rather than a symbolized one.

If a known person, consider whether you've been feeling distant, and the dream is telling you it's safe to draw nearer or that you feel closer than you realized. Have you been concentrating too much on long-term goals and need to consider more immediate ones?

See **close; distance/distant/in the distance; position(s)**.

nearsighted

Limited perspective, possibly only a small part of the picture, rather than an overall/broader view; failing to plan/look ahead, or to consider the consequences of your actions.

See **eyeglasses**.

neck

Messages about the relationship between the mind/intellect (head) and the body (physical). It may be that they're cut off from one another (by a necklace or other adornment?), suggesting that you rely too much on your intellect and don't acknowledge your feelings as much, or vice versa, depending on other emphasis in the dream. The neck is related to control of yourself/others. It can represent willpower, or self-restriction, possibly a need to control your feelings more and not be overwhelmed by them. Do you "choke back" the expression of your feelings, maybe have a "lump in your throat"? Perhaps you are, or someone else is, too angrily expressive ("jump down his throat"). Have you been too conservative and need to "stick your neck out" more, or have you been taking too many risks? Maybe you're involved in a "cutthroat competition," or have been "breaking your neck" for someone who's not sufficiently grateful. It may be a "necking" or sexual dream, especially if someone else's neck is involved.

Metaphysically, the neck houses the throat/communication chakra, which is related to clear hearing and true listening. Associated with expressiveness, it is, naturally, a major chakra of creation/creativity.

See **body**. If applicable, see **choke; strangle; swallow(ing)**.

necklace

As an adornment for the neck, it shares some of its same symbolism. If emphasis is on finding a lost necklace or on jewels in a necklace, see **jewelry** and **jewel(s)**.

See **amulet(s); neck; pendant**.

necktie

Neckties, and difficulties with them, often figure prominently in the dreams of engaged men who are close to "tying the knot" (Siegel). A necktie can be a phallic symbol, but consider also the appropriateness of the tie, its color/design, for additional clues.

See **appearance; pattern/design**.

needle

If a sewing needle, it may relate to repairing or creating things; pulling things together; union. If embroidery or other decorative needlework, consider the colors/design. It could refer to adding special touches to something that's relatively plain to transform it into something beautiful. Are you having trouble finding the "needle in the haystack," or is someone "needling" you?

If referring to a needle used for injections, see **injection; syringe**. See **embroidery; sew(ing); thread**.

Negro

See **Africa/African; person, dark or dark-skinned; shadow**.

neighbor

Neighbors offer a good hook for projection of inner material/needs (von Franz). If known, they may reflect some present issue between the two of you or within you. How do you feel about neighbors, especially in a negative sense? Your dream may be expressing a need to develop new friends/resources, or to become closer or more active in some "neighborhood" or community of your life. Do you suspect/fear that some neighbor is a hood or acting like one, or that some aspect of you is a "hood"?

What's it like to be a neighbor? In what waking-life situation are you having similar reactions? Neighbors can be characters offering you a solution to a present situation/attitude. Your interaction with them might suggest how you could interact in a waking situation.

nest

Safety; protection; birth; female genitals; emotional/physical security; your home. Do you need to think ahead and "feather your nest"? Is it time for you, or someone in your family, to "leave the nest," accompanied by all the feelings that involves?

net

If you're in the net: entanglement; caught in a trap, possibly of your own making. Consider the symbolism of anything else also caught. Fish/water could relate to emotions/unconscious ideas, for instance, wild animals to trapped/repressed instincts. You feel trapped by them—or have a strong need to keep them in check—or perhaps it's your own feelings that are trapped (unable to be recognized/expressed).

A net can pertain to your ability to contain/gather/harvest, and the work needed to accomplish it; to security, especially if it's a safety net such as that used beneath high-wire performers. Are you "walking a tightrope"; having difficulty, or success, balancing something in your life?

See **spider web**.

new

A new opportunity, idea to consider, or way to respond; present situations/issues as opposed to old ones; strengthened confidence/self-esteem. It could represent new aspects of the personality emerging, especially if a new room or some new part of something old, or already owned, is discovered (Siegel). New clothes might symbolize new attitudes, a new way of expressing yourself, a change in your persona.

New Year

A new project/relationship/cycle of your life; a new beginning or fresh approach; a situation/relationship that's going to take 12 months to accomplish/mature.

See **celebration**.

newspaper

Gossip; seeking knowledge/answers; a new idea; possibly information you've ignored that your psyche is now pointing out. Perhaps you need to make headlines; express yourself more openly; make your skills/abilities more known; get the message out. Are there any puns related to the name/article/section of the paper?

night

Dark/unconscious shadow aspects of yourself; hidden aspects of yourself threatening to, or working to, emerge; lack of awareness/insight; secrets. Night is also related to lunar/feminine symbolism. Is the moon present or absent in the dream, and is there any significance to that? The Egyptians believed that night occurred when the sun god descended into the underworld; hence, night is also related to sleep; death; winter; exploring the depths of personality.

See **dark/darkness; day; death; moon/moonlight; time**.

nine

Numerologically, nine signifies a magnified completion, or, as some say, a triple completion; the number of wisdom resulting from the completion of a full cycle before we begin again with 10. In alchemy, this meant a synthesis of the physical/intellectual/spiritual within a cosmology that also had three separate planes of existence (3 x 3). In Christian tradition, nine symbolizes the Holy Ghost and, often, a group/choir of angels. In mystic Hebrew tradition, nine symbolizes truth.

It is the ultimate (we "want the whole nine yards"); the elaborate ("dressed to the nines"); the ego (*I* is the ninth letter of the English alphabet). It can refer to the nine months of pregnancy; therefore, to the conception/birth of anything.

See **number(s)**.

no/saying no

Consider how the experience of "saying no" in a dream compares to your actual ability in waking life. Sometimes in family therapy we say that a family doesn't approach being healthy/functional until everyone in it can say "no" and make it stick. Is that something you need to learn? Possibly the dream is showing you how. How comfortable/capable were you in the dream? How did it feel (good, scary?)? Could your dream be saying that you've been saying "yes" too much and are depleting your inner resources?

nobility

See **royalty**.

nomad

See **wanderer**.

noon

Midlife; a need for a break or nurturance. If your association is "high noon," it may symbolize a crisis/deadline for you. It can symbolize being awake/aware, as contrasted to being emotionally/intellectually unaware.

noose

A threat/danger; anxiety about restrictions or responsibility ("a rope around my neck"; "my head's in a noose''; ''dangling at the end of a rope''). Because a noose customarily goes around the neck, it can have some of the same restrictive, controlling qualities as ''neck,'' ''necklace,'' and ''necktie''; therefore, also anxiety about that control.

See **hang(ing)**.

north

Metaphysically, north represents the direction of earth/reality. Presumably magnetic/psychic energy currents run north and south, so the north/south orientation is considered to be harmonious with earth currents. North/south often carry the same symbolism as up/down, top/bottom, head/genitals, consciousness/awareness, and unconscious/instinct. North, considered the ''land of discovery'' and the direction of initiation (actually, north by northwest), can symbolize going forward, in general or esoterically. With its connection to the North Pole, it can mean emotionally cold/indifferent. If you suspect this, see **cold; frozen; ice**.

See **direction(s)**.

nose

Intuition (''I have a nose for this''); curiosity. Although we have largely lost the ability to do so, animals use their sense of smell to learn about the world, so your dream may signal you need to learn more about something by ''nosing around,'' or that you're already being too nosy. Perhaps you ''smell something fishy'' or ''smell a rat.'' Maybe you need to ''raise a stink.'' Then again, you may be missing something that's ''as plain as the nose on your face.'' In Freudian terms, the nose is a symbol for the penis. Because it's related to one of our senses, nose can also represent a sensual experience or reflect a need for sensual stimulation/gratification.

See **dog/puppy**.

note

See **letter; music/musician**.

notice

If there's something you especially notice/observe, consider whether your psyche is signaling that this is something you need to pay attention to. From a Freudian sense, however, special emphasis may mean that the real message of the dream pertains to something else comparatively insignificant within it.

See **attention; look(ing)/looked at; see(ing)**.

nuclear attack/explosion

See **atom bomb**.

nude

See **naked/being naked**.

number(s)

Numbers often appear in dreams as the age of a person, amounts of money, important dates, certain number of persons, floors of a hotel, or time. They can symbolize any kind of interrelationship. Their meanings are often quite elusive.

First, consider specific references in your life/family to the number in the dream, such as births, deaths, anniversaries, numbers of siblings/children, a specific age. What financial significance might the number have? Does it enhance your understanding of the number to turn a whole number into a fraction (4 = 1/4 or a quarter), or to turn a fraction into a whole number (1/32 = 32)? Break down numbers over ten into their separate integers (32 = 3 + 2 = 5), or add all the numbers in a dream to arrive at a total.

Second, consider any cultural meanings—possibly sexual lingo—that the number has. Finally, consider some of the archetypal meanings of numbers reported in this dictionary. Cirlot calls numbers "idea forces." Numbers also can refer to putting things in order, especially their "proper" order; organizing/arranging. Are you experiencing some chaos/instability in your inner/outer life?

While the age of a person can represent the dreamer at that age, when the age of a younger person is known in the dream, in the Delaney/Flowers dream interview method it may represent some aspect of the dreamer/dreamer's life/another person who was "born" that number of years ago (Flowers).

See specific numbers.

nun

Duty; service/dedication, especially to higher ideals; belonging to a structured/organized community; obedience; making vows and living up to them; spiritual aspirations; celibacy and its secret wish for the opposite, therefore the virgin/whore theme; a sibling (sister). If you once thought of becoming a nun and didn't, she can represent unfulfilled ambitions; roads not taken. Because so few people know about life inside a convent and because a nun wears or "takes" the veil, she can also be a symbol for secrets, hidden knowledge/mysteries. If she's dressed in a black habit, she may represent an energy drain or a shadow aspect. She can be a pun on "none/nothing," with its many implications, or a sexual pun that says a person "ain't had none."

nurse

A caretaker looking after the helpless/ailing aspect of you; a healer, and therefore, a need for healing; a source of nourishment. Possibly you're feeling overwhelmed and need/wish you could give up some of your efforts for a little ''nursing'' (at the breast?). Thus, the nurse can be a ''mother'' symbol. Being nursed can relate to a wish to return to less responsible times; lack of eagerness for taking on new responsibilities; fears/anxiety about being helpless/incapacitated. If you're the nurse, then your dream may be saying that you're ready to nurture yourself, or to take on a service responsibility.

If applicable, see **doctor; hospital; injection; needle; syringe**.

nut(s)

People who seem crazy to us are sometimes called ''nuts,'' and therefore, nuts in dreams could represent the craziness (nonsensical aspect, ridiculousness) of a waking situation; the crazy (inappropriate, one-sided) way you're viewing a situation/relationship; the way in which you are, or someone else is, ''making you crazy'' (keeping you mixed up or confused); a crazy aspect of yourself.

As a source of food, it can signify a *basic* need; potential; a kernel of truth; the need to get to the truth/core of something. In Christian symbolism, the kernel sometimes stands for the soul or for the divine nature of Christ.

Is there some endeavor in which you need to start with the basics, then lavish care and work hard so your ideas will flourish? Is it a ''hard nut to crack,'' or do you simply need to ''get down to the nuts and bolts'' of the situation? In sexual slang, nuts are testicles, so consider some allusion to sexuality/potency, or to a male.

See **acorn; seed(s); squirrel; tree(s)**.

nymph

See **elemental being; water nymph**.

oak tree

As with all trees, it may symbolize the dreamer, and/or the world axis. Because it's strong and sturdy, it may especially symbolize those attributes within yourself, or others with those attributes. Thus, it can symbolize the personal father; the archetypal father/masculine authority; the cosmic source. (The Greeks believed the human race sprang from the oak tree.) As a sign of long life, it may represent some long-lived person/attitude. Its compensatory meaning could indicate that you've been feeling weak/powerless.

See **strong; tree(s)**.

oar

In Freudian symbology, a phallic symbol, so rowing would symbolize sexual intercourse. "Masculine" strength dipping into the waters of the feminine; consciousness dipping into intuition/the unconscious; a traditional symbol of creative thought and the cosmic word (Cirlot). By its action, it can raise awareness/disturb tranquillity. It suggests that something is "making waves"/ripples in your awareness, but it *is* energy/action at work. Consider who's using the oar (more power/energy there), and the ease/difficulty of the action. A broken oar might reflect limited capacities/handicaps. Are you "paddling your own canoe," or "resting on your oars"? Being in a boat without oars suggests you're at the mercy of the unconscious or the "currents" of life; you're not in control ("up the creek without a paddle").

See **row(ing); sailing**.

oasis

A promise of, or need for, respite from your physical/emotional labors or efforts; a signal that you've been extending yourself too much and a possible wish for an end/rescue; emotional resources; the potential for growth during a time of emotional/creative barrenness. Consider the distance from the oasis and any difficulties/limitations with it for clues to the extent of your stamina, or any attitudes you have about whether an end is in sight and whether you deserve it.

See **desert; shade; water**.

oats

As a grain, oats are a basic food and can refer to basic nurturance needs, especially a need to attend to your instinctual/sexual urges (if fed to animals). They are related to the harvest (autumn) and to the gathering of resources. You may be expressing a need/wish to "sow your wild oats."

See also **grain(s)**.

obelisk

Its shape makes it a definite phallic symbol, but it also reaches toward the sky and can, therefore, symbolize union with, or reaching toward, the divine; union of spirit/matter; the alchemical formula "as above, so below." It's related to the sunray and illuminating Light (Cirlot). If you've traveled to a country (Egypt, Italy, England?) where you've seen an obelisk, it may relate to that experience. In ancient Egypt, the obelisk served to glorify the pharaoh who erected it. Are you needing some attention, or have you already had enough and are feeling like royalty? Consider the symbolism of any writing or decorations.

obese

See **fat/fat person/being fat**.

object changes into something else

See **transformation.**

object comes alive

New potentialities.

observe/observing

See **look(ing)/looked at**.

obstacle

Inhibitions; reluctance; issues of conscience. Consider the age, sex, role, and other prominent characteristics of a person who's an obstacle, or is preventing you from progressing forward. Is it some aspect of you, especially at an earlier age; attitudes formed earlier and still held? It might represent someone in your present/past. If man-made, what aspect of you, or a waking-life situation/relationship, could it represent? Why is it appearing *now* to slow you down or halt your progress? Has it appeared in other forms/ways earlier that you've not recognized until now?

Perhaps you've been "barreling ahead" without careful thought and need to "take a breather" or consider other possibilities/options. A natural object suggests you may need to do some basic psychological work—expend some emotional effort—to bring about inner change. If appropriate, see the symbolism of the specific object. A human obstacle suggests interpersonal/relationship issues from your past/present.

See **detour**.

occupation

See **business/work**.

ocean

Ocean carries much of the same meaning as sea. Our vast unconscious reserve; the collective unconscious; the depths of our emotions; memories; the mother or primordial womb; the cosmic source or primordial mother. It can symbolize universal life; transitional forces at work; endless possibilities/potentiality (Cirlot). Ocean relates to the expansiveness, potential, and storehouse of our being. Depending on how it appears, it may serve as a barrier to access of, or protection from, something on the other side, another world of awareness.

See **sea; water**. If applicable, see **boat; ship/shipwreck**.

octagon

As an eight-sided figure, it's related to the symbolism of eight. Not quite a circle and not quite a square, it can symbolize transition/regeneration.

See **eight**.

octopus/squid

A water animal that emits an inky substance when threatened, it can represent threats to the unconscious; shadow aspects; clouded vision. As a creature with eight arms/tentacles, it's related to the symbolism of eight and to the symbology of the spider with its many legs. It can refer to grasping; greediness; a need for accumulation (related to a feeling of not having enough?); frantic or seemingly aimless reaching or searching without an organized plan; caught in the unfoldment of a process, or in the grip of a potentially dangerous situation.

See **spider(s); water**.

odor

Related to the sense of smell, odors can signal a sensual/sexual dream. Odor can refer to genital/excremental odors; secrets; curiosity. A musty/stale odor may refer to some aspect of your life/personality that's old, ignored, or not used very much, possibly hidden wisdom or a special truth. Are you needing to "sniff out the truth" of some situation? It can suggest there's something that "smells," a situation that stinks. Or perhaps your dream is reflecting the "sweet smell of success."

See **nose; perfume; smell**.

office

Your work/profession, or status within it; mental activity; emotional effort; creative ideas/accomplishments. Actual colleagues in your waking workplace may symbolize aspects of your relationship with them, including difficulties/support. Were things tidy or messy? Could your dream be referring to order, or lack of it, in your life; or your ability to handle/take charge of a situation?

See **business/work**.

officer

A real-life authority figure; your sense of justice/morality; your conscience; that aspect of you that allows you to coordinate/direct your life/activities, i.e., your *inner* director/authority. The officer could represent you at an earlier age; bullying (inner tyrant)/benevolent aspects of yourself; false security (if ineffective, immature). His/her presence can suggest a need for control, possibly because current attempts at inner control are not working; or a need to examine elements of inner "control" (where they came from, whether they're still useful) and revise them.

See **colonel; military; police**.

ogre/ogress

Mythologically, the ogre symbolizes the "terrible parent," especially the father, and often represents a warning to attend to this—in fairy tales (Cirlot). In folklore, ogres are frequently large, stupid, gullible, and easily frightened—an attempt to render them less harmful and more controllable—although they are small trolls in Norway. This dream figure is always an excellent one to dialogue with (see Dreamercises #3 and #10, Part 1) or to retell the dream from the ogre's perspective (see Dreamercise #4) to determine why he/she is appearing in your dream now.

Depending on your ogre's appearance, see **elemental being; giant; monster(s)**.

oil

Consider what kind of oil and how it's being used. It may represent an anointing/healing (Hopcke), or be smoothing the way for something to occur. The dream could be saying that you need to assert/express yourself more ("the squeaky wheel gets the oil"); need to "oil the wheels" in order to "keep the wheels turning"; need to ease the friction in some situation/relationship.

ointment

Ointments are often used for healing, so your dream in itself may have been a healing one; or it may suggest that healing is needed. Consider the symbolism of the body part to which ointment was applied. If applied to a known person, does it refer to healing that needs to take place in that relationship, or, if an unknown person, to an aspect of yourself?

old

According to Jung, everything old hints at some change about to occur, something coming, a transition. How did you feel about the person/object that was old? If an object, what condition was it in and how did you react to that? Is there something in your waking life that you need to value more, repair, or renovate?

See **ancient; antique(s)**.

olive/olive tree

A longtime symbol of peace and considered, mythologically, as a dream promoter. Odysseus (Ulysses) made his marital bed for Penelope, a famous dreamer, from olive tree branches. Consecrated to Jupiter and Minerva (Greek, Athena) by the Romans, the olive tree may symbolize aspects of their mythology or represent knowledge/mental acuity (because of its sacredness to Athena). Since olive oil was often used in lamps, it has become a symbol for light; enlightenment; and cosmic Light.

one

The beginning of an activity; the point at which a decision must be made; wholeness; unity; individuality; uniqueness ("I'm Number One"). One is a symbol of the cosmic divine (the One) and the divine within us; the highest spiritual stage (Christ/Buddha consciousness).

See **circle; number(s); zero**.

oneself

See **dreamer/dream ego**.

onion(s)

Consider whether there's a situation that has more layers than you've suspected. You may need to peel away some of them for insight, especially if the situation is one you're "crying over" or unhappy about. Compared, however, to deep-felt pain/sorrow, "onion" tears are rather shallow and may represent a situation in which there's lack of depth/emotion; suggest they're the only kind of tears you can allow or that are acceptable, i.e., give you an excuse to cry. Folk wisdom says that to dream of onions means good luck, possibly because many folk tales tell of the use of onions to ward off disease or to draw it out of the body/sickroom.

opal

Because of its translucent colors/luminosity, it can represent higher knowledge, or connection with the divine/spiritual realm. In reality, the stone is quite fragile and breaks easily, which characteristics it also can symbolize. Traditionally, it symbolizes hope and is the birthstone of someone born in October.

See **gem(s); jewel(s)**.

open

Consider first the symbolism of the object that's open/opening. How might any of the following apply: access to ideas; potential; movement/progress; secrets revealed; lack of defensiveness; a way out?

See **closed**.

opening

In Freudian terms, an opening in a natural/man-made object suggests the vagina and access to the womb. Depending on its appearance, it could symbolize a wound or old scar, possibly from a psychological trauma; access to new ideas/information/opportunities; an altered perspective. If it appears safe, use your imagination to go forward into the opening and finish the dream (see Dreamercise #11, Part 1).

See **access; cave; door**.

opera

Expressed passion and high drama. Consider whether you were a member of the audience (see **looking/looked at**) or a performer (see **actor/actress**). Your action may be related to active or "onlooking" behavior in waking life, or to a theme you are living out in your life. If you're viewing a known opera, consider how its story is related to your own.

If you're a performer, you may have a need to succeed; display your talents/abilities; sing your own praises. It may signal that you're capable of successfully undertaking a demanding challenge. Many opera plots hinge on misperception/misunderstanding. Could this refer to a waking situation? Do you want/need more drama or passion in your life?

See **movie; music/musician; theater**.

operation

See **surgery**.

opponent

First, consider your opponent as another aspect of yourself. Depending on appearance/activity, your opponent may be a shadow aspect, or a little-accessed wisdom resource. He/she may be someone opposing, or in competition with, you in waking life. How you cope in the dream may give you clues about your confidence/self-esteem. A victory may erase any lingering doubts, while a loss suggests you may need to rethink plans regarding a waking situation, unless the loss is a relief and the dream shows you how to live with it.

See **game(s); shadow**.

opposites

The union of opposites in the Hermetic vessel was a critically important alchemical task and relates to perfecting our human vessel/body and acquiring inner harmony. It's the search for the Grail, the hero/heroine journey, the lifelong process of individuation.

Your dream may be pointing out that there are choices available; or it may show you how you can reconcile/combine two viewpoints into a creative solution.

Even if opposites are not depicted in your dream, it may alert you to an inner conflict if you consider what the *missing* opposite may be (see Dreamercise #7, Part 1).

One of the most mythologically important consequences of the reconciliation of opposites occurs when Athena refuses to agree with Apollo in banishing the three Furies. She accepts them, welcomes them into Athens, and they are transformed into the Eumenides, the three graces.

See **Grail; shadow; standing opposite**.

oracle

A message from an oracle is most likely a direct message from your unconscious/inner wisdom, and/or a message about the mythology active in your life. Worries about future goals/projects/activities may have prompted the dream, and its message may offer direction/clarification.

See **crystal ball; fortune-teller/fortune-telling; medium**.

orange [color]

Balancing; creative expression; cutting through/penetrating; female strength (Epstein). According to Epstein, the appearance of orange in a dream sometimes indicates a physical abnormality, which should be checked out by a physician.

See **color(s)**.

orange [fruit]

As with all circular fruits containing seeds, it's a symbol of fertility and promise. Associated with the sun, it suggests consciousness. The tree's fragrant blossoms, often used in wedding bouquets, symbolize purity/chastity.

See **fruit(s)**.

orchard

Filled with cultivated trees that bear fruit, it can symbolize your own efforts; the fruition of your ideas or the need to cultivate some. The condition of the orchard can provide additional clues.

See **tree(s)**.

orchestra

The activity/interactions of a group that form or result in a harmonious whole; inner integration. Members of the orchestra may represent various aspects of yourself, inner resources. The orchestra could symbolize your family; working/professional relationships; any group with which you're involved, and with whom you "make beautiful music together."

See **band; music/musician**.

orchid

Since antiquity, the orchid has been regarded as a fertility symbol. It can represent the exotic; courting or love magic (connected with its cultivation in warm, moist locations or in greenhouses); a project/relationship that takes careful cultivation/attention. As a beautiful flower that often grows wild in the jungle, it can represent the Self or the individuation process; the expression of individuality/uniqueness in the wild mass of society.

See **flower(s); jungle**.

order(ly)

Things arranged in an orderly fashion may suggest chaos in your waking life, and the need to consider/organize your inner/outer life. Perhaps your unconscious is sorting out and organizing issues/emotions, especially if you've had a recent trauma. Inability to organize materials/things in a dream may reflect waking anxiety or self-confidence issues.

ore

See **mine; minerals**.

organ

A sexual pun for the penis and/or your need for sexual gratification; any organ of the body. As a musical instrument, it may represent the music of life; i.e., your being/existence, resources for harmony or for ''striking just the right chord'' in your life.

See **music/musician**.

organize(r)

See **leader/lead(ing); order(ly)**.

orgasm

At the 1993 meetings of the Association for the Study of Dreams, researcher Gayle Delaney (see bibliography) reported that at some time in their lives, 40 percent of women and 80 percent of men dream of having an orgasm. For the male dreamer, this does not necessarily result in ejaculation (a ''wet dream'').

For more information on sexual dreams, see **sex**.

orientation

See **direction(s)**.

orphan

See **abandon(ed)**.

ostrich

Its feathers were an attribute of the Egyptian goddess Ma'at, symbol of truth, justice, cosmic order. Because of its practice of burying its head in the sand, it may suggest denial; unwillingness to examine/accept a situation.

See **animal(s); bird(s)**.

otter

Playful part of Self that can acknowledge/draw upon unconscious material and enjoy it.

You may need to stop taking your situation so seriously and develop a new perspective, especially one wherein you accept your feelings, and trust your emotions/intuition.

See **animal(s)**.

out of control

See **control/controlled/out of control**.

outside/outdoors

If outside a room or apart from a group and unable to get in, it may symbolize rejection or being out of the mainstream (by choice, accident, chance?). Being outdoors suggests a lack of restriction (therefore, too much restriction in waking life?); a need to connect with your basic or inner nature; a need to take time out for relaxation or introspection. What in your life needs to be integrated/resolved for wholeness or acceptance?

See **landscapes/settings**.

oval

The vagina; the aura of magnetic energy that surrounds living matter.

See **aura; halo; mandorla**.

oven

Female genitals; the womb, especially of a pregnant woman ("one in the oven"). The glowing furnace/oven can represent spiritual gestation (Cirlot); transformation; death/cremation.

See **baker/bakery/baking; cook(s)/cooking; bread** (if applicable).

owl

Longtime symbolisms include death; spiritual darkness. Related to activities of the night—sexual or otherwise ("night owl")—it therefore shares some of the same symbolism as night/moon. It is the symbol of Athena (Greek goddess of learning/knowledge) and of Athens, the city named for her, and can be related to the Wise Old Man/Woman archetypes. Some of our idioms suggest its relationship to wisdom or balancing intellect/judgment against pure emotion ("wise as an owl") and to craftiness ("wise old owl").

See **bird(s); moon/moonlight; night; Wise Old Man; Wise Old Woman**.

ox

Strength; burdensome work/task; self-sacrifice; carrying the yoke of others' actions; cosmic forces (Cirlot).

See **bull(s)**.

oyster

Unnecessarily closed off; being unaware of the consequences of your actions; withdrawal to work on inner growth/development; female genitals. As a shelled creature that lives in water, it can symbolize defenses against emotions or emotional material. However, it's the oyster that creates the pearl, symbol of the Self and of enlightenment, so it may symbolize ongoing tranformative work. More mundanely, it may indicate a hard-shelled attitude or be saying that at last, "the world is your oyster."

See **clam; pearl(s); shellfish**.

pack

See **baggage; luggage; knapsack**.

package

Hidden or "wrapped away" emotions/resources; mental or emotional gifts/treasures (attitudes, skills, love?) received from others during your life; anxiety about a surprise. How you deal with the package may reflect how you cope with the unexpected in waking life. Does the way it's wrapped provide additional clues? To receive a package is to acquire emotions/resources; to send/give one is to offer them to another, or to project them on to another.

If applicable, see **box; container**.

packed/packing

At its simplest, packing a suitcase may reflect anxiety about upcoming travel. Packing dreams can refer to inner growth/movement; the readiness for/fear of/ability to handle change or new input; storage/acquisition/retention issues ("packing up" old ideas, memories, roles no longer applicable or needed?); ignoring or hiding emotions/issues; a need for adventure; ending relationships ("send someone packing"); a new stance in life ("pack up all my cares and woes," "pack up your troubles").

Where applicable, see **box; clothes/clothing; container; luggage; travel(ing)/journey**.

paddle

See **oar; row(ing)**.

padlock

See **key/keyhole; lock(ed)**.

pager/being paged

Accessibility; being interrupted; identification/identity issues; the need for being always "on call" in some situation/relationship.

pain

It may refer to actual physical pain about to occur or, more likely, to emotional pain and/or the avoidance/repression of emotions or of the recognition of a problem. The symbolism of that part of the body in pain may offer additional clues/puns as to the source/meaning of the pain, such as someone in your life who's a "pain in the neck."

See **ache**.

pain medication

Dreaming of aspirin or other pain-controlling medication may express a need to reduce the affect of the dream message, or of your associations to its images. If you discover this to be true, take it easy; be gentle with any judgments you may make about your insight.

See **medicine/medication**.

paintbrush

Creativity, possibly repressed or unacknowledged.

painter

He/She can represent the animus (if male) or the personal/collective unconscious because of the artist's ability to project symbols/ideas (Jung).

painting

Meanings can differ depending on whether you're creating the painting, considering owning it, or viewing it. You may be expressing/considering a different viewpoint/perspective. A painting can represent emotions more safely expressed or contained (framed), which you may, of course, buy (acknowledge) as your own. If you're the artist, the painting can symbolize self-expression; creative abilities; feelings/anxieties about being judged.

Are you "hung up" in some relationship or expression of yourself? Depending on what/how you're painting or something is painted, it may be a cover-up; express a need to get rid of outdated/unacceptable ideas/attitudes; refer to sprucing up an old relationship. Perhaps you have a need to "paint a rosy picture"?

See **art; artist; craft(s)**.

palace

A need for recognition, i.e., to be treated like royalty. It may be related to goals/ambitions/desires for success; having limited access to the inner world of authority figures, possibly parents. If your dream palace was a fairy-tale one, it may reflect a need for escape; to be lavishly entertained; for exotic, sensual delights; a wish for a happy ending.

palmist

See **fortune-teller/fortune-telling**.

palm(s)

To hold something in the palm of your hand is to possess it, if only temporarily. Thus, one of the symbolisms of the palm of the hand refers to ownership/power/control ("have someone in the palm of your hand"). However, the magician palms cards to create *illusion*, while the gambler does it to *cheat*. The dream may be related to a financial issue/situation ("cross my palm with silver"). Open palms, or palms up, show no deception or hostility; where else in the dream might it be expressed/hinted at? In physical and spiritual healing, the palms of the hands are senders and receivers of energy, as in the "laying on of hands," or in experiencing the safety/security of being in the palm of the hand of God.

See **body; hand(s)**. For sweaty palms, see **perspire**.

palm tree

Exotic or Mediterranean location; Florida; California. It can be either a masculine (because of its tall shape) or a feminine/mother symbol (if its nourishing fruits such as bananas, dates, and coconuts are emphasized)—or the union of both principles. Its shape and vertical growth symbolize the soul and/or the anima in a woman's dream (Jung). In Babylonian myth, it was the tree of life in the primal garden (Walker). Able to bend with the wind, it can represent flexibility; the ability to sway with circumstances; a warning that you're too easily swayed. If you're aware that palm trees often harbor rodents, your dream symbol may be a negative one. Then again, you may know that unlike many trees, the palm tree's current growth is *inside* rather than on the outside, so it may refer to protected inner growth or to your inner core. Ecclesiastically, palm branches symbolize victory; eternal life; resurrection; Palm Sunday.

See **tree(s)**.

pan(s)

It can be a feminine symbol, especially if related to food/

cooking (fertility, nourishment). If you're familiar with Greek mythology, it may refer to the woodland god Pan, a horned/hoofed satyr. A fire in a cooking pan may refer to something in your life that's merely "a flash in the pan."

See **cook(s)/cooking; container; saucepan**.

panties

See **underwear**.

panther

As a feline animal, it refers to instincts, especially lust; feminine wiles or power; cunning; stalking. Its blackness relates it to the night; secrets; the dark side of an issue; the shadow aspect.

See **cat/kitten**.

pantry

Emotional reserves; nurturing resources.

See **food**.

pants/trousers

Short pants may refer to immaturity or an immature outlook on life; long pants to masculine power/authority ("wearing the pants in the family"). Losing or not being able to find your pants may refer to feelings of vulnerability; exposure; open to ridicule or "em-*bare-ass*-ment"; being "caught with your pants down."

See **clothes/clothing**.

paper

Blank paper may refer to unexpressed feelings; the moment of opportunity; the creative moment before expression occurs; inability or lack of desire to communicate. Consider any decorations on the paper, its condition (burnt, tattered?), and its kinesthetic feel (rough, slippery, parchment?). Decorative wrapping paper may refer to the facade you present to others; anxiety about a gift you owe. A "plain brown wrapper" may mean sexual issues/anxiety; a need for privacy; be related to low self-esteem. Wallpaper suggests something that needs beautifying or covering up ("paper over the cracks"). The first wedding anniversary is a paper one.

parachute

Protection during risk; "time to bail out"; adventure. It can be one form of flying, or of falling.

See **airplane; fall(ing); flying**.

parade

The parade is related to holidays, special occasions; therefore, to cycles, the passage of time, rites/rituals. It may represent some special time in your life. Mardi Gras parades can symbolize a release of inhibitions, the flaunting of social customs/values. Could the symbolism of whatever figures/animals are in the parade reflect a need to possess or, conversely, to control those attributes? Do you need to be seen or to "strut your stuff"?

See **march(ing); procession**.

paradise

Dreams of paradise are connected with early feelings of being in the womb or of having your every need taken care of as an infant. Therefore, they often refer to wishes/needs to let go of responsibilities and be carefree, possibly as a result of waking burdens. If it's not possible to let go of them at this time, your dream may be a compensatory one, giving you what you cannot have in waking. It may represent a country you've visited; a time in your life that you consider to be paradisiacal. A "paradise flavor" often appears in the dreams of older women (Garfield).

If applicable, see **heaven**.

paralyzed

See **immobile/paralyzed**.

parasite

Some attitude/anxiety that's draining your energy; a person who's not carrying his/her load; a hanger on, i.e., someone you can't get rid of; feelings/issues related to dependence/independence.

See **bug; insects**.

parasol

See **umbrella**.

parcel

See **package**.

parents

Your childish consciousness; issues with your actual parents or childhood issues recently reawakened, which may now need to be considered with adult consciousness (Jung); aspects of parents that you're like; parental knowledge/teaching; the wiser/more mature aspects of yourself; archetypal parents (see **Wise Old Man; Wise Old Woman**).

See **father; mother**.

parlor

In the United States, the parlor has been superseded by the living room, so to dream of one can refer to old-fashioned ideas/attitudes/ways; little-used resources; a relationship with an elder relative who did have a parlor; entrapment ("come into my parlor," said the spider to the fly").

See **house; living room**.

parrot

Gossip; repetition of ideas/points; someone with no new ideas/initiative; a messenger symbol, something noisy or colorful in your life.

See **bird(s); pet(s)**. If applicable, see **pirate**.

party

See **celebration**.

passage

If a passageway, see **hall(way)**. If related to travel (book passage), see **abroad/traveling abroad; travel(ing)/journey**.

passenger

"Going along for the ride"; not being in charge of your decisions/actions; letting someone else make choices related to your life; not taking direct responsibility but rather being "a backseat driver," or possibly a silent partner/director.

See **drive/driving; vehicle(s)** and the particular vehicle.

passive activities

Passive activities—which Calvin Hall classified as talking, sitting, standing, looking, watching, seeing—account for about one fourth of our dream activities. If you have determined a waking situation/attitude to which the dream refers, how does your dream behavior relate to it? Is it typical/atypical, show how you contribute to the problem, or offer new alternatives? To compare your action over time, use Dreamercise #15. If you don't like your dream behavior, use Dreamercise #3, #4, or #10 to understand it better, and Dreamercise #11 to practice new/different behaviors. All dreamercises are in Part 1.

passport

Your personal/national identity; ability to traverse various conditions/situations; new perspectives open to you.

See **abroad/traveling abroad; travel(ing)/journey**.

past

Past situations or experiences can refer to unfinished business; old conflicts/anxieties reawakened by a present situation; emotional ties to which you're clinging; older ways of handling a situation. If known persons from your past, it may be related to your relationship with them; someone in your present life who resembles them; some similar aspect of yourself. Sometimes your past, or issues from the past, are symbolized by old objects, objects in the background or distance, a historic date/experience.

pastor

See **minister/pastor**.

patent

Creativity; your uniqueness; a need for control/ownership/protection of your ideas, and therefore, possibly anxiety about a waking situation that has the potential to deprive/deplete/rob you; your ability to invent solutions to problems/issues.

See **invent/inventor**.

path(s)

Your direction/goals in life or those related to a current project/relationship. A narrow path suggests feeling there's not much leeway or room to maneuver, not a lot of choice. Consider whether the path turns toward the left (affected by past attitudes and ideas; need to activate/rely on feminine aspects?) or the right (future possibilities; need to activate/rely on masculine aspects?), or whether you've lost your sense of direction. Has someone led you "down the primrose path"? A "well-worn path" suggests you've been this way before and could refer to repetition of a problem/issue; inability to see new ideas/directions; the security of knowing your way.

Metaphysical/spiritual teachings are often referred to as "the path." Do you need to attend to this aspect of your life?

See **road; travel(ing)/journey; walking** (if applicable).

pattern/design

A pattern may appear in any object, but especially fabrics, rugs, and baskets. While a design may refer to the general pattern/design of your life, consider also its specific elements for the symbolic meaning of its form, color, or function. Scottish tartans, for instance, reflect clan membership, an aspect of identity.

peace/peaceful

Resolution of an emotional issue/conflict; the end of a cycle and the pause before a new cycle/endeavor; acceptance of your inner nature; inner calm; the end of a time of grief/loss/change and a new level of stability.

peacock

Associated with the mythological phoenix, it is, therefore, an early symbol of resurrection/the soul/rebirth. It was the bird of Juno (Greek, Hera), the Roman Great Mother goddess whose name meant soul, and whose month is June, making her the goddess of marriage/families. The bird's multicolored tail is a symbol for blending and for the concept of totality (Cirlot). More mundanely, it may represent a person who's "strutting like a peacock," and be related to ego inflation; pride; bragging; displaying one's sexual wares/prowess.

See **bird(s)**.

pear

Because of its shape, it can often symbolize a female/the womb/uterus. It is associated with the Virgin Mary. If ripening, it may symbolize pregnancy or a desire to become pregnant.

See **fruit(s)**.

pearl(s)

As a treasure from the sea, the pearl often represents the Self for women. Associated with water (the unconscious), pearls often represent inner/ancient knowledge, insight ("pearls of wisdom") from our depths. When Aphrodite, Greek goddess of love (Roman, Venus), rose from the sea, she carried a pearl in her hand, so pearls can represent feminine wisdom, especially about love and relationships. Broken/damaged pearls may signal that you're unable to rely on/trust your feminine instincts and need to do some psychological repair. It is the birthstone of someone born under the sign of Gemini (May 21–June 20).

See **jewel(s); oyster; treasure**.

pedestal

Who/What is on the pedestal? In a positive sense, it can mean honor; recognition; adoration. Negatively, it may signal that you've given some of your own power away by projecting an aspect of yourself on to another ("put on a pedestal") and subjecting yourself to his/her will or whim. Could the dream be suggesting that you need to "knock someone off the pedestal," or that one of your idols has "feet of clay"?

See **above; below; position(s)**.

pelican

An early symbol for Christ/Christianity. In medieval writings its body shape was sometimes used to represent the alchemical vessel where distillation occurred, thus representing the growth toward wholeness, individuation.

See **bird(s)**.

pelvis

See **lower body**.

pen/pencil

Communication; record keeping; documenting past/present

activities; power ("the pen is mightier than the sword"); the need for any of the preceding. In Freudian terms, both are phallic symbols.

See **point(ed)**.

pendant

If hanging at the neck or near the breasts, it may symbolize the energy of the throat chakra (see **neck**) or the heart chakra, respectively. The latter is related to love/relationships; emotional touching and being touched; the desire for unconditional love.

See **amulet(s); jewelry; necklace**.

penguin

As a flightless bird, the penguin may represent being weighed down by your emotions or by a negative (cold) situation, unable to soar. Its black and white coloring could refer to a need to balance opposites or to achieve harmony.

penis/phallus

In Jungian terms, the appearance of a phallic (elongated) symbol often represents creative potential; the power of healing; fertility; an archetypal symbol that Jung called the "creative mana." Shown in a deep, possibly underground, location, it represents the God-image in a state of transition; the inner person awaiting creative release (resurrection).

From a Freudian view, an especially large penis or erection may be related to doubts/anxiety about a male dreamer's maleness/sexual drive. The changing nature of marital sex during pregnancy often leads to an increase of both virility and impotency dreams for men, including situations in which penis sizes are observed/compared (Siegel).

See **ball; body; lower body; sex.**

people

Known people may reflect aspects of your relationship with them; or, as with any dream figure, known/unrecognized, aspects of yourself; resources to draw upon. Depending on their actions, they can represent positive or negative opinions/judgmental attitudes/new perspectives; feelings of acceptance/rejection, and therefore, related to self-esteem or self-confidence. Consider their characteristics (appearance, speech, actions, nationality) especially prominent, emphasized, or distorted ones—for additional clues. The number of people in the dream may be symbolic. For instance, two people other than the dreamer may represent the parent/child relationship or a sexual rivalry situation.

See **crowd; persona;** and the various "person" entries.

pepper

Something that's an irritant; that "puts a little spice in your life"; sometimes a slang for penis ("pecker"). Are you needing to be more of a "hot pepper," or to warm things up in some situation?

perfume

Self-stimulation; sensory stimulation, and therefore, possibly a sexual dream; seduction; erotic; possibly a woman in the life of a male dreamer; an elusive woman or the elusive presence of feminine aspects. Do you need to "throw someone off the scent"?

person, color change of

Cross-coloring dreams—in which the dreamer or other characters change color/race—often relate to anxiety about changing roles/identities in waking life.

person, dark or dark-skinned

If you're not dark-skinned, the appearance of a black/brown/dark-skinned person may represent your shadow, especially if the person is large or you can't quite see his/her face. If a female person, see also **Black Madonna**.

In some instances, a black person represents basic, primitive, or wild instincts within you, and, as such, may represent the recognition or beginning of the individuation process. Negative/dangerous attitudes/behavior attributed to the black person may reflect your own prejudices or societal stereotypes, and in this way express not only your unsolved problems but those of society as well (Ullman).

Estés writes of the "dark man"—not related to skin color but in terms of deeds, i.e., terrorist, rapist, thief, etc.—who appears in women's dreams and has one of three purposes: to (1) alert her that something's wrong in her world, (2) signal that her creative energies are being depleted, (3) announce the liberation of a "captive" function in her psyche. In the latter instance, he heralds the imminence of a change from one level of functioning to another, more mature level.

See **Africa/African**.

person, dead

Dreaming of deceased people, especially family members, can be a way to keep alive your relationship with them. It's a normal aspect of the mourning process if the death is a recent one. Deceased friends/teachers may symbolize some aspect of them that's a part of you or that you need to incorporate; or suggest that you've lost that quality in yourself that they represent.

See **ancestors; death**.

person, fair-skinned

A fair-skinned or fair-haired (blond) person can: be a pun for a fair-weather friend; suggest you need more frivolity ("blondes have more fun") or sexuality ("gentlemen prefer blondes") in your life; represent a person who's racially unbiased (Adams), or a dark-haired or dark-skinned person about whom you have conflicting feelings, and whom you made "light" in order to express actions/feelings you otherwise couldn't.

person, famous

We rarely know the actual famous person, but rather a persona he/she portrays; hence a famous person suggests that whatever your beliefs/understandings about him/her, something in your waking life has triggered issues about those traits/behaviors regarding you/another, or about the institution/principle that person represents for you.

When the dream character is a relative of a famous person, your dream message may be saying that you've been, or are, close to fame/greatness, but not quite. Is this an unfulfilled dream, or perhaps a continuing theme of your life ("almost, but not quite")?

Hopcke says famous people are the closest things we have to gods/goddesses today and may, therefore, represent archetypal figures. They may represent personal issues embedded in the archetypal motifs of hero/heroine, mother/father, masculine/feminine, as well as wisdom and shadow figures. Consider whether there are any puns embedded in the person's name, as in Chevy *Chase*, Ron *Moody*, Sondra *Locke*, Victoria *Principal*, Fannie *Flagg*, or *Harry* (hairy or harried?) Morgan.

If none of this rings a bell, use Delaney's dream interview questions and ask yourself, "Who is . . . [Victoria Principal, for instance]? What is she like?" Then describe the actress as if you are speaking to someone who has never heard of her.

See **actor/actress; royalty**.

person, foreign

Some foreign/distant aspect of yourself (unconscious material; shadow?) that's attempting to make itself known. Do you like/dislike, enjoy/fear the qualities of the foreigner? How are those qualities similar to/unlike your own?

person, historical

Some aspect of your personality, possibly the major/predominant characteristic of the historical personage, wearing the costume/facade of another.

person, known

Something in you is hooking into something about that known person, or the dream issue involves your relationship with that person. What were you doing yesterday/recently that's like that person or your experiences with that person? What aspect of the person is like you? If someone well-known, it likely represents some quality the person expresses that you've overlooked or not noticed (Signell).

If someone from your remote/past history or someone you don't like, it can be an expression of your shadow aspect; other unacknowledged aspects of yourself (Signell). It can represent a waking situation that's evoking feelings similar to those from the past relationship; or some general principle/situation in which you're presently involved (Faraday).

See **shadow**.

person(s) merging with/changing into another

This often calls attention to an idea/concept, rather than an aspect of the Self/another. Look for the commonality (personality traits; feelings; attitudes) of the persons. It can reflect emerging or changing attitudes (L. Weiss) or trying on different roles. Notice any change in emotion that accompanies the physical change.

For person changing his/her sex, see **sex change**. For person changing his/her race, see **person, color change of**.

person, special

People with special or extraordinary abilities/insight/power may symbolize that ability, responsibility, or concept, i.e., a judge may represent judgment (Krakow and Neidhardt); an archetypal symbol.

person, unknown

If you're relatively unknown in your own dream (in a crowd?), it can symbolize unrecognized aspects of yourself, especially ones you've downplayed for the sake of others or for your own needs. Has someone slighted you recently? It can symbolize one who is so unnoticed that he/she can wander through the crowd and obtain secrets; thus a person who's more important than he/she may seem. An unknown young girl/woman may symbolize the Self in women's dreams, and the anima in men's dreams (Jung).

See **name(s)**; and **shadow** for persons totally unknown but having a prominent, possibly dark/hidden/veiled part in your dream.

persona

The persona (Latin for mask) is an archetype expressed through any of the public faces we put on to interact with one another. It's revealed through the ways we present ourselves: the roles we play, clothing we wear (in fact, clothing itself is one symbol of the persona), hairstyle, our comportment, and, for women, their makeup. We cannot live in a society without our personas—we need to act appropriately for the situation—but we needn't be fooled that they are the real or total Self. The "collective persona" is carried through the "public" faces of our various institutions, governments, flags, and other national symbols. You may wish to make a list of the various personas you exhibit in your dreams over time (see Dreamercise #15, Part 1). What do they say about who you are, or who you're becoming? Do you need to expand your repertoire?

perspire

Anxiety; a time of waiting ("sweat it out"); stress/fear/nervousness ("sweaty palms," "a cold sweat"); effort ("sweat of one's brow"). It can refer to a kind of cleansing or ridding of toxins; a need to "cool off" emotionally.

pests

Emotional distraction; an annoying person/situation that's "bugging" you or that you'd like to eradicate.

See **bug; insects**.

pet(s)

Civilized instincts; a need for love/acceptance; a need to be playful; intuition. Dead pets may appear as themselves or in the guise of other animals and may help you grieve their loss. Pets may serve as dream guides directing you toward, or imparting, new information/wisdom; be a pun for sexual behavior ("petting"); suggest that you need more stroking/touching/attention.

See **cat/kitten; dog/puppy**; or other specific animals. For talking pets, see **animal(s)**.

petticoat

See **underwear**.

phantoms

See **ghost(s)**.

phoenix

A mythical creature with characteristics of both the eagle and the pheasant, it has long symbolized transformation; resurrection (death-rebirth theme); regeneration; the completion of a project/process and the readiness for another. It also symbolizes need for, or promise of, a new beginning or chance; making a comeback; regaining your innocence, thus, a new perspective; getting at the essence of something; "trial by fire."

See **bird(s)**.

photograph

Memories; a false or rigid image, possibly locked in from the past; illusory security; clinging to past attitudes/positions. If a family photo, your family environment, influence, or heritage (if past or birth family, rather than present family). If a self-photo, it may relate to needing a closer or more objective view of yourself; or if a retouched photo, to a need to put across a different, likely more favorable, view/aspect of yourself. If you're taking photos, it can refer to a need for focused attention to some situation (consider what you are photographing for clues); a need to capture/recreate/awaken the moments of a relationship or of your own inner nature. If black-and-white, it may be emphasizing a need to consider opposite values/positions and to reconcile them; dogmatic attitudes (it's either "black or white"); a need to add more color/life to a situation/relationship.

physician

See **doctor**.

piano

Making music or harmony in your life, unless the piano needs to be tuned, in which case your dream may be saying you need to make some repairs, hire a consultant (therapist?), and get your life back in tune. Is there something "dis-chord-ant" in your life?

See **music/musician; organ; rhythm**. As an instrument with eighty-eight keys, see **eight**.

pickle

To preserve something; to change the character of something; the penis, and therefore, possibly a sweet or sour situation/relationship; anxiety/fear/realization that you're going to be in trouble ("in a pickle").

picnic

Informality; reduction of formal rules/authority; letting down your guard; possibly romance. It may refer to a situation/relationship that's relaxed and easy, or to one that's tough ("it's no picnic"). Consider the symbolism of the location.

See **eating; food; landscapes/settings**.

picture

A situation succinctly expressed or disguised ("a picture is worth a thousand words"); consequently, consider carefully its details, especially anything that's emphasized or distorted, for additional clues. It may refer to perfectionistic tendencies ("picture-perfect"); unwillingness to face change; need for an expanded perspective ("the big picture").

If applicable, see **art; artist; draw(ing); painting; photograph**.

pie

Desserts/rewards of life. Pie à la mode may represent an especially satisfying reward; a temptation if you're on a diet; or may be related to a need for maternal nurturing (ice cream = milk), which may also be true of cream/custard pies. Particular kinds of pies can be related to holidays (pumpkin = Thanksgiving; mince = Christmas?) and your experiences/feelings about them. Are you reaching beyond your abilities ("pie in the sky")? Is someone in your life being "crusty"? Do you need to put your life in "apple pie order"? If whole, the pie may represent a mandala, the Self.

See **sugar/sweets/candy**.

pig(s)

Uncivilized; undisciplined; low class; someone with sloppy eating/dressing habits or rude manners; gluttony ("pigged out"); greed; a woman who's sexually indiscriminate; sexual slang for the police; someone who's stubborn ("pigheaded"); a man with a "pork belly"; financial responsibility ("bringing home the bacon"). It's also related to the sense of smell; the ability to root out/sniff out hidden aspects of a situation. Yet, in Tibetan symbolism, the pig represents unconsciousness, lack of awareness.

In many early cultures the pig was a symbol of fertility and was associated with, or was an appropriate sacrifice for, fertility/mother goddesses. In fairy tales/legends/folklore, the pig, especially the sow, represents the womb; fecundity; the mother in her devouring aspect. The only creature who was ever able to tame the fiery Hawaiian volcano goddess Pele was the pig god Kamapua'a.

See **animal(s); boar**.

pill(s)

See **medicine/medication; pain medication**.

pillar

A masculine symbol, especially of strength; stability; durability; the ability to uphold values/morals. A pillar is representative of the world tree and its symbolism, and sometimes of the spinal column, especially in Egypt, where it is the *djed* pillar, associated with Ptah, creator of the world, therefore with fertility/agriculture and the continuation of life.

pillow

Consider how the pillow is used. For instance, if under the head, it could be a mental support; something to soften an intellectual position. If behind the back, it could represent supporting energy; stamina; the need for support/resources. Are you having some battle/conflict in your waking life that's really only a "pillow fight"?

pimple

Negative emotions erupting; feelings about your self-esteem or self-image; feeling immature/awkward in some situation/relationship. If you're an adult, has a waking situation activated feelings you had when you were an adolescent?

pin

If a straight pin that's sticking you, it may represent an irritating situation/relationship, possibly involving a male (phallic symbol) or someone who's being a real "prick." It may refer to a situation that's falling apart or otherwise unstable; that you feel anxious about or feel the need to hold together. You may be feeling trapped or immobilized ("pinned down"). To be "pinned" refers to a romantic relationship and commitment. According to Estés, Sleeping Beauty's prick led to sleep (a dip into the unconscious), awakening awareness, and Prince Charming (masculine aspect, wholeness).

If decorative, see **jewelry**. If applicable, see **sew(ing)**.

pine tree

Ever green, it symbolizes immortality. Its cones (as fruit/seeds) symbolize fertility (Cirlot).

pink

Romance; love; a traditional symbol of baby girls; feminine immaturity; good health ("in the pink"). As a pastel, it may represent a diluted emotion (red), i.e., one you have difficulty expressing or dealing with, or that's reduced in intensity.

See **color(s); red**.

pipe(s)

If a man's smoking pipe, feelings about men who smoke pipes; a romantic male or one of authority; someone you know who smokes a pipe; old-fashioned virtues/values.

If a conduit, it may represent the transmission/reception of ideas. Consider the type of pipe, the way it's connected/disconnected (your connection with others?), where it's located, the contents/material it conducts. For instance, a sewer pipe may have a more negative connotation than water pipes, but when new and/or large enough to crawl into, it can represent a need to hide/escape. If related to a house, it can represent your inner plumbing (circulatory system, gastrointestinal tract?) and possible difficulties there.

Any kind of pipe may suggest "pipe dreams." If bagpipes, feelings/relationships connected with England/Scotland/Ireland or someone of those nationalities.

If applicable, see **plumber/plumbing**.

pirate

As a plunderer of ships at sea, the pirate may symbolize some person/situation that's adding chaos to your emotional life. He may represent freedom; defying authority/socialization; some person/action that's out of the mainstream; someone who has violated your integrity or creativity.

If applicable, see **parrot; sailing; sea; ship/shipwreck; thief/theft**.

piston

Sexual drive/energy; sexual intercourse (because of its motion; a pun for "pissed on."

See **engine**.

pit

If you're in the pit, it may represent feelings of being trapped. If a pit in the ground, it may refer to feelings/issues related to a maternal or maternal-like relationship. If elsewhere, consider the meaning of the location (basement, jungle?). It may refer to a negative waking situation that's "the pits"; feelings of being depressed ("down and out"; "in the pits"); involvement in a situation that's so messy/complicated, it's like a "snake pit." Do you fear there's a "pitfall" ahead?

See **cage**.

pizza

Abundance; choices; access to variety; group/family socializing or celebrating; deprivation of/need for any of the foregoing. If round, it may be one form of a mandala (see **mandala; Self**).

See **bread; eating; food**.

place(s)

See **city/cities; country/countryside; foreign country; landscapes/settings**.

plains

It may be a pun for Oklahoma ("where the wind comes sweeping down the plains") or any midwestern locale; your relationship with someone living in a "plains" locale; something that's homespun; a person who's plain, wholesome, without frills; smooth going (no mountains/gullies).

See **landscapes/settings**. If applicable, see **farm(er); field(s); grass**.

plait

To plait or intertwine things together suggests interdependence; cooperation; affiliation; an intimate relationship; possibly entwined in a situation/relationship that's more complicated than you originally thought; strength in unity, i.e., uniting different efforts/ideas/influences to create something new.

See **knot(s); rope; weave(ing)/weaver** (if applicable).

plan

A need for a plan; therefore, possibly feeling insecure or without sufficient direction. It may give you some actual ideas for a waking situation.

plane [action; tool]

Yours or another's skills/abilities at smoothing and easing situations/relationships; a need to make something fit; an idea/concept that needs to be refined; training/educating ("taking the rough edges off") someone.

See **carpenter**. If a vehicle, see **airplane**.

planet(s)

To dream of more than one planet may refer to someone you know who's involved in astronomy/astrology. It suggests that your dream may have a cosmic/spiritual/archetypal theme. If you're traveling to a planet, it may refer to a need to escape; be free of/distance yourself from some person/situation. If a single, or specific, planet, it may refer to the unconscious (the unknown); someone born under the sign of that planet.

In astrology the following planets are considered to influence specific attributes of our lives; metaphysically they are associated with the chakras/energy centers:

Mercury: Associated with the sixth chakra (the ajna center or third eye); the antenna of the five senses and ruler of the rational mind. Horoscope attributes relate it to communication, thinking, learning, consciousness.

Venus: The fourth/heart chakra; the key to emotional reactions; relates to what you value and to your sense of values.

Mars: The third/solar plexus chakra; the energy principle; action based on sensory and emotional impressions; relates to initiative, aggression, sexuality, courage, impulsivity.

Jupiter: The seventh/crown chakra; the capacity to recognize and react to opportunity, especially with optimism; relates to abstract learning.

Saturn: The first (sexual, base, or root) chakra; the self-preservative, species-perpetuating principle; relates to defensive/aggressive/ambitious responses to outer situations.

Uranus: The fifth/throat chakra; relates to creative originality; individuality; self-expression; sudden, unpredictable change that stimulates you to break away from old patterns.

Neptune: The second/spleen chakra; relates to strong, deep feelings; inherited mentality; unconscious influence; idealism; decision making from deep, almost intuitive knowledge.

Pluto: Relates to extremes of any kind and links the themes of sex/death/rebirth; recognition of the spiritual; your perspectives; ability to get to the core of an issue.

See **earth; globe; moon/moonlight; sun/sunlight; universe**.

plank

Consider the condition of the wood (good, needing repair/polished, rotting?) for ideas about areas in your life that may need work, or shoring up. Also consider its location or function, i.e., in an old house (some aspect of you or your identity?), on a pier (emotions?), in new construction (personal potential or the basis for new ideas?), hiding secrets beneath it (the unconscious; hidden aspects of yourself?). Working with wood of any kind is related to the symbolism of the tree; therefore, to yourself and to the next level of your creation/development. Unless, of course, you're in trouble and having to "walk the plank."

See **tree(s); wood**. If applicable, see **carpenter**.

plant(s)

Growth or potential for growth; energy; spiritual development; fertility; the expression of loving care. The opposite of the foregoing if dying or not in a good condition. Possibly one's children, especially if estranged from them (otherwise, they're usually not disguised).

See **garden; gardener; vegetation**. If applicable, see **flower(s); vegetable(s)**.

planting

See **sowing**.

plaster(ing)/plasterer

A need for repairs; hiding or denying problems in a situation/relationship; covering over faults, weaknesses, or gaps in the truth. Perhaps you "got plastered" recently, with whatever subsequent feelings.

plate

What's on your plate may relate to what has been "dished up" for you in waking life. Perhaps you're feeling lazy or envious and desirous of having something handed to you "on a silver platter." An empty plate, while others have food, can indicate emotional impoverishment; no "goodies"; feeling left out. A plate piled full may, again, refer to being so emotionally impoverished that you can never get enough. However, if you have been struggling with food issues, and your plate is empty, or not quite full, by choice, it could indicate new control and/or priorities. Food on a plate can refer to sexual appetites or any other sensual urge. Consider who else is in the dream and the effect of their presence/actions. For a different viewpoint, use Dreamercise #4, Part 1.

See **food; eating**.

play(ing)

A need for recreation; entertaining new ideas; masturbation issues ("playing with yourself"); competition issues; emotional/sexual situations ("make a play for"; "playing hard to get"; "playing the field"); feeling overwhelmed by a waking situation or responsibilities; a need/desire to practice new skills without customary consequences. Is there something you're being asked to "play along with"? Many idioms using "play" show its relationship to attempts at manipulation/control: "play along with," "play cat and mouse," "play fair," "play for time," "play ball with," "play your part," "play it cool," "play up to" someone. Does one or more of these attitudes or stances connect with some waking situation? In *Games People Play,* Eric Berne describes a number of ways we avoid intimacy through our communicative styles and messages. Are you "playing it safe" and only playing at closeness, or are you "playing with fire"?

See **game(s)**.

plowing

Fertility; preparing/working for change; laying the groundwork for a new beginning or approach; awareness that a hard, but potentially fruitful, task is ahead; sexual intercourse; archetypally, the union of the masculine/feminine. The plowed field may refer to the female genitalia; the personal mother; the archetypal Great Mother.

See **sow(ing)**.

plumber/plumbing

Gastrointestinal or urinary problems; possibly trouble "digesting" or expelling some noxious situation/information/attitude; having to deal with "shit" in your waking life; some aspect of your life that's stopped up and not flowing smoothly.

plunge

Taking a risk; taking a dive or loss; anxiety about a waking situation that may not be clear, or in which your own role/position may not be clear; a need to be more adventurous/experimental; a need for more recognition of your unconscious influence (plunge into the water). What present situation is too dull or restrictive for you, causing you, perhaps, to feel like acting a little recklessly?

If applicable, see **descend(ing); fall(ing)**.

pocket(s)

As a container, it's a feminine symbol (the womb, vagina?), but that meaning will change depending on whose pocket it is. Trouser pockets may symbolize masculinity or male possessions, for example, while apron pockets may refer to nurturing. In general, pockets refer to things hidden or not obvious (secrets?); ideas not considered openly or not yet in the open; information about yourself not revealed in a relationship. Consider the contents of the pocket and whether it's in good shape or needs repair. Do you suspect that someone has his "hand in your pocket" or someone else's, or is "lining his/her own pockets" at your expense? Perhaps you've had to "pocket your pride."

See **clothes/clothing**.

point(ed)

Although from a Freudian perspective, anything pointed can be a phallic symbol, and inserting a pointed object into an opening (a pencil in a sharpener?) can represent intercourse, your dream could be saying that there's a point you need to see or to make (''get to the point''). Perhaps there are some rules you need to attend to/establish (''point of order''). It can relate to commitment or having reached the ''point of no return'' in a project/relationship, with all that implies for you, positively or negatively.

pointing

Consider whether you do the pointing or are pointed at, and whether your feelings about the situation are positive (honoring?) or negative (anger, embarrassment?). Is it an act of aggression, identification (''point him out''), recognition? What needs to be ''pointed out'' to you?

poison

A toxic relationship; an activity that's repugnant/dangerous; negative attitudes; gossip or other activities that adversely affect someone or influence others' attitudes (''poison their minds''); a waking situation in which nurturance has been withdrawn.

pole

Because of its shape, a masculine/phallic symbol. In Christian symbology, Christ is sometimes the ''fixed pole'' around which the church calendar revolves. This is related to the *axis mundi*, the world axis/pole and life energy, often symbolized by the Maypole. As the point around which everything turns, it can also represent the Self. If it's the North or South Pole, it may refer to someone who seems to have a magnetic attraction; needing a sense of direction; a frozen or too distant emotional situation; far-off dreams/ambitions.

police

In general, the principle of order and control; therefore, that part of yourself that's able to bring this about, or seeks control/order. Police can represent messages from your conscience, indicating you already feel guilty, or that an action you're considering will result in feeling guilty. It's common for police to represent our parents; the morals/prohibitions taught by parents or other authority figures; issues of obeying/defying authority and independence/dependence.

See **officer**.

polish

Consider the symbolism of what needs to be polished, what you're polishing, or what already is polished. What aspect of you needs more polish; or is someone "shining you on"?

If applicable, see **housework/housekeeper**.

pomegranate

Because of its many seeds, it symbolizes fertility; immortality through progeny; an invitation to sex; procreation; the vagina/womb; love/energy (because of its red flesh). It is a Judaic symbol of faithfulness to the Torah, while in Christianity, it's associated with Mary and with hope. It is related to blood and sacrifice; and is a symbol of oneness and the recognition of diversity in unity (Cirlot). It was a pomegranate seed that Persephone ate—condemning her to spend half a year in the underworld (Hades)—thus connecting it to germination; cycles; death-rebirth themes (see **grain(s)**). The national emblem of Spain, it may represent your relationship to Spain or someone of Spanish descent.

pond/pool

See **lake**.

pope

Religious authority/doctrine; code of religious behavior; a revered male role model; personal or archetypal father.

See **priest**.

poplar tree

A waking experience/locale where this tree existed. Because one side of the leaf is dark and the other quite light, it can symbolize opposites, especially dark/light, therefore night/day, sun/moon, positive/negative.

See **opposites; tree(s)**.

porcupine

A strong need to be left alone or to be protected against intrusion; the power (long, pointed quills = masculine symbol) to protect/defend yourself. In American Indian tradition, porcupine often accompanies the trickster/coyote figure. In some folklore, he is blessed with powers to control witches/evil forces. What has you bristling, and can you handle it by adopting porcupine's ways, perhaps using your own sense of humor? Use Dreamercises #3, #4, and #10, Part 1, to get to know your porcupine better, and to ascertain his skills and gifts to you.

position(s)

Your position in a dream, intertwined with your actions, suggests your attitude toward the dream situation and toward the waking situation to which it relates. Reviewing your positions/

postures over time (see Dreamercise #15, Part 1) may give you some idea of typical/habitual positions, as well as those that are unique/different for a given dream scene. Positions can be a reflection of striving toward goals and your feelings about your ability to achieve them.

See **above; behind; below; beside; close; distance/distant/in the distance; down; front/in front; near; opposites; standing above; standing opposite; up**.

postman

See **messenger**.

posture(s)

Postures can relate to our stance (open; defensive; protective) or to attitudes. They are probably not too important unless unusual or something in the dream calls your attention to them. For more insight into the posture, assume it in waking life. Attend to how you feel, what your thoughts are, and especially what your next movement or posture might be (how the posture wants to continue, its natural follow-through).

See **body; jump(ing); kneel; prone; position(s); rotating/revolving/turning; run(ning); sit(ting); stand(ing); walk(ing)**.

potion

See **magic drink**.

pot(s)/potter

If circular, it may represent a female/womb symbol. The flatter it is, the more it may suggest a mandala. Because potters work with clay, considered by the folklore of many cultures to be the basic material of humans, they often are considered the creators of the world, or of the first humans, therefore connected with cosmic creation (an archetypal theme); the divine; spirit. More mundanely, it may refer to smoking marijuana (''getting potted'').

If you were creating the pot, see **artist, craft(s); create(ing)/creative**. If a cooking pot, see **saucepan**.

power/powerful/powerless

To be powerful, or have power, refers to growing skills; confidence; self-esteem; inner strength, especially if you've been in therapy or have been doing growth work. Feeling powerful can be a compensatory dream for a recent situation in which you felt powerless. If the power is without compassion, however, it suggests issues with/about: authority, independence/dependence, adequacy/inadequacy, approval/disapproval. If you feel powerless in the dream, consider a waking situation that may have evoked that same feeling or feelings related to any of the preceding issues, which you were unaware of at the time.

See **competitor/competition; helpless**.

prayer

To be praying or hear a prayer suggests spiritual aspirations; a need to connect with the divine or with your spiritual life; opening to your inner guidance/wisdom or holiness; willingness to allow unconscious material to emerge. Look for other clarifying clues, i.e., a request or expression of needs, giving thanks or honor (which may relate to needs for approval/affection). Consider to whom the prayers are being offered for clues as to whether it relates to a male/female figure from your past/present life, since holy personages can, at times, also represent parental/authority figures.

If applicable, see **church**.

precipice

Feelings of danger/foreboding; a waking situation in which you feel unsafe, or on the edge (perhaps fearful but not necessarily negative).

See **abyss; canyon; cliff; edge**.

predator(s)

Predators (people or animals) often symbolize injured instincts; aspects of yourself that need to be repaired. They can represent negative aspects of yourself, the naysaying or critical functions—what Estés calls our ''inner stalker''—that developed and grew as others wounded, criticized, or were inattentive to your more creative functions.

If dream predators have become recurrent nightmares, work with them in Dreamercises #3, #9, #10, and #16, Part 1; and do some of the creative quests mentioned in Chapter 6.

pregnant

If you're not pregnant or wishing to be, a pregnant woman—or a statue/figure with a huge, rounded belly—can symbolize a developing idea/project, or, negatively, anxiety about a situation that's growing out of control. A pregnant figure/character larger than life may represent the archetypal Great Mother.

For some of the specific kinds of dreams of pregnant women and their husbands, see the subsections on men's and women's dreams in Chapter 4, Part 1.

See **baby**.

prehistoric

A need to break away from some present situation; someone who's behaving in a primitive way; an "ancient" (childhood) authority or situation, whose influence is still active within you; your own primal urges and instinctual drives.

present(s)

See **gift/giving; package**.

present time

The most common time in dreams is the present; however, the appearance of a person/situation from the past suggests that even though occurring in the present, the dream, or some aspect of it, is rooted in, or refers to, past experiences/issues.

preserved

Depending on its condition and the object itself, it may reflect something that you value; something (belief, personal/cultural values?) that you've held on to too long; some aspect of your life that's crumbling or that needs more attention and care, possibly repair; something from your past still active in your present functioning.

See **mummy**.

preserves

See **jell/jelly/gelatin**.

president

A need for recognition; leadership ambitions/abilities; personal/archetypal father; authority issues; a power or a puppet, depending on your own biases or position.

See **director; leader/lead(ing); officer**.

priest

Spiritual/religious needs; religious beliefs/affiliation; possibly feelings of guilt, especially if needing to go to confession; the personal/archetypal father. The priest may represent the archetype of the Wise Old Man, or the spirit, which can appear in dreams when you need information that your waking resources can't provide. For generations, priests have been healers, so don't overlook the possibility that your dream is signaling some aspect of you that needs healing, or that a healing takes place in the dream.

See **church**.

primates

Primates are often a disguise for a triangular relationship in waking life, especially between men and women, but also including any kind of threesome (Krakow and Neidhardt). This situation may replay the early oedipal relationship between baby, mother, and father. Women in their third trimester of pregnancy often dream of large animals such as monkeys (Siegel) and gorillas (Garfield).

See **ape; monkey**.

prince

If a male dreamer, the prince can represent himself when young or an infant, when he was supremely important (Jung). Possibly a need to feel that important/honored once again; recognition of your royal potential. If a female dreamer, it can represent her brother; a boyfriend; wishes for romance or the perfect lover; the animus.

See **king; royalty**.

princess

If a female dreamer, herself; possibly the need to be rescued. If you're the princess in the dream, you may have recognized your royal potential (the development of your full character), but also your need to grow more. Or is the dream telling you that you are behaving like a demanding/spoiled princess? For a male dreamer, she can represent his sister; wishes for the perfect/ideal woman; the anima.

Fairy-tale princesses are often related to the hero/heroine myth, since they're imprisoned or are the victim of a spell, and they, or someone else, must perform certain activities before they're awakened to full potential. The heroine descends into, then ascends from, the depths of her unconscious into consciousness.

See **queen; royalty**.

prison/prisoner

We are all imprisoned by some attitude/belief/fear/training, often from childhood, that limits the development of our full potential. It's possible that your jailer is your shadow aspect. Review recent occurrences, particularly within the last 24 to 48 hours, for ideas as to what they may have triggered with respect to being restricted, emotionally or physically limited, incapable/inadequate, guilt feelings, feelings about authority.

See **cage; cell; imprisoned; jailer**.

prize

Recent praise; a need to be rewarded, hence, feelings of not receiving enough acknowledgment; sexual prowess issues.

See **trophy; victor/victory**.

procession

Related to parade, it refers to a more serious or solemn situation/occasion. Thus, it may refer to actual academic/professional/religious situations, or to graduation to a new level or way of life. Derived from the idea of pilgrimages and progress (Cirlot), the procession is, therefore, related to cycles and time.

See **parade; rite/ritual**.

professor

See **teacher**.

profession

See **business/work**.

prone

Lying down can relate to relaxation; rest and recovery; retreat; and, of course, to sexual or relationship situations/issues. It may refer to health issues/anxieties; concerns about "standing up for yourself" or taking an aggressive position. If one person is standing and another is lying down, it may refer to a caregiver position/attitude or to a power (one up/one down) posture, depending on who the people are and what action is occurring.

See **position(s); posture(s)**.

propeller

Movement or motivation in your life, most likely from an outside influence/source; a situation that's been speeded up, possibly going too fast for you; a need for more control or to be the driving force in some situation/relationship.

See **engine**. If applicable, see **airplane; boat**.

prostitute

If a male dreamer, it may relate to feeling sexually needy; feelings of social/sexual inadequacy; negative/demeaning attitudes toward females or sex; possibly guilt feelings for sexual urges; a wish that sexual relationships were simple, straightforward transactions.

If a female dreamer, it may relate to fantasies about what being a prostitute is like, i.e., possibly more sexual freedom/expression, less inhibition. It may refer to inner feelings of guilt; negative attitudes toward men; "whorish" feelings. Was there some way you sold yourself or your ideals recently?

prune

Inasmuch as prunes are a notoriously effective laxative, they may represent excremental functions and be related to a recent situation about which you have hostile feelings, or a need for an emotional clean-out. Because of their appearance, they may represent aging ("wrinkled as a prune"); a negative attitude ("prune face").

See **food; fruit(s)**.

psychic

See **fortune-teller/fortune-telling**.

psychotherapy

See **therapy**.

pub

See **bar**.

puberty

See **adolescent/adolescence**.

pull(ing)

Taking action; asserting authority ("pull rank"); influencing others, or being influenced by them or your own emotions ("pulled in different directions"); a group/community effort ("pull together"); using strength rather than intellect to get your way. Conversely, perhaps you need to be a little more sneaky and "pull some strings" to "pull something off."

See **move(ing); push(ing)**.

pulse

Feelings/anxiety about your health; getting/needing the sense/essence of a situation; being in charge and/or monitoring a situation ("have your finger on the pulse of it").

punish(ment)

Being punished relates to our conscience, moral/societal values, and to guilt about adhering to them. It may be related to low self-esteem; self-doubt about your capabilities; an unequal situation/relationship in which one person has more power/authority than the other and uses it unkindly, hence, also childhood situations in which there was verbal or physical abuse by an adult. If you're punishing another, it may refer to feelings of anger; a need for retribution; a projection of your own negative feelings onto another.

puppet

Someone easily controlled (you, another?); not feeling in charge of a situation or feeling powerless; acting a role you're not involved in; speaking for another; a situation with strings attached. If you're watching a puppet show in the United States, it may represent childhood feelings/conflicts. If in another country, it may represent your feelings/relationships with that country or its people. Puppet shows frequently have archetypal themes. In Bali, the puppet master *(dalang)* is a priest. He prays and engages in other sacred actions before the show to enlist the help of the spirits in presenting a traditional, archetypal drama.

See **marionette; movie**.

puppy

See **animal(s); dog/puppy**.

purple

The color of royalty and regalness; the personality or instincts sublimated in the service of the spirit; intuition; wisdom.

See **color(s)**.

purpose

Having a clear sense of purpose suggests having similar feelings, or wishing you did, in waking life. A strong purpose, or feeling good about your purpose, may be expressed in dreams after you've done some inner growth work (therapy?) or near the completion of a crisis/grief situation. The less clear the purpose, the more ambiguous some waking situation/attitude may be.

See **direction(s); plan**.

purse/wallet

In Freudian terms, a purse symbolizes the womb. Both purses and wallets can symbolize female genitals. They're common symbols for our persona or our identity. Losing them suggests fears you have about losing some part of your identity or individuality in a current/upcoming situation. If you're pregnant, dreaming of finding or losing a purse, wallet, or other womblike container may reflect concerns about your condition, or about your adequacy to carry out upcoming responsibilities.

pursued/pursuer/pursuing

Pursuit dreams are a fairly common type of anxiety dream. Consider what's pursuing you for clues as to whether it relates to alien aspects of yourself (aliens/monsters?), primary or sexual urges (animals/monsters?), or perhaps to an inner battle with societal values (mobs/crowds?). Although quite frightening, from Jungian and Gestalt points of view, the pursuer may actually be an unconscious or rejected aspect of yourself that's trying to make contact with, or be recognized by, waking consciousness, and may become more frightening if you resist its efforts. To recognize and attend to it and its purpose, consider honoring it with Dreamercise #3, #4, #10, or #19, Part 1.

If you're pursuing someone/something, it may refer to your goals/ambitions; to pursuing the expression of elusive emotions; inner action/development that's taking you forward into the future; or, if pursuing an animal, to the freer acknowledgment/expression of instinctual urges.

See **followed**.

pus

See **abscess; infection**.

push(ing)

Effort; energy; a new drive or "push" in your life; perhaps the feeling that you, or some person/situation in your waking life, is a "pushover." If you're being pushed, it may refer to feelings of being pressured/coerced; not having enough time for yourself or enough time to complete something to your satisfaction (related to perfectionistic tendencies?). Perhaps there's someone to whom you need to give a little push or encouragement

See **move(ing); pull(ing)**.

puzzle

Solving a puzzle relates to a test of your intellectual skills/stamina/awareness. As a self-challenge, it's a symbol of the hero/heroine's journey toward seeking an answer and therefore toward wholeness/enlightenment. If a picture puzzle, it may represent trying to understand/uncover the elements of a situation; a need to get the overall picture; trying to put together elements that will make a situation work or come together. If a crossword puzzle, it may relate to a quarrel or "cross words." Puzzles can represent a known person who likes to engage in the kind of puzzle in your dream.

For another archetypal understanding, see **labyrinth/maze**.

pyramid(s)

Ancient symbol for the *axis mundi*/world mountain; a holy mountain or high place of God. To the ancient Egyptians it represented a stairway to heaven for the deceased, as well as the sun's rays descending to earth. It was, thus, a threshold symbol. More mundanely, as a pointed object, it's related to the phallus. The square base and four sides relate it to the square and the number four. The shapes of the sides also relate it to the triangle and the number three. It may represent a wider awareness, especially as related to spiritual issues; the mysterious unknown; spiritual initiation; Egypt, Mexico, and other countries with pyramids and your relationship with them.

See **Egypt; four; stair(s); three; triangle; world mountain**.

quail

As do all birds, it symbolizes the union of sky and earth. Since the quail most often hides on the ground, it can symbolize impulses/emotions that need to be, or are in the process of becoming, raised to higher levels of understanding or spirituality. Often hunted, it may symbolize a part of yourself that feels hunted, oppressed, singled out, desirable, insignificant. We often think of quails as having a family (a covey), so it may symbolize nurturing; following maternal advice; being too rigid in the way you're proceeding; needing a definite focus/plan of action. In China the quail symbolizes spring, hence creativity; renewal.

See **bird(s)**.

quarantine

Alone; separated; unable to utilize resources; having limited access to information; cut off from various aspects of yourself (a form of imprisonment). Usually we are quarantined because of a contagious disorder, so the dream could symbolize some idea/aspect of yourself or a secret that you "shouldn't spread around," or that you're afraid will infect someone else. It could mean being ostracized because of something over which you have no control. Are you comfortable (being cared for) or distressed? If you're trying to reach/contact someone, consider what relationship it pertains to, or what part of you that person represents.

See **cage; cell; imprisoned; prison/prisoner**.

quarrel

If not someone with whom you are actually quarreling in waking life, it can symbolize hidden/unexpressed anger or resentment toward some person or aspects of yourself that the image represents. If with someone with whom you *are* quarreling, does the dream suggest new insights/behavior?

See **anger; fight/fighter**.

quarry

The search for the feminine; unconscious information ready to emerge. If empty or played out, it can symbolize grief; emotional barrenness; repressed feelings; a woman's realization that she's going through menopause. If something is being done to change the face of the quarry, it may symbolize a new project; creativity. Archetypally, it can represent the Earth Mother, or the search-for-hidden-treasure motif (a Self/individuation symbol).

See **dig(ging); gem(s); rock(s); stone(s)**.

quake

See **earthquake; fear**.

quart(s)

Although a measurement, we usually think of a quart of something as being fluid and in a container, so it can symbolize the feminine, or the union of masculine/feminine, depending on the fluid being measured. Is your quart container empty, full, being filled? A quart of milk could symbolize either mother; nurturance; breasts; semen; some life-giving aspect of yourself. "A quart low" refers to someone not using or not having full mental capacity; someone who's a little less than a complete bullshitter. Anyone you know?

See **container; milk** (if applicable); **measurement**.

quartz

Quartz is one of the most common and well-known semiprecious minerals, so consider, first, what quartz means to you (maybe the heart of your watch, therefore something that's timely or passing, cycles?). Then consider whether or not something is made from the quartz, and whether it's being mined, used in a ceremony, received as a gift (sacred?).

Australian aborigine tribes consider quartz to be a rain stone. Cherokee Indians used them as divining stones, while other tribes have used them to make cutting weapons such as arrowheads or knives. Some tribes, and contemporary metaphysical healers, use them as a healing stone, a conduit of energy.

Quartz can refer to something that has, or is becoming, crystallized (rigid, "crystal-clear"?). In thin sheets, it can be used like Kerlian photography to see the aura around a person, hence, a medium for seeing a person's energy or for knowing ordinarily unseen things about him/her.

The shape of most quartz crystals is definitely phallic; however, coming from the earth, they also retain a feminine quality. So quartz can symbolize the union of masculine and feminine energies/ideas. It may be a pun for "quarts."

See **crystal; minerals; quart(s).** If applicable, see **clock; time; watch**.

quay

See **dock; harbor**.

quicksand

Being stuck, overwhelmed, drawn into something dangerous; feelings of inadequacy. Deceptive because it looks like ordinary sand, quicksand can symbolize being caught unawares in an unstable situation. It can symbolize the negative aspect of the mother image: devouring, sucking your life/creative energy.

See **marsh**.

quilt

As a craft, making a quilt represents the transforming of unconscious energy into consciousness; transforming separate pieces of energy ("scraps" of information) into a new whole that has an image/identity of its own. Consider any symbols/designs on the quilt. As something often handed down in families, or made by grandmothers/elders, it can represent familial/cultural wisdom or caring; a relationship with your ancestors, your heritage, or with another culture. It suggests covering; shielding; protecting your inner self/values/ideals. The condition of the quilt may indicate how successfully it is performing its function.

See **craft(s); sewing**.

quince

A somewhat tart fruit, the quince makes good, exotic jelly, and thus can symbolize transformation. In its natural state, it symbolizes good fortune; love, and is sacred, naturally, to Aphrodite, Greek goddess of love/beauty.

queen

Your personal mother; the archetypal mother; the personification of the good or bad mother (depicted in fairy tales as a stepmother or wicked queen).

See **princess; royalty**.

quiet

Quiet is associated with peace; calm; meditation; having time for yourself; going inward (connecting with unconscious energies). Is your dream telling you that you need more, or have too much, of one of these in your life? Is there a secret about which you need to be ''quiet as a mouse,'' or is this an admonition of your childhood (possibly ''children should be seen and not heard''?) now activated by some waking situation? Quietness in nature (''deathly silent'') often precedes a disaster (''the quiet before the storm'') and can symbolize anxiety/tension; night; death.

See **death; destruction** (if applicable); **night**.

rabbi

Spiritual/religious needs; situation that awakens issues related to religious beliefs/affiliation; a source of, or need for, spiritual comfort. As an administrator, the rabbi is related to business and to authority figures/issues. As a teacher, the rabbi may be associated with personal learning/performance experiences or issues. A rabbi is connected to ancient wisdom/knowledge—the keeper of tradition—and may represent the archetype of the Wise Old Man.

rabbits

Rabbits are associated with procreation/fertility; softness; vulnerability. In numerous symbologies, the rabbit/hare is associated with the moon; the earth; timidity; vigilance. In Japanese symbology, the hare represents long life, and according to one of the country's legends, the rabbit keeps the moon clean. In ancient Egypt, the hare represented the very essence of life/being. Given all this, dream rabbits most likely deal with basic/elemental emotions/attitudes/activities. They can reflect issues of intelligence ("dumb bunny"); someone who's cuddly; the need for more cuddling; someone named "Bunny." In Jungian theory, the rabbit/hare can symbolize the mother archetype. Jung's *Archetypes and the Collective Unconscious* displays a photograph of a window in the Paderborn cathedral in Germany. Three hares move clockwise within a circle, which Jung says represents consciousness "scenting or intuiting" the unconscious and the center/Self.

See **animal(s)**.

race/racing

Running in a race suggests daily/business life (the "rat race"). Depending on how you're doing in the race, consider whether the future looks good (you're winning or "ahead of the pack") or bleak. The dream may refer to issues concerned with ambition; career; competition; skills/abilities; prowess; winning/losing. Racing a sports car is related to the preceding and, according to Freud, to sexual urges (as is racing a horse).

See **competitor/competition** and, if applicable, **bicycle; car; horse(s); run(ning); sailing; vehicle(s)**.

radar

Your intuitive antenna; the ability to "read" people; a need to be cautious; possibly feelings of guilt or of being out of control. It may represent a waking situation in which you hope your feelings/actions will, or will not, be noticed, depending on dream content/action.

radio

Depends on your values/attitudes about radio, and whether it relates to the past (before television) or the present. Pay attention to the show, which may also indicate whether it relates to past/present issues, and to the message/theme, whether verbal or musical. It could refer to the ability to "hear things out"; your capacity to fantasize, conceptualize, sort, or organize from what you hear (analytical/intellectual skills); a situation in which you've recently been unduly influenced by the spoken word (gossip; someone else's ideas?). Is there a situation you need to "tune in" to, or one in which you have recently "tuned out" something? If the message is powerful and your feelings positive and strong, the radio voice could be the equivalent of the disembodied voice (see **voice**).

See **ear(s)**.

railroad

Your life route. Are you "on track" or derailed? Is your train cautioning you not to "get off track"? It may suggest that you've "lost track" of your goals or directions; that you've been lazy and need to "make tracks." Is there some situation in which you feel like you are on, or come from, "the other [wrong] side of the tracks"?

See **train(s); travel(ing)/journey; vehicle(s)**.

rain

Rain is related, first, to your attitude about it, and to the kind of rain it is (light spring shower; downpour; storm?). General symbolism includes: fertility; renewal; wiping your slate clean; and shares some water symbolism (see **water**). It can be considered a message/influence from heaven or the divine. It may refer to unexpressed tears; the need to cry/mourn, and the fear that if you did, the shower would turn into a storm; the need to turn inside, be alone, introspective, or put aside your usual activities.

See **thunder/lightning; storm**.

rainbow

One of its symbolisms is that of transition; hence, dream rainbows may represent a reordering of psychic/emotional material. Its seven colors have been used variously to represent the seven virtues, the seven vices, the days of the week, the seven planets of early astrology, and the seven chakras/energy centers—anything related to seven. For Jung it represented wholeness, becoming one's true Self (individuation).

In ancient Greek and Egyptian mythologies, it was a link to the gods. In Norse mythology, Bifrost, the rainbow bridge, connects the realm of the gods (spirit) to the human realm (matter). In Judeo-Christian religion, the rainbow represents God's promise to never again destroy mankind with a flood. More mundanely, it could be indicating that you've been "chasing rainbows."

See **rain; seven**.

raincoat

Protection against emotions; having the ego strength to consider or experience emotions at your own pace; condom; sexual prowess.

See **clothes/clothing**.

rake/raking

The need to clean up or organize; the need for stability or to get a handle on things. Is there a chaotic situation you need to tidy up? It may refer to a male who is debauched or irresponsible, or one with a dashing, jaunty appearance/personality.

ram

Someone born under the sign of Aries (March 22–April 20). A symbol of the Egyptian god Amun, it traditionally is a symbol of masculine power/strength. Many gods have been depicted as ram-headed, notably the Egyptian creator god Khnum and the Roman god Jupiter.

See **animal(s); sheep**.

ranch

A need to get in touch with or corral your animal nature; need for a new/wider/more expansive viewpoint; a need/desire to get away, possibly for rest/ recreation; getting in touch with your basic and unpretentious, possibly earthy, nature.

If applicable, see **bull(s); calf/calves; cow(s); cowboys; horse(s); sheep**.

ransom

If for you, it may refer to your self-worth, or your fears/anxieties about what others might think you're worth. It may reflect your wish for someone to rescue you. If you're paying the ransom, it suggests being coerced into buying/paying for a relationship; possibly that the cost of some situation/relationship is too high.

rape

If benign, emotionless, or even with tinges of romance, it may refer to a common female fantasy of being sexually overpowered (but not hurt), or of the romantic/powerful stranger. It may refer to a need to not be sexually aggressive but nevertheless have exciting sex; attitudes about sexual technique or about sexual relationships and emotional/sexual openness.

If violent/frightening/nightmarish, it may be associated with an actual rape situation (post-traumatic stress dream), or serve as a clue to the existence of repressed memories of childhood sexual abuse.

See **sex**. If applicable, see **attack; incest**.

rat

Although in Western/European countries the rat is usually considered a sign of filth/poverty (U.S.) or illness/evil (Europe), in Asian countries it's a propitious sign, signifying fertility and wealth (Japan), or good luck (China). It may refer to a person who has recently treated you badly, or who is untrustworthy.

raven(s)

According to mythology, ravens were white until they brought bad news to Apollo. Being black, the raven is psychologically akin to the shadow and to death; however, it's not likely a symbol of your own death but rather what death means to you—perhaps the death of a relationship, feeling, conflict, or problem. In folktales, the raven is often the bird that seeks out information and is akin, therefore, to the hunter archetype. They can represent dark thoughts; sudden illumination (von Franz). In some American Indian traditions, he is a trickster/shadow figure. In Nordic mythology, the two ravens Hugin (thought) and Munin (memory) were associated with the father god Odin. British legend says the kingdom will disintegrate if the ravens of London's White Tower leave.

See **bird(s), black; crow(s); hunter/huntress; shadow; trickster**.

reaching out

Need to give/receive; the ability to assert yourself to ask for, or move toward, what you want/need; the need/ability to connect with/contact others; needing/asking for help—and any difficulties/inhibitions related to the preceding. It is related to goals/ambitions and how you succeed or are thwarted in your efforts. Have you extended yourself too far recently, or been too closed off and need to extend more?

See **arm(s); hand(s)**.

read(ing)

Depending on the kind of book, it may reflect a need for intellectual/academic stimulation or for entertainment. Its contents may relate to someone you know connected with that topic. Pay special attention to unusual or out-of-place items in the book. Do you need to "read" people better?

See **book(s)/looking at books**.

rebirth

The death/rebirth theme is expressed in a variety of symbols in dreams, because it's related to all the symbols we use to express our life's journey/quest and any significant growth or change.

When people with cancer or other potentially terminal diseases are in remission, they often have definite rebirth dreams, dreams of miraculous recovery, or dreams with renovation themes (Siegel). People who are completely cured are less likely to have such dreams.

receiving

See **gift/giving**.

receptacle

See **container**.

recluse

A need to be alone, escape, withdraw, or protect yourself from emotional/physical intrusion, possibly because of depleted energy; a need for introspection and to draw upon your inner resources; anxiety about, or a need to distance yourself from, some person/situation. Has someone recently invaded your privacy or inner world?

See **hermit**.

record/cassette

Two sides to a situation; getting in tune with your inner state. If for learning or for listening to books, it may refer to a need for intellectual stimulation, or a message/insight close to consciousness (see **radio**). If music, creating a mood; a need for enjoyment/sensual experience or distraction. A particular music may refer to a specific experience/person.

See **music/musician**.

red

Life energy (blood); fiery passion (''red-hot''); the emotions of embarrassment (''red-faced''), anger/rage (''see red''), and therefore, related to the symbolism of fire (''hotheaded,'' ''hot under the collar''). Your dream may be reminding you of an upcoming ''red-letter day.'' In alchemy, it represented the fourth stage in transformation, the reddening or *rubedo*, in which the illuminated/aware life process was now ruled by the enlightened, ''spiritually objective'' self. It preceded/foretold of the completion of inner work.

The appearance of red sometimes indicates a physical abnormality, which should be checked out by a physician (Epstein).

See **color(s); individuation**.

reflection

It may refer to introspection; an attempt to understand a situation or see it from a different view; a situation that's ''topsy-turvy''; opposites or reversals of any kind (see **opposites**). If in water, it may refer to reflecting on an emotional situation. If in a mirror, see **mirror**.

refrigerate/refrigerator

Chilling emotions; a need/wish to put something (feelings, issues?) on hold or in cold storage; time to cool down, ''play it cool,'' or ''chill out''; sexual coolness or frigidity, especially referring to a female; a need to take the passion/energy out of a relationship or situation, recognition that it's already gone, anxiety that it's diminishing.

See **cold; ice**.

rejected

It's not uncommon for expectant fathers to dream of feeling left out/rejected from a variety of situations, including sexual ones. Siegel suggests this may reflect feelings of not being included in the pregnancy experience, as well as old sensitivities about rejection now activated by fears of being displaced by the baby.

If you're a female dreamer, being rejected can refer to your own feelings of self-worth; to earlier situations of sibling rivalry or other envy; or can be stimulated by recent situations that have activated old anxieties related to approval/acceptance, especially by authority figures.

relatives

Family issues or feelings. One relative can substitute for your entire extended family; for another relative with whom he/she was particularly close; or for some aspect of yourself, possibly an inherited one.

See **ancestors; family**; and, if applicable, specific relatives.

religious themes

Dreams with religious themes will be related to your own religious beliefs/experiences, with all their positive/negative qualities. They may be stimulated by recent experiences that activated religious/moral/ethical issues, by events that involve a religious activity/situation—what Siegel calls *turning points* (weddings; baptisms; confirmations; death/grief/mourning situations). Even if you don't think of yourself as religious, dreams with religious themes may occur as a result of inner growth, or development of the Self, for that is, after all, what religious rites were once designed to honor and celebrate.

rent(ing)

Anxieties about money or "keeping a roof over your head"; some aspect of yourself (values, ideals?) that you're considering, or intrigued with, but have not yet made your own. If renting an object/furniture, consider its specific symbolism for you.

repair(ing)

Does what needs to be, or is being, repaired refer to incapacity or lack of functioning in your inner/outer life or to health issues? If you're making repairs, it may refer to skills or abilities; mastery and self-confidence; changing attitudes; efforts toward, or need to take care of, some situation in waking life. If beyond repair, perhaps it's time to give up holding on to some situation/relationship, or old, worn-out positions/attitudes.

reptile(s)

As a cold-blooded creature, a reptile may represent someone with frozen emotions or who has recently behaved in a cold-blooded way; the autonomic nervous system (Jung); primitive impulses from the older part of our brain (the brain stem, also known as the reptilian brain).

If applicable, see **frog(s); lizard(s); snake(s); toad(s)**.

reservation

Anxiety about upcoming travel (difficulty/problems with hotel/travel reservations?); security needs (having something on hold or in reserve?); a situation that you have some concerns (reservations) about. Perhaps you're reserving the right to your own opinion.

rescue

Coping; successfully combating/acknowledging certain emotions/characteristics symbolized by the person rescued; feeling lost/overwhelmed/inadequate and wishing to be rescued; feelings of needing to rescue a particular situation/relationship. If recurrent, persistent fears; a compulsive need to always be rescuing/enabling someone.

restaurant

Need for, or realization of, the existence of a variety of sources/resources for nurturance/energy; the need for options; ability to sort out information/emotions and make choices; feeling overwhelmed by emotions or choices (too many goodies to choose from?); social stimulation. Consider the various people/foods for clues to what you hunger for.

See **eating; food**.

restrain/restraint

Consider who/what is being restrained, by whom, and how, for clues as to whether it relates to a relationship/situation in your waking life; some inner aspect of yourself that's too inhibited or, conversely, out of control; long-standing attitudes/issues recently stimulated. It could refer to a need to hold back verbal/emotional expression; wishes to control some person/situation; a curtailing of abilities; some way you feel you're being hampered/limited or otherwise unable to be all that you can be.

revolving

See **rotating/revolving/turning**.

rhythm

Rhythmic motions of any kind are often symbolic of masturbation or sexual intercourse. Rhythm expressed in music can refer to sexual situations as well, but can also refer to life energy and interactions (''rhythm of life''). The first rhythm we were aware of was our mother's heartbeat, so it may refer to a maternal relationship/issue; but our most basic rhythm is our own heartbeat. Thus, it may refer to matters of the heart, or to emotional/physical heart problems if there's a lack of rhythm or rhythmic difficulties.

If the beat of a drum, see **drum(ming)**. See **music/musician**.

ribbon

It can represent girlhood; however, its more traditional meaning has to do with binding/loosening in relationships; bonds voluntarily accepted. It may refer to the beginning of a new project/situation ("cutting the ribbon") or a winning one ("blue ribbon"). Consider the color of the ribbon. If red, it may refer to anxiety about AIDS, or someone with AIDS.

rice

In Asia its meaning/value is similar to that of wheat for European/Western countries; therefore, it refers to abundance; riches/richness; basic nurturance. In Western countries it may relate to Asian ideas/countries/people. Commonly thrown at weddings to symbolize fruitfulness, it may, therefore, be associated with marriage/commitment; fertility.

rich(es)

Feeling emotionally/financially impoverished, or, conversely, inner abundance; truth or wisdom; the need to acquire/accumulate, possibly compulsively (therefore related to hoarding, insecurity).

If applicable, see **jewel(s); money**.

rides/riding

Consider the meaning of the vehicle/animal you're riding in/on. One of the issues with riding is whether you're in control or are a passenger. It could reflect a need to "ride herd on" your emotions. Is there some situation/relationship that's presently a "rough ride," or wherein you feel you need to "ride it out," possibly because someone is "riding roughshod" over you? Then again, it may relate to a situation in which you have no say, are indifferent, or are just "along for the ride."

See **animal(s); vehicles(s)**; and the particular vehicle or animal. If a carnival ride, see **carnival; fair**.

rifle

See **gun(s)**.

right

Conscious reality; rational action. Movement to the right/clockwise may represent conscious movement, movement away from the unconscious. It can signal the "rightness" of an idea/plan/concern; the place of honor; a need to avoid blame or to be perceived as following the rules ("doing the right thing"; "getting off on the right foot"; "keeping on the right side" of someone). It could refer to an inability to admit or perceive that you've been wrong; to feelings you have about being politically conservative, especially if you have recently been in a situation in which that might not have been the most propitious position to take. Is there someone you need to "set right"?

See **direction(s); east**.

right side of body

Traditionally the right side of the body is considered the active or masculine side; still, what would you "give your right arm" to have?

See **body**.

ring [sound/tone]

Promise/hope ("give me a ring sometime"); joyous or sexual interaction ("ring my chimes"); enlightenment/insight/understanding (that "rings a bell"). Is there a recent situation that does, or doesn't, have the "ring of truth" about it? If a church bell, it may be a call to attend to your spiritual life (see **church**).

ring(s)

As a circle, the ring is associated with eternity; wholeness; the mandala. Has someone been "running rings around" you? As jewelry, it can represent affiliation (a class ring); promise or romance (engagement ring); commitment (wedding ring). Rings can indicate that the activity you perform with your hands is one you highly value and/or wish that others will see it likewise.

See **vow(s)**.

rite/ritual

Transition ("rite of passage") into a new phase or way of life; connection with inner awareness; connection with "tribal" (familial) heritage; intense but structured (ritualized) feelings/activities; connection with universal creative powers/energies and cosmic mysteries, i.e., moving into and through the unknown or the unconscious. Cultural rites of renewal are attempts to abolish the separation between the conscious mind and the unconscious, i.e., to reunite the participant with his/her instinctive makeup. (Jung). In a play on words, it may represent a situation in which you feel you're correct; "Mr. Right"; some person/company named Wright.

See **celebration; ceremony; initiation**.

river

Fertility; flowing or fluctuating feelings; the course of your life (''river of life''). Are you ''going with the flow'' or ''swimming against the current''? If you're not in the river, is it a barrier? In some instances, it may symbolize the flow of urine. A raging/flooding river suggests disruption, possibly uncontrolled emotions.

See **water**. If applicable, see **boat; canal; channel**.

roaches

It may be slang for smoking marijuana; represent an undesirable aspect of yourself that needs acknowledgment. As one of the oldest insects on earth and one of the hardest to eradicate, it may refer to tenacity; longevity. Consider retelling your dream from the viewpoint of the roach (see Dreamercise #4, Part 1).

See **insects**.

road

A sense of direction; your life's path. Its condition and the ease/difficulty you have traversing it may reveal how much you feel in charge of your life, or provide clues to changes you need to make. If beside the road or having difficulty getting on it, how have you gotten sidetracked? Consider your mode of travel and see **run(ning); walk (ing); vehicle(s)**.

Emphasis on the middle of the road suggests feelings regarding your adequacy (about average, nothing special?) or taking a neutral stand with its associated feelings (comfort, anxiety, guilt?). Are you wavering about, or have not yet made, a decision? A fork in the road may refer to an impending decision or choice. A curve may refer to new events or changes and their associated anxiety, especially if you can't see what's ahead; but it can also refer to middle/old age and your feelings about ''rounding the bend.'' Back roads may refer to an alternative way of life, or to a need to explore/return to old or more traditional ways. Any road not taken may represent a missed choice. Consider any puns in the name of the road/street. A dream occurring on ''Main Street'' could refer to a central issue/problem (Whitmont and Perera); a major idea/concept.

See **crossroads; path(s)**.

robber/robbery

See **thief/theft**.

robe

A robe can symbolize power/authority (royalty), secular or spiritual; however, the robe of the priest also protects from the powers/energies being invoked. A bathrobe or other informal robe may refer to intimate or sexual situations; a casual attitude; privacy needs/issues.

See **appearance**.

robot

Mechanical attitudes/actions; childhood conditioning/training; acting without thinking or, possibly, without feeling, hence, feeling dead inside.

rock(s)

Steadfastness; solid personality ("solid as a rock"); the stable, inner house of wisdom, as in the rock that Moses struck which flowed with the water of life; obstacles or stubbornness. Does the dream relate to a "rock-hard" attitude, or to a situation in which it's hard to move around? Where in your life are you "between a rock and a hard place"? Rocks are slang for diamonds (romance, wealth, the Self?) and ice cubes (related to drinking or alcoholism?).

A single or especially striking rock—or one that's all that is left after a ravishing fire—may symbolize the Self; wholeness; vitality (what von Franz calls "psychic totality").

See **stone(s)**.

rocket

If going into outer space, it may relate to the need to break free of physical/mental/emotional limitations (related to the past, or to present responsibilities?); a desire to escape worldly problems/situations; a need to connect with the spirit or divine; a wish to soar to new heights (related to emotions, ambitions); cosmic concerns. It can be a phallic symbol and refer to ejaculation.

If it explodes on the ground, see **destruction**.

rocking chair

Expressing, or experiencing, your inner rhythm/pulses; being in tune with the ebb and flow of the universe; a need for childhood comforts; anxieties/perceptions about aging.

rodent

If a tunneling, underground creature (see **nest; tunnel**), it may be related to the unconscious, or to earthiness. Otherwise, see **mouse; rat**.

See also **animal(s)**.

rodeo

Are you an active participant or an observer? It may relate to taming the wildness or animal instincts within; challenging, testing, or displaying your skills/abilities; a need for control/dominance.

If applicable, see **audience; bull(s); competitor/competition; calf/calves; clown; cow(s); cowboy; crowd; horse(s); rope**.

roles

In Jungian psychology, the persona is an outer layer of personality, the mask/facade we show in public, the role we play. Roles are not necessarily negative; indeed, many are important for social interaction/survival. In addition to the variety of personas and disguises you can wear in a dream (remember, various aspects of yourself can appear as other people, animals, objects), there is the question of whether you're taking an active part (initiating or participating in some action), behaving passively (something is being done to you and you don't resist), or observing.

With respect to a given dream, is the behavior typical of your approach in a waking situation; a fear that you've been too one-sided; or showing you a way you need to behave? If exploring a series of dreams, can you discern a pattern in your behavior/approach to situations?

See **persona**. For other clues to identifying the expression of a particular persona/role, see specific occupations and **actor/actress; animal(s); appearance; car; clothes/clothing; house; stage; theater**.

roof

A need for protection; a feeling that you're unprotected (decaying or damaged roof?); a need to connect with the spiritual or divine; awareness of your intellectual limitations/boundaries. It may refer to an advanced, possibly spiritual, stage in the formation of the Self.

See **home; house**.

room(s)

Rooms, and the actions within them, often represent a particular characteristic of the dreamer or a particular relationship. Discovering/building new rooms, or finding that a room is larger than you thought, can symbolize undertaking new roles; developing new strengths or parts of your personality; emotional expansion. It may signal the end of a grieving period; coming out of depression; readiness for new relationships. A barren/empty room may relate to dead feelings; the onset of menopause.

See **architecture; home; house**.

rooster

See **cock**.

roots

Roots of a plant, especially those of trees, show our connection to the earth, to our personal family, and to the archetypal Mother Earth. They represent our heritage/ancestry and your ability to take nourishment from that; stabilizing/grounding factors in your life; tenacity; some aspect of your life that's tangled or being choked by other roots (persons, relatives?); a need to get at the root of some situation or to "root out" a troublemaker.

See **plant(s); tree(s); vegetation**. If root vegetables, see **vegetable(s)**.

rope

If tying someone up or being tied up, a situation/relationship that you feel is restricting or holding you back in some way (how are you "tied down"?); emotional or sexual restraint (especially if roping animals); inhibitions of any kind, including sexual; but also, conversely, a need to, or for, control. It may refer to a situation you feel you've been coerced or "roped into"; one in which your "hands are tied"; one in which you "know the ropes." Then again, you or another may be getting "enough rope to hang yourself"; may be "on the ropes" or "at the end of your rope."

For an additional meaning of rope, see **plait**.

rose

A symbol for the Self (Jung); a common symbol of the Western mystic/wisdom tradition. The rose in an enclosed garden is similar to the Grail quest, to the search for paradise and wholeness. In Christian symbolism, the rose is the supreme symbol of Mary, the mother of Jesus. Roses are related to love/romance and were sacred to Aphrodite/Venus.

See **flower(s)**.

rotating/revolving/turning

Greater point of view; widening of horizon; awakening of new consciousness; possibly spinning out of control.

round

See **circle**.

row(ing)

Asserting your will; overcoming resistance; movement in your physical/emotional life; determining the direction/course of your life. If another person is in the boat, it may refer to power/control, caring/romance, or emotional strength issues in that relationship. If rowing in a competition, see **competitor/competition**. If related to fishing, see **fish/fishing**.

See **boat**.

royalty

Kings, queens, princes, and princesses may well be archetypal symbols whose message you need to pay attention to. Do they appear to you in person or on television? Since we most often see royalty on television, engaged in worldly activities, they may simply symbolize a more worldly characteristic of yourself, which you need to elevate (or wish you could). If you saw the dream figure recently, what characteristics was he/she exhibiting that relate to you or a waking situation, especially one concerned with responsibility or social standing? They can represent an authority figure in your life, especially parents (from the time when you were a little princess/prince); a lofty idea/ideal; inflated ideas of self-importance and grandeur.

A king/queen (prince/princess) appearing together may symbolize the unification of—or need to unify—opposite values or masculine/feminine aspects in your psyche or waking life. In Freudian theory, kings and queens represent parents, princes and princesses represent siblings.

See **king; person, famous; prince; princess; queen; television** (if applicable).

rubbers

See **contraceptive**.

ruby

In alchemy, rubies and garnets were equated with the mineral cinnabar, which stood for the red *(rubedo)* stage of the transformation process. The garnet is the birthstone of someone born in January, while the ruby can represent someone born in July. Ruby may also be someone's name.

See **gem(s); red**.

ruins

Old ways; past bonds/ties; outdated attitudes that no longer serve you well; something you've recently ruined, possibly a relationship; a relationship that has not been kept up/maintained; aspects/patterns of your personal/family/cultural history.

See **ancient; architecture; city/cities**.

run(ning)

Meanings will differ depending on whether you're running for health (jogging), running toward some person/object, or running away. Running with ease suggests you're "on the right track.'' Difficulty running can refer to feelings of helplessness; being held back by negative attitudes/fear of success/assertiveness; feeling ''rundown'' or ''out of steam.''

If running for health/training, it may refer to health needs or to your general state of energy. If running for competition, see **competitor/competition**.

Running toward some person/object may refer to ambitions/goals; willingness to undertake responsibility; a positive attitude (if the goal is positive). If a negative goal/situation, it may refer to situations, such as addictive or codependent ones, to which you're inevitably drawn even though the results may be disastrous. Running away can be related to avoidance; issues of responsibility; guilt; new strength to avoid what's negative for you. If running from pursuers, see **pursued/pursuer/pursuing**.

Have you had a recent situation in which you ''ran up against'' an obstacle; were ''out of the running''; or someone ''ran out on you''?

See **body; movement; posture(s)**.

rust

Being worn down by life elements; not being used, or able to be active, to your full capacity; feelings of being neglected/ignored; situations or relationships you've not taken good care of/nourished; aging or the passage of time.

sack

Consider the materials the sack is made of, its contents (secrets? resources?), and who gives it to you, if applicable, for initial clues. It may refer to someone who has the power to "give you the sack"; therefore, anxiety about your job situation. As a container, it may represent the vagina/womb; putting something in a sack may refer to sexual feelings/intercourse.

See **container; knapsack**.

sacrifice

Is there a recent situation in which you feel you have, or someone else has, been sacrificed for another's glory, or have been compelled (literally, psychologically?) to give up something you enjoyed or from which you would have benefited? It can refer to current/long-standing guilt or low self-esteem, which causes you to give up enjoyment/pleasures, possibly feeling you don't deserve them. Thus, it may be related to a habitual stance or approach to life. Conversely, your ego may have been so pompous in recent waking times that this dream is attempting to provide some balance. Cirlot reminds us there is no creation without sacrifice. What are you ready to give up in order to achieve something else?

saddle

If you're in the saddle, riding a horse, it may refer to sexual wishes/urges, or to a need to control them; needing a sense of direction or to exert more control over your life; recognition that you are indeed "back in the saddle again"; a need to dominate/control a specific waking situation/person, possibly someone whom you perceive as a "horse's ass." Conversely, if someone has "ridden roughshod" over you recently, your dream may now be giving you the chance to "take the reins."

See **horse(s)**.

sadism

Depending on who is performing the sadistic act and upon whom it's being inflicted, it could represent feelings of anger/rage toward someone; feelings of guilt and a need for punishment; lack of self-worth. If a particularly brutal or nightmarish dream, it may be a clue to the existence of repressed child abuse experiences. If recurring, you may wish to consult a therapist.

sadness

It's not unusual for dreams in which there is sadness and separation/loss themes to occur within one to three years after the loss of a loved one, according to Canadian psychologist Don Kuiken.

Called *existential dreams,* they often produce the kind of insight that helps carry the bereavement forward to conclusion.

safari

If observing animals, the dream can refer to your need to recognize/express your animal instincts/urges. If hunting/shooting animals, it may refer to a need to suppress/control those same urges. It can reflect a need in your life for more wildness; freedom; expression; expansion (open space). For additional clues, consider the animals, natives (see **aborigine/aboriginal**), and others on the safari. Could they represent resources, or people/situations in your waking life that you'd like to wipe out or conquer as a trophy for your ego?

sails

The sails on a boat are related to air/wind; therefore, the breath, and the out-breath, of God. A lack of wind would refer to lowered energy/motivation/spirit. In medieval times, wind sometimes represented the Holy Spirit. Do the colors/decorations/numbers on the sails offer clues?

sailing

Your movement through life, especially through emotional situations. Determining whether you are the captain, part of the crew, or a passenger will give you an idea of how much you're in charge, need some help, need to turn to other resources, or whether you want someone else to do all the work. The ease ("smooth sailing") or difficulty ("sailing against the wind") of the trip will also give you some clues as to whether you're meeting emotional/internal pressures or issues well, or having difficulty coping.

Are you/another "sailing under false colors"? Would you like to "take the wind out of [someone's] sails" (anger, revenge?); or has someone done exactly that to you, and you're still feeling the effects?

See **boat; captain; sails; sailor; ship/shipwreck**.

sailor

Are you or someone else the sailor? It may refer to your own role as an actual sailor (navy experiences?); to someone you know who is similarly connected; your ability to "sail through life," dealing with its "ups and downs" (rolling sea) and "weathering its storms." What situations are you working on or need to take charge of?

See **boat; navy** (if applicable); **sailing; ship/shipwreck**.

salad

Could the kind or name of the salad relate to situations/experiences from your past/present? Is anything missing? It may suggest something you're hungry for or need to add to your life, literally or emotionally. It may be a visual pun for something that's "rough" or "bulky." The "dressing" may be a pun for clothes or a role, possibly a recent anxiety about how to dress/appear, what final touches to add. The dressing might also represent a need to spice up your life or to listen to some "seasoned" advice.

See **food; vegetable(s)**.

saliva

Semen; sexual/sensual appetites; someone/something you're "drooling over" or hungering for; a mouth-watering situation; creative energy. If the saliva of an animal, it may refer to the intensity of your animal urges, or to anger/rage (a mad dog). If a person drooling/slobbering, it may refer to anxieties about losing physical/emotional control.

See **digestion; mouth/lips**.

saloon

See **bar**.

salt

A basic element of life, it may represent any other basic/necessary element required for life. It can refer to feelings about work/effort ("salt mine"); someone's worth or value (''worth your salt''); a bland situation/relationship that could use some seasoning, or one that needs preserving/purifying. It may relate to someone who's earthy or vulgar (''salty''), or trustworthy and generous (''salt of the earth''). As something that's extracted from water, it can represent change; or dried-up emotions. Related to tears, however, it may refer to a situation in which you've not mourned sufficiently. A ''grain of salt'' represents the merging of individuality into something that's greater, possibly spiritual/divine, but can also suggest that you're placing too much importance or focus on some issue.

In Roman and early Christian times, salt stood for kinship and was a symbol of blood; therefore, a substitute in sacrifices, dedications, and anointings. In the book of Numbers, the Bible speaks of a ''covenant of salt,'' which cannot be broken. It is a sacred word in Hebrew because its numeric value is the same as that of God's power name multiplied three times (Walker). In Hopi tradition Salt Man is a war god. For the Dineh (Navaho), Salt Woman is a variant of Changing Woman, a moon goddess who can, at will, adopt the appearance of any stage of womanhood.

salve

See **ointment**.

sand

Infinity; the passing of life (''sands of time''); shiftlessness/instability/unreliability (''don't build on shifting sands''); avoiding or ignoring an issue (''bury your head in the sand'').

See **beach; desert**.

sapphire

The ancients believed sapphires were the key to understanding the sayings of the oracles, i.e., to decoding unconscious or metaphorical messages. They were thought to bring divine favor. Probably because of their blue color, later tradition associates them with the lapis, the philosopher's stone of alchemy and the metaphor for wholeness. Sapphire is equated with heaven; spirituality; and is the second foundation stone of the New Jerusalem (Book of Revelation). Analogous to the Hebrew tribe of Reuben, it relates to the emotional impulse to seek the truth and to the love of truth. As the birthstone of September, it may represent someone born in that month.

See **gem(s); jewel(s); jewelry**, if applicable.

Satan

See **devil**.

satellite

If located in the heavens, it may represent a need for an overview; the communication of ideas between your higher/spiritual self and your more mundane/worldly aspects; the need to control/watch over others; possibly voyeuristic needs. If still on the ground, it may represent anxieties/thoughts about launching an impending, probably major, project.

See **flying**.

saucepan

As a container, it may represent the feminine/womb. Consider the symbolism of its shape (round, square) and anything in it. It's also related to food (unless something else was in it) and cooking; therefore, to transformation. What's cooking in your life? What situation/relationship is or needs heating up?

See **cook(s)/cooking; food; kitchen** (if applicable); **pan(s)**.

sausage

Depending on its shape, it may represent the penis/male sexuality. Round and flat, it may represent a mandala. It can refer to something spicy or that needs to be spiced up. Usually made from several ground-up ingredients and flavorings, it may represent amalgamation/union/transformation.

See **food**.

savings

Anxiety about money or the future; hoarding/acquisition needs; issues related to financial/emotional security; inner or outer resources or potential. Is there something you're running out of, or don't have enough of?

See **money**.

saw(ing)

Because of its shape and being a tool, the saw is a phallic symbol; but it can also refer to the ability to cut through difficult/long-standing issues. Depending on what's being sawed, it may be a reference to sexual intercourse; masturbation; angry/hostile feelings. As a pun for sight (what you saw), it may refer to an insight/awareness you haven't quite recognized or assimilated (possibly because the information is destructive?).

If the saw is being used to create some new project/object, consider its characteristics for additional clues (see **craft(s)**).

See **tool(s); wood**. If sawing trees, see **tree(s)**.

saying no

See **no/saying no**.

scales

Anxiety about weight (especially if you're on a diet), or about being held accountable (with accompanying guilt?). An issue/situation that's weighty; one in which you're going to have to weigh various aspects before making a decision; a need to find some kind of balance or balance point; something that's "tipping the scales." It may be a pun for the scales of a fish or for some person/situation that's "scaly."

See **balance(d)/balancing; fish/fishing; justice**.

scales of justice

They are related to all concepts/situations/issues of fairness/unfairness, truth, justice/injustice, and judgments. Look to other clues in the dream to determine if this is a present/past (long-standing?) situation, possibly awakened by a recent event. In Egyptian mythology, scales were used to weigh the heart (individuality, personality) of a dead person against the feather of truth (Ma'at, symbol of the right order; law). If they balanced, the deceased was considered "one" or whole (balance between the conscious or unconscious), and could enter the netherworld of eternity.

See **balance(d)/balancing; justice; scales**.

scar

Memories; the effects or influences of past injuries/woundings, emotional and physical.

See **wound(s)/wounded**.

scarab

A traditional symbol of immortality, the scarab beetle is related to death/rebirth themes; anxiety about death/aging; experiences with Egypt or its people.

See **manure**.

scared

See **fear**.

scepter

See **staff**.

school

If you're presently in school or contemplating going back to school, it may relate to anxieties about performance/abilities. If long out of school, are you the teacher/student, and how are you performing/coping? It is likely that some recent situation awakened old anxieties/insecurities about skills/abilities. It may be related to an authority situation in which you feel that you're being treated like a student again, or one in which you feel you're being tested (see **exam(s)/examination**). It can be connected with some new learning situation, especially one wherein you will be evaluated/rated.

Is there something you must "school yourself" to do? Could it refer to someone who is "of the old school" or who's "telling tales out of school"?

If applicable, see **graduation; teacher**.

science/scientist

To dream of being involved in a science project, or of a scientist, may refer to an actual situation/person; represent the need to experiment with/try out several solutions to a situation/relationship; suggest that you need to set up an established or organized order/process. It may refer to the need to intervene and then "wait and see" or document the results before you take your next step; the need, related to ambition, to make an important discovery, or to pass on your achievement/knowledge to others (service/fame/immortality issues?).

scissors

What is being cut and how? Scissors may refer to some situation/relationship you need to "cut out" of your life, or from which you need to separate; something in your life (especially if cloth, the fabric of life), that needs to be shaped (cut?) and transformed into something else. Scissors can refer to death if they cut the thread of life. Metaphysically, a pair of scissors refers to crossroads and therefore to union/conjunction.

See **crossroads**. If applicable, see **thread; sew(ing)**.

scorpion

It may refer to someone born under the astrological sign for Scorpio (October 24–November 22). Negatively, it may refer to a stinging situation; one that has the potential to inflict pain.

scratch

A minor irritation, or perhaps one that began as minor but has the potential to become worse; anxieties about having to begin something "from scratch"; a situation/relationship in which you've just begun to "scratch the surface." Because it's related to itch, it may refer to sexual urges, or something else you "have the itch" to do.

screen(s)

Screens, such as window screens, can serve to protect from insects and outdoor elements (annoyances, natural urges); shield from information you're not yet prepared/trained to receive. Like a veil, screens can conceal secrets/higher wisdom. They may refer to an evaluating or separating process; therefore, to judgment about skills/abilities. Has someone been creating a "smoke screen"?

See **veil**.

screw(ing)

A screw or inserting a screw can refer to manual labor (see **construction; repair(ing)**); to the need to hold some situation/relationship together; a situation/relationship in which you were cheated, deceived, or in some other way didn't get what was best for you. It is too common a pun for sexual intercourse for that possibility to be ignored. It can refer to a situation in which you didn't do your best ("screwed up"); a lack of mental/emotional capacity or good judgment (someone "has a screw loose"). Is there someone in your life who is "all screwed up" or whom you would like to "put the screws on"?

scythe

A longtime symbol of the harvest; therefore, of cycles; passing time; aging; new hopes; rebirth (a new or emerging season/cycle).

sea

A natural body of water, the sea often represents our emotions ("stormy seas" or "a calm sea"), and our unconscious. As a pun, it may represent perception/understanding ("I see"). In this time in your life, is it rough or smooth sailing? Because of its "unfathomed depths," Jung said the sea represents the collective unconscious. It can represent the original source of humankind; the womb; our personal mother; the archetypal or primal source/mother of us all. More mundanely, it may refer to a situation in which you're "all at sea," or feeling "lost at sea." You may need to reassure yourself that there are "plenty of fish in the sea."

See **ocean; water**. If applicable, see **drown(ing); tide(s)**.

séance

A need to "see beyond," to have foresight/awareness/insight/intuition; questions or anxiety about life after death; contact with the unconscious through projection of your own inner information onto the medium/spirits.

See **medium**.

search(ing)

Whatever you or another is searching for may indicate something missing in your life. Are you moving toward a goal or does it continue to be elusive?

What have you lost recently; or how often do you go through life feeling lost? Perhaps you're taking the position of not knowing ("search me").

See **lost**.

searchlight

A pun on searching for enlightenment/awareness; possibly a need for recognition; fear of failure/embarrassment in front of others; fear of being found out (related to shadow or sexual aspects?); performance anxiety (adequacy, confidence issues?). Who or what is eluding you?

See **light; look(ing)/looked at**.

seashells

Seashells, especially the cowrie shell, symbolize the vulva and the birth/rebirth theme. They can represent the outer shell/persona we adopt to protect ourselves from threat; therefore, not showing the inner person/feelings, or being emotionally closed off. It may be linked to the symbolism of the pearl (see **oyster**). In Christianity the scallop shell is the symbol of the apostle James the Elder, brother of John, because tradition has it that he baptized with a scallop shell, although, in fact, this is unlikely.

See **spiral**.

seasons

The season, or a change of seasons, may represent change/movement in your life; growth of the Self; cycles; the flow of feelings within the psyche.

See **autumn; spring; summer; winter**.

secret

Having a secret, being privy to a secret, or being given a secret may symbolize being an initiate, knowing part of the mystery that leads to spiritual growth or individuation. As a member of a secret society, it may symbolize belongingness; eliteness; being one of the chosen. Keeping/having secrets may refer to sexual issues, or to a fear that others would belittle you if they knew your secret; therefore, related to shame.

If a nightmare or unpleasant dream, the secret may refer to sexual or child abuse, which you had to keep secret to survive, and which is now threatening to make itself known. If so, you may want to consult a psychotherapist.

security system(s)

The modern equivalent of the "drawbridge" or walled castle, a security system of any kind probably relates to your feelings of emotional security; a need to be well fortified. Does it protect you? Is it outdated/weakened? (You may need some emotional support.) Are you able to skillfully bypass it (ready to break away from old fears/restraints?), or does someone else (vulnerability)?

sedative

A need to withdraw from/avoid something; a need to reduce anxiety/energy.

See **medicine/medication**.

seducer/seduction

A feeling/fear that you've been lured/lulled into doing something you might not otherwise have done, i.e., easily influenced; a person who's a "sweet talker." If you're the one seduced, it suggests giving up your critical thinking ability or power of choice.

See **sex**.

see(ing)

Eyes are one of the major sense organs with which we incorporate or understand information, so it's not uncommon for seeing or looking to occur in dreams. For it to be significant, it would have to be especially emphasized in some way. If that's so, then consider the symbolism of what you're observing/seeing and how it relates to insight; your perspective; a rigid/limited viewpoint; another's viewpoint; possibly something you've only glanced at and need to "take a closer look." It may relate to voyeuristic needs in terms of sex, or with respect to learning secrets/gossip.

See **look(ing)/looked at**.

seeing through [objects, walls]

This skill may call attention to your ability to clear the way for a new project, or to see the inner workings of a situation. Is there a waking situation you need to look into more closely; or is the dream connecting insights about a past (parental?) relationship to a current one? "Clear sight" is the term metaphysicians use to designate the ability to see the truth; the essence; the relatedness of some actions/persons/situations.

seed(s)

A time-honored symbol for fertility; genetic heritage; the continuation/continuity of life; cycles; ancestral ghosts (von Franz). They may refer to sperm; your progeny; the wisdom/learning one implants in younger persons; therefore, it may also relate to parenting, educating, or mentoring. It was the hidden purpose of alchemy to fertilize and nurture the inner seed, the mystic center, already present in the human psyche/soul; thus, it relates to essence, as well as spiritual, physical, and intellectual potential (Jung). Seeds may refer to the growth or potential of any type of project/situation/relationship.

Self

A complicated and expansive concept, the Self is at once the totality of the psyche; the potential each of us has for becoming all that we can be; and the regulating "center" of the psyche as experienced by the ego (itself the regulating center of conscious awareness). It is unknowable except through its symbolic productions, that is, drawings, dreams, etc. Each dream, then, is a kind of dialogue between the ego and the Self—or the Guiding Self, the term Whitmont and Perera use. We get our first hunch of the Self around the age of eight years (von Franz).

Because it's enduring, the Self may be symbolized in its early dream appearances by indestructible items such as stones, gems (diamonds), circular forms (precursors to its later expression as a mandala). Any object of high value in a dream may also be a symbol of the Self. The Self is intricately tied to the Jungian concept of individuation, the process of seeking wholeness, the push for the development of higher consciousness. As the individuation process—growth of the self and the Self—continues, Self representation comes more and more to resemble the mandala.

See **diamond(s); gem(s); mandala; pearl(s); sheaf; stone(s)**.

semen

Masculinity; fertility; the potential for growth.

See **sex**. If applicable, see **ejaculation; orgasm; penis/phallus;** and the discussion of tadpoles under **frog(s)**.

sentry

See **guard(ing)**.

serpent(s)

In mythology/folklore, a serpent usually means a snake. As analogies for heroes, serpents often have magic powers and are themselves associated with dragons. Thus snakes/serpents/dragons share some of the same meanings, i.e., healing; transformation; renewal. One of the most famous winged serpents is the Aztec savior god Quetzalcoatl. Like most archetypal deities, he was two-sided, being a god of creation (corn was his symbol) united back to back with his brother Death. Pachamama, a Peruvian/Bolivian goddess, often associated with Mary, is said to be of the Amaru or serpent/dragon race. As an earth mother goddess, she is associated with fertility, agriculture, and tilled fields.

See **dragon; snake(s); reptile(s)**.

servant

Although included in this concept is the need to serve or perform some kind of service, it has become associated with an unequal position and is, therefore, also related to any kind of inequality; lowered self-esteem; wealth (or lack of it); authority issues; possibly a need to "put someone in his/her place" (or the signal that someone has done this to you); a need to be taken care of (issues of independence?). If it is a compensatory dream, it may occur as a result of too much recent ego inflation or a feeling/fear that you have been/will be abandoned.

setting of dream

See **landscapes/settings**.

seven

One of the most sacred numbers, it represents victory; the highest stage of illumination; initiation (perfection); the ending before the beginning of a new, more mature phase; an evolutionary process (von Franz). It represents the seven stages during which the sacred mountains of the world arose and, as told in the biblical Book of Genesis, the day on which God rested after creating the world. Therefore, it can also symbolize rest; regeneration of energy; or a need for it; an evolutionary process. A symbol of creative and intellectual cycles (seven orifices in the head), it may refer to patriarchal leadership. According to the Talmud, a chandelier of gold containing seven branches, each with a name of one of the seven patriarchs (Adam, Noah, Shem, Abraham, Isaac, Jacob, and Job), hung over the throne of King Solomon. Seven is involved in the alchemical process of "three into four," sometimes thought of as the divine (trinity) entering the form (four earthly elements).

We live with constant reminders of the importance of this number in folklore/mythology/our daily lives, i.e., the seven days of the week, seven notes in the musical scale, seven colors in the rainbow.

See **number(s)**.

sew(ing)

Creation and creativity; need for, or ability to make, repairs/

amends; a situation that you feel responsible for keeping together, that you're afraid is coming apart, or that needs to be mended. It may refer to sexual intercourse, especially if using a sewing machine. It may be a pun for "sowing" and relate, therefore, to planting ideas; fertility; inner growth.

See **knot(s); mend(ing); thread**.

sex

In its broadest Jungian sense, a sex dream symbolizes the attraction to, and urge to merge with, polar opposites (Whitmont and Perera). Therefore, it can refer to psychological completion; union (of ideas, aspects of yourself). Frightening, oppressive, or unpleasant sexual dreams often relate to repressed/unresolved spiritual problems, says Taylor, who believes that the sexual and spiritual are intertwined. Some authorities believe that violently explicit sex dreams/nightmares, or negative sexual dreams, can be a marker of earlier sexual abuse.

Dreams of having sex and/or orgasm (with or without emission for men) are normal for both males and females. Although sexual dreams can pinpoint sexual/physical problems, they are just as likely to be symbolic of your own masculine/feminine aspects or attitudes, especially if dreamed immediately after intercourse.

It's not uncommon for people approaching a wedding to experience especially erotic adventures with partners other than their intended spouses (Siegel). This kind of dream probably represents the intensity—and possibly the newness and variety—of your sexual passion. A series of nightmarish dreams at this time, related to sexual experiences, may relate to fears about your changing identity. The pending experience may have stimulated anxieties from the past about fears of abandonment, rejection, intimacy. Dreams in which you're sexually rejected are common during recovery from divorce/separation.

From a Freudian perspective, most, if not all, dreams will disclose some underlying infantile sexual wish/attitude. Waking events (day residue) won't enter your dreams unless related to deep-seated feelings or attitudes. Any conflicts about sexuality will be reflected in sex dreams (Natterson and Gordon). Many sex dreams are heavily disguised as other activities. For instance, going in or through a back door can represent anal intercourse.

Dreaming of having sex with a parent, when this has never happened in waking life, may symbolize feminine/masculine aspects of yourself or of archetypes (Mother Earth, Wise Old Man). Dreaming of sex with a male or female authority figure may represent a disguised parent/parent substitute. Having a parent visible while you're having sex with someone else may relate to the sexual roles or mores that parent taught you, possibly an attempt to overcome them. Or the visible parent may serve to restrain/inhibit you in some way, a form of control that can be positive or negative.

Sexually explicit dreams can be understood on three different levels (Natterson and Gordon). The dream can: (1) relate to an overt sexual need/issue; (2) tell you something about waking relationship issues with others; (3) reveal perceptions about your sexuality in the context of your social/political society. They can reflect early feelings/teaching about sex, marriage, love, and male/female roles.

How you feel in the dream—happy, satisfied, being forced (ambivalence?), or fearful—may give you some clues about your attitudes toward sex, possibly values learned from your parents. Risqué (for you) sexual behavior freely engaged in may symbolize a wish to be free of waking sexual inhibitions/guilt. Dreams with sexual conflict may really be about establishing waking boundaries for yourself (Delaney).

A sex partner known from your past (not necessarily a sex partner at that time) may relate to aspects of that person you need to incorporate into your waking life; unfinished relationship issues; conflicts about a customary way of relating that have been activated by a recent experience.

See **anima; animus; ejaculation; genitals; homosexual; masturbation; opposites; orgasm; shadow**.

sex change

Dreams in which one or more figures change their sex within the dream are common (Delaney). They can suggest someone in your waking life who has two qualities, especially feminine/masculine qualities. If the change is pleasant, it may represent a quality you'd like to embody. If negative or causing a problem, it may point to an underlying issue in your waking life. If you, the dreamer, change your sex, then when you work with the dream, ask, "How do I feel as a man [or woman, if a male dreamer]? In what ways can I evolve that perspective in my waking life?"

See **person(s) merging with/changing into another**.

shade

A need for protection from intense energy/power; anxiety about your social/professional status; a need to hide or be less noticeable; shadow aspects of yourself; feelings about being overshadowed; attitudes or unfinished situations from the past that prevent you from shining. Do you think someone in your waking life is, in fact, a "shady character"?

See **shadow**.

shadow

Most simply, the archetypal motif of the shadow can be understood as the dark part of our personality, whatever it is that we're afraid to face or would prefer to believe is not a part of our personality. Robert Johnson calls it the "dumping ground" for characteristics we don't acknowledge, the "unlived" side of our human potential. Jeremy Taylor defines it as the threshold between conscious self-awareness and the unconscious.

Like the anima/animus, it's an aspect of ourselves that's usually neglected in the first half of life as we develop our conscious personality. The shadow appears in dreams as our same sex, often portrayed as a sinister, unlikable, dark-skinned (if you are light-skinned), or unknown figure. It may appear as a lurking or hidden animal/person (behind the bushes, curtains, or the dreamer), or an unknown mass/force/shape (shades of science fiction!). A shadowy quality in someone well-known to you may represent his/her shadow, while an obscure person from your past can represent your own shadow (Signell).

A positive side of the shadow is creativity that we don't realize we have; a creative desire we haven't acknowledged, perhaps since we were children; some noble aspect of our personality that's not permitted expression in our particular culture. Demands for growth, therefore, often come from our shadow aspect (Jung). Somewhere in the dream in which a shadow aspect appears, or in a subsequent dream, is something representing the gift of the shadow, the potential for wholeness.

The shadow is sometimes portrayed in fairy tales/myths as the youngest, or fourth, son, who bests his brothers with the help of animals (instincts).

See **Black Madonna; four; person, known; person, unknown**.

Śhakti

See **Great Mother; snake(s)**.

shampoo

A need to clean out old ideas/attitudes/ways of thinking or anything else that interferes with your intellectual functioning. If the shampoo accompanies a new hairstyle (especially for females), it may refer to self growth; a need for a new approach to a situation/relationship; a desire to present a new persona/image to the world.

shape(s)

Existent in all of nature and reproduced in artistic works/physical structures, basic geometric shapes refer to our own basic nature; our connection with nature/the universe; the way our inner/outer worlds are shaped, i.e., our own basic structure/attitudes. Shape/form is often a symbolic way of connecting spiritual/physical (inner with outer); therefore, if it appears in a dream simply as an abstract shape, possibly luminous, it likely refers to the archetypal meaning of the shape (Jung).

See the specific shapes: **circle; cross; cube; diamond** [shape]; **spiral; square; star(s); triangle**. For the crescent, see **moon/moonlight**.

shark

Uh-oh. As a voracious/vicious predator, it may represent someone in your waking life whom you see as particularly greedy/unscrupulous; your own appetites; anger/hostility (someone you'd like to "take a bite out of"); frightening emotions.

See **fish/fishing; predator(s)**.

sharp(en)

If elongated, it may be a phallic symbol and related to anxiety about a particular male or sexual relationship, or male/female issues in general. If you're sharpening an object, it may refer to aggressive/assertive/protective actions and the feelings from which they arise.

See **point(ed); knife**, if applicable.

shatter

Some aspect of yourself/another that's quite fragile; vulnerability; an unexpected happening that evoked strong emotions, possibly feelings of shock/heartbreak.

sheaf

A sheaf of wheat/grain indicates integrated psychic forces; the process of integration of the unconscious (individuation); the natural order. It shares some of the same symbolism as fruit that grows in a bunch. In Egyptian hieroglyphics, it defined the concept of limitation (Cirlot).

If bound or tied together, it may relate to **knot(s)**. See **bunch; corn/cornfield; wheat; Self**.

sheep

The idea that humanity could be symbolized by a flock of sheep with its shepherd first arose with the Egyptians, later becoming a common Christian symbol. Are you just one of the flock or do you stand out in some way? What is the "sheepish" part of you and how is it being expressed in a waking situation? Like Little Bo Peep, have you lost your sheep (ideas, insights)?

See **animal(s); lamb**.

shell

See **seashells**.

shellfish

They are related to the symbolism of shells in the sense of protection; defense; vulnerability or lack of it, especially as related to emotions/emotional situations.

See **fish/fishing; seashells**. If applicable, see **clam(s); crab(s); lobster; oyster**.

sheriff

See **police**.

shield

Protection; defending or defensive. Are you protecting yourself or shielding someone else? Can what is on the shield (a design, a coat of arms?) provide information regarding your ability to invoke protection? If circular, it may refer to the mandala/Self. Mythologically, the shields of sun gods served to reflect the light of the spirit/divinity.

shine/shiny

Related to the symbolisms of sun/light/reflections, it can refer to awareness; consciousness; personal energy; illusion (reversed reflection of an object); a need to impress, or put something over on, someone ("shine up to"; "shine him on"); abilities ("outshine"); a need for attention.

See **aura; light; reflection; sun/sunlight**.

ship/shipwreck

Sailing over large bodies of water, a ship symbolizes the journey across/through the unknown/unconscious. As a large vehicle that sails on larger, more extensive bodies of water, it's more related to the process of transformation/individuation than a boat. If you're on the ship, how do you behave? Where are you going? How do you relate to those other aspects (other passengers) of yourself? Is the journey easy or does it have troubles? A shipwreck would relate to difficulties with the preceding concepts; feeling/fears of being overwhelmed by emotions or by circumstances beyond your control (nature, fate, destiny?).

See **boat; sailing**.

shirt

As a cover for the upper torso, it relates to emotions/emotional situations. It may also refer to someone in your waking life who is a "stuffed shirt"; self-sacrifice or generosity ("give the shirt off your back"); a financial risk or anxiety ("lose your shirt").

See **appearance; blouse; clothes/clothing; upper body**.

shit

See **excrement; defecate; toilet**.

Shiva

See **dancer**.

shiver

Feelings of fear/excitement/anticipation, possibly sexual ("shiver with delight"); something that's creepy ("gives you the shivers"); a signal that you need to distance yourself from some person/situation, or that you need to "come in out of the cold."

If related to temperature, see **cold; ice**.

shoes

As with feet, shoes may relate to grounding or connection with the earth/world; therefore, to your life position/attitude, your approach to life. Removing your shoes in certain situations can be a sign of respect; reverence; humility. Because shoes cover our feet, they represent convictions about our beliefs; understandings and the ability to act on them (Estés). They may refer to spiritual issues (sole = soul?).

Consider the quality/condition/design of the shoes. High heels may relate to especially feminine attitudes or to sexual wishes or issues, while slippers may refer to the bedroom or to informal attitudes/approaches, as might sandals. Perhaps you're living out the Cinderella myth, at least in some aspect of your life, waiting for Prince Charming to find you. Have you, or someone else, become "too big for your boots"? Are you trying, or have anxiety about trying, to "fill someone else's shoes"? Perhaps "if the shoe (situation) fits, you should wear (acknowledge) it'' in waking life.

See **clothes/clothing; foot/feet**.

shoot(ing)

Expression of aggression/hostility; need/ability to protect/defend (yourself, another?); feelings about having been, or fear of being, injured; a need to destroy or ''take potshots'' at some aspect of yourself. (Consider what you're shooting.) It can be related to skills/abilities/competition; therefore, to training/discipline. Since a gun is considered a phallic symbol, it may refer to intercourse or, if you're a man, to aggressive attitudes about women/sex. Archetypally it's associated with the hero/heroism; therefore, with your own personal life journey and goals (targets), as well as with hunting/the hunter role.

Is there a goal you're shooting for (''have your sights on'')? Are you afraid that something you want to try, or have tried, is merely ''a shot in the dark''? Perhaps there's a situation in which you need to ''give it your best shot,'' or, indeed, ''shoot for the works.'' Is there a situation you'd like to ''take a shot at''; would you like to be the one ''calling the shots''?

See **gun(s); hunter/huntress; target** (if applicable).

shop(ping)/shopkeeper

Needs in general, but especially needs for acquisition/ownership; possibly greed related to inner feelings of emptiness/unfulfillment; the ability to make choices/decisions and to compare values/merits; relationships and your need to ''shop around''; anything you're seeking in waking life. Consider the meaning of what you're shopping for. For instance, it may refer to a need to change your image if shopping for clothes/makeup. If you are in reality a shopkeeper, it may relate to waking anxieties/experiences.

See **marketplace/grocery store; business/work**, if applicable.

short

Loss of stature/status; feelings of powerlessness; some way that you're ''coming up short,'' possibly related to finances, or to childhood issues/feelings.

See **size**.

shoulder(s)

Strength; burdens or carrying burdens; ability to labor (''put your shoulder to the wheel''); responsibility, including guilt (''shoulder the blame''). Shoulders can refer to nurturing; supporting abilities/needs (''shoulder to cry on''); camaraderie (''rub shoulders with''); taking a group/community stand (''shoulder to shoulder''); personal/territorial space and/or invasion of it (''shoulder room''). They can refer to a posture of bravery (pull your shoulders up); depression/sadness/feelings of inadequacy (drooping or sagging shoulders); the ability to ''shoulder your way through'' (aggressive action, determined perseverance?).

Psychologically, shoulders are related to ''shoulds,'' so you need to consider whether you have guilt pertaining to your shoulds and whoever laid them on your shoulders. Karen Horney wrote about the ''tyranny of the shoulds,'' those that we establish which, by their very nature, are unobtainable or unachievable, thereby lowering/eroding self-esteem.

See **body; upper body**; also, if applicable, **carry(ing)/carried; load; yoke**.

shovel(ing)

Digging yourself into/out of a situation/relationship; digging into your inner self and recovering memories/insights or hidden/unconscious issues. Shoveling can relate to clearing or making a path for yourself; burying issues you don't want to face. If using the shovel to dig a hole, it may refer to feminine issues related to mother, women, birth, sex, and/or the work that's necessary to make you whole. In slang, it may refer to someone in waking life who's a fast talker or puts people on (''shovel the shit''), or someone who can speak the truth (''call a spade a spade'').

See **dig(ging); hole**.

show/show off

Need for approval/recognition; a distraction from expressing/connecting with other emotions; self-revelation or revealing something to others. Is there a recent waking situation in which you were feeling insecure/inadequate/insufficiently acknowledged?

See **approval; attention**.

shrink(ing)

The dreamer or others (as aspects of the dreamer) shrinking can signal that the dream issue stems from childhood, or it can refer to a recent situation in which you felt embarrassed or small; lowered self-esteem. Objects that shrink suggest their impact/value is being reduced or is not as important as it once was, especially in nightmares. Shrinking may allow access to something you've previously been unable to understand/perceive; a new perspective. It can refer to a person who is a shrink (psychotherapist, psychoanalyst), or to the need to see such a person.

See **small**.

shutters

Shutters can be for pure decoration and thus related to the persona, or to the ability to bluff someone. They can serve as protection against adversity and foul weather (attitudes); possibly a need to "batten down the hatches," or to shut out things (ideas, emotions?) you don't want to acknowledge.

See **home; house; storm**, if applicable.

sick

Anxieties about health/illness; a situation/relationship that you are "sick and tired of," "sick to death of," or that "makes you sick"; the illness preceding healing/transformation.

See **vomit(ing)**, if applicable.

side

To have someone at your side, or to be beside someone, is one of the most frequent positions in dreams. If we are to make anything of it at all—assuming the postures aren't threatening, it suggests feelings of equality/camaraderie. Consider the people beside you as outer resources or inner aspects of yourself that you can draw on. It may imply opposites in the sense of right side/wrong side; their side/our side; choices ("take sides"); judgments/morals ("seamy side").

See **left side of body; right side of body**.

sign

Identification; a need for direction; calling attention to a message. (Consider the possibility of puns.)

signature

Your identity; giving permission/agreement, and therefore, willingness to engage in some action.

silence

A need to hide or not be noticed, and therefore, anxiety about receiving attention or about being able to express yourself; feelings of inadequacy; feeling stunned; withdrawal; unspoken feelings; a need to focus attention.

silver

As a color, silver is associated with, and can represent, lunar/spiritual aspects or yourself. It may refer to something extremely valuable/precious (the Self); anxieties about aging (silver-haired); a situation/relationship that has a "silver lining." Metaphysically, a silver thread/cord is said to connect the etheric/energy body to the physical body for out-of-body journeying. It's the metal for the alchemical stage of whitening.

See **color(s); individuation; moon/moonlight; white**. Also **coins; money**, if applicable.

sing(ing)/singers

See **song(s)**.

sinking

Feelings of being overwhelmed; lowered self-esteem or confidence ("I'm sunk"); determination ("sink or swim"); attitudes that are pulling you down; fear/anxiety; loss of energy/enthusiasm ("sinking feeling"). Consider the symbolism of whatever it is that's sinking or that you're sinking into.

If applicable, see **drown(ing)**.

sister

If an actual family member, she may symbolize some aspect of your relationship, or serve to remind you that someone in your waking life has characteristics similar to your sister. Have issues of caring or sibling rivalry been awakened? Her appearance may also signal issues related to your family role; kinship; belongingness ("sisters under the skin").

If not an actual sister, she may symbolize characteristics of yourself, possibly ones you need to activate; the anima (for a male dreamer); the Self (for a woman without a sister). A "sister" is also a religious person, a nun, and may symbolize spiritual issues.

See **brother; family; girl**.

sit(ting)

Along with standing, probably the most common posture/position in a dream; therefore, probably not significant unless emphasized or having difficulty. Consider where you're sitting and with whom to decide whether it refers to equal/unequal status. It may refer to someone holding a "seat of authority"; "sitting down on the job." It is a more relaxed posture than standing. Consider whether you're "sitting back and letting it happen"; withdrawing; feeling or behaving passively, indifferently, or ambivalently ("sitting on the fence"); sitting up and giving attention; "sitting this one out." Are you "sitting in judgment" or "sitting at someone's feet"? Maybe you just need to "sit tight." The dream may also refer to a need to get to the seat (origin?) of an issue/situation.

See **position(s); posture(s)**.

six

The completion of a creative process (outer project or inner work?); achievement; perfection; harmony. Its geometric representations are the hexagon and the hexagram, as seen in the six-pointed Star of David (Solomon's Seal). In addition to a possible religious meaning—its connection with Judaism—the hexagram can symbolize the union of masculine/feminine (in ancient times the upper triangle represented fire and the lower represented water); wholeness.

See **number(s)**; and snowflake under **snow**.

size

In Freudian terms, the size of a person/object, especially if the emphasis is on big/little, may be a disguise for the size of someone's penis (a male dreamer, lover, father?). Size is related to the importance we attach to objects/persons; the power, or lack of it, we perceive them to have over us (thus related to our own feelings of power/powerlessness, one up/one down, topdog/underdog); emotions attached to any of the preceding; emotional or ego positions/postures.

See **measurement**.

skate/skating

Being able to maintain balance in your life's journey; ability or energy to propel yourself along. If you're actually learning to skate, it may refer to feelings/anxieties about recent efforts. If not, consider first whether you're skating on ground (your pathway), ice ("skating on thin ice"?), or in a rink, which, if circular, may refer to a mandala, or can suggest that you're "going round in circles."

skeleton

Something that's not fully developed; feeling overworked or understaffed ("a skeleton crew"); a need to "get down to the bare bones" of a matter, the basics; the underlying structure/support of a situation; a secret/scandal ("a skeleton in the closet"); a loss of substance/power/energy ("a mere skeleton of his former self"). It may refer to attitudes or anxieties about illness/death (someone who's "just skin and bones"); a situation/relationship you now realize is long dead.

See **bones; death; ghost(s)**.

skin

Protection of our innermost being; physical boundary (how permeable or impermeable is it?); ability to sense/feel the physical world; sensitivity ("thin-skinned") or lack of it ("thick-skinned"); your front/persona; someone who's superficial or shallow ("only skin-deep"); surface issues. What has "gotten under your skin" recently, "made your skin crawl," or "given you goose bumps"?

Wearing animal skins (see **tail**) relates to acquiring the characteristics/energy of the animal; therefore, also to rejuvenation.

See **body**.

skirt

Femininity; as a covering for the lower body, skirt shares some of its same symbolism, i.e., physical/sexual needs. What's your own understanding of the length of the skirt (short = sexy, stylish, young? long = modest, old-fashioned, dressy/formal experience?)?

See **clothes/clothing**.

sky

Sky relates to heaven, the realm of the gods, and therefore, to spirituality; the union of spirit/matter (sky connects to ground). A clear sky could refer to clear thinking. Looking up at the sky may relate to self-esteem (feeling insignificant or in a "down" position and needing reassurance); cosmic issues (feeling a small part of a whole). Something coming from the sky may relate to a wish/need for divine intervention if positive, or to something that has the potential for destruction or to create havoc in your waking life.

A pale blue sky is a well-known symbol for the unknown after death/the beyond/eternity, but from a Jungian point of view, a blue sky can also signal potential that has yet to be realized. Consider the color of the sky for setting the time of day; for its relationship to sunrise/sunset/midday or other times; and for setting the mood/theme of the dream.

You may want to look up information on the Egyptian sky goddess, Nut, or any other sky goddesses, to see how they may be at work in your psyche, or self-development process. According to Egyptian legend, the sun passes through the body of Nut every day. In conjunction with her brother Geb, the earth god, Nut was a mother goddess, creating Isis, Osiris, Nephthys, and Seth.

See **air; blue; weather**. If applicable, see **clouds/cloudy; day; night; storm**.

slave

It's common for a depressed woman, unhappy in her marriage or going through a divorce, to dream of herself as a slave (Cartwright).

See **servant**.

sleep

See **asleep**.

sleeve

Shares some of the same symbolism of arms and that of the garment that has sleeves. It can suggest unconscious perception that someone has "something up his/her sleeve."

small

Diminutive figures may represent feelings of insignificance; an attempt to reduce some dreaded person/feeling to a size you can cope with ("knock them down to size"). If the dreamer is smaller than usual, it may refer to a younger age/time period (Hall).

See **dwarf(s); little; size**.

smell

See **nose; odor; perfume**.

smoke

Passing through, or surrounded by, smoke—especially pleasantly aromatic smoke—with no fear, is a sign of ceremonial smoke that is always cleansing, protective, and strengthening. It has a feeling of movement around and through you. A cleansing may be called for in waking life; the dream may be a cleansing one, or be saying that you've already done the work, and now comes the celebration/acknowledgment. If not ceremonial, smoke may be calling your attention to a situation that needs to be taken care of before it develops further ("where there's smoke, there's fire"), or in which you or someone else has/needs to "put up a smoke screen"; or that you need to give up some fantasy ("smoke dreams") and get more realistic.

See **fire; fog/mist**.

smoking

Smoldering emotions (especially if you don't smoke in waking life); anxieties/concerns about the habit of smoking; addiction (see **addict(ed)**) or control/willpower issues; a physical need for nicotine (if you've recently given up smoking).

smooth(ness)

A need to "smooth over" something; someone who's a "smooth talker," or a wish that you could be; a well-worn situation/relationship. If your first association is "smooth as a baby's butt," it may be related to an attitude of innocence; childhood issues; infantile/immature wishes/fantasies.

snail(s)

Slow but dedicated progress; a need to slow down or speed up; secretive or sneaky; doing things in the dark (sex?). Snails are lunar creatures, therefore related to moon symbolisms. In mythology, the snail is associated with the cosmic labyrinth or spiral; therefore, with growth and cycles. Metaphysically the snail symbolizes the cyclic activity of matter. Some folklore relates the snail to the female genitals, and to fertility; pregnancy; all female mysteries. It is a Christian resurrection symbol.

See **labyrinth/maze; moon/moonlight; spiral**.

snake(s)

Snakes have quite complicated and varied symbolism, depending on personal experience and any cultural/mythological history with which you are acquainted. Consider emphasized characteristics, such as whether and how it's moving, whether or not it's threatening/entangled/twining, and the number of snakes.

Winding/twining snakes, as on the caduceus of the medical emblem, can signal an especially healing dream (the snakes of Asclepias). Because snakes are often found in dark places or near water, they can represent occult/magical forces; our own primal energies/instincts, as the personification of the unconscious.

They symbolize kundalini energy, which originates at the base of the spine and rises through chakras (energy centers) to culminate in wisdom and a higher state of consciousness. Many relate the kundalini snake to rising sexuality; also to Śhakti, the feminine principle.

In mythology, the snake in/climbing the tree symbolizes the process of becoming conscious, another meaning of the Adam and Eve story. According to Jung, mythological snakes may be hero counterparts. The snake swallowing itself, the uroboros, is related to the wheel; cycles; the Great Mother archetype.

Snakes can suggest feelings about deviousness (a "snake in the grass"), or temptation (the Garden of Eden snake). They symbolize self-renewal/resurrection because they shed their skin. Their renewal meaning often connects them with water symbology (see **water**). Since women shed their menstrual blood once a month, snakes sometimes represent feminine attributes, especially the ability to move/glide through life easily/gracefully.

Because snakes have had such positive and negative meanings culturally and mythologically, they can point to people/experiences about which you have ambivalence.

See **animals; lizard(s); reptile(s); serpent(s)**.

snow

If skiing, sledding, or building a snowman, it may refer to fun/relaxation. If the tone is negative, it may refer to feeling "left out in the cold"; cooling emotions/passion; concern that you've been given a "snow job." Are you feeling "snowed under" with work?

If you're inside, looking out, it may refer to a new, clean/fresh perspective; feeling protected against someone's coldness toward you. If pristine, see **white**. If animal tracks in the snow, it may refer to a beginning, but not wholehearted, acknowledgment of your basic nature/urges. If human prints, see **footprint(s)**.

Snowflakes are closely related to the mandala (see **mandala**), the growth or expression of the Self (see **Self**), and to six (see **six**).

See **winter**. If applicable, see **cold; ice**. For North/South Pole, see **pole**.

soap

A need to wash away something (memories, emotions?) in either a positive/negative sense; needing to rid yourself of feelings of being dirty emotionally, of guilt; possibly a need to confess or make amends ("come clean"). It can be a disguise for some intense or continuing emotional/dramatic situation in your life, as in a television soap opera.

See **clean(ing)/cleansing**.

sock(s)

A single sock may be a pun for hitting someone, or having been hit with information that surprised you.

Otherwise, see **stockings**.

solar plexus

Located just below the breastbone and above the stomach, it's the area where we often feel emotions first, or store unexpressed emotions. It can be a healing center if wisdom figures (personified ideas) touch/heal there. Emphasis suggests that held-in emotions may need to be explored/released.

soldier(s)

Camaraderie; belongingness; warring or peacekeeping aspects of yourself, depending on your conception of soldiers. What is your rank, i.e., do you have authority or not, and does this relate to a waking situation? If you're a former soldier, what recent situations evoked feelings/conflicts similar to those you had when in the military? Consider what activities soldiers are engaging in, their location, and the outcome of their actions.

In mythological motifs, it's not uncommon for the soldier to represent the negative forces of nature or of humans (Estés).

See **military; war; warrior**.

solstice

A turning point in the inner activities, symbolized by the season when it occurs.

See **seasons**.

son

For a female dreamer, it may refer to your actual child; parental responsibilities; the undeveloped masculine within. If a male dreamer, it may mean the same, but also immature aspects of yourself; memories/experiences of when you were younger; unfulfilled possibilities/ambitions you once had; hopes you wish will be fulfilled in your son. Having a son may evoke male feelings of pride/envy/rivalry issues, which may be expressed in dreams. It may be a pun for sun (see **sun/sunlight**), especially if the dreamer has no children.

See **boy; family**.

song(s)

Songs are magic. In ancient/primitive traditions, the gods gave the songs/chants; singing them can, likewise, call the gods to return, heal wounds/illness, and even produce spellbinding powers. A song is a call to awaken the psyche; to attend to inner wisdom, or the wisdom of the song, and apply it to a waking issue.

See **music/musician**.

sore

See **abscess**.

soup

As with all food, it relates to emotional hunger or nourishment. It's often a comfort or healing food. Consider whether the soup is rich/nourishing (basic needs) or thin; the possible symbolism of its contents; who made it or gave it to you (self-nurturance or from another?); with whom you are eating it. Is there something you are ''all in a stew'' or ''in the soup'' about? Perhaps some situation/relationship is ''as easy as duck soup,'' ''as thick as pea soup,'' or so complex, it's ''everything from soup to nuts.''

See **eating; food**.

south

Emotionally, south refers to love; warmth; passion. If referring to the southern United States, it may mean relaxed living and/or the prejudices/biases of the South. Metaphysically, south represents life; questions; expectations. See **north** for the north/south alignment.

See **direction(s)**.

sow

See **pig(s)**.

sowing

Fertility; plans/ideas for the future; sexual frivolity and freedom (''sowing your wild oats'').

See **plowing**.

space

Consider the kind of space (tunnel, the sky, a room, outdoors) as a reflection of your inner dimensions. You may want to observe over time how it narrows/expands/changes, and tie that to waking experiences. Empty space may refer to potential, or negatively, to feelings of emptiness.

See **boundaries; edge; open**.

space travel

Journeying through, and exploring, inner or psychological spaces; seeking new awareness; a wish/need to escape worldly burdens/turmoil.

See **find/discover; flying; galaxy**.

spear

See **lance**.

spectacles

See **eyeglasses**.

speech

If attending a speech, it may reflect your need for emotional/intellectual stimulation; affiliation with certain ideas/principles (see **audience**). If delivering one, you may have a pent-up message to deliver; a need to teach/instruct others about the way a situation should be, possibly because you've not been receiving enough acknowledgment. Do you need to ''tell it like it is,'' or to ''set the record straight''?

speed

Energy, especially that needed to accomplish a task/project (''full speed ahead''); a compulsion (being driven) to complete something; going too fast (out of control?) in a relationship/situation; slang for amphetamines or drugs that result in a ''high.'' What feelings are associated with speed in the dream?

If applicable, see **fast; vehicle(s)**, the specific vehicle involved, and **addict(ed)**.

sphere

See **circle**. If applicable, see **ball; globe; planet(s)**.

sphinx

Union of masculine/feminine powers; riddles; mystery; strength; endurance; Egypt and your association or experience with the country or its people.

See **Egypt**.

spice

A need for variety to revive/enliven (''spice up'') your life; a new flavor, and therefore, a new perspective/approach; a need for sex/pleasure. Is there a pun embedded in the particular herb/spice (sage = wisdom; thyme = time?).

spider(s)

Negatively, a female spider can represent a devouring mother/female; the feminine power to possess/ensnare (especially in a man's dream). Contrary to the negative attitudes we have about spiders in Indo-European or American cultures, in American Indian mythology the spider frequently is a helpful, healing figure. For some Dakota tribes, the spider is a creator; in Pima and other tribes, he's a trickster figure.

See **insects; spider web**.

spiderweb

An archetypal symbol for weaving, and of weaving our life energies together—our growth/life process. From ancient times, the spider and web have been associated with spinning and with the Greek goddess Arachne, who had the power to spin our fate. In Dineh (Navaho) mythology, Spider Woman created and spun the universe into being from two connecting threads.

The shape of the web may represent the mandala/Self. Its appearance may signal a situation/relationship in which you feel trapped; suggest it's time to examine an old pattern of behavior and spin a new one. A tangled web may refer to secrecy/deceit, as Shakespeare well knew (''what tangled webs we weave, when others we practice to deceive'').

See **weave(ing)/weaver**.

spine

See **backbone**.

spiral

One of the most fundamental movements in nature and life, the spiral is a microcosmic/archetypal symbol representing the movement of life in general and your own particular life movement. In addition to designs on walls/clothing/jewelry, the shape of fancy foods/desserts, don't forget to observe it in spiral stairs, the spiraling flight of birds/planes, spiral pathways up/around mountains/hills, and spiral seashells (Taylor).

Metaphysically, the creative spiral rises; the destructive spiral descends. Spiritual growth, personality development, awakened/new consciousness, are all often described as a spiral—the cycle comes around full term but at a higher, more enlightened level. The center is always our Self. A single spiral sometimes represents rising kundalini or sexual energy.

The double spiral represent the in-breath and out-breath of God, or of creation; cosmic or worldly involution/evolution; the interrelation of opposites; the element of water, which is able to transform/regenerate; the double-headed snake of healing (the caduceus).

See **ascend(ing); descend (ing); labyrinth/maze; Self; shape(s); snail(s)**.

splinter

A different view; association with a divergent group ("splinter group"); division/separation ("splinter off"), which can be productive or negative; a personal wounding; negative attitudes/viewpoints that are irritating; a surprise hurt/wounding, possibly felt but not necessarily realized right away; a dent in your protective abilities.

If applicable, see **hurt; pain; wound(s)/wounded**.

spoon

Giving/receiving nourishment. If being fed, it may refer to childhood needs/memories; infantile wishes to escape responsibility; being given special information/treatment ("spoon-fed"); someone who's wealthy or gets all the breaks ("born with a silver spoon in his mouth").

See **eating**.

sporting events

From a Freudian perspective, active, physical sporting events can be a disguise for attitudes about sex as an aggressive act: Boxing relates to box/female genitals; soccer can be a pun on "sock her"; baseball can relate to "base" feelings and "balling" (Natterson and Gordon). The spectator may be a vicarious voyeur, or may be watching parental/other forbidden sex acts.

For different perspectives, see **baseball; football; game(s)**. If applicable, see **competitor/competition; team/team player/team sports; victor/victory**.

spring [season]

All seasons are related to cycles and the death/rebirth theme. Spring is especially related to new life/new beginnings; revitalized/increased energy; creativity; fertility; the emergence of, or fruiting/budding of, potential or dormant ideas; childhood/youth.

See **seasons**.

spring [water]

The bubbling up/emergence of emotions; ability to make your feelings known even when others are trying to cover them up; hidden or reviving sources of energy; inner/emotional resources. Some springs have magical, sacred, or special healing powers.

square

The four elements of the universe. In sacred geometry, it's connected to the four and to Hermes, who's associated with three *and* four. Mythologically and metaphysically, a four-sided figure marks off the boundaries within which transformation can take place.

Together the square and the circle form a mandala, the Self symbol. If you divide a square with a diagonal line from either upper corner to the opposite lower corner, you have two triangles (the number three), so the square/four also encompasses/embodies the battle and/or union of opposites, i.e., lower/upper, conscious/unconscious, shadow/ego, the upper trinity of God/the lower trinity (mind, body, spirit) of man.

Our idioms suggest that the square symbolizes fairness ("a square deal"); something that's substantial/nourishing ("a square meal", "three squares a day"); that you are, or someone in your life is, being too conventional/unbending ("he's a square").

See **four; mandala; shape(s); three**.

squid

See **octopus/squid**.

squirrel

Domestic or financial affairs, especially acquiring a larder (resources/money) for the future or for hard times; a need to hide/bury something; an industrious and/or forgetful person; someone who's odd ("squirrelly"). Is there something you need to hold on to ("squirrel away")?

stab

See **knife; sword(s); wound(s)/wounded**.

stable

Where horses are kept/trained; therefore, the maintaining and civilizing of—possibly holding back or repressing—your animal/sexual impulses. It can represent someone who can be counted on; a staff of loyal workers, possibly on contract. Your dream may be dealing with regret or hindsight. ("It's too late to shut the stable door.") Or do you feel like you're just "shoveling shit"?

See **horse(s); manure** (if applicable).

staff

A symbol of power (the king's/pope's scepter) and order. Staffs displaying flags/banners may symbolize identification with a country; prayers/petitions to the gods; a pun for business personnel. In some biblical and mythological stories, the staff is transformed into a snake or has a snake twining about it, which relates the snake/staff to healing and self-renewal. In Icelandic literature the *völva*, a seer and healer, especially of women in childbirth, always carried a staff decorated with precious stones.

See **snake(s); wand**.

stag

A symbol for Jesus because of its capacity for self-renewal; the urge toward individuation or wholeness.

stage

Your roles or performance in life; an act you are, or someone else is, putting on, and therefore, a facade, persona or false pretenses; a project you're trying to arrange or "stage"; gossip ("a stage whisper"); a need for more, or a feeling of having too much, drama in your life; performance anxiety ("stage fright"); recent feelings of having been overlooked. It may refer to the order, sequence or process of something—the stages it has to go through from start to finish—therefore, associated with cycles and/or with a stage, or the stages, of your life. Who can you bring in from the wings to help you "set the stage"?

See **actor/actress; play(ing); roles; theater**.

stairs

Ambition ("climbing your way to the top"); the steps you have to take to progress toward a goal; false hopes/fantasies ("stairway to the stars"); the "ups and downs" of life. Stairs going nowhere may represent a memory of the birth process (Hopkins). Stairs can be a pun for staring/voyeurism. Like elevators/escalators/ladders, they may symbolize different levels of awareness; the dream's message may be that it's time to move from one level to another (Woodman). Don't forget to consider the structure within which the stairs are located for additional clues.

See **ascend(ing); climb(ing); descend(ing)**.

stamp(s)

A need for communication; if in a collection, they may relate to money/security/hoarding issues. Consider the symbolism of the stamp's shape, objects/persons it depicts, its amount, and the country of issue.

stand(ing)

Probably the most common posture in dreams and not unusual, unless called attention to, such as an inability to stand. In general, it refers to our posture ("stand tall"); position in life or with respect to a given situation or issue ("know where you stand"); values ("what we stand for"). It may be emphasized if there's a waking situation in which: you're not quite sure where you stand; you've been "left standing"; you've had to "stand alone" when someone did not "stand by" you. You may have anxieties about "standing down" or "standing aside." Are you feeling a need to "stand firm," "stand your ground," or "stand up for someone"?

See **position(s); posture(s)**.

standing above

Standing above someone/something may reflect superior feelings; feelings of fear/courage, if you're looking down, for instance, into an abyss. It may be the position that gives you a wider/greater perspective and reflects using your intellect or consciousness rather than your emotions. If you're alone, could it be that you've used your intellect/intellectual position to distance yourself from others or to "look down on" them? If the dream is compensatory, it may, in fact, reflect recent feelings of inferiority.

See **above; position(s)**.

standing opposite

If you're standing opposite someone, consider your stance (posture) and the action/conversation to determine if this is a person with whom you are in opposition, or have some resistance to understanding/engaging in a relationship. It may be the counterpart or "devil's advocate" to some waking position. It can represent having the capacity to confront opposition. Consider whether the same holds true for sitting opposite, for in some instances (dining, playing cards) the person sitting opposite may be considered your partner.

See **opposites; position(s)**.

star(s)

The five-pointed star, the pentacle, represents humans (five limbs) and/or our hopes/wishes; feelings about destiny ("it's in the stars"). It can represent the spirit of man. Associated with the number five, a star can mean your senses are being elevated to a higher level of awareness. As slang for a famous/well-known person, it can represent your wish to be noticed.

See **actor/actress; five; shape(s)**.

starfish

While sharing some of the symbolism of the star, as a water creature, it's more closely related to emotions or emotional experiences.

starvation

Mental/emotional impoverishment; some aspect of yourself/another that's being ignored (emotional or family issues?). If you're dieting or have a food disorder, it would not be an uncommon dream.

See **eating; food; hunger/hungry**. If applicable, see **homeless**.

station

Your position of authority (or lack of it); socioeconomic status in life; possibly your relationship with people (depending on your behavior in a station).

If stranded in a station, see **travel(ing)/journey**. If applicable, see **crowd**.

statue

See **idol**.

stealing

Negatively, it may represent anger/hostility toward the person you're stealing from, if known. While it may suggest you aren't feeling adequate about your skills, conversely, it could be saying you're feeling so competent that "it's a steal." In a positive sense, if you're successful, it may represent newly developing confidence, which you possibly feel is not quite legitimate or can't quite claim as your own yet. If you're feeling inadequate/anxious about some waking situation, you may wish to "steal the show," or "steal someone else's thunder."

If someone is stealing from you, it can relate to feelings of inadequacy; being undeserving;

feeling cheated/violated in some way. It can be a pun for steel.

See **steel; thief/theft**.

steel

Toughness of spirit; inflexibility; a need to prepare yourself for an emotional situation or against weakness (''steel yourself''); sometimes cold/emotionless (''steel-hearted''). A pun for stealing.

See **metal; stealing**.

steam(ing)

Feeling and/or the need to express anger (''all steamed up,'' ''boiling mad,'' ''letting off steam''); a need to raise your energy level (''get the steam up,'' ''steam ahead''); sexual arousal; passion. If you are steaming something, consider the symbolism of what it is (food, clothes?). It may be related to **fog/mist**.

See **emotion(s)**.

steeple

See **church**.

step(s)

See **stairs; walk(ing)**.

sterilize

Feeling dirty or guilty; a need/wish to clean/purify yourself; anxiety about infection; killing off emotions; protection from invasion (of emotions, attitudes?); a need to remain inviolate in some aspect of your life.

stiff(ness)

Rigid attitudes; unbending approach to situations; holding yourself back; inability to be spontaneous; the body armor that results from the preceding; also, the penis in sexual arousal.

stockings

As coverings for the legs/feet, socks/stockings share some of the symbolism of shoes: support and protection of our foundations and understandings. If sexy, they can refer to sexual arousal/stimulation. If bobby sox, they may refer to your actual teenage years; memories or dreams, especially unfulfilled ones; younger, more immature ideas. A Christmas stocking implies a need for, or to give, gifts/recognition.

See **clothes/clothing**.

stomach

The beginning of the transformation process; therefore, also any difficulties with change/acceptance, as in a situation that you ''can't stomach.'' The ability to ''digest'' life's experiences; whatever you ''hunger for''/desire; something that ''turns your stomach''; repressed/stored/swallowed emotions and words (indigestion?).

See **abdomen; body; digestion**.

stone(s)

Unity; strength; values/attitudes/beliefs that are, either positively or negatively, unchanging (''etched in stone''). They can be a symbol for what is sacred or magical. Consider the shape, size, and number of stones present. If extremely large or enduring (menhirs), they may be: an archetypal symbol for the Self; related to a need for more ritual/spiritual activity; a phallic symbol (related to power). If shattering/crumbling, they may indicate impending infirmity; you may want to see your doctor.

Stones may be related to issues of moral judgment or guilt. (''Let he who is without sin cast the first stone.'') Or you may need to ''leave no stone unturned'' in your efforts.

The mystical philosopher's stone of alchemy symbolized the merging of unconscious/conscious material for personal perfection. Thus, stone, particularly a rough stone, represents the personality/character that needs to be hewn or developed and perfected (individuation). What superfluous attitudes do you need to cut away as your next step toward self-knowledge?

In early times, the decoration/placement of stones often represented the navel/center of the world. Among the world's most spiritual stones is the Black Stone of Mecca. Resting inside the Ka'aba, the center of the Muslim world, it allows direct communication with God. Another well-known stone, relating to sovereignty/inauguration, is the stone from Scone (the Irish Stone of Destiny), which forms the base of the coronation throne, located in Westminster Abbey, of the sovereign of Great Britain. In some legends, the Grail is a stone rather than a vessel.

Still, your stone may be a bit of the Blarney Stone, representing the gift of eloquence (as the Irish say), or an exaggeration of the truth (as the non-Irish say); your associations with Ireland or someone who's Irish.

See **gem(s); rock(s)**.

stork

In folklore, the stork is the carrier of new life; therefore, it could represent a new baby, or wish for one; any new project/situation that's in its infancy.

storm

Negatively, a storm can represent unexpressed fears or seething emotions, especially anger/rage; depression; turmoil; attack ("take them by storm"); knowledge/awareness, possibly suppressed in waking, that suggests a devastating shock/loss. In its positive aspects, it can represent the rising of spirit within; the ability to withstand whatever comes ("weather the storm"). Don't forget to consider any pun contained within the name of a hurricane.

See **emotion(s); weather**.

stove

See **cook(s)/cooking; oven**. If applicable, see **fire; hot; melt; warm/warmth**.

strangers

See **person, unknown**.

strangle

To have someone by the throat; i.e., in your grip/power ("stranglehold"); holding back the emergence/expression of feelings (see **choke**). Because the throat chakra is related to clear hearing/insight, it may refer to stifling of awareness/creativity.

See **neck**.

straw

As dried/dead grass, it can represent cycles; transitoriness. Often spread on the ground to make a nest, it may symbolize earthiness; nesting/homebuilding instincts; comfort with your more base instincts/urges.

See **hay**.

stream

Shares symbolism of the river, with the implication of less energy/flow; therefore, possibly less emotion/passion about a situation; problems that are easier to overcome. Is your stream clear and fast, slow and lazy, muddy or murky? Are you flowing comfortably, or are you dammed up in some way? Ease of progress might be implied by "flowing downstream," although it can also have the implication of erosion/cutting away at something. If your association is to "stream of consciousness," it may refer to your connections with others or their ideas; free association; the collective unconscious. Within the stream, or associated with it, can be resources (see **fish/fishing**); refreshment (food, water); spiritual knowledge (cleansing/purification; the "stream of God's law").

See **river; water**.

street

See **road**.

string

Strings/cords/ropes are all related to binding, cohesion, and joining; therefore, the strength of the string may refer to: the strength of your involvement in/commitment to a project/relationship; feelings of being constricted; your ability/concerns about holding some situation/relationship together. Perhaps you need to "pull some strings," or you realize that someone else already has. Does some situation/offer come "with strings attached"? Maybe you're angry enough to wish someone "strung up," possibly because you suspect or fear you're being "strung along." Then again, it may refer to feminine/maternal influence ("apron strings"). If drawstrings, consider the contents of the purse/pouch, which might lead you to ponder who "holds the purse strings." Don't forget that wonderful proverb "The string of a man's patience pouch is tied with a slip knot." In sexual slang, the uncircumcised foreskin of the penis is called the "dickstring."

See **cord; knot(s); thread**. If a string of jewels, see **necklace**. See **silver** for the metaphysical meaning of the silver string/cord.

strong

Newly found courage/confidence/capability. If a compensatory dream, you may have been feeling not so strong recently.

stumble

See **balance(d)/balancing**.

submarine

Exploring the emotions or unconscious material with safety/protection; a different perspective/understanding; getting at the depths/core of a situation.

See **below; water**.

subway

See **under/underneath; underground**.

sucking

Need for emotional nurturance; a need/wish for time-out from your daily responsibilities; sexual urges/demands. If you're being sucked on by humans/creatures, consider who or what they represent that's presently an energy drain ("bloodsucker"). What are you afraid you're being "sucked into," or is there someone you are, or may need to be, "sucking up to" (with all its resultant feelings for you)?

If a sexual dream, see **sex**.

sugar/sweets/candy

Sweets can represent sensual/sexual pleasure; joys/special treats in life; and, sometimes, a lover (your "sweetie"). They can represent indulgence (have you been depriving yourself of some pleasure?); a forbidden pleasure; goals/ambitions of various kinds, i.e., "the sweet smell of success," or a "sugar daddy."

suitcase

As a feminine container and one that can carry clothes, it may reflect some aspect of your outer/inner identity and/or a challenge to it. Pregnant women dream about finding/losing suitcases as reflections of their changing identity; as concerns about being a parent; as representing a container (womb) for the fetus (Siegel).

See **luggage**.

summer

Midlife; the ripening of a situation/relationship; a time of energy/growth/development; fruition; need for relaxation; vacation memories.

See **seasons**.

sun/sunlight

The divinity of the self; wholeness; the source of life; immortality; vital energy; consciousness/awareness; enlightenment. It may be a pun for your son, or that of another. Mythologically the sun can represent the *anima mundi*, the world soul. While the sun usually represents masculine power, in Japanese Shinto tradition, it's feminine and is personified by the goddess Amaterasu, the spirit of the universe.

sunrise

See **dawn**.

sunset

The ending of a situation/relationship; aging; the final years of your life.

See **evening**.

supervisor

If not an actual waking person, he/she may represent an authority figure in your life; attitudes toward authority; potential for restriction/development of your skills; ambition; the ability to take charge of/control life events, or the need to exert such control; your inner controller, and therefore, possibly societal rules or regulations, your conscience.

See **boss**.

surgery

Concerns about an upcoming surgery or about your health; the opening of the Self; the influence/intrusion of someone else, possibly an authority figure, into your life; a need for emotional healing; something that needs to be "cut out" of your life. (Consider the body part/area for additional clues.)

If applicable, see **doctor; hospital; nurse; wound(s)/wounded**.

swallow(ing)

It may refer to a recent/impending situation related to "swallowing your pride," or to swallowing some information "hook, line, and sinker" and now feeling rather foolish. It can be related to having to "eat your words"; holding back your feelings/words; a long-standing habit of swallowing your anger.

See **neck**. If it refers to food/fluid, see **drink(ing); eating; food**.

swamp

See **marsh**.

swan

Swans mate for life, so it may refer to a romantic situation or a lifelong commitment; the end of some situation or relationship in your waking life (a "swan song"). It can refer to some person/situation that seems to have begun as an ugly duckling and that you hope will emerge into a lovely swan; thus, in this instance, it's also related to patience; potential; transformation; inner rather than outer beauty. As a water bird, it may refer to an emotional situation, especially one with a positive/calming influence. In ancient Greece, the swan symbolized initiates of the mysteries; divine power; knowledge of the future. It was sacred to Apollo and to Orpheus, who represented the esoteric/secret doctrine as revealed through music. According to von Franz, the swan can represent a spiritual aspect; intuition/hunches; sudden ideas/feelings that seem to come from nowhere and fly off again. Negatively, she says, they represent the flighty, inhuman quality of the anima.

See **bird(s)**.

sweep(ing)

Cleaning/clearing away mental/emotional debris ("making a clean sweep"); taking a new stance/attitude; ignoring facts or intuition ("sweep it under the rug").

See **housework/housekeeper**.

sweets

See **sugar/sweets/candy**.

swelling

Something that's swollen/swelling may represent the penis/sexual urges; pregnancy. Otherwise, see **abscess; infection**.

swimming

According to Siegel, pregnant women in their third trimester often dream of swimming in channels or downhill, while at the time of conception, it's not unusual for a woman to dream of fish, or other small, aquatic animals, swimming *up* narrow channels. For Freud, dreams of swimming represented memories of/wishes to be in the womb again, and may occur at stressful times when reassurance is needed. As a movement, it's one wherein you're making headway under your own power ("swim with the tide"). Because you're in the water, it could refer to emotional work/energy; becoming aware of unconscious material (especially swimming underwater); a wish to be "in the swim of things."

Any resistance—swimming upstream ("against the tide"), sitting beside a pool, standing on the shore—suggests difficulty/hesitancy in dealing with emotional issues (a specific situation?) or the challenge of the unknown; resistance to foolhardy behavior ("jump/dive right in"; "sink or swim").

Being in shallow water may represent feelings/anxiety of shallowness/insecurity/tentativeness toward an emotional situation; concern about getting closer/going deeper; making sure you're safe and not overwhelmed.

See **dive/diving; lake; underwater; water**.

swing(ing)

A wish/hope for sexual variety; masturbation; romance, if two are on the swing. It may symbolize cycles; movement going nowhere; the ebb and flow of energy. Do you need to "get in the swing of things," or are you already "in full swing"? Swinging/rocking are movements that seem to be soothing to the nervous system. Often related to childhood/infant memories, they may relate to the freedom of the womb or of childhood; therefore, to a need for relaxation or to escape from present responsibilities. Mythologically, mechanical swinging/nodding movements are often attributed to demons, the archetypal idea of nonredemption (von Franz).

See **rocking chair**.

sword(s)

The processes/feelings of ambition/competition/competitiveness (''take a stab at''); aggressiveness; hostility; protection/power (especially masculine power, since the sword is definitely a phallic symbol); old-fashioned chivalry. Has some relationship or situation become a ''double-edged'' sword, or has someone recently ''stabbed you in the back''?

If applicable, see **attack; defend/defender**.

syringe

From a Freudian perspective, the needle and its contents may symbolize the penis and intercourse. Consider, therefore, what is in the syringe and who gives it, or an injection, to you. Does its contents—and by analogy the giver's influence—empower you, or sap energy?

See **injection**.

table

Social/family connections and your place within them (your place at the table); authority/control; wisdom or power (the "head of the table") and its extension into your personal life/community/country (as the law of the land); attitudes/ideas that are on hold ("table the proposal"); something you can't hold any longer and have to bring to the table. (Consider the symbolism of specific articles on the table).

As with all pieces of furniture, its condition, the material it's made out of, and activities occurring may offer additional clues. One of the most famous archetypal tables was the Round Table occupied by King Arthur's knights, defenders of the Grail. Circular, and with the Grail as its mystic center, it actually becomes a mandala.

See **furniture/furnishings**. If round, see **circle; Grail; mandala**.

tablet

If a pill, see **medicine/medication**. If for writing, see **messenger**. If a stone tablet, see **stone(s)**.

tadpole(s)

See **frog(s)**.

tail

If appearing on an animal that's supposed to have a tail, and is not unusual or out of the ordinary, it's probably only related to the significance of the animal; therefore, see **animal(s)** and the specific animal. If appearing as a part of, or worn in the form of, an animal skin, it suggests a meaning similar to that when ancient Egyptian pharaohs and priests wore them, i.e., animalistic traits and the power conferred when their skins are worn; strength; special honor. If appearing as part of a human, it may refer to our early ancestors and, therefore, our long line of heritage; the devil/shadow aspect; the penis or sexual energy. It can suggest someone who is "tagging along," "tailing behind," or who's following (tailing) you in some fashion.

tailor

The measure of your worth; new/changed goals, ambitions, skills/capabilities; anxiety about whether or not you "measure up" to some situation; or you may be altering your appearance (attitudes, behavior?) *to* measure up. Is there something you wish would be "tailor-made" for you? How has your waking status changed recently?

See **clothes/clothing**; if applicable, **lower body; upper body**.

taking a trip

See **travel(ing)/journey**.

talisman

See **amulet(s)**.

talking/thinking

Talking and thinking occur about equally in dreams; hence, their occurrence is not unusual unless it's in some way bizarre (speaking a strange/unknown language), what you're saying/thinking is unusual/strange, the conversation or thoughts evoke strong feelings or behavioral reactions, or conversation/thought is totally absent.

Difficulty talking may refer to the inability to make yourself heard or to express yourself adequately; the habit of "swallowing your words" and/or hiding your feelings. As with any dream interaction, you need to consider your place/position in the dream (equal or not?), the actions occurring around or implied by it, and how your messages are received (or not).

If lecturing or teaching, see **teacher**. If applicable, see **leader/lead(ing)**. If a talking animal, see **animal(s)**.

tall

Having stature/authority; pride/bravery (either genuine or a facade, i.e., "walk tall and carry a big stick"); ability to have an overview, overlook things, or oversee projects; something (project, deadline?) or someone that's "looming over" you or whom you have invested with power;

possibly someone who exaggerates or tells "tall tales."

See **giant; size**.

tame

See **animal(s)**.

tangled

Entanglement in a situation/relationship; confused thoughts/ideas; a situation that's in a mess and needs to be straightened out. Do you cope with the tangling successfully or with difficulty? If successful, it may reflect a waking need/ability to take charge of some situation and exert order, or possibly get at the truth. If unsuccessful, it may relate to self-confidence; feelings of being overwhelmed, or caught.

See **roots; vines**.

tank

As a container, it relates to the feminine/womb, possibly your emotions if filled with water (fish tank, aquarium). If referring to a tank truck, consider the contents of what's being hauled (gasoline=energy; milk=nourishment; toxic gas/fluid=depletion of spirit/creativity?). If a storage tank, consider the contents. It may relate to resources; hoarding or acquisition needs. If a military vehicle, it may refer to a need for protection, defensiveness, or to aggressive/hostile feelings.

If applicable, see **container; vehicle(s)**.

tap

A signal or call to attention, possibly coded (secret message); the expression of nervousness/boredom/anxiety; the ability/need to "tap into" resources, other aspects of yourself, monetary funds.

If tap dancing, see **dancer; dance/dancing**.

tapes

See **record/cassette**.

tapestry

Your life flow or some part of it ("the tapestry of life"); some aspect of personal/familial history/heritage; a connection between your life history and world history (the cosmic connection?).

See **art; history; weave(ing)/weaver**.

target

Have you gotten off the track in some situation, or in your life direction (goals, ambitions?), and need to get "back on target," or pay more attention to the target (goals)? Perhaps your analysis of some situation is "right on target"—you've hit the "bull's-eye." You may be feeling there's something you have been targeted to receive, pleasant or unpleasant. Are you feeling that you're the target of someone's hostility (a "sitting duck"); or would you like to target your own feelings/anger more directly? If you hit the target, do the numbers you hit have any significance in your life?

If a round target, see **circle; mandala**. If mounted on straw, see **hay; straw**. If applicable, see **aim; bow and arrow; competitor/competition; gun(s); shoot(ing)**.

taste

Your personal preference; yearnings; the possibly negative aftermath of an experience ("left a bad taste"); societally/culturally appropriate behavior (tasteful; tastefully done); learnings (acquired taste); a sexually attractive female ("tasty dish"). Any dream that refers to one of the senses may reflect a need for sensory or sensual stimulation/gratification.

See **eating; food; mouth/lips; tongue**.

tattoo

Consider the color used, the part of the body, and the object tattooed onto it for additional clues. Tattoos carry the ancient meaning of blood sacrifice (Cirlot); therefore, protection from danger; identification; recognition; allegiance; a need for attention. For some it's a dramatic/unusual way to communicate or get attention; memories that are hard to get rid of, i.e., indelible.

See **appearance; decorate/decoration**.

tax(es)

Pushing (taxing) the limits; someone who's irritating or bothersome; being stressed ("taxed to the max"); financial anxiety; what we owe to some person/organization and our feelings about whether or not it's fair.

taxi

Are you the driver or the passenger ("just along for the ride")? If the passenger, it suggests letting, or a wish to let, someone else take action or take charge for you; needing help finding your way. It can represent being "carried off" or "carried away." (Your taxi driver might be the modern equivalent of Prince Charming.)

See **car; vehicle(s)**.

tea

Need for a time-out, possibly to "drink in" recent experiences; therefore, a need for rumination/reflection. It can refer to a need for a stimulant or anything stimulating or energizing (friend, project, idea?). If afternoon/formal tea, it may be related to your experiences/associations with England or someone you know who's English; Asian-related experiences/persons; any other tea drinker known to you.

See **coffee; food**. If reading tea leaves, see **fortune-teller/fortune-telling**.

teacher

The need for advice or new learnings; seeking a new path. In Jungian terms, the appearance of a teacher may signify the archetype of the Wise Old Man, the spirit, who fills in information you need for the next step in your development. If female, she can also symbolize the Wise Old Woman; the Great Mother; the personal mother who hands down information/tradition.

See **school**.

team/team player/ team sports

Being a player on a sports team suggests issues related to a group, possibly your job/professional affiliation, or to society. The dream may be signaling that you have anxieties about: where you fit into the team; needing approval from peers; how dispensable/indispensable you are.

If applicable, see **sporting events**.

teddy bear

Lost security, comfort, companion; need for cuddling or reassurance; regression to an earlier state, and therefore, a need to be young or taken care of; childhood memories/nostalgia; an immature relationship.

teenager(s)

See **adolescent/adolescence**.

teeth

Strength and aggressiveness (''chew him up and spit him out''); greed; devouring instincts; envy; overconfidence or overestimation of your abilities (''bite off more than you can chew''). As tools that break down food, teeth can symbolize the breakdown of psychological information in order to digest/understand/integrate it (''get your teeth into it''). They can, however, also indicate that there's something—an attitude/feeling/situation—that you're having trouble incorporating (digesting) in your waking life. In Freudian theory, the loss of teeth is related to anxiety about the penis, possibly castration fears.

Dreams of losing teeth are common as we grow up and older. They may symbolize transition and/or the aging process; loss of power/potency (also typical with respect to a work situation); emotional injury (Siegel).

See **body; dentist; face; mouth/lips**.

telegram

Signals/messages you're sending out in your daily life; a situation/relationship that carries with it anxiety or a sense of urgency; possibly a crisis.

See **messenger; telephone**.

telepathy

Dreams in which you convey your thoughts and receive those of another person/animal without speaking suggest a "magical" experience, and may, therefore, signal a mythological theme.

telephone

Telephoning—or any image of indirect/exotic communication—can symbolize telepathic communication. It may reflect a connection of any sort (good, bad, fading, intermittent?) with a situation/relationship. It can suggest a relationship that you wish to hold or keep at a distance; anxiety about facing/confronting someone; a need to "get in touch" with some aspect of yourself/another.

telescope

A need to see into the future; anxiety about what's coming; considering, possibly magnifying, what's "on the horizon" (upcoming); a need to take a closer look at something. Inasmuch as telescopes are used to view stars and outer space, it may be related to the symbolism of stars as planetary bodies; fame and/or the need/desire to be the center of attention; a need for a spiritual connection or to expand your spiritual life. What do you need to see more clearly?

See **binoculars; galaxy; planet(s); star(s)**.

television

Passive contact with the world; your inner news/story; a safety valve, i.e., putting distance between you and the situation. In a positive sense, this could give you a more objective perspective, so you could "get the picture." Negatively, it may help you ignore issues by attributing them to someone else ("it's only a story").

See **look(ing)/looked at**. If a television personality, see **person, famous**.

temple

Is it ancient or modern? If ancient, it may refer to your religious/spiritual heritage or to associations with the country where it's located. If modern, see **church**. It may refer to your body, as the temple of the soul, or be a pun for the temple of your head (see **face; forehead; head**).

If applicable, see **worship**.

temptation

Consider who/what is tempting you. Most likely it refers to inner conflict and/or ambivalence. It could refer to needs to disobey (related to authority, guilt, dependence/independence issues?) or collect/hoard; sexual rules/restrictions; restriction of/confusion about choices.

See **boundaries; devil** (if applicable).

ten

Balance; unity or a return to unity; marriage of opposites, or of the masculine (one) and the feminine (zero); the end of a cycle.

tennis

Meaning changes depending on whether you're an observer (more passive behavior, vicarious enjoyment/sensation; voyeuristic needs?) or a player. If a player, meaning changes depending on whether for recreational or tournament play (see **competitor/competition; team/team player/team sports**), singles or doubles (related to team cooperation, utilizing resources?).

In general, playing tennis refers to an expression of personal energy; to actively asserting yourself. It may be related to evaluation/judgment; control issues; feelings about having someone else "call the shots." One of the scores is "love" and may, thus, refer to a romantic situation, but tennis may also refer to a situation that seems to you to be a racket.

See **ball; game(s)**.

tent

A need/wish for outdoor recreation if you like living/sleeping in a tent; a need to make contact with nature or commune with your inner nature; a need to get away; a temporary, impermanent, or unstable (no foundation) aspect of yourself/another. It may refer to a whole constellation of memories of military/other experiences in which tents were used, or be related to mobility and wandering (see **wanderer**).

See **camper/camping**.

termites

Something eating away at/undermining your inner foundation

or self-confidence; a waking situation that causes you worry.

See **pests**.

test

Initiation; feelings about your value/worth; anxiety related to a life situation in which you feel you're being tested/judged/evaluated; anxiety about your qualifications or performance in some situation; possibly a need to correct some mistake from the past.

See **exam(s)/examination**. If a medical test, see **examined** and, if applicable, **doctor, hospital; injection; nurse; syringe; X ray(s)**.

testicles

Male energy or sexual drive/power/fertility, i.e., creativity; anxiety about your sexual prowess; wishing for/needing a lot of nerve to accomplish some task.

See **body; penis/phallus**.

texture(s)

See **emotion(s)**.

Thanksgiving

See **holiday(s)**.

thaw(ing)

Warming up to some person/situation; coming around to another's way of thinking; the melting or letting down of some aspect of your defenses.

See **cold; ice; warm/warmth**.

theater

If observing a performance, consider how it relates to your life story or clarifies some aspect of your life drama/mythology (see **audience**), especially if it seems you've seen it before. Each character may represent some aspect of you, or some role that you play or have played. Possibly one or more of them is showing you a new role you might play. If acting in the theater, see **actor/actress**.

See **stage**.

therapy

Dreaming you're in some kind of therapy, especially psychotherapy or counseling, when you're not suggests a need for, or movement toward, healing and transformation, toward becoming all that you can be, hence self-development. If the therapy relates to the body (massage, physical therapy?), consider the symbolism of the applicable part of your body and what it tells you about needing (kneading?) to be healed. What is your relationship with the healer? The therapist may represent the archetypal mother or father, in positive or negative aspects.

If applicable, see **body; doctor; nurse; hospital**.

thermometer

Anxiety about health; a reading on the mood of a situation/relationship (hot, cold?), or of your inner nature; the "ups and downs" (changing emotions) of a situation/relationship; looking for normalcy.

thief/theft

An aspect of yourself, possibly your shadow (especially if dressed in black), that threatens to rob you of important energy if not attended to; some way you've been emotionally robbed. Consider what the thief is attempting to take. Edinger says dreams of having committed a crime can represent taking the fruit in the Garden of Eden; therefore, the development of a new stage of consciousness. Freud considered robbers/burglars as infantile memories created from bedside visits when one's father looked in on his sleeping child.

See **intruder; shadow; stealing**.

thighs

The capacity to do things; endurance; power, especially of movement (inner or outer); strength.

See **body; leg(s)**.

thin

Feeling flimsy; fragile; possibly transparent; old and worn (if a thin cloth, for instance), but also agile/flexible/energetic. If a person, it may reflect anxiety regarding aging/illness; self-appraisal and/or criticalness, possibly related to social appearance/acceptance.

See **appearance**.

thinking

See **talking/thinking**.

thirst(y)

Urges/longings (for knowledge awareness, insight?); a need for sensual/sexual experience, or for more emotional satisfaction.

See **drink(ing); water**.

thorns

A situation that's dangerous/difficult (a "thorny issue"); a need for defenses/defensiveness; someone in your life who's a "prick." If on a flower, they may refer to the danger lurking behind an otherwise beautiful/benign situation.

If applicable, see **splinter**.

thread

In the myth of Ariadne, the thread serves to remind her of her duty, and is also her link with the past. She gave one to Theseus when he entered the labyrinth on Crete, establishing and symbolizing his guideline out of the dark unconscious and his connection with consciousness.

See **sew(ing)**.

three

In numerology, three is considered a masculine number, thus, symbolizing masculine or fatherly aspects or needs; consciousness. It's a number of completion; the resolution of the duality of two; a union that produces a new reality (1 + 2 = 3). Its correlating geometric shape is the triangle, which symbolizes the trinity of God and the three aspects of man (mind, body, soul); however, in Egyptian hieroglyphics the triangle is a symbol for woman.

An alchemical formula attributed to Maria Prophetissa, sometimes called the sister of Moses, says that out of three comes the one as the fourth. So three and four are forever related to the *process* of individuation, the development of the Self, and its masculine or feminine attributes (see **four**).

In Jungian psychology, three is a restless number, symbolizing urgency and striving. It can symbolize the beginning of a destined psychological course or the gathering of creative energies prior to actual creation.

Mythological time expressed in threes (three years, three months) represents the time of transition or the transformative moment (Estés); but the three-legged animal often represents the shadow.

Three is also associated with the three Norns, the German goddesses of fate who evolved into the three Graces; the three phases of personal time (past, present, future).

In Freudian terminology three is associated with the oedipal situation (mother, father, child) and may be related to attitudes toward authority, competition, dependency, and sexual interaction.

See **number(s); Self; triangle; x**.

threshold

A time for decision; a pause to reconsider a decision; an opportunity for choice. As a stepping-off point for something new, it's related to cycles, concerns about risk taking, the unknown. As a boundary between two worlds or states of being, it's a place of unusual potential/creativity.

throat

See **neck**.

throne

Authority or someone sitting in judgment, and attitudes/feelings about that; a wish/need to be more acknowledged/recognized, to elevate yourself; recognition that you have the capability to undertake a new project/situation. In sexual slang, the toilet is often referred to as the throne (see **toilet**).

If applicable, see **chair; king; queen; royalty**.

throw up

See **vomit(ing)**.

thunder/lightning

Sudden enlightenment; change of attitude; an unexpected change in psychic energy; something overpowering; spiritual illumination.

Every culture has stories about who/what makes lightning/thunder. Mythologically the thunderbolt and the blinding flash of lightning have long been divine signals to *wake up*. They also symbolize power; Zeus threw thunderbolts to vanquish his enemies. It was *Mjöllnir*, the hammer of the Norse deity Thor, that produced lightning; the rolling wheels of his chariot produced thunder. Thor is also associated with law, justice, and oaths past/present. ("May lightning strike me dead if I'm not telling the truth.") Because lightning and thunder are associated with rain, they may represent fertility. (Thor was the god of farmers and of the boundaries of their land). More mundanely, dreams involving lightning/thunder (especially during a storm) may represent feelings/situations in which you feel threatened/endangered/overwhelmed, or new strengths or abilities, if coping well.

See **storm; tower**.

ticket

The cost of an experience/relationship; a sacrifice or the consequences of your actions ("the price you pay"); power/control, or confidence ("write your own ticket").

If applicable, see **audience; game(s); movie; sporting events; theater; vehicle(s)**, and the specific vehicle for which you hold a ticket.

tickle

Feeling overwhelmed by your responsibilities and, possibly, needing to release tension; the ability/need to laugh at life's situations; a sense of humor; letting down your defenses. If someone is tickling you, consider whether it's pleasant (prelude to sex or intimacy?) or hostile. Or are you merely tickled about something, i.e., enjoying your own perspective?

See **laugh/laughter**.

tide(s)

Changing emotions; the "ebb and flow" of life or of a relationship; cycles, and therefore, change; a woman's menstrual cycle; anxiety about aging/life energy (if the tide is out, ebbing). Do you need a little money/food/emotional support to "tide you over"?

See **ocean; sea; water**.

tie

See **necktie**.

tied up

See **cord; plait; rope**.

tiger

Female sexuality and aggressiveness; power; leashed/unleashed anger (depending on situation). If chasing you/another for the kill, what is there in yourself that you are trying to get rid of?

See **animal(s); cat/kitten; lion(s)**.

time

General references to time may refer to a particular time in your life, now past; to the present; or may suggest you're having "the time of your life." They may be saying that "now is the hour" for you to take some kind of action/make a decision. A specific time can serve to remind you of something you need to remember (an appointment?), or a "timely" piece of information.

See **clock; watch**.

time of day

Where you are in your life; an expression of the mood/emotional content of the dream; sometimes unexpressed/unrealized aspects of yourself.

See **dawn; day; evening; morning; night; noon**.

toad(s)

Negativity; earthy or earthbound attitudes; inability to transform your life; lack of creativity; a follower (a "toady"); hidden abilities that you can't access, possibly as a result of selfish or thoughtless attitudes/behavior. In fairy tales, the prince is often under a spell to be a toad until someone loves/kisses him; hence, also related to an ugly facade that covers something of value.

toilet

If clogged, it suggests emotional material/feelings/needs unable to be expressed; self-expression that's prevented, possibly by others' attitudes/opinions.

A toilet can sometimes represent shameful/rejected aspects of ourselves (shadow); also ridding ourselves of them or flushing them away.

See **bathroom; defecate; excrement; urine/urinate**.

tomato

Occasionally known as a love apple, and therefore, sometimes related to romance/sexuality; breasts, or if especially ripe, female genitals; also slang for a female. When cut, it forms a mandala.

See **food; fruit(s)**.

tomb

A need to bury old ideas/attitudes; connection to, or need to acknowledge, your ancestors/heritage; attitudes about death. Related to the symbolism of the womb, it may refer to birth/rebirth issues; to being "born again"; the unconscious (because of its darkness). For Pythagoras, the body was the tomb of the soul, which was set free during sleep to travel upward and communicate with higher beings.

See **catacomb; cemetery; grave**.

tombstone

See **gravestone**.

tongue

The pleasure of/ability to taste, and therefore, sensual ability/needs and discrimination (see **taste**); ability to sift through the sugar or salt of a message and get its real meaning/essence. Communication, often messages of anger or wrath ("speaking with a forked tongue," "having a sharp tongue"); possibly a reminder to "watch your words," "hold your tongue," or anxiety/shyness about how to get a message across ("cat got your tongue?").

See **mouth/lips; swallow(ing)**.

tool(s)

Resources; skills/abilities/training ("the tools of your trade"); a need to build/create in a new direction; a need to repair a situation/relationship. Tool is also slang for penis, so a broken tool could symbolize impotence or sexual anxiety; the action of tools often represents sexual intercourse/masturbation.

See **hammer, saw(ing)**.

topaz

In Hindu tradition, the topaz symbolizes long life and beauty. It's the birthstone of someone born in November. As the ninth foundation stone of the New Jerusalem (Book of Revelation), it corresponds to the tribe of Issachar and refers to growth accelerated by a desire for understanding, to the divine good of truth and the truth of good, and to charity toward others. (The Rev. Carl Yenetchi of Wayfarers Chapel, Palos Verdes, California, suggests that Pliny's description of *topazion*—the gem indicated in the Greek version of the Book of Revelation—most likely refers to what we know today as peridot.)

torch

Purification through illumination and truth (Cirlot); romance/passion ("carrying a torch for someone"; "torch song"); insight/awareness, i.e., "shedding light on a situation" (see **light**); inspiration or leadership ("lighting the way"; her "torch burns bright").

See **fire; flame(s)**.

tornado

Emotional turmoil/upheaval/terror; something (ideas, relationship?) that has potential for destruction in your life; sudden change; someone who sweeps through your life like a tornado (enters, does damage—maybe sweeps you off your feet—and then moves on). Is there a dramatic, possibly potentially destructive, change on the horizon about which you feel powerless?

See **storm; weather; wind(s)**.

torpedo

Unconscious anger/aggression; unexpressed sexual drive or anger at females, if a male dreamer; anxiety about sex, or anger at—or fear of—males, if a female dreamer.

See **submarine; weapon(s)**.

torso

See **lower body; upper body**.

tortoise

See **turtle**.

torture

People who have actually experienced torture may have post-traumatic nightmares about it. Otherwise, it may represent attitudes/memories/guilt that you call upon to be hard on yourself, possibly related, therefore, to recently awakened negative feelings about yourself.

totem pole

Consider the kind of figures/animals and whether you're observing or carving the pole. Totem poles put us in contact with spirit beings and gods (connection with the divine), and with our ancestors (connection with heritage). They refer to honoring/remembering, as well as to the creativity involved in carving them.

See **wood**.

touch(ing)

Making physical/emotional contact or the need to ("touched my heart"); something you need to "get in touch with"; molding/creating/infusing with energy. If you deliberately avoid touching someone/something, consider the symbolism of that person/object to determine who, or what aspect of yourself, you are avoiding or failing to recognize. Your dream may reflect anxiety about having "lost your touch," being "out of touch," or having "touched bottom."

See **finger(s); hand(s)**. If sexual touching, see **sex**.

tower

Consider which images are up in, and which are down from, the tower. If you're in the tower looking down, it may symbolize ego inflation, a so-called superior position ("tower over") from which you have been viewing some person/situation/yourself. Conversely, it may signify a lack of self-esteem and wish for elevation.

If someone's in the tower looking down at *you*, it may signify someone you look up to ("a tower of strength"), possibly falsely. Conversely, it may signify that you secretly think you are better than he/she. Ascent and descent within the tower may symbolize (like **elevator; ladder; stairs**) an attempt to bridge the gap between you and God, between the spiritual and the mundane. It may represent the rising/descending of the spirit within you; unconscious ideas coming close to consciousness; an overwhelming feeling/experience.

A tower can symbolize a place where our emotions (our heart, our feminine aspect) are held captive, or the ivory tower where you hope to be relieved of worldly responsibility and protected from suffering.

See **Eden, Garden of; thunder/lightning**.

town(s)

See **city/cities**.

toy

A playful or immature attitude; acting without seriousness; considering an issue/idea ("toy around with"); insincerity; a need to play more/have more fun.

See **doll; play(ing)**.

track(ing)

The need to get in touch with another aspect of yourself, related to insight or awareness. Meaning changes depending on what you're tracking (animal urges, people?), or whether you're being tracked, i.e, someone is "hard on your tracks" (implying a need for care/protection/defense). Other clues include the time of the year or day and the temperature. Hot weather may refer to sensual/passionate aspects of yourself. Tracking in the snow may refer to trying to track down elusive cold/dead/dying feelings. You may fear/wish to get "off the beaten track," or perhaps there's something you've "lost track of" (person, goals, ideals?). Do you need to "blaze a trail"?

If applicable, see **follow(er)/followed; footprint(s)**.

train(s)

As a travel vehicle, it can symbolize the present state of your life's journey, or your approach to life (old-fashioned/streamlined? smooth/derailed?). The train station may reflect an attitude about your position (station) in life; tracks can reflect a rigid/unchanging pathway through your life. If you move from one car to another, consider each of them as some aspect/perspective on your life. Movement within the train may suggest that although an overall goal/direction is fixed, you're moving on your own energy, or at your own pace, through the plan.

A train can be a pun for teaching or regulating behavior (see **training**). If stranded in a station, see **travel(ing)/journey**. If having difficulty boarding the train, or you miss it, see **airplane**. See also **depart(ing)/departure; travel(ing)/journey**.

training

If you're actually in some training program, it would not be unusual to dream about that situation and about learning the appropriate material. Obtaining training can reflect a need for new information/insight; lack of self-confidence, possibly about skills; anxiety about your ability; a wish to change your status/position (inner or outer); a need to make new, possibly more knowledgeable, plans.

See **business/work; school**; and, if applicable, **exam(s)/examination; teacher**.

tramp

Someone toward whom you feel either disgust and wish to reject, or compassion and wish to help (depending on dream actions/feelings); an irresponsible or whorish aspect of yourself; a broken ("I'm broke") or wounded aspect of yourself.

transcendent dreams

See **grief**.

transformation

Transformation dreams refer to change: a need for change; change that's occurring or about to occur. They can take a symbolic form, as in food being cooked/eaten/digested. They also include dreams in which characters/objects change within the dream or over a series, which both Rossi and Corriere connect with expanded awareness; inner transformation; deep-level personality development.

Corriere and associates identify four kinds of transformative or "breakthrough" dreams: (1) those that move from confusing, distorted content to realistic, clear, and nonsymbolic content; (2) movement from no feeling to full feeling; (3) movement from no human characters or content to human interaction; (4) movement from a passive, observing dreamer to an active one who initiates action and interaction.

See **sex change**.

transparent

Some person or situation in which motives are obvious, at least to you, or one in which no one is trying to keep anything hidden (openness); ability to perceive and understand the dynamics of a situation/relationship; intuitive ability; possibly vulnerability, especially about being mocked or made fun of. Are you afraid that someone will "see through" you (self-confidence issue?), or have you seen through another's actions?

transsexual

If considering or awaiting transsexual surgery, presurgical dreams can give you clues as to your anxiety about the surgery, recovery, and life after surgery. If you're not considering surgery or are not a transsexual, then the dream most likely symbolizes anxiety/ambivalence about, or reluctance to deal with, masculine/feminine roles or passive/aggressive behavior. It can indicate feelings that masculine/feminine aspects of your psyche have been damaged (by parents?). Consider how satisfying/frightening or disgusting (shadow aspect?) the dream is for other clues.

See **sex change**.

transvestite

See **clothes/clothing; sex change**.

trap(ped)

Being trapped suggests coming up against your own boundaries/limitations; rigid ways of thinking by which you have boxed yourself in or limited your choices. Consider the symbolism of who/what is trapping you. Being trapped in an abyss suggests attitudes toward mother/women; trapped/surrounded by mountains may refer to idealistic goals. Trapped in an elevator suggests an inability to "rise above it all" and get a different, possibly more spiritual or enlightened, perspective. Walls in a house may reflect family limitations or beliefs that you have difficulty giving up. It's common for women in their third trimester of pregnancy to dream of being trapped in small places (Siegel).

travel(ing)/journey

If the dream refers to an actual trip you've made, were there people/ideas you failed to attend to, or perhaps characteristics of others that you now need to adopt?

If not an actual trip, it may refer to your way of life; your current pathway; or indicate that you're still seeking your personal goals/aims in life—especially if you're searching for places/objects. What does your dream destination mean to you?

It can represent your progress toward a particular goal/project; new ideas; a need for change; a need to break free or break out of some situation, or to assert yourself and feel like you're "on top of the world." Your speed/direction of travel may reflect your potential (efforts); confidence; control, but it's modified by whether you're walking/driving, or someone else is in charge.

Events/people you encounter may represent aspects of your waking interactions, or aspects of yourself that make life's journey entertaining or troublesome. Being stranded (in a railway or bus station, airport, town) suggests you may be caught between, or have ambivalence about, two people in your life, two choices, two stages/phases of your life. If you made a deliberate stop/detour, it may reflect that you have reached another level in your emotional/physical life and need to pause to enjoy, reflect, rest, or review before you continue or change direction. Wandering on a journey can suggest you've lost your sense of direction; you are searching for new goals/possibilities; you're open to exploring opportunities (see **wanderer**).

How easy/difficult is the journey? Is it an "uphill battle" or "downhill all the way"? Obstacles encountered may symbolize discontents or emotions that are blocking your quest. Assuming there's no difficulty, walking (see **walk(ing)**) suggests independence; self-generated goals;

restoration of balance (left and right); understanding (feet).

If driving, look for clues as to how well you're handling yourself (within acceptable limits, speeding?). If traveling on public transportation, you may be pursuing the goals/values of others, particularly family or another kind of community. Or perhaps you're "all in the same boat"? Is the driver known or unknown (unconscious)?

Missing a bus/train/plane suggests missed opportunities. As a pun, "taking a trip" may refer to some way in which you perceive yourself as having fallen in someone's eyes; been "tripped up"; are about to take a fall. An accident may express "derailment" from your path, or a sense of being overwhelmed. Do you need to go "full steam ahead," or slow down? Arriving at your destination speaks of success, or the need for/opportunity to make a decision (will you get on or off?).

Archetypally, travel can refer to the development, or movement, of the individuation process—the theme of the hero/heroine's journey or quest, the seeking of truth or wholeness.

See **abroad/traveling abroad; direction(s); movement; Self; vacation**. If applicable, see **vehicle(s)**, and specific vehicle.

treasure

Skills/abilities; anything you value; your own value/worth. In Jungian theory, the treasure that's hard to find refers to the Self.

See **jewel(s); Self**.

tree(s)

You and your state of psychological or physical health; your cyclic energy; the process of self-development/individuation. Consider the tree's condition. Its parts may symbolize various aspects of yourself (roots = heritage, unconscious, feet/legs; branches/limbs = branches of the family, arms/hands; twigs = younger relatives, fingers; fruit = maturation/development).

Traditionally, trees symbolize stability; renewal; capacity for endurance; immortality; wisdom. They can represent the personal mother and Mother Nature. Because of its branching, the tree is archetypally related to the labyrinth. In mythology, two trees are often the opposite of one another, thus, a sign of duality. Consider the specific kind of tree and puns on its name for additional clues.

See **Christmas tree; forest; labyrinth/maze; opposites** (if two trees); **roots;** and the specific kind of tree.

trespassing

Anxiety about whether you've crossed some imaginary or actual boundary in your own life or another's; reactions to a recent transgression toward you by someone else; feelings about whether you deserve a recent success/promotion; possibly a feeling that psychologically you are an imposter, i.e., that you are masquerading as more successful/capable than you inwardly feel.

trial

See **court**.

triangle

Aspirations; potential; truth; a sexual triangle in your life; the childhood/oedipal triangle of mother, father, child. Spiritually, it's often a symbol of the triune nature of God, as well as the trinity of man (body, mind, spirit). It's the geometric symbol for the number three, and any cycles or orders/arrangements that appear in threes. With the apex pointed upward, it represents masculine virility; fire; movement toward consciousness/awareness. Pointed downward, it becomes a feminine symbol and represents water; unconscious material.

See **shape(s); three**.

trickster

The trickster archetype is the one that surprises. When anything in your dream upsets or breaks into your preconceived notions, the trickster is at work shifting perspective, restoring wholeness. In dream theory, the trickster is often a symbol of unexpected growth, possibly in a new/different direction. In his purest, mythological form, he dupes others and is usually duped himself. She may appear in animal form, often as a coyote, or be the impulsive character you have a hard time pinning down. She holds up the past, or lower aspects of ourselves, so we won't forget how things once were. Jung calls the trickster a "primitive cosmic" because he frequently has superhuman qualities; still, she often acts without thinking and from the unconscious rather than with logic/reason.

In Shakespearean plays and Balinese dramas, the trickster figure often acts as the alter ego, saying what the king/others cannot say, expressing insights. Acting instinctually, the trickster can be an expression of your more primitive nature; an essential expression of boundless life energy—playful, restless, footloose.

He/she may be an expression

of either too restricted ("act more like me") feelings or a fear that you've acted too impulsively; a desire for a quest; possibly, greater consciousness.

See **clown; shadow; zero**.

trophy

Depending on its shape, it may be a masculine or feminine (cup) symbol. Whatever its appearance, it can refer to sexual prowess; self-confidence; a need for, or acknowledgment of, success.

See **award; prize; competitor/competition; sporting events; victor/victory**. If applicable, see **game(s)** and the particular game/sport.

trousers

See **pants/trousers**.

truck

Trucks can symbolize heavy work, or tasks too heavy for you (overloaded?). Have you taken on too much responsibility; or do you have more potential/energy than you realize? Pregnant women dream of trucks or driving trucks, possibly as an expression of their growing bodies (Garfield).

See **vehicle(s)**. If a tank truck, see **tank**.

trumpet

Triumph; exaltation or high energy; a call to attention, therefore a need to make your skills known ("blow your own horn"); a reference to the angel Gabriel or to the state of your spiritual life.

tunnel

The vagina/womb (depending on what's at the end of the tunnel); therefore, possibly a need for security/nurturing, or an opening to a new awareness. Hopkins suggests that a dream of going through a narrow tunnel, especially with a light at the end of it, may be a memory of the birth process; however, it can also refer to impending death if ill (von Franz). It may refer to a limited perspective ("tunnel vision"); hope ("light at the end of the tunnel"); endeavors ("tunneling your way through"); a need to escape ("tunnel out"). Consider how easy/difficult (life struggles?) it is for you to make your way through the tunnel. Are you getting too big for this?

See **cave; hall(way)**.

turkey

Someone who's not very bright; voracious needs/appetites

(gobble, gobble); a reference to Thanksgivings past/present.

See **holiday(s)**.

turning

See **rotating/revolving/turning**.

turquoise

The birthstone of someone born in December. In gem lore, it's a stone of good luck/fortune; it's said to ward off evil. It has similar meanings in American Indian tradition, where it's also associated with the sun, fire, male power. Believed to have balancing/healing energy and to act as a unifying force between the spirits of the earth and the air, it's therefore used as an offering. In those Indian myths that depict Turquoise Woman as a variant of Changing Woman, she then becomes the ancestral mother of the Dineh (Navajo); the creator of humans for the Indee or Apache—the archetypal Great Mother.

See **gem(s)**.

turtle

Long-lived; sluggish, slow/plodding; withdrawal (into the shell) for defensiveness/protection; independence. When withdrawn, it can be a female (round) symbol, yet with all appendages extended, it can be a male symbol. Therefore, it can also be a symbol of homosexual or transsexual inclinations, and of the union of opposites (Jung). Some turtles are able to live on both land and water, which would indicate the ability to be comfortable with both conscious and unconscious material. In many cultures/traditions, the turtle symbolizes the earth or material existence (contrasted to birds); eternal life.

See **animal(s)**.

twelve

The zodiac and/or the months of the year; cycles and the passage of time; various traits/energies of the archetypal zodiac that we must accomplish in our self-development; the tribes of Israel, whose representative stones are placed in the foundation of the New Jerusalem (Book of Revelation); the disciples of Jesus.

twig(s)

Your progeny; someone you're teaching or mentoring (''bent twig''); a new/fresh perspective; new energy with respect to a relationship; small learnings or yearnings. If thrown for divination, anxiety about the future. If used for dowsing, anxiety about your emotions or an emotional situation, possibly a need to feel secure about it.

twilight

See **evening**.

twin(s)

Strong psychic processes at work, often healing ones. In mythology, one of the twins is often mortal while the other is immortal; thus twins often signal the *emergence* of unconscious (immortal) material into consciousness (mortal). They can also symbolize ambivalence. Sometimes the shadow appears as a hostile twin. Twins represent the battle between the opposites of our psyche that we must encounter to become whole. In that battle, it is our heroic task to ascend, although we may sometimes have to descend temporarily into an "underworld" to survive and ultimately "win." In Egypt the process is represented by Horus and Seth. Astrologically, twins represent Gemini (May 22–June 21).

See **double/duplicate; shadow; two**.

two

Separation; polarity; any opposite function or action, such as inner/outer, conscious/unconscious, masculine/feminine, beginning/end; the cosmic Alpha and Omega—and the awareness that comes with recognition of any of the preceding. It can symbolize a need for balance (between two points of view/issues), or that a balancing is in progress (a compensatory dream in Jungian terms).

Two of the same animal/creature often indicates movement/change in the unconscious that will soon be available to consciousness. Two can symbolize a relationship; a marriage of opposites, and therefore, healing; possibly awareness through acknowledging opposites.

See **number(s)**.

UFO

To dream of a spaceship, and/or an alien within it, can symbolize creative ideas; willingness to, or suggestion that you need to, entertain unusual ideas, get a different perspective. Look to the shape of the ship (circular = female, anima; elongated = male, animus?) and any decorations for additional cues. As a mandala, a circular UFO, and its travels, may represent the Self and the journey toward self-awareness and self-development. Thus, flying saucers signal change, namely, the breakdown of the old order and the *potential* of the new (Taylor). It is not uncommon for a pregnant woman to dream of spaceships, which represent her body with its unknown visitor.

See **vehicle(s)**.

umbrella

Protection from things of the sky (sun, water); a solar/masculine symbol; a symbol of the canopy of heaven. In some countries, it symbolizes royalty (so sacred or special, they need protection from the sun); the solar wheel above the Buddha's head. Does its color, decoration, or condition (new, torn, with holes?) give you any additional ideas?

umpire

An authority figure, especially as related to competition. A need for you/someone else to play by the rules, or to exert control (become an authority figure?); possibly anxiety about either.

uncle

If an actual uncle, he may represent some aspect of your family heritage (traits, characteristics, attitudes), or of that particular uncle whom you've not been fully acknowledging. If not an actual relative, he can represent masculine aspects of yourself, positive or negative, depending on how "Uncle" behaves toward you. Uncles have the power to bestow gifts (new ideas, emerging awareness).

See **family; father**.

under/underneath

As a *direction*, under symbolizes the unconscious; entering the depths of the unknown; the mysterious; shadow aspects. Associated with earth, or depths, it can symbolize the womb (Mother Earth) or death/rebirth issues.

Descent into the underworld and return is the hero's/heroine's basic journey; therefore, being underground or riding the "underground" may refer to examining earlier issues in one's life that you've ignored/left unresolved. In folk lore/mythology, descent into the underworld represents descending into the realm of illusion; the darkness of our material nature. Ascent, then, refers to returning to the light of understanding (M. Hall).

Under as a *position* may refer to feelings/issues of oppression ("under someone's thumb"); status (underdog); protection ("take someone under your wing"); something sleazy/illegal ("under the counter," "underhanded"); hostility (something said "under your breath"); pressure ("under fire"). We are advised to keep secrets "under our hats" or "under wraps," while government agents often work "undercover" to infiltrate "the underworld."

In Gestalt therapy the "underdog" aspect of ourselves will sabotage other, more rational efforts if ignored and is, therefore, related to the Jungian shadow.

See **above; descend(ing); direction(s); shadow; underground**.

underclothes

See **underwear**.

underground

Hidden emotions/instincts; the unconscious; death or death/rebirth issues; buried (repressed)/ ignored aspects of yourself. If synonymous with a subway or mode of transportation, it may refer to travel; speedy communication; a need to make a hasty getaway or to get somewhere (ambitions, goals?) fast.

See **dig(ging); under/underneath**.

underwater

Swimming underwater may refer to your ability to delve into your emotions; a need/readiness to become aware of unconscious material. If you're able to behave normally (speak, walk) underwater, consider the dream as expressing a mythological theme. If you're having trouble, see **drown(ing)**.

See **swimming**.

underwear

Some aspect of your, or another's, personality not usually shown, possibly attitudes related to sexual identity, other sexual issues, body image, or self-esteem, but also to any other hidden prejudices/ideas/habits. Consider their appearance and condition for other clues, i.e., torn underwear may relate to negative/critical feelings, or feeling of inadequacy. If more fancy/sexy than you ordinarily wear, it may refer to wishing/feeling one way while outwardly behaving another way. Perhaps you're finally coming to acknowledge/recognize an aspect of yourself not previously expressed.

See **clothes/clothing**; or for a pun, see **briefs**.

undine

See **water nymph**.

undress

If a voluntary action, it can refer to revealing your emotions; expressing closeness or a need for intimacy; sexual desires. If being undressed, especially unwillingly, it can refer to situations in which you feel you've been humiliated, stripped of your power/integrity, or emotionally violated, i.e., invasion of your personal space. It may refer to a waking situation from which you need to "re-cover," or one in which you need to investigate and "un-cover" more information.

See **naked/being naked**.

unearth

See **dig(ging)**.

uniform

Lack of individuality; being robbed of your identity; expectations of group/organizational behavior; lack of spontaneity in interactions or self-expression; peer or other pressure to shape up. Or it can indicate a sense of togetherness; identification with a profession (related to acceptance and recognition/prestige issues); a need to be part of something greater than yourself (a higher/larger cause?); a need to get things organized and precise, especially if you've experienced some recent trauma/chaos.

universe

If the dream carries with it a feeling of profoundness, it is likely related to your own cosmic concerns, possibly to theological/spiritual questions with which you have been wrestling; to expansion/development of the Self. It may give you an entirely new view/feelings about yourself and your relationship to the world, or to eternity. However, dreams that imply or present the secret(s) of the universe have, for the most part, actually been quite mundane. They may relate to our need for secret knowledge, which in Freudian terms would be bedroom/sexual secrets, but might also refer to a need for ego inflation or feelings of superiority.

See **galaxy; globe; world**.

university

See **school**.

unkempt

Someone who's ragged, dirty, disheveled, or otherwise unkempt may refer to a dirty, possibly shadow, aspect of yourself (sexual attitudes, negative feelings, guilt?); increasing awareness of that aspect in someone in your waking life. If you, it may mean the same as above, but can also refer to feelings of low self-esteem/unworthiness; how you believe you really are inwardly; anxieties about financial security. If a compensatory dream, it may serve to balance recent issues/feelings of pride/ egotism. Use Dreamercise #3, #4, #10, or #11 to rid yourself of some of that repressed dirt and to release creative energy.

See **appearance; clothes/clothing; dirt(y)**.

unknown

Anything unknown in a dream (different from not remembering), or clearly missing, may reflect unconscious information, possibly shadow or anima/animus aspects. It suggests boundaries and opposites: what is known versus what is not known, consciousness/awareness versus unconscious material.

unknown person

See **person, unknown**.

unlock

Freeing/loosening of old rigidities; releasing repressed energy; freedom; opportunity; feelings of comfort/anxiety about the unknown or the future. Consider the symbolism of whatever is unlocked or being unlocked. It may refer to issues about secrets; boundaries; restrictions; or lack of them, depending on what's unlocked, what and how much is visible on one side and on the other.

See **key/keyhole; lock(ed)**.

unopened

Something unopened has the possibility of being positive or negative, so consider any feelings you have about whatever it is that's unopened. If positive, it may refer to unexplored possibilities; potential; anything yet to be achieved or envisioned. If negative, it may reflect a state of denial (unwillingness to see); the threat of danger; withholding; closed-off attitudes; sexual unwillingness (especially if a box or container). Unopened mail may refer to unwillingness to communicate or to receive information; closed-off attitudes (possibly by a "male"?).

unravel

A waking situation that's coming apart; getting at the core or beginning of an issue/situation; a need to untangle a mess.

unusual

See **mystery/mysterious**.

up

Being up/upright is the most frequent dream position. Up movements/positions or objects definitely above something can refer to an inflated ego. Conversely, if you've been "feeling down," your dreams may compensate by including up references. It may be a signal that you're emerging from some sad/grief situation. It can reflect the idea of being happy; high on drugs. Jung believed anything coming up or rising related to material emerging from the unconscious. It may be a signal that you're "one up" on someone, or a wish that something is "on the up and up." Then again, you may be "up to the hilt" in work; or recent experiences may have left you "up a creek."

See **above; ascend(ing); high/height; position(s)**.

upholstery

The need/ability to put a new face or outer covering on an old structure, i.e., to change your own image or that of a relationship/project. Depending on the symbolism of the upholstered object and its condition, reupholstering can suggest giving a new look to something that still has a sound/solid (experienced?) structure; preserving past experience. Negatively, it may say that even though you do this, you still have a frame that's no good.

See **pattern/design**.

upper body

The top half of the body is

related to consciousness and awareness, to thinking (especially the head), and to feeling/emotion (heart). For this to be true, however, there must be specific emphasis on the upper body; or on a belt or other article around the midsection that makes a definite division.

urine/urinate

We often dream of urinating when our bladders are full. Freud considered this an excellent example of attempt at wish fulfillment wherein we dream of going to the bathroom so we don't have to wake up and go. This type of dream seldom results in actual bedwetting for adults; however, children may dream of peeing as they actually wet the bed. In adults, the dream may symbolize hostility ("pissing on someone"); feelings of inability and futility ("pissing away your life"); letting go and expressing our emotions; or, conversely, holding back. Who or what are you "pissed off" at?

urn

As a container, it is a feminine/womb symbol. Consider its color/contents for additional symbolism. If a container for flowers, see **flower(s); vase**. If containing ashes, it may represent the negative, devouring mother or refer to a deceased person; anxiety/concerns about aging/death; a recent cremation and your feelings about it. As a repository for cremains, it may carry some of the symbolism of the grave.

uroboros

The tail eater, the mythical snake (or sometimes a dragon) who swallows his tail and transforms himself. This symbol, which itself sometimes symbolizes the cosmic egg or eternal time, represents one of the symbols of the Jungian concept of the Self because it is a form of the mandala. Being represented by the mineral cinnabar connects the uroboros to red gems.

See **ruby; serpent(s); snake(s)**.

vacation

A sense of relaxation; allowing yourself relief from pressures; pleasure that you've earned . . . unless you have troubles/difficulties arriving at, or during, the vacation. Then the dream may suggest that you have anxieties about an upcoming vacation; can't turn off your waking attitudes/stresses; can't let yourself off the hook, even for a little while. Perhaps you feel you're not deserving enough for a hedonistic experience, or that you can't relax because of repressed feelings/urges (sexual?) that may arise if you do. What part of you is ever vigilant?

vaccination

See **injection**.

vagina

It's unlikely that you will have a dream with emphasis on the vagina specifically, unless it is a sex dream and related to masturbating or having sex, which may be simply a pleasure or release-of-tension dream. It is likely, however, that you will dream of many images that can represent the vagina/womb (hollow containers/vessels, long-necked gourds, small furry animals, flowers with long necks).

If you're a woman, consider first what these dreams convey about issues of femininity/being female, with their short- and long-range implications. Being a daughter, remaining single, menstruation, marriage, motherhood, career, menopause, are some possible issues. Then consider the dream's message with respect to sexual or procreation attitudes/needs.

If a male dreamer, consider what the dream is saying not only about your sexual urges/needs but about your feelings/relationship with a particular woman. Carry it further to consider what it may be saying about your ability, in general, to create friendly, close, or sexual relationships with women, and how that's connected to your relationship with your mother and other female authority figures.

See **womb**.

valentine

Romance; old-fashioned sentiment; tradition; heartfelt acknowledgments or acknowledgment of the heart. It may relate to the date of February 14 (Saint Valentine's Day), with associated past/present occurrences, or a reminder that it's upcoming.

valley(s)

A mountain-enclosed valley can represent protection; security; but also isolation; imprisonment; a feeling that you've been overlooked. A broad valley suggests openness to feelings, new ideas, or spiritual experiences. As a site for rivers and transmitted soil, valleys can represent fertility (creativity); life energy; the womb/vagina. As a symbol for depth/descent, it can relate to deepening your knowledge/experience.

valuable

The Self, especially if it's something valuable enough to be hidden away in a safe or elsewhere (hidden treasure); the essence of your personality; your moral/ethical values; ideas/beliefs that you treasure.

vampire

Food or drug addicts, or people in addictive relationships, may dream their blood (life) is being sucked from them (Woodman). If you're the vampire, you may be sucking in life energy, or aspects of another, that you need to complete yourself.

Negatively, it suggests you're being drained of your life energy/autonomy by another, or by repressed instincts. The Freudian view is that vampires or "evil" creatures represent repressed infantile feelings toward sex, especially incest, and in this case, toward "sucking" and "biting." The sharp teeth may represent anger/aggression, your own or another's. The vampire can represent the devouring mother, or your fear of her; a negative/unacknowledged aspect of the anima/animus.

See **teeth**.

vanish(ed)/vanishing

Some person/thing vanishing suggests you may not have given sufficient attention to those characteristics/qualities of that person/object that are within yourself; feelings that you can't count on someone; fear/anxiety that you're alone and responsible; loss of a previous support; an immature part of you that's afraid you can't cope, especially with sudden, inexplicable loss. Consider your behavior when you discover the disappearance.

See **disappear(ance)**.

vase

The vagina/womb, especially if tall/slender or filled with water/flowers. Pouring from a vase can symbolize an offering to a god; generosity or sharing of wealth; hospitality; the dissemination of knowledge. The water pourer is the symbol for the zodiac sign of Aquarius (Jan. 21–Feb. 20). Pandora's box was originally a vase from which she poured blessings. It became a box due to a mistranslation during the medieval years (Walker).

Vatican

As the seat of the Catholic church, the Vatican may symbolize divinity in an archetypal sense (the Ultimate Divinity), or, more mundanely, may represent religious/spiritual authority. Access to much of the Vatican is forbidden to the public, so it may represent that which is mysterious/hidden, possibly the collective unconscious.

On the other hand, until the fourth century A.D., the temple of the Great Mother goddess Cybele (Demeter) stood where Saint Peter's basilica is today (Walker), so it may represent feminine energy/instincts (love?) conquered or overcome by masculine power.

vault

As a container, it symbolizes the womb. If containing treasures/secrets (bank vault?), it may symbolize life energy; the process of self-fulfillment; anxiety about finances. Also associated with tombs, vaults can refer to death/transformation. Therefore, either a bank vault or a tomb can be related to anxiety or concerns over aging and the future.

See **container; death**. If you're locked in a vault, see **cage, prison/prisoner**. If applicable, see **money; wealth**.

vegetable(s)

Consider first your associations to the vegetable and the action that's being taken regarding it (watered, pulled, chopped, cooked?). As a type of vegetation, it can symbolize nourishment; cycles (winter/summer, life/death); fertility; abundance.

They can, however, also symbolize a lower form of life; the unconscious; your vegetative (autonomic) functioning. Vegetables sometimes symbolize derogatory attributes from our childhood ("carrottop"); a dull person or one who's not using his or her intellect ("cabbage head"). The length/shape of the vegetable can symbolize masculine (long) or feminine (round) attributes, or sexuality.

Root vegetables may be saying something about your family heritage; background; stamina; hidden attributes (buried deep in the ground); or indicate that you are well grounded. Onions, or any other fruit/vegetable that has layers that can be peeled away, can represent complicated situations; the gradual exposure, or hidden aspects, of a situation ("there's more than meets the eye"); the processes of intimacy, self-revelation, self-growth. In what way are you vegetating?

See **cook(s)/cooking; eating; food**.

vegetation

Growing things (grasses, forests, bushes, flowers) can be images for our own vegetative or basic physiological functions; mortality; transitoriness; and, sometimes, resurrection/renewal. It's not unusual for vegetation images (grass, wheat fields) to appear in the dreams of terminally ill people (von Franz).

vehicle(s)

Your body; your passage/progress through life; a relationship; your job/profession. If you're in the process of buying/selling a vehicle, the dream can represent anxiety related to that situation. Vehicles are associated with the central mood/energy of our psyche, which transports us from one endeavor/idea/thought to another (Estés). Jung says the vehicle represents movement or the manner in which the dreamer lives his/her psychic life, i.e., whether individually or collectively (tram, bus?), spontaneously/mechanically.

Consider, then, the state of the vehicle (whether or not it needs repairs), who owns it (symbolizing psychic force/energy), the ease/difficulty and quality of the journey (safe, terrorizing, enjoyable, tension-ridden?), and whether you're in control or someone else (urges, instincts, unconscious material?) is driving/piloting. What do you need to do to be more in charge; or is it better, for now, if you let someone else be "in the driver's seat"?

Does the vehicle have good control (brakes) or do you need some attention there? Are you able to see (headlights) where you're going or are you "in the dark"? A vehicle that won't start may signal that you're feeling depressed or powerless.

See the specific kind of vehicle: **car; boat; bus; ship/shipwreck**.

veil

Ignorance; the separation of worldly knowledge from divine knowledge; hidden or private truth; disguise. For something to be veiled indicates its energy or symbolism is intensified. Lifting the veil, or entering a veiled/heavily curtained gateway, may symbolize access to divine secrets or to the sacred mysteries of life. A transparent veil unites opposites: It both reveals/hides, hints of the known/the mysterious or unknown, thinly separates consciousness and unconscious feelings/energies. It can symbolize ambivalence. (Part of me wants to hide something, part of me doesn't.)

In many countries the veil is a symbol for modesty, chastity, or marriage—all pertaining to hiding or protecting sexuality. From a Freudian perspective, a veil/curtain often represents denied entryway into the parents' "hidden" bedroom, and feelings of being excluded from the secrets/activities that go on there.

In the Grail quest, the knight Perceval's ("pierce-vale") search (journey toward enlightenment) was the way of love and dedication (E. Jung and von Franz).

vertical

Something that's vertical, upright, or moving vertically can symbolize the penis; sexual intercourse; the relationship/union of opposites (up and down, above and below, heaven and earth).

Vertical movement on a tree suggests movement along the cosmic axis (*axis mundi*) or world tree (see **world tree**), and involves the spiritual realm. Metaphysically, a vertical direction may refer to the spine, therefore to courage/integrity; the movement of kundalini energy (sexual and life energy); the vertical path of the initiate seeking enlightenment and soul/spiritual development. Vertical movement means breaking out of our restrictions and moving toward freedom or, in a spiritual sense, toward transcendence.

See **ascend(ing); descend(ing); direction(s); down; flying; up; world tree**.

veterinarian

Someone who notices, is comfortable with, responds to, or heals our basic nature (feelings/wishes) or material rising from our animal instincts/needs (unconscious issues); a therapist, or a need for one. Someone who has "animal" wisdom (Hillman).

See **animal(s)** and any specific animals.

victim

If you're the victim, it may relate to your own feelings of being a victim or victimized regarding life in general or a recent waking experience. It may refer to feelings of self-hate, unworthiness, or low self-esteem; or to a lifelong role you learned early, possibly as a result of childhood wounds (emotional/physical), that now represents some aspect of your usual stance (persona).

In "The Myth of Masochism," a paper presented at the 1993 meetings of the Association for the Study of Dreams, psychoanalyst Walter Bonime stated his belief that humans don't really enjoy suffering, but that some of us *can and do* enjoy what our suffering does to someone else. We "win" by suffering. Does this connect with your dream experience?

If you're victimizing someone else, it may refer to feelings of anger toward, or a wish to be powerful over, some person/situation in your waking life (a sexual or cultural subgroup?).

See **aggression; murder(er); wound(s)/wounded**.

victor/victory

Victory is often symbolized by other images: crowns, wreaths, trophies. It's related to competition; vanquishing the enemy; reward for efforts; triumph (or failure, if you're not the victor) of consciousness/willpower over unconscious material (instincts?). Depending on who is the victor, it can be a symbol of power/strength versus inferiority and may relate to a self-esteem or self-confidence issue. If you're the loser, it may be a projection of your shadow aspect.

video game

A need for recreation, diversion, vicarious excitement, or to get away from more serious responsibilities—in either a positive or negative sense.

See **competitor/competition; game(s)**.

videotape, watching a

See **look(ing)/looked at; movie**.

view

Your viewpoint or perspective (changing, stable, inflexible?); ideas about the past/present/future; your position (close, far away?) with respect to the dream issue.

See **look(ing)/looked at; see(ing); vision**.

vigilantes

Anger; aggression; need for power/control; emotions out of control; behaving out of control; fears about your own abilities, possibly about being overwhelmed by group influence; peer pressure.

villain

The power/strength of the unconscious shadow (Jung).

See **intruder**.

vine(s)

The potential for nourishment (honeysuckle or fruit vines?); fruitfulness (grapevine?); flowering life energy; tenacity (a "clinging vine"); entanglement. Consider the condition the vine is in. A grapevine may also symbolize a communication or rumor to which you have paid too much, or not enough, attention; gossip that needs to be corrected. The dream may be suggesting that your hierarchy of inner priorities/messages needs listening to (or, conversely, to be reordered). How are you like a vine?

See **grape(s); wine**. If applicable, see **tangled**.

violence

It may reflect feelings of anger/rage, so consider the symbolism of who is enacting, and who/what is receiving, violent action. It can sometimes be a marker of repressed memories of child abuse. If a recurring nightmare, review National Nightmares, Chapter 5, Part 1.

violet [color]

Intuition; royalty, hence feelings of being treated royally or wishes that you would be; wishes/needs for recognition; feelings of confidence/ability, or lack thereof.

violet [flower]

In Christian lore, the violet is dedicated to the Virgin Mary, while folklore associates it with delicate love. In ancient times, violets were thought to induce sleep; eating their roots would bring pleasant dreams.

See **amethyst; color(s)**.

violin

A female symbol because of its shape. Played with a bow (masculine symbol), it may reflect romance; courtship; sexual intercourse; "making beautiful music together"; someone you know who owns/plays a violin; actual experiences associated with the violin. As a fiddle, it is often used to accompany folk dances, western/square dancing, and may, therefore, be related to the backwoods; down-to-earth attitudes/feelings; releasing energy in recreation.

In musical/mythological lore, the fiddle is a magic instrument that can entrance/charm/bewitch humans and summon the inhuman (spirits, fairies, animals, demons). In some United States folklore, the master fiddler is the devil; therefore, dancing or listening to his music holds the possibility of endangering your soul.

virgin

Innocence; unsullied; an unmarried person; sexual morals/attitudes; wholeness; naïveté, especially sexually; your own girlhood if a female; anxieties about a young daughter; someone born under the sign of Virgo, the Virgin (August 24–September 23). If you've been feeling in some way "whorish," to dream of yourself as a virgin may be reassuring and restorative. It may refer to "maiden" aspects of yourself, positive in their innocence, or negative in their lack of development; the Virgin Mary, and therefore, to spirituality, or, archetypally, to the primal mother. Consider any myth you know involving virgins to determine how it might match your waking life.

vision

Were you farsighted or did you see things close at hand? The dream could be saying that your sight is limited and you need to change your perspective; or it may refer to inner vision, insight, intuition.

See **eye(s); eyeglasses; look(ing)/looked at; see(ing)**.

voice

An unknown/unseen voice speaking in a dream usually expresses some truth or condition that's beyond doubt, according to Jung. Considered a message from the deepest layers of the psyche—the personification or voice of the Self—it often comes at decisive psychological moments. If the message is critical or negatively judgmental (as is common with addicts before and during early stages of recovery), it's a message from the superego. Spoken words/phrases are typical of the content of non-REM (NREM) dreams.

volcano

As a cleft in the ground, volcano is related to magic and oracles; visions from the underworld/unconscious; the primal mother or creation. However, we usually think of volcanoes as erupting/spewing; hence, they often symbolize volatile emotional energy (rage?) bubbling in the unconscious; pent-up sexual energy. Is the volcano dormant (repressed energy) or smoking (potential for eruption)? Do you behave in an appropriate or inappropriate manner regarding it; and how do your actions relate to waking behavior or your personality? A volcano has the potential for both destruction and construction (new land/shapes). In Hawaii volcanoes are the personification of the goddess Pele; it's dangerous to cross her; however, volcanic eruptions are common in the dreams of pregnant women about to deliver. Cartwright and Lamberg speculate they are anticipating the labor contractions.

See **destruction; explosion; lava**.

vomit(ing)

Ridding oneself of hostile, sexual, or other repressed feelings (guilt?). If someone vomited on you, it may symbolize dumping unacceptable feelings. Then again, perhaps there is something in your waking life that you "can't stomach." What is your reaction during and following the dream (satisfied, scared, disgusted?)? What were other people in the dream doing and what authority figures might they represent (mother, father, boss?); or did this happen alone (vomiting up secrets?)?

voodoo

Exotic magic, therefore symbolic for many people of evil. It can symbolize primitive/unconscious rituals for calling upon divine powers or warding off evil; a primitive/shadow aspect of yourself. More correctly known as *vodun* or *vaudou* by practitioners, it has become an amalgamation of Catholic and Haitian beliefs, and can symbolize, therefore, the dilution (in a negative sense) or the joining (in a positive sense) of spiritual or cultural beliefs/attitudes/practices.

See **magic**.

vow(s)

Often symbolized by a ring, especially a wedding ring. Consider what aspect of yourself, including an archetypal figure, gives you the ring, and to what purpose. If you're giving the ring to another, what vow/commitment do you wish to make to, or receive from, that person? Dream vows may refer to childhood vows you made (I'll *never* do that again; I'll *never* allow that to happen to me) that have been awakened by a current situation, or that are now outdated but still influential. Childhood vows may be expressed as a primitive vow, which is often sealed/acknowledged with human blood, or a blood (animal) sacrifice. If your dream involves this kind of ritual act, it can be indicative of the emotional strength attached to the vow.

voyage

See **travel(ing)/journey**.

vulnerable

If you're especially vulnerable, it can mean you've been feeling the same way regarding some actual situation; or, conversely, that you've been insensitive, hard-hearted, or callous.

vulture

Your own associations are foremost here. Then consider that a vulture can symbolize something/someone that picks/pecks at your wholeness; the dark, shadow side of all that the eagle represents. In ancient Egypt and some American Indian cultures, it's a solar symbol (as are all birds), therefore related to fire/light/life (the opposite of black/bleak), and was the protector of pharaohs. One of the oldest totems of the Egyptian Great Mother, the vulture-headed goddess Nekhbet was recognized as a protecting goddess of births. As a mother goddess, she became associated with the Virgin Mary in Christianity. Because it cleans bones, the vulture more commonly is regarded as a symbol of death; regeneration; transformation; completion of a project/process, or the suggestion that it's time to finish it.

See **eagle; death**.

waiter/waitress

A need to serve, or be served, depending on who is the waiter/ waitress. If of the opposite sex, it may reflect your general attitudes toward that sex. Part of the meaning resides in your own perceptions of the status of this occupation, as well as how the status is depicted in the dream. What are you waiting for?

If applicable, see **eating; food; restaurant**.

waiting

How do you feel in the dream? Are you impatient, possibly having to wait in relationship to someone else (issues of power/control; dependence/independence?)? Are you happy or content to wait for leadership/direction? If waiting for something to happen, it may relate to expectations and anxiety about the unknown; a feeling of equanimity and indifference ("just have to wait and see"). Perhaps you've been rushing in waking life, and the dream is compensating, reminding you it's time to slow down ("they also serve, who stand and wait").

If applicable, see **time**.

wake up

See **awake(n)**.

walk(ing)

Using your own energy, self-confidence, and drive to get through life. Consider whether: it's easy/difficult; you know the way or are lost; you're tired/ energetic; where you're walking, i.e., what your goal is; whether you're well on your way or still need to "take that first step." Do you need to "tread carefully" or is there a pending situation in which you should "avoid putting your foot in it"? You may have anxieties about having to "walk the line," "walk out on someone," "walk all over someone." It may relate to feelings you have about someone you had to "step over" or "step on." Is there a situation/project in which you're making, or wish you could make, "giant strides"? Walking erect suggests the alignment of the upper (divine, consciousness, mind) with the lower (earthly, unconscious, matter).

See **travel(ing)/journey**.

walking up stairs

See **ascend(ing); climb(ing); stairs**.

wall(s)

From a Freudian view, a wall may represent feelings of being excluded from the parents' bedroom and the sexual activity/secrets that occur there. Walls separate and organize functions (such as thinking from emotion); restrict or set limits; protect (related to both defensive and security issues); create privacy or isolation. Have you "walled off" your emotions or put a barrier/distance between yourself and another?

walled city

In ancient literature, poetry, and art, the walled city was often a symbol for our spiritual center, although, negatively, its walls can symbolize unchanging dogma. Likewise, in Jungian psychology, a walled city/courtyard—square or circular—can represent the mother protector, or the Self.

wallet

See **purse/wallet**.

wallpaper

As a surface decoration, it's related to clothes/persona/outward appearances; dealing only with surface appearances or awareness rather than digging deeper. Its design may suggest a mood/emotion, or say you are "too busy." Are you involved in a "repeating pattern" in your life? Like paint, it can suggest a "cover-up," or the need to brighten your environment.

wand

Being an elongated object relates it to a phallic symbol. If a magic wand, it directs power and energy, thus representing authority or special power/influence granted, earned, or taken. It suggests a situation/relationship in which you may feel enthralled, emotionally helpless, or hopelessly in love ("cast a spell").

wanderer

Searching/looking for direction; a sense of being lost; lack of motivation/goals. In myths/fairy tales, the wanderer represents the death of one kind of life and the beginning (or future potential) of another. Therefore, it's related to the death/rebirth and resurrection/transformation motifs.

war

If not a post-traumatic stress dream, and you have been in military combat, something in your recent life may have evoked feelings similar to those you had in combat. If you've never been in a war zone, it may reflect anxiety about someone who is in one; hostile and aggressive feelings; warring and/or ambivalent feelings; personal threat and the need to defend; a struggle to be free/victorious; the wish/need to break free from some inner or outer restriction or unwanted aspect (the enemy within?)

See **battle; destruction**.

warehouse

As excess storage, it may refer to stored energy or resources; memories; aspects of yourself or ambitions put aside (in storage); a need to acquire or hoard (related to security/insecurity and self-confidence issues?). Consider the symbolism of whatever is stored in the warehouse. If vacant, perhaps your inner resources are temporarily depleted, and you need to take time off to replenish yourself and restore your reserves.

warm/warmth

Because we are usually comfortably warm in dreams, this likely has little significance unless it refers to a definite change in room/body temperatures. If only part of the body, consider the meaning of that part. Other possible meanings include: security; nurturing; relaxation; comfort; beginning to like some person or situation ("warming up to"); a thawing of emotions. It may suggest you're coming close ("getting warm") to some discovery/insight.

See **cold; emotion(s)**.

warn(ing)

Warning dreams are adaptive if, in reality, you're in a dangerous situation. They keep you from sleeping too soundly, thus ensuring you're more able to react to waking danger (Weiss).

Otherwise, your dream may be alerting you that something is amiss in your inner or outer life that you've not noticed/realized.

If applicable, see **voice**.

warrior

You; your journey through life, especially if a male dreamer; need to defend/protect/conquer; defending, or fighting to overcome, the old/established order, including your attitudes and childhood training.

See **battle; fight/fighter; military; war**.

washing

See **bath(ing); clean(ing)/cleansing**.

washing machine

Washing machine dreams are common for both men and women during pregnancy. Siegel speculates they may represent the womb and/or ultrasound experiences. Since a washing machine cleans clothes, it may be related to changing your appearance or outward behavior. If washing sheets/towels, it may refer to cleaning up sexual matters.

wasp

A waspish (petulant, bad-tempered, spiteful) aspect of yourself or another; WASP (white Anglo-Saxon Protestant). The wasp is the natural predator of one cycle of the cabbage moth. What pest in your life is the wasp trying to take care of that prevents you from unfolding, as does the cabbage?

See **insects**.

waste

What you can't handle or utilize; something not useful; nonconservative attitudes; wasting your energy; someone who is "wasting away."

If applicable, see **defecate; excrement; garbage**.

watch

Sharing some of the same symbolism as clock and time, a watch suggests you're even more tied to time, since you take it with you. If a wristwatch, it can symbolically accent or restrict wrist functioning or flexibility, and is related to the symbolism of hands and arms. If a pocket watch, it may refer to old-fashioned attitudes; respect/appreciation for old-fashioned ways; relationship to someone who owned one, especially a family member (family heritage?). What needs to be taken care of in a timely fashion?

See **clock; time**.

watching

See **look(ing)/looked at; see-(ing)**.

watchman

A guide or guard; protective and/or vigilant aspect of yourself; a need for security/protection. What do you need to watch out for in waking life?

See **guard(ing)**.

water

The living essence of the psyche; the flow of life energy; fertility. In its positive aspect it's considered the fountain of life, the primal waters from which all life emerged. Negatively, it can represent illusion; the underworld; chaos. Metaphysically, the waters of life symbolize secret doctrine or esoteric teachings.

Frequently water symbolizes the unconscious and emotions. Thus, a gentle wave may symbolize incoming (coming into recognition) emotions. A flood, huge wave, or wall of water can represent a rise in unconscious energy or overwhelming emotions (sexuality, fear, anger?). However, waves are common images in the third trimester of pregnancy.

A constructed lake is likely to represent the personal unconscious, while a large body of water (ocean, sea) may be an archetypal symbol for the collective unconscious (Jung). Although often considered a feminine symbol, during the Renaissance, water was personified as the god Neptune. The Hawaiian god of life waters is the father god Kane. A person carrying water may represent the astrological sign of Aquarius (January 20–February 19).

waterfall

A progression from higher to lower; from the surface to the depths of the unconscious; from movement to rest; a surge of energy. If you're in water, approaching a waterfall, it may refer to feelings of danger or peril (long-standing or related to a waking situation?); or fear of being overwhelmed (carried away) by emotion. Do you need to make a splash for yourself?

water lily

See **lotus**.

water nymph

In esoteric and metaphysical thought, water nymphs (undines) or fairies often symbolize elemental spirits related to water; fleeting emotions.

See **elemental being**.

waves

See **water**.

weak

Depleted life force/energy; lack of purpose/direction; loss of, or lack of, self-confidence; feeling controlled/dominated, or a need to do so yourself; a need to take care of someone weaker (nurturing? hero?).

wealth

In addition to referring to money, it may refer to inner wealth; the ability to value things other than money, i.e., family, friends, nature, God.

See **money**.

weapon(s)

A need to defend/protect from inner or outer attack.

See the specific weapon; **bomb/bombed; gun(s); knife; lance**.

weather

Weather often symbolizes our emotional state; emotional material from the unconscious.

See **storm; wind(s)**.

weave(ing)/weaver

Uniting/combining different influences/elements in your life; the warp and woof of life; alternating phases or possibilities in your life; bringing together natural elements in a certain order; giving birth (von Franz). Consider the fabric being woven and any meaning related to its pattern.

Weaving is tied to the mythology/symbolism of the web (see **spiderweb**). Arachne attained such skill in the arts of spinning, weaving, and embroidery that the nymphs would leave their groves to watch her. Minerva (Athena), the goddess of spinning/weaving, became angry at Arachne's skill and her presumption (engaging in competition), and transformed her into a spider. Another classic weaver was Penelope, the wife of Ulysses, who wove the robe for her father-in-law's funeral canopy by day, unraveling it at night because she had pledged to choose one among her many suitors when the canopy was finished. Do either of these myths fit your life?

web

See **spiderweb**.

wedding

Union of masculine/feminine aspects of yourself; joining spirit and matter; a wish/need for a harmonizing balance; transition; change. If you're planning a wedding, the closer you get to the date, the more wedding dreams you will have, but don't be surprised if many of these turn into nightmares in which the worst possible thing happens. Siegel says these dreams point out anxieties/fears about changes that will occur in your identity/role; how you will perform as husband/wife; issues related to independence/commitment.

Engagements and weddings, especially radiant or ecstatic ones, sometimes appear in the dreams of people who are ill and/or close to death. Von Franz calls this the death-wedding motif.

weeping

See **emotion(s)**.

weld(ing)

Joining, especially by heat (passion); therefore, it may symbolize commitment, marriage, or a joining of two things (people, partnership?) that, when their efforts/energies are combined, results in something stronger and more enduring than when separate. Also repairing a weak/cracked aspect of yourself or a relationship.

well(s)

Going down into or drinking water from wells has long been a symbol for deep spiritual nourishment (the "wellspring of life"). They can represent wishes/desires; primal feminine nourishment; but if you're sinking in one, it may represent that you are in the dark, beginning phase of individuation.

west

Expansion of abilities or opportunities ("go west, young man"); untamed/wild aspects of yourself (instincts/urges); fulfillment. Because the sun sets in the west, it may refer to death/dying; aging or old age; the end of a cycle.

See **direction(s)**.

whale

As a mammal, the whale is a distant relative that lives underwater and needs to surface from time to time; therefore, it represents periodic contact with our unconscious, the underworld, or our shadow. It can represent intuition, which lies "down under" and surfaces occasionally. Sometimes it's an archetypal symbol for the Great Goddess/Great Mother.

See **animal(s); Mary, Virgin**.

wheat

Death/rebirth/resurrection; cycles; spring or fall of your life (depending on the nature of the wheat); germination (of an idea, relationship?). Cutting wheat may represent the end of a cycle with respect to life or a project/relationship. As a major component of bread, wheat can refer to sustenance (emotional or physical). Is there a recent experience/situation that's "grist for the mill," or in which you need to "separate the wheat from the chaff"?

See **grain(s)**.

wheel

The circulating process; ascending/descending; the rotation of the sun; cycles; the zodiac. Being round, it relates to the mandala and the Self. A potter's wheel may refer to humans in general; creation/creative abilities; and, archetypally, to God or the cosmic creator.

See **balance(d)/balancing; circle; mandala; Self**.

wheelchair

If you're in the chair, it may reflect seeing yourself in a position of weakness or invalidating yourself. If someone else, what aspect of you does that person represent? How do you cripple/immobilize yourself?

whistle

A signal calling for attention; sexual interest (wolf whistle); a call to romance/sexual behavior ("if you want me, just whistle"). Whistles tell us when to begin/end actions (time to get to work or stop working so hard?). If someone is whistling a song, it may refer to happiness; a need to change your mood or entertain yourself/another. Are you afraid that you or someone else is just "whistling in the dark"?

white

Purity; newness; awareness; the lightening of a previously drab, dreary, or depressed inner/outer life; sometimes death. Noble/special figures wearing white may represent the anima/animus. In alchemy, whitening was the third stage of the transformation process and represented new knowing.

See **color(s)**.

widow/widower

Hostility toward your mate; anxiety about the death of your mate, especially if he/she is ill; anxiety about your ability to cope without a mate. If your mate has recently died, it may refer to your new reality. It can reflect lack of reliance on, or ignoring, your masculine/feminine aspects; in effect, rendering them dead.

wife

If a man, dreaming of your own wife may relate to relationship issues you're dissatisfied with. Consider how you and she behave for clues about the roles you've adopted that enhance/interfere with trust/closeness. Dreaming of having a wife when you don't, or aren't engaged, could relate to needing to add any of the following to your life: stability, romance, closeness, nurturing—whatever characteristics you associate with a wife. A wife can be a reflection of your anima (feminine aspects) and suggests a need to acknowledge that part of yourself, a need for balance.

If a woman, issues in your marital relationship; the various roles you play as a wife and the feelings you have about them.

wig

Vanity; a need to change your appearance or the way you come across, especially with respect to your power/energy (hair) or intellect/ideas (head). After marriage, an orthodox Jewish woman wears a wig (a *sheitl* or *shaytl*), the original purpose of which was to not appear attractive to other men.

wild/wilderness

Both wild animals and a wilderness area can refer to untamed instincts; uncultivated social/sexual behavior. A wilderness can relate to a need to recognize/honor both our inner nature and the world of nature; a need to commune with the spirits of nature or the inner/outer spiritual; a chaotic or aimless emotional state; a need to throw off restrictions/inhibitions and live a little more freely.

See **animal(s)**.

will [document]

Finishing a cycle; generosity or greed; your heritage (financial and otherwise); anxiety about an impending death, your own or another's; delegating responsibility and resources; readiness to give up attachments/possessions.

win/winning/winner

See **victor/victory**.

wind(s)

Although winds can represent a stormy time in your life (''rough sailing''), they also blow in seeds/new ideas, thus representing new consciousness material from the unconscious; new passion or creativity (''winds of change''); ''smooth sailing''; someone who's verbose (''windy''). They may represent transitoriness and change, because of their capacity to change direction. Is there any significance in the direction of the wind? Could your dream be reminding you that you need to check out ''how the wind blows'' in a particular situation?

See **air; weather**.

window(s)

Consciousness; awareness; intuition (''windows of the soul''). Looking out a window suggests the opportunity/need for a new view. Looking in may reflect your inner view. Being in a windowless room may indicate feeling trapped; the inability to shift viewpoints; a situation in which you ''can't see your way out''; feeling fully protected.

See **architecture; home; house**.

window shades

Depending on whether they're open or shut, and who is outside or inside, they can reflect privacy, isolation, or openness. If a silhouette seen through the shade, it may refer to your shadow aspect, or to unknown (hidden) aspects of yourself/another.

See **window(s)**.

wine

Life; the spirit; good times, either in terms of a celebration or prosperity; transformation, possibly to a higher level of consciousness. (Jesus turned water into wine; wine is changed into the blood of Jesus in the Eucharist.)

If applicable, see **drink(ing); grapes; vine(s)**.

wings/winged

Wings added to any non-winged image indicate intuition and/or sacred potentiality attempting to rise and make itself heard. It suggests sublimation of the inner energy represented by that image and its expansion into wider, possibly community, activities. Could your dream be saying you now have the skill, or shouldn't attempt, to ''wing it''?

See **bird(s)**, if applicable.

winter

The implied duality or struggle between opposites (good/evil, sleep/awaken) that prepares us for transformation (Jung). Aging/old age; an emotionally barren time; cooling emotions toward a situation/relationship; the pause before the next cycle, and therefore, a resting/formative time.

Wise Old Man

An archetypal figure who represents spirit, in contrast to matter, and gives knowledge/insight not available in waking life but that may be necessary to accomplish psychological tasks. He can appear as any authority or wisdom figure: priest, teacher, elder, healer, winged gods. In folklore he sometimes appears as a wise dwarf or helpful animals that speak and display superior knowledge.

See **animal(s); dwarf(s)**.

Wise Old Woman

Like the Wise Old Man, she represents the loving and wise aspects/possibilities of ourselves. She may appear as any authority, wisdom, or elder figure—priestess, teacher/professor, witch/sorceress, doctor, grandmother, queen—and is one form of the Great Mother. Sophia, worshiped by the Gnostics as the Mother of All and by early Christians as the Holy Spirit, is an archetypal female wisdom figure, often believed to be the cocreator of the universe. Her Hebrew name is Hohkma.

witch/witchcraft

Thematically, the witch and her evil activities represent negative aspects, or one polarity, of the mother archetype, what Jung called the "loving and terrible mother." Estés is one of the few Jungians who sees the witch figure as positive in that she symbolizes the wild woman archetype, the instinctual, inner-knowing Self that has to be protected and nourished. From the Freudian point of view, witches, and other "evil" creatures, represent repressed infantile feelings toward sex and toward incest with our parents.

See **crone**.

wizard

Recognition of, and ability to control, your own inner nature; a need for control/manipulation; wish for magical/supreme power; the ability to mobilize a variety of resources, including your own, to bring some situation/project into existence.

See **magician**.

wolf

A wolf is often a symbol of loyalty. If in your associations you consider the wolf as similar to a wild dog, then the wolf represents a more primitive aspect of your dog or animal instinct. In American Indian cultures, he is traditionally a pathfinder and may be pointing the way. In Norse mythology, wolves were the hounds of, and therefore associated with, the three Norns or Fates. A wolf/wolf dog can represent death or the animus, especially in fairy tales, in which it takes the form of a devouring desire to eat up everyone and everything (von Franz). For Estés, the wolf is the wild woman aspect of females, that part which, as a result of her searching and inner work, is able to choose when it is appropriate to throw off the shackles of culture and rely on her own learnings, intuition, and collective feminine wisdom. It is a woman's *basic* feminine strength.

See **animal(s); dog/puppy; fate** (if applicable).

woman/women

If known to you, she can refer to concerns/issues/feelings you have about her. She can represent another, possibly new, woman in your life, suggesting similar aspects between the two that you need to consider. If unknown, she can represent your ideal woman (anima) if you're a man; aspects of yourself, possibly inner resources (whether you're a male or female) such as values, emotions, creativity, intuition. If you're female, she may represent aspects of yourself, including your inner Self, or your shadow. To look for archetypal content, consider whether your dream women represent movement upward or downward (possibly symbolized by depiction as goddesses), and any of the following bipolar dimensions of feminine energy: strong/weak, old/young, mother/daughter, queen/princess, goddess/whore; good fairy/witch.

womb

It is unlikely that you will actually dream of yourself in the womb. However, any circular object that can contain something or does (especially water), or in which you are hiding (especially crouched down or bent over), frequently represents the womb.

wood

If you/another are working with wood (carving, shaping), consider whether the object is beautiful, purely ornamental, or useful. If shaped by your own hands, it may represent a power-giving, creative act. Many cultures still consider wood—once living trees—to be sacred or to contain spirits and vital energy. Therefore, any actions with wood and/or resulting objects are also related to energy and the spiritual. Conversely, something made of wood may refer to feeling dead inside or emotionless; behaving automatically ("woodenly") without emotion (sometimes after trauma); acting unthinkingly according to earlier training/conditioning.

See **carpenter; craft(s); forest**.

woods

See **forest**.

wool

Wool may refer to: the winter season; protection from the cold;

expensive clothes (appearance) that have to be carefully cared for and protected from moths (annoyances). If you were working with wool—carding (unraveling tangles and/or organizing thoughts in your life), spinning (refining chaotic thoughts, creating your life thread), weaving (see **weave(ing)/weaver**), or knitting (see **knit(ting)**)—consider the symbolism of these actions or the garments being created.

Perhaps you've just been "wool-gathering" or realize that someone has tried to "pull the wool over your eyes." In the nursery rhyme "Baa Baa, Black Sheep," the three bags of wool are gathered as offerings/appeasements for the mother, father, and child aspects of ourselves. Could this apply to your dream?

If applicable, see **clothes/clothing; lamb; sheep**.

work

See **business/work**.

work clothes

A need to get down to work on some inner/outer situation; attitudes/feelings about your actual work; your professional persona. Depending on the work clothes and accompanying behavior, you may be: digging into the nitty-gritty of a situation/relationship; raking out the old; planting or constructing new ideas—"cleaning up your act" in some way.

world

Confidence in your abilities; someone who's worldly; a more wide-ranging or global perspective.

See **globe; planet(s); universe**.

world mother

An archetypal motif of the Great Goddess, the collective unconscious. Sometimes symbolized as the ocean.

world mountain

An archetypal motif similar to that of the cosmic egg, it refers to the original mountain/structure that arose out of cosmic waters so that all other beings could crawl upon it, survive, and develop.

world soul

See **sun/sunlight**.

world tree

A mythical/archetypal motif wherein the axis/axle of the world *(axis mundi)* a stabilizing and controlling force—is often symbolized by a tree or a pole. It is the central point in the cosmos, and therefore, eternal or inexhaustible life energy or process; an enduring principle (the Tree of Life in the Garden of Eden). In Jungian psychology, it refers to the growth of the Self. It is the meeting point for the three cosmic zones: heaven, earth, and underworld.

In shamanistic terms, it is an opening into alternate realities. Probably the most famous world tree in folklore is Yggdrasil, on which Odin, the Norse god of winds and spirits—the Allfather or essence of spirit—hung upside down for nine nights in order to receive the secrets of the runes. This myth also embodies the archetypal myth of the "willing sacrifice." Jung points out that man can become whole only with the cooperation of the spirits of darkness.

See **backbone; tree(s)**.

worm

Traditionally it represents earth; earthiness; the underworld or death (Jung); crawling; knotted energy (Cirlot). But as we now know that earthworms are good for the soil, enrich it, and change its composition—can transform old vegetation into compost—a more modern concept might be that worms can represent unconscious enrichment leading to change or the foundation for new growth. It may represent a reprehensible person ("a worm"); a need to "wriggle or worm your way out of" some situation. An inchworm may be a reference to perseverance; working your way through a situation "an inch at a time"; slow, careful efforts; something that needs to be considered carefully, and "every inch" of it reviewed.

worship

Attending/observing a religious service suggests a need to open yourself to more spiritual development or influence in your life; to listen to the voice of your inner self. If worship is already part of your life, consider what support, or facets of yourself, others in attendance symbolize.

See **adore(d)/adoration; church; prayer**.

wound(s)/wounded

In one sense we have all been wounded, so wounds can refer to the reawakening of old, family wounds; recent ego wounds; current physical sensations/conditions that you've been unaware of in waking life. Repeated dreams of a wound/

wounding in one particular area of the body may symbolize an impending illness. Dreams of wounded children may refer to the wounding of your inner child and can point to a need to heal.

In many myths, the male is wounded in the genitals, or more commonly, in the thigh, which symbolizes a wounding in his ability to generate and sustain relationships (the Fisher King in the Grail myth). Wound dreams are related to the archetypal theme of the "wounded healer," the shaman or other person who must be wounded/handicapped in order to develop healing capacities.

See **bandage; injury**.

wrap(ping)

A way of decorating (gift wrap); protecting (as in wrapping a bandage); readying something to send on; hiding something; a successful conclusion ("that's a wrap"). It may be related to generosity (see **gift/giving**) or to special occasions/holidays. (Consider their symbolism, if applicable.) Depending on how something is wrapped, it may relate to tying and to knots (see **knot(s)**). Esoterically, any wrapping represents matter, as contrasted with spirit. For the Chinese, the four points of the paper covering a central object represent the number five and the center of the world (Herder). It may be a pun for a garment, a wrap, and relate to clothes (see **coat; clothes/clothing**) or to temperature and comfort (see **cold**).

wreath(s)

Is it for decoration, related to a specific holiday (consider your associations to that holiday) or to a death (see **death; funeral**)? Also consider how it's made and of what materials (flowers, vines, grasses, cloth?). At its simplest, a wreath is related to the symbolism of the circle and the mandala.

See **circle; mandala**.

write/writing

Communication; self-expression; possibly a need to sort out/organize your thoughts/ideas. If writing a poem/story, it may refer to creativity, but consider whether the type of story relates to your life story, or to a theme presently active in your life. If writing your life story, it may refer to a need to ponder past actions to get new perspective, or to leave some legacy/wisdom to your family/friends.

See **letter; mail; messenger** (if applicable).

wrong

Doing something wrong, being in or going into the wrong place, suggests engaging in behavior that's not in line with your conscience.

X

If "X marks the spot" of buried treasure, this can symbolize the individuation process; transformation; metamorphosis. X is related to crossroads; divergent paths; the issue of roads taken/not taken; decisions needing to be made; a change of attitude. It can also symbolize the inversion energy or urge, i.e., something seeking to manifest itself in its opposite form (black to become white, below to become above; unconscious energy to consciousness). The inversion process is related to things that hang upside down (the acrobat, the bat), and to the numbers two and eleven. It shares the same symbolism as the cross of Saint Andrew, i.e., intercommunication between upper and lower worlds (Cirlot).

See **acrobat; bat** [mammal]; **crossroads, eleven; two**.

X ray(s)

Seeing beyond what's consciously known (intuition?); "seeing through" someone's actions; gaining new insight or perspective.

yacht

See **boat**.

yard

Consider the yard's condition (in ruin, well kept?) and whether or not it's fenced for additional clues. If it needs to be mowed or repaired, it can symbolize a burden, or that you need to "clean up your act." If associated with a house, the front yard may symbolize the face you show to the world, your persona, or that you're being "up front" about something. The backyard suggests secrets; hidden facets/aspects of yourself (the shadow, the unconscious?). If it has a playground or children's play equipment in it, it may symbolize recreation; freedom from restriction or authority; sex.

A train switching yard may reflect a need to change your plans or lifestyle. How have you been "sidetracked"?

See **architecture; door; fence; garden; measurement**.

yeast

A fermenting idea; increasing energy; transformation, hence a spiritual search or inner work.

See **bread; double/duplicate**.

yell(ing)

Anger; aggression; fear; need to be rescued or to make a dramatic statement. Consider who it is you're yelling at. If no one is there, are you feeling ignored, a lack of support, or helpless in some waking situation?

yellow

Shares much of the symbolism of gold, especially as related to transformation. It is, thus, associated with light, the sun, consciousness, and is linked to maturity (gold being an autumn color). In China, yellow and black together symbolize the unity of opposites, while yellow alone symbolizes the center of the universe and royalty (the emperor). Since colors often indicate emotions, yellow can symbolize cowardice ("a yellow streak"). Associated with the signs for discount stores in the United States, yellow may reflect feeling discounted, or something you should discount. Road signs, printed in yellow and black, refer to caution; a need to pay attention or get the message.

According to Epstein, the appearance of yellow in dreams sometimes indicates a physical abnormality, which should be checked out by a physician.

See **color(s); gold(en)**.

yoga/yogi

A spiritual guide; contemplation/meditation; balance of physical/mental; flexibility; spiritual/mental discipline and/or development—and the need for any of the preceding. If you're learning yoga, it would not be unusual to dream of some of the new postures you're learning, but consider, as well, what they could mean in terms of activating old issues/feelings. A yoga teacher may represent a specific teacher in your waking life, or, in general, a teacher or wisdom figure.

yoke

Having to shoulder a burden; enslaved; suppression of instincts. If the yoke of clothing (blouse, shirt), consider the symbolism of the garment and any decoration.

youth

See **boy; girl**.

zero

An eternal number that's both "nothing" and "something," and therefore, a paradox; the "no-thing" that is beyond comprehension. Being circular, it can represent the ideas of immortality (never-ending); the cosmic origin; perfection; wholeness; unchangeability; the planet; the womb; the sun (therefore, warmth and power); or the mythical, magic circle (King Arthur's round table) that often has protective powers. It represents "the One" (God or the divine self), quintessence; the philosopher's stone of alchemy. In numerology, when zero follows another number, it amplifies the meaning and power of that number.

"Zero hour," with its accompanying tension, implies that a decision or important activity (possibly emerging unconscious material) is at hand; an impending attack; a countdown (losing or reversing time?). There may be some situation you need to "zero in on," examine, and take a stance.

See **circle; double/duplicate; mandala; number(s); one; shadow; sun/sunlight; trickster; uroboros**.

zipper

Consider the symbolism of the article in which the zipper is inserted (clothing, pillows, purses?), and whether it's open or closed. Zippers can enhance privacy; relate to modesty or social morals; reveal and release; protect and secure (as in a purse); draw together. Use Dreamercise #3, Part 1, and become the zipper, for it may relate to your ability to be open (receptive) or closed (defensive). Have you been talking too much and need to "zip your lip," or, conversely, need to be more open and expressive?

zodiac

The cycle of time; the wheel of life; enduring. It can be one form of the mandala. In its most mundane sense, the zodiac simply can be a signal that you desire or need answers, guidance, or wisdom. Since it embodies all the signs—all the intellectual and emotional phases—it also symbolizes the total creative process and the great cycle of creation, which always includes involution and evolution, inbreath and out-breath of the Creator. It presents the myths of man in a connected pattern that reflects how man and God interact. In its entirety it can symbolize the cosmic wheel; cosmic man; or the collective unconscious (von Franz). Individual signs may symbolize personal or archetypal characteristics.

See **uroboros**.

zoo

All animals represent instinctual and basic urges/energies, so what better to represent the totality of these, the unconscious, than with a zoo. Consider what's happening to the animals, how they are handled/treated, their condition (well cared for; neglected?), and happenings with specific animals. Are they caged, or in a simulated natural environment where they have room to roam and grow? A dream zoo may suggest that your thinking, or some waking situation, is mixed up or disorganized ("this place is a zoo"; "it's a zoo out there"). It may be a signal to establish some priorities and a return to order.

See **animal(s);** the symbolism of specific animals; **cage** (if actually in your dream or if implied).

Bibliography

Adams, Michael Vannoy. *Racial Identity Dreams: "Colorism" and Multi-Cultural Psychoanalysis*. Paper presented at the Tenth Annual Conference of the Association for the Study of Dreams, Santa Fe, N. Mex., June 1–5, 1993.

Alexander, Ron. "A Peaceful Night's Sleep? Dream On." *New York Times,* Jan. 8, 1989, 40.

Allen, Henry. "The American Dreams: Fear of Falling and Other Long National Nightmares." *Washington Post,* July 7, 1982.

Angier, Natalie. "Cheating on Sleep: Modern Life Turns America Into the Land of the Drowsy." *New York Times,* May 15, 1990, C1, C8.

Ansbacher, H. and L. *The Individual Psychology of Alfred Adler*. New York: Basic Books, 1956.

Armitage, Roseanne. *Dreaming, Stress, and Major Depression*. Paper presented at the Tenth Annual Conference of the Association for the Study of Dreams, Santa Fe, N. Mex., June 1–5, 1993.

Auerbach, Loyd. *Psychic Dreaming. A Parapsychologist's Handbook*. New York: Warner Books, 1991.

Beaudet, Denyse. *Encountering the Monster: Pathways in Children's Dreams*. New York: Continuum, 1990.

Bolen, Jean Shinoda. *Goddesses in Everywoman*. New York: Harper & Row, 1984.

———. *Gods in Everyman*. New York: Harper & Row, 1989.

Bonime, Walter. *The Clinical Use of Dreams*. New York: Basic Books, 1962.

———. *The Myth of Masochism*. Invited address presented

at the Tenth Annual Conference of the Association for the Study of Dreams, Santa Fe, N. Mex., June 1–5, 1993.

Borbély, Alexander. *Secrets of Sleep*. New York: Basic Books, 1986.

Bosnak, Robert. *A Little Course in Dreams*. Boston and London: Shambhala, 1986.

Breger, Louis; Hunter, Ian; and Lane, Ron W. *The Effect of Stress on Dreams*. New York: International Universities Press, 1971.

Bunker, Dusty. *Numerology, Astrology & Dreams*. Westchester, Pa.: Whitford Press, 1987.

Campbell, Joseph. *The Hero with a Thousand Faces*. Princeton, N.J.: Princeton University Press, 1968.

Campbell, Joseph, ed. *Myths, Dreams, and Religion*. New York: E. P. Dutton, 1970.

Cartwright, Rosalind, and Lamberg, Lynn. *Crisis Dreaming*. New York: HarperCollins, 1992.

Castaneda, Carlos. *The Art of Dreaming*. New York: HarperCollins, 1993.

Choi, S. Y. "Dreams as a Prognostic Factor in Alcoholism." *American Journal of Psychiatry* 130 (1973): 699–702.

Cirlot, J. E. *A Dictionary of Symbols*. New York: Philosophical Library, 1962.

"Clue To Depression Sought in Sleep." Science Watch. *New York Times,* March 13, 1990, C2.

Conty, Patrick. "The Geometry of the Labyrinth." *Parabola,* 17, no. 2 (May 1992): 4–14.

Corbett, Lionel. *The Numinous Dream*. Paper presented at the Tenth Annual Conference of the Association for the Study of Dreams, Santa Fe, N. Mex., June 1–5, 1993.

Corelli, Rae. "An Awakening Debate. Uncovering the Secrets of Dreams." *Maclean's* 103 (April 23, 1990): 41–43.

———. "The Mysteries of Sleep and Dreams." *Maclean's* 103 (April 23, 1990): 36–40.

Corriere, R.; Karle, W.; Woldenberg, L.; and Hart, J. *Dreaming and Working: The Fundamental Approach to Dreams*. Culver City, Calif.: Peace Press, 1980.

Corriere, Richard, and Hart, Joseph. *The Dream Makers: Discovering Your Breakthrough Dreams*. New York: Funk & Wagnalls, 1977.

Cosgrove, Cindy. "Dreamlight Diary.'' *Whole Earth Review* (fall 1991): 13–14.

Crawford, John. An Interview with Aaron R. Kipnis, author of *Knights Without Armor. Dream Network 11*, no. 2 (1992): 6–7, 30–31.

Crossley-Holland, Kevin. *The Norse Myths*. New York: Pantheon Books, 1980.

Cunnginham, Scott. *Sacred Sleep. Dreams & the Divine*. Freedom, Calif.: The Crossing Press, 1992.

Davidson, H. R. Ellis. *Gods and Myths of Northern Europe*. London: Penguin Books, 1964.

Delaney, Gayle. ''The Dream Interview.'' In Delaney, Gayle, ed. *New Directions in Dream Interpretation*. Albany: State University of New York Press, 1993.

———. *Living Your Dreams. Using Sleep to Solve Problems and Enrich Your Life*. Rev. ed. San Francisco: Harper & Row, San Francisco, 1988.

———. *Sexual Dreams*. Invited address presented at the Tenth Annual Conference of the Association for the Study of Dreams, Santa Fe, N. Mex., June 1–5, 1993.

Domhoff, G. William. *The Mystique of Dreams. A Search for Utopia through Senoi Dream Theory*. Berkeley, Los Angeles, London: University of California Press, 1985.

Donner, Florinda. *Being-In-Dreaming. An Initiation into the Sorcerer's World*. New York: Harper & Row, San Francisco, 1991.

Dossey, Larry. *Dreams and Prayer*. Invited address presented at the Tenth Annual Conference of the Association for the Study of Dreams, Santa Fe, N. Mex., June 1–5, 1993.

Edinger, E. F. *Ego and Archetype*. Boston and London: Shambhala, 1992.

Ellman, Steven J., and Antrobus, John, eds. *The Mind in Sleep. Psychology and Psychophysiology*. 2d ed. New York: John Wiley & Sons, 1991.

Epel, Naomi. *Writers Dreaming*. New York: Carol Southern Books, 1983.

Epstein, Gerald. *Waking Dream Therapy*. New York: Human Sciences Press, 1981.

Estés, Clarissa Pinkola. *Women Who Run With the Wolves*. N.Y.: Ballantine Books, 1992.

Fagan, Joen, and Shepherd, Irma. *Gestalt Therapy Now*. Palo Alto, Calif: Science and Behavior Books, 1970.

Faraday, Ann. *Dream Power*. New York: Berkley Books, 1972.

Feinstein, David, and Krippner, Stanley. *Personal Mythology*. Los Angeles: Jeremy P. Tarcher, 1988.

Fincher, Susanne F. *Creating Mandalas for Insight, Healing and Self-Expression*. Boston and London: Shambhala, 1991.

Flowers, Loma. ''The Dream Interview Method in a Private Outpatient Psychotherapy Practice.'' In Delaney, Gayle, ed. *New Directions in Dream Interpretation*. Albany: State University of New York Press, 1993.

Freud, Sigmund. *The Interpretation of Dreams*. New York: Avon Books, 1965.

Fromm, Erich. *The Forgotten Language*. New York: Grove Press, 1951.

Gackenbach, Jayne, and Bosveld, Jane. *Control Your Dreams*. New York: HarperCollins, 1990.

Gackenbach, Jayne, and LaBerge, Stephen, eds. *Conscious Mind, Sleeping Brain. Perspectives on Lucid Dreaming*. New York and London: Plenum Press, 1988.

Garfield, Patricia. *Creative Dreaming*. New York: Simon & Schuster, 1974.

———. *The Healing Power of Dreams*. New York: Simon & Schuster, 1991.

———. *Pathway to Ecstasy: The Way of the Dream Mandala*. New York: Prentice-Hall, 1989.

———. *Your Child's Dreams*. New York: Ballantine, 1984.

———. *Women's Bodies, Women's Dreams*. New York: Ballantine Books, 1988.

Gofen, Ethel. ''Sleep. More Than Meets the (Shut-) Eye.'' *Current Health 2,* no. 17 (January 1991): 4–11.

Goleman, Daniel. ''Feeling Sleepy? An Urge to Nap Is Built In.'' *New York Times,* September 12, 1989, C1, C5.

Gross, Augusta, and Rousso, June. ''What Children Really Think About Their Dreams.'' *Dreamworks 5,* no. 3/4, (1988): 193–200.

Gutheil, Emil A. *The Handbook of Dream Analysis*. New York: Grove Press, 1951.

Hall, Calvin, and Van de Castle, Robert. *The Content Analysis of Dreams*. New York: Appleton-Century-Crofts, 1966.

Hall, James A. *Patterns of Dreaming. Jungian Techniques in Theory and Practice*. Boston and London: Shambhala, 1991.

Hall, Manly P. *An Enclyclopedic Outline of Masonic, Hermetic, Qabaalistic and Rosicrucian Philosophy*. Golden Anniversary Edition. Los Angeles: The Philosophical Research Society, 1975.

Harary, Keith, and Weintraub, Pamela. *Lucid Dreams in 30 Days: The Creative Sleep Program*. New York: St. Martin's Press, 1991.

Hauri, Peter J., and Linde, Shirley. "Can't Sleep? Tired? Tense?" *Redbook* 175 (May 1990): 156-162.

Hillman, James. *The Dream and the Underworld*. New York: Harper & Row, 1979.

Hobbs, Joanne. "My Lord Who Hums: Revisioning the Insect/Human Connection." *Dream Network 12,* no. 2, (1993): 14–17.

Hobson, J. Allan. *Sleep*. New York: Scientific American Library, 1989.

Hopcke, Robert H. *Men's Dreams, Men's Healing*. Boston and London: Shambhala, 1990.

Hopkins, Linda. "The Use of Dream Material in Reconstructing Birth Experiences." *Dreamworks 4,* no. 3 (1984-85): 201–203.

Horney, Karen. *Self-Analysis*. New York: Norton, 1942.

Hoss, Robert. *Add a Little Color To Your Dreamwork*. Workshop presented at the Tenth Annual Conference of the Association for the Study of Dreams, Santa Fe, N. Mex., June 1–5, 1993.

Hudson, Liam. *Night Life. The Interpretation of Dreams*. New York: St. Martin's Press, 1985.

Jacobi, Jolande. *Complex Archetype Symbol in the Psychology of C. G. Jung*. Princeton, N.J.: Princeton University Press, 1959.

Johnson, Robert A. *Owning Your Own Shadow: Understanding the Dark Side of the Psyche*. San Francisco: Harper & Row, San Francisco, 1991.

———. *She*. New York: HarperPerennial, 1989.

Jones, Richard M. ''An Introduction To Dream Reflection.'' In Barry McWaters, ed. *Humanistic Perspectives: Current Trends in Psychology.* Monterey, Calif.: Brooks/Cole, 1977.

———. *The New Psychology of Dreaming.* New York and London: Grune & Stratton, 1970.

Jouvet, M. ''Does a Genetic Programming of the Brain Occur During Paradoxical Sleep?'' In Buser, P., and Rougeul-Buser, A., eds. *Cerebral Correlates of Conscious Experience.* Amsterdam: Elsevier, 1978.

Jung, C. G. *The Archetypes and the Collective Unconscious.* Princeton, N. J.: Princeton University Press, 1969.

———. *Dreams.* R. F. C. Hull, trans. Princeton, N. J.: Princeton University Press, 1974.

———. *Man and His Symbols.* Garden City, N. Y.: Doubleday, 1964.

———. *Memories, Dreams, Reflections.* New York: Vintage Books, 1989.

———. *Psychology and Alchemy.* Princeton, N. J.: Princeton University Press, 1968.

Jung, Emma, and von Franz, Marie-Louise. *The Grail Legend.* 2d ed. Boston: Sigo Press, 1970.

Kalweit, Holger. *Dreamtime & Inner Space. The World of the Shaman.* Boston and London: Shambhala, 1988.

Kamberg, Mary-Lane. ''The Sound-, Light-, and Sleep-Show in Your Room.'' *Current Health* 2, no. 15 (January 1989): 26–27.

Kennedy, Alexandra, and Kramer, Kenneth. *Naked Messages from the Underworld: Dreams of Dying and Grieving.* Video presented at the Tenth Annual Conference of the Association for the Study of Dreams, Santa Fe, N. Mex., June 1–5, 1993.

Knapp, S. ''Dreaming: Horney, Kelman, and Shainberg.'' In Wolman, B. B., ed. *Handbook of Dreams: Research, Theory, and Applications.* New York: Van Nostrand, 1979.

Kolata, Gina. ''Light Resets Body Rhythms for the Night Worker.'' *New York Times*, May 3, 1990, A18.

Koukkou, Martha, and Lehman, Dietrich. ''A Model of Dreaming and Its Functional Significance: The State-Shift Hypothesis.'' In Moffitt, Alan; Kramer, Milton; and Hoffmann, Robert, eds. *The Functions of Dreaming*. Albany: State University of New York Press, 1993.

Krakow, Barry, and Neidhardt, Joseph. *Conquering Bad Dreams & Nightmares*. New York: Berkley, 1992.

Kramer, Milton. *Freudian Dream Theory*. Paper presented at the Tenth Annual Conference of the Association for the Study of Dreams, Santa Fe, N. Mex., June 1–5, 1993.

Kuiken, Don. *Reactions To Stress: Loss and Dream Impact*. Paper presented at the Tenth Annual Conference of the Association for the Study of Dreams, Santa Fe, N. Mex., June 1–5, 1993.

LaBerge, Stephen P. "Lucid Dreaming. Directing the Action As It Happens." *Psychology Today* (January 1981): 48–57.

LaBerge, Stephen, and Rheingold, Stephen. *Exploring the World of Lucid Dreaming*. New York: Ballantine Books, 1990.

Langs, Robert. *Decoding Your Dreams*. New York: Ballantine Books, 1988.

Lansky, Melvin R., ed. *Essential Papers on Dreams*. New York and London: New York University Press, 1992.

Leach, Maria, ed. *Funk & Wagnalls Standard Dictionary of Folklore, Mythology, and Legend*. San Francisco: Harper & Row, 1984.

Lortie-Lussier, Monique; Simond, Suzanne; Rinfret, Natalie; and De Koninck, Joseph. "Beyond Sex Differences: Family and Occupational Roles' Impact on Women's and Men's Dreams." *Sex Roles 26*, no. 3/4 (1992): 79–96.

Lortie-Lussier, Monique. *Women's Dreams and the Crossroads of Social Change*. Invited address presented at the Tenth Annual Conference of the Association for the Study of Dreams, Santa Fe, N. Mex., June 1–5, 1993.

Lowe, Wendy. "Summoning the Sandman." *Better Homes and Gardens* 67 (June 1989): 39–40.

Mahrer, Alvin R. *Dream Work in Psychotherapy and Self-Change*. New York and London: Norton, 1989.

Markley, Oliver W. "Why Do We Dream?" *Whole Earth Review* (fall 1991): 10–12.

Maybruck, Patricia. *Pregnancy and Dreams*. Los Angeles: Jeremy P. Tarcher, 1989.

Meddis, Ray. *The Sleep Instinct.* London: Routledge and Kegan Paul, 1977.

Meier, C. A. *Healing Dream and Ritual.* Einsiedeln, Switzerland: Daimon Verlag, 1989.

Mendel, Werner. "The Tactical Use of Dreams in Psychotherapy." *Existential Psychiatry 6,* no. 23 (fall 1967): 332–344.

Miller, David K. "Dreaming, Poetry, and Dream-Poetry." *Voices. Journal of the American Academy of Psychotherapists. 14*, no. 1 (spring 1978): 49–51.

Mindell, Arnold. *Dreambody.* Boston: Sigo Press, 1982.

———. *Working with the Dreaming Body.* London: Routledge and Kegan Paul, 1985.

Moody, Raymond. *Life After Life.* New York: Bantam Books, 1976.

Morrison, Reed. "Dreams Mapping Recovery from Chemical Dependency." *ASD Newsletter* 5, no. 5 (Sept./Oct. 1989): 1–3.

Nadis, Steve. "Mathematics of Sleep." *Technology Review* 90, (Feb./Mar. 1987): 13–14.

Natterson, Joseph M., and Gordon, Bernard. *The Sexual Dream.* New York: Crown, 1977.

Norman, Dorothy. *The Hero: Myth/Image/Symbol.* New York and Cleveland: World, 1969.

O'Connell, Kathleen R. *The Dream and the Recovery Process.* Invited address presented at the Tenth Annual Conference of the Association for the Study of Dreams, Santa Fe, N. Mex., June 1–5, 1993.

Passell, Peter. "Sleep? Why? There's No Money in It." *New York Times*, Aug. 2, 1989, A1, D6.

Progoff, Ira. *At a Journal Workshop.* New York: Dialogue House Library, 1975.

Rawles, Richard. "Visionary Dreaming." *Dreamworks 4*, no. 3, (1984-85): 190–199.

Redmountain, Alex. "Nineteen Things To Do with a Dream in the Post-Freudian Era: A Guide for Creative Clients." *Voices. Journal of the American Academy of Psychotherapists* 14, no. 1 (spring 1978): 63.

Reed, Henry. *Dream Solutions. Using Your Dreams to*

Change Your Life. San Rafael, Calif.: New World Library, 1991.

Reik, Theodor. *Listening with the Third Ear*. New York: Grove Press, 1948.

Rinfred, Natalie; Lortie-Lussier, Monique; and De Konick, Joseph. "The Dreams of Professional Mothers and Female Students: An Exploration of Social Roles and Age Impact." *Dreaming* 1, no. 3 (1991): 179–191.

Rosenthal, Elisabeth. "Pulses of Light Give Astronauts New Rhythms." *New York Times*, April 23, 1991, C1.

Rossi, Ernest L. *Dreams and the Growth of Personality*. 2d ed. New York: Brunner/Mazel, 1985.

Royte, Elizabeth. "Sweet Dreams Are Made of This." *Mademoiselle* 93 (January 1987): 82.

"Salt and Sleep." Science Watch. *New York Times*, July 4, 1989, 16.

Sanford, John A. *Dreams. God's Forgotten Language*. Philadelphia and New York: Lippincott, 1968.

Siegel, Alan B. *Dreams that Can Change Your Life: Navigating Life's Passages through Turning Point Dreams*. New York: Berkley, 1992.

Siegel, Lee. "You Can Dream Your Way to New Skills, Scientist Finds." *Orange County Register*, Oct. 28, 1992, 1, 18.

Signell, Karen A. *Wisdom of the Heart. Working with Women's Dreams*. New York: Bantam Books, 1990.

Smith, Carlyle. "REM Sleep and Learning: Some Recent Findings." In Moffitt, Alan; Kramer, Milton; and Hoffmann, Robert, eds. *The Functions of Dreaming*. Albany: State University of New York Press, 1993.

Snyder, Fred. "Toward an Evolutionary Theory of Dreaming. *American Journal of Psychiatry 123* (1966): 121–42.

Stone, Merlin. *When God Was a Woman*. New York and London: A Harvest/HBJ Book, 1976.

Stukane, Eileen. *The Dream Worlds of Pregnancy*. New York: Quill, 1985.

Sullivan, Kathleen. *Beyond Dream Ego—What Does the Dream Really Say?* Paper presented at the Tenth Annual Conference of the Association for the Study of Dreams, Santa Fe, N. Mex., June 1–5, 1993.

Tanous, Alex, and Gray, Timothy. *Dreams, Symbols, and Psychic Power*. New York: Bantam, 1990

Tauber, Edward, and Green, Maurice. *Prelogical Experience. An Inquiry into Dreams and Other Creative Processes*. New York: Basic Books, 1959.

Taylor, Jeremy. *Dream Work. Techniques for Discovering the Creative Power in Dreams*. New York: Paulist Press, 1983.

Tedlock, Barbara, and Tedlock, Dennis. *Dialogues Among Dreams*. Paper presented at the Tenth Annual Conference of the Association for the Study of Dreams, Santa Fe, N. Mex., June 1–5, 1993.

Teillard, Ania. *Spiritual Dimensions*. London: Routledge and Kegan Paul, 1961.

Ullman, Montague. "Dreams, the Dreamer, and Society." In Delaney, Gayle, ed. *New Directions in Dream Interpretation*. Albany: State University of New York Press, 1993.

Ullman, Montague, and Limmer, Claire. *The Variety of Dream Experience*. New York: Continuum, 1987.

Van de Castle, Robert L. *Effect of Birth Order upon Percentage of Male Characters in Women's Dreams*. Paper presented at the Tenth Annual Conference of the Association for the Study of Dreams, Santa Fe, N. Mex., June 1–5, 1993.

Vaughan, Alan. *The Edge of Tomorrow*. New York: Coward, McCann & Geoghegan, 1982.

———. *Patterns of Prophecy*. New York: Hawthorn Books, 1973.

von Franz, Marie-Louise. *Dreams*. Boston and London: Shambhala. 1991.

———. *The Feminine in Fairy Tales*. Boston and London: Shambhala, 1993.

———. *On Dreams and Death*. Boston and London: Shambhala, 1984.

von Kreisler, Kristin. "The dream that haunts you." *Redbook* 178, no. 5 (April 1992): 108–113.

Walker, Barbara G. *The Woman's Encyclopedia of Myths and Secrets*. San Francisco: Harper & Row, 1983.

Ward, C. H.; Beck, A. T.; and Rascoe, E. "Typical Dreams: Incidence among Psychiatric Patients. *Archives of General Psychiatry* 5 (1961): 116–125.

Warner, Carol D. *The Many Roles of Dreams in the Recovery Process*. Paper presented at the Tenth Annual Conference of the Association for the Study of Dreams, Santa Fe, N. Mex., June 1–5, 1993.

Watkins, Mary M. *Waking Dreams*. New York: Harper & Row, 1976.

Weiss, Joseph. "Dreams and Their Various Purposes." In Melvin R. Lansky, ed. *Essential Papers on Dreams*. New York and London: New York University Press, 1992.

Weiss, Lillie. *Dream Analysis in Psychotherapy*. New York: Pergamon Press, 1986.

Wernick, Robert. "From Out of the Past Come Thundering Hoofbeats of the Demon 'Nightmare.' " *Smithsonian* 19, no. 9 (March 1989): 72–82.

Whitmont, Edward C., and Perera, Sylvia Brinton. *Dreams, a Portal to the Source*. London and New York: Routledge, 1989.

Windsor, Joan Ruth. *Dreams & Healing*. New York: Berkley, 1991.

Wiseman, Anne. *Nightmare Help*. Berkeley, Calif.: Ten Speed Press, 1986.

Woodman, Marion. *Dreams: Language of the Soul*. Audiocassette tape no. A–131, 1991. Available from Sounds True Recordings, 735 Walnut St., Boulder, CO, 80302.

———. *Rolling Away the Stone*. Audiocassette tape no. A-095, 1989. Available from Sounds True Recordings, 735 Walnut St., Boulder, CO, 80302.

Index

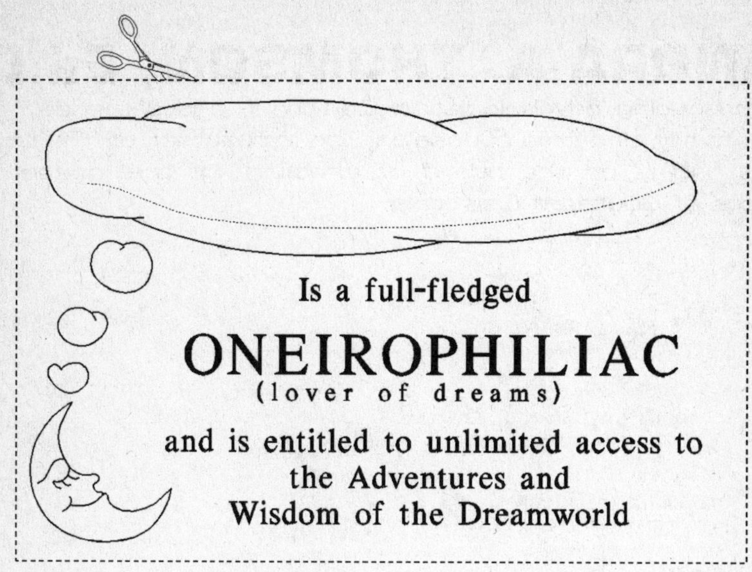
Is a full-fledged
ONEIROPHILIAC
(lover of dreams)
and is entitled to unlimited access to
the Adventures and
Wisdom of the Dreamworld

SANDRA A. THOMSON, Ed.D., is a practicing psychologist in California, and a licensed marriage, family, and child counselor. She is coauthor of *The Lovers' Tarot* and is on the board of directors of the Independent Writers of Southern California.